Sheyne Rowley has worked extensively with children and their families for nearly 20 years—the first ten years as a childcare worker and teacher in schools, kindergartens, daycare centres and the home environment, both in Australia and abroad; the last nine years with distressed families, dealing specifically with what appears to be unsolvable cases of significant sleep dysfunction in children aged up to six years. Her unique strategies have seen parents from across the globe contact her to enlist her help in resolving their child's sleep-time issues, which she can do in as little time as three days.

Sheyne's remarkable success rate has seen her secure regular appearances on Channel 7's *Sunrise* since March 2003, where she is known as 'The Australian Baby Whisperer', as well as appearances on Channel 9's *Mornings with Kerri-Anne* and the ABC's *7.30 Report*. In 2008, she was delighted to speak in Parliament House at the launch of PACAN (parliamentarians against childhood abuse and neglect). Sheyne is also a popular choice as ambassador for many peak bodies.

This is Sheyne's first book and it is for babies aged six to 24 months. She is writing a further volume designed for children aged two and over. Her website is www.dreambabyguide.com and it is an interactive site designed to complement this book.

This book is dedicated to:
my own mother and father who gave me such a great foundation,
my precious family, for their endless love and support,
and to all the beautiful babies, mums and dads
I have been blessed to work with.

You have all taught me so much that I could
write a book about it!

Sheyne Rowley's
Dream Baby Guide

**Positive Routine Management
for happy days
and peaceful nights**

ARENA
ALLEN&UNWIN

This book is intended as a source of information, not a medical reference book. While every care has been taken in compiling the information contained herein neither the author nor the publishers can be held responsible for any adverse reactions to the suggestions offered. The reader is advised to consult with a medical health professional for any concerns they may have before they embark on any of the suggestions contained herein.

First published in 2009

Copyright © Sheyne Rowley 2009

ARENA, an imprint of
Allen & Unwin
83 Alexander Street
Crows Nest NSW 2065
Australia
Phone: (612) 8425 0100
Fax: (612) 9906 2218
Email: info@allenandunwin.com
Web: www.allenandunwin.com

National Library of Australia
Cataloguing-in-Publication entry:

Rowley, Sheyne, 1972–

Sheyne Rowley's dream baby guide : positive routine
management for happy days and peaceful nights / Sheyne Rowley.

9781741753257 (pbk.)

Includes index.

Child rearing.

Infants – Care.

649.122

Set in 11/13.48 pt Bembo by Bookhouse, Sydney
Printed by South Wind Productions, Singapore

10 9 8 7 6

Contents

Must read . . . Understanding my philosophy

You cannot use the methods outlined in this book without first reading this chapter. Whether you are purchasing this book to repair sleep dysfunction and family harmony, or to simply implement balanced communication to maintain your already established healthy sleep patterns and family harmony, I can only impress upon you that it *is* important to read this first chapter. This book is about establishing a strong family philosophy. It is not a bits-and-pieces manual, where you flip to page whatever and all your answers are there in a two-minute blurb. It's about deciding on the direction you would like your family to head in, and working with your wisdom using the tools outlined throughout this book to lay down a respectful and balanced path in words for your family to travel along. It's about achieving a great day every day for today, tomorrow, next week, next year and next decade.

I want to challenge your old ways of thinking about sleep and communication. You need to understand that how you manage your family's day ensures you and your little ones are equipped and empowered with the emotional tools to achieve great sleep through happy, healthy days. It's about understanding that an imbalance at sleep time is a direct reflection of an imbalance somewhere else during the day, and learning how to identify where that imbalance may be so you can respectfully correct it. Therefore my *Dream Baby Guide* is about moving away from the old way of thinking that sleep needs to be managed with the stock-standard routine suggestions or control crying, all done in isolation of daytime environment, play, communication, nutrition and emotional stability. It is about enlightenment—about understanding your child's world and body from their perspective, and assuming a confident and respectful parenting approach that will see your family develop true harmony.

Looking in the right place

After working in this field for nearly 20 years, the last seven years on Channel 7's *Sunrise* program as 'The Australian Baby Whisperer', I have received tens of thousands of emails asking for help. Some in absolute desperation and fear; others with simple questions. In all these emails, however, there are two common elements. The first is the order of the points in each email, and the second is the primary reason given for the possible problems. Here is an email I received this minute, as I write this chapter, as an example:

> Hi Sheyne,
> HELP! My baby was a great sleeper but isn't now. I was hoping for a one-on-one consultation with you. My baby has reflux and allergies and is a poor eater / sleeper. Do you provide home visits?
> Regards,
> Catherine

Upfront in all these heartfelt emails parents always plead for help. Then they tell me one of two things: 'My baby was a great sleeper until _____ then it all went to ribbons'; or 'My baby has never been a good sleeper'; and these lines are usually accompanied by a medical-based reason for the sleep problems. The medical condition outlined might have occurred during the child's first few weeks of life, or be from an illness three months ago, or an ongoing difficulty with reflux, or even something as simple as teething. Whatever the reason given, it appears that the first place a parent looks when a problem arises is medical. Whether this is out of fear—a genuine concern their baby is in discomfort—or pride ('please don't tell me it's something *I'm* doing that's causing this'), there is one thing that is a fact: medical-based issues are generally not the cause of sleep-time disruptions. In all my years of caring for children, I can count on one hand—that's right I said 'one'—how many times sleep disruption was the result of a medical-based issue.

While there is no denying that reflux, irritated airways and general illness and discomfort can contribute to sleep difficulties, these are all usually quite manageable and preventable discomforts. Everyone is very quick to highlight them and the things they have done to correct them, but very few people will say 'I can't lie my baby down to change their nappy because they are impossible to manage', or 'I can't put my baby down to even play or they cry', or 'My baby won't let me feed them', or 'My baby won't sit in the high chair / car seat / pram or bath', etc. Ironically, however, it's these areas and many others like them that are the main places I look at first, and are almost universally the real causes of sleep-time disruption. In assessing sleep problems I tend to look in all the other places to find the cause of sleep-time disruption—everywhere else but medical. In looking elsewhere I get a clearer and more balanced picture of how significant any issue of possible discomfort might be playing in a child's sleep-time or daytime behaviour.

To highlight just how different my way of thinking about this problem is, for every single family that comes to seek my guidance I have an assessment process called 'Dream Baby Profile' (DBP), where I interview mum and dad for a full hour to determine where the key areas of

> I want to challenge your old ways of thinking about sleep and communication.

disruption are for their little ones. In compiling my DBPs I am very reluctant to talk about any actual sleep problems until the end of our discussion. I say to parents at the beginning of each consult:

> Okay, I am going to ask you to run through your day from their wake-up time till bedtime at night, but please don't skip to the night, or only talk about the sleep problems, because your little one's challenges aren't there . . . the sleep problem is only a symptom of the actual imbalance. So once I have assessed the day correctly, I should be able to tell you what is happening during your nights.

Most parents agree happily but within two minutes there we are in the middle of the night, talking through what happens then. So I take a breath and haul them out of their night-time stories of frustration and exhaustion back to the days and their little one's behaviour around eating, playing with and without someone present, being guided, communication, nutrition, etc. Within a few minutes, however, we're back talking about the nights again, as if all the problems can be found there. Well they can't.

Once I have established a child's DBP it's easy to know what's going on at night. This is when I say 'Okay, based on your baby's DBP this is what you are experiencing at sleep time: _____'. At this point most parents interrupt me with incredulous looks and lines like 'Have you been talking to my friends?' or 'Have you been secretly watching me?' or 'Are you psychic?' Fortunately, I have not partaken in any of the above. There is no need. Each child's unique DBP shows me very clearly what they are experiencing during the day, and that view provides far clearer information about the symptoms the child will be displaying at night. Much like a doctor sees a series of symptoms in a patient and runs tests to determine the cause of them, I see the symptoms, such as sleep-time disruptions, but need to view the daytime activities and environment first (my tests) to determine the cause of those symptoms.

What's in my DBP?

With a DBP I am able to teach a family how to address any sleep-time issues in the same manner that I address them: by understanding the cause and repairing that, rather than trying to put a Band-Aid on the symptom with any of the typically imbalanced one-size-fits-all routines and control crying approaches. This means that families almost always come back to me within a month of starting their program, when their sleep is restored and the house is flowing harmoniously, and say 'Now I get it, I didn't at first, but now I see how everything lies in how *I* manage and guide my family's day'. This is what I am hoping this book will do for you: change your mindset and give you a clearer view of the path you need to walk and lay for your family.

You need to be able to develop your own Dream Baby Profile for your child. The DBP looks at each area of your child's day to ensure the emotional skills and flows of communication needed for them to grow are being acquired, and that nutrition, sleep requirement and environmental factors are balanced. It is an individual picture of your baby's situation, highlighting their areas of strength and weakness. The form in the box (see page 5) is a guide to help you compile your DBP. Don't worry if it doesn't make much sense to you now, it will as you navigate this book and gain a clearer understanding of the areas in your child's day that may require encouragement before you embark on your new routine and your repair program.

The DBP encapsulates each area of my personal philosophy, which I call 'positive routine management' (PRM). My PRM philosophy ensures balance is created within the home. More over, it ensures you have a balanced view of their entire day when assessing possible triggers for sleep issues, either those presently experienced and which might need repairing, or those that might crop up in the future and need rebalancing. This will create your own PRM philosophy and by the time you implement your PRM, your baby from six months onwards should be able to:

- go to sleep after a gentle snuggle and a song, a loving tuck-in and good night, and then fall asleep all by themselves . . . every time . . . without tears

Dream Baby Profile
List all members of the family (including pets): _____

Sleep requirement assessment
How much sleep does your baby need?   high / average / low

Association around sleep
Is it parent- or child-governed? _____

Child's routine
Daily: _____
Settling: _____
Resettling: _____
Waking: _____

Family's communication mode
Child-governed   _____ percentage of the time
Parent-governed   _____ percentage of the time
Negotiated   _____ percentage of the time

Creating independence
Emotional tool kit input: _____
Cot environment: _____
Play environment: _____

Meeting nutritional needs
Iron, vitamin / mineral intake: _____
Milk intake: _____
Water intake: _____

Environmental factors in bedroom
Light: _____
Noise: _____
Movement: _____
Comfort: _____
Temperature: _____
Use of comfort items: _____

Interpretation
How do you interpret your child's cries? _____
How do you help them if they are upset? _____
Do you understand the Sleep Bus? _____
Do you understand the ripple effect? _____
Do you understand sudden wakings? _____

- sleep right through the night for 11 to 12 hours without the need for feeds or intervention (unless there is a professionally diagnosed medical reason to pursue night feeds, although I have only encountered three instances of this in my career)
- eat well throughout the day
- play happily with or without you
- cope with you putting them down on the floor or in the cot, and even stepping out of the room without stress
- sleep a minimum of two and a half to four hours during the day, with at least one of those sleeps being one and a half to two hours in length, if not two sleeps of that length
- be co-operative at the end of the day from 5 to 7 p.m., albeit tired and ready for a full night's sleep, but not miserably unhappy and unsettled.

Now if you're thinking, 'I've tried everything, I've been to sleep school and I've had people come into my house and nothing's worked. How could this work?', then rest assured. Many families have sought the help of lots of the hard-working services available to them in both the public and private systems—often being whizzed through a referral process where each service offers the same solutions—but appear to have achieved only inconsistent results, if any. Then, when parents report a failure to achieve results to the next service assisting them, they are informed they are either not doing it correctly, or they 'just have a baby that won't sleep', or that they are not being firm enough with their child. If this is you, and you have tried but failed to repair your sleep issues in the past, don't fret or feel despondent: this program has much to offer that you will not as yet have been exposed to learning.

What is positive routine management?
Let's pull that phrase apart to understand it better:

- Positive—constructive in intention or attitude
- Routine—a sequence of actions regularly followed
- Management—the dealing with and managing of the situation.

As a parent, you govern the routine events in your child's day and night, and you need to implement the transitions in your little one's day in such a way that your child sees the experience as a good thing. This underpins my philosophy in providing the life tools your baby learns so they can, for instance, go to sleep independently when you put them to bed. It allows them to know what you expect of them by listening to and being guided by you throughout the day.

At what age should I start guiding my baby?

Between the age of six months and two years, a parent should be laying the foundation for a strong, trustworthy and loving style within their family. (Under six months your baby is rapidly changing and respectfully this age group needs its own complete book—see page 517 for more.) If your child is under the age of two, your emphasis will be strongly directed towards learning how to communicate to your baby and helping your baby to understand you. I find that because all parents are busy learning how to cater for their babies' emotional and physical needs, it is only when their baby starts to display a little bit of a sprightly spirit and gets cross about certain events (such as when it's time for a nappy change, meal or sleep) that a parent feels the need to learn how to actively communicate with their baby in the true sense of the word.

> The primary goal of parents with children under the age of two is to *be understood*. There are no consequences to think through, no discipline to be done, you simply need your child to be able to understand you.

This means, some parents have to start to actively communicate with their little ones from six months of age, and other parents at 18 months. No matter what stage your baby is at in that under-two age group, the foundation you need to lay down to establish true communication remains the same.

The sooner you start a balanced approach to parenting the better. Ideally, and this book assumes, you will start when your baby is six months old. But if your baby is 12, 16 or 22 months of age, don't worry, you can start then, but you will need to begin at the basics set down here for six month olds. On the upside, your child will learn the skills more quickly the older they are. The method is the same when they are six months as when they are 24 months: a consistent approach so they can look to you for clear guidance, and thus you can help them develop the communication skills they need to live happily through every day and night.

Can my baby really understand me from six months of age?

Most certainly! If you create a pattern of routine communication (called 'language cues') during an everyday routine event (such as nappy changing time, when going to bed and at meal times, etc.) then you develop predictable associations around those cues. Your baby will be able to learn any new process or language in less than 12 hours. By the time your beautiful baby is six months of age, your ability to have a well-balanced and well-defined style of communication that is understood by your baby can be quite extraordinary.

Understanding the causes of sleep disruption

A baby can and does have the ability to sleep, even if they are struggling because of a lack of sleep. The fundamental problem with most help services available for parents is, more often than not, simply a misunderstanding. What they don't realise is that there are two, not one, main groups of children suffering from sleep disruptions:

1. those with classic routine and association issues
2. those with significant communication and behavioural difficulties, particularly in the area of emotional security.

The current systems are effective for the first group and this is where they report most of their successes. The general system available is invaluable to many in this situation, and should be praised for it. But in the second group, despite the children often having loving, intelligent, attentive parents, they just need a little extra guidance from mum and dad. This second group I call 'special care' families, and they need a parental philosophy established in order to facilitate daytime harmony, which ultimately establishes sleep.

My program offers a balanced and gentle approach to all children needing sleep repair, and is therefore extremely effective and respectful for both groups. But by treating those in the second group the same way as those in the first can, in some cases, actually contribute to exacerbated symptoms of daytime and sleep-time disruption, rather than help. There appears to be a lack of understanding or assessment process to identify or help the children and families that fall into this second group and this is why I have been run off my feet for years working with them. Without help, it is easy to assume the possible short-term and long-term effects of an unbalanced parental philosophy could be:

- early childhood health problems
- parental mental and physical health problems
- ADHD (attention deficit hyperactivity disorder)
- obesity in children
- school-bullying and confidence issues.

Long term, the issues that may arise include:

- depression
- drug and alcohol abuse
- crime
- employment difficulties.

In order to repair these special cases of sleep dysfunction a daytime management and communication plan must be implemented. Therefore you must not ever address sleep in isolation from the rest of the daytime activities. Sleep dysfunction mirrors imbalances during the day in areas of psychology, physiology and communication.

The skills required to help a child fall asleep peacefully in their cots and beds and sleep well at night are in fact the same life skills a child needs to be developing in general to equip them with a strong and dependable personal 'emotional tool kit'. This kit will allow them to grow up feeling comfortable in their own skin, to feel respected and autonomous, to be respectful and reliant on wisdom, to be flexible, and to make wise choices based on learnt wisdom. In my opinion, they will also have less propensity toward struggling emotionally in early childhood and adolescence.

The sleep problem for group two can be so much bigger than simply the loss of sleep in early childhood. It's interesting to note that the above long-term effects are far more prevalent in males than females and a large proportion of my client base are male children under five years of age. That said, I have my fair share of little girls, but I find our beautiful, gentle, snuggly little boys are quite sensitive and need lots of clear guidance, and predictability and reassurance in their days. Put simply, a solid parenting philosophy being established initially will not only facilitate the pathway to healthy sleep before problems begin, but also to healthy communication and emotional development for our children not just for today but, as I said earlier, for tomorrow, next year and next decade.

Looking more closely at sleep-time disruption

As outlined above there are two main causes of easily correctable sleep-time disruptions. While there are many other reasons a baby may experience disturbed sleep, these are the two most basic and common causes of sleep-time disruptions that parents and carers can identify quickly, and therefore develop a plan to respectfully empower the child with the skills and understanding they need to enable you to repair their sleep.

What is association-based sleep-time disruption?

As a child under the age two has no concept of time lapsing or sleep, all they know is the feeling associated with going to sleep, which is feeling tired. When they feel tired they often express a level of discomfort and ask their mum or dad one simple question: 'What should I do?' How you respond to that question is how they learn their sleep-time associations.

What do you tell them they need when they are feeling tired? Do you say they need you to help them cope with that feeling, or have you been able to place them in their cot / sleep environment and have them be calm and relaxed enough, about that environment and you leaving the room, to find some self-soothing strategies for coping with the sensation of tired? I find several kinds of associations that families fall into:

- parent-assisted settling and resettling association, which requires a parent's intervention for the child to go to sleep and to go back to sleep
- self-settling abilities but assisted resettling association, where a child can self-settle to initially fall asleep but requires a parent's assistance to go back to sleep if they wake early from a nap or through the night
- parent-assisted settling and self-settling association, where the child requires a parent's intervention to initially go to sleep but can resettle independently.

Parent-assisted or parent-governed association means basically anything that requires your intervention: patting, rocking, putting a dummy in their mouth, sitting with, singing, feeding, putting covers on, rolling them over, lying them down, appearing at the door, calling out once / twice, pushing in a pram, running, jumping, driving, etc. The full list of parent-governed responses are too numerous to list but just know that nothing is odd, and if your little one requires your assistance in any way whatsoever, it is considered a parent-governed association.

Child-governed / self-settle associations are anything your child does automatically when they start to feel tired and these do not require your intervention: twirling hair, thumb sucking, turning head from side to side, rubbing head / ears / eyes, moaning, playing with the tag on a blanket, cuddling / holding / touching / looking at any kind of comfort item, etc. Again the list of child-governed associations is very long but nothing is too odd. If your little one requires no assistance from you, it is considered a child-governed association.

There are also some variations on the above patterns where we might see a child have the ability to self-settle and resettle independently during the day without the need for a parent's intervention, but may be unable to self-settle or resettle at night. This is because different parts of the daily routine signify different actions from parents. As the evening approaches, something as simple as a bath time may indicate that soon you are going to feed them to sleep when breastfeeding, which can create a different set of expectations and therefore associations. A child might be able to self-settle and resettle through the day and night without the need for intervention, however cannot sleep anywhere else but at home or will only go to sleep for one person, and cannot resettle for others, even their other parent.

This is because there are two kinds of routines that people can work with to create associations and they are:

- an environmentally based routine
- a language-based routine.

An environmentally based routine is where you set up the indication cues for your little one that it's 'almost time to sleep' using the environment around them. That means it's about that cot, and that chair, and that person, and that picture on that wall, or that window and those puppy dogs you wave goodnight to, etc. The problem with this kind of routine is that you cannot pick it up and take it with you, and you tend to become house bound. Or your baby will sleep effectively only at home, making vacations and sleepovers something that can be stressful for all, and something that can pose a real risk to ruining your home sleep permanently as the child might become fretful around sleep if exposed to a foreign environment.

A language-based routine is where you set up the indication for your little one that it's 'almost time for sleep' using a series of language cues and events. The beauty of this routine is that it is transportable and can be moved from one location to the next with ease, and can be transferred from one carer to the next with minimal fuss or confusion. This means daycare workers, nannies, mum *and* dad, grandparents, aunts, uncles, etc., will be able to settle your child even when you aren't there, and in another environment from the one they are used to. You can create a predictable pattern that makes your baby feel empowered by knowing what to expect and how to cope with it, which ultimately means they will feel safe and secure even when you are not there with them.

Why are associations such a big deal? Well, you might also ask why can't we just put them to sleep the way that seems to work the fastest or how they think they would prefer to go to sleep. The reason a pattern of just parent-governed associations for a child's sensation of feeling tired can pose a problem comes back to that one simple fact about your child's understanding of sleep: they have no idea about the concept of sleep or about time lapsing at this age, and they only know that when they feel tired they have been told they need others to cope with that feeling. And, because a child will naturally wake throughout the night, they need the same factors in play as were there when they first went to sleep.

This means that a child falling asleep at 7 p.m. (with a parent-governed association) will need the same associations when they wake naturally between 10 and 11 p.m. that they needed to go to sleep initially. This will occur again at around 2 a.m., and again between 4 and 5 a.m., before they wake up for the day between 6 and 7 a.m. So it is crucial to make sure your child is empowered with the tools to cope independently with feeling tired so they can resettle themselves happily. During the day, these cycles can occur as often as every 20, 30 and 40 minutes roughly and can cause significantly disruptive sleep if your little one is needing to wake up and call out for assistance constantly to achieve more sleep.

The constant wakings often lead to a profoundly overtired baby who, by the end of the day, is often so unsettled that they require assistance to go to sleep in the first place. Once this pattern becomes well established, a baby or toddler who should be sleeping very soundly from the age of six to 24 months can become overtired by the need to call out multiple times a night, and may ultimately become profoundly overtired. This could lead to your baby no longer waking just at these key partial-waking windows between deep solid sleep blocks, but hourly or, in some of the worst cases I have seen, every 20 to 40 minutes right through the day and night.

Second key cause of sleep-time disruptions

The second key cause of sleep-time disruption comes up around common sleep requirement and routine miscalculations. This is one of the most common problems I come across. There are two main sleep groups for young ones:

- average to high sleep requirement, those who take around 14½ to 16 hours of sleep in a 24-hour day
- low to average sleep requirement, the group that takes around 13 to 14½ hours sleep a day.

Males on average have a naturally lower need for sleep each day, and females typically need a little more. There is, sadly, a common myth that a child who sleeps more is a 'better' or 'good' baby, and the child who doesn't sleep marathon naps is not. In all honesty, a child with a lower sleep requirement can sleep less and still be as vibrant and happy and delightful as the big snoozer so long as you are catering to their routine needs. The main problem here is that in all the literature you read on babies and sleep there is generally only one sleep routine suggested per age group, and this clearly does not cater for the varying sleep needs of children.

It's not appropriate to expect every single child to need to sleep to a certain hour each morning and still require two long morning and afternoon sleeps. Indeed, it's totally unreasonable and the constant sleep problems experienced by our little people, despite 'professional' intervention, are a testament to that fact. It can be the main reason why babies cry for so long when you are trying to force them into a sleep routine that does not suit their actual needs. I always say to parents that they will see a dramatic improvement within three days of commencing their new parenting program *if* the child's sleep requirement routine is correctly assessed.

Generally, those children with lower sleep requirement are at a higher risk of having developed strong parent-governed associations as a direct result of the use of an inappropriate daily routine. This means the baby / toddler is an extremely tired little person by late afternoon / early evening and requires both assistance to go to sleep and, because they are so overtired, wake frequently, requiring multiple assisted resettles through the evening.

Occasionally, a child who needs an average-to-high sleep requirement becomes so overtired that they are virtually unable to have their sleep repaired on a high sleep requirement's routine. However, once they have begun the sleep repair process on the low-to-average sleep requirement routine (also known as a 'sudden repair routine'), they can then start to sleep more soundly and eventually progress on to the higher sleep need plan without disruption. In the process, tears are reduced dramatically while you provide a healthy amount of sleep without expecting too much.

Resolving sleep-time disruption respectfully

As you can see by this part of my general philosophy, it is inappropriate to use a strategy like control crying as a sole solution to sleep-time difficulties. You cannot start to ask your child to go to sleep at a certain time, nor ask your child to stay asleep for any particular length of time, without first knowing how much sleep they are truly capable of taking, or when they will actually need to be sleeping to encourage appropriate sleep at night or at more important sleep windows through the day. Clearly then, the first two steps in identifying the things you need to do to start resolving significant sleep-time issues are to first assess what sleep requirement your child has, and then plan to adopt an appropriate daily routine to suit their needs. After that you need to look at developing a consistent sleep-time settling, resettling and waking routine before you go any further.

If you want your little one to be relaxed about a particular event of the day then you need to make sure it is consistent, predictable and something they have seen you do many times before. If you think about the things your children enjoy the most, they are things that they have had repeated to them many times and can therefore predict, like a nursery rhyme or a favourite book. They are also things that they have seen us do many times a day, such as handle our car keys, handbag, shoes, remote controls, mobile phones, pots and pans, the broom, sitting in the driver's seat of the car, etc. Essentially anything that they have seen us do, they would like to do themselves. Therefore planning your settling program around your little one's need for predictability is really important. You do this by simply following the suggested settling, resettling and waking routines available in this book, and role playing this with a teddy several times a day for a few days prior to and while you are commencing your repair program.

I often hear parents tell me of the many types of settling techniques they have developed to suit each of the different times of the day. They describe different day settling techniques to night settling techniques, and then go on to relate a series of different resettling techniques based on how their child is reacting on that particular day or night. This usually amounts to a very unpredictable routine and therefore a very unsettled little baby who is making up their own routine to suit their need for a more predictable routine when they are feeling so vulnerable. This is where a parent looks to a child and asks 'Do you want / need to go to sleep?'

It is important to note here that sometimes babies get locked into a set of conditions that they have initiated which is not at all appropriate or good for them. This is where your baby is the last person who should be guiding you as to the best way to help them go to sleep. I always say 'Ask a question, expect an answer'. I have to add, when it comes to health and safety I do not believe all babies will naturally fall into a healthy pattern without proper guidance from their parents, so you need to ensure that you are able to govern sleep time so they don't feel as though they need to govern it themselves.

Again, to do this we create three separate routines:

- settling routine
- resettling routine
- waking routine.

You can adapt the examples in this book of these types of routines to suit your needs but it's important to not include any of the old things you used to do with your baby pre sleep repair as they are tied up in your child's mind with different associations and expectations. A totally new routine will ensure your little one will have this routine defined with its true meaning and there is no confusion for them.

Communication

There are three guiding lines of communication that we use in early childhood, middle childhood and adolescence. They obviously become more complex as a baby develops into a child and adolescent but the undercurrent remains the same: child-governed line of communication, parent-governed line of communication, and negotiation. Understanding these three lines (see page 29) is your key to successful communication within your household. Understanding the importance of balance within these three lines of communication is the key to developing respect and empowering your child's emotional tool kit.

In the child-governed line of communication a little one will say (through the use of cries, sounds, gestures or words) 'I would like to do / have a cuddle / feed / play / that toy / nappy change', etc. This is where a child makes a request. I have to say, parents are awesome at this line of communication—to a fault! Parents often say to me 'I don't know what they want because no matter what I do they still cry'. They are not fully interpreting the problem or cause of tears. They are very good at understanding what a child is asking for at any given time but the problem lies in the child being impulsive and not yet understanding consequences. All a little one knows is what they have been shown, so they will often ask for and request things that do not necessarily resolve the difficulty they are experiencing. It may simply mean that they need you to direct them on to a path that is more likely to have a positive outcome for them, even if they do not always understand your rationale at the time. This requires confidence and trust in yourself as a parent, and it's important to use your wisdom to help your child achieve good outcomes.

> Meeting a child's every demand does not always mean you are meeting a child's every need.

In the parent-governed line of communication, a parent / carer will say 'I would like to change your nappy / feed you / put you down to play / dress you / put you in your cot or pram or high chair or car seat', etc. This is where a parent makes a request and a child *learns* to understand and happily obliges by meeting those requests. Parents often need a little help and guidance for this line of communication because their child may resist their suggestions. They don't do this because they are cheeky or challenging you or are being (dare I even use the inappropriate label) 'naughty'. It is mostly because they do not understand what you have asked for. They don't understand language or you have not learnt how to define your statement. Being little creatures who are impulsive, and enjoy living in the moment with no concept of consequences, they often do not see the importance of changing their nappy, eating a meal, or moving from one location or activity to another. They could stay at the park all day as far as they are concerned.

The importance of establishing this line of communication is about equipping them with the ability to tune in and see value in your language and therefore form a desire to begin developing their own.

The negotiating line of communication is established once the first two foundational lines have been laid and well established. When your child is between 12 and 18 months of age (it varies from child to child) simple negotiations are offered at casual times of the day so the child does not feel stressed or overburdened. To truly master the art of negotiation you must be sure that every negotiation does not turn into a child-governed line of communication or your little one will not have the opportunity to learn how to engage in a negotiation with someone else and could lose the ability to be flexible and open to suggestions. It is vital that a child has positive examples of effective negotiation with positive outcomes reached by both the initiator and the participator. This line of communication is also often used in place of a parent-governed line as a passive form of governing, yet negotiation leads to confusion when not balanced with both parent- and child-governed lines of communication being truly understood and respected by both parent and child. Negotiation at no point should become the dominant line of communication in any household, but should be balanced in its frequency of use and in its outcomes.

These three lines of communication should be respectfully established at home, where the child is known best, loved most, and the people engaging in the interaction are patient, loving and empathetic. It is the most gentle and effective way for a child to begin their journey into being good communicators, confident in their ability to engage with others on a social level, with the ability to offer suggestions autonomously, respectful enough to source and appreciate the wisdom and suggestion of others, and flexible enough to make the most of every interaction with not only their peers, but with adults as well.

Independence

This is one of the most important areas to consider when looking at helping a little one feel comfortable and relaxed enough in their cot to fall asleep peacefully without the need for intervention and assistance. By independence, I'm not suggesting that a baby be left to their own devices. Essentially I'm talking about a way in which you can equip your little one with some important information about the normal range of emotions and feelings we all experience each day. As previously mentioned, I call this their emotional tool kit.

Being such emotional creatures, we experience a huge range of emotions on a daily basis, and a lot of them are not as simple as happy or not. There is a grey area where we may experience feelings that do not fall into the happy or most pleasant range yet are feelings that are perfectly safe and normal to have, and it is because of these that it is vital to empower your child with some information regarding those feelings, and it is crucial to ensure that you are empowering them with a variety of coping skills for each of those emotions that don't involve just us.

Picture a child running in a park. They are having a great time until they suddenly fall. Having not injured themselves physically they go through a series of emotions that fall into the grey area of feelings. Their immediate response to these feelings is to look to their parent to assess the situation. The parent will usually do one of two things:

1. Wince and pull a face and say 'Ooooooooooooh' in a slightly unsure concerned voice . . . at which point a child will go 'I knew it' and burst into tears. Usually after a five-second cuddle and kiss they stop all their crying and concern, and squirm out of your arms to go and play as if nothing has happened.
2. Offer an encouraging statement and suggestion like 'You're okay, up you get' . . . at which point the child will usually get up and dust themselves off or, occasionally, if their little hands start to smart and sting, will come over to mum or dad offering their hands as if to say 'these don't feel normal, or pleasant, are you sure I'm okay?'

Your response here shows us how you can skill your child for the task of going to sleep without mountains of stress or tears.

Because your child will have had the opportunity to have learnt, through your loving guidance, that the feelings they have when they have to 'wait', or 'be in their cot', or 'cope with you leaving a room', or 'feel tired' are all safe, familiar and normal feelings to have; they are things that they can deal with—with your presence, or without. You do this by providing opportunities throughout each and every day that involve developing these skills, and you reassure them by the way you respond to their concerns (just like the child that falls).

Why is this so important? Because the most basic skills a child needs to have developed in order to go to sleep without tears and stress are the ability to:

*   cope with being in their cot awake
*   cope with you leaving the room

- be comfortable with the skill of waiting calmly
- cope with you not picking them up every time they demand it
- cope with the feeling of being tired in a relaxed way.

You achieve this by:

- practising playtime in the cot
- developing a trustworthy predictable short-term absence cue and practise leaving the bedroom or playroom or kitchen for short periods of time, then reassure them by remaining confident and relaxed and not always solving everything for them by picking them up
- practising playtime in the high chair, sitting and waiting in the pram, playing on the floor while you do chores, and sitting quietly on your lap while you read to them
- not picking them up every time they get bored or get tired of waiting— teach them to challenge the environment around them for stimulation as well as expect to be entertained and stimulated by you
- having them sitting on your lap for two to three stories when they start to feel tired so they can learn to relax into the feeling of being tired without the need to feed, fight it, become hyper-stimulated or be excessively assisted to cope through actions like patting, rocking, pacing, singing, etc.

As your baby's emotional tool kit for dealing with the sensation of being tired increases more and more each day, you will quickly start to see them coping better and better when faced with other normal everyday occurrences. This will help you tremendously when it comes to asking your baby to go to sleep for you at night time.

Environment

Environmental elements impact on a baby's ability to sleep. This is one of the areas that *must* be addressed when you are deciding on the best plan of action to help your little one feel safe and be in the best position to not only fall asleep, but to go back to sleep quickly, at the point of a typical partial waking during the night, without your intervention. There are four main areas I work on environmentally:

- movement—that is, wrapping a child so their movement is restricted or not
- light in their room
- noises they may hear
- temperature.

When your little one has not had the opportunity to ever actually learn how to sleep effectively in the first place, I tend to make sure I start teaching them sleep from the very beginning. In the case of a baby that is ten months old, for example, who has never been able to self-settle or resettle without assistance, their skills for that task are equivalent to those of a newborn. Therefore I will often go back to basics when it comes to environmental aids to get sleep happening.

Please bear in mind that any environmental aids introduced for the purpose of helping repair babies' sleep are literally a short-term aid to assist the baby while they get used to the new conditions around sleep. Once those new conditions have been embraced and baby is feeling more autonomous with the skill of going to sleep and back to sleep without the need for assistance, these aids quickly become redundant. You can start to wean them off each one in a timeframe that the baby feels comfortable with. There is no rush. If baby is happy, why change things?

Nutrition

Dietary intake and sleep go hand-in-hand. There are a few simple principles that must be acknowledged when trying to repair sleep-time difficulties. Food provides fuel and the capacity to sleep and sleep provides fuel, and the capacity to eat food. The two therefore work together. Balancing food with sleep is a tricky business. Knowing that food can take the place of lost sleep, or detract from a child's ability to take an upcoming sleep is an important skill for a parent to have. Understanding the impact low iron intake has on your baby's ability to stay asleep however, is a necessity. Understanding how to balance your meal times so you can achieve great sleep and great meal times is a vital part of your sleep repair program. Understanding the behavioural elements of meal times and how to manage them will transform your child's ability to eat and therefore promote great sleep. Great sleep will reduce the behavioural elements of meal-time difficulties, thus sustaining great sleep.

Understanding your baby's cries and the process of sleep

This area must be understood clearly before you can progress with any kind of sleep repair program. Currently, there is a movement keen to do away with control crying and all hybrids of it, and I must agree with that. Sadly, I am also seeing that same movement with nowhere else to turn other than to eliminate all crying and fully assist a child to sleep. This I cannot agree with. I see both of these methods at either end of the spectrum when it comes to extreme approaches, and I also see both creating their own version of learnt helplessness in a child.

The approach I advocate is about balance. If crying is a child's only way of communicating, it's important we learn how to understand them and communicate with them. This sleep repair approach advocates a balanced strategy where all your child's needs are met well before you even embark on beginning the independent sleep. This means that by the time you start to show your little one how to sleep, the vital skill set, environmental factors, appropriate routine and healthy balanced communication are in place.

This essentially leaves us with a simple task. Babies don't like change. Anything slightly new will evoke a reaction and a need for the child to ask you if they are okay and if this is normal, healthy and safe. It's how you respond to those questions that needs a balanced approach. This combined with understanding how your child's body falls asleep, stays asleep and how often they can wake, and how long it could take for them to be able to fall asleep again, are all vital elements in repairing sleep.

What is a dream baby?

A dream baby is a baby who has a balanced life. A dream baby is a baby whose individual sleep needs and nutritional needs are met on a daily basis; a baby who feels emotionally settled and able to cope with the general flow of their day. A dream baby is a baby who feels safe and comfortable in their environment, and is equipped with the right emotional skills both to enjoy playing by themselves and interacting with others. Most importantly, a dream baby is a baby who can be heard and feels that their needs can be met, and who can understand and predict what their carers are asking them to do. A dream baby has parents who understand their children's needs and, based on their own wisdom, can help their little ones achieve a happy day based on that wisdom every day.

So, where to from here?

This book is to be used by dividing your repair plan into two distinct areas. The first is what I call 'your homework'. The second is what I call 'creating harmony'. You must never start creating harmony until you have completed your homework. To do so would be imbalanced and unfair to your little one, and yourself. You may also find that in starting your homework, some of your family's harmony is naturally created within one to two weeks without the need for further action, and therefore there is no need to move ahead with step two. For others, however, your homework is vital preparation time for your baby to become skilled and ready for the second part of your repair plan, which is creating harmony.

Your homework

For those experiencing sleep-time and daytime behavioural challenges

You will need to read through the sleep section in this book carefully to determine if you need to start a sleep diary (see page 534) or not. If you do not need to keep a diary then the only difference between you and the parent who does, is recording and calculating your child's sleep requirement, or not. Either way you will both need to follow the homework section carefully by reading through the entire book and developing your own personal dream baby profile. As you progress through the book you will identify areas where you need to work on skilling first yourself, then your baby with all the tools you and they need to be able to repair their sleep and daytime imbalances respectfully and permanently, and to create a truly harmonious home.

Homework will include developing your communication skills and the ability to respectfully guide your baby, promoting independence through play and equipping your child's emotional tool kit, balancing their nutrition, correcting their sleep environment and practising your swaddle or tuck-in technique, if appropriate, while you practise the all-important new sleep-time routine role play for your baby. Once you have completed this portion of your repair program, you will be able to go back to your dream baby profile to see if you understand and have / are catering for each area carefully before determining whether you and your baby are now finally ready and skilled to embark on your permanent repair by creating harmony.

For those experiencing daytime behavioural challenges only

You will begin by reading through this book to develop your own dream baby profile. As you progress through the chapters you will identify areas where you need to work on skilling yourself first, then your baby with all the tools you and they need to be able to repair their daytime imbalances respectfully and permanently to create a truly harmonious home. This homework will include developing your communication skills and ability to respectfully guide your baby, promoting independence through play and equipping their emotional tool kit, balancing their nutrition and correcting their play environments. It is also worth ensuring that your sleep is set on a good language-based foundation so it remains permanent and achievable even when you are not in your home. Once you have completed this portion of your repair program, you will be able to go back to your dream baby profile to see if you understand and have catered / are catering for each area carefully before determining that you and your baby are now finally ready and skilled to embark on your permanent repair by creating harmony.

Creating harmony

For those experiencing sleep-time and daytime behavioural challenges

You will need to set your date to put in place a new daily routine, and settling, resettling and waking routines for the first time. Until this point you will maintain your *old* routines and settling techniques while you completed your homework. This means do not make any routine or sleep-time change until you have completed your homework first. I cannot *stress* strongly enough the importance of waiting until you finish your homework before you start to make any sleep routine or settling technique changes. Your homework *must* be complete before the date you have set to commence the routine arrives so you *fully* understand how to interpret your child's cries, how to assist them with their sleep, and how to manage everything carefully. Once your homework is done and everything and everyone is ready, go to your final night's checklist (see page 27) for instruction, then at 6.30 a.m. the following morning your new routines and support techniques will begin. This is an exciting time and opportunity. Embrace it as a real chance to *teach* your baby how to sleep. Allow three days for a bit of hard work, bearing in mind 'The communication learning ladder' (page 67), and then three full weeks to lock your new great sleep into place.

For those experiencing only daytime behavioural challenges

You will need to set your date to put in place your new approaches in the areas of the day that your little one is finding the most stressful or difficult through the strategies outlined in this book, including the 'SURE' encyclopaedia sections. Once you have achieved positive results with your daytime communication and harmony you can then start to consider role-playing any language-based changes you may have decided to make to your child's sleep-time settling routine, to ensure it is permanent. This is an exciting time and opportunity. Embrace it as a real chance to *teach* your baby how to communicate with you and how you communicate with them. Allow five days for a bit of hard work, bearing in mind 'The communication learning ladder' (page 67), and then always maintain your new communication by re-reading the communication section every month or so until you are confident with your child's rapidly changing communication skills.

Get excited mums and dads, you are about to become a baby whisperer!

Part 1
Communication, independence and play
for happy days

1
The importance of communication

People often think it is too challenging a task to communicate with a baby, but it's not when you have the right tools. And as I've said, and will say many times throughout this book, you cannot repair disrupted or poor sleep patterns and daytime behavioural problems until you can communicate well with, which means respectfully guide, your child during the day and night. I cannot stress enough how important good communication is to harmony when it comes to creating a balanced family environment. It enables you to have true and lasting understanding and co-operation in your home and, when there is stability within the family home, the natural bonuses are children who have deep, healthy restorative sleep, are not fussy at meal times, and can happily explore and play and therefore learn and grow.

Good communication makes up a substantial 85 per cent of my parenting philosophy, and there's no big secret to it. Good communication simply means being trustworthy, which becomes apparent to your child when you are predictable and consistent. Communication starts with a simple flow of predictable information that accompanies a set pattern of routine events at regular times of the day (events), such as meal times, nappy changing times or bath time. Being consistent means you always use the same style of a clear, well-defined language that your baby not only recognises but is also able to fully understand at all times. Using predictable and consistent ways of communicating with your baby throughout the day is the only way to reduce or eliminate tears significantly when teaching them a new routine around sleeping, eating, or playing independently.

By the time your little one has reached 18 months of age the use of words will become the more dominant portion of your conversations. At this stage of your child's development, if you have developed a good communication base with your child from an early age, other people may be surprised at how amazing the bond is between the two or three or all of you, and how easy you make parenting look!

What's your communication style right now?

Good communication always involves clear, repetitive language. It guides you and your child from one part of the day to the next; the ability to verbally lay down this path is called a 'governing' or 'parent-governed line of communication'. This is where you guide your child with routine words and phrases so they can happily follow instruction from you, and your little one feels in control of their day as these words and phrases are predictable for them and they move through their day with ease. This is a win–win situation. You make the decisions about key areas of your child's day based on your wisdom and desire to meet their best long-term needs but your child feels in control of it all. When this balance is not struck we see tears and tantrums from not just the baby, but from a tired and confused mum and dad too. As I see it, there are four typical styles of communication I encounter when I go into a house where parents are experiencing significant difficulties at sleep time or with daytime behaviour:

1. Basic communicators with no definition

Those who talk clearly about the upcoming events, and state a clear expectation of behaviour, but fail to follow through and define the statement; for example, 'Nearly time for a nappy change, Charlie'; then 'Time for a nappy change, lie down'; followed closely by the child rolling over when placed on the change table. The baby then spends the next few minutes trying to crawl away and crying each time he is laid down again. It means the statement by the parent, 'lie down', has not been defined, and Charlie has not been shown what it means to not try to get up. Charlie thinks 'lie down' means 'roll over' because that is what he is allowed to do each time that statement is made.

2. Delayed communicators

Those who do not talk clearly about upcoming events, or state expectations. This is generally because they do not think their baby will be able to understand them so they don't tend to use language consistently enough until their baby starts to talk to them. These mums and dads generally feel they have never been much for talking, and occasionally they state that they feel like they are being fake or insincere. These parents think through everything clearly in their head but rarely share the information with their baby or toddler. They will, however, say indirect statements like 'Come on, let's go!'

3. Nervous and uncertain communicators

They are the parents who turn every statement into a question. They either make everything a question automatically, without even thinking about it, or make it a question because they have predicted their baby or toddler will get upset at the statement and impending transition. Good examples of this are: 'Are you ready to lie down for nappy change?' 'Do you want some lunch?' 'Do you want to have a bath?' 'Should we go inside?' or 'Do you want to have a sleep?' This is not to say that there is anything wrong with asking questions; in fact you are encouraged to ask questions at appropriate times for at least one-third of a baby or toddler's waking day. It's just that you need to refrain from asking a question around an event that needs your guidance.

Using predictable and consistent ways of communicating with your baby throughout the day is the only way to reduce or eliminate tears significantly when teaching them a new routine around sleeping, eating, or playing independently.

Often, when I ask these parents to make a clear statement, they attempt to do so but use a downward inflection (see page 59), which makes the statement sound uncertain or like a question. If you know your baby or toddler has to come inside from the garden, or needs a nappy change, or has to sit down and have their dinner, or a bath, or to have a sleep so they can feel better and enjoy their day, then you will need to guide them confidently by saying it in a more appropriate way, like 'It's time for a sleep / to have lunch / to go inside / to have your nappy changed'. That full stop is symbolically important here.

4. Confusing communicators

Now, while some people are real talkers and naturally use a forewarning stream of language as well as offer clear pre-empting cues (see page 40), they are not necessarily routine with their style of communication. Unpredictable communication that is clear but not repetitious is more difficult for a baby to grasp, and therefore it may take much longer for your little one to understand you and be relaxed with you guiding their day; for example, 'Time to change your nappy' said one day, then 'C'mon, let's get rid of that poo' the next, followed by 'Let's get you some new pants, Mr stinky bum!' the day after.

The flow of communication approach (see page 40) ensures you are using your language appropriately, and that your actions in defining that statement help your little one to learn what you are saying, and then to understand what each of your language cues actually means. This is how you empower your children with the feeling of control over a situation that you are governing. They feel in charge because they can predict what you will do, and what their role during that time actually is. Once you have learnt the appropriate flow of communication, it's important to dig a little deeper to fully understand the importance of your language in your baby's life.

How well do you communicate?

This checklist will give you an understanding of where you are now and what you need to consider to ensure you are truly ready to start communicating clearly with your under-two year old.

Do you understand and believe in your motivation for guiding your little one?	YES / NO
Are you willing to be consistent, therefore trustworthy?	YES / NO
Are you being specific with language?	YES / NO
Are you being specific with the praise you give?	YES / NO
Are you conscious of your role in building their self-esteem through language?	YES / NO
Do you fully understand separation anxiety, and ways of reducing the stress to your baby?	YES / NO
Have you learnt how to communicate and teach your little one through role play?	YES / NO
Have you and your partner established your family boundaries together?	YES / NO

Some of these points you will have already considered, while some will be new concepts for you. This means that for the new areas brought up, or indeed with questions you may not understand, there is much to be discovered as you read more in this communication section of the *Dream Baby Guide*. When you have completed reading the section on communication, come back to this checklist and do it again, and see how different your understanding will be. By the time you are well into your new style of communicating with your child you will have considered all of these questions, will understand them, and will be using them with ease.

Make the time to make it work

Between the ages of six and 12 months, your baby will need quite a bit of repetition communication from you in order to learn to understand your statements, which means you need to stay with them and repeat your statements and be patient. I always make sure that when I know I need to teach a child of this age not to touch the oven door, I ensure I don't have a million other things to do that will distract me, or get frustrated by the time it may take to teach the baby to understand that 'no touch' means 'no touch'. It may only take two to five consistent statements and true definition for your little one to learn the message but each one of these sessions will require your full attention and real patience.

By 12 to 15 months, you will still need to be repetitive and follow through, but the process will be much faster, so you won't need to allocate as much time to teaching them something new. From 15 months all the way up to two years, if you are having trouble establishing your parent-governed line of communication, you need to be a little prepared. You will encounter a far more behaviourally motivated resistance from your baby, which means you will need to stay calm, compassionate and ultra-confident while still appearing to have all the time in the world to achieve the stated request and outcome.

> Make sure you allow the time to set your child up and equip them for coping in the big wide world so they can confidently and happily engage with their peers and their carers.

Remember, you're on their team and helping them, and have to understand that for them this is tricky. You should not be at loggerheads with you child . . . ever. Empathy is your key here.

I always say that you should manage your child with the same amount of spirit and determination as they possess, but always stay on their side and be empathetic and compassionate while you follow through. If they are bold and confident then that is wonderful, and you should parent them with the same boldness and confidence. If they are overly bossy and entirely inflexible however, then they need you to be strong, clear and absolutely consistent, all without going into battle with them.

I can assure you now that if you do not take the time to teach your child to co-operate and be flexible, then their little friends and teachers at kindergarten will do this, and that might be a bit of a shock to your child. Make sure you allow the time to set your child up and equip them for coping in the big wide world so they can confidently and happily engage with their peers and their carers. To allow them to throw a tantrum or scream when faced with an event that isn't governed by them means you are leaving them ill prepared to cope outside the home when interacting with others.

I know that, given the choice, any parent would prefer to be the one to help their toddler to learn how to be a little flexible and to have some basic social skills as far as elementary communication goes, rather than leave it to the kindergarten playground or a childcare professional. If followed, the flow of communication (see page 40) will do this for you, and for your child.

The three lines of communication

Life as a child is full of new and challenging things, and the ability to be a loving tour guide to them during these early years of life, where you can share your wisdom, is one of the most balanced and caring things you can ever do when preparing your little one for the big wide world. This involves three simple lines of communication:

1. A **child-governed line of communication** is where your child makes a request and you happily oblige. The child governs the outcome of a situation. This is healthy and balanced and it is good for learning communication skills and independence. To be balanced, however, it should constitute only about one-third of a child's waking day from when they are six months old onwards.
2. In a **parent-governed line of communication** you make a request and they happily oblige. This is the parent governing the outcome of a situation. This too is healthy and balanced, and is good for their learning of communication skills, social skills and for developing their emotional tool kit.
3. A mutually agreed-upon line of communication, called a 'negotiation', is the final communication line introduced, and it comes into play most often after a child is 12 months of age. You must establish clear child- and parent-governed lines of communication before introducing a healthy balance of negotiation opportunities. This should constitute one-third of a toddler's waking hours from 12 to 15 months onwards. This line should never replace a parent-governed line, but rather be additional to it.

These three lines of communication are what you must start to use with your child from four to six months of age all the way through to school and beyond. Ultimately they should be used equally throughout a day and there should be respectful boundaries set around each member of the family to ensure that each person can speak and be respectfully heard.

I find that just about every parent I work with is really good at listening to their child's governing line of communication, and is happy to oblige their beautiful baby's every whim, almost to the point of collapse. While a good portion of your language throughout the day will consist of a child-governed line, and although as they reach toddlerhood the negotiating line of communication will kick in, there are many repetitive times during each and every day when you need to guide your child because they are simply too little to appropriately run the event without your intervention. This is the one line of communication everyone seems to neglect, yet is absolutely crucial when asking your baby to, say, go to sleep and stay asleep, or eat or play at particular times. This is the parent-governed line of communication and it enables you to be a loving guide and teacher who knows that meeting a child's every demand is not meeting their long-term needs and best interests.

Time to be a teacher and a guide

Ideally, while your baby is still young and at home with you, you want to be the one to teach them what it's like to be guided, to have to wait, to sometimes have to do things differently, or to sometimes just trust others. To never provide those opportunities through your loving and patient guidance at home means you will be leaving these important life lessons to others who will not know your child as intimately as you, or not have as much time or patience to gently help them through this time as you would. This is obviously a crucial line of communication, especially for sleep, for a series of reasons.

We need to be able to ask our children to look to us for guidance, and to co-operate when we put them to bed if we are to correct any typical sleep-time problems. They are learning to trust the emotions they are feeling when we are guiding them, and learning that those emotions are normal and safe. If they are to sleep through the night or for a significant period of time during the day, they have to be able to let you put them into bed and leave them in the conditions they will encounter multiple times throughout any sleep period, which is generally being tucked into their soft warm bed in their own little room, and without you in the room.

They need to understand that you are consistent with your parent-governed line of communication, and that these situations are not designed to be a negotiation. After they have had the opportunity to practise this routine event of you guiding them at various other times of the day, each day, they will be empowered with all the information they need to recognise what is required of them at sleep time. They have to be comfortable with relinquishing a little control of certain aspects of their day to someone else . . . and that takes some practice. You need to ask your children to be co-operative at sleep time and at other event routines where you govern the situation, so you need to give them every opportunity during the day to understand the parent-governed style of communicating from the age of four to six months so they have a chance to get used to this normal situation.

Evidence of communication imbalance

If your communication is lacking in the area of the parent-governed line, your baby will not cope terribly well with you transitioning them from one part of the day to the next. These are some classic signs that you are inconsistent or behind in the parent-governed line of communication:

- Nappy changing time—they try to roll over and crawl away. Most parents without a governing line in place have felt they needed to do away with the change table altogether by around eight to ten months for safety reasons.
- Getting dressed—they arch their back, flail around and get very upset until you pick them up or stand them up.
- Getting in the high chair—they become stiff, arch backwards and try to kick off the seat so you can't sit them down.
- Staying in the high chair—they scream and throw everything off the table before demanding you get them out within three to eight minutes (their attention span) whether they have eaten adequately or not. They often won't let you put a bib on them.
- You feeding them—they shake their head, wave their hands, hit the spoon, pull the spoon out of your hand, cover their mouth with their forearm, or put their mouth on the tray or back of the seat, all while pulling those impossibly cute but quite relentless 'you can't feed me!' faces.
- Getting into the car seat—they become stiff, and slide out of the seat towards the floor as you struggle to get them into a sitting position so you can do up the buckle.
- Getting into the pram—they become stiff like the high chair scenario, and often get very, very cross at you (even at eight months). However, they may still settle fairly fast if you move confidently.
- Staying in the pram—they insist on being carried, and if you don't pick them up quickly, they squirm out of their buckles and try to stand in their pram. If they are unable to stand yet, they will cry and this is often

accompanied by them turning to face you and gesturing to be picked
up with little up-stretched arms.

- Not stopping the pram—they will cry if you do stop it or, if old enough,
they will attempt to move the pram by rocking their little bodies forward
repeatedly. If you do not go quickly, they get cross. This is often
accompanied by them turning to face you and gesturing to be
picked up.

- Demanding to be picked up all day at home and crying continually
until they are on your hip is very common if it is an option for them—
it's their way of doing the 'but please, please, please can I, please, please,
please'–type of relentless badgering that an eight year old is very good
at . . . come on, you all remember doing it! They will go and go and
go unless you say a very definitive 'yes' or 'no'. They crawl to your legs
and precariously try to stand up, often trying to squish between you
and the kitchen bench, pushing you out of their way and crying until
they either fall over at which point they become very, very upset, or
you pick them up.

- Playing with things you don't want them to—they reach for the curtains,
the TV and remote controls, around the pot plants, rubbish bins, etc.,
and you are always having to go over to the baby and to move them
physically away or to take every possible item out of their reach. Parents
who have not set forward expectations for their baby by the time they
are crawling, typically find it difficult to set boundaries around these
sorts of items.

- Not playing independently—they demand your constant attention and
cling on to you. I call these little ones 'Velcro babies', as they are
permanently attached at the hip to mum or dad. In the most extreme
cases they look like a little monkey when you attempt to sit them on
the floor, and when you try to put the baby down without sitting with
them it results in tears. These babies may still squirm down and venture
off to play on their own terms, but that is a child-governed line and is
very different to when you ask them to play.

- Sitting happily on your lap—they are unable to keep sitting and focus
on a task. They insist on standing, or try to slide down your arm
confused that they may be meant to have a breastfeed. Most of the time
you need to stand up with them, or allow them to stand on your lap or
they become very unsettled.

- Can't drift off to sleep—they become upset when you attempt to put
them into their cot, which results in you having to assist them to sleep.

The assistance often includes milk feeds, nursing, rocking, patting, shushing, lying next to them, holding firmly, etc.

- Going back to sleep—if you are having to assist your baby to sleep, they will obviously need to be assisted back to sleep when they wake up too early.

In addition to the above areas of difficulty, we could expect a toddler between 12 and 15 months of age who is experiencing difficulties with communication and guidance to also have problems in some other areas. Some examples include:

- not coming inside after playing outdoors
- not packing away toys and books or other play things
- not holding your hand when you're out and about
- pinching or scratching or smacking others when they feel cross
- not listening and paying attention—they have learnt that when someone speaks, it generally means they can continue to do what they were doing, which means they have not learnt how valuable communication is, so simply tune out
- not letting you watch your television shows.

Does any of that sound familiar? These are just some examples of the more typical daytime problems that arise from an underdeveloped parent-governing line of communication.

Without a parent-governed line of communication there is no way in the world you should be embarking on any form of sleep training where you expect them to allow you to guide them without expecting a lot of stress and tears from your baby or toddler. You need to address and establish this basic foundation of communication first and foremost. By not having it you definitely cause the child stress and confusion during any sleep-time attempts. This is why those basic crying management routines, regardless of what form is suggested, are incomplete and unbalanced. You need to established a good parent-governed line of communication before all else.

It is in the first two years of a child's life that the emphasis on their responses to you and the environment around them is aimed squarely at their ability to understand, predict and therefore trust their mummy and daddy.

You will quickly be able to recognise if your child is feeling overburdened with running the day, because you will notice the symptoms above. It's not hard to turn this around. Anyone who has worked with me has seen how remarkably quick a child's ability can be to understand a really simple request or flow of events. People are amazed at how happy and content they can become and how quickly an unsettled baby can relax and settle with a good parent-governed line of communication put in place. Taking the time to learn how to talk to and with your baby or toddler is one of the most loving and considerate things parents can do for their child.

It is in the first two years of a child's life that the emphasis on their responses to you and the environment around them is aimed squarely at their ability to understand, predict and therefore trust their mummy and daddy. At no point would a child between the age of six months and two years of age ever be deliberately not listening or deliberately not co-operating with you. That's not to say that they won't clearly express a desire to not do as you have asked sometimes, if they think that there is another option. If your child is having difficulties during the day, you need to look very closely at your parent-governed line of communication to be certain you are developing the environment they need to trust and feel safe with you running any portion of their day. To not develop your language skills means your child may feel vulnerable, and will therefore struggle against your guidance or anyone else's.

Children are always so very happy to accept guidance when asked confidently, but it is perfectly natural that they will try to challenge you if they are tired. This is where you need to take the burden off them entirely, as far as decision making goes. If your parenting style is clear and direct when they are tired, you can avoid major behavioural problems because they will be able to relax and trust that you will guide them. Once they become tired, children are desperate for predictability and will tend to become boisterous and bossy to retain the governing line of each situation. This is why we need to teach them about boundaries, so we can bring them back into our care and guidance, and help stop them feeling so overwhelmed.

2
Be a respectful and loving guide

Taking the time to establish a clear and predictable style of communication with your baby is so much more valuable than just establishing good sleep patterns. Sleep-time disruptions are a direct reflection of some form of imbalance during the day, be it a routine, the way you communicate, at meal times or perhaps any number of causes. By adopting a balanced and healthy parenting philosophy, where your gaze is fixed firmly on conveying your wishes and intentions clearly to your baby or toddler, you can open simple, easy-to-understand and trustworthy lines of communication. This will promote happy playing, no-fuss eating and a predictable flow to the day that helps you and your baby relax and get the most out of this extraordinary first two years of their life. In turn it also ensures your child feels empowered. They will have a clear understanding of each situation through familiarity and you will have the confidence that your precious baby has had the right balance of food, sleep and stimulation throughout the day to encourage a full undisturbed night's sleep.

It is possible to see many unfortunate examples of controlling parents who have left their children damaged or ill prepared to cope with the complexities of life as an independent adult. As concerning to me, however, are the equally extreme parenting philosophies that wholeheartedly promote beliefs in exactly the opposite in a bid to redress the past. Sadly, these give a growing child, who is new to the world, nearly 100 per cent control, which will result in a generation of children who are unable to accept guidance, who disregard authority and who are inflexible and controlling of all those around them. This is not a good thing either. What will happen to this generation of controlling and inflexible children when they become parents? Will they grow up and be controlling of their children and repeat a generational cycle? Without thought and intervention, our society then shifts from controlled children as the result of controlling parents, to controlled parents as the result of controlling children. This can become a perpetual cycle in some families and be extremely destructive. Then there are parents who adopt a balanced middle ground, where their child is respected and able to make decisions and control certain aspects of their life but who still provide the guidance crucial for a child to be safe and able to grow up to be a contributing, conscientious and empathetic member of society. They are also ensuring their child will be a great future parent to their grandchildren: a truly amazing gift to pass on.

> By adopting a balanced and healthy parenting philosophy, where your gaze is fixed firmly on conveying your wishes and intentions clearly to your baby or toddler, you can open simple, easy-to-understand and trustworthy lines of communication.

Where lies the balanced middle ground then? Where and how do you ensure you are able to retain a healthy concern over the direction of your children and family without being controlling, and giving your children the same level of healthy personal direction and control without letting them become controlling? For me, it lies in those moments when a child anticipates what they are required to do when they move from one daily routine to another. This is where you have taught them what to do so they feel a level of control and personal direction, yet you established the original event routine based on wisdom.

Being predictable

The predictability of each and every event in a child's day is what helps them settle down and enjoy the transitions that naturally occur when you complete one part of the day and move on to the next. Babies transition dozens of times a day, and it's during these times they feel most vulnerable. This is for a couple of reasons. Firstly, they are impulsive and see no reason to move on from one activity to another. Secondly, babies are intelligent and like to look for patterns to follow—humans are classically creatures of habit. If you do not tell your child what to expect, everything suddenly becomes chaotic for them; they feel unsafe, which usually results in tears or clingy and demanding behaviour. By becoming demanding, a baby aims to restore a sense of control and predictability to their day, no matter how inappropriate their behaviour may be to achieve it.

Almost all the tears I encounter outside basic needs like hunger, tiredness, comfort and love occur during transitional episodes of the day when a parent is guiding the event without adequate communication being put in place. The tears from their child are obviously behaviour based. The baby feels out of control and it is making them feel uncomfortable, angry or frustrated. Almost every parent I work with misreads these tears and looks for some form of medical reason—teething, tired, sore tummy, food allergy, colic, reflux, for example. I am not saying that these conditions do not exist, or that they do not cause discomfort; you simply need to make sure you are assessing the cause of the tears based on their pattern of behaviour.

Notice how tears at transitional episodes occur only during a parent-guided time of the day; never when the baby requests a transition themselves, like when they squirm out of your arms to be put down on the floor to play. Clearly they are aware of the change that is about to occur when they guide it, but it is when you instigate a change without adequate communication in place, or for the first time, that you will see them become unsettled. Can you imagine how uncomfortable you would feel if you stayed at a friend's house and no one told you where you would be sleeping or what they have planned for the day and night? You would feel on edge and probably wouldn't be able to relax because you'd need to watch your hosts to work out what's what and what's expected when. Imagine how this must feel for a baby or toddler every single day if no one was keeping them informed.

Because all children are unique in their personality, there will always be some babies who are not terribly affected by others guiding them throughout the day, remaining relaxed and easygoing with or without clear instruction. On the other hand, I have been absolutely run off my feet for the last ten years because there are so many babies who find it extremely stressful and unsettling to be without clear communication throughout the day. By adopting a simple flow of communication you can empower your baby with the insight of knowing what you expect of their behaviour during an event. This allows you to guide them during the day, which then ensures they attain the vital coping tools they need to be comfortable with what you and they are doing at sleep time.

I believe that as parents it is our role to create predictability around routine daily events, such as meal times, bath time, sleeping times, to teach our babies the way to do these things. When someone asks me, 'When is my baby going to learn how to sleep?', my only answer is, 'When you teach them!' You must be able to guide them, and in order to guide them you must be able to communicate clearly with them. It's not difficult, but it does mean making a deliberate effort on your part. The reward of watching your child confidently picking up these skills far outweighs any effort you might put in.

Without a doubt—and I say this with the experience of explaining to many parents how to do this—the ability to understand and subsequently communicate with your baby on a deep and intimate level are achievable goals for any parent. All the families I have worked with over the past 15 years, regardless of the severity of the disruption they are experiencing, have been able to quickly learn effective communication skills to understand their babies or toddlers and to restore harmony to their home in as little as two to five days. The challenge after that lies only in maintaining a confident style of parenting and communication.

> When someone asks me, 'When is my baby going to learn how to sleep?', my only answer is, 'When you teach them!'

Once you have embarked on your new confident communication approach, you will need to give yourselves and your little one a good three to four weeks to feel absolutely comfortable with it. The bulk of the learning will happen for you within a five-day period, but learning to be consistent parents will take you far longer. Go easy on yourself and don't get frustrated. As time progresses, you will see baby or toddler settle right down and relax as they learn that you are predictable enough to trust, and you will feel more ably equipped to guide this beautiful little life on a healthy path to middle childhood.

Finding the balance

The only way to ensure we break the nexus from one generation of controlling parents to the next generation of controlled parents is to create a balance in our communication streams. When I talk about communication I know many people think, 'I don't really understand what my baby is trying to tell me'. Let me show you where this is not quite the right philosophy when you are dealing with a baby or toddler.

People invite me into their homes because they are desperately trying to help their baby by listening intently to everything their, very often, upset little one is telling them. They give them all the feeds they demand, they pace with them for as long as they ask, and pick them up every time they request it. This, they believe, means they are *hearing* what their baby is trying to tell them. After all, the baby knows when it's hungry, has a full nappy, is feeling a little sore in the tummy, or simply wants a feed to feel happy even when they aren't hungry. Once the parent has addressed all of their child's demands and the little one is still upset, they start looking for medical reasons for the tears. Surely if they have done everything the baby has asked, then wouldn't that make the baby happy?

Well, doing everything a baby demands does not equal a happy baby. While listening to your baby is still extremely important, and usually a well-established skill for most parents when I'm called in, to just listen is not a balanced approach. It's often the baby's level of crying that makes a parent think they must be very bad at interpreting what their little one is saying, but that is absolutely *not* the case.

The main problem is you can't always look to a baby for guidance about how to make them happy because they actually don't often know what they need. A baby might stay up all night if you let them guide you, but it is certainly not what they need and it won't ultimately make them happy. This is because a baby is impulsive and does not understand consequences. A baby may refuse solids and opt for what they know—breast or bottle milk—but their subsequent hunger during the middle of the night and their grumpy moods indicate that drinking just milk is insufficient.

I'll give you an example from an adult's perspective. I have just entered a distressed family's home. I observe the scene. The baby is upset, the parents are looking desperately to their baby for guidance to make her feel better but they are getting nowhere in helping settle their little one down. I always ask the same thing: 'Okay, you've called me in as an authority on this situation, what exactly do you want from me?'

The parents almost always look at me desperately, often on the verge of tears: 'We have never done this before, we desperately need help, we don't know what to do. Can you please just tell us or show us what to do?'

Now I do have some wisdom in the area of making babies happy that I could share with them, but imagine if I didn't share it. How much confidence would a parent have in me if I then spent our entire day together asking them what I should do to improve the situation they are in, or look to them for guidance? They would lose faith in me altogether, they would become upset, and they would probably get frustrated or angry at me.

Well BINGO!

This is *exactly* what a baby is saying to a parent when they are upset: 'Help me feel better, mum and dad. Tell me what to do, I just don't know.'

I am constantly finding parents wanting the best for their baby but only ever looking to their child for answers. This is an incomplete communication style. You are the guide. You must make executive decisions for your baby that you *know* will improve the situation so they can feel happy in the long run.

Your baby only knows what they have experienced. What have you taught them to do when they are tired—be feed, patted, lie on your shoulder while you pace with them? Then that will be all they know. They do not have the logic at this early age to think of a better way. So this is where you need to help them. Not only do you need to show them how to do things better, but you need to take the burden off them.

When I walk into a house and spend time with a new family with very little experience at parenting, I take the burden off them immediately. I say look to me for guidance, I will show you a better way. And each time the parents or the baby does something that I feel will make theirs or their baby's life stressful, I correct them and show them a new way. Sometimes that brings tears, sometimes not, but it always means that if a brand new solution can be learnt then there will not be any more tears in that area.

When there are tears from the child or the parent, I don't crumble into a heap; I am confident. Why? Because I know I know more about this particular scenario than they do because I have more experience than them. And this brings us to another part of my philosophy: as parents, you need to learn to trust yourselves. You know you love your baby and you know you would never make a decision for them from a place other than love. So build your confidence on that platform and you can help your baby to be happy.

Your flow of communication

Ultimately, you are aiming for a framework for communication that you can use at home, take to grandma and grandpa's or playgroup, take on vacation, and essentially use anywhere, but, more importantly, it will mirror the style of language that your little one will encounter when they are no longer under the protective shelter of your wings. Essentially you want a flow of communication that is basic in application and simple to understand; a way of saying 'here we are now', 'this is where were going next', and 'this is the expectation of your behaviour' to ensure that the upcoming event is pleasant and stress free for everyone. When you reach the next location you begin again, 'So here we are now', 'This is where you're going next', and 'These are my expectations of your behaviour'.

I call this 'laying a path in words' and in a nutshell it contains six steps (see box on page 41). You govern, they control, and everyone wins. This way you can impart wisdom on to your children about the best ways to go about doing things, and how to cope with the feelings that come up at certain times in the most effective way. This is the beginning of developing social skills, and it ensures you start to equip your precious baby with their vital emotional tool kit.

Your primary intention when communicating with children under the age of two years should be fully focused on *being understood*. This means you must be 100 per cent accountable for what you say, and the clarity you

The six steps of the flow of communication

For a baby to get comfortable with you providing a predictable style of language, you should start it when your baby is six months old—a great parenting plan.

These six steps are very important for children ranging from eight to ten months of age and absolutely vital for 12 to 15 month olds plus. Remember that it is a better plan to use this flow of communication in all aspects of their day, not just the areas with which they are having difficulty. This way your child can develop good associations with this style of language and feel confident that understanding is achievable.

1. Pre-empting
State what you are doing now and what you will be doing next. For example: 'Now we are ___A___, but soon it will be time to ___B___.'

2. Forewarning
Provide a final warning to baby that transition is about to take place: 'Last one bubby, nearly time to ___B___.'

3. Stating event and expectation
For example, you can say 'Time to change your nappy, time to lie down and wait for mummy'.

4. Defining your statement
Define each and every statement with its true definition; for example, 'Lie down and wait' does not mean roll over and get on your knees; it simply means, 'lie down and don't try to get up'.

5. Following through
Regardless of their reaction to the request or statement made, you continue enthusiastically until the task is completed. For instance, your baby must realise they are to stay on their back and not roll over on to their side, let alone get up on to their knees. Otherwise your statement and conflicting definition will confuse your child and they may think that 'lie down' means 'roll over and get up'.

6. Completion
Wrap up the event with a clear statement that indicates it's all finished now and they can guide you again.

These six steps are important and you should refer back to them often. A good idea here would be to flag this page with a Post-it Note so you can find it easily.

give to each statement. Let's look at the six steps of the flow of communication (as outlined in box) in more detail.

1. Pre-empting

This is where you state the task your child is involved with now, and what they can expect to happen next: 'Lachlan can help daddy feed the puppy dog now, but then it's time for a bath. *Nearly time* to sit down and wait for daddy. Now, where's that puppy's food?' If you look at this pre-emptive dialogue you will see it involved three stages:

1. stating the current event the child is involved in: 'Lachlan can help daddy feed the puppy dog'
2. stating the upcoming event and your expectations of their behaviour: 'Then it's going to be time for a bath; time to sit down and wait for daddy'
3. and finally finishing on a positive by redirecting his attention back to the what he was engaged with: 'Where's that puppy's food?' This final redirection can be helpful where a child is unhappy with the next event, that is the bath. This final stage will enable you to prepare them for the next event, and quickly get them back into the current enjoyable task to avoid tears and tantrums. This means that by the time you mention it next, it won't be such a big surprise and is unlikely to trigger as strong a reaction as it might have if simply sprung on the child.

To use a pre-emptive line of communication upfront is being considerate because it ensures you empower your child with an understanding of what's going to happen in their day before it unfolds. This prevents tears because they don't feel unsettled or frightened by any unexpected changes in their daily routine. During the first two years of a child's life they like to know exactly what is going on and, let's face it, can be a little more assertive than any of us ever expect; however, because of their age, they don't always make the most appropriate choices.

What we are aiming to do by pre-empting is to reduce the amount of time you will have to spend either correcting inappropriate behaviour or dealing with it. By providing a routine for your child that you have actually established yourself, you will create a predictable timetable that your baby will ultimately feel they own and control because they can pre-empt the next stage of the day. This is a win–win situation; you are able to appropriately structure the day based on your baby's true needs, and they will still feel in control of their day because you have made it predictable for them. This is the key to a content and happy baby or toddler.

Now a 24-hour routine structure obviously does not allow your little one to predict all the changes in their day, and it's because of this that tears—and, by 12 months of age, full-scale tantrums—can start to appear. It's so easy for adults to know their next movements and forget to let their child know. Be sure to always articulate your plans for each section of the day, 30 minutes in advance. Imagine if you had just sat down and had grand plans to finally read the paper and your partner took you by the hand and put you in the car and you had no idea what was going on or where you were going. You would be really put out by this, and rightly so, so it's important to remember that your children are exactly the same.

By using your pre-emptive language consistently and making it a simple part of your communication style within your family unit, you will create harmony instantly. You will also teach your children to be open, expressive and respectful of your desire and need to be involved in their plans for the day. This respectful, open and sharing style of communication will follow them right through their childhood, adolescence and into their adulthood.

Hot tip! Always use your flow of communication prior to predictable trouble times, such as meal times, nappy changing times, when going to bed or to daycare / someone's house. You'll be reassuring your baby and getting them ready to smoothly transition from one event to another.

2. Forewarning

This is where you transition your child from one event to another smoothly with a two- to five-minute warning of the upcoming changes. This ensures your baby has a last minute to prepare and knows where they're moving to next, thus empowering them with general control of their day and preventing tears or the dreaded tiny tantrum. While you govern it, they own it and feel in control of it.

From this point on, get into the habit of always articulating your plans for your child at each transition of the day, two to five minutes in advance. Just like pre-empting, state the current event, state the upcoming event and your expectations of their behaviour, and finish on a positive by giving them something to look forward to so that you encourage them to co-operate. For example, if you plan to pack away the toys and sit them down for lunch, say 'Lachlan, last one, then it's time to pack away toys so we can sit down for lunch. Blocks in the box. Yummy chicken and vegetables and your favourite Wiggles spoon.'

When you plan to wipe their face and hands, and then take them to change their nappy, it would sound a little like this: 'Okay Lachlan, it's nearly time for mummy to wipe your face and hands and then it's time to change your nappy, nearly time to lie down and wait for mummy. I wonder which toy you're going to play with today while I change your nappy.'

3. Stating event and expectation

As opposed to the 'nearly time to' of the pre-emptive step, this portion of the flow says it's now 'time to' transition into your next event. This is where your little one may resist you a little, but with lots of forewarning you can help them understand what 'it's time to' actually means. You would take your little one to their, say, high chair and pat the seat, saying 'It's time to sit down and wait for mummy'.

Be sure you are careful about how you manage this stage of flow. If I say to a child 'Sit down and wait' I do everything I can to not confuse them and to ensure they get the true meaning of that statement by always getting them to sit down for me. Don't you get confused here: you're not negotiating. You don't say 'Would you like to sit down and wait?' because you are open for their answer, and it might just be 'No'. This is a clear parent-governed event and it is not up for negotiation. This is how you teach a baby to know when to relax and allow you to guide them. If you taint your parent-governed statement here by saying 'when I say it's time to sit down, it means sit down . . . but if you cry, arch your back, hit me, you don't have to', then you will literally be encouraging tears every time you ask them to sit down, or ask them to do anything for that matter. This is why you need to define your statement.

4. Defining your statement

Defining your statement is the difference between being a good communicator or being someone who makes little sense to your baby. The ability to be aware of exactly what you have said to your child, and then being considerate enough to show them what that statement actually means, is far more simple than dealing with the fallout that occurs when your baby or toddler cannot listen to you because you make no sense to them. So think about what your style of communication is teaching them.

When you say 'No touching daddy's computer' what are you actually defining with that statement? Do you pick them up and move them somewhere new? If you repeatedly do this, a baby either gets upset because they weren't finished playing with the object, or simply turns and heads straight back to the object to continue with their play. This is when I find most parents become frustrated and think their baby is not listening to them. In fact, you haven't taught them what your original statement actually meant. Simply taking them away from an object appears the easiest thing to do, but it does not teach them what 'no touch' means. It is just a short-term solution and will not prevent this same scenario playing out over and over again, particularly if your baby has taken a real shine to the colourful buttons that everyone else seems to be allowed to play with.

Try to see it from your baby's perspective. Imagine you are relaxing after a long day, sitting on the lounge and flicking through a magazine. Your husband then says to you, '*Ne lisez pas ce livre*'. You look at him and he just looks back at you with raised eyebrows, then looks away. You have no idea what he just said but you figure, as he looked away, it mustn't be important. You carry on relaxing but then he come over to you and repeats, '*Ne lisez pas ce livre*', before taking you to the kitchen to look at the coffee machine. You look at the coffee machine for a while because he is pressing all the buttons for you. It's quite interesting, but when you have finished looking at it, you automatically go back to what you were doing before, which was relaxing with your magazine. This is where your partner sighs and comes over again and repeats, '*Ne lisez pas ce livre*', before enthusiastically taking you to see the new alarm clock in the bedroom.

Each time you have finished looking at what your partner has shown you, you simply go back to doing what you were enjoying. The statement, '*ne lisez pas ce livre*', has no meaning to you because each time he says it, he takes you to see something different. By now you have stopped listening to him; it's just easier to look out for where he is going to take you next, or if he is going to take you somewhere new. So what does '*ne lisez pas ce livre*' actually mean? I'm going to show you how to define this statement in a way that will teach you what its true definition is.

Imagine again you are relaxing after a long day, sitting on the lounge and flicking through a magazine. Your husband says to you, '*Ne lisez pas ce livre*'. You look at him and he comes over to you and taps the magazine, shakes his head and repeats, '*Ne lisez pas ce livre*'. He takes the magazine out of your hand and places it on the coffee table repeating, '*Ne lisez pas ce livre*'. You look at him then reach out to pick up the magazine again but he waves his hand in front of the magazine and repeats, '*Ne lisez pas ce livre*'. Each time you go to reach for the magazine he blocks your hand or waves over the magazine and repeats, '*Ne lisez pas ce livre*' as he shakes his head. He then hands you the remote to the television and says '*Vous pouvez regarder la television*'. He gives you a hug, points to the magazine and shakes his head again and says '*Ne lisez pas ce livre*', then points to the television and smiles repeating, '*Vous pouvez regarder la television*'.

It is quite clear that he doesn't want you to read the magazine but suggests you watch some television instead. His actions and persistence of communication and intervention define his statements for you. This is exactly how your children learn. You must speak and define the statement by physically encouraging them to stop touching the computer until they understand what 'no touching daddy's computer' means.

The other mistake people make when it comes to defining a statement is to give a statement an incorrect meaning, and then get upset with their child for doing what they have taught them the statement means. A classic example is when you say 'Lie down while mummy changes your nappy', but then allow the baby to roll over and get up on to their knees. You have taught them that 'lie down and wait for mummy' actually means 'roll over and get on your knees'. Another classic line is 'Sit down for morning tea', but the parents allow the child to stand up and walk away with the food in their hand. Here you will have taught them that 'sit down for morning tea' means 'stand up and wander around with your food'!

They are not doing these things because they think they can get away with it, they are not deliberately not listening to you, they are actually doing what they think you have told them to do. It's most distressing to observe parents berating toddlers at shopping malls for acting in a manner that the child has been taught is correct. The child is only following their parent's original instructions and then getting into trouble because the parent has inadvertently directed them to act this way in the first place. Each time I observe this kind of communication the child is clearly confused and often looks heartbroken at the parent's sudden annoyance.

An example of this is a child at a mall walking next to their parent and the parent says 'Hold my hand, please'. The child glances at the parent, then continues walking without taking the parent's hand. The parent continues walking, thinking, 'Oh well, I guess they are okay to not hold my hand', and doesn't follow through on that simple statement. A few minutes later when their toddler, distracted by their surroundings, walks into another person the parent repeats 'Come and hold mummy's hand, please!' Again the child is allowed to continue walking without taking the parent's hand. The statement clearly means to the child, 'nothing changes when mummy says this statement'. When the mother and child reach an escalator, the need to hold the toddler's hand is now a must for safety reason, so the mother repeats the statement impatiently, 'Hold mummy's hand!' The child follows through on its taught definition, 'nothing changes when mummy says this statement', and continues walking without taking their parent's hand. They are doing as they have been shown. Suddenly, the mother grabs her toddler's hand, squeezes firmly, frowns and says 'I said hold mummy's hand' in a firm or cross voice and impatiently pulls the then-shocked baby towards the fast-moving staircase. You can imagine the rest of this event.

One of the most unfair things you can do is to teach your child to not listen, or to think your statements mean something else, and then get upset with them for doing what you have taught them. It's confusing, unfair and why I am so totally and utterly against smacking. Can you imagine if the frustration in this last story culminated in a smack? I do not agree with enforcing co-operation through fear, anyway, but given the fact that communication is a complex issue and easy to inadvertently confuse a child, the idea of smacking them means you are blaming them for the problem that has arisen, and this is almost always never the case. Communication should be viewed as a progressive part of your relationship and, as such, should always be assessed and managed respectfully and compassionately.

Now that you can see the importance of actually defining a statement with its true meaning, the next important thing to do is to feel confident about teaching your child what you mean when you speak. As a parent you have a right, if not a duty of care, to teach this brand new life entrusted into your care about the normal expectations we all have of people's behaviour, and about the boundaries they need to know when they are out of their house and, eventually, out of your immediate care. No matter what parenting style you adopt, the vital skills around defining a statement are the most basic and courteous language tools you can employ to ensure you are acting as a loving and wonderful teacher for your child to learn from.

5. Following through

Once you have defined any language with its true meaning, you need to follow through for as long as it takes to ensure your baby understands this definition fully. This does not mean harping on about it for hours on end; you simply follow through with your words and actions until they stop trying to do anything other than what you are defining, or they acknowledge what you have said.

The way an eight to ten month old will acknowledge your request is by getting cross or upset at being prevented from doing their chosen thing. This is different to not understanding you are making a request of them. When they don't understand you are asking something of them, they just busily repeat the same action over and over regardless of your intervention. It's when they stop and look at you and get cross or upset that they have identified the fact that you are intervening. At this point, you can acknowledge this and say 'Good listening' then repeat your statement, 'No touch the power point', before moving them away to a new activity.

What we are looking for in older babies is recognition from them that you have asked them not to touch the object, or not to do anything other than what you have stated. In crawlers, this often comes in the form of stopping the action of trying to touch the object, sitting on their bottom and looking at you and the object, and then you again. They may hold their hand out without touching, in which case you will say 'That's right, good listening, mummy said no touch' in a calm, patient manner. You can then clap, or kiss them or just smile warmly. At this point you can move them on to a new activity.

If you have asked them to lie down, then you will obviously want to follow through and continue to prevent your baby from doing anything other than lying down until they stop resisting. You will be offering distractions and staying calm as you reassure them while you follow through with your definition. Once they have understood and accepted the request you can carry on and complete the nappy change or dressing at that point only, but if they start to resist again, you will need to stop focusing on changing the nappy and manage their behaviour.

Remember, your primary intention when communicating with children under the age of two years should be to fully focus on being understood. This means you must be 100 per cent accountable for what you say, and the clarity you give to each statement.

The reluctance of a strong-willed little bossy boots does not mean you rush to finish your task. Be cautious to not make the mistake of being rushed along by your baby's temper or you will teach your baby to get stroppy at you to make you hurry up. Carry on with your task, activity or request consistently and patiently until you come to the natural end and then move to the next step of your flow of communication. When you are dealing with a toddler who is quite determined and gets extremely impatient with you, you need to be absolutely consistent, patient and carry on until your little one is listening. Do not rush. Keep a steady pace and stay confident and reassuring.

It all comes down to patience. Just because you are asking your child to listen, it does not mean you should be aggressive, really bossy in your tone or impatient in turn. You can be compassionate: 'Mummy knows it's hard to lie down and wait, I know you feel a little bit cross', but remain consistent with the definition of the statement 'lie down and wait'. You can be patient and sound warm and friendly even when they get cross the first time you ask something of them.

By the time your baby gets to around 15 months of age, their ability to understand and learn is quite extraordinary and you will find you only need to define a basic boundary and follow through a couple of times and they will always understand that boundary from that point on. By the time your beautiful baby is heading for the very exciting and clever 18 months of age, they will be able to learn to happily accept a new boundary with a simple clear request, often without even challenging you if you use clear pre-emptive and forewarning language and role play (see page 631).

The important thing to remember when you are following through with your parent-governed line of communication is that this is meant to make up one-third of their day so don't feel like you are being too bossy when you guide your little one by laying a path in words for them. This is the only and best way for your child to learn the skill of communication. This is a normal healthy balance that will ensure your little baby can relax and not feel burdened with having to run an entire household. The parent-governed line is always the most neglected line of communication because it's the most difficult line to establish, and it is subsequently far too often the point of origin for all crying at sleep time. So, please make sure you invest the time it takes to get this working well for both you and your children.

6. Completion

If you are wanting your child to look to you for guidance, you need to be trustworthy and reliable. In order to be trustworthy and reliable, you need to be consistent, and this is where the completion of the flow of communication becomes absolutely vital. Imagine you correctly take every single step in the flow of communication but then forget to wrap up the event with a line of parent-governed communication. You will be inconsistent with the message you are delivering.

I'll give you an example. At sleep time, you ask your baby to go to sleep, and you define that statement, and after a little grumble or a big protest they go to sleep. Then they wake sometime during the night and cry. You once again ask them to go to sleep and you follow through. Then in the morning when they wake and cry you think to yourself, 'Great, they have had enough sleep', so you walk in and pick them up. Your baby doesn't know 7 a.m. from 2 a.m. so by not allowing them to govern communication at 2 a.m. but allowing them to do so at 7 a.m. is a complete contradiction for them and it only teaches them to always cry just to see what will happen. Can you see how your child will be confused about whether they need to cry to ask you to pick them up? If you did this in the morning, why won't you do it when they wake in the middle of the night?

Your baby / toddler will always be looking to you for guidance to go to sleep, to go back to sleep and about when it is time to get up (see page 605). You cannot say, 'look to me for settling and resettling, but cry to let me know when you want to get up' because this is a completely mixed message and will, in fact, only teach a child to cry. It is up to you to let them know when it's time to get up. When you establish a parent-governed line around all sleep times, you teach your baby that when they wake up they can have a chat or a play, and can trust that you will come in to them in due course and get them up. These little ones don't feel the need to cry out, they are simply happy to be awake in their beds, and happy to have a little chat or play until someone comes to get them up.

3
Step-by-step guide to communicating

Parents who struggled with their first baby always seem to say to me when baby number two comes along: 'Our first baby was two and a half years old before they were able to sleep through the night. I didn't know what they wanted from me as they couldn't talk. I don't want to go through that again. Can you help?' Well, I have never met a six month old who could possibly, even if they could talk, tell a parent how to help them sleep better or to show them how to behave. It's a parent's duty to teach their children how to achieve these basic skills of life. It's essential that you realise this from the very beginning; you are your child's guide.

Helping your baby to, say, sleep peacefully at an early age is far more effective than two years of unsettled, disturbed nights. This is where you need to become your baby's whisperer. In order to have predictable patterns around routine times of the day you need to create a set of conditions that your baby or toddler can, well, predict. These conditions ultimately make them feel in control.

When to say it
We now need to look at creating predictable patterns around routine times of the day. This is called an 'event routine'. These are times when you create a set of conditions that your baby or toddler can predict, and ultimately feel in control of because they know what to expect. Some examples of event routines would be when:

- changing the nappy
- getting dressed
- eating a meal
- getting ready for sleep
- playing independently
- during bath time
- getting in the pram / car / high chair
- coming inside from outside.

As an example of when to say things during a event routine, your flow of communication would run like this:

1. **Pre-empting**, you might say 'Let's read our books, then we go nigh', nigh's'. You go to the couch with two or three books, sit him on your lap facing the books, and have a lovely read for about ten minutes, or until five minutes before the sleep time.
2. The **forewarning** cues throughout your reading experience would be, 'Nearly time to pack away books, nearly time for nigh' nigh's'. Five minutes before bed, you would put the books away and say your sleep cue, 'Nigh', nigh'', and have a cuddle and a kiss with him, and he might then say goodnight to everyone in the room. Keep forewarning him during this routine and say 'It's time for nigh', nigh's' as you walk him or carry him towards his room.
3. Once in his room, close the door, go to his cot and give him a big squishy cuddle and kiss, **stating the event and your expectation** of him by using your cues for sleep. You might sing 'Twinkle twinkle little star', twice through, while you gently and slowly sway with him.
4. Quietly give him a kiss and **define your statement** with your goodnight cue: 'Time for sleep. Mummy and daddy love you. Nigh', nigh'.' Say 'Lie down' before you lie him down.
5. **Follow through** by saying your settling cue and by stroking his hair gently or patting him until your cues are complete. Make sure he is settled in, and ensure he hears your cue, 'Nigh', nigh''. This should be the last thing he hears before you turn and leave the room.
6. At the end of sleep time, use your waking routine to **complete** your flow of communication.

It is important to note here that this above example is not the instructions you follow for settling your little one into bed, it's just as example of applying the flow of communication to your settling routine. The more consistent you are with the way you run all your routines, the actions you make and the words you use, the sooner he will pick up on your cues. Then, you will be effectively communicating with your child.

How to say it

When you start to teach your child you need to ensure the way you deliver a statement is not confusing to them, and you need to be able to deliver it with confidence, so they can relax and trust that you are clearly directing the next portion of the day. This is how you prevent tears from starting and, if they do start, it's the quickest way to see them end. My personal line of communication is so clear and so confident that I am able to develop an immediate bond with a child and assume a primary carer's role within an hour of meeting the child, and they absolutely love me and the guidance I give them. They watch me, and they crawl after me like a little shadow, and they giggle when I talk, or pull one of those beautiful little concentration faces as they listen intently to what I am saying.

> My personal line of communication is so clear and so confident that I am able to develop an immediate bond with a child . . . they absolutely love me and the guidance I give them.

How you communicate with a child is extremely important and how you do it is what could make the difference between success and failure in a communication venture. You need to be able to use your new parent–governed line of communication with confidence. Let's reverse the tables for a moment and put you in the hot seat.

You have a new boss at work. She is clearly your superior, and you need to look to her for guidance but you do have the freedom to make suggestions and offer alternative ideas. There is potential for a balanced, open style of communication within this structure that ensures someone with more experience oversees the running of the business so that safe and sensible decisions remain the focus of all your interactions. Your new boss seems lovely, warm and completely accepting and patient. But from the moment she arrives, every single decision she makes is posed to you as a question:

Do you want to write that report for me?
Should we have a meeting?
Do you want to work late?
Is it okay if I work in my office now?
Can I go home now?

This would indicate to you that your new boss was not confident in her ability to guide you, and quite possibly needs a little help and guidance herself.

Imagine your office was responsible for landing a huge deal, and there is a lot riding on this deal. As a consequence you are anxious about it. If you were more confident and assertive than your boss on a general day-to-day basis, then you would quickly assume a leadership role and offer great suggestions on how to move forward with this deal, and confidently guide the people around you. If your boss then suddenly became assertive for the first time and started to move in a different direction to your plan, you would naturally step down, but find it extremely stressful not knowing what she was doing or how this was going to turn out.

One of two things will generally happen in this scenario. You will either become extremely stressed, demand to know the plan and what you can do to keep the momentum going and grumble about the fact that you had a better plan; it upsets you thinking about how inconsistent your boss can be. Or, you completely spit the dummy, try to continue on your path and lock horns with your boss, hoping she will back down and be less assertive like she usually is. After all, this is all you really know from her, so it's just easier if she assumes her usual social role again.

Well, this is what happens when parents make all their statements a question and only occasionally become assertive. The important thing to become aware of when establishing your parent-governed line of communication, is that sentence structures involving words like 'can I', 'should we', 'could you' are not the only way that you can change a statement to a question. Sometimes all you need to do is simply change the inflection, the pitch of your voice, at the end of a sentence. Try it yourself!

First, say 'Lie down and wait for mummy / daddy' out loud as though you are talking to your child. Now say it again but lift the inflection at the end of the statement. Then say it again but drop the inflection at the end of your statement. Comparing your three tries, which inflection did you naturally use when you first said the statement out loud? If you lifted the inflection, it was a question. If you dropped the inflection, then pat yourself of the back; this is a confident statement. You can understand clearly by the example that an upward inflection turns a statement into a question and the downward infection keeps the statement as a statement.

I live by the rules of respectful communication so, if you ask a question with the use of what grammarians call 'modals'—those words that create the mood of a verb like 'should we', 'could we'—or via the use of an upward inflection at the end of a statement, then you have to expect an answer. You should then respect the answer you are given. If your inflection has indicated that the child can choose to say either 'yes' or 'no', and they have chosen 'no' before you have had a chance to correct your inflection, then you must respect that answer. You can hardly start to establish a respectful two-way open language stream within your house where only your language is respected.

If you catch yourself turning a statement into a question, you can quickly correct yourself by repeating the statement with a clear downward inflection if your child hasn't answered you yet, as they can do with a clear and predictable 'wwaaaahhhhh' as a 'no thanks', or a cry when you go to move them to the new activity, or a clear head shake, or an even clearer 'no' in an older baby and toddler. Once that has occurred you will need to go back to your flow of communication and start again in a few minutes from your forewarning step with a simple statement like 'Okay bubba, last time and then it's time to _____!' statement, with a downward inflection.

If they get cross at that point, then stay confident and follow through as usual with your parent-governed line of communication by defining that statement: 'Last time, and then it's time to sit in your pram' does not mean 'last time, and then it's time to sit in your pram . . . but if you cry then you don't have to sit in your pram', it literally means 'last time, and then it's time to sit in your pram'.

Always remember: ask a question, expect an answer. And respect the answer!

Go easy on yourself. The first step is simply hearing yourself using inappropriate inflection, or using a question style of sentence structure when you are trying to guide your child with a parent-governed line of communication. The second step is hearing it in yourself and quickly correcting it. The final step is thinking it, correcting it, and then saying it correctly. Most parents get a little frustrated with themselves but please don't. It's better to just get on with it and know it's normal to go through a learning process around something that has become automatic. It generally takes about five days of hard work to correct your inflection and sentence structure. Ask your partner to point out any obvious slip-ups. By working together as parents, it helps both you and your partner and encourages you to be tuned into your communication.

The way you respectfully use a parent-governed line of communication with your child is very important to the way your child perceives your guidance, and therefore perceives the vital guidance of others throughout their lives. Just because you are governing a certain part of the day, does not give you the right to be anything other than confident and respectful as well as encouraging and thankful. Just as a toddler can stand and dust themselves off after falling over because his parents have reassured him he is okay, so must we adopt this same reassuring confidence when our child is uncertain in a new routine flow or situation. This is about learning to assess a situation from an adult's perspective and to reassure your little one that they are just fine, even if it feels a little new and uncomfortable to them. This is done through smiles and happy reassuring confidence that is designed to help them recover from tears or fears quickly. This should all be expressed not only in words, but through your enthusiasm and sense of humour, the tone of your voice and even your body language.

Enthusiasm

This is the first point for communication with a child under two. A ten year old once told me I reminded her of a kid on red cordial as she cuddled my arm. It's possibly the best description for how I interact with children. I am excited about life. I can honestly say that I see the world as wonderful, and I have never lost the ability to understand the feeling of joy or wonder or enthusiasm that happens when you experience something new, just as a child does.

Try hard not to ever lose your sense of humour, your enjoyment of watching your beautiful baby's clever way of working out how the world works, your love of life and your desire to be the best possible parent or carer you could ever possibly be. I often sit and listen to a parent say the most unkind and untrue things about themselves, and sit crying in front of their child who looks on wide-eyed. By feeling worthless and allowing shattering inner dialogue to impact your self-esteem around your baby, you simply bully yourself into a place of no confidence. Your baby will be unable to relax if you appear upset as they will instinctively read this as potential danger for themselves and will need to cling to you and try to govern the day to create predictability to calm themselves down.

> The way you respectfully use a parent-governed line of communication with your child is very important to the way your child perceives your guidance . . .

This may sound difficult for some mums who are struggling with postnatal depression, or dads who are terribly concerned for their wife and baby. But what I do know is that it is so easy to speak to yourself in a way that you would never tolerate from anyone else, and it often impacts on your ability to even try something. Your baby will never judge you and no one expects you to be perfect. Disregard all the negative inner dialogue while you are with your baby, and always try to appear happy, confident and full of love and enthusiasm. Even if you have to fake it till you make it, you need to learn how to fall off the path, then get straight back on and try again.

My predominant style of communication is enthusiastic; I usually enjoy most aspects of the day, I have a sense of humour about most events, and I only become more serious when I need to define a statement and help a little one learn a new cue or routine that they are struggling with. Humour is particularly valuable with babies from the age of ten months, and toddlers respond beautifully to quick humour in a stressful situation, where they might normally cry or feel a little anxious. It's possible to change a child's immediate response to certain emotions with positive input. Particularly with a toddler who gets easily embarrassed, it's lovely to help them giggle at some of the things that may happen by sharing the experience and the response with them.

Take every opportunity to make a baby or toddler laugh every chance you get. This is the language of under-two year olds. They love repeated sounds, love to laugh at things that are a little overwhelming and, if caught quickly enough, will laugh as a response to an overwhelming emotion when encouraged by a carer, as much as they would cry when not helped. Take the time to get them giggling, then snuggle in for a kiss and hug as often as you

Defusing meal-time tears

Imagine you have a ten month old who is looking like she might just be getting a little grumpy about the concept of eating dinner tonight. She is tired, has had a big day and has lost all inclination to be patient. She gets a little frown on her face and lowers her chin into her chest with a little pout. We know she is just on the brink of losing it and, finally, she gives a little kick and squirms in her chair as she grizzles a complaint straight at you. You're on the threshold of meal-time hell. Do you become tense?

I see parents in this situation try to distract their baby, often overwhelming the baby with choice. While distraction is sometimes a helpful tool, it is also generally well known for escalating a situation, and frustrated crying and tantrums follow closely. My suggestion for dealing with a tiny tot in this situation, where you can see they are getting a little edgy, is to try to defuse it all with humour. How?

When she does her little kick and grizzle at you, respond with a little surprise jump in your seat (blink and shake of the head included) and offer a high tone, 'Oh!', and stop and smile at her, and wait for her next move. She now has your attention and she can see you are waiting for her to respond. This will change the flow of what is starting to occur, but you're not out of the woods yet. You now need to lock it in by being repetitive. Your baby will likely repeat the behaviour because you were responsive, and this is when you simply repeat your response. If she is responding well, get a little more dramatic with your surprise. Raise your hands, jump a little higher, anything to make her interested in your little interaction. This should start a meal-time laugh session. Then it's official, you have defused the situation and this will allow you the opportunity to start the meal with one of those gooey laughs (all food and gums).

can every day. These are the precious times, so a tickle with a raspberry on the neck at a random time of the day just makes them happy and always leaves them bright-eyed and expectant when you are about to interact with them.

Tone

Learning how to use a tone that is encouraging and reassuring, as well as gentle and loving when guiding a child, appears to be a slightly lost art. Because of the extreme parenting views expressed these days, some parents confuse guiding a child with a strategy involving frowning and growling, or being apologetic and overly concerned. This is parenting from the extremes of the parenting pendulum and not from a place of real balance. Guiding a child in a way that is compassionate and understanding through the use of happy upbeat tones and confidence is fulfilling your loving duty of care towards your little one. This tone should remain as you define your statements and requests, even when your child is a little unhappy with your consistent guidance on those first few attempts.

Defusing an embarrassing situation

Imagine your 22 month old bumps her head on the table and plops down on her bottom. There are three people sitting nearby watching, and all react with a little 'Oo-ohhh' when she does it. The bump wasn't so hard, but the emotions that have come up around that event are potentially overwhelming when all eyes are suddenly on her. Most people pre-empt what will follow and rush forward when they can see she is about to cry. Others in the room offer a hand as well and it all becomes too much for the toddler. This sudden overload of input tips her over the edge, and tears and shying away from the crowd begin. These episodes can take a while to recover from. Toddlers tend to want to hide their face, and sit still with their parents for quite some time, and can become a little clingy afterwards. Rather than risk this scenario, it's important to try and defuse the situation on a one-on-one level if you can. How?

If you can see it is going to take more than an 'oops, up you get' and a 'hurray' clap and cheer, then keep her close, make eye contact and act as though you got the bump like her. Pull a funny face, lift your tone, look a little surprised and say 'Oh bump' as you touch your head. Repeat it a few times and gauge her response. At this point she might laugh, in which case the people around her join in, and she thinks she is quite funny. On the other hand she may just cry or shy away anyway. This is normal with an older age group, and at least you can rest assured that you gave it a try. If they do react poorly to the situation, all focus should be removed, and a quiet cuddle with mummy while she chats to the guests should take the pressure off your baby. Once she is calm, you can offer a distraction but don't be surprised if she does not want this, preferring to sit snuggled into your lap. Many mistake this for being tired but it is just a normal response from a toddler to others seeing them hurt themselves.

Many people wrongly perceive that guidance or parental instruction should come in the form of tough parenting. This is absolutely not the case. In fact, that form of aggressive communication will only teach your children to make each of their requests in a tough or aggressive way towards not only you, but all others who are close to them. You are setting an example for your children, so the feeling that is associated with them being co-operative, and therefore contributing and important members of a family, should be one that evokes a sense of pride and pleasure at making their mum and dad happy, just as their mum and dad are thrilled to listen and interact with their baby and toddler when requested.

You should always be happy, and ask politely, but be confident in your right and need as a parent to make requests or guide your baby and toddler. If you are nervous about them being cross at you or becoming upset, then you will likely lift your inflection in a hope to achieve a happy answer. This means your statement is a question—and remember, if you ask a question expect an answer. If your baby or toddler gets very stroppy about you governing certain times of the day, the only way to correct that

What tone is that?

Say 'Lie down and wait for mummy' using different tones. First, say this statement as though you are talking to your child. Now repeat the statement like you are concerned they are going to cry and resist your guidance when you ask them. Did your inflection lift, was your voice low and soft, did you skim over the words, did you pull a funny face where your eyebrows went up in the centre and down at the ends? Imagine this from your baby's perspective. You look like something bad is about to happen, and that you feel bad about it. This means that every time they are asked to do something, they assume the asker is doing something awful and feels bad. How unpleasant would it be for your baby to be asked to listen then feel?

Now try it with a bossy tone. Did you sound angry? Did you frown and open your eyes? Did you finish the statement with a pout and retain your frown and stare? Imagine this from your baby's perspective. Your simple request looks like you are angry at them. This means that every time they are asked to do something, they assume that the asker is angry. How would you react if someone asked you to do something in that way?

Now try and say the statement politely. Did you smile? Did you make clear eye contact? Did you sound happy with a naturally higher tone right through the sentence? Did you raise your eyebrows and open your eyes? This last way is how I would like you to deliver every single parent-governed line within your PRM. This will ensure respect through guidance, and establish a positive and healthy association and attitude for your baby towards education. It will also benefit your child in the long term by encouraging healthy expectations from friendships and relationships in the future.

scenario and help them feel more comfortable with this healthy balanced line of communication is to adopt a confident, matter-of-fact and respectful tone, and practise this often.

Body language

When it comes to communication, your words are not the only thing a child under two years of age reads when trying to understand what people are telling them. Ensuring your body language matches your verbal language is a little more challenging than most would have imagined or even contemplated, but often, when establishing confident communication, you might be saying the words but what your baby is reading is an entirely different story. Body language essentially consists of eye contact and the actions of your full body. It's important to be conscious of your body language and to not confuse your child with a body language that may indicate something that is not going to eventuate.

The most important thing to watch is that your verbal language matches your body language. When we ask our babies to trust us so they can relax and allow us to govern them through certain parts of their day, we need to make sure we change things from a visual-based environment (where the baby feels they need to watch your actions to predict your movements) to a verbal-based environment. To do this you need to be great with your language and to be both honest and confident.

Firstly, to be honest, if you are trying to establish trust between you and your baby, moving around a lot will not encourage a child to relax while they get used to being a separate entity from you, particularly if they are immobile. If you are just starting out with independent play management (see page 136) for example, it's important to stay in one particular area. Walking in and out of the room will make your child nervous and make them feel as though they need to watch you all the time. This will obviously discourage play and the child will not enjoy that most basic of early childhood desires and needs, which is to explore and challenge their environment.

Does this mean you need to stay still? Absolutely not! It just means you should plan to work in one area of the house at a time. Tidy the kitchen, prepare the food for the day, gather any clutter into a basket on the bench ready to put away later. If you were to move around the kitchen bench, to the other side, your baby may interpret your body language as suggesting you are going to leave the room, and they will cry and ask to come with you. Try to work through one room, then move to the next with clear language as you transition, so they can learn to trust the fact that you will always tell them when you plan on moving from one room to another, rather than leave them to try and read your body language and guess your actions. Being conscious of your predictability enables your baby to trust that you won't just flit in and out of the room without telling them, which means they can focus on their toys and trust you will tell them of any planned changes.

It's also important to be cautious of disrupting good play with your body language. When you walk over to your baby to offer them a toy to play with, how do you do it? I find most parents straddle over their baby, who is lying down, and then they reach forward with both hands to retrieve toys and make clear eye contact. The visual message the parent is offering the baby is something like 'I'm about to pick you up'. The baby's legs kick, and their little arms go up and down in anticipation of being picked up. The parent then offers their baby a toy, which the baby pushes aside as their eye contact is now clearly fixed on their mum or dad and the anticipated action of being picked up. The parent then thinks 'Uh-oh, they don't want to play' and attempts to stand up. At this, the baby bursts into tears and the parent, in a bid to calm baby down before leaving, bends over again and places their hands under baby's arms as if to say 'I know you want to be picked up so maybe this pretending pick up will make you happy'. This is even more confusing, as you are really saying 'I'm pretending to pick you up to make you happy, but I'm not actually going to pick you up'. The baby strains his or her stomach muscles, and lifts their head off the ground to be picked up, but nothing happens. Now mum has become unpredictable. This is when a baby will become very vocal and demand to be picked up because your unpredictable actions are making them feel uncomfortable.

Instead of this scenario you need to look for ways of ensuring your body language does not send *any* mixed messages. To do this you have some simple rules. For example, if you do not plan on picking your baby up, but would like to tidy up their play station, or offer them a new toy:

- avoid eye contact as you approach, instead look to the toys
- approach in a less direct way, perhaps side on, and via the head rather than the feet
- stand, bend or squat side-on to baby
- use only one hand and avoid reaching over the top of baby
- keep the focus of your baby's eye contact on a toy rather than just you
- do not make the play with the toy all about *you*
- watch the volume of your voice; keep it happy, gentle and encouraging.

If baby is trying to make eye contact and asking to be picked up (usually indicated by pushing the toy aside and kicking very fast with solid eye contact), and your intention is to not pick baby up (which is a perfectly reasonable thing for a baby to experience), then eye contact could be confusing for your baby at this time. Try placing the toy between your eyes and theirs. This is a good way to clearly encourage play with the toy.

If your baby is a crawler, encourage her to follow you back to their play area rather than always pick her up and carry her everywhere. If you have a toddler, the trouser tug (see page 374) is one of their good strategies, so be aware of how to handle it. Always use your up cue (see page 76). The one thing you must never do is to say 'no' with your mouth but 'yes' with your body—I can't make it any simpler than that.

I often see a parent trying to use a parent-governed line of communication and asking their baby to wait in the high chair, but as soon as the baby gets cross or demands to be picked up, the parent says 'Wait' but puts their hands under their baby's arms and leans in to cuddle them, or goes a million miles an hour and picks them up without defining the request. This is unfair and confusing. This is not being confident, or predictable. If you have embarked on a routine event using a parent-governed line of communication and your little one, whether eight months or 18 months of age, is having a really hard time learning to allow you to govern the end point of the event that they used to be in charge of, your body language *must* remain clear and be the same as your verbal language, and you must remain confident.

The idea of how to appropriately use your body language and, most importantly, your eye contact is one that needs to be addressed carefully if you are to ensure the messages you are sending your child are consistent with your language. The most important time to establish the 'no eye contact' rule is when you are using your governing line of communication and their behavioural response to your guidance indicates they are not going to co-operate. To then stare at your child once you have stated your request and closed the verbal lines of communication would suggest you are open to a negotiation, or you are looking to your baby for guidance. This is a conflicting message. You do not ask a child to do something, and then look to them to tell you what they would rather do instead. You should carry on with your chores or task and deliver a clear message that your request stands and there is no negotiation opportunity.

Once you have decided that you are governing a line of communication, it's important to carry on and be extremely mindful of your eye contact as it will definitely encourage loud crying or tantrums, which is your child's way of telling you what to do. If you say 'Wait for mummy' then you have made a clear request. If your child then starts to try to regain control of the situation and request something else, it is less confusing for your child if you just carry on without engaging in eye contact until they settle down.

If you find your baby is very upset however, and needs a little reassurance, then you should make eye contact and repeat your request confidently. It's important to acknowledge them if they are finding something difficult, and to reassure them that you understand how they feel. Something as simple as a stroke on the face, eye contact and an 'it's okay, bubby, mummy just needs you to wait. I know you feel cross, but you're okay.' This should be done only occasionally because the moment you make eye contact they will tell you to pick them up, or try to guide you. Always remember that your motivation when you reassure them is *not* to fix it but to just let your little one know you can hear them; you know they are upset but they are okay and your request still remains.

Be certain to not torment them with many eye contact reassurances. Only do it if they are having a very difficult time and your attempts to carry on have not proven helpful in getting your little one to calm down a little and accept your guidance. Always remember that eye contact almost always means you intend on saying or asking something. When was the last time your brother or sister just walked up to you and stared at you? What would you do if they did? You would not be able to continue your task because it would be a little off-putting. At the very least it would take your focus off what you were doing, and direct it right back to them. It would also encourage you to engage in conversation, or ask if they wanted to engage you in conversation. If you were upset with them however, it could possibly provoke a less pleasant reaction, so be mindful of your eye contact with your child only when they are challenging you with big tantrums.

Equally, when you want to make sure your little one has heard you, or you want to let them know you have heard them, eye contact is a vital component of good communication. The first place a child's gaze will drift towards from birth is the human face, and it is a great way to get their attention, or to ensure they have ours. The idea of avoiding eye contact when a toddler is challenging your communication is based on a simple philosophy that if you intend on following through with your communication, you do not want to get into the sibling-type argument of 'yes', 'no', 'yes', 'no',

> Always remember that your motivation when you reassure them is *not* to fix it but to just let your little one know you can hear them; you know they are upset but they are okay and your request still remains.

with your little one. You are best to make your statement and then avert your gaze, or they will say 'no' (verbally or through crying) and you will be encouraged to be consistent and say 'yes', which of course is likely to only receive the same answer from your child. Where does this end then? It is better to simply make your statement, and carry on without confusing the parent–governed line by looking to your child for guidance.

Please do not misunderstand this. The diversion of eye contact is just for occasional use and only when you have a very cross child screaming and arching to be picked up out of the high chair, pram or cot, or wherever. This is not a daily strategy, or something that is done for prolonged periods of time. It is designed to help a child, who thinks they need to scream or tantrum as a form of communication, to learn a new way of communicating.

The case of baby Corbin

One of the most upsetting things I encounter when working with young mums and dads is the misinformation, or misunderstanding of information, that occurs when parents are told about body language and the importance of and appropriate use of eye contact. I had a first-time young mum come to listen to me lecture at Newcastle University. She approached me at the end of my lecture to tell me about her tiny five-month-old son who was only able to sleep for 15 minutes at a time, 24 hours a day. He was sitting quietly in the pram, and when I got down to his level to greet him, he made no eye contact. In fact, not only did he make no eye contact, he deliberately avoided my gaze. I sat next to his mother and talked with her about the situation. I observed her communicating with her son. Neither looked at each other, much to my surprise, and when he became upset he looked away as she patted his tummy looking at the floor.

I asked her to communicate with little Corbin more directly, so she said his name, touched his hands, reassured him, but continued to avoid eye contact. If she did look at his face, she was averting her gaze, and visa versa. When I enquired about the avoidance of eye contact she informed me that she was told by a healthcare professional to avoid eye contact and to be like a robot and he would settle down. The only result of avoiding eye contact all together, however, was an emotionally unsettled little baby.

Strategies were immediately put in place to encourage an intimate connection with eye contact, baby massage, swimming lessons and lots of songs, nursery rhymes and one-on-one focus playtime . . . with lots of eye contact. That day, she went home, had a bath with her baby, and talked while he lay on her chest for over an hour. They connected and Corbin got the giggles. For four days straight Corbin giggled every time his mother looked at him.

Corbin's first sleep after that intimate and close interaction was established, as well as a few other basic routine adjustments, was for three hours straight and right through that first night. I had encountered this only once previously, and the same level of unsettled behaviour accompanied this pattern of body language.

Motivation for communication

Communication with children under the age of two years is an intricate and detailed process that sees most parents instinctively equipped with all the right tools to happily interact effectively without the need to research strategies. But it is becoming apparent that the role of parenting is fraught with fears or stresses about whether the mum or dad are doing the right thing by their children. While it is vitally important we remain accountable for our actions and we educate ourselves, the perils of such an endeavour can be a little confusing. Many strategies are conflicting, and many parents are starting to lose contact with their basic instincts and rely heavily on others to instruct them on how to be a parent.

Now this may sound ironic coming from me, but I highlight it because I really want you to find a complete parenting approach that does not entirely skip the important element of communication. I find there are two strategies in particular that people tend to offer. The first is the kind that focuses on strict sleeping times, meal times and management of sleep times, but misses the foundation to all interactions with the children. The second is often encouraged through frightening scenarios of what might happen if you don't follow their particular strategy, and the motivation for adopting this approach is focused squarely on fear over common sense. As a result, balanced and loving parenting and boundary setting are being replaced with strategies borne out of fear or guilt.

Before you can get back in touch with your natural parenting tools, you need to address the motivation for your communication in the first place. Learn to listen to your instincts. When trying to learn more about a confident parenting philosophy, it is so important that the literature or information you are hearing is 'common sense' broken down into a practical set of tools that you know you possess and can now tap into. If what you are hearing about communication does not make you say 'Oh gee, that is so obvious, why didn't I think of that', then you can bet your bottom dollar the strategy is flawed in some way, shape or form.

When you are out and about and you see or meet other people and their children, what are the things that make you go 'I don't want my child to behave like that?' I'd wager that it is the child that screams and demands, refuses to listen, cries endlessly, is aggressive in any way shape or form with their parents or other children, won't let their parents do anything for them, or accept anything the parents suggest to them (even sleep when they are tired or food when they are hungry or a nappy change when they are soiled), or are clingy. These are not the children that possess the qualities you desire for your child.

What about the children that make you think 'That's a beautiful little boy / girl. I would love my child to be content and happy just like that.' I bet they're the ones with sprightly, clever personalities, who are cheeky but will accept guidance from their mum and dad if they get a little too cheeky, who play happily, engage in busy interactions with either their mum and dad, other children or those around them, are verbally engaging either through babble or by attempting to use words, and show clear socialising patterns. I bet they're the children who will go to sleep for their parents when they are tired, and will eat reasonably when they are hungry and who can accept a simple 'not now' or 'no' from a well-meaning parent and possess the skills and confidence you would want for your own child.

Then pay attention to what motivates you here: the desire to have a positive relationship with your child so that they have the best opportunity to be the happy child you want to raise. There are certain behaviours that should not be perpetuated or allowed to continue or it starts to work against the child and the parent. There are certain healthy boundaries that need to be set to ensure everyone can enjoy themselves, including the child, their parents and the others around them, and there is a certain level of clear parental guidance that is needed to help keep everything running smoothly. Your ability to feel confident enough in your own personal hopes and desires for your entire family to make decisions based on those principles, because you know it is the right thing to do even if it causes a few little dramas when you initially set the boundaries, is what sets you apart from someone who is trusting their intuition, and finding a parenting solution based on that, or disregarding their intuition and only trying to work to an ideology.

4
The communication learning ladder

How do you correct a poor cycle of behaviour during the day? Well, I'm about to give you a ladder analogy that effectively describes the steps a child needs to progress through to learn a new style of communication or routine event. At no point can you put off teaching a baby the process, or skip any of the steps. Once each step has been learnt and effective communication has been achieved, the only thing left to do is to enjoy your happy and content baby and maintain your positive communication by being consistent.

The rungs of the ladder

Your primary goal in communication, with a child under the age of two years, is to simply be understood. The ability level of a child who is six months old is obviously going to be different to that of an 18 month old, but the ability to understand a simple request during the normal flow of a routine is equally as complicated a task for both age groups if effective balanced communication streams have not been introduced.

The listening tasks I have developed during the daily routine (event routines and language cues like the up cue (see page 76), wait game (see page 74), and consistent language you will encounter in event routine) are all achievable from the age of six months, so regardless of the age you begin, the ladder to learning their new routine expectations still needs to be climbed and then maintained. I am not terribly interested in making a day more challenging communication-wise as a child grows. I am more interested in establishing basic healthy two-way communication in a wisdom-based parent-guided house where a child's voice is respected. For this reason, the style of communication established at six months of age remains the foundation for all your communication until they are two years old and beyond. Once your child is functioning happily with the rungs of the ladder that I am about to highlight, there is nothing further that needs to happen other than to continue to evolve your communication and expand your baby's vocabulary.

The bottom rung of the ladder

This is the beginning, where an inappropriate child-governed line is the dominant form of communication. This might be when you try to lay your child down to change their nappy and they roll over, refuse to stay in one spot, become emotionally overwhelmed resulting in a tantrum, arch their back, cry, anything rather than what you want them to do to ensure the event is a pleasant one. When you remove their nappy, they put their hands in their poo repeatedly because it seems interesting and you are unable to manage their positioning while cleaning their hands. This is when it reaches the point where it seems easier to do away with the change table and try to change them on the bed or the floor. You become a master at changing their nappy while they crawl around.

> Your primary goal in communication, with a child under the age of two years, is to simply be understood.

Achieving this transition from bottom rung to top rung does not happen without your child having to go through a natural learning process. Remember to be realistic and fair with your little one: it might take a day, or sometimes two or three days to become familiar enough with a new flow of events before they feel they can truly relax and trust the process is predictable and, therefore, safe.

Steps in between

On the second rung your child is unfamiliar with the new routine and fights, but you remain consistent and confident, even if it feels a little uncomfortable to initiate the change. Keep your eye on the top rung for motivation.

By the third rung your child will be familiar with the routine but needs repetition and consistency to trust the new process and relax. You will still experience some resistance but as soon as you repeat your cues and appear confident they settle quickly.

On the fourth rung your child is familiar with the routine and trusts your consistency. They will start to relax and play with their toy. Towards the end of the event they will become a little unsettled as they try to pre-empt the end. You need to stay calm, maintain a steady pace, and complete the event appropriately.

The fifth rung sees your child managing the new routine through predictability. If your little one is not mobile, they will look towards their room, gesture to lie down, look for their toy in its usual location and play happily until the nappy change is complete. If they are mobile, they may crawl or walk to their room, and will follow the actions of a non-mobile baby.

The top rung of the ladder

The pinnacle is when an appropriate parent-governed line of communication is in play, when your child is empowered with the flow of the event and ultimately feels in control of the routine as they can pre-empt the sequence of events that you have taught them. This is a win–win situation. You lay your baby down, and they lie still, happily playing with a little toy while you complete the nappy change, blow some raspberries on their tummy and sing some cute nursery rhymes while they giggle at your crazy antics. You clap your hands and say 'Up, up' and your baby waits for you to pick them up. You have a cuddle and thank them for being so helpful and lying still for nappy change and you turn out the light together on your way out the door.

How you may feel during their climb

Teaching a child something new is a thrill to me, because I know how well it will turn out. I often say to a parent when they say 'This is hard, they are really cross' that 'I know how this story ends, I've read the book thousands of times. This is like the boring first chapter that you need to read to establish the characters and once you get past that, the rest of the story just flows and is easy'. For parents, however, they don't know how it ends. They are stuck on the first rung of the ladder, and it's because of fear that they fail to climb further. I would like to reassure you that these strategies work! I use them every day, and if they didn't work, I wouldn't have a career. Stay calm, stay confident, be your child's solid ground to stand on by being steadfast and seeing it through. You will be absolutely amazed at your under-two year old's ability to listen, understand, learn and master a new skill in an amazingly short period of time.

This learning process is only short lived, but while you are going through the transition, most mums and dads find it virtually impossible to see past this brief period when their baby or toddler is crying or having a tantrum about the new set of unfamiliar conditions. I find most parents assume that their baby is feeling fear, pain or neglect. In reality, most little ones are just uncomfortable with the unpredictability of the event, and in an effort to stop feeling like that, will try to go back to their old set of conditions (no matter how inappropriate they were). When they have been unsuccessful at achieving those old conditions they become frustrated, angry and eventually upset at their lack of control. When this happens you must remember to always assess the situation from an adult's perspective:

- Where are they?
- Who is looking after them?
- What am I asking of them?

If you are teaching them to lie down while you change their nappy, sit and wait in their high chair until the meal is finished, sit on your lap for a story, and lie down in their soft cot, in a house where they are loved, and you are creating a new and improved way to do something, then the answers to all three questions are simply, 'at home', 'mummy / daddy—so no one better' and, 'to change their nappy'. This is all safe and reasonable and nothing to feel anxious about pursuing. You were the one who taught them how to do something a certain way in the first place, and you are now simply teaching them something new once again. Be patient and don't expect your child to get it immediately. Give them a day or three to be fair, and stay optimistic and confident so your baby can feel reassured.

> Always remember the transitional window is just that: a transition.

Be careful to not make any change or reaction to it about yourself. Your baby is new to this world, and while they learn something new it can feel a little uncomfortable until the routine becomes familiar. In this time, I find that mums and dads can get as upset as their child. This means your baby has no one to reassure them. Don't bicker amongst yourselves when your child cries. It's important to put your needs and feelings aside. Stay strong, confident and reassuring to ensure a swift transition for your child rather than a drawn-out process by misleading your child to believe that this new routine makes you uncomfortable or angry too. They will never relax if they anticipate this may occur.

When your child resists guidance

It's perfectly natural and normal for your child to resist guidance initially when you first implement a parent-governed line of communication. As you can see above, there is a whole series of rungs that need to be climbed before you achieve the ultimate relaxed style of guidance, from changing the lines of communication from a child-governed to a parent-governed one. Once this is in place and you and your child have become confident with that balanced flow, you can incorporate your third line of communication, negotiation, and you will have a parent- and child-governed home. This change is challenging for your little one, and is naturally met with a little or, sometimes in the case of a few toddlers, a lot of resistance.

When a child struggles with being guided, I tend to spend a good three weeks completely guiding the child, by using my language cues even when things are going really well. This gives the little one the opportunity to feel comfortable and get used to being guided at happy times, as well as at challenging times. This creates more positive associations with guidance, and once the resistance stops, I gradually reintroduce choices. If your child copes well with the more open style of communication (negotiations) by happily accepting the responsibility of making some choices without trying to govern all areas of the day again, then you are fine to continue guiding them and offering more choices, but slowly does it. Do not confuse your child and lead them to believe you are looking to them for guidance again, or they will feel burdened and feel the need to again create a trustworthy predictable day by governing it themselves through often inappropriate behaviour. Always retain a confident parental guiding role in your child's life.

Whether the resistance from your child is driven by their strong character and naturally assertive or even bossy nature, or because they are feeling uncomfortable with a new or foreign set of conditions, your response should always be the same. It is perfectly natural for your child to feel the whole range of normal healthy human emotions. In fact, they should feel them. There is nothing normal or healthy about a child only ever feeling happy. That is an unrealistic expectation. Your child also has a right to express the way they feel when they feel those emotions. They are only new to this world and, even for an adult, the feelings associated with frustration, unfamiliarity or anger are generally overwhelming and need to be vented. Your child's daily moods and reactions to certain events are not directly proportionate to your parenting ability.

Do not make their normal emotions about you or you risk creating a culture in your family where your child cannot be honest about the way they are feeling for the fear it may upset you. Never discourage a child from feeling or openly expressing their emotions. Never avoid a normal situation simply because it may evoke emotions. It is your response to your child's expression of emotions that tells them if they are still safe under those circumstances, despite their feelings at that time.

It is so very important that your child can rely on you to be the solid ground on which they can stand when they feel uncertain and uncomfortable in a particular situation. Imagine how it must feel when you have asked them to sit in their high chair, and you are following through and defining that statement for the first time in their life. They will be unsure and may become very upset at the unpredictability of the situation. Then imagine how they might feel when you smile, stroke their hair and say in a confident and loving voice 'It's okay, bubba, it's just time to sit down, you're okay!' then carry on with your chores until they settle down.

While your child may still feel cross or upset about the situation, you have said by your actions and language that you are not concerned for them.

> The important thing to be conscious of is your response, and the subsequent message it is conveying to your child.

Since they determine whether they are at risk based on your response to their reaction, they can simply feel cross or upset about the situation without feeling as though they are in harm's way. A great example of this is when you see a toddler running at the park, and then they suddenly fall over splat! If they haven't seriously hurt themselves, they look for their parent immediately and more often than not, a parent will react in one of two ways: 'Awwwwwwwwwwww, ouch' with a look of real concern, extended words, the v-shaped eyebrows and a contorted mouth; or 'Oops, over he goes, you're okay little guy, up you get, yeah'.

If the parent looks or sounds concerned, as in the first scenario, the child drops their little head and the crying begins almost immediately. They will often need a cuddle of reassurance before they are immediately better and off they go again. If the parent looks more confident about the event, the child will often get up, rub their smarting hands or knees and carry on safe in the knowledge that their mum and dad don't think they are at risk.

This is an important example to highlight because when you are helping your child work their way through a new learning process, which will often only take a day or so, they *will* express themselves if they are not pleased about the change to their day, and they will look to you to gauge if they are okay or not in this new situation. Your role now as a parent is to assess the situation from an adult's perspective. If you assess a situation from your child's perspective, meaning you react by becoming upset too, then you will be misleading them and delivering the wrong message about this new routine and basic request to your child.

If you have assessed that your child is in a safe location, is loved, and only feeling uncomfortable about learning something new, then you need to let them know that they are safe, and they are not at risk by remaining completely confident and reassuring. You are their rock, and they need you to be steady and confident to feel safe. They are permitted to get upset, and even allowed to have a full-scale tantrum if they feel totally overwhelmed, but you do not get the luxury of bursting into tears and having a tantrum right alongside them. The important thing to be conscious of is your response, and the subsequent message it is conveying to your child. You can empathise confidently without looking guilty or extremely concerned that your child is upset. If you need to practise this, take the time while you are having a shower, or driving in the car alone (if that ever happens) to put yourself in that situation and verbally practise responding in an empathetic but confident and reassuring way.

Remember to follow your flow of communication, and always remember that it only takes one or two positive and confident sessions to teach your baby something basic and new like nappy changing without tears or tantrums. Once you have established the language cue around that event you will be able to forewarn your little one of your expectations and their response to that situation will become more and more positive and a reflection of your response.

Responding to their resistance

Right from the time when their baby is eight months old, I encourage mothers and fathers to be mindful about what their actions are when teaching their baby. Be extremely cautious about giving currency to inappropriate behaviour, like back arching, screaming or hitting out, or undesirable communication, such as screaming and tantrums. If you carry on with your request and ignore these behaviours (by cleaning the table while you wait for your little one to calm down, or adjusting the buttons on your shirt while your child vents) without making eye contact or changing your actions, your child quickly learns that you only respond to their calmer behaviours, and they are picked up when they are *not* screaming, hitting or back arching. This can only result in your baby finding a more positive way of asking to be picked up, and will therefore not feel they need to scream or worse to get your assistance.

To respond with communication or body language to any of those inappropriate or undesirable patterns of behaviour is literally teaching your child to continue to do them in order to make you listen to them. When your child goes into a style of behaviour that is clearly caused from impatience or bossiness that you do not wish to see continue (and yes, they can be a little bossy from time to time, bless their little hearts), you need to disengage physically by making no eye contact (apart from occasionally reassuring them in a confident manner if you feel it is necessary) then carrying on. If the behaviour continues, then turn your body side on or away from them until they settle down. This is how we say 'when you scream, back arch, hit, kick, etc., mummy will wait until you calm down before we carry on'. It helps them understand that as soon as they are calmer, mummy and daddy will come back and help them. It strongly discourages that very common pattern of behaviour where they eat for three minutes then throw everything off the tray and insist on getting down immediately. This strategy helps us teach them to stay in their high chair longer, and thus improves their ability to eat a more balanced meal, which ultimately impacts on their sleep.

If you feel stressed about your child's tears or the origin of those tears, remember to always go back to assessing the situation the child is in from an adult's perspective, not a child's perspective. Waiting for you to tell them when it's time to get out of the high chair, or off the change table, is a perfectly reasonable expectation to encourage right from six months of age.

The wait game

There is a very specific waking routine for little ones who have completed their sleep time, but for most other times of the day, when we are needing to guide them into, through and out of an event routine like nappy changes, or getting dressed, or getting out of the pram, I tend to use a fun game to help the baby / toddler learn to look to me for guidance so they don't think they need to cry to be picked up. I call the strategy 'the wait game'. The wait game is a highly valuable tool that not only gives you practice at governing the outcome of a situation, but also ensures your baby or toddler understands that this is normal, and quite a fun game.

This game incorporates a subtle form of my own version of a simple sign-language cue. The added convenience of this is when you are out with your little one, or they are very focused on making a racket and can't hear you, a quick flash of this basic visual sign will enable them to understand your request. This game is conducted in response to certain behaviours and needs to be incorporated at the end of all parent-governed times of the day.

Making the sign

The sign is simply done by making an L shape with you thumb and first finger. Start with a closed fist, and angle your hand so your bent-over fingers are facing towards them. Open your forefinger and thumb to make an L shape so they can see it briefly then withdraw your hand as you close it to a fist again. This is designed to be a brief flash that just catches their gaze without irritating them, or stopping them from doing what they are doing.

Your child may not necessarily look at your hand, and is likely to make eye contact with you. This does not mean they do not register the sign in their peripheral vision, and quickly learn to understand it. I tend to rely heavily on the word 'wait' after the first few days, and only offer the sign at the end of a request, when they are in the correct position. When you are first playing the game however, you may chose to offer the sign as they start a particular behaviour you wish to correct, and again after you have re-positioned them correctly.

How to play

This simple but essential verbal and visual cue can be incorporated into the array of parent-governed events of the day. It should essentially be played as a fun game that is based on anticipation and a little bit of excitement about what is about to happen at the end of the game, which is generally a fun snuggle or tickle. You play this while introducing and following through on the expectations of their behaviour. For example, when your child is in the high chair and you have wiped their face and hands and removed the tray, quickly flash your sign and with a big cheeky smile say 'Waaaaaiiiiiiiit! Wait.' This can be followed with a laugh or a giggle of excitement from you so they start to associate that request with warm and fun feelings that they trust and actually enjoy.

While you are asking your child to wait, you need to undo their buckles, and remind them to still wait for you as they are not to govern when you pick them up. You are trying to practise a situation where your child gets the opportunity to start feeling comfortable with you governing the outcome of the event. If, while your little boy is waiting for you to pick him up, he raises his arms or leans forward in a gesture to say 'pick me up', you need to define your statement and tell him what 'wait' actually means. This would require you to take his little hands and put them down in his lap while you say 'Hands in lap, wait for mummy / daddy', or gently push him back into a safe sitting position saying 'Sit back, wait for mummy'.

Continue to make him wait until he is sitting as you would like. This may cause tears as he gets annoyed or feels uncomfortable with you being in charge, but like everything else in early childhood, practice makes perfect. He needs to progress through the natural ladder of learning and you need to be patient and confident until he starts to recognise and therefore enjoy the process. Once he is sitting with his arms down and waiting for guidance from you, you can use your up cue with him by clapping your hands, offering your hands and picking him up while saying 'Up, up'.

When you have picked him up, you can raise him in the air and say 'Good waiting, my darling', while blowing raspberries on his cheek and having a little bit of baby fun. This way, when you are in the supermarket and he gets stroppy about waiting in the checkout queue or demands to reach the sparkling lolly wrappers carefully designed to make every parent's shopping trip impossibly painful, you can quickly flash him a smile and your wait sign without even opening your mouth and your little boy will sit back, put his hands in his lap and look at you with a big smile. This will give you the chance to change the mood, and offer a valuable break to give him a toy from his bag of tricks (see page 369) to distract him.

If you have a little baby between six and ten months of age, it is important to try and play the wait game in a fun and consistent way. If you have followed all the basic instructions and your baby boy is struggling to calm down, try to distract him with a great toy. The moment he calms down or is distracted, then use your up cue and pick him up.

The up cue

The up cue is a very simple way of helping your baby rely on a verbal environment more than a physical one. You walk past your baby a hundred times a day and if your little one has to look at you to determine whether you are going to pick them up or not every single time, then they will be getting distracted from their toys over and over, and no doubt, getting unsettled and eventually upset. This usually results in your child being uninterested or unable to focus on play, and wanting to be carried around all day simply because you are so unpredictable. By introducing a verbal cue like 'up, up' each time you plan to pick them up, they will be able to play, knowing that they don't need to anticipate you picking them up unless you say 'Up up'.

There are two important things to remember when using the up cue. Many people say 'Up', but then offer their hands and ask the baby if they want to get up and wait for their baby to lean forward and gesture up. What happens? The baby cries. The idea of using the up cue when completing a parent-governed line of communication is to tell your baby that you govern when they will be picked up, and not their tears or tantrums. To then ask a baby to cry to be picked up is encouraging tears and defeats the purpose of completing the event. Pick your baby up without asking permission after you have stated your cue and be happy and confident.

Be aware of your child's reaction when you pick them up. If they stop crying immediately then they are clearly using a behavioural cry. This cry, which you may have interpreted as an emotion-based cry, is in fact your baby's only way of saying 'pick me up now'. Learn to listen, and classify your baby's cries. Some of them are literally only their way of saying 'can I have another Cruskit, please?' even if they sound deeply distressed. This is your child being a tiny bit bossy, and if they are being bossy, be sure to follow through with the wait game until they stop demanding to be picked up. Don't teach them to cry to be picked up.

Answering their questions

From the earliest age, your baby is able to clearly communicate with you. And while a parent struggling with their child's behaviour won't agree, I rarely ever meet a parent who does not understand what their baby is saying or asking for, be it feeling uncomfortable, needing a nappy change, being hungry, needing to be picked up, or feeling tired. The natural ability to understand your baby's communication is not rocket science, but knowing what to do when they ask for something that you would prefer they didn't have, or would prefer them to allow you to do differently, is when things start to get a little more complicated . . . and this is often where the confusion lies for parents about how well they are understanding their child.

I have no idea why they call two year olds the 'terrible twos', because it's actually in the age group from 12 to 24 months that things start to get a little hairy if baby doesn't like the way things are happening. This is when difficulty in guiding your little one becomes apparent. The challenge for you in being able to help them do something without tears and protests tends to start at around eight to ten months, but I have seen it in children far younger. This is when you need to introduce clear and honest lines of communication quickly if you haven't already done so.

Learning to live with their emotions in this second year of life, when they have a clearer idea of what they want or desire is when you are far more likely to see, and have to deal with, your beautiful fluffy-haired, pink-cheeked, soft and kissable baby turning into a fiery little ball of anger in a mere nanosecond. I have to admit, whether I see an eight month old or an 18 month old bright pink with fury because they have to sit in their pram or high chair, it is often a little reassuring that the biggest problem in their day is sitting in the pram when they would rather be carried. Though this is small comfort to a parent dealing with a steaming-mad child, it's a quick reminder to always assess the situation from an adult's perspective.

Once your child is good at telling you what they would like, or where they would like you to take them, there will definitely be times when their desires actually conflict with their true needs and you will have to deal with your child wanting something they can't or shouldn't have. It's when you fail to assess their true needs and confidently assert your right as a parent to guide the next part of the day that things can go pear shape. This means your child, with very little life experience and certainly no way of consciously resolving a situation, is burdened with telling you how to do things. This is often where a baby will have a mother breastfeed them from 2 to 5 a.m. as a means of going back to sleep, or where a toddler will go to bed at 11 p.m. at night and get up at 4 a.m., ready to start the day, or a 14 month old will not eat a proper nutritionally balanced meal but snack on biscuits, juice, milk and cheese sticks all day.

Under 12 months of age the resistance might be about getting carried everywhere, or not being picked up as soon as they demand it, or the request for 15 breast feeds in a six-hour period, or about wanting to play with the fan switch while daddy holds them there all day, or simply because they want to play with any of the general no-touch zones of the house like power points. Over twelve months of age though, it might be to go outside at all hours of the day and night, to insist they hold your hand as they walk everywhere because they are not able to walk yet, to have another ride and another, and another, and another in the Wiggles car at the shops, to walk instead of being pushed in their pram, to eat some food they can't or shouldn't have, or to have the biggest and most expensive toy off the shelf at the toyshop.

The first strategy I find most people use if they don't just buckle and give in immediately to their little one's demands (which is healthy and natural on some occasions) is the good old distraction technique. While this is a great strategy, and has its place in a balanced parenting approach, it should never be the only way to deal with a baby asking for something, or doing something you don't want them to do. First of all it's important to lay appropriate foundations for play and behaviour during the day. Don't set them up for play or daily activities that they cannot achieve on their own. If you make their whole day about walking when they cannot yet walk by themselves, then you will be telling your baby they can do nothing without you. Create a balance and don't always allow them to make you stand and hold their hand so they can walk everywhere. This example can be applied to many different scenarios.

When it comes time to say 'no', that's right, I said 'no', don't be so scared of the word that seems to frighten everyone these days. Well, perhaps not everyone, but certainly the families I have to work with are fearful of it, which says a lot. Sometimes babies need to know that you have heard them, and that you do not intend to do what they want or give them what they are demanding right now. To only use the distraction technique often sees a baby throw a tantrum out of pure frustration because they think you haven't heard them or don't understand what they have wanted. I often see parents buckle if they have to acknowledge what their baby wants, even when the parents really don't want the child to have what

Sebastian wants a biscuit

I stayed in a house with a family in Melbourne who had 19-month-old twins, Lucy and Sebastian. The mother was concerned about how many tantrums Sebastian was having, and just how difficult she was finding it to manage his behaviour. Sebastian was a very poor eater, had a low iron-absorption rate and low iron stores and was struggling to cope during the day and unsettled every night. His biggest problem was snacking, so we were working very hard on establishing a balanced eating plan to encourage better overall nutrition to naturally improve his general demeanour. There was going to be a two-pronged approach here: we needed to be clear with our communication to ensure we weren't triggering the tantrums; and we also needed to correct his eating habits to restore a balance to his system so he wasn't so depleted nutritionally, so that his threshold for coping with normal emotions wasn't so low.

On the first day I observed little Sebastian approach his mother at the kitchen bench and ask for a biscuit. As his mother was serving dinner at the time, I had instructed her to make sure there was no snacking before meals. Sebastian stood with his feet firmly together, one hand in the air pointing to the biscuit tin and his eyes clearly fixed on his mother. 'Biscuit,' he said. His mother looked at me a little horrified.

'Look Sebastian,' she said, 'mummy has made some yummy dinner, chicken, your favourite.' Sebastian looked at the food, which smelled lovely and was making him feel hungry, and then continued to point to the tin. 'Biscuit!' he repeated. This time his mother sighed and said, 'Here you are, can you take your spoon to the table for mummy?' Sebastian took the spoon and dropped it on the floor. Then dropped to his knees and bounced as his frustration clearly started to grow.

'Biscuit,' he insisted, just about to cry. His mother took his hand and said, 'Come on, let's go and wash our hands for our yummy dinner,' and tried to lead him out the door. At this point Sebastian continued to point at the biscuit tin and tried to look back at it as he was guided out of the room, crying. He then dropped his weight and went into a full tantrum before they reached the hallway.

The problem for Sebastian was that he was trying to tell his mother something, but she didn't acknowledge that she heard or understood his request, and never answered his question. This avoidance strategy only frustrated the child, and made him ask more and more passionately. This common communication error often happens when a parent is nervous and not sure how to say 'no'.

they are demanding. Many only buckle because they are nervous of saying 'no'. Let's get honest here! Saying 'no', and then explaining why, is normal and healthy when it comes to establishing boundaries, and not saying 'no' is just confusing, and a little tormenting. Consider the scenario in the box about Sebastian asking for a biscuit.

Another commonly used strategy that parents use when answering a child's question that also lands them in hot water if used is:

Child: 'Biscuit!'
Parent: 'You want a biscuit?'
Child: 'Yes.'
Parent: 'No biscuit now, it's dinner time.'

Broken down, what you are saying to a child is asking, 'Would you like a biscuit?' They respond, 'Yes', but you say 'Well you can't have one'. Very confusing! This turns a clear parent-governed line of communication into a question, which creates a child-governed line of communication, and ultimately the child's answer is not respected. Always remember: if you ask a question, expect an answer, and respect that answer. This is what happens when you are not confident with your ability to make choices for your child.

A further common mistake is when you try to be less direct:

Child: 'Biscuit?'
Parent: 'You can have a biscuit later.'
Child: 'Biscuit!'
Parent: 'Soon you can have the biscuit.'

The child continues to ask for a biscuit and eventually, frustrated at not being handed one, will drop to the floor in a tantrum. What's happened is that the parent has answered the child with what appeared to be a 'yes', but it's not. A child this young does not understand the concept of 'later'. Later could be in one minute, or five hours. All that's heard is a positive response, what sounds a little like the child might get to have a biscuit.

Until your child is five years of age, you will need to be far, far more specific and give them daily routine landmarks to predict what 'later' is and not leave your little one hanging. A far more honest and fair answer is a clearly stated, 'No biscuits now. All gone, bye bye biscuits.' This does not mean you can't offer it later. It just means you answer them clearly and don't lead them to believe that you might give them the biscuit soon. It's just not fair.

It's important to be able to indicate to your child that you have heard what they have said. Pre-empt any possible problem areas within the flow of their day. If you know they may ask for a biscuit when they smell food cooking, then tell them what they can expect before you start to cook and tell them your expectations of their behaviour and what they can expect of you: 'Mummy is going to cook your dinner now, yummy chops and mashed potato, nearly time to sit down at the table for your chops and veggies. No biscuit, all gone biscuits, yummy chops with dippy sauce.'

The ability to say 'no blah now my darling, it's time for blah' is a vitally important clear line of communication that must not be disregarded or erased from the parent's vocabulary. It's vital to retain because babies need simple, clear acknowledgement and answers.

Creating patterns of routine communication

As discussed previously, there are within a normal day or week many events—nappy changing and dressing times, time to sit in the high chair or car seat, time to have a bath or sleep—that occur multiple times. These events are often the transitional triggers that cause tears for your baby or toddler, and stress for you. One of the most sensible things you can do when developing a balanced line of parenting is to make sure you and your partner are parenting from the same page. By this I mean you have discussed a general plan on how you think things should be done in your house, you have established the boundaries or house rules, and you are both going to be consistent in the way you manage certain parts of the day to ensure you precious little bub is not confused or stressed by events they have to experience over and over and over again.

Never repeat a toddler's request back if you do not want them to have something. This is tormenting to a child and is only going to result in tears.

Each of these events should be made predictable and consistent for your child. This is how you lay the important foundations for trust through communication, which means you have a manageable set of conditions to deal with each time you encounter a routine situation. It also ensures your baby feels completely in control of the event because they can pre-empt and therefore feel they own each step, even when mum, dad, big sister or granny change their nappy.

The power of creating patterns of routine communication within your daily routine cannot be underestimated. Imagine your 18 month old has a really cool little red car that they like to ride in. It sits in the garage alongside your car, and each time they have to get into your car, they reach for their car, and then get upset when it appears you haven't understood that they would like to play in their car. This turns into a tantrum and getting them into your car becomes a huge drama. While you're getting your child ready to go to the car you put your flow of communication into full practice.

Use pre-emptive and forewarning language: 'It's nearly time to go in mummy's car.' Be honest and tell your little one that they are not going to ride on the red car: 'We will say bye bye, red car, Jeff is going in daddy's car.' Tell them what they are going to do instead: 'Daddy has a special book in the car for Jeff, and it has lions in it, and they say "Roaar".'

Olivia learns a new way

Little Olivia was ten months old when I worked with her mother and father to help her sleep. Olivia and her mummy were having a terrible time when it came to going to sleep, and an equally as difficult a time throughout the night when it came to resettling. Olivia had been guiding her mother through a settling routine that was clearly not working as her mother needed to breastfeed for up to three hours to get her to sleep. This was making both mum and baby exhausted, and wasting precious energy on an event that simply did not need to be so difficult.

We set about developing a new routine for sleep time. From the day we were to start the new routine Olivia could predict the following events:

- breastfeed on couch
- cooing and cuddles with mum and dad
- kiss daddy goodnight (he would learn to settle her in a week)
- walked up to mum and dad's room to be wrapped (one arm out to suck her thumb)
- into her room
- a cuddle and a song
- a kiss on the cheek
- into her cot to be tucked in
- cues
- mummy leave room so Olivia can put herself to sleep.

We role played for a couple of days leading up to the first day, and had been working very hard on our communication. Olivia was ready to try it all by herself.

Olivia's mum called me on the second day of their new routine. She was crying and finding it a little hard to talk. Concerned, I asked her if Olivia was okay and she told me yes. The reason Olivia's mum was crying was because little Olivia was not only comfortable with the routine, but had taken full control of it. After her mother has given her a cuddle and sung 'Twinkle twinkle little star', Olivia stretched up and sucked her mother's cheek, the way she kisses, then reached out to her cot to be laid down. Her mother couldn't believe that by creating a predictable routine, she had actually taught and subsequently empowered her little girl with a lovely way to go to sleep that suited both Olivia and her family.

Then follow through your statements for the actual event. As you walk to the garage say 'It's time to go in daddy's car.' And tell them they are not going to ride on the red car again: 'Say bye bye, red car, Jeff is going in daddy's car now. Bye bye, car.' Then move them on to the next activity immediately: 'Where is your special car book? Let's find it.'

New basic cues

Here are some simple language cue suggestions to use in some of your event routines:

Pre-emptive

'Now we're doing _____, but soon we will _____.'
'Nearly time to _____.'
'Sit /lie down, and wait for mummy.'

Forewarning

'Last one, nearly time to _____.'
'Time to pack away.'
'Time to sit /lie down, wait for daddy.'

Saying 'no' when you have other plans

'Say bye bye, _____'

Boundary setting

'No touch. Hot / break/ hurt / sore.'

Request to keep shoes and socks on as you drive in the car

'Socks on. Shoes on.' But remember to define this!

Distraction or redirection

'Where's your _____ (sound effects are sometimes good here: buck buck beguck, for chicken')

Self-help skills for feeding

'Scoop it up, in your mouth.'

Retaining a governing line when your baby is challenging you

'Daddy do it.'

Meal-time management

'Hands down.'
'Fingers out of mouth.'
'Bite.'
'Mummy / daddy do it.'

Asking them to give you something or put it somewhere

'Ta for mummy / daddy / toy box.'

Offering them something

'Ta for, (baby's name).'

This is the basic principle flow of communication for their entire day. Through this you can convert the line of communication from them governing the event to you governing the event. This style of communication is adopted for the entire day, even when they are happy to co-operate. In fact, to use this language when they are happy to co-operate actually enables you to quickly develop a good set of associations with the conditions around listening.

Specific language and specific praise

I often hear parents with a child 12 months to two years of age using very broad terms when it comes to communicating or praising their baby. It's important to be extremely specific and break down your language when it comes to highlighting your expectations and appreciation of specific events. 'Good listening' may not exactly be grammatically correct, but it is a very specific term for praising purposes, as are 'good eating', 'good sitting', 'good waiting for mummy'. It's equally as important to be conscious of what you are saying to your baby and how potentially empty a statement can be. Define, 'Please be good for mummy'. What exactly is good?

Some other common examples of empty statements may be 'eat nicely', 'behave', 'be nice', 'play nicely'. All these statements are far too broad for your average under-two year old to understand. I would be more inclined to use the following statements to describe each of the above more clearly to a baby or toddler. 'Eat nicely' would need to be broken down into understandable tasks like 'Pick up your spoon, scoop it up, in your mouth! Good eating with your spoon!' or 'Cup on tray! Good listening, Bella. Look [point], cup on tray. Yeah!' and clap.

'Behave' would need to be broken down into understandable tasks like 'Good sitting, bubba'. 'Be nice' could be broken down into understandable tasks like 'No hitting, be soft to daddy', as you encourage baby to stroke daddy's face with their hand. 'Nice being soft, bubby. Ohh soft.'

'Pack away please' could be broken down into 'Time to pack away. Joshua, pick up the block [point to the block], in the bucket, ta for the bucket, letting go of the block! Good packing away, Joshua. Good putting the block in the bucket! Pick up more blocks, in the bucket, let go.'

Each one of these specific styles of communication requires you to physically help them the first few times until you can see they understand what the terms mean. Whether you start using this style of communication at ten months of age or at 18 months of age, your child will still need to go through the same learning process. There is no fast tracking when it comes to children learning language. They cannot skip a step simply because they are older or have a more advanced understanding of language. You need to start at scratch no matter what age your baby is, and once this style of communication is achieved successfully, then you need to remain consistent to avoid slipping back.

Building their self-esteem through language

Communication is one of the most powerful tools you own when it comes to working with children, whether you are a parent, nanny, sibling, teacher, carer, or baby whisperer. Each child is a clean slate, a tablet yet to be written on. Research shows that most people have formed the bulk of their opinions on life by the time they are 16 years of age, and rarely revisit those opinions and assess them from an independent adult's perspective. Because of this I really need to stress the absolutely vital role you play in shaping the self-esteem and self image of your child. I need you to imagine that every single time they look at you they are asking: 'Who am I?' 'What am I like?' 'What do I like?'

I need you to hear what you are telling your child directly, or indirectly. This style of mindful communication should be something you actively practise from their earliest age, but most certainly something you use from when they are the age of six months, and most definitely put into practice from the time they are eight months of age. If they shudder when they taste a super sweet pineapple for the first time, is your automatic response 'Oh, you don't like that', or do you say 'You don't want that'? Perhaps a better response would be: 'Oooh, sweet new taste. Look mummy try it too! Nice and sweet.'

When they are crying at bedtime, do you take them out into the lounge room and say to your partner, 'He doesn't want to go to bed, he hates his room, he is scared'? When you are frustrated with your toddler do you say 'Why don't you listen? Why do you always cry? Why won't you play, sleep, be happy?' When you feel tired and deflated do you say 'I'm sorry I am such a terrible / silly mummy. Mummy is terrible!'?

All of these statements are common, and they all mark your child's slate. I need you to imagine that your language has the power to change any situation from negative to positive. If a child is having difficulty in any aspect of their day, that's when you need to be encouraging with comments like 'Let's go and see your beautiful room, where there's that big blue car on your sheets', and remain confident while you enter into the child's room. This way your baby can see that you are okay, which means they are okay. This continues even when your child cries. You need to re-lay his impression of that room, his cot and the entire sleep environment with positive language, happy confident tones and persistence.

Each time you make a statement such as 'He doesn't seem to like _____', 'He only drinks _____', 'He won't eat for me', 'He hates having a bath', 'He doesn't like his father bathing him', 'He gets upset when he sees grandma', 'Dogs frighten him', 'He doesn't really like to share his toys', you are literally building your child's profile of themselves and the world around them. Change your statements immediately to build a positive profile of your child and the surrounding world.

Consider the impact of 'Charlie did good listening for daddy today, mummy', 'Charlie did good lying down and waiting for daddy when I changed his nappy! Yeah.' This is the language you should use, even if this was a challenging first day with your new cues. We want to tell our children they are good sleepers, love their cot / room, good eaters, love vegetables, like water, like to play with their toy, love bath time, are beautiful, are happy, good listeners, a good friend, funny, love to be active, are good at sitting and waiting . . . the list goes on and on.

Your responsibility is to build your child's self-esteem and self-profile and this starts with the communication you have with them about them and grows into what you tell them of the world and those in it around them. Remember: Who am I? What am I like? What do I like? The way you verbalise to your child about your child, your parenting, their siblings and their relationship with them, their teachers, school, friends, extended family and the world around them will ultimately pave the path for them, and equip them with the tools they need to move forward in life as a calm, relaxed, and positive human being.

5
Tools for equipping their emotional tool kit

Consistent! I hear this word a lot in early childhood development.

'Are you consistent?'

'Oh yes, I'm definitely consistent.'

'Me too! I'm consistent.'

'Oh yes, I heard that consistency is the key, I try to be consistent whenever possible!' 'Oh my husband isn't as consistent as me, but I am definitely consistent most of the time.'

It's one of those words that is said but rarely truly understood. I often observe these 'consistent' patterns, and the only thing I find to be consistent is that most parents are only consistent when they are not busy or preoccupied. In other words, if they aren't on the phone, at the shops, at a friend's house, having friends over, in a rush, busy cooking, cleaning or talking with their husband or wife.

This means that they are not consistent, and just about every single family I work with is guilty of being inconsistent. Now this doesn't mean I or anyone should wag a finger at you. If anything, you probably need a hug because, if your little one is very unsettled, this will make things a lot more challenging. It's a difficult balance to strike but I encourage you to do your absolute best to help your baby settle down quickly.

To be consistent means you remain 100 per cent available to your child's needs, even when you have guests over, you are having a conversation, the doorbell rings or you are cooking dinner. Being consistent does not mean 'only when you are 100 per cent focused on your child'; it means regardless of what else is happening, you are always aware of your child and their needs and actions, and consistent with your language, with your expectations, and with your definition and follow through, regardless of anything else that is happening. This means, your baby comes first. You keep your main focus fixed firmly on the communication streams between you and your child, and everything else fits in around that.

If you teach your baby that occasionally they need to listen, but sometimes they don't, you have suddenly taught your child to wait until you act several times to know whether they need to listen to you this time. This is where the troublesome and flawed, 'I'm counting to three'–type strategies start to evolve.

The problem with one . . . two . . . three

If you are inconsistent, by the time your baby is almost two years of age they have been taught to listen to you only when you repeat yourself over and over. This means your baby is being taught on a social level to not actually listen to someone when they ask the first time respectfully, but to wait until someone gets frustrated with them. I often find parents employ a home-grown one, two, three strategy when their child is around two years of age. This is where we inadvertently reinforce the request to listen only when someone loses their temper or patience.

> Be emotionally available. Consistency means your baby comes first no matter what else is happening in your world.

Being consistent means your baby learns to listen to you, and learns to follow through when you talk and ask respectfully, and not only when you lose your temper. This is a two-way street, so when your baby asks you to listen to them, you need to be attentive to their needs and to not put them off for a hundred other chores, or drop them the moment the phone rings.

Be consistent and predictable for your baby by always defining your statements when you make them. This establishes a respectful style of listening and communication in your family that few actually achieve simply because they do not understand the importance or true definition of being consistent.

What communication are you encouraging?

Your baby is an amazingly complex and intelligent person. They experience the same emotions that we do. They can have clear ideas on what they would like to do, and when they would like to do it. Because they are just grasping the concept that they are separate entities from those around them, they tend to get a little annoyed when you don't automatically know what they are thinking or, indeed, want to do exactly the same things that they want to do. This means your baby will not hesitate to communicate with you for a moment, and will spend most of their days trying to express how things make them feel.

As your child's brain develops, so does their ability to not only make choices but to act upon them, whether it is to pick up and shake a rattle or to have a piece of cheese out of the fridge. And your baby will use crying as a way of talking as well as expressing their emotions. When you interpret all their cries as fitting neatly into only a few set categories—where the trigger is thought to be either emotionally or medically based, like fear or distress, pain or hunger—you fall well short of truly understanding what a complex and clever little person your baby is. Obviously, good proportions of babies between the age of six and seven months rarely display a real need for clear parent-governed lines of communication, which is often expressed through their language of being very unsettled, grizzly, grumpy, or distressed. However, the need to listen carefully to your baby, when aged seven to eight months, becomes an important observational skill to ensure you don't encourage crying or tantrums by misreading your baby's bold and confident attempts to guide those around them.

By the time your precious baby is celebrating their first birthday, they have a very strong understanding of their abilities, of what they would like to do, and have become very efficient at communicating those needs to their primary carers. Be sure to always give your child a clear indication that you have been able to understand their cry by a verbal sentence or definition. This helps your baby start to learn early phrases. An example of this would be when your baby cries and gestures to be picked up. You respond by saying 'Alex wants up. Mummy pick you up', before using your up cue (see page 76).

When responding to your baby's cries however, be extremely cautious about giving a certain style of inappropriate or undesirable communication from them, like back arching, screaming, head banging, or hitting, a value in their vocabulary. Imagine you are asking your baby to wait in their high chair while you wipe down the tray and complete the meal time. If your child was to start screaming, or back arching, or hitting the tray, then your automatic response might be to remove them from the situation that is upsetting them. But ask yourself:

- Is it appropriate that they learn to wait while you wipe down the tray? (Yes.)
- Is it asking too much of them? (No.)
- Is it a skill that will be useful to them in other situations as a life skill? (Yes.)
- Should they scream, back arch or hit the tray at the end of each meal to get picked up? (No.)

If this behaviour does occur, then you should always be conscious of the outcome you would like to achieve during the completion of the event. If you would like to discourage behaviours such as tantruming, screaming, crying, hitting, back arching, etc., then it's vitally important to not give these behaviours a definition or predictable positive outcome for your baby. You should strive to do the opposite of what they expect the behaviour will achieve, such as wipe down the kitchen table, casually put your hair up, pat the puppy dog, or talk to a bird outside on the windowsill until the behaviour subsides. With under-two year olds you should not leave the room, or move around the room too dramatically or to where they have difficulty seeing you. Just stay in the room and carry on with your chores until your little one stops the behaviour. This could take a little bit of time so you need to stay calm and patient. But in the longer term your child will learn that you only respond to their calm behaviours, and they are picked up when you say the words 'up, up' and *not* when they are screaming, smacking, or back arching.

To respond with body language—such as looking at them, moving faster to complete the task, leaning in to cuddle them in a bid to stop their tantrum—or to pick them up when they do any inappropriate or undesirable patterns of behaviour is to literally teach them to continue the behaviour and you will co-operate with them. This obviously does not apply to a baby who has got a sudden fright, who is extremely excited when someone they love has come home unannounced, or they have accidentally hurt themselves or been hurt. We are only talking about not teaching your little one to behave in a manner that will ultimately have people scowl at them, make you exasperated or frustrated with them, or pigeonhole them as a certain type of child, which impacts on their self-esteem. Be honest with your expectations and teach them that you will always follow a routine flow of events to complete a task, and their inappropriate styles of communication are not how you talk to one another in your house.

If your baby is happy and content then continue to use your language and simply praise, praise, praise a positive outcome. This will help them associate this style of routine language with rewarding and enjoyable outcomes. Right from the time their child is eight months old I encourage mothers and fathers to be mindful of what their actions are teaching their little baby by:

1. disengaging physically—making no eye contact apart from occasionally reassuring them if you feel it is necessary in a confident manner, and turning your body in a different direction and simply carrying on with doing something else—when your child goes into a style of behaviour that you do not wish to see continue
2. turning your body side on or away from them until they settle down if the behaviour continues
3. distracting them once they settle down with a toy or a story until the behaviour stops entirely.

Then you can pick them up or offer them something that you know they were asking for. This is how you say 'when you scream, back arch, hit or kick, mummy / daddy / nanny will carry on with something else, but when you are calm mummy and daddy will come back and engage with you and get you up or give you what you want'.

Remember to always assess the situation the child is in from an adult's perspective, not a child's perspective. Waiting for you to tell them when it's time to get out of the high chair or off the change table is a perfectly reasonable expectation to encourage right from the age of six months.

Parenting from a place of love

This is often where confident parents stands out from the crowd. Being able to make good decisions for your baby or toddler and empower them with a series of solutions for the normal healthy emotions they are experiencing, without being fearful or concerned that you may lose their friendship or those around you might judge you are rightly motivating for boundary setting and a solid ground to stand on as parents. This is parenting from a place of love and self-assured confidence, because you know it is the right thing to do for your child.

This is in stark contrast to parenting from a place of fear or pride, where parents are concerned they are 'being mean' or 'breaking their child's spirit' or '[insert latest emotionally scary buzz term here]' by asking their baby to lie down for a nappy change, or teaching them to listen or co-operate occasionally through the day. To parent from a place of fear is difficult, but when parenting from a place of pride you are more focused on appealing to other adult's standards or falling prey to the ever-judgemental eye of the public, family and, sadly, friends rather than catering solely to your child's true needs.

Parenting from a place of love is where you take your child's overall needs into consideration and set appropriate boundaries and life lessons based on those needs, even if your child doesn't always agree with you. Parenting from a place of fear or pride is where you are factoring in your needs and fears as well as the ideals of others as the reason for your style of communication. It's these personal needs that often cloud your judgement when it comes to assessing a child's *true* need versus a child's short-term demand.

Guilt when parenting

Setting boundaries is a part of your duty of care towards your child. While some children seem to thrive without boundaries there is equally as large a proportion of children that are profoundly unsettled by a lack of guidance or predictability in their day. You need to acknowledge the vast and varied emotional needs of your children.

The children that do not cope without clear boundaries bear the unique fingerprints of being overburdened, which classically appears around a basic area of need where the parents would like to guide the child but find it especially difficult without going to extreme lengths. These symptoms include difficulty at bedtime, playing independently or sitting still to eat or do anything that involves waiting for you to complete a task for them. Each child reacts differently and may experience significant difficulties in only one area, or in all three areas and beyond.

To not take each individual child and assess them on their own unique set of strengths and weaknesses is parenting to cater for your need to meet an ideology, and not your child's actual observable needs. For children who are more sensitive, and keener to have a say in the flow of their day, to be denied the emotional safety nets that many boundaries represent, is to not meet some of their most basic needs in early childhood. A child may want to touch a hot oven door but, because it is obviously dangerous, you tell them it is a no-touch zone. This is safe, loving guidance and clearly not emotionally damaging. Nor are the clear, safe and loving boundaries set around really basic listening and co-operation right from a very precious but amazingly aware six months of age.

To fall prey to guilt, which appears to be the parental curse of just about every mother and father, means you may be creating patterns of poor or inappropriate behaviour simply by overcompensating or mismanaging them due to guilt. You not only have a right as a parent to guide your children respectfully and safely until they are of an age where they can make appropriate decisions and healthy life choices for themselves (based on all you have taught them), but you also have a duty to not burden your children with having to run an entire household of adults and possibly other siblings. I always ask a mother and father, 'If *you* don't know what to do when your baby is upset, how on earth would they know?'

Children only know what you have taught them, so you have a choice to teach them how to deal with normal daily life scenarios in a way that will empower them with the emotional tools they need to cope in the future, or you could teach them that the only solution is you or a breastfeed, or to be carried everywhere, or to simply avoid any situation that will evoke emotions. No parent would really want to hold their child back or limit their ability to explore and feel safe in this world by not exposing them to the normal life conditions that they will encounter every time they interact with someone outside the four walls of their house, or outside the loving and protective arms of their mummy and daddy.

Separation anxiety

Understanding basic separation anxiety and the important role your communication plays in developing and maintaining trust through that particular communication is one of the more important tools to equip yourself with as a parent. This is one of the most obvious areas of concern for your baby when it comes to learning how to go to sleep independently. If you cannot leave a room during the day when they are playing happily, then how can you expect them to cope with you leaving them in their dark room when they are worn out and tired?

Up until the age of around four to six months, your baby is generally quite content to be left in the care of others, but as they grow they start to develop a sense of 'object permanence'. This is where your amazing little baby learns that things and people continue to exist even when they are out of sight. This is them learning and understanding that they come to an end and you come to a beginning. Once they develop an understanding that they can call out to you from a neighbouring room, and you occasionally return at their insistence, they start to look for a more permanent pattern during these events. The problem starts when your baby can find no predictable pattern within these absences. In fact, the patterns are so varied that there are some days you do not return for hours, while on other occasions you return within minutes. To make matters worse, they spend a little time gazing lovingly at their best friend (mum or dad) before happily starting their play, but when they look up to watch you again you have suddenly disappeared altogether and they cannot see you anywhere in the room. You are now being inconsistent for them.

This is where a child might feel more comfortable guiding you rather than being in a situation where they cannot predict you. Focusing on play becomes difficult because they start to be more focused on where you are, and as a result play becomes a challenging task. It is simply easier for them to ask to be taken everywhere with you, comfortably perched on your hip so they can predict what you will do rather than risk being left feeling vulnerable and unsure of their environment. Unpredictability around your movements and absences triggers anxiety in your baby as they lose trust in the process of you staying in the room, as well as around you leaving and always coming straight back. They naturally start to try and avoid that situation from repeating itself. The signs of separation anxiety vary from child to child based mainly on the consistency of the communication provided by the parents. Some children can still clearly be experiencing real stress around a primary carer leaving their line of sight well into the second year.

This is a normal and healthy stage of development but one that is difficult to work through for most parents or full-time primary carers. The sense that your baby is clearly upset and calling to you can be a very difficult thing to deal with, whether you are running to the bathroom for 30 seconds, or leaving your child in the care of someone else for a short time or the whole day. As your baby has no concept of time, it's difficult for you to be able to explain to your little one the difference between you only going to the bathroom for a minute or two, or you going to work for the day and, consequently, they won't see you until the following morning in some cases. This is where you need to look at ways of being honest, and creating some kind of predictability for your little one to be able to trust. This is where your language cues and the associations you develop around those cues become extremely valuable tools. By implementing the following short- and long-term absence cues, and then working through the emotions that occur around those events, you can develop trust with your baby in as little as one to three weeks.

Short-term absence cue ('I'll be back')

In the early stages of building trust there are many variations that occur when you leave the room. Each time you leave, your baby may become anxious because they will be unsure whether you are leaving the room for a short time or a long time. The unpredictability of this can make your baby or toddler a little clingy because it's easier for them to stay with you than to be unsure of when you are going to leave the room, or how long it could take you to return. To help them through this period until they begin to understand the rhythm of the house, you need to establish a short-term absence cue.

The aim of this cue is to make your little one relaxed about you leaving their line of sight during play or other 'alert' times of the day, as this is what you will need to do at each sleep time. There is a series of emotions that will come up around this event for them, so it's really important that you give them the opportunity to feel those emotions and for them to learn that they are safe feelings to have, that they can cope with them and that you are always predictable around these absence cues.

Obviously, the worst thing you could do is to act nervous when they react to you leaving the room; that is, you race back into the room to fix their distress. Always remember to assess the situation from an adult's perspective. A parent going to the bathroom under predictable conditions is most definitely *not* something they need rescuing from and certainly not the message you want to deliver to your baby. It would be debilitating for a baby or toddler to think they are 'not okay', or 'cannot calm down until you have held them and fixed it each time you re-enter the room'. This is not teaching a baby appropriate coping strategies to normal emotions.

Often I see parents, with only love and the best of intentions, being their child's complete emotional solution throughout the day, and then expecting the child to be totally self-soothing at night. You need to make sure your requests during the day are equal to those at night. You need to give your little one every opportunity to practise and learn how to cope with the sensations experienced when you leave the room during the day and to understand that you always come back quickly when you use this cue, which will give them a chance to learn what to do to help themselves feel better. This means your child gets the chance to learn how to cope with the sensation of you leaving the room during the day in brief intervals with lots of positive reinforcement and allows them to build confidence around this event, long before they experience it at sleep time. This means they can relax into their new settling routine without the added stress of separation anxiety.

So what is the short-term absence cue? Each time you leave your child's line of sight, simply say, 'I'll be back'. The first time you do this, make your absence short. Each time thereafter, gradually leave for longer and longer periods of time. Be cautious to not say the line or communicate through walls, that is from one room to the next, or you will encourage your baby to focus on keeping you in their auditory 'sight'. This defeats the purpose because the conditions they encounter when they are going to sleep should not include them hearing you through the door, or thinking they can call out to you all night and you will respond each time. The intention of creating these cues at a non-sleep time is to prepare them for sleep-time conditions, where you will want your little one to feel comfortable in a room on their own. So during the day you will want them to carry on with their task, to trust you will reappear, rather than be anxiously looking at the door and listening for you.

> For your short-term absence cue you should always say 'I'll be back', each and every time you leave their line of sight. As well, you should say 'I'm back', each and every time you re-enter the room.

The importance of developing these cues is essential to establishing their trust in you when you leave a room, which in turn helps them adjust to and feel comfortable with the emotions that happen when you leave them in their bed. Obviously your short-term absence cue is vital in developing their coping strategies for sleep. That said, to teach your child to talk to you, or you talk to them through doors and walls during your short-term absence cues, means you are encouraging your child to call out from their cot at sleep time which, for most babies, means crying. Be careful to always think through the broader implications of what you are teaching your baby.

It's easy to be lazy with this one. You should always say 'I'll be back', each and every time you leave their line of sight. To complement this, you should also say 'I'm back', each and every time you return. This is just being courteous to your little one to let them know your movements so they can relax and do what all babies so love to do: explore, play and learn, rather than feel the need to watch your every move.

Long-term absence cue (saying goodbye)

This is where the bulk of the stress around separation anxiety arises. When you are absent for what feels like an eternity and your child frets, this will then occur each and every time you leave their line of sight throughout the day. If you plan to be away for a long period of time, such as when you go to work, the gym for a few hours or the hairdressers, then it's very important to say a proper goodbye.

There is a tendency to think babies are too young under the age of 12 months to understand or be bothered by you leaving, but I can assure you, if you don't pre-warn them when you are leaving for a substantial period of time, they will have a cry every time you leave their line of sight, even when you quickly go to get something in the other room. This obviously creates poor associations with you leaving the room, and impacts significantly on your ability to settle them at sleep time. There are so many mums and dads that can't even venture into the bathroom in peace because their children can't trust or predict when they might return.

Even if saying goodbye results in a few tears, it's still very important that you go through the process of allowing them to feel the emotions tied up in someone they love leaving them for a substantial period of time. This ensures they don't lose trust in you. It is obvious there will come a time when your baby or toddler is very sad to say goodbye for an extended period of time but it's okay for them to feel those emotions. These are normal feelings to have and nothing to shelter them from. It's so much more important to be honest with your baby and let them feel a little sad for a few moments than allow them to lose faith in you. Be honest and tell them when you plan on going for a substantial period of time.

It's always a nice idea to have a little goodbye routine. If daddy or mummy goes to work, take the time to allow the baby to walk them to the door or car, and to kiss and cuddle everyone goodbye. Wave to them, and involve them in the final part of the routine so they actually complete the farewell process themselves. This could be something as simple as closing the door, the window, or the garage door with you. This is important for a couple of reasons. It gives a child a sense of control over the situation, enabling them to govern the end of the event so they can move on. It also gives the child something routine to look forward to while doing something they may find difficult.

Troubleshooting

Q Do I need to use the short-term absence cue every time I leave their line of sight?

A Yes, certainly if you are leaving the room, but if you are both in the kitchen and you are ducking into a cupboard to find a pot, simply tell them you are looking for a pot. If they are prone to becoming a little stressed initially when you disappear, be a little vocal as you search for the pot as it will help them relax.

Q Do I need to use the short-term absence cue when they leave the room, and exit my line of sight?

A No, when they leave the room they are aware they won't be able to see you so there is no element of surprise or trust-damaging process when they exit the room.

Q What about my other children, do they have to use the short-term absence cue?

A Only if they are old enough. But as your other children are not your baby's primary carer, your baby's means of survival, it may only be a little irritating or upsetting when their sibling leaves the room unannounced, something they will become accustomed to. If your child is old enough to understand what you are doing, ask them to just tell their baby brother or sister they are going to leave the room out of courtesy.

They will absolutely love the predictability of a routine event like this. If you look for the things that babies enjoy the most you'll find they are repetitious patterns that get the most laughs and the most relaxed demeanour. A great example of this is when you take your baby or toddler to grandma and grandpa's house, and grandpa always takes them to enjoy the same rose bush outside, and to turn on the same tap, and grandma always sings the same knee-jig nursery rhyme, and your baby quickly begins to expect and love this pattern of events.

To create a predictable end to the goodbye routine develops strong positive associations with the event for your child; it teaches them how to move on, and enables them to learn how to cope with this normal life event in a positive way.

Developing trust during separation

The first rule in developing trust with your little one around separation anxiety is: be honest. Try to *never* walk out of a room without saying goodbye or 'I'll be back'. Imagine how you would feel if you looked up and your baby was gone, and you called out and heard nothing, so you went looking and found nothing. It would leave you frantic. Obviously, our fear as adults would be a justified fear but, remember, for a baby it feels the same way when you disappear. They look up from what they were doing, and you are gone. So they call out, and nothing, so they look for you and find you have vanished. This is just as frightening for a baby.

After teaching in kindergartens and childcare centres for years, some of the worst things I have had to deal with are the result of a parent who has snuck off without saying goodbye because they didn't want their baby to cry. What they failed to realise was that when the child looked up and around, and then got up and looked for them and couldn't find them, their child got upset anyway. And worse, not just a little upset as they would if they'd said goodbye, but extremely upset and, in some cases, frantic. The most difficult thing for these children was the confusion that followed. They would continue to cry and look for their parents for at least an hour and in some cases the better part of their day, compared to children whose parents were honest and said goodbye. These children often cried for between 30 seconds and five minutes and then were able to carry on with their day.

The children whose well-meaning but misguided parents had snuck off without saying goodbye would turn up to kindergarten the following day clinging desperately to their parents' legs, feeling uncertain about their environment because it was now associated with uncomfortable feelings from the previous visit. This same situation happens in the home environment when you or others that the baby loves and trusts fail to be honest about leaving. At no point are you doing your baby or toddler any favours by being dishonest and not telling them when you leave, be it for a short time or a long time.

Positive feedback

Be your child's emotional safety net. When you tell your little one that you plan on leaving their line of sight for a short period of time, your intention is to try and create a auditory-based environment that means your baby can carry on playing, trusting that if you leave the room for a short period of time you will let them know, and tell them when you return so they can carry on playing undisturbed. This basically means they don't need to stop playing just because you are scooting out of the room for the moment because their need to watch you to predict your movements is negated by your verbal cue and the associated events that always follow your actions. This means they know your movements and the outcome of them, without even looking.

When you use your short-term absence cue you should casually say it without trying to take their attention off what they are doing. Initially, while they are learning to trust that this new cue means you always come back within a short period of time, they will obviously look up, and perhaps cry, but over time as they start to trust this cue their need to look up will diminish and they will continue to play. This is your ultimate goal, so the way you say 'I'll be back' casually, without even looking at them, tells them that you are very relaxed and not concerned for them, and this fills them with a sense of security.

Remember what we said about eye contact. To engage your baby in eye contact could suggest you are about to talk to them or play with them, so to make eye contact as you say your short-term absence cue but then leave the room will be a confusing message. The short-term absence cue should be said casually as you confidently walk at an even pace out of the room regardless of their reaction. Spend a brief period out of the room, and then re-enter confidently, regardless of their reaction. Your response to their reaction when you return to the room is what tells them if they are okay or not when they feel that way. What are your actions telling them about the way they should feel about you leaving the room?

You should always try to walk in confidently, say hello in a happy tone and offer a warm smile. Sometimes you will carry on with your chores and verbally reassure them by confidently saying 'You're okay, bubby', then redirect their focus, 'Where's your car?' If, however, you feel your baby has found this a really difficult task, then you should sit down casually beside them and without fixing it for them (by picking them up, patting, shushing, rocking, etc.) try to show them how to calm down through play. If you have an attitude that everything is okay and feel confident that despite their tears they are in fact okay, then they will be able to assess that they are okay.

Remember how a child reacts when they fall over and looks to their parent to assess if they are hurt or not, and the parent's reaction ultimately determines if they start to cry or dust themselves off and carry on happily. It's the same in all situations where the child feels uncomfortable. Don't make them think that you leaving the room is a bad thing by being frightened or overly reactive to their reactions.

If your baby is mobile and they follow you as you leave the room, allow them to follow your voice while you stay happy, even if they crawl or walk after you crying. This tells them that you are not concerned, they are not in any danger, and ultimately means that they can feel comfortable being able to express the way your movements make them feel without being given the wrong messages about those feelings.

At no point while you are on your journey should you change your action from your original plan unless they hurt themselves. This means they learn that they can follow you, but you are not going to pick them up on these chore or toileting journeys. You should still close the bathroom door as planned and you should still walk back into the original living area that you left once you have completed you chores and say 'I'm back' without carrying them in with you. It's perfectly normal for a child to want to be near you and, if they can move, then they are fine to follow you, but don't teach them that you moving around the house means they need to be carried everywhere because it is totally unnecessary and it limits their opportunities to explore and discover their environment.

Don't taint your cues

Remember that the golden rule of all communication is consistency. If you want your child to trust you, you must be predictable; if you want to be predictable you must be consistent 100 per cent of the time. So always use your short- and long-term absence cues, always be reassuring in your response to their reactions and consistent in the messages you deliver at the their expression of those emotions and don't adopt an 'I'm too tired to do this today' attitude because all yours and your baby's hard work is compromised by inconsistency. Try to be as consistent as possible. If you are too tired however, pick your battles. Instead of presenting a parent-governed line, offer a negotiation, and, if they say 'no', then accept it. If you do not have the energy to work through a short-term absence, simply take them with you. Just be sure to be consistent when you do use a cue.

It's normal to get tired and to not have as much enthusiasm and energy every day of the week, and it is for this reason that I simply suggest you don't push the envelope for either yourself or your baby on these days. Therefore, if you don't feel you have the energy, then simply carry on with your day and don't ask anything particularly challenging of your baby. It is more important to maintain the expectations around your cues than to damage the trust your child has in them by you changing their definition halfway through a routine. To taint a cue could mean you change the definition of, say, 'I'll be back' and the associated expectations your baby has of your behaviour around that event. This would mean you were unpredictable and therefore untrustworthy, and this will result in clingy behaviour in your child.

Remember, you can teach a baby very quickly to cry to get you to come back in the room, rather than play and wait for you. And you do not want to teach a child to cry when you leave a room to make you come back because you are clearly not going to be able to maintain this, and it is a destructive strategy to use around your baby's sleep time.

Triggers for episodes of anxiety

Now that you understand the root cause of some basic separation anxiety in the home environment, it's important to understand the things that may disrupt the carefully balanced conditions of trust within your new language framework. If lack of trust is the cause of the tears, and communication to create predictability in their environment is the solution, anything that disturbs this predictability could easily disrupt the flow and trigger episodes of anxiety in your baby again.

On days when it's clearly not working, your ability to confidently guide your baby with strong clear parent-governed lines of communication is one of the most reassuring tactics you could adapt to re-establish trust, along with your pre-emptive and forewarning cues. You will soon see it is a quick and helpful strategy to help them settle down quickly and trust your guidance again. When they are feeling anxious, you allow them to govern fewer areas of the day, depending on how unsettled they are. They are simply unsure of your predictability again, and you need to quickly establish their trust.

Some of the triggers could be things like a sudden change in the environment like the arrival of a new sibling, a sibling going to school after being home for the weekend, a change in carer for the day, a sneaky exit by you, someone being unwell, tradespeople in the house, daddy arriving home from work, or going to a family barbeque where your little one is passed around a lot. Obviously the big guaranteed triggers include a hospital stay, a holiday, or moving house.

During these times remain consistent, retain the ability to guide your baby or toddler, and follow your flow of communication by laying a path in words for each transition of the day until your little one calms down. The more you learn to understand your child the better equipped you will be in being consistent.

6
Learning to understand your child (to avoid tears and tantrums)

Now that you have looked at ways of establishing a balanced guiding role as a parent within your household, and discovered how you can actually create a peaceful and smooth flow to the day by unburdening your children, it is possible to safely look a little deeper into what your child is trying to tell you at all the remaining times of the day. But at this point I need to make something very clear. The intention of this communication style within a loose or, in some cases, strict routine is to create days that almost guarantee every one of your child's needs are met without them:

- getting frustrated
- having to ask for food when they are hungry (which usually means they are being fed a little too late)
- indicating they are so tired they aren't coping well (which usually means they should already be tucked up in their bed and starting to drift off peacefully).

A simple parent-governed line of communication with a daily routine offers a child the opportunity to relax and not be burdened with needing to ask for fluid, food, stimulation, predictability, love, fun, interaction or sleep.

The benefits of guiding your child well
A well-governed day ensures your baby is fed before they become too hungry, go to bed before they get too tired, are active and stimulated when they need to be, and are still and relaxed when their bodies are weary. You

take the stress out of transitioning from one event to the next and provide predictable patterns of guidance around every regular event of the day. Already, before the day has begun, the usual triggers for tears or stress that cause unsettled behaviour are not present. This allows your child to be a child. They can spend their days busily playing, exploring, challenging their boundaries and learning to communicate through your solid examples while discovering all there is to know about themselves, their family and the world all around them.

Early childhood is a formidable time for discovery. To waste even a moment of that through unsettled, difficult-to-manage days for either your child or yourself is a waste of a very precious and wonderful time in all our lives. By creating event routines within the day, you equip your children with the tools they need to cope with, predict and own every typical scenario they will experience every day of their early life (nappy change, meal times, bedtimes, pram time, playtime, etc.), making all the normal daily tasks pleasant language-rich opportunities to learn from and enjoy for both child and parent.

By working together and learning vital communication and life skills through these event routines each day, you are able to prepare your little one for just about every other scenario they may encounter, simply because they can trust your guidance. Through this they will be able to:

- play with their toys better
- confidently play on their own
- like their room and their cot
- trust you when you leave the room for short periods of time
- sit down patiently, wait and be relaxed
- accept the sensation of being tired and know what to do when they feel like that
- sit down for a meal without stress
- happily eat their food at meal times.

You will have developed rich self-esteem building days though positive communication and predictable, simple-to-understand language. You are always working past areas your child finds challenging to help them achieve a sense of confidence in all areas of their life. You are encouraging positive forms of communication from your child, and role modelling excellent communication within your family. You have eliminated fear-inducing stress from the day. Your little one's sense of their new positive routine management (PRM) enables you to guide your children to prevent tears and stress. They can predict you. They can trust you. They can understand you. Their every possible basic need has been met, and now you are left with the normal communication that remains when a child is not burdened.

This is what it should be like for our children. A confident parent guides a child throughout their day so they can relax and be a baby, rather than having to feel tired, hungry, upset and overwhelmed before trying to tell their mummy and daddy what they need to feel happy. No matter how mild or extreme your little one's anxieties are, a good-fitting routine and a confident parent-guided day will eliminate tears permanently within five days and make understanding your child a much easier task.

Does this mean there are not times when they are going to get upset, or have other needs they have to express to you? Not at all. Babies communicate through crying and, just like us, there are different things that affect them every day. The entire idea of the routine and flow of communication is to make sure it is not a basic need being missed that has triggered the tears. This means that you need to just look at individual situations and the environment around them at the time of their communications to better understand their personality, likes and dislikes.

Excluding a genuine and obvious symptom of illness or discomfort, all other tears are the result of things happening around baby. Obviously, there will be times when your little one feels overwhelmed by a situation. Because they are so new to this world and the intense emotions our bodies and minds are prone to experiencing, there will always be a need to read their feelings, and to possibly help resolve a problem with them. Once you know your child is eating and sleeping when they need to, and can accept guidance, then the ability to observe what is truly bothering a child is far more simple.

The five behaviour-based crying triggers

The trigger for their emotions is what allows you to determine the way you can help them through the situation. Before a child reaches the point of being completely overwhelmed, there are usually signs that they are starting to feel upset. This will manifest in many different ways, and rarely are these triggers isolated. They are often common triggers repeated throughout the day. There are five cry responses to watch for once you have catered for all your child's basic needs through routine and communication:

1. distressed cries or tantrums
2. frustrated or angry cries or tantrums
3. impatient cries or tantrums
4. bossy cries or tantrums
5. attention-seeking cries or tantrums.

Distressed cries or tantrums

This is when they are saying: 'I'm not coping' or 'I'm overwhelmed'. Always reassure them when you first identify this trigger to their daytime concerns, and then look at the best way to help them cope better the next time they are introduced to that same scenario. Here are some common causes and solutions for distressed crying and tantruming.

Cause	Possible solutions
Someone leaving the room	Short-term absence cue (see page 94)
Someone leaving for work	Long-term absence cue (see page 96)
Grandma going home	Pre-emptive cues (see page 40)
Someone popping in unannounced	Soothing and enthusiastic tones (see page 58), plus time to warm-up to the situation
Overwhelmed after a large function (over-handling can be too much for many babies under 15 months old)	• Pre-emptive cues • Keep them close • Short-term absence cues if you are leaving them with others at the function
Foreign environment (holidays for examples)	• Pre-emptive cues and role playing • Keep them close
Transition of carers	• Pre-emptive cues • Going-to-work event routine (see page 762)
Transition from one event of the day to the next (bathing to getting dressed, play to meal time, park to car, home to shops)	Pre-emptive cues
'I'm tired / hungry / thirsty'	Meal-time routines / management (see pages 216 and 242)

Once they have become upset, stay close, stay positive, give them lots of cuddles and lots of reassurance. Make sure your response to the situation fills them with feelings of security and give them positive feedback. These events may be very stressful for a young child who is particularly sensitive or overtired. Each may trigger a slight loss of trust in the predictability of their environment. By remaining a clear guide and outlining each event of their day and breaking it down into simple steps, even if they are just eight months of age, you will make their day predictable once again and they will be able to relax.

Once you have identified the cause of the stress, such as the examples given above, then your main focus should become preventing the tears the next time. Always look to avoiding a distressing situation from occurring in the first place by being aware of your child's triggers and staying conscious of upcoming events and how they may affect your child. This is how you stay 100 per cent emotionally available to your children. And, this can be achieved in a family with one child, or a family with eight children.

In toddlers, the above situations can easily trigger tantrum episodes when they are trying to tell you what to do to help them feel better, but don't know what they want or need to feel better. This is a common response to a child feeling as though they can't predict the changes around them. Often their automatic response is to try to establish control of that environment. When the parent doesn't know what the child is saying, the child's behaviour will quickly spiral into a full tantrum simply because they are feeling overwhelmed.

> Being aware of your child's triggers and staying conscious of upcoming events and how they may affect your child is how you stay 100 per cent emotionally available to your children.

Practice makes perfect! It's a hard job learning how to communicate clearly and respectfully with your child, but if you get into the habit of following two simple steps, your day will be virtually tear free:

- be consistent by articulating their day in small steps through the use of the PRM approach
- think a step ahead of them the whole time; watch for triggers and stay emotionally available.

Always ask yourself what could go wrong, and what could they find difficult about the upcoming events in the day. Then ask what you can provide for them to do instead. An example of this would be walking through a shopping centre while your toddler sits in the pram. You know you are about to pass the hot chip shop or that luring Wiggles ride, and that they will demand their way. And when I say demand, I mean demand, especially when they are allowed a ride. Their response to getting off is almost as bad as their response to not being able to ride in the first place. For those of you who have experienced this, you know it can be an extremely stressful and confidence-shattering event where you are left questioning your ability to communicate with your little one at all!

Not all parents have to endure the hour-long crying session that can be triggered by such an event. If you know you are not able to give them a ride, then a balanced approach would mean you could either offer a ride or equally be able to politely say 'Not today, bubby' and still have a happy baby. Yes, it is possible. It takes work for some parents to help their little ones to settle down, but it is definitely a relatively quick process to work through if you remain confident. I do it for a living, and children are always happy to accept the condition if you have given them plenty of forewarning before they see the trigger and decide to ask for something.

The secret lies in pre-emptive language. Once they have asked, it is a little more of a challenge because they will become frustrated that you appear to not understand them, which usually results in a more frantic insistence before they become overwhelmed and start to tantrum. The

'Woke up on the wrong side of the bed' babies

Alex was the beautiful 18-month-old baby boy of two very loving, working parents. He had recently experienced a significant trauma when introduced to a childcare centre without the usual orientation and gradual introduction to his new carers and the environment. This had, after four days, left him so completely unsettled that he cried for two days straight. Despite a lengthy stay and every test their local hospital's emergency department had to offer, Alex was sent home with a clean bill of physical health. But he was far from emotionally healthy. He was screaming, and continued for 48 hours straight. No breaks, no sleep, no food or water, just inconsolable crying from a baby who had crossed from the emotional line from distress into the realm of trauma.

His absolutely distraught parents rang me utterly consumed about what could possibly have happened while he was in the centre's care to cause this reaction. As a childcare worker myself, I have helped orientate and adjust thousands of children into daycare, and have only once before seen a reaction so strong from a child. As I got to know Alex over the next week, what had happened at his childcare centre became very clear.

Alex was a child who needed time to warm-up to his environment, and the extra people in it, even at home. He was still young and he interacted predominantly with one carer at a time prior to childcare. As his parents shared his primary care equally, he was comfortable with both parents nurturing him. When Alex shifted from one location to the next, from sleeping to coming out to be with the family for instance, he would become very distressed. People would try to talk with him, offer him toys, everyone would look and fuss, try to make him feel better and, when all that failed, they would assume he must feel sick. Well guess what? He just needed to sit, get comfortable in that space without too many people focusing on him, and be gently encouraged to start playing by the person who brought him into that situation. That was it.

Alex was not ready to interact with others until he had had a little adjustment time, even at home. Imagine how he would have felt being taken to childcare for the first time, with no warm-up days when his parents would be with him, no time to get to know his carers, no orientation to get to know the environment, no time to watch the other children play and see how much fun they had, and without his favourite teddy. He was just taken there, and at the ability of pre-empting a possible trouble time for your child is one of the most important parts of avoiding tears and tantrums. So, before you even get out of the car at the shops, you should be preparing them for the fact that today they can't go on the Wiggles car. You say 'Bye bye, Wiggles car. No sitting on the car today, just waving. Wave bye bye to car.' And you prepare them for the thing they can do instead, 'We can see a balloon / puppy / baby'. This can simply be in the form of a picture, a window display, a can of pet food, a picture of a child, or other babies in prams just like them.

centre staff's encouragement, was simply left there. Clearly this was a traumatic event for him; in fact, an event that is easily stressful for any child under two.

The centre claimed they 'forgot' his orientation process. They apologised for their error. Alex regained his trust within five days of starting this program and now attends a new daycare centre after careful preparation. He loves it. Our strategy to help him through this 'stage' of his life at home was simple. When being introduced to a new scenario he needed lots of forewarning. We would tell him in happy tones who he would see, and what toys there were to play with, and let him know he could have a cuddle with daddy / mummy until he was ready to play. As we entered the room, we would play a little peek-a-boo game, asking the other adults in the room not to respond to our entry. Then, casually, we would enter the room and keep it fairly low key. Unless he indicated he was ready to say hello to other people, we didn't push it for a few minutes.

His initial response was always the same. One finger in his mouth, head tilted looking shy (even with his mother or father) and firmly attached to whoever brought him into the room. This included me. Once he was sitting, we encouraged the adults to start natural communication with one another and just leave him be. He would sit, listen quietly, and eventually start to look around the room. When we saw this we would slowly point out his toys. This was usually done with a little bit of humour. We didn't offer the toys to him though. He would stay on our lap, and we would have a little silly play with the toy but leave it on the floor.

Within moments he would be giggling at our crazy play, and then suddenly pop down, still holding one of our legs and reach for his toy. If he couldn't reach, we would hold his hand and with gentle encouragement he would slowly step away from us, and then come back with his toy. He would generally start to play at our feet, and the other carers could talk about the toy from that point on. As soon as he was ready, he would respond to the other carers and suddenly feel completely relaxed and move on as though nothing extraordinary was happening.

This was Alex's warm-up time. It took about two or three minutes for Alex to adjust to a new environment each time he entered it initially. Within three weeks, the need to warm up had disappeared completely because he always knew he had the time he needed to adjust without the pressure of everyone overwhelming him. He had regained his trust. While Alex's case was extreme because of the childcare centre incident, it is actually a common phenomenon in early childhood when you observe children's behaviour carefully.

On the final run, as you get closer and closer to the Wiggles car, before you have even seen it, make sure you keep reminding them, 'Nearly time to wave bye bye to Wiggles car. Soon, no sitting on the car, just waving, then we can find the balloons.'

As you turn the corner, stay happy and confident, 'There's the car. Wave bye bye. Good waving, now where's that balloon? Let's go find those balloons'; and keep walking confidently, keeping their focus on their new target. Once you have successfully cleared the object that usually causes your child stress, offer lots of praise for their good behaviour. Stop the pram for a moment, tell them that they did 'good waving', and 'no crying, yeah', then repeat your suggestion to find the balloon. Talk about that event several times through that afternoon and show them that it was pleasing and they are actually very good at waving to the car.

Once you have mastered this skill, and your child is able to happily wave to the car without becoming stressed, you can offer them rides, making sure they are well pre-empted in much the same way you taught them to wave. In this case, while you are on your way to the shop, you can start to tell them, 'Today, Sophie can have a ride on the Wiggles car. Mummy will undo buckles, and Sophie will sit down and wait for mummy on the ride. Fun!' And as you get closer to the ride remind her: 'Nearly time to have a ride on the Wiggles car'.

If you know they have a particularly difficult time getting off the ride again, then be sure to pre-empt the end of the ride and tell them what they need to do: 'Sit down, wait for mummy in your pram, then say bye bye to Wiggles car.' If your little one tends to have difficulty when grandparents arrive, coming out of their bedroom after a nap, going to a party or when friends arrive, to name a few scenarios that I call 'woke up on the wrong side of the bed' syndrome (see box on page 106), then be patient. They are only little. Most people are irritated by this behaviour, but it needs patience and gentle guidance. Use clear pre-emptive communication, paying careful attention to letting them know who they are going to see, and what they can do. For instance, after you've changed their nappy say 'Let's go and have a cuddle on the couch. We can play with your truck if you like.'

As you leave the room and turn off the light make it a fun peek-a-boo game. When you turn the light off say 'Where's that mummy gone, shall we see if we can find mummy?' If they react strongly and indicate they do not want to 'find' mummy then reassure them confidently and simply say 'Okay, let's go and sit down on the couch', and skip the peeking game. If they are okay with the peeking game, then continue to play it together and stay really happy. Say 'Peek-a-boo mummy', then hide again, and repeat once more. Their reaction gives you a chance to gauge how they might feel about seeing someone else and enable you to enter the room and decide whether to engage the other carers' attention or not. Sometimes it just takes a simple sit on the couch and time. Allow them to cuddle you while you chat with others in the room. Direct your child into play and allow them to move away from you in their own time by using lots of silly play and encouragement.

Frustrated or angry cries or tantrums

Here your child is saying to you: 'I'm really cross or irritated' or 'I'm overwhelmed'. Some common causes of frustrated or angry crying or tantruming are as follows.

Cause	Possible solutions
Toys not doing what they would like them to	• Leave them and see if they can resolve it themselves first • If you need to intervene, empower them by showing them how to resolve it without just fixing it for them • Role play with the toys (see page 132)
'My mum and dad don't seem to understand what I'm asking for.'	Answer their questions and acknowledge what they are saying (see page 77)

Once they have become upset in an event like a toy causing frustration, it is better that you let the moment pass without getting too involved. It's often out of necessity that a child will try different solutions to resolve the problem they are experiencing. They will never feel the need to try themselves if you always run and fix it for them immediately. If it becomes clear that they are going to be unable to resolve it themselves, and you have given them a minute to try, always show them step by step how to resolve the situation. Break it down into simple language cues for each action, ones that you will be able to offer them next time from a distance, such as 'turn the truck', 'lift the car', 'build it up again'.

I usually try to use a sense of humour here. If a moving truck is stuck in the corner of a wall I tend to make a funny noise, and say 'Uh-oh, truck stuck, doink doink doink' as I bounce it off the wall, showing that I am experiencing the same frustration that they are experiencing. This empowers them with a different response to the situation next time, and tells them that when that happens it's normal and okay and nothing to become really stressed about.

Once you have identified the cause of the stress, such as the examples given above, then your main focus should become preventing the tears the next time. Have a one-on-one play session with them at another playtime and show them how to resolve that situation through role play (see page 132). Incorporate your new language cues into your play, and deliberately experience and resolve the same problem that they experienced. This means the next time your child encounters that situation, they will be able to respond better; you will have given them appropriate problem-solving skills, and if they still need a little help, you can encourage them from a distance with your new verbal cues. This will allow them to feel confident with their abilities, and encourage active problem solving when they encounter an obstacle in the future rather than feeling helpless in that situation or needing to call out for help. Please remember that you should be offering toys that are age appropriate.

Remember, this is not about an academic scholarship. Play is about enjoyment, exploration, learning and growing. They shouldn't *have* to know how to use anything, but if they want to play with something, and you are able to show them how to do that better, then that is a great motivation. These episodes are generally short-lived, and an important reminder of why it's so important to always introduce a new play with a parent-guided one-on-one role-play session before they embark on independent play with the activity.

Impatient cries or tantrums

Your child is saying 'I'm really bored, hurry up', or 'I have something else in mind, and this isn't it'. Here are some common causes and solutions to this situation.

Cause	Possible solutions
They don't think you understand what they want	Answer their request honestly; if you can't do so right now, then tell them that (see page 77)
You are doing a parent-guided activity	• Keep them informed so they don't feel in limbo; use your flow of communication (see page 40) so they know what is coming next and how long they will be at the shops, in the car, at a restaurant, in the pram, high chair, shop, etc. • Use the wait sign and game (see page 74) • Be cautious about what communication you are encouraging and don't teach them to scream, squeal, back arch or tantrum to make you do what they want; wait until they have stopped crying or tantruming, then say 'Okay, Jake feels better now. Let's go.'

Cause	Possible solutions
They need to sit in the high chair, pram or car seat	• Keep them informed so they don't feel in limbo, using your flow of communication (see page 40) so they know what is coming next • Use the wait sign and game (see page 74) • Use your bag of tricks (see page 369).

If you have answered their request honestly and they have become upset, it's better that you let the moment pass without getting too involved. Often, once you have answered them they just want to express how it makes them feel, and can then quickly accept this boundary and wait. If you over fuss or intervene, you run the risk of dragging it out, and it almost always escalates. Don't feel the need to stop them from feeling what they are feeling. It's okay if they feel cross when you say 'Sit down, wait for mummy, I have to pay the lady / I have to change your nappy', and you should not stop them from expressing themselves.

It's also okay to empathise without over fussing, 'Oh gosh, I know it's tricky to wait Joshy. You're okay, mummy won't be long, then we can go and see birdies in the trees'. Offer a quick cuddle if their crying or tantruming has been going for a little while, but if it continues I tend to take a bit of a no-fuss approach and move on to something else to break the cycle before I do as they demand. This means that I then just carry on with my journey, leaving them in the pram, high chair, etc., without communicating or rushing, until the situation comes to its natural end as it would if they were not crying. But always be cautious of the communication you are encouraging. You don't want to teach them that if they would like us to move, they need to squeal, scream or tantrum. In this case, I stay patient and help them calm down through distraction, only then do I end the event or oblige them.

> Once you have identified the cause of the stress then your main focus should become preventing the tears the next time.

Once you have identified the cause of the stress, store it away as a trigger for tears and tantrums. If you know they dislike stopping in the pram, or waiting in the high chair, then you need to practise that skill in a calm environment. Take your little one for a walk around the block rather than try to establish better communication at the shops. Develop some cues that enable your child to predict when you might stop for a while, and when you might go again, such as 'stopping, wait for mummy' or 'let's go, good waiting for mummy'.

Always take your bag of tricks (see page 369) and practise your high chair play (see pages 192). Get good with your flow of communication. Be confident. Practise at a time when you are unlikely to buckle under the immense strain of the ever-judgemental eyes of complete strangers so that your little one can be empowered with how to cope, with what to expect, and with the ability to relax at those times in the future.

Bossy cries or tantrums

'I don't want to' or 'I insist' are two phrases that come to mind to describe this reaction. One of the best tools you can have here is a sense of humour if you are dealing with toddlers, and always use a confident tone if it is an appropriate time. You can try something like 'Okay, daddy will wear your shoes / hat. Come on daddy, time to put shoes on now.' There are some cases, though, where I find that communication needs repairing before we can use a humorous approach as it can only serve to upset them more. If this is the case in your house and your little one is being extremely resistant to any form of guidance, then correct the behaviour using your flow of communication first, then re-introduce humour only if it is helpful and effective with your little one.

Remember, this is about balance, so be sure to work through and past tantrums that are the result of real resistance when you have used your flow of communication well. Here are some triggers and solutions.

Causes	Possible solutions
Wanting to go outside, for a walk, to grandma's when it not possible	• Prevent it by telling them something within a suitable time bracket—they don't understand time terribly well so if you tell them they are going to see nanny and poppy this afternoon during breakfast they will be waiting at the door all day • Use the wait cue and game (see page 74) • Use distraction as a tool
Not wanting to hold hands near a road, or in a busy mall	Refer to holding hands (see pages 341)
Not wanting to wear hats, shoes or socks, or put clothes on	• Refer to hats on (see page 335) • Refer to nappy changing (see page 287)
Standing up in the bath	Refer to sitting in bath (see page 319)
Not wanting to pack away	Refer to packing away (see page 330)
Demanding food	Refer to answering their questions honestly (see page 77)

Once you have answered their request honestly and they have become upset, it's better in this case that you let the moment pass without getting too heavily involved in trying to get them to calm down. Again, they may just want to express how the situation makes them feel, and can then quickly accept this boundary and wait or settle down if you give them a little space. If you over fuss or intervene, you drag it out, and it always escalates. Don't feel the need to stop them from feeling. It's okay if they feel cross when you say 'No outside, bubby, time to play with your cars' or 'Wait', and you should not stop them from expressing themselves.

Move on as quickly as you can, and perhaps distraction is your best option here. This is either by you getting on with the task you were doing when they started to make the request, or by looking for something saying, 'Where's that puppy dog gone?' for example, or 'Can you hear a birdy, I can hear a birdy?' or 'Let's go and find your truck'. It's okay to empathise every now and again, and offer a cuddle if it has been going for a little while, but if it continues take a bit of a no-fuss approach and move on to something else to break the cycle of the demands.

Don't try to fix it, just stay confident, and stay busy doing your chores and every now and again offer a distraction. If this upsets them, you should respect that and leave them be. Sometimes a tantrum needs to run its course and people trying to talk a child down will only overwhelm them even more. It might come down to how well you have defined a parent-governed line in the past. Did you inadvertently teach your child to respond in this manner by eventually giving in to them in the past? This often means a child thinks that they are meant to cry for a long period of time if they really want to do something.

In this case, you will have to be very calm, really patient. If they will let you, eventually try and use distraction and be sure that you are consistent until they learn they don't have to cry for a long time to change the outcome. Be fair and make sure that once you have said that they can't do something right now, that they calm down completely, and move on to something else entirely before you would even consider obliging their demand.

If you have identified the cause of the stress, store it away in your mind as a trigger for tears and tantrums. If you know they always demand to go outside, or insist on going to the car, etc., and you are about to enter an environment that may trigger that episode, don't get nervous and hope it won't come up. Think ahead, use your flow of communication and tell them what is coming, what they can do, and put forward an expectation of their behaviour. Then repeat what they can do and get them involved in the play or activity or daily event immediately. For example, if your child always wants to go out to the back yard but it's raining, and you are about to go into the laundry where the back door, your child's usual access to their beloved back yard is, then you need to be fair and tell them before they see the door and get any funny little dancing-in-the-rain ideas into their head. Using your flow of communication, here's one way to do that:

Pre-emptive: 'Lovely playing with your blocks, bubby. Soon mummy is going to put the washing on. Emma can help mummy pick the clothes out of the basket. No going outside. Bye bye outside. Mummy / Emma close the door and say bye bye outside.'

Forewarning: 'Ok Emma, last one then mummy needs to put the washing on, no going outside, bye bye outside, close the door, we'll get Emma some clothes?'

State event and expectations: 'Okay, up up, time to help mummy with the washing. Let's go say bye bye to outside, Emma can close the door. Say bye bye outside, wave, Emma close the door.' Then help her close the door, even if there are tears. Move on quickly without feeling the need to stop her expressing herself, and remain sounding happy and confident. You remaining calm and confident is the fastest way to calm her down, and the easiest way to help calm her mood: 'Now, where's the clothes? Oh look, here they are.' Pop your bubby down and let them play with a few clothes.

If the tantrum continues, then it's time for a no-nonsense approach. Carry on with what you are doing, and stay calm and reassuring.

Attention-seeking cries or tantrums

Here's what they are saying: 'I think it's funny / interesting watching you when I do this', or 'What happens when I do this?' or 'Notice me, please'. They are testing you, and are repeating the action over and over and over again; for example, putting their foot on the table, standing in their high chair during the wait game and crying, then stopping and sitting before you attempt to sit them down and correct the position. They tend to do this when you are tyring to govern a line of communication and you cannot resolve it. My advice is to choose your challenges wisely. Only ask them to do something that you can define and achieve as an outcome. And watch what you are teaching them to do. Attention, good or bad, is still attention, and some patterns of behaviour need to be totally ignored to stop them from happening. Walk away, look away, or just pretend you never saw it. This can be combined with moving them to perhaps prevent them from doing it again. Make sure the only time they get your attention *isn't* when they are calling out, or acting out for it. Acknowledge all their positive times of the day, and try to not give currency to the less desirable behaviours.

Here are some other solutions to common attention-seeking crying or tantruming.

Cause	Possible solutions
They are putting their foot on the table or standing in the high chair or exhibiting other attention-seeking behaviour	• Move them away from the table • Ignore the behaviour • Do their buckles back up and replace the tray • Clear away the table until the pattern stops, then start again
When they want to do something that you cannot or should not allow	• Answer their question (see page 77) • Ignore the behaviour

Imagine that you have asked your 20-month-old son to sit down in the high chair during the wait game (see page 74) at the end of a meal time. You ask him to wait while you wash his hands and remove his tray and buckles, and he stays sitting down on request, then before you have suggested it's time to get up, he tries to get up just to see your reaction. You lean in to help him sit down again and he quickly sits on his bottom without needing your help and smiles a beautiful grin. If this becomes a game for him, when you are not able to define your statement 'sit down and wait', then you have a few strategies to choose from. The one you choose depends on your confidence with guiding your little one, and his natural temperament.

Firstly, pretend you don't see it and carry on if it feels like a one off. Or, pop his buckles back on calmly and say 'uh-oh, that's not good sitting. Buckles on bubba', and replace the tray. Now is the time to ignore the behaviour by pretending you're not looking and are busy wiping the table until he gets bored. Be patient, it could take a while. Once this behaviour stops, praise him with 'Good sitting. Okay, wait for mumma', and move on to something entirely new through distraction, before going back to your wait game.

You could use distraction by saying 'Sitting down, wait for mummy. Heeey, do you think we should find your big blue ball? Wait for mummy!' As soon as he is distracted and still sitting, praise him, 'Good sitting, Nick. Up up', and pick him up. Go and look for your ball together.

Another strategy is humour if they think they are pretty funny and they are old enough (18 months plus). Make a joke out of the behaviour so it gets a little bit of focus as they would like, and have a bit of a giggle together, then ask them to stop. You will need to be confident with your governing line to use this style of management, but it is more fun this way. Perhaps wait until you are more comfortable with your communication before you progress to this strategy. You could say something as simple as 'sitting down, wait for mummy', then pause for their cheeky antics, pull a funny face at them and say 'Ohh, that's not sitting' and tickle their tummy. Repeat 'Sitting down for mummy, waiting'. If they do it again, you can say 'Ohh, that's not sitting, you tricking mumma, funny Nick'. Then make your last request, this time using forewarning language: 'Last one, then it's time to wait. Sitting down, wait for mummy.' Have one last giggle and then say with a more serious face a clear stop: 'Okay, no more, sit down'. Say 'Wait for mummy, no standing' and be ready to physically intervene and stop them from standing this time. When you stop them, they will quickly see the game is over, and you can move straight to the distraction strategy mentioned above.

Troubleshooting

Q What if it is not going well, and he is just challenging me?

A If the behaviour continues relentlessly despite ignoring it, distraction and starting over, and he is clearly challenging you and about to tantrum, then you will need to address the pattern with a clear request to stop. Add some kind of physical intervention to prevent him from repeating the pattern again: this could be by not allowing his feet to hit the foot rest until he has stopped trying to push off it.

Without doubt, attention seeking is a little more challenging to deal with. It can be one of the cheeky, fun parts of early childhood and it still has me trying hard not to laugh at their antics. Naturally, I do my absolute best to not confuse them by laughing, but you can be forgiven for having to pretend you're having a cough when you are in fact laughing heartily on the inside at your beautiful baby's clever new trick. Any parent who has worked with me on developing communication will know this is always a fun part of the day, but it occasionally goes pear-shaped.

To deal with it you need to remain as consistent as possible. Try not to confuse your language streams by laughing or giving in. Be cautious and ignore as much of this behaviour as possible because your time would be better spent having a fun game with them later, rather than battling with them now.

Learning to negotiate

Learning how and when to negotiate is possibly one of the more confusing areas for a mum and dad to work through. Negotiations should really start to happen from around 12 months of age onwards. The ability for a child younger than this to recognise that they are being given a choice is questionable. Until this age, you are simply working on understanding your children's requests (child-governed line of communication), and being understood by your baby (parent-governed line of communication). But negotiations and choice are important, so when and how do you introduce them into your communications streams?

The answer is not so hard: when you want to offer your child choices, and you know that you want them to become autonomous with their decision-making skills. However, it's important for them to learn to make both good and not so good choices, but it's best to wait until an appropriate time to introduce negotiations for two very important reasons. One, you don't want to overburden them, because they will become exhausted and will often feel the need to guide you. And, two, you don't want to leave them open to losing faith in their ability to make a choice that will have a positive outcome for them.

The art of negotiating is about starting slowly and then building up your confidence and theirs by working together to reach a *mutually* agreed-upon outcome. You start by offering a negotiation or choice around an object. This is where you teach a child about the choice between one thing and another thing. This is a visual early learning tool about choice, which ultimately builds in to the next stage of your negotiations. You then offer negotiations or choice around an *event*. This is where you transfer their knowledge of a choice of this or that into a broader concept.

Your starting point

Always start with a choice around objects such as:

- between two books
- which finger foods on their tray to eat first
- a series of play stations on the floor
- to go from your arms into someone else's arms, or not
- to have a ride on the swing or slide at the park, or not.

The choice should never be about routine times of the day where their health, happiness or wellbeing is at question. Don't offer choice about going to sleep, giving a biscuit with no nutritional value before dinner versus a meal of high nutritional value later, whether to lie down during nappy change, whether to have a bath or not, or a water instead of juice. All too often I see parents offering negotiation streams around every event of the day. This is indicated with comments like:

- Should we?
- Could we?
- Can we?
- Do you want to?
- How about?
- Are you ready to?
- Ready?

And also when you use the following terms with upward inflections on the end of the closed statement:

- Lie down?
- Sit down?
- We go in the pram?
- We have a sleep?

All of the above styles of communication are a negotiation and they need to be used appropriately.

Once a child becomes overtired and overburdened, their ability to cope with the choices being offered ceases, and then all negotiations turn into child-governed lines of communication. Then is when a child cries because they don't know what they need to feel better, and the parent loses confidence in their ability to communicate and guide their baby. This is why you need to start slowly, building your confidence in deciding what is and isn't appropriate for a child to govern, then slowly build your negotiation repertoire.

It's important to be conscious of what you are saying. If you overuse negotiations they lose their value and completely lose their meaning to a child. They just become confusing questions where their answers are respected sometimes, and disrespected at other times.

To negotiate or not

Once you are ready to take the next step, it's also time to be conscious of offering one of the negotiating lines mentioned above around events that you are not terribly fussed about:

- Do you want to go for a walk, or play with your truck?
- Do you want to come outside now, or play with your toy first?

- Shall we go to the letterbox?
- Mummy feed you, or Alexis do it?
- Do you want socks on, or bare feet?
- Do you want to sit in the pram, or walk?

Always remember, that just because these above events were offered as a negotiation today, it does not mean they are always up for negotiation, and this is where people get nervous. Our children learn very quickly, so it could be easy for them to assume the next time you 'asked' them, using a parent-governed line of communication, to sit in the pram that they have an option of saying 'no thanks'. This is where your ability to communicate correctly, make a clear statement and then define it, comes into play.

The use of the flow of communication will give them ample opportunity to understand your request. Once you have included your negotiating line of communication, you will have a complete, well-balanced and respectful style of communication that will become the foundation for all interactions within your family. And the good news? It will all be happening by the time your little one is two years old. A guaranteed happy family strategy!

Negotiations to encourage a good choice

You know that there are times when you would like to offer your toddler the opportunity to make a better choice, and this is often represented with the famous 'my way' or 'my way' negotiation. This can be an effective tool for parents when it is used appropriately and can be used when your child is around 20 to 22 months old. It is a positive alternative to an immediate 'no' answer, and it offers a chance for a child who is perhaps a little reluctant to co-operate to retain the line of communication through what looks like a negotiation. The parent appears to be negotiating without changing the original request.

An example of this is: 'It's time to turn off the TV. Alexis do it, or mummy do it?' This is what I like to call a 'passive parent-governed line of communication'. The only trick with this negotiation would be in the time it takes your child to respond. Your communication should always be about asking your child to listen when you ask them politely, and not after you have repeated yourself three times, or counted to three or lost your temper. This means, you offer a passive parent-governed line of communication *once* only. If it is not accepted, then you proceed with, 'Okay, mummy do it!'

I generally find that once we say 'Okay, mummy do it' in a calm polite voice, they are then willing to co-operate, but it's too late! This is the eleventh hour. Don't fall for it. You don't want to teach them to wait until the last minute to listen. Once you have said a simple and polite statement, there is no going back. You are teaching your little one to listen when you ask. So reduce the time you might spend fussing with endless negotiations, and leave more time in your day for the fun stuff.

An appropriate passive parenting line of communication does not replace the flow of communication you learnt earlier, but complements it. Here are some good examples of how they fit together:

- 'Okay, time to say bye bye to the park now. Let's go find froggie. Quick, Jordi walk or mummy carry you?'
- 'Okay, it's time to turn off the TV. Press the button. Quick, Jed turn it off or mummy do it?'
- 'Okay, sitting down for your drink, show mummy good listening. Quick, sitting down or mummy help?'

When I'm out and about, I hear quite a few examples of inappropriate passive parenting lines, such as when it involves a lie or a blind threat, and here are just a few:

- 'Sit down in the pram or we're not coming back to the park again!' but the child runs to the car and the family do return to the park the next day.
- 'If you're not gentle we are going home', when a child hits a friend with a saucepan in the sandpit and then the child is allowed to stay and play until end of the play session.
- 'Last time or mummy will take it away', repeated six or more times and mummy never takes it away, child gets bored and wanders off.

As you can see, the gap between the appropriate and inappropriate forms of communication is vast. Be conscious of only using this final form of negotiation once you and your little one have found a comfortable balance with your object and event negotiations.

Happy negotiating!

Working through and past the tantrum

So your little one is very cross, or upset. They have gone a deep shade of pink, are flailing around in a little heap on the floor, and are desperately confused because they are wanting you but pushing you away, but needing help, but too angry to accept it. They are officially overwhelmed!

This is nothing to be frightened of. This is normal. When you think about what they have to cope with, it's no wonder they decide it's all too much sometimes and have a great big vent. These precious brand new lives arrive, bundled into the fairly tight-fitting complicated space suit that is their body, and haven't been given a manual on how to use it correctly. As they grow, their new-found mobility and growing comprehension of the world around them complicate matters rather than making them easier. Add to that the complexities of emotions and the way we learn to cope with them based on the environment around us and, well, sometimes it needs to be cried about.

It's not about stopping your child from feeling normal emotions, and most certainly not trying to stop them from expressing themselves, but they do sometimes need our help. This is where you assess the final stage of your intervention with tantrum management. Obviously, this is a slightly difficult area to generalise too heavily about, but the basic principle will help you assess how to best manage your little one's moments of being overwhelmed. Nothing can truly replace your instincts however, and if you feel as though they are having ongoing difficulties (continued need for similar managements for five days without relief), then you will have to use your instincts to learn how to better defuse the situation in future ventures.

When and how to intervene

If you are following through with a parent-governed line of communication and you need to correctly define a statement (see page 44), simply complete your request despite your child's tantrum or crying. Use this practical strategy suggestion and continue until you achieve the outcome you need. This is about not confusing your child, or teaching them that a parent-governed line is an opportunity to negotiate. To buckle means you will encourage your little one to cry each time you enter that particular routine event. The alternative is to put them down if they are in your arms and let them have their tantrum about the situation until it passes, without letting them move away, then continue with your request exactly where you left off.

When they are desperately trying to get you to do things for them then pushing you away, and wanting you but not wanting you, it can often result in you needing to pick them up and distracting them by going for a walk and talking about everything you can see in the garden until they have calmed down. To allow them to continue would only prolong the situation and they are indicating that they do want help, but don't know how to accept it when they are feeling so overwhelmed. At this point, stepping in and taking over and holding them while staying confident so you can reassure them and help them calm down is an appropriate strategy. Alternatively, you can sit down and hold them firmly while you read a book to them or watch one of their DVDs. Keep them with you even if they fight it and remind them they are okay. Talk about the DVD or the book until they calm down. When your child wants to be picked up, then wants to be down, and is all over the place, they are a little like a rag doll. They are feeling out of control at this stage so holding them will provide the emotional and physical safety nets they need to feel less stressed by the situation. This is the same strategy you need to adopt when they look like they may hurt themselves.

When they are not happy with one of your decisions and you have tried to distract or calm them but they are very upset and demanding a different

Max and the great 'carry me' debate

Young 19-month-old Max had taken quite a liking to being carried. Not just carried here or there, but everywhere. He would not go in the pram, he refused to walk, and he would not let mum put him down to play unless she sat down while he clung desperately on to her, then sat on her as soon as she sat. He was officially glued to his mother's hip unless he decided otherwise, which was a rare event. His mother was six months' pregnant and not sure what she was going to do over the coming weeks if this behaviour continued. As he grew and his weight increased, so too did the stress on mum's shoulders and she ended up with severe shoulder strain, resulting in significant pain. She was instructed by her doctor to not carry her son at all.

This was clearly going to be a challenge for both mum and me. Max would throw an intense tantrum if his mother did not carry him in exactly the position he preferred. This was putting her back and her unborn baby at risk, so we needed to help him to learn how to accept the boundary of not being carried everywhere. This was all about balance, so we said that we would sit down for cuddles, but mummy couldn't carry him. We set up a new management plan by pre-empting the situation. We explained that mummy had a sore back and a sore shoulder and couldn't lift him, and soon he would be able to have a lovely play with his toys while mummy did some cooking. We set up play activities for him near his mummy, showed him how much fun they were by playing with them for a few minutes, and then popped him down to have a play. Mum stayed for a few minutes then informed him that soon she would stand up to do some cooking. Finally, as promised, mummy praised his lovely playing then told him she was going to cook and that she wanted him to play with his toys.

Max stood up at the same time and asked to be picked up. His mother reminded him she couldn't pick him up but that she would sit down for a cuddle on the couch. This was not what Max was demanding and a huge tantrum ensued. He pulled at her arms, tried to push her to stand, tried to push her off the chair and refused her gentle offers of a cuddle.

This is a good example of when you need to adopt a no-nonsense approach. Once you have made your decision, offered a sensible solution and patiently given your child a minute to accept, there is nothing more to be done. To stay would only drag out this process, and outcome, give them space. If they are being extremely demanding or bossy, or completely impatient, simply follow through with your request despite the tantrum or crying.

Seeing a management through

When it comes time to work through one of your new parent-governed lines of communication, there is the learning process to go through (see page 67). To work through the tears, and sometimes the tantrums, and reach the other side may be a little tricky for even the most determined of mums and dads, but the effort is worth every moment of the learning

to pick bub up would not resolve the situation. The only thing left to do is go back to your chores and ignore the behaviour, and give him three to five minutes to calm down.

These were the new boundaries I asked Max's mummy to set:

- If he pulled at her, and hung off her hands, then she was to lie him down on the floor and release his hand from hers and say 'Okay, Max is too cross, mummy is going to do her jobs'. Then she was to stand up and go back to her chores.
- When she was to lay Max down, she had to provide a soft area with pillows, soft toys and books.
- He was not allowed to grab her hands, drag her, move her, push her or make her do anything. She had to keep busy with her chores, and occasionally remind him, 'No, Max, mummy can't pick you up now, when you feel better mummy will come and have a cuddle on the couch', then offer a line of redirection like 'Where's your books?'
- When the three to five minutes were up, she was to try again by suggesting 'Okay, Max, let's have a cuddle on the couch?' before going and sitting on the couch with an offer of arms.

If the tantrum repeated itself, she was to repeat the above sequence. Once the tantrum subsided, Max would either accept the cuddle or not. If he accepted the cuddle, she used the flow of communication so he knew that after the cuddle it was time to go back to his toys and play again, because there was more cooking to be done by mummy. She persisted with this strategy for two days until there were no more battles. Max was able to predict the times he would be playing, and knew that if he needed a cuddle he could ask for one.

This is the kind of response—ignoring a tantrum or just letting it take its natural course without actively intervening or trying to fix it—that will help the situation come to an end much quicker than it would if you were intervening. If they are just upset with what you have said, and it was a reasonable boundary, then ignoring the tantrum for brief intervals will allow it to subside. When they are being very stroppy because they are impatient or demanding you pick them up, or reject your offer of toys on the high chair, etc., then you are best to just pretend you didn't see the tantrum behaviour begin. If they are very cross, then sit quietly near them doing something else until they calm down. You can suggest to them, 'Too loud for mummy's ears. When Max feels better, mummy get you up.'

process for your child and for you. The other side of the tears or tantrums when learning something new is nothing short of beautiful. Your child now has a more relaxed way of coping with the situation compared to before, and is able to trust that you will show them a better way in the future if something similar happens.

Have your little battles or your big ones, be patient, stay respectful and confident, and your child will come through the other side with a new ability which creates a calm, and pleasant experience, rather than a stressful battle.

Destructive communication

This topic has to be touched on. I encounter destructive communication far too often, and am never shy to point it out to parents when I see it. Most parents appreciate the input, even if it is difficult to hear initially. There is nothing more destructive to a child's entire life journey than to start out forming opinions about the world around them based on a set of negative untruths, or manipulative innuendoes intended for someone else in a moment of anger.

Every child has a fundamental right to grow up feeling loved, wanted, safe and secure. They should be free from the burden of your relationship's highs and lows, the emotional insecurity of an adult, or a negative view of the world. Remember they are a clean slate, and it is your responsibility to write on that slate. Always be conscious of the fact that every time they look at you they are asking, 'Who am I?' 'What am I like?' and 'What do I like?'

The following is a list of destructive communication styles that will negatively impact on a children's relationship with their mother or father, as well as impact their relationship with their siblings.

Destructive input while they are within earshot
Examples of this are:

- 'He hates sleeping, his room / his cot / being put down.'
- 'He doesn't like to go in the pram / car.'
- 'He doesn't like his daddy bathing him.'
- 'He never lets his father feed / dress him.'
- 'He likes his mother more than me.'
- 'I'm the only one that can do anything for him.'
- 'Why do you make me cross?'

- 'Why do you always cry?'
- 'Why can't you play nicely with your brother?'
- 'Why do you and your brother always fight?'

Competitive parenting: children as pawns

Here you are competing for your child's affections with subtle verbal inputs that can destroy relationships. These generally occurs when one parent is upset with the other:

- 'Naughty daddy should be home now!'
- 'Mummy doesn't like bathing you does she?'
- 'Oh forget it, daddy doesn't want to play with you, he'd rather watch the television.'
- 'Let's leave daddy alone, he doesn't want to talk to us.'
- 'Forget it, we'll do it ourselves, daddy / mummy can't do anything.'
- 'We don't want daddy / mummy to help us anyway do we?'
- 'We don't care if daddy / mummy doesn't like to spend time with us.'

This can manifest in a non-verbal way, too. It comes in the shape of undermining the other parent by always taking over when the child demands it. To not offer your spouse and their baby the opportunity to find their own way is to limit their relationship potential. Your partner will never be able to do it just like you, but that's because they aren't you. Give them time to find their own way together without always coming in and 'rescuing the baby' from their parent. This kind of undermining is destructive in two ways: it makes the child think daddy / mummy can't do it, and it makes the parent attempting the task think they are not a good parent. This then directly impacts on the time and interaction that parent has with the child, risking their bond.

Bickering with your child like a sibling.

This is the, 'yes', 'no', 'yes', 'no', argument. It's tormenting and toxic communication. You are the adult. State the answer, and then do not bicker with your child.

Negative input about their sibling relationship

The lines go something like:

- 'Stop annoying your brother.'
- 'Why can't you play together?'
- 'You're so rough with your brother.'

- 'He doesn't want to play with you.'
- 'You two are a nightmare together.'

Undermining yourself or others
- 'I'm a terrible mummy.'
- 'Naughty mummy.'
- 'I'm sorry, I'm a bad dad, mate.'
- 'Is mummy so terrible that you don't want to _____?'
- 'Do you hate being with your dad so much that you _____?'
- 'Daddy can't do it.'
- 'We don't like granny coming over do we?'

Responding to your child with an eye-for-an-eye attitude
- 'They bite you, you bite them back.'
- 'They hit, you hit back.'

Trying to teach empathy through guilt
This is the situation where your child pushes you away when you come to play with them because they are playing on their own or with someone else. They don't do it to be mean: it's just that sometimes they are very busy and they are not yet at the stage of co-operative playing. Often in their minds the arrival of an adult mid game can represent the end of a play session, which naturally may not be what your little one wants if they are very absorbed in their activity. This apparent rejection can feel a little hurtful for some mums but more often it happens to dads. And, because you feel hurt, the next time they come to play with you, you push them away so they can feel how hurt you felt.

Be very aware, they will not link the two situations. By using emotional guilt because they hurt your feelings when they appeared to reject you, you try to hurt them in the same way. But this won't actually teach them empathy at all. In fact you actually *will* hurt them, because they are only children. Most children will wonder why you are behaving like this. They are then likely to role play that behaviour back to you because they are learning how to interact socially with others, and you will have started a vicious cycle of negative interactions.

Teasing, mocking or laughing at your child when they are angry
Do I need to elaborate? It's just cruel.

Wanting to be wanted

This creates a pattern of dependency so you can feel important to or needed by the child. It encourages tears when you leave them at daycare. One of the worst things I see when working in the field of early childhood is a parent who hovers and says goodbye as many times as it takes the child to cry before they feel satisfied and can leave. This appears to stem from a need for validation that they are loved. This is an unfair burden to give a child. It is not a child's responsibility to love you, it is your responsibility to love them. They already do love you; they will miss you. Needing tears to feel as though you're important to your child is a toxic form of parenting stemming from low confidence in your parenting ability. Have more faith in the absolutely irreplaceable role you have in your child's life. You are the most important person in the world.

7
The development of play

As babies grow, so does their ability to play. In the following chapters, you will discover the developmental stages of play that your baby is capable of, and then the most appropriate forms of play you can encourage at home to foster a sense of pleasure and enjoyment. The most important thing I need to remind you about play is that it is not a *goal* or something they have to *achieve*. Play is not about being successful at something: it is about a journey of discovery, of fun, of laughter and of opportunities to develop their skills. It is about discovering what your child enjoys, and building upon those experiences. It's about opening up the world around them and helping them build the confidence to explore it.

Ways to engage in play

The variety of ways in which you can engage in play with your baby is based loosely around their age and developmental capacity. Between six and 12 months, the first style of play you will see is called 'solitary play', sometimes known as 'independent play'. Solitary play often remains an important and active style of play well into the third year of life and can be clearly identified in young babies. It is simply play in which a child shows no interest in the activity of others. A study by Mildred Parten in 1932 also identified periods of a transitioning to a more social type of play during this early age and she called it 'onlooker play'. These brief interspersed episodes of onlooker play are those times when your little one shows moderate interest in the activities of others, despite being unable to actively participate yet.

As children get older and start to toddle about on their feet, they begin to engage in a form of play known as 'parallel play', when they play happily alongside you or another child doing a similar activity (such as digging in the sand pit), but not in a co-operative or engaging fashion. This play is again a wonderful way to take your child's lead in their interests, to learn from them, and to observe and then emulate a similar form of play back to them, and gradually expand that play through offering some new ideas as they observe your interactions with that particular activity.

Styles of play

Understanding the types of play that your baby is capable of engaging in will help you understand your little one better, help you balance their learning opportunities and make watching your little one learn a truly eye-opening experience. Once you understand the styles of play your child has a natural propensity towards, you can feel reassured that their way of playing is normal and confident about establishing a play environment that caters for their needs. Most importantly, once you understand the function of the stages of play, it will help you to play with your child, ensuring you are aware of the different elements of play that will need to be achieved to strike that all-important balance.

One-on-one play

One-on-one play is the close, intimate play you engage in with your baby. It generally involves eye contact, physical closeness and time. This style of play is a favourite with parents, siblings, extended family, friends and baby alike. This area has rarely needed further encouragement from me during any intervention I have been involved with during my career. It is usually well developed in most homes, and a healthy bond and strong sense of trust has always been beautifully fostered as a result.

During one-on-one play you can engage in many different activities. This time can be dedicated towards doing normal household things together like cooking, putting on a load of washing, making the bed (when there is more fun involved than bed making) or watering the garden. It can be a more specific kind of one-on-one play where you dance together with coloured scarves, or sing songs and they watch or learn the actions to those songs. It could be a one-on-one play experience where mummy and / or daddy role play on how to use, explore or extend a new toy, or help your little one to more effectively learn how to use the toys they have shown an interest in.

One-on-one play can even be a special trip to the post office or the local fruit shop. These trips can become a language-rich one-on-one interaction, so long as your focus on these outings is to have a fun playtime, when you are not actually distracted and frantically shopping. You can't claim all your trips to the shop as one-on-one play, but you could definitely make some of those little greengrocer trips a really fun adventure. This style of play and interaction should and does happen regularly throughout each and every day.

Role play

This is the style of play you often see an enthusiastic parent engaging in when they introduce a new toy, or when they come home from work after missing their baby or toddler all day. This play almost always involves a toy and generally follows a simple path: the adult attempts to show the baby how to use the toy by using it themselves with lots of enthusiasm and fun. What the play actually is generally follows a child's interest; a parent is naturally inclined to offer an activity for enjoyment's sake, as much as for learning's.

This is an extremely important and valuable style of play as you are now teaching a child how to use their toys in a way that will be more enjoyable and challenging. This ensures your child can get the most out of their play, and empowers them with play strategies for the more challenging but equally important solitary or independent play. There are two great reasons to encourage you to engage in this kind of play. Role playing is ideal when your baby is happy and content, and it is also helpful as a tool to calm an unsettled or stressed baby. So which of the two styles of role playing you adopt—actively engaging their attention or playing enthusiastically by yourself next to your child—depends on how your baby is feeling at the time of play.

Actively engaging their attention is perfect for when your baby is happy and enjoying the flow of their day, but be mindful of the developmental ability of your baby. To ask them to play *with* you is just too difficult a task for them when they are little. It's more important that you take their lead and then enjoy their current area of interest together. Their preference can then be explored further through your participation and obvious enjoyment of the activity too. Engaging their attention like this is extremely delightful for your baby and toddler. They will stop and watch you, and may even attempt to take the toy so they can play with it, but once they have watched you play or taken the toy, you will see them go straight back to solitary play.

A blend of solitary play interspersed with moments of onlooker play while you are with them is normal and natural. As they develop into toddlerhood, they will play alongside you doing a similar thing, such as digging in the sandpit at the same time as you, but not necessarily playing with you. This progression into parallel play is normal and healthy, and they will actively engage your attention and take you to a play location to do this together as much as you will actively engage their attention for the purpose of play too.

As you play with their toy, remember to only play with it in a way that they can copy. In other words, use it appropriately and know that whatever you do with the toy they are likely to role play and try to master later. This is where some gorgeous but slightly over-enthusiastic daddies need to be reminded that placing a toy plane on the fan and turning it on is not exactly the most effective or appropriate play strategy to teach your baby. That said, it's pretty funny to see the cute little rituals that parents create with their little ones. This is not about being a rigid play machine, it's just about providing a healthy balance of learning and exploring opportunities for your child. So be sure that, as a rule of thumb, you play with their toys appropriately most of the time!

> The most important thing I need to remind you about play is that it is not a *goal* or something they have to *achieve* . . . it is about a journey of discovery, of fun, of laughter and of opportunities to develop their skills.

Playing enthusiastically by yourself next to your child is excellent when your baby or toddler is unsettled or not pleased about the way things are going. Most people stand and jiggle and shush and rock, but confident positive role playing with a toy could quite possibly be one of the fastest ways to calm a baby. Their tears could be around a request to sit in the bath, stay and play in their cot, stay in their high chair, or play on the floor without being picked up. Finding a balance at these times of the day could be through play sessions like these.

As you start to use this style of play, it's important to keep in mind that you are not confronting them with yet another request. They are likely to be unsettled in the first place because they are not comfortable with the original request you made, so imagine their reaction if you then indicate that you want them to do something else like 'look at this toy', particularly if it is clear they are saying 'I refuse to play in my cot'. The constant demand to look when they are feeling cross only frustrates them, and they are likely to become even more upset.

The idea of this play is to help you make a simple request, then give you the opportunity to stay with them and role play a good alternative for them to use at times when they feel cross or upset (without actively trying to engage their attention). This means you are saying 'When you feel like this, this is a good idea', and showing them that by playing happily with their toy they can calm down and feel happy again. This is equipping your baby's emotional tool kit. This is obviously vital for sleep, so your confidence and consistency here will mean your little one will learn that all–important 'lie here calmly until you fall asleep' skill. It will be something that you have both already worked through at a less stressful event, like daytime play, where they learn to listen when they are not feeling tired.

Simply sit down near them, stay calm and confident, and have a really enjoyable play with one of their toys. It is necessary to remind you at this

Playing to find emotional solutions

You are equipping your baby with emotional coping tools when you foster role-playing strategies. I call this their 'emotional tool kit'. This means that they can they feel an emotion, and they can go to their emotional tool kit to find a solution to resolve the way they feel. If they open it up and the only tool they have to use is mum or a cuddle, then this can leave them extremely disempowered, especially if you are not with them 24 hours a day. What may seem a reasonably simple solution now—giving them a breastfeed when they are angry that they need to stay in their cot to play—is not going to be of much use when they go to daycare or start kindergarten, spend the day with daddy, go to granny's, or if you go have to go to hospital to have the another baby or get ill. You won't always be there to give them a breastfeed then.

Think about what other tools / skills you have empowered them with to cope in these situations. Mummy, daddy and a good old cuddle and feed offers the most basic and important solution, but because we are looking to provide balance, you want to ensure that you are empowering them with more than one solution to a problem. Their emotional tool kit holds a variety of coping skills / tools you have helped them to learn in order to empower them. These skills / tools will be used by them on a daily basis, and are a combination of learnt and instinctive coping and resolution strategies around certain types of feelings and emotions.

Naturally, there will be some emotional response to their surroundings and they will have an instinctive need to be close to a primary nurturer. These are typically around illness and basic dependency needs, such as hunger, warmth, love, comfort, fear and so on. When you respond to these emotions with physical intervention, you tell your baby that they must have your help and this is something that they cannot resolve on our own, yet. This enhances the foundation to all bonding, growth and development. When you lump every single emotional response they have into that emotional dependency basket, however you are not truly listening to your child, and you are limiting their ability to start to understand a normal range of human responses, and you leave them disempowered and vulnerable.

It's normal to have to wait, and the feeling of impatience is not an indication that they are emotionally at risk and, therefore, not an emotion they need to be rescued from all the time. It is better to equip them with appropriate coping strategies instead. In this case, learning to challenge the environment around them and start to play is an appropriate response. To always stage that you are *not* trying to get them to look at you or the toy, you are not saying their name, you are not waving a toy under their nose, or saying 'Look' in a hope of stopping the tears, you are just playing in a solitary or independent fashion right alongside them until they calm down, become distracted and then settle. Play like you would if you were them, or their age. Play with the toy in a way that they can copy. This could involve banging two blocks together, spinning the wheels on a car or scratching the textures on a toy. For toddlers it might involve building a little tower of three blocks, knocking them over and looking surprised and excited.

rescue them from these normal feelings (like impatience) is to tell them that those feelings are not safe, and should not happen, and mummy / daddy is the only one to make them feel better. This is not the case, and you are teaching them that they can't cope with a simple non-threatening feeling. It is important to truly watch and listen to your little one and ensure that your responses are appropriate and on a graded scale of intervention.

When I was teaching in the daycare and kindergarten settings, I would often see little people (two to three years of age) come into centres and find it extremely challenging to cope on their own. Even the most basic of feelings had always been resolved for them by being picked up and having their immediate demands met. This created an unrealistic transition into a normal social environment. I often observed these same children make a request to their little friends (who are all developmentally egocentric at this age) and when their friends didn't oblige, they became upset and began to tantrum. This scenario is also not so uncommon in other settings.

Children are often surprised then frustrated when their new little friends lack the willingness to meet their demands as their parents have been doing most of their new lives, but it's when they reach into their emotional tool kits to find the tool they should have been empowered with, and discover that tool is missing, then things can become quite stressful for them. Some children are taught to cry, or tantrum, if they really want their parents to do as they have asked. Often the parent's reasoning for this is because it's just too hard to do it any other way. Sadly, these little children then try to use these tools at kindergarten and have a tantrum when their friends, who look on momentarily with interest, then walk away to continue playing. These children find it difficult to integrate and socialise initially, and often need much assistance from carers to learn the basics of normal social interaction and balanced expectations around communication.

Egocentricity in early childhood is a natural stage of development that lasts well into a child's school years. But what tools are we teaching our little ones right from this early social stage of development? To not provide multiple tools for coping with the multitudes of emotions or typical situations children experience is not only unfair, but also neglects our duty as carers: to impart our wisdom on to our little ones, and prepare them to cope and integrate into a social world where they are creatures independent of their mummy and daddy.

Whatever you chose to do, however, it should always involve up-beat tones and vocalisation (which will look like you are talking to yourself or the toy), so use a happy voice and bright vibrant expressions.

Your child will be most responsive to a repeated pattern of behaviour and sound. This is what is likely to distract them and indirectly draw their attention more than anything else. Often, even when they are having a little protest or a big old cry, they will stop momentarily and have a little chuckle at a repetitive action and sound, when play is done enthusiastically, before resuming their crying.

The final part of this strategy is to be patient and consistent. Often a mother and father will say to me once we have worked through tears or protests for a good period of time, 'I'm so glad you were here, because I would have given up a long time ago and never seen that it was possible to get them to calm down that way'. Each time you use this strategy to help them calm down you will see it becoming easier and easier for them to calm down quickly and start to play. Eventually, you will be able to use this form of play to defuse a situation that you believe may result in tears, or they will settle down quickly once you introduce this play if tears have already begun because you are teaching them a new way to calm down.

Think about it: if the only thing you do to help them calm down is pick them up or breastfeed them, then they are taught that that is the only way to calm down. But that is only a learnt pattern. So why not empower them with more than one way to calm down, and make at least one of their new calm-down strategies a routine that they can use that doesn't completely rely on you? This means that if you need to go out and leave your little one with your mother, husband, wife or sister, your baby has coping strategies. More importantly, if you say goodnight and leave the room, and they get cross momentarily at the request (which is pretty common), they know how to calm down quickly and don't think they can't cope unless you walk in and pick them up or breastfeed them.

Independent play

This is the one area of play that I find often needs a lot of encouragement by the time I enter a home environment. That encouragement is not only needed for the baby to start to try to play without constant role play or one-on-one play, but for the parents to establish a pattern for letting them play without being fearful of their baby not coping. I find the parents' fear of walking away actually creates babies who can't play independently because they see their parents are fearful, and therefore believe they must be in an unsafe situation.

I always ask parents in this situation: 'How will they ever learn to play independently if you never give them enough time and space to really practise and get the hang of it?' This is about parenting from a place of love, based on their child's true needs, and not about parenting from a place of fear, based on their short-term demands (see page 91). Your baby's true need is to be given an opportunity to experience the balance of all styles of play, which then gives them the opportunity to learn how to play independently. To not nurture this will create a clingy baby who is unable to cope outside your arms or your immediate eyeshot. This is not balanced, and as much of an imbalanced strategy as never playing with your baby.

To not foster independent play means you never work on developing a strong language-based style of communication between you and your child, or foster one of trust in their ability to predict your movements, which even when you're not right in front of them empowers them with a sense of confidence in their own space. This one style of play is the most basic skill your little one needs to develop to feel safe and comfortable in their cots for sleep. This is about them learning to feel comfortable in their own little space and learning to trust that, even when you step away, you will always be there for them, and the first time they should be practising this should be during playtime, not sleep time.

Most babies by six months of age, when not exposed to this style of play, start to feel very uncomfortable with the idea of you stepping out of their line of sight. This is because they have not developed trust in your communication or had the opportunity to feel the emotions associated with playing at room's length from their primary carers. This means that your baby starts to 'play it safe' and cling on to you because they have not learnt that there is any other way. Often, by the time I come into someone's home, some babies are so anxious about their mummy or daddy walking away because they feel powerless, that they are terribly overburdened with trying to tell their mum and dad what to do most of the time.

This immediately creates a snowball effect where the parents who, obviously unable to understand all the thoughts and desires their baby, may now have a little one who is crying and unsettled more often than not. This generally results in a loss of confidence in their parenting ability. This is when I find a parent will look to their baby and say 'Then what do you want? I'll do whatever you want, just please don't cry bubby, I only want you to be happy.' This is when parents start to look to their babies for guidance, and the baby is now burdened with the massive, overwhelming and exhausting job of running the flow of their house. And this often becomes too much, and everyone becomes overwhelmed.

If this is you, it's okay: it's repairable no matter what age your baby is, but the strategies are particularly effective with children under two years of age. This style of independent play and parent-guided play should take up a balanced one-third of your child's play opportunities during the day, including a concentrated hour of play each morning when they are at their absolute best. Remember, it is about balance. Not all play should be independent. That is entirely unbalanced too. You are looking to encourage an hour of independent play throughout the day, then allowing your child to choose between playing with you, or pottering off and playing on their own, if they like, at any other time of the day. That is a balanced approach to playtime in the home environment.

The complexity of play

In the early stages of play, between six and 12 months, a child will start holding a block (fine motor skill) and with jerky movements begin to connect one block to another (eye–hand co-ordination, spatial awareness and physical development). Through practising this challenging task, the baby's ability to control their motor skill, develop their eye–hand co-ordination, become spatially aware, and learn to understand and cope with the sensation of frustration, develops the vital skill of patience, which will result in them being able to learn how to eventually build a small tower.

Clearly, even the simplest forms of play are the cornerstone of physical, cognitive, language, social and emotional development and are essential to fostering healthy overall development in your child. One-on-one play gives a parent the opportunity to provide language-rich experiences, by role playing through any areas that they may feel their little one is experiencing difficulty understanding or coping with. This style of play also promotes important parent–child bonding, and provides teaching opportunities to encourage a positive association with play through fun, laughter and learning what is interesting to your child.

Play provides opportunities for your little one to make lots of noise, to express themselves freely, to be entertained and have lots of fun, all while developing the important skills of patience, repetition, persistence, completion and transitioning, right from the tender age of six months. These skills are all needed for confident socialising when they begin to spread their little wings and become creatures independent of their parents in that first exciting social environment of childcare, playgroup, kindergarten or preschool. Play provides opportunities for your child to be in control of their surrounding in an appropriate way that enables them to also feel empowered.

Socially, the importance of play is clearly geared towards developing patience, independence and co-operation and, as they get older, is part of learning to share. They discover that they may not always get the outcome they want and that compromise is a helpful tool. It teaches them to ask for help, and begins the tremendous journey towards developing the important communication and social skills essential for integrating confidently into any normal social environment.

Good challenging play is also thought to be a great sleep inducer. We know from personal experience that if we are met with a really challenging situation during the day, we are likely to dream about it that night. In fact, not only are we going to dream about it once, but we are likely to dream about it over and over again. Although a popular school of thought on the purpose of dreaming suggests that a dream state enables the child to process on a subconscious level some of the more challenging things they experience through the day, it is speculated that the ability to truly know about a child's dreaming is virtually impossible at the moment. However, babies have not developed an imagination, it is proposed they can only dream about the things in their day that they have experienced. The 15 years I've spent encouraging an environment rich in opportunities to explore and play has yielded nothing short of staggering results in the area of sleep development and maintenance. After years establishing and refining these strategies I strongly believe in the importance of creating a fun play environment filled with challenging and interesting opportunities to explore and play every day at home.

Are toys important?

All too often I walk into a house and a parent says to me, 'They will play with me, but they will not play on their own. Why is that?' or 'They never play with their toys, they just want to sit on my hip all day, why?' I always remind them that 'you are interesting and responsive, offer physical, cognitive and language opportunities to challenge their development needs as well as provide key social and emotional role modelling for them to learn from'. However, playing independently is an entirely different skill set altogether, and requires far more planning and assistance to help some little ones even to show an interest in playing on their own.

When it comes to independent play, if play is the route to balanced healthy development, then toys and a stimulating environment are the direct pathway to the desire to play. Remember, this is about balance so it is important for a child to be able to explore: they need a play environment that is interesting and encourages exploration through the use of toys.

Toys encourage longer attention spans for playing alone, which promotes an elevated interest in play because of previous successful and fulfilling encounters during these episodes. By providing an environment that is rich in age-appropriate challenging activities, you will encourage a child to want to explore their environment more.

By providing both one-on-one enthusiastic playtime between yourself and your child, your child will develop strong and confident play strategies based on adult-directed role play, and develop warm and happy associations with each particular item or toy you have previously established with them. By introducing a toy to your baby, then backing it up with a simple example of how to utilise that toy, your child learns how to use the toy and is then keen when given the opportunity to practise their skills. This enables them to discover what they like, and what they are like. Therefore variety in play, such as a good selection of toys, will help facilitate healthy independent play.

The problems with achieving play in modern-day parenting

For many of the families I've worked with, the root of their sleep-time and daytime behavioural issues is firmly anchored in their little one having difficulty around the ability to be in their own space and still feel safe: issues which need to be worked through on a daily basis. A long time ago I was quoted in the newspaper as saying that the convenience of easy home maintenance and white goods as causing all manner of problems with our children's sleep, but it didn't go any further into explaining my claim. That day so many people questioned me about what I meant. It's really quite simple, and it is the main reason why our parents keep saying to us, 'We never had these problems when you kids were young, and now it seems like everybody is suffering from this same thing'.

Once upon a time, in the 1970s and '80s when we were kids, few homes had the conveniences we now take for granted—microwave oven, dishwasher, four-minute cycle washing machine and a super-effective vacuum cleaner. The equipment we had was good, but not that good, and so a daily vacuum or Bissell carpet sweep was a common and time-consuming task. Pre-made high-quality baby food in the refrigerator section of our local well-stocked supermarket was not yet available. Baby food in jars was certainly an option but many mothers preferred to shop and cook their baby's food. The meat came from the butchers, the fruit and vegetables came from the greengrocer and our normal weekly food supply came from the supermarket, rather than from today's one-stop shops, which made a trip to the local shops back then another time-consuming task. Our parents would make the baby's food before making the rest of the family's dinner as the option of a takeaway was a rare treat. Household bills had to be paid at the local post office or via a long wait in a huge line at the bank. You could of course send a cheque, but that needed to be written, addressed and stamped, followed by a walk to the local post box. All these time-consuming tasks are in such stark contrast to our modern online or telephone banking facilities, supermarkets and massive 'everything you need in one place' shopping malls, pre-cooked baby food, takeaway meals, and convenient home maintenance items, that the time-restriction comparison for parenting in the past compared to now is not even worth highlighting.

It is clear that our parents did not have as much time as we do to spend sitting and playing with their children. Our parents were, however, a well-organised bunch and a daily routine or schedule (whether intentional or not) was almost essential in ensuring the chores were done. I distinctly remember my mum crawling around the floor with me and my sisters, but I also remember adventuring all over the house while mum busied herself with the normal chores. I remember making the trip with dad to the bank each week and waiting and waiting and waiting while he paid the bills and organised the family finances step by step with a cashier. Now I am thrilled that technology has improved and we have more opportunities to spend with our families, but I believe this additional free time has triggered a disturbing new epidemic sweeping the current generation of parents.

We have so many products designed to make our lives easier and to give us more time, but the downside of these time-saving devices is that the most simple of skills a baby once learnt as par for the course is not now being developed effectively in our little ones, particularly our first child. What is that skill? The ability for your baby to just play on their own without the need to be entertained.

So what about subsequent children? Have you noticed that children who come second in the family are far more effective at playing independently? This is because first children consume a portion of mum and dad's time, meaning the second child has far more opportunity to practise independent playtime. I find a number of parents say of their second child, 'He did cry now and then, but he just had to wait because I was toileting my toddler, and by the time I got to him he was happy and playing'. Clearly then, all our children need is space and time to develop independent play.

In many of the homes I visit today, babies struggle when put down for just a moment, and become quickly stressed if their mum or dad stands up and walks one or two metres away to grab a glass of water. What the parents need to do is bring back the crucial balance of interaction into their children's lives and some of the lost opportunities that our fast-paced impatient natures have created by time-saving products. They also need to give babies the chance to discover the joy of a quiet play with their toys, and empower them with the ability to feel comfortable and safe to be on the floor or in a play environment where their children can still see them without feeling anxious.

There are even more compounding factors to be considered today. Family dynamics have changed, and guilt from a dual working family can often create an entirely different set of complications with communication streams that are designed to compensate for parents not necessarily always being there with their baby. We appear busier than ever, despite every possible time-saving device at our disposal and all their apparent convenience. We still feel rushed and exhausted at the end of every day. Time appears to be a precious commodity, so every opportunity we get to be at home, we sit on the floor or on the couch with our baby and play. This adds to the difficulties babies are developing around play right from an early age. Even if your time is limited, to not create a balance of opportunities for your baby when in your company means they learn that when you *are* around they should *always* be playing with you, and they should not be away from you. What impact do you think that may have on a child's feeling about going to sleep in their cot? It's vital that even when you are working full time, you still make sure that when your baby is with you, you provide balanced play opportunities so they can still develop the independent skills they need when in your care.

As a childcare worker I often found parents were stunned to learn that their baby could play on their own in daycare, yet this skill was not transferred to home. If you are hoping that a teacher will teach your child valuable skills that you have not yet had the opportunity to teach them, then you are in for a little bit of a surprise. For each environment, your baby will need to be taught the set of conditions relevant to it.

Always be conscious of finding the balance at home so your little one can feel confident both playing on their own or with you, making playtime and sleep time an event that does not invoke feelings of anxiety, stress or unfamiliarity.

8
Getting organised for play

Under the age of 24 months your baby is obviously new to this extremely interesting and often slightly overwhelming world. When we look at a baby's ability to identify and be drawn to a specific area of play designed for them, we need to look at the general state of the home. Too much stimulation will often overwhelm a child and cause tears. This is generally where a baby will start to insist that you carry them.

If you would like your baby to play, then a clean, clutter-free home, or at least play area, is the very first thing you need to focus on. If your lounge room has accidentally become part office, part storage room, part laundry, then you need to quickly work out a way to find some sensible storage solutions to create neat areas with clearly organised sections so clutter does not build up again. If you are keeping the old printer and computer on the floor in the corner, it's time to tuck it away in a spare room, cupboard or the garage or, better still, make a few dollars and sell it. If it is time to sort through and throw out things that are broken, or to fill a bag with things you no longer use and drop it in to a charity shop, then there is no better time and no more excuses.

Your baby will benefit tremendously from the sort out. Often parents say to me, 'We know we need to clean this up, but we don't have time because the baby is awake and demanding so much of our time that we just can't get around to it'. Well, if you are waiting for the child to start playing before you begin your spring clean, you are going to be waiting a terribly long time. Your baby needs you to create a clear, simple and clean environment for them before they will feel comfortable enough to step away from you and want to explore that space. No more waiting for them, make the decision yourself so you can guide your child into happier play.

Organising their play areas within the house

In the same way that a cluttered and unorganised home will prevent a baby from playing, excessively over-furnished rooms can create visual obstacles between you and your little one, and bubby may feel you are very far away from them, or inaccessible because of it. On the other hand, just as an overfilled or unorganised space may be overwhelming, a vast open space may leave them feeling exposed, vulnerable and isolated. Both these conditions will make it almost impossible for a parent struggling to establish independent play to step away and give their baby the opportunity to learn a new, considerate and, therefore, enjoyable routine. This often creates a sense of failure for the parents around their ability to teach their baby something new, when it is actually not them at all but the environment that is creating difficulties for their little one.

> Your baby needs you to create a clear, simple and clean environment for them before they will feel comfortable enough to step away from you and want to explore that space.

There are very few homes that I go into where I don't become a room redecorator. I am always looking for a clear pathway between baby and parent to create a visually open environment to foster an emotional sense of closeness. I prefer to have a kitchen bench to be the only large obstacle between baby and their parents. If your baby is one of those little people struggling with being put down then move furniture about to create clear visual and physical walkways between spaces.

If you find that you have extra dining chairs or large one-seaters overfilling the room, move them about so you create the illusion of more space. You could also remove them from the room entirely while you spend a few weeks teaching your unsettled baby how to play. Neatly tuck dining chairs in under the table to reduce the space they are occupying and, if you have an extendable dining table, reduce it to its minimum size. Tidy up the position of footstools, magazine racks and coffee tables.

On the other hand, if you have a vast space to fill, it's important to try and create a slightly more intimate play area near your kitchen. Utilise larger items of play to create the feel of a big playpen but don't block your child's path to potter off and explore if they feel comfortable to do so. Large soft pillows, baby play frames and soft floor coverings spaced at a close distance will create a warm, safe and inviting space to occupy while mum, dad or carer busy themselves in the kitchen.

Defining your baby's play area

Defining each area of play, what I like to call 'play stations', requires you to create a predictable set of conditions for your little one to know. By having a simple mat, some nicely displayed well-spaced activities with clear open walkways between each play station, you create a routine that your child learns to expect and, ultimately, feels safe and empowered within. The simple idea of setting up several play stations in a room in well-spaced positions creates a flowing, inviting, continually refreshing environment for your child, and helps them to learn how to transition from one activity to another.

Transition here occurs when the baby gets bored with one activity station and when that happens they begin to crawl to their parent for entertainment and company. On the way to the kitchen where you might happen to be, baby must pass a series of inviting, clear activity stations and invariably will become distracted and stop to engage in a whole new form of play. This extends their attention span and builds a healthy association with play and independence. This early naturally learnt transitioning skill will be a vital and well-established one for them by the time they reach school age, and it will draw praise and acknowledgement from their teacher about your child's self-direction, which immediately will empower your child with confidence, instantly enhancing a positive self-image and inner dialogue about their ability to achieve in the classroom.

You are teaching your children right from an early age how to set up their own play in addition to learning how to transition. By three years of

Set their sights on play

Overly colourful and busy play mats may be disruptive to play. Primary colours are often used in the design of children's toys to make them eye-catching and attractive. However these same primary colours are also used in the design of baby play mats. All too often I see parents, with the best of intentions and the desire to create an inviting environment, place a brightly coloured mat, pattern side facing up, with multi-coloured toys on the top and then wonder why their baby either cries immediately when placed in that environment or will only play with their fingers, barely touching the toys. Unfortunately, their beautiful and eye-catching toys are now camouflaged on their overly busy play mat, and it is all a bit too much.

Always remember, less is more when it comes to children's play stations. Turn over the play mat to see if there is a single colour underneath and use it that side up so baby can see the colourful toys on top of it. And reduce the amount of toys you provide for each play area to ensure that when you offer your child toys, they will be easy to see, and inviting to play with.

age children who successfully transition in play are confidently and beautifully setting up their own play stations in a way that will promote optimum play for them. This creates children who have established clear leadership play skills and who draw the attention of other children in a positive and healthy way. The benefits of simply setting aside 15 minutes on your part each day to create a play environment for your child are astounding—and well, well worth the trouble.

Establishing a good play environment

The design of your house is actually a really important part of your little one's ability to play happily. Obviously at a young age, your baby's ability to play without being able to see you is extremely challenging for them, and to expect them to play in a separate room for a prolonged period of time can often create a situation where you find they become anxious around play in that particular environment because they know that you will often leave their line of sight. If a baby is to feel comfortable enough to play they need to be certain that they do not need to watch you to ensure you won't suddenly disappear on them.

I am a strong believer in initiating independent play in the morning while a parent busies themselves with cooking and chores. For this reason, I always suggest you plan your play stations around the kitchen. Obviously, the kitchen itself is not necessarily a safe environment while you are cooking, but the areas around the kitchen actually provide many ideal locations for your baby to safely explore and play without the stress of not knowing where you are.

If you live in an older dwelling, there is a good chance your kitchen will be a separate room to the main living area. The challenge of creating a play area that your baby will feel comfortable enough in so they can focus on toys and not worry about you will be slightly more tricky. Look carefully at the space outside your kitchen. If this is a dining area, you can simply move the chairs out of the way and use the floor space around and under the table to create a fun play location that still ensures your baby can see you as they play. Because you will find you are limited with the space you have with this kind of design, you may need to utilise the far ends of the kitchen, away from the actual cooking area. This may mean you need to move the bin or the small breakfast table for a few months until your little one has become more comfortable with playing while you are busy.

If you live in a house of modern design you are likely to have a kitchen that overlooks a main living area. In this case your play stations need to be evenly spaced around the main living area, from a distant location and slowly progressing closer and closer towards the kitchen entrance, basically following your baby's natural crawling path. The philosophy behind this kind of simple design is to establish an environment that will help provide exciting distractions as a more mobile baby makes the usual beeline for your legs while you stand in the kitchen preparing vegetables (see page 374). This also ensures your little one can gradually move closer and closer towards you as they become more and more tired with the progression of the morning.

If your baby is not mobile, the design of the toys is carefully planned so the more difficult or less popular style of play, and in almost all babies this is tummy play, is the activity furthest away from you, and is the first location for play. This ensures you offer the most challenging task when they are at their best, usually after a sleep and a meal, and when they are truly ready to be down and playing. Gradually, as the morning or play session progresses, you will move their location and change their position, keeping play feeling fresh and having appropriate expectations for them around play, taking into account their concentration spans of five to 15 minutes.

Depending on the size of the space that you have to work with, I would generally set up three to four play stations. A play station is an area that has been clearly defined with a play mat. Each mat is equipped with around four age-appropriate toys, and each mat will target a specific style of play, meaning each of the four toys should come from the same developmental area. The four toys should be evenly spaced in the play station, with one toy on each corner on the mat.

The simple idea of setting up several play stations in a room in well-spaced positions creates a flowing, inviting, continually refreshing environment for your child, and helps them to learn how to transition from one activity to another.

If your baby is not yet mobile, you will provide different styles of play at each of the four mats, based on the position you plan on placing your baby. As I've discussed above, you probably should start with tummy-time floor play, and slowly progress to less physically demanding styles of play to ensure you don't ask your baby to be in a position that will be difficult for them to maintain as they progress through the play stations. You should aim to achieve a total of one hour of independent play for your child with around ten to 15 minutes at each station. After they have played for a period of time, go and join them, play for a few minutes, then transition them to the next area. Spend one to two minutes establishing them at the new station then go back to your chores using your flow of communication. After ten to 15 minutes, move them to the next play station.

Setting up your play stations

Each set up consists of four play stations and you will use the same ones for about a week as repetition is the key to mastery of skills: the more familiar your little one becomes with their toys, the more skilled they become making play a truly enjoyable experience. As weekends tend to be busy family times, you will probably not do these activities then unless you are having a quiet one, but you will need to decide on the coming week's activity stations on the Sunday night. These will need to be fresh and new for your baby, so get inventive and imaginative (see page 154).

Play stations to encourage independent play should be designed to be set up once a day and then packed away at the end of any session to mark the passage of that part of the day and the next, such as lunch then sleep time. For the remainder of the day, play is less formal and deliberate as your child will potter happily among their toys or with their family. In the following pages I will give you examples of the kinds of play you need to establish for your little one for a single week. Please note that the toy suggestions are merely suggestions and your choice of toys can be based on what you have at home or on your child's interests.

Play stations for a non-mobile baby aged six to seven months

At this early age, targeting specific areas of development is not as easy as it is with the slightly older group as many types of play and equipment designed for home play offer blended developmental opportunities.

Furthest play station away from parent

Development target: Blended developmental opportunity
Position: Tummy
Duration: 15 minutes (rotating baby once to encourage seven to ten minutes at each end of mat)
Toy examples:
- A Lamaze First Mirror placed to one side of baby so they are encouraged to support the weight of their head and use their upper-body strength to investigate the beautiful little face looking back at them
- A Fisher-Price Tappy The Turtle to encourage reaching, pushing for a response and problem solving
- A texture snake/dog by Lamaze to encourage reaching, discovery through exploration of textures and sounds while they rub, squeeze and manipulate the toy's varied textured sections
- Small water-filled ball with a duck floating on the water to encourage pushing, pulling, reaching

Next play station moving towards parent

Development target:	Blended developmental opportunity
Position:	Back
Duration:	15 minutes (rotating position of A frame on mat once, encouraging seven to ten minutes at each area of play)
Toy examples:	• Fisher-Price A frame / Lamaze crossover mobile play gym equipped with three evenly spaced but different-length hanging attachments directly over baby so the toys hang down over their chest
	• Fisher-Price A frame placed beside the baby so the spinning, fixed side attachments become the baby's main visual focus
	• Activity board on opposite side propped up safely

Next play station moving towards parent

Development target:	Blended developmental opportunity
Position:	Seated on Baby Bumbo seat (never use on elevated, raised or uneven surfaces, on other seats or in cars or baths—use only on the floor surrounded with pillows)
Duration:	15 minutes (rotate the position once at ten minutes if necessary)
Toy examples:	Play gym with hanging activities of varied lengths, sound and texture emphasis

Closest play station to parent

Development target:	Blended developmental opportunity
Position:	Seated
Duration:	15 minutes
Toy examples:	Safety 1st Bouncing Baby Play Place—the activities fixed to station are adequate
	(The beauty of this activity centre is its longevity; when baby is old enough it turns into a large figure-eight train set and all the fixed items on the activity centre, like a little train with moving parts, a silo, a little house with door bell and doors that open, and a moving see-saw with children on it, then come off and complement the train set)

Play station for slightly mobile baby aged eight to ten months

Once your baby becomes more competent with sitting, their frustration around lying on their tummy and back begins to grow. This is particularly obvious in babies in busy homes where there is an older sibling. Despite their ability to sit, it's still important to encourage the skills they need to develop crawling and sitting themselves up. At this age, targeting specific areas of development is becoming easier, but many types of play and equipment designed for home play still offer blended opportunities developmentally. The general idea at this age is to put a little thought into your set up and not just put out random toys in a pile on their play mat.

Furthest play station away from parent

Development target:	Blended developmental opportunity
Position:	Lying on back
Duration:	15 minutes (rotating baby once, encouraging seven to ten minutes at each end of mat)
Toy examples:	• Lamaze Chime Garden to encourage reaching, grabbing, spatial awareness, eye–hand co-ordination and problem solving
	• Lamaze textured snake / dog to encourage reaching, discovery through exploration of textures and sounds while they rub, squeeze and manipulate the toy's varied textured sections
	• Small water-filled bottles with glitter to encourage pushing, pulling, reaching
	• Lovely responsive shakers / rattles

Next play station moving towards parent

Development target:	Blended developmental opportunity focused on problem solving
Position:	Sitting up with pillows behind for support and safety
Duration:	15 minutes (rotating angle after ten minutes but ensure they are facing towards you)
Toy examples:	• Lamaze Multi-Sensory Clutch Cube
	• Fisher-Price Activity Board lying on floor in front of or next to baby or Fisher-Price Brilliant Basics Walker-To-Wagon parked within reach

Next play station moving towards parent

Development target:	Blended developmental opportunity
Position:	Sitting up with pillows behind for support and safety
Duration:	15 minutes (rotate the position of the seat once at 10 minutes if necessary)
Toy examples:	• Baby play nests and baby play donuts and cubes
	• Fisher-Price Discovery Beads
	• soft toys with textures to explore and a material book placed in their lap and around the sides of the mat to encourage reaching

Closest play station to parent

Development target:	Physical development
Position:	In a Jolly Jumper (please follow manufacturer's safety guidelines carefully)
Duration:	10 to 15 minutes
Toy examples:	Activity provided by the station adequate

Play station for a crawling, cruising or walking baby aged ten to 12 months

Once your little people start to move about you face a new set of challenges. Your task is to ensure your baby finds their environment more challenging to stimulate them and encourage them to play independently rather than walk to you. Once they become mobile, their access to you can make play something that some babies are not willing to consider unless you invest a little more time in ensuring the environment represents an exciting and distracting invitation to explore. Obviously, if you have a baby who is single-minded about perpetuating a self-directed routine of sitting on your hip, setting clear boundaries and expectations about their behaviour for this one hour of play each day, as well as closely examining your communication style with your child, will help you change a difficult task for your baby into a fun, predictable play routine in a matter of days.

At this age, targeting specific areas of development is much easier with clearly defined types of play and equipment designed for home play which are easy to come across.

Furthest play station away from parent

Development target:	Cognitive, problem solving
Position:	Sitting upright and they happily reposition themselves
Duration:	Self-directed for any duration or parent-guided for ten to 15 minutes
Toy examples:	• Fisher-Price Pop, Push and Slide toy (many other manufacturers make this kind of toy; you are essentially looking for an animal pop-up toy where you push, slide or turn a lever to have any one of four animals pop up)
	• Fisher-Price Cookie Jar Shape Sorter
	• Lamaze Musical Spin 'n' Stack Rings
	• A simple transfer task (as in from one container to another)

Next play station moving towards parent

Development target:	Language
Position:	Sitting up, crawling
Duration:	Self-directed for any duration or parent-guided for ten to 15 minutes
Toy examples:	• Tent with tunnel attached
	• Books made of material
	• Hardback books
	• Soft toys and pillows

Next play station moving towards parent

Development target:	Gross motor, music
Position:	Beside coffee table or on couch for cruisers or floor mat if they are not cruising
Duration:	Self-directed or parent-guided
Toy examples:	• crocodile xylophone
	• shakers, like maracas
	• bells
	• tambourine

Closest play station to parent

Development target:	Blended developmental opportunity
Position:	Sitting upright, crawling, repositioning themselves
Duration:	Self-directed or parent-guided for ten to 15 minutes
Toy examples:	• LeapFrog LeapStart Learning Table—activities fixed to station are adequate
	• Cooking utensils like big spoon and bowls as they come towards kitchen

Play station for a crawling, cruising or walking baby aged 12 to 18 months

The same principle of setting up four play stations at intervals through the main play area for this age group still applies, however, position is no longer an issue as they will likely be mobile and self-positioning by now. As they will be able to access things from a standing and sitting position you can utilise many different surfaces and areas to create a fun exploratory environment for your little one. Chairs, coffee table, couches and floor activity stations will keep them entertained and exploring for a long time. Each play station should target a specific area of development so they can transition from one activity to another at that particular station and be able to adjust to playing with it simply because it is challenging the same skill set or problem-solving area of the brain.

Try to target a different area at each station. The many areas of play you can target could be cognitive problem solving, social / role play, construction / destruction, discovery, music, fine motor skills, gross motor skills, language, and simple concepts like colour, shape, size, weigh, movement, texture.

Play station for 18 month to two year olds

This is where play becomes great fun. All your foundational work has gone into establishing great skills and therefore true enjoyment in exploration and play. These activities have until now, and should continue to be, been both store-bought toy activities and imaginative homemade ones designed to encourage explorations. You have spent a lot of time playing with them and allowing them to govern play or deliberately role-playing play skills with each activity while you govern play. You need to create balanced independent playtime with one-on-one activity time as your little one is starting to get entertained by simply exploring the world around them and learning from those they see every day.

Now is the time to turn your attention to role play in all its forms. While activities and stimulation to encourage all areas of development should be encouraged, once your child reaches this age there is a natural desire to do as they see, which usually means they like to get domestic—bless them. They will have areas of interest that you can use as your cues for activity ideas, and while it's important to offer lots of different experiences for them around play, their keen interest to focus on one activity and master their skills should not be interfered with.

Each of the areas for play remains the same, only you are starting to offer more challenge and learning how to extend their play experiences by perhaps combining activities. This will teach your little one to start blending activities and make the most out of their play environment.

For cognitive / problem solving

- Coloured pegs with four plastic pots—attach a coloured piece of paper at the base of each pot and start to show them how to sort and categorise their pegs by colour; they can either place the pegs in the pot or attach them to the side.
- A bucket full of autumn leaves and some large plastic insects—show them how to find and collect the bugs in a bucket and offer a safe, large magnifying glass to extend the play if you like, showing them how to use it by using it yourself.

- A long piece of sticky contact taped upside down on the coffee table, sticky side facing up, and lots of different textures, themes and pictures in a container for your little one to stick on the tape—try coloured circles one day, pictures of healthy food another day, felt another day,

Toy / activity inspiration list

Here are some ideas for toys or activities at various play stations to keep you moving. Try to catalogue your toys on your own list to get you thinking about specific areas of development and how to plan the stations.

For cognitive / problem solving
- Simple three- to-ten piece puzzles with large handles (gradually make more challenging as baby's skills increase)
- Posting boxes and shape sorters
- Nesting cups
- Stacking rings
- Earlyears Inside Out Cube
- Fisher-Price Pop and Slide Animal Pop-up Board
- Bead puzzles
- Fisher-Price Peep-a-block 2-in-1 Activity Wagon

Social / role play
- Fisher-Price Little People Yellow School Bus
- Toy mobile phone
- Fisher-Price Chatter Telephone
- Mega Blocks, My Musical Farm
- Amazing Animals Sing & Go Choo-Choo

Physical development
- Laugh & Learn Stride-to-Ride Learning Walker
- Homemade pillow pit (made with your couch cushions)
- Cars
- Balls
- Pull-along toys
- Activities that encourage throwing, rolling, stacking or transferring
- Different handbags (your old ones or from an op shop) with different clasps—zipper, magnetic stud, drawstring, twist clasp—containing coloured scarves in one, blocks in another, spoons in another, small soft toys in another

Construction/Destruction
- Large Duplo
- Large foam blocks
- Simple, light, wooden stackable blocks
- Fisher-Price Peek-a-Blocks
- Any activity that can be pulled apart / put together
- Plasticant Mobilo Building and Construction Toy (for those 18 months of age)
- Four 1.25-litre bottles filled with coloured water with added sparkles or other interesting additions with lids Super Glued shut—show them how to roll the bottles down a simple homemade ramp

Language
- Puzzles
- Books (hard-backed)
- Small tent filled with pillows and hard backed books
- Magnetic storyboards (Maisy) for the fridge or white board
- Soft toys
- Puppets

or cellophane. You can name and date their art and stick it to the window or glass door at home for them to admire and show to others.

Social / role play
- Fisher-Price Little People range (in particular, the farm).
- Toys'R'Us Just Like Home activity sets such as broom / mop / dustpan set, toy microwave, 120-piece food set, crockery set with plates and cups, shopping trolley, cash register.
- Old wallet with old discount cards or a handbag and simple dress-ups items like hats and shoes.
- A dolly's / teddy's pram, bath, high chair, capsule, change table with accessories.
- Their own little kitchen area with pots and a small table and chair set.
- Simple homemade cloths line (set up in the corner of a balcony so they can't walk into it) with pegs, a bucket of bubbles and some clothes—remember to supervise any water play.

Construction / Destruction
- Extend block play by adding toy animals, and coloured paper for water or grass.
- Toys'R'Us wooden block puzzle train.
- Large Duplo with cars.
- Fisher-Price Pop-on Busy Tabletown.

Language
- Add magnetic numbers, colours and shapes at a safe size if popped in mouth.
- More complex books.
- Safe cubby house / tent retreat as their quiet language corner—set it up under the dining table or on the couch with a clear boundary of bottoms on seats to keep them safe from toppling off.

Making each play station look inviting

Some babies are happy to have a few toys thrown on a play mat and seem to be able to play anywhere their parents take or put them, while others require far more stimulation, encouragement or careful planning to achieve this same simple task. Most parents who experience difficulties with baby's daytime play say their bubs have displayed this tendency from a very early age. Many of the parents who make their way on to my waiting list are the only mums in their mothers' group whose baby has 'never played on the floor like the other babies do', or 'has never just drifted off to sleep mid play or on a pram ride'. Most of these parents have little ones who have always insisted on sitting on their parent's lap, even from the earliest age, so they can join in with all the social chatter the mothers are engaged in while all the other babies play happily on the floor.

It is these mothers and fathers who will need to invest a little more time creating an environment that will draw their baby's attention and encourage an active interest in their surroundings. Each play station should look lovely. Fan the books out and place one on a big teddy's lap, open and clearly role modelling reading. Their Fisher-Price Peek-a-blocks can be in a semi-constructed tower with the posting giraffe half filled, and a few remaining blocks inviting baby's attention. Nesting cups should always be a complete set and semi-constructed, or towered, or in a straight sequential line. Each activity you set up should be semi-constructed and look nice. At no point would you just chuck a toy on the floor willy-nilly for independent play.

By spending a little more time creating a fun play environment, you increase the chances that play will start to happen without much more intervention and without the need to work through any difficult behaviour.

Choosing appropriate toys

When it comes to setting up play stations for babies, I always tell the families I work with that 'if there is an overwhelming choice of toys, then your baby will be too overwhelmed to make a choice'. This same principle applies to adults. Think about how you feel when you walk into a toy shop for the first time with the intention of buying your child something that they will enjoy and you're met with aisles and aisles of toys, floor to ceiling. You might feel more confused than ever. When it comes to purchasing appropriate equipment I am always conscious of a few things:

• Don't get caught up in products that claim to make your baby super bright and highlight the typical benefits of play with that particular toy. All the bells and whistles in the world with grand statements claiming that the toy will make your child somehow attain a higher IQ for the experience does not necessarily mean it's a particularly great toy or holds any more benefit for the child than exploring a cardboard carton. Try to remember that all play is valuable and encourages healthy development.

• Look for multiple tasks in a toy for babies ten months plus. A toy where they need to work out how to make something happen with an action is far more valuable than a toy that does all the stuff for them with the simple and somewhat unchallenging push of a button or single insertion of a small ball. If that's all the baby needs to do to trigger the bells, lights and whistles of some super fancy-looking toy then, despite its appearance on the outset, they will actually quickly tire of the toy and lose interest in playing with it altogether because it is not challenging, just entertaining to look at—much like a TV!

- Look for longevity. Ask yourself, does it provide multiple levels of skill requirements appropriate to several age milestones? A good example of this is the Safety 1st Bouncing Baby Play Place. It starts as a fun play walker then converts to an early stage figure-eight train track. The Fisher-Price school bus starts out as a fun problem-solving exploratory, action response toy for babies, and then turns into a small social-play piece of equipment that matches the Fisher-Price little people range designed for toddlers and preschool-aged children alike.
- Search for less busy-looking toys with softer colours (see box on page 145), which is often a better idea for those under ten months of age. Look for activities with this age group that incorporate basic concepts like colour, shape, texture and sound.
- Buy quality.
- Think about the things you do the most and buy similar things. If you always talk on the phone, get them a phone as they will have had so many role plays of how to use this toy from you that this form of play will be extremely desirable to them.
- Make toys using everyday household items. Familiar objects are always the things they enjoy playing with the most.

Physical positioning for play

Positioning can make a tremendous difference for a baby when it comes to being able to play effectively on their own. If you are struggling with establishing play for your little one and they are immobile, unable to sit, or have a tendency to get frustrated after a short period of playtime on their own, then you need to consider how you can make the most out of your baby's time, and provide a series of positions to ensure play can be comfortable and enjoyable for a much longer period.

I see many people get stuck on a rigid set of rules with babies, without actually stopping to consider the baby's comfort. Sitting your baby too early is often frowned upon—come hail or high water, your baby must lie down until they can crawl. I have to say I agree that babies need tummy time every day, but the idea that we cannot provide multiple positions for a baby's play session is simply too strict and unrealistic. By ensuring a balance of tummy time, back time and assisted sitting, provided your baby is able to sit effectively with little to no intervention, you can create an ideal, enjoyable, fun and empowering play session and encourage a healthy attitude about play.

At any one time, you should encourage around ten to 15 minutes of play per play station and position before you go over, give them a cuddle, relocate them to a new play activity and position if required, and then spend a few minutes playing with them. Obviously, if your baby is very engaged with their play, then there is no need to go and remove them from that situation but it is important to be conscious of the need to not push your baby to play beyond a reasonable length of time in any one place. To create a situation where you always leave them too long, and they feel the need to cry to have you come and move them, only teaches them to cry during playtime. If, on the other hand, you provide an environment where they trust that you will come and play or come and give them a cuddle or move them to a new environment then your baby can happily focus on play and confidently wait for you. This will quickly increase their attention span, create a situation where they are more likely to play for longer without a need to continually try and engage your attention through crying, and develop strong positive associations with play.

Lying on their tummy is not always a favourite for many babies but it is essential for many reasons. Apart from the obvious developmental benefits highlighted in just about every baby book in the universe, tummy time offers babies the opportunity to practise letting their mummy and daddy put them down. This may sound trite, but if you have a baby who is struggling at sleep time then the simple task of lying down your baby can be something that is extremely difficult and often confusing for the baby and parent alike. The ability to pop your baby down on their tummy or back for floor play becomes a crucial element that assists you to establish realistic expectations for baby settling on their back at sleep time. It is far more beneficial to develop this ability at a non-confrontational time such as play time, when you are there to guide and reassure them, rather than at sleep time, when they have a low threshold for coping. This means you are actively developing a style of communication during the day that is consistent to your baby's night settling and resettling needs.

To not lie your baby down during the day causes confusion and develops inconsistent communication streams about this particular situation and feeling. Think about it. You establish a play area, you ensure you baby is well fed, rested and comfortable and you eliminate any possible causes of stress, such as furniture blocking their sight of you, then you put them down slowly and gently on a soft comfortable surface and try to establish play time. Sounds easy right? In most cases the baby will burst out into loud crying, complete with flailing arms, kicking legs and an inability to open their eyes until they are picked up again. Now let's look at your response to this situation.

The baby cries in this safe and comfortable environment so, confused by their sudden crying, you pick them up, hold them upright and calm them down. This happens over and over again and after several attempts you give up. Remember, despite all the initial changes you have established, your baby has not yet had the opportunity to experience the improved new conditions and establish their trust yet, so there is always a little work to do. This is their need to establish trust in the new environment. To not help them through this means you are not catering for their true need and forgetting your important role as a wise, patient and loving parent by leaving them emotionally stagnated in a place of anxiety.

If you respond to a baby's association of anxiety around being put down you create the following communication about the new safe environment:

- You reinforce the idea that lying down under any circumstances must be as bad as they think, and you must always rescue them from this position.
- You teach them to cry to be picked up without even stopping to admire the toys around them.
- You teach them that you will always pick them up even if you assess the conditions to be safe. This will be particularly confusing for them at sleep time and is often the cause of sleep problems.
- You tell them that they can't calm themselves down, and they always need you to do that for them, but that is simply *not* the case. You are teaching learnt dependency here where they would be better equipped with blended solutions of both dependent and independent, with the view to empowering them to cope fully on an independent level.
- You never give them the opportunity to learn how to work past an initial concern, or through a negative routine pattern (crying) in response to an old event to create a new routine pattern (play) to the same event.
- You promote upright positioning as positive and an emotional solution, and associate lying-down positioning as negative and irresolvable on their own.

As parents, you need to assess your baby's true needs. The ability to be put down is a simple and important one. All too often I see a learnt pattern being developed around this skill that says, 'if you cry when lying down, I will always pick you up'. And, as I've said, this usually then goes hand in hand with sleep problems, and out of exhaustion and desperation a mother or father will embark on control crying in isolation as a strategy to resolve sleep-time blues, when in fact positioning is your first area to repair.

Can you imagine the challenge for the baby when a parent never pursues tummy or back playtime through play because it makes your baby grouchy, but then makes the baby cry it out and solve it on their own at sleep time? Alone in their cots they will be tired and feeling vulnerable without the skills they need to cope in a situation like that, because the only skill they have been taught is to ask to be picked up so you can fix it.

If, after carefully assessing the situation from an adult's perspective, you think tummy or back playtime in this environment is a reasonable request and still important (which it is in most cases, if you take all the above-mentioned things into consideration), then now is the time to work through and past those tears and old patterns of behaviour to achieve a new positive association and outcome at playtime.

Why do some babies dislike lying down?

This is a fairly common problem and one that needs a little refection in order to solve. Some of the most common reasons could come from a simple positioning pattern established when they were younger. If your baby was a windy baby, there is a high chance that you held them upright in your arms to help them release air. So lying on the floor can be a long, long, long way away from what they are used to. Sitting upright is also clearly a far more interesting position for many babies.

If your baby had colic or reflux, then quite often poor associations were developed when the child was laid down and experienced discomfort or pain within a short period of time. Even though the colic or reflux symptoms may well have passed, the association and mistrust in that environment may still exist well past its expiry date if you have not worked through and re-established trust in that environment once the pain or discomfort had gone.

Sometimes an early pattern of sleeping upright on mum and dad during the day is established with BabyBjörn-style products or even a baby sling that allows the baby to sleep upright. It is a warm environment next to you, with restricted visual stimulation, but in a cot environment it is not possible to replicate because it does not represent the safest conditions. These upright sleep conditions during the day create a strong sleep association for the baby of sleeping on their tummy and upright. The task of then sleeping lying down on their back, without your extra warmth and where they can see everything and move without restriction, is almost a foreign concept for baby. It is often impossibly difficult for your baby to adjust within a few short months or sometimes weeks of upright sleeping during the day.

Should you still use these products? Sure, of course you should, but everything in your baby's life should be in balance. Sometimes they will need to sleep in a sling, other times in the pram, other times in the cot or crib. These styles of sleep environment will need to be addressed whether you are at home or out and about. Just because one is easier it doesn't mean it should be your first option every time, or your baby will start to require that sleep environment day and night and become inflexible with unbalanced skills.

The same thing occurs for babies who only sleep on their mother or father during the day. If this is you and you're stuck on that couch every day for as long as your little one needs to sleep, please know you're not alone, and know that 'positioning' is the first place you need to start. For other children, though, it could be siblings creating an unpredictable environment, and the need to set appropriate boundaries around your baby may be essential in reducing stress so your little one can stop worrying and start to play happily without interruption. This may mean that you have a basic-sized mat that your baby plays on through the day and their sibling cannot step on the mat unless they ask first, and there is no running past the mat, only walking. These simple boundaries means a baby can relax and trust that their loving and adoring big brother or sister will not invade their space, smother them in mountains of toys or lather them in kisses. This alone helps a child settle down very quickly and ensures that while they cannot speak, you are sure to speak on their behalf.

For some babies it could be that renovations on your house are occurring and they see many strangers walk past them, in which case you would need to keep them closer. If, however, your child still shows clear signs of feeling unsettled by the intrusion of strangers in their house, the need for a simple partition to create a visual division between the baby and the workers' walkway will help them settle and develop a trust that those workers will follow a predictable path, reducing the stress immediately. A partition could be something as simple as a baby gate with muslin over the side that they never cross. This means baby can trust that the workers will come no further than the gate and always walk the same paths. Gradually your baby's trust will come back and they will focus more on play and become used to the changing environment. Then you can take away the muslin by inches, and eventually remove the gate.

For some babies, putting them down on the floor may always indicate to them that you are about to leave the room. If this causes stress then don't avoid putting them down altogether because you know your baby will cry. You need to look at establishing a short-term absence cue (see page 94), and ensure your playtime environment is suitable (see page 146). If you are in the habit of just wandering off without telling your child in the hope that leaving while they are distracted will prevent tears, then you need to actually think in an entirely different way because that strategy is in fact the number one reason why playtime can become so difficult for a baby. If you don't create an auditory-style environment with a predictable stream of communication like the short-term absence cue, 'I'll be back', your baby will never feel comfortable to just focus on their toys and play. They will feel they have to watch you for indications of your movements.

Sitting

A baby sitting up is a very complex task, and it can take quite some time for them to master it. Babies can occasionally overbalance from the sitting position and topple over when they first start to sit, which can be frustrating and,

The case of James

Seven-month-old James was a very tired, overstimulated and anxious little boy when I arrived to help him and his family find a little peace. His mother had carefully filmed James' play prior to my arrival, and as I sat on the floor getting to know little James, she showed me what it was like on a normal day to try and put James down on the floor for even the most simple of playtime. At this stage his mother was suffering from a strained shoulder and was finding it extremely difficult to hold him all day, every day, but James would not have a bar of being put down on the floor.

I watched the video, which showed a brief example of the problems they were experiencing. It showed James sitting happily on his mother's lap, feeling safe and secure, watching his beautiful and very theatrical three-year-old sister dance and sing and rolly polly over everything. Mum would then lift him out of her lap and lie him down right next to her. He would burst into tears immediately and become frantic, kicking and flapping wildly. His sister would lean over to try and help him stop crying and would try and tickle his tummy, which would only upset him more. His mother would get frustrated with big sister and use a firm tone to ask her to 'just leave him be'. His mother would then lie down next to him and offer him toys and shake his rattles in front of him to try and distract him. He would try to hit them away kicking and crying, all the while watching his sister dancing. He then started to rub his eyes and cry in long deep howls. Within two minutes of being put down to play, his mum now commented that he was obviously tired and that was why he couldn't play, sometimes in some unfortunate cases, a bit ouchy. Generally, most babies develop the ability to sit at between four and seven months of age. This usually coincides with achieving skills like holding their head up or rolling over. Even the most seasoned sitter will have the occasional topple when they are distracted or preoccupied, but by around seven to eight months, 90 per cent of babies will be able to sit up unaided for an extended period of time.

To ensure your baby's association with sitting independently is not one that evokes a fear of toppling over and bumping their head, or a feeling that it is just better to be picked up and carried as there is no risk of anything unpredictable like falling and hitting their head happening, you will need to do three things each time you sit them down:

1. distribute their weight by ensuring the centre of their weight is balanced on a solid sitting base.
2. check the environment for safety and comfort when falling
3. be considerate of your child's personal space.

Balancing their weight is very simple. When you sit a baby up, they have a tendency, particularly when wearing bulky nappies, to either sit with their bottom tucked under them a little too far, or to rely on the bulk of the nappy behind them to have the same level of support that a pillow

and proceeded to pick him up. As she picked him up, his crying stopped immediately and a little smile appeared as she perched him on her hip. James was often put to bed because the situation was being misunderstood and this created serious sleep-time problems as well. I often encounter a misunderstanding of the dislike of environmental conditions being interpreted as tired signs.

What I could see from this simple video was a whole series of other things causing little James stress and frustration. Firstly, he was not given any warning that he was going to be laid down on the floor. So the first new rule of communication needed was a consistent pre-emptive cue to indicate he was about to be put down before it was done. The second very clear problem was his concerns about his very gorgeous but overexcited sister playing mummy. She would cramp his space all of a sudden, tickle his tummy and make a lot of noise. Some clear boundaries needed to be set around him when he was playing by himself on the floor. Then we looked at positioning. When his sister was around, sitting him up was far more appropriate than lying him down as this left him feeling less vulnerable. The problem he had with sitting was that with very little practice, he was not very good at staying upright, which would result in him falling, which then created a poor association for him.

It took us one morning with the new boundaries and positioning rules in place to regain his trust and establish positive independent play. The results for him and for his family, as you can imagine, were wonderful. This highlights the need to try to look at all aspects surrounding the problem to help resolve a baby's daytime blues.

would have. Each time you sit your little one, grab their nappy from behind and give it a firm pull to help baby sit on their lower bottom and upper legs rather than further back on their bottom. This will immediately create a very straight back, but with the extra height to ensure they are balanced. Instead of having their legs close together, you will need to push their legs out so their feet are at the same distance or slightly more apart than their hips. This creates a solid triangle base for them to sit on. Once they are positioned well, then you can put some toys between their legs to encourage them to lean forward into their sitting position. Immediately you will see them able to stay more balanced on their new solid sitting foundation.

If your baby has become resistant to being put down at all, then sitting is the best location for them initially when re-establishing floor play. Sit behind them, and pop them between your legs. Position them correctly and support their back, and establish play. It is quite normal for a baby who has lost trust in the process of being put down to continue to lean back on you initially, but gradually, as they build their confidence, you can place their toy at reaching distance in front of them so they are encouraged to lean forward and support their own weight. This has been a quickly resolved problem in the many homes I've entered and only takes one day to correct. It may sound obvious but this one loss of trust in being put down can be the foundation of all playtime disruptions. Often, this is never revisited as the parent just thinks that their baby hates being put down and that's that. To never revisit this though means your baby will be stuck in an old association that could be easily resolved with a parent's wise guidance.

The second area you need to ensure is maintained when establishing correct positioning for sitting is the safety nets you put around your baby. One safety net should be created with pillows. This is where you can ensure that no matter what happens or how bold they become with their movements, if they do fall over, they don't get hurt. You also need to ensure that the area that you put them in to play does not have a coffee table leg, wall or any other hard object to fall against.

The final safety net is consideration. As parents you need to ensure you set clear considerate boundaries around your little one's personal play space by giving any older sibling clear boundaries about what is and isn't appropriate around the baby.

Varying positioning for playing

There are many positions in which to place your baby to create a fresh feel around play. This enables them to play for longer periods and develop a good feeling around the challenge of exploring their environment. These include:

- lying down with toys in reach
- lying down with toys out of reach
- sitting down with toys in reach
- sitting down with toys out of reach.

The different challenges you provide for a child in early or advanced stages of lying-down and sitting-down positions vary from toys in close proximity to a more distant reach position. Initially start with toys within reach, then you can gradually place some at an adequate distance to promote reaching, or tummy shuffling. As the child becomes more and more competent with sitting, you can go from putting a toy in their lap to several toys within reach. Ultimately you provide a harder challenge by putting toys at a distance, which would require some problem solving and repositioning by the little one to access that toy.

Another great sitting strategy is to look at how you can utilise hanging mobile frames used when baby could only lie down. By placing visual, textured and sound-responsive toys on the frame, either in front or beside your baby, they will be able to enjoy these toys in a different way and find new challenge in the task of playing with a fixed object. This all makes for an interesting variety in the types of play stations you can provide for your child.

Maintaining safety while cooking or ironing

Obviously, while I encourage a parent to do their chores in the morning while baby practises their independent playtime, it's important to remember all the safety hints for keeping the kitchen safe and sound for busy little people and busy parents. The Safety 1st website (www.safety1st.com) has many tips on how to make your entire house safe for little people and their parents.

Advantages and disadvantages of playpens and gates

I am not a big advocate of playpens. I generally don't ever see the need to incorporate them in any home maintenance program I implement and more often than not eliminate them entirely from play sessions when I am re-establishing effective independent play. I find that babies' play is limited in a playpen and their entire home time, unless in adult's arms, is generally behind the bars of a cot or a confined pen. I also find that playpens tend to get messy with an accumulation of toys thrown into it in a haphazard manner during a general tidy up, and this rarely offers great opportunities for effective and challenging play. Finally, I find that when a playpen is used for older more mobile babies it is generally used in place of effective communication streams, such as setting simple boundaries by saying, 'Wait for mummy', 'I'll be back' and 'No touch' or by providing a practical and child-safe environment.

If you are too frightened of your baby following you or getting up to no good when you duck into the laundry for a moment or two, then you may need to establish clear two-way communication that still enables you to achieve the same response from them; that is, playing independently, while you do the chores. By using the very foundation of communication with the simple use of language cues you won't need to confine them to a playpen. As usual however, I am not a zealot for anything in particular and if your baby is extremely happy to play in the playpen, and all is well with this strategy and you and your baby's communication, then there is no need to eliminate it if you feel it is a positive element of play for your little one.

The use of gates is an extremely effective tool for setting safety boundaries if you are concerned your little one will get into mischief in certain location, or when you cannot see them. A gate can often make cooking safer, and it is a good idea to use gates to keep play outside the kitchen, so long as they can still see you. Gates can be useful to stop patterns of crying. Think of a time when they will classically always follow you to the bathroom and cry at the door. By simply establishing a new pattern, such as a short-term absence cue, and by placing a toy at the gateway, you will discover that your baby will start to follow you crying, but then be distracted by the lovely toy at the gate and sit and play while they wait for you to return.

Gates also offer older children the opportunity to play with their toy without fear of having it destroyed by their baby brother or sister. This typical playtime dilemma is often what causes upsets and can motivate snatching, pushing and tantrums from older children as well as fuel mistrust about play in little ones. The use of gates, however, is often interpreted as an unpleasant necessity and this is commonly reflected in the way a parent will talk about the gate. If you have a baby who is cruising, you cover the gate in sparkly, well-fixed stickers and get really excited about its installation, fostering warm positive associations with this helpful parenting tool, and ensuring that baby has something to do each time they encounter it. If you always make a habit of pointing to the stickers and counting with a big happy smile, you will see your baby reflect this pattern and enjoy the encounter rather than seeing it as something that just prevents them from reaching something or someone momentarily.

As I've said above, always make a habit of placing a favourite toy at the gate, and then once you have walked through and closed the gate behind you, lean over it briefly to have a little tinker with that toy. This will encourage your baby to focus on the toy, rather than on you leaving, and help prevent tears. If your baby is very relaxed and content about you leaving, there is no need to do anything other than use your short-term absence cue.

Play stations and siblings

If you are wishing to establish play stations for an older child as well, then similar principles apply to the stations but you need to keep in mind a few extra simple rules. Remember to consider the example you and your older child are setting for your baby. Your older child cannot constantly be demanding your time and attention while you establish a different set of expectations for your baby, which is independent play. A continuum of care and expectation should be established so that both your children are part of the same parenting philosophy.

Your older child should also have three play stations set up for them, one of which would include some form of activity for any child aged two or over in the corner of a room, what I call 'a home corner activity'. An example of this would be a mothering corner with a dolly or teddy, for boys and girls alike. Children this age like to copy whatever they see their parents doing and as you have a younger child, the older sibling will be mimicking you looking after a baby. The area would contain a baby cot (made with a box if necessary), a baby high chair with bowls and spoons (use one of their seats from their tiny tots table-and-seat set if you don't have a toy high chair), a change table with nappy, empty pots of cream and a couple of singlets (use a foot stool as a change table to save money). This can easily be set up a good distance from your little baby's play stations to give them space apart.

Another play station can be put up high on the dining table to prevent an overzealous crawling sibling from destroying it accidentally. This could be a basic problem-solving activity like puzzles, or basic construction sets, such as Duplo.

The final play station could be in your older child's room, on the floor at a distance from baby brother or sister, or even in an adjoining room. Music and movement make a fun activity which is a favourite with two year olds plus. Offer a small CD player with their favourite music playing on it. Provide instruments like bells, a tambourine and a xylophone.

Incorporating a small language area for baby and toddler is a lovely quiet activity to encourage them playing in the same space without the risk of conflict or distress. Big soft pillows, some hard-backed books, a couple of favourite teddies and a request to 'sit in the quiet corner' and 'use soft voices' is a must. Initially, when putting your children's play areas together, you need to gain your baby's trust in playing with their older sibling. It is important to sit with them both and establish a 'no touch the baby' policy until the boundaries are understood and they are both settled and content. When you can see that your toddler understands these boundaries, then you will be able to step away, allowing them to play together (parallel) again. Always keep an eye on your toddler and always define the statements above (see page 44).

Any loud or physically active play, such as music and dancing, should be isolated to a specific area away from your baby, or to the next room.

The case of James and Oliver

James was a sweet little eight-month-old boy who had a lovely older brother called Oliver. Oliver just loved the company of his mother Sarah and his baby brother James. But baby James was finding it extremely difficult to be put down at any time during the day. While it was difficult for her, Sarah reasoned it wasn't too bad because sleep time was not an issue in their household. But within a month of the dislike of his mother putting him down during the day, James started experiencing the same concerns at sleep time. Some investigation on my part revealed that this pattern of behaviour began during play time.

I sat on the floor and got acquainted with Sarah, James and Oliver. As Sarah and I sat and chatted, little Oliver sat playing quietly on his mum's legs showing me all his favourite toys. I asked Sarah to show me what she normally did when it was time to put James down. She rolled her eyes and said 'Okay, cover your ears'. She briefly turned James to face her and gave his a little kiss then said 'C'mon little man, time to lie down and have a play'. I was pleased to see she was using clear pre-emptive language with him.

James was placed carefully on the floor but he laid stiff, straining to look down towards his toes. There were no tears, but he was clearly watching for something and his tummy muscles were straining. He had absolutely no interest in the toys his mother was offering him but I could see James watching his brother. Oliver, having seen his brother being put down, immediately set about gathering up toys in the room and then placing them on his baby brother's tummy.

This had become a ritual his mother claimed. She hadn't wanted to damage the strong bond developing between her two beautiful sons so Sarah initially fostered this behaviour by rewarding Oliver. She was so pleased to see him being so kind and generous towards his sibling. Within a few short months though, she went on to explain, this pattern of behaviour

This ensures your older child has as much freedom to express themselves as possible, and that your baby is not disturbed or stressed by the wonderful hullabaloo your older child is creating. If your little one has been stressed during independent play and you are trying to re-establish trust in playing again, always invoke the 'no touch the baby' boundary. Your older child can play with the baby when you are able to supervise but personal space boundaries must be established when you are not there to protect your baby from an albeit well-meaning but very fast and overwhelming big brother or sister.

With that in mind, it's important to be cautious about how you set your boundaries. At no point should you raise your voice. Politely make your request and, if they do not listen, then simply remove them from the play zone. They can only return when they are willing to listen. It's that simple. If they return and do not do as you have politely asked, remove them from the play zone again. Each time you remove them, go back and play with your little one. Repeat this until they cease the undesirable behaviour.

got completely out of hand and was now causing his little baby James considerable stress. It had also become stressful for Sarah.

Oliver had now gathered up a fair few toys for his brother, and Sarah said, 'No more toys, Oliver', as she watched him continue to gather even more. Thirty seconds later James was becoming excited with the amount of toys, but was still not crying. 'Oliver, mummy said no more, now listen to me', Sarah said in a firm voice, but Oliver continued to offer more toys, just one at a time now. James started to try to roll towards his mother and moan. Sarah raised her voice sharply, 'Oliver, that's enough. Now mummy's cross!' By now James started to cry. As Sarah picked him up she said, 'I'm sorry, Oliver keeps spoiling your play'.

My observation of what was happening was slightly different to Sarah's take on events. As I watched, the same pattern repeated itself over and over again. James was not terribly concerned about his brother bringing him toys; in fact, he was quite used to it and watched with great interest. What was bothering him was the fact that his mother was yelling every time she put him down. Because Oliver always got James toys, and his mother had accidentally defined the statement 'no more toys' to mean 'get more toys until I yell and pick him up' by not following through, Sarah yelled every single time she put James down. This meant James, being a baby and not understanding her behaviour, was getting a fright each time he was out of her arms. As this didn't happen when he was in her arms, he had decided to stay in her arms so he didn't have to get yelled at.

Together we worked on the flow of communication, at rebuilding James' trust in play when put down. Within 24 hours, James was sleeping and playing without a hitch. This highlights the importance of setting boundaries politely and consistently with an older sibling around the baby without raising your voice.

The reasons for not raising your voice are obvious as far as setting a good example and establishing appropriate communication skills in your house. It's also important to remember that if you raise your voice, you have officially lost control of the situation. This makes it difficult for your baby to confidently allow you to guide them as you immediately become unpredictable.

Twins

When working with multiple births, the same scenarios appear in each home for those aged between six and 24 months. There is generally one twin who is far more reliant on the company of their sister or brother for comfort than the other. While this is perfectly natural, I often find the way parents manage the more reliant one is to *always* ensure they are close to their sibling. This is good up to a point, but the independent twin will begin to be burdened with the responsibly of keeping their sibling happy at playtime. It's important to continue working on empowering both your children with the vital skill of being able to sometimes play on their own.

I often suggest using strategies like head-to-toe play, or feet-to-feet play to ensure both your babies' needs are catered for. I am conscious of one

The case of Andrew and Olivia

Andrew and Olivia were beautiful six-month-old twins who kept their adoring mummy and daddy on their toes every night with two-hourly bottle feeds. Every time mum fed one twin, she would feed the other just so she didn't have to get up in ten minutes' time but they often then stayed awake for hours during the night, needing snuggles and reassurance. During the day, the babies were tired but happy. The babies had spent a lot of time awake each day; they were classic catnappers.

Olivia was content to play and enjoyed the company of her brother but didn't have difficulty playing on her own. Andrew on the other hand was a very adoring big brother. He would snuggle and smooch his twin sister endlessly, and would be at his happiest when he was right on top of her sucking her cheek. Olivia loved him very much but found this arrangement most unsatisfactory because she clearly had toys to explore, and a slobbering brother was slightly cramping her style. Eventually she would get upset by her brother's antics, and her frustrated cries would send her adoring brother into a complete emotional meltdown. This ultimately meant that play sessions were over within 15 minutes and both babies needed to be held until the next feed or nap time.

The general strategy I work with when dealing with unsettled twins is to offer graded exposure to a less dependent form of play at least once a day. We decided they needed time together towards the end of an hour-long play session, as this was when they were both less able to cope on their own and were truly ready to be together. So their first play station was designed to encourage a visually close environment where they could coo and smile at one twin rolling on to and happily smooching their baby sister or brother lovingly, but ensure I also take the recipient's need for space in mind too.

The case of Andrew and Olivia highlights the need to provide twins with a graded exposure to one-on-one playtime simply to ensure both babies have a good opportunity to fully explore and enjoy their environment. The close physical relationships of twins are almost always fostered, as they should be, but too often the need to empower both babies with the practice and skills they need to be individuals is given very little thought and rarely seen as important. All children, regardless of their background, who are being raised in an emotionally supportive and loving home environment, should be exposed to a balanced set of conditions, which they will encounter as they grow and enter the big social world of childcare, kindergarten or preschool.

A typical sequence of play stations for non-mobile babies would follow a simple path:

- visual connection but playing separately
- feet-to-feet play
- head-to-toe playing beside one another

another but from a slight distance. This resulted in Olivia chatting away happily with an occasional smile for her brother, and Andrew gazing starry-eyed at her, the love of his life, while still playing happily with his toys.

Gradually, we would bring them closer and closer together in 15-minute intervals. The second play station offered them feet-to-feet playtime. This was absolutely delightful to watch. With bare feet they could touch each other and would lock toes immediately, and both of them would play and chat happily without visual contact, content knowing the other was near. Next we progressed them to head-to-toe play where they would lie next to each other but at opposite ends. Eventually, they would play alongside one another and Olivia, having had her delightfully busy free play, was more content to play and smooch her brother in return. Play became a more settled and enjoyable event for both babies and Andrew learnt that he could be as content just looking at his sister, as he was when he was sucking her cheek.

One of the most empowering aspects of this form of play for Andrew was to be seen at sleep time. Andrew found it very stressful if he was unable to see his sister when he woke up so he would often cry until she woke up and cried too. When he was able to hear her crying, he would settle down immediately and go back to sleep. Unfortunately, this now meant his little sister was wide awake and cross about it. Once these play strategies were incorporated into his day, and some careful adjustments made to their sleeping arrangements, Andrew was content to sleep without the need for tears or disrupting his sister.

- head-to-head play (where they are cheek to cheek without actually touching)
- lying beside one another (parallel facing the same direction allowing for their typically adorable smooching and spooning opportunities).

As children get older and stronger and able to sit, the same principle applies to the graded exposure of play but you incorporate the positioning strategies slightly differently:

- floor play where they have a visual connection but play separately
- sitting up with feet-to-feet play
- Bumbo seats, where they can reach each other's hands next to one another but facing different directions with their own toys on suspended mobile on each side
- Donut play seat, where they can sit next to one another and have full access to one another.

Troubleshooting

Q They don't play with the play stations I have set up. They actually prefer to play with other things instead. Is this still ok?

A Yes, yes, yes! The main reason that we set up a lovely play environment is to help promote an interest in the environment so your baby will want to play in the first place. If your baby takes an interest in their environment and becomes self-directive, then that is a perfect outcome.

Toy storage to promote better playing and easy packing away

One of the first things I like to do when working with an older toddler (18 months plus) is to set up a great toy storage area. This helps them and you pack away quickly, and makes it easy for your toddler to quickly learn how to pack away without too much intervention. A good toy storage area empowers your child with being able to go and access specific tasks with little difficulty, making play more interesting. To help you understand why it's important to set up a simple toy storage area it's best to look at the function of toys at this age.

Most toys for children aged 18 months and onward are designed to have a specific problem to solve, or sequence of events to process, or contain an interesting role-play (Duplo, little people, cooking) opportunity for them to work through. The desire to spend time with an activity comes from a place of real interest and challenge in that toy. If that toy is always incomplete however, the child will often never learn how to complete a task unless guided by an adult and will be more likely to wander, demand television, or hover around after mum or dad bored, or as many parents describe, 'Whinging'. This can often lead to them disliking time spent indoors, always wanting to play outside, often making a parent want to spend more time out of home. The desire to play with a toy often comes from their feelings of enjoyment, which comes from mastering an activity, and their ability to concentrate comes from their desire to do an activity they feel confident they can complete, or engage, and successfully grasp its concept.

When toys are all thrown into a toy box however, it often takes me up to an hour to find a series of completed activities, and it is therefore an impossible task for your toddler. So a small amount of time invested in the way you pack away will have lasting benefits. In order to establish effective play and easy packing away within this age group, I work with a simple system: no stackable crates and no huge toy boxes unless they are only for cars, dolls or dress-ups, which is a complete task isolated to one area.

I use a series of four small, removable, lightweight drawers in a light plastic frame on casters. These drawers are available from hardware and storage shops. Before you get too excited thinking about pretty wicker pull-out drawers in wooden shelves, remember you need to achieve two things with these drawers:

1. Safe, lightweight removal of a drawer by your child without the constant need for your intervention.
2. The ability to attach a visual prompt on the front of the box so your child knows where to go to either find or pack away their toys. This could simply be a picture of a play station containing some of the toys within that drawer.

A series of drawers means you can circulate the toys you provide, keeping play fresh and exciting.

The areas that each drawer can hold could be broken down into the following types of categories, which can simply be adjusted to suit your toys:

*   construction, such as Duplo
*   puzzles and problem solving—nesting cups, sequence rings, pop-up toys and puzzles
*   role play—cooking and pretend food / mobile / laptop / car keys / crockery
*   transport—trains, planes and automobiles
*   Fisher-Price little people

- animals and small life accessories such as trees, rocks, floor car mats
- language—books, felt board, magnetic stories
- music
- balls
- dolls and dolls' accessories
- junky toys.

Once you have arranged your toys into appropriate drawers, it's time to label them in a way that will be easy for your little one to recognise. To do this I set up each area of play so it looks nice then take a quick picture and print it up. Stick each picture on the front of your toy storage area with clear contact and your little one now has easy access to great complete play stations, and setting up and packing away will become a joy for all.

9
Independent playtime in the cot

I firmly believe playtime in the cot after a baby has woken up from a sleep is one of the main strategies available to underpin long-term sleep maintenance. It is important for even the best sleepers to establish this skill so they can maintain good sleep when there are little hiccoughs along the way, such as illness or holidays. I feel it is also vital for a child to be adept at happily playing in their cot to ultimately help them to learn how to sleep there with as few tears as possible. Playing should always be a part of their bedtime ritual until the age of four or five years, and it's *never* too late to establish this simple sleep-time boundary, even when they are happily sleeping in a bed at five years of age.

Playtime in the cot is, of course, an important listening-skill learning tool as well. You make a simple request and you govern the outcome of that request. You're creating a predictable pattern for your little one so that the routine will become familiar for them and they will be able to pre-empt this part of the day, empowering them with the feeling of being in control. This feeling of control enables them to develop great comfort around the skills needed to go to sleep in their cots and be able to cope with a request to go back to sleep if they have woken early and need you to attend and leave again. If you can't ask them to have a little play in their cot when the lights are on and they are fresh after a sleep, how can you possibly ask them to lie quietly while their body drifts off to sleep?

Independence and happiness

When there are sleep disruptions, there is generally an expectation on the infant's part that, on most occasions when they need attending to, you will come and pick them up to feed them, pat them, hold them or take them out of the room to start the day again. This alone makes it very difficult for them, and for you, to establish realistic expectations when it comes to resettling during the night. It creates a situation where, when you do need to attend to them at night, they become extremely upset if you don't immediately pick them up as they are expecting or demanding, particularly if you have taught them that you always pick them up when they request it during the day. This simply means that they have learnt that this is a normal way to ask you to pick them up. You have actually taught them to 'cry like that if you want to be picked up'. So can you see why babies often cry at night when this is the accidental pattern of communication developed during the day or post sleep? This is where communication can become confusing and inconsistent for little ones and it is a prime reason for them to become unsettled and clingy through the day and cry excessively through the night when you attend to them.

Cot playtime after sleep establishes a pattern of behaviour where your baby wakes up feeling happy and will play for 15 to 20 minutes without you needing to go into their room at all.

By getting them to play in the cot you are looking for an outcome where it won't feel unusual to your little one if you don't pick them up during a resettling. Ultimately, this will allow you to come and go from the room for short periods of time without causing them distress, and they will be developing self-settling strategies. This is the most basic skill they need in order to go to sleep without tears—at each and every sleep time. It's also a good opportunity for you to practise your little one's vital listening and co-operation skills at a non-sleep time so you can spend time reassuring them while they learn to co-operate. That is why you need to practise these important and often challenging skills after a sleep when they are at their best, and also why you target this skill development during a play session. This way they don't have to experience this feeling and learn how to cope with it for the first time when they are tired, it's dark, and you've left the room.

Another reason for developing cot playtime after sleep is to establish a pattern of behaviour where they wake up feeling happy and will play for 15 to 20 minutes without you needing to go in at all. This will be how you will know they are awake and it is important because some babies have prolonged wakings through the night from time to time for any number of reasons. Perhaps a growth spurt, a mild daytime sleep miscalculation where they have overslept, or even the local garbage truck triggering a night waking that will take some time to get past. You need to ensure they are always happy to just lie there and have a little chat to themselves or a little play. This means that as the natural sleep pattern continues to cycle through the night they are going to simply drift off to sleep contently without needing mountains of fussing from their parents, which can overstimulate them, or without waking their exhausted mummy and daddy unnecessarily.

You may have achieved cot play after one sleep from your little one but don't be surprised if you experience them having a slightly inappropriate routine after another sleep. When a child wakes you are looking for clear signs that they have had enough sleep, and you do this by listening for them playing happily or chatting after the expected sleep time is complete. If they are not chatting and playing, they might resettle themselves if they have not had enough sleep. If they are on a LSR routine (see page 515) and they wake up at a reasonable time you would *never* ask them to go back to sleep as this could create a pattern that communicates to them, 'if you don't want to sleep just cry until I pick you up'. This is because after they have slept the specified amount of time you are unlikely to have a successful resettle. This style of communication accidentally teaches them that they need to cry before you get them up. This then becomes a learnt pattern of behaviour to achieve an outcome. They are not being naughty or trying to be disobedient but if you ask them to go back to sleep when it is unlikely that they can, you simply start to create a poor cycle of waking and crying. This is generally the cause of waking and crying when in a routine.

Consult your routine details once you have determined your child's sleep requirement (see page 534). Any waking after the specified time should be accepted as the completion of their sleep cycle and no efforts or request should be made of them to resettle unless they do so without your intervention. Therefore, leave them for as long as you can, or as close to the maximum sleep time designated for your routine type before you go in. If it becomes clear that this is not going to be possible because they are crying an emotion-based cry, then simply wait your natural ten-minute pause (please see page 674) before going in and establishing cot playtime.

If you are going to re-establish playtime in the cot and they need a little more time to relax into this routine on waking, you will probably need to establish the play yourself until their existing crying routine is replaced with a more appropriate play routine. The important thing to remember when re-establishing cot playtime is to not *rush in* just because they are crying. You should try to enter the room with your waking cues during a lull in the crying episode and ask them to sit down immediately if they are standing, as not standing in the cot while you are in the room is another defining statement you need to work on. If they are crying because they are still a little tired or haven't fully woken yet, it is vitally important for you to adhere to your allocated waking pause (see page 700) to ensure they are fully awake before you enter the room. If they are still crying, even once you've established playtime in the cot, you should always encourage them to calm down and start to play by sitting by the cot and playing yourself before you begin packing away to get them up. This is where your positive bubbly attitude and confidence will help them settle.

You need to be cautious with your body language (see box on this page). Once you have said your waking cues with a big smile on your face regardless of their reaction when you walk in the room, say 'Mummy / daddy will get you some toys' and establish playtime by placing the toys in the cot within arms reach and then hand them one. A good tip here is to hold the toy so it interrupts your eye contact so they focus on the toy and not you. If they are standing when you enter the room, ask them to sit down immediately using your 'sit down, wait for mummy' cue. If you have established playtime in the cot without much drama, casually and confidently use your short-term absence cue, 'I'll be back', before stepping out of the room for a minute or two. If your little one makes a noise and starts to cry when you go to leave, don't hesitate or turn back, just keep going. To hesitate or turn back will teach them to cry every time you go

Body language

Initially, it is common for little ones to have expectations that you will pick them up, so you need to ensure you don't confuse them with your body language.

- Don't lean over the cot with two hands, like an invitation to them to ask you to pick them up.
- Only ever stand side on to the cot to talk to your baby, and only use one arm in the cot at a time until your bub is used to playing after sleep rather than being picked up immediately when you enter the room.
- Don't try and offer a semi-hug over the bars or by placing your hands under their armpits as this will appear to your child that you are going to pick them up when that is not going to happen.

If your little one can't start to play, or starts to kick excitedly misreading your intentions, simply sit down or stand side on to the cot and chat to them through the bars and keep your hands busy by perhaps folding a towel.

to leave the room if they would like you to stay. If you never leave they won't discover that they will be perfectly okay, and that cot playtime can be a really enjoyable time of the day.

Remember, their cot is the only place in the entire house that is truly their space. Don't be so frightened of the learning process that you deny them the opportunity to discover the joys of playing quietly in their cot. Wait 30 seconds to a minute after you have left the room if they are very upset, then reassess if you need to go back in to them after this short pause or if you should give them a little more time to calm down (see page 700). If they are still crying and you feel they need some reassurance, step back in the room casually and confidently, saying 'I'm back' and ask them to sit down and either go back to pottering around the room, or sit by the cot and re-establish cot play again. When re-establishing play using the method outlined above, always stay confident, as your response to their crying tells them if they are safe or not.

When and how often should baby play in the cot?

If you are in the full recovery mode, then cot play will need to happen as often as physically possible. If you are in maintenance mode, just being able to govern your baby at the completion of sleep time is the main aim, so if you can offer one cot playtime a day and they are content to play, and content to let you leave the room, then it is not necessary for you to do it at every sleep. If, on the other hand, your little one gets upset when you try to govern the outcome of sleep, then this is where sleep can fail after an illness, when you go on holidays, or if there has been the occasional hiccough that results in a night waking. Because of this I suggest you maintain cot play as often as you can until your bubby is happy to play for you again.

If you are in full recovery mode then you should stick to the recommended suggestion times for your new routine. If your baby has woken early and you are not going to attempt to resettle, then it's important they have a longer cot play. If they have woken and are playing happily in their cot for a good period of time before you have to go into them, then they can easily have a short cot play for just a couple of minutes if you are in a rush. Regardless of how well they woke and played independently, I recommend you always have a little cot play after you have entered the room to keep their expectations realistic for the middle of the night should the need to resettle arise.

If you are in maintenance mode, then cot play should go between ten and 20 minutes, or longer if they are enjoying it. All children should have a quiet cot or bed play after waking until they are five years of age. As soon as you are unable to make this simple request, the language governing sleep time is no longer governed by you, and sleep will not be successful or maintainable until this crucial line of communication is restored.

Still struggling to establish play?

If your little one is having a really tricky time because you are not picking them up as they are demanding, you need to establish a more gradual approach. Sit down next to the cot if they are unsettled. Stay confident, even if inside you feel unsettled by their cry. Be patient and don't get frustrated with them. They are only little and are learning a big new thing. They will mirror your response, so if you just get on with playing, using happy tones and expressions, they will start to be distracted by their toys.

Do be careful with eye contact—they read it very well—and if you are uncomfortable with them crying at this time, they will know and become more upset, thinking there is something wrong, when in fact there is nothing truly wrong, they are simply being asked to play in the cot. Occasionally, eye contact can be problematic for them as they see it as an open invitation to communicate and may boisterously ask you to pick them up. Even after you have clearly answered them with an honest response it's best to make it clear with your simple 'sit down, wait for mummy' strategy, then only look at the toys while *you* play on your own in an attempt to distract them. Always look like you're having fun, regardless of their response.

Be realistic about what you are asking them to do. If they are in a loving, safe home, a simple request, if done in a respectful and consistent manner, is absolutely within reason and well worth working through.

When babies want to be picked up, they often get irritated if you act as though you don't understand their request. Constantly saying 'Look at the toy' will indicate to them that you don't understand them when they say 'I don't want to play with that toy, mummy, I want you to pick me up', and they will only get more frustrated with you. If you simply play with the toy yourself after saying 'Sit down, it's playtime now', it is more likely that they will calm down and become distracted by the toy you are playing with. Please note, you are not demonstrating the toy to them, you are playing with the toy by yourself and they can see you doing this. Only play with it in a way that they would. This could be spinning the wheels of a car or banging two blocks together while you make a repetitive 'u-u-u' or 'e-e-e' sound. You wait, they will be instantly interested in what you're doing if you play at their level. Once you have their attention, don't look at them too quickly or ask them to join in or the crying may begin again. Just take it slowly and move in baby steps as you stay happy and busy playing.

Once they have calmed down and started watching you, casually and quickly place the toy in their lap without even looking at them, then quickly pick up a new toy and continue playing enthusiastically on your own. This way, they are more likely to pick up the first toy and copy your actions, which mean they will start to play with the toy by themselves. From the point of greeting them and establishing playtime, you are now playing parallel to them, rather than co-operatively with them. You need to talk to yourself, and play by yourself to role play the type of play they should be doing in their cot. They may get very angry and try to stand up holding the cot bars and if so you will need to follow through and ask them to sit down.

Remember to define your language. If you ask them to sit down, don't even allow them to grab the cot bars as this will confuse the actual request. 'Sit down' does not mean 'try and stand up', it means 'sit down', so don't confuse them by being inconsistent. Simply block their hands from reaching the bars and even if they get cross, continue on with your play strategy. Make sure your vocalisations are enthusiastic and chatty enough to distract them from their little mission and to catch their eye.

As they become more confident about playing in their cot on request, you start to gradually pull back your involvement. Over a three-day process, pull back by:

- stopping verbal chatter while you sit next to the cot playing parallel
- starting to play on the floor with your toy rather than through the cot bars
- sitting side on to the cot and folding washing or reading a magazine while they play
- crawling over to the change table to tidy the bottom shelves.

If you can stand for a while at the change table, even if they have a little cry, just keep busy and allow them to calm down. Make sure that if they start to try and stand you use your language and clearly ask them to sit down and wait for mummy / daddy. Your language should be consistent enough by now that they will sit when you ask them without needing your physical intervention. If they challenge you and don't sit down and you do need to go over to them, and just tap their hand with one finger while repeating your sit down cue so they know you want them to let go. If they still won't let go or they don't seem to understand your request, simply release their hands from the cot bars by sliding your thumb under their palm, so they have to sit down. Thank them for sitting even if they are cross at you, offer them some toys by having a little tickle with one momentarily then go back to the change table even if they are having a little cry.

Next you start to move around the room without talking to them, even if they have a little cry. You can sing quietly to yourself so you appear confident and okay, which will mean they can learn to feel okay about having that feeling that comes with not being able to control your actions. This is setting appropriate feedback to your baby about their natural emotions and feelings (equipping their emotional tool kit) and telling them which ones are fine to have and which ones need extra reassurance or intervention to resolve. Be realistic about what you are asking them to do. As you are asking them to have a little play in their cot while you are in the room, don't for a moment think you are asking too much of them. It simply isn't the case. If they are in a loving, safe home, this simple request, if done in a respectful and consistent manner is absolutely within reason and well worth working through.

Once you can move around the room, start to come and go from the room for one- to two-minute intervals using your short-term absence cue,

Troubleshooting

Q Why do you need to stop them from standing?

A For a few reasons actually. Firstly, because it often causes them to cry. If they stand, they usually demand to be picked up, whereas when they are sitting down they are more likely to start playing and won't be so demanding. More importantly however, when it is habit for them to stand in their cot, they tend to stand up the moment they even stir in their cot which wakes them up, and it's difficult for them to sit themselves down in the middle of the night, meaning they often need help to resettle. I want it to be normal to not automatically stand up when they wake. It's also easier to settle a baby back to sleep quickly when they automatically sit down when you enter the room, and finally it's important to make sure you are always practising your governing line of communication around all things pertaining to the cot. This means a baby is used to you guiding them in the cot, making asking them to go to sleep or lie down a much simpler task for both parent and baby.

Q Is there any exception to the rule?

A Yes, there are always exceptions to the rule. If your baby stands and plays happily and doesn't cry as you come and go, then they are okay to stand while they play if, and only if, you have no standing issues at sleep time. If your baby never tries to stand in the middle of a resettle but stands and plays happily at cot playtime (which is unlikely) then they are fine to play standing in their cot, so long as they aren't crying.

'I'll be back'. Increase your absence time gradually. Be careful to not run back in when they cry as this will simply teach them to cry to get you to come back. If they stand when you leave then don't react, just pretend you don't see. This way the only response they get from standing is you leaving the room, which will discourage the standing in the first place.

When you re-enter the room, don't come back in in a way that looks like you are saving them from playing in their cot, because the situation (when correctly assessed) is not one they need rescuing from, even if they are upset that you aren't picking them up. It's no different to your child being told to not touch an oven door because it's hot, and getting cross when you will not let them do as they desire. This does not emotionally scar the child, and nor does following through on something as simple as a little play in their cot. So walk in with a big smile and tell them 'I'm back' in a happy tone. Remember, don't use a sympathetic tone or you deliver the wrong message to them about cot play and what *you* think of it. If you are apologetic, it means you are asking them to do something awful, when this is clearly not awful. Simply and confidently ask them to sit down if they are standing and sit or go straight back to the change table and keep yourself busy. You can go back to singing to yourself but don't get too involved in having a big conversation with them unless they are very settled and happy to play. If you try to chat while they are still demanding of you, then you allow them to govern the outcome of the situation. They are likely to ask you to pick them up once you open up a line of communication again. Remember you have answered them honestly with a 'sit down, it's playtime now, where's your toy', and so now you just need to get busy trying to get them to play independently by defining that statement.

It is not necessary for them to be frightened of playing in their cot because it's a lovely warm comfortable place for them to be, and your reactions to their environment will tell them that that is the case because you won't be frightened for them.

Finally, if they are now playing and happy at cot playtime, you can chatter and interact intermittently, remembering this is still meant to be an independent time, but you can go over and join in playing from time to time, and go and get extra toys from another room. A great strategy to get the slightly older baby more enthusiastic about you leaving the room for short periods of time is to have a series of small toys that they really enjoy at a non-sleep time. These toys could be something like a special car that goes 'brrrrm brrrrm', or a little cow that goes 'moooooo'. Once you have established these funs toys with predictable names and sounds at normal daytime play, the simple suggestion of 'where's your cow that says moooooooooos, where's it gone?', and a confident 'mummy go get it, I'll be back' will be enough to see them happy about you leaving the room. Head out of the room saying aloud (not to the child but just so they can hear you are still about) 'Moo cow, where are you, Jake wants to play with you'.

Be cautious when you initiate a strategy like this that you don't accidentally start a pattern of dialoguing to each other outside the room. I always ask myself, how can this be misunderstood, is there ever going to be a time when I don't want to do this, or to teach a child to do this? In this case, when your child is in their cot, the answer is fairly simple, you do *not* want them to learn to talk to you through the door or walls. At sleep time, it's time to chat to themselves, play by themselves and that way they will be comfortable to drift off to sleep by themselves.

Deciding when it's time to pack away

When you have decided it's time to pack away you need to create a predictable end of play routine that your baby can recognise as the transitional window that always precedes getting out of bed. This is vital for a number of reasons:

- you govern the end of sleep time which prevents them from becoming confused during the night
- they feel in control of the situation because they are able to predict your behaviour
- they can predict the end of sleep effectively, so at no point during the night do they expect to get up until this process is completed
- you can practise listening and communication skills.

I always suggest that the decision to pack away should be made by the parents. To hand the control of this time to your baby will simply tell them that you are waiting for them to cry before you start packing away. This will only cause them to become upset when you do not respond to their requests at other cot management times.

If you look to your baby for guidance about an appropriate time to end playtime it may indicate that you are asking them or giving them permission to guide you at cot time. As all sleep times of the day are a parent–governed line of communication you don't want to confuse them for any night resettling attempts, so be consistent with your guidance until they are out of their cot. That said, if you can see that your baby is playing happily and there are no problems with this task for them, you can easily decide on the end of cot play whenever you choose.

It's important to remember that playtime in the cot is actually a really lovely time for your little ones because they are in the one place in the entire house that is theirs. Don't assume that because you might not enjoy this kind of activity that your baby doesn't like it. If they like to play in their cot, then let them. Watch them for cues about what they think of the activity, and always provide positive feedback about the play. Your attitude about cot playtime will fuel their attitude about cot playtime. If you act like they must hate it, then they will. If you treat cot playtime like it is lovely time then they will enjoy it.

Creating a predictable pattern for bubby

The pack-away routine should always follow a predictable pattern like your baby handing you the toys and you popping them in the same place such as under the bed or in a little toy basket. Then you should fold up any wraps or loose sheets and pop them on the end of the bed. Finally, you arrange any extra accessories into their usual location for the next sleep; for instance, if your baby has a dummy, have them pop the dummy 'back in the pot / hat' as dummies are reserved for 'cot time only'.

If, while you're in the early days of establishing your cot playtime routine, they start to cry when you stand up to start to pack away, be patient as this is a normal response to you moving and becoming unpredictable for them. They need to learn to wait, and you need to stay calm and confident as you follow through on your plan to establish a predictable packing-away routine. Don't move faster than you would if bubby was cooing happily at you; you need to be really cautious to not teach them to get cross or cry at you to get picked up sooner.

If you have waited the allocated time for cot playtime to end and your baby has been playing happily for a little while, it's a good time to forewarn, 'Okay, lovely playing my darling, it's time to pack away!' Watch your inflection (see page 58) as you say this so as to cause as little confusion about your meaning as possible. If your baby is sitting and quite happily watching you for guidance, it's lovely to develop a two-way chat here so you can teach them to participate and open up a deeper level of communication, where you both understand and can pre-empt each other.

Teach your little one to pack away by saying 'Ta for mummy' and holding out a hand before then pointing to a toy then offering an open hand again. Repeat this action a few times until your baby picks up the toy, and looks at your hand. You can then either wait for them to put it in your hand, or guide your hand up to theirs and take the toy saying 'Ta for mummy'. When you have the toy in your hand clap and cheer and repeat the process with all the toys in the cot. If at this point your baby is having a little trouble understanding this concept, either pick up the toy yourself and pop it in your own hand and say 'Ta for mummy' then clap 'Hurray', or help them pick up the toy and pop it in your hand while saying 'Ta for mummy' then clap 'Hurray'. Repeat by offering your hand after pointing to the next toy and say 'Ta for mummy'. Very quickly they will be handing you toys and helping you pack away, and clapping and cheering themselves as they go.

Getting them up

Now this may appear to be a very easy task, but while you are refining your communication you need to be cautious during this early learning stage of the routine to not confuse your baby at all. This is a time when you should play your wait game (see page 74), like at all other times when completing a parent-governed task. Once the wait game is complete, pick up your baby using the up cue with a big huge smile and fun snuggle and carry on with your day.

When introducing cot play, if the parent who doesn't normally get the baby up wants to visit the child during playtime in the cot, it's important to make this as easy as possible for baby as this is a brand new routine you are introducing. If you are the one establishing the boundaries around sleep time—you have asked your little one to look to you for guidance for when it's time to go to sleep, go back to sleep and wake up, and get up—and your partner has not yet had the opportunity to experience your new waking routine management, then it is likely that your baby will have clear expectations that they will be picked up immediately when your partner walks in the room. If there is a chance of this happening, then be cautious to not put your little one in a situation where, when they are slowly learning to trust and become comfortable around one parent's governing line of communication, they have to get used to two of you saying 'It's not time to get up yet'. This is clearly overwhelming and difficult for your baby.

The best way to handle it on those first couple of weeks, if you are on a full recovery routine system, is to generally allow no one but the settling parent to attend during any cot time at all, including settling, resettling, waking and playtime, until your child has been introduced to the settling process through role play. If you are on maintenance, then it's best to gauge

Practice makes perfect, and repetition is a parent's best teaching tool.

your child's response to the situation. Don't allow your partner to enter on the first few days of establishing this new playtime routine unless you are in the room, so you can guide them if the baby becomes unsettled. If you do attempt to introduce the second parent to the situation and things don't go smoothly—your baby becomes very upset, or angry and asks to be picked up—don't allow your partner to do the instinctive thing; that is, run away or to try to rescue baby by picking them up. This is where you get your partner to stay calm, and come and sit next to the cot, and follow through together as united parents to help your baby understand that the boundaries are consistent. Once your little one calms down, or your playtime is drawing to a close, keep your partner sitting while you complete the routine with a happy pack away (even if they are cross at you) before *you* get them up, and all three of you leave the room.

If bub is settled then your husband can use the up cue to take baby, then have a cuddle and carry on. If bub is unsettled, or in older babies, a little cross that dad is not doing what he is instructed (as in 'pick me up'), then you need to wander off once you get them up and calm your baby down before you head back to daddy and have him use a really quick up cue before he picks bub up and has a cuddle and continues happily with the day. You need to be cautious here, while you are developing new lines of communication and setting some new boundaries, as you do not want to teach your baby that if they cry long enough or hard enough you will change the conditions. You are best to go to the end of defining your new routine, particularly on those first few days when it feels new and a little uncomfortable, rather than teach them that if they don't want to do something (and remember it's only playing in their cot), then they will need to cry for a really long time to get picked up. This would obviously be a confusing mixed message and clearly only teaches your baby to cry for a long time before you change the new conditions back to the old. If you were going to do that, can I suggest you don't start it in the first place, because it's a waste of your baby's precious time and energy to go through all the learning of a new routine only to discover that crying is what they needed to do.

If your baby has shown clear signs of needing a little more time before there are two people to have to understand at cot play time, then you would not introduce the other parent until they were clearly a part of the sleep-settling process and had role played those new expectations several times. It's also important here to ensure that your partner is working very hard on developing a balance of communication through the day at non-sleep times, and giving your baby the opportunity to learn and understand those new cues at a non-confrontational time of the day like playtime.

If, on the other hand, your baby is happy for your partner to come and say hello, then have a little play before using your new short-term absence cue and leaving again with no concern from your baby, then there is clearly no problems with that additional parent coming in to see the baby during playtime in the cot.

Finally, it doesn't matter what toys you introduce to cot playtime. The more fun and enjoyable the better, I say. Just be sure to not place toys in the cot that they can climb on to as this would be a fall and injury risk.

Troubleshooting

Q How can I tell what is causing the crying after a few days of working very hard at cot playtime?

A Be aware of their true response to the actual play experience. If they cry only when you leave the room, then their issue is you leaving not the cot playtime, therefore you need to practise leaving often to develop their trust in your short-term absence cue at other times of the day as well as during cot playtime. If your baby can play while you are there, but can't when you are walking around the room, then it is not the cot playtime they are uncomfortable with, it is the unpredictability of your movements, therefore your daytime communication in that area is what you need to work on. If your baby will play happily for daddy and not for you, then your little one is a bossy boots with you and you need to be cautious of them feeling overburdened with needing to guide you to create predictability. Tighten up your communication throughout the day by using lots of pre-emptive and forewarning flows of communication, as well as talking through a lot of the things you are doing and practising lots of parent-governed lines of communication like the wait game. You will need to ensure you are following through with your language, because to not do so means you don't make sense, and therefore your baby has to watch you to predict your actions. This would mean they couldn't start to play. Lastly, if your baby is not sleeping well think about whether you are implementing everything *but* a complete or correct routine. If this is the case, give the routine suggestions (see page 515) a try as they will make your baby and you so happy.

Q Can I lean over the cot to cuddle them during cot play to help them feel better?

A If your little one is on the full recovery routine management (see page 541), predictable communication is crucial at this moment so, while this might feel like a bit of a challenge for many parents, the answer from a communication point of view is do *not* hug them during playtime in the cot when they are in the 'learning to sleep' phase of the routine. You do not want to confuse the lines of communication here. Sleep time and all cot time is to be a parent-governed activity. To allow your child to ask for a cuddle swaps the lines of communication. Can you imagine the confusion for them then if, during the night, you do not allow for a language stream change, which we obviously can not allow at this stage? By letting them occasionally govern cot playtime, you are being inconsistent and I promise you, it will only result in tears when they stir at night as a hug will be their only solution.

Hugs are reserved for when they get up, until they settle down with this new routine. For now, ask them to sit down and have a play. Often I will greet them with lots of rubbing and stroking, and eye contact and touch, but the request to stay sitting is maintained. If, while I'm looking over the top of the bars, they reach up thinking I am available to pick them up, I then drop down and talk, play and touch through the bars so they do not become confused. It would just be too difficult for a child of this age to understand just 'one' cuddle. If you say 'yes' to one, and then 'no' to another, or worse, 'yes' to all the cuddles, they will spend their whole time cuddling you over the bars and they will never have the opportunity to discover the joy of playing in their own little space or that they can cope without a cuddle every time they wake at night. When you get them up, they can cuddle you for as long as they like, we just don't complicate the in-cot expectation by including cuddles. We have provided a settling routine rich in snuggle time.

Once everything has settled down, and your baby is not waking at night and can play happily in their cot, a snuggle is a lovely idea before you ask them to sit down and play, so long as you don't confuse them. If you are simply establishing cot play as maintenance, because your baby already sleeps well, then a snuggle without picking them up when you come in the room is okay before you ask them to sit down and play, so long as you don't confuse them. Confusion could be indicated by them crying after the cuddle when you ask them to play. If this occurs, then just stick to play time until they are a little older and can understand the communication streams better, then introduce cuddles after that point.

Q How do I handle monkey grips during cot play?

A As I have already stated, babies are such little creatures of habit, and in the initial stages of establishing your new cot play, they may not be too comfortable with the changes they are experiencing. These new experiences could easily make them a little unsettled and their usual response to this is to want to sit on your hip. This generally ensures there are no surprises for them but also means your little one never gets the opportunity to experience these normal changes that occur in our lives. To never allow them to experience some change means that they become inflexible, clingy and a little bit bossy as they embark on the insurmountable task of controlling all those around them so they don't have to experience anything unpredictable.

The whole idea of this guiding and language-rich strategy is to ensure that we teach them to predict us, so that no matter how many changes happen in their lives, they can safely look to us for guidance and they will feel safe. If they have grabbed on to you, don't reluctantly try to pull away, it's a mixed message. Either allow them to hug you or don't. If they have got a monkey grip on you, say 'Hi bubba, it's time to sit for playing, thanks for my cuddles' as you reach around to find their hands and quickly release their grip on you. Give them a kiss while continuing to hold their hands to prevent little octopus arms continually grabbing you and sit them down. Some mothers say their babies are 'too strong' and my only answer is 'not that strong'. You're an adult; get them to let go quickly so your message to start playing is clear, and you don't drag out the inevitable.

The most important strategy, however, is prevention. Don't let them grab a hold of you in the first place. If you know this is a typical pattern with your little one, and their little arms are outstretched from the moment you walk in the door, then you need to plan ahead. As you walk in the room and start your waking routine and cues, warmly ask them to sit down as you head to open their curtains. Once you head back to them, reach out and take their hand as you approach with a big smile and say 'Good sleeping my bubba' and give their hands a kiss while still holding them firmly enough. If they do break free and go for the monkey hold, ask them to sit down. If they challenge this or do not understand this request because this is your first day teaching them the new routine, then help them sit down.

Sometimes it's helpful to turn them around to sit them down if you can't use their hands to help them sit. Turning them around stops the grabbing at your clothes and enables you to quickly move forward with your brand new playtime. Once they are sitting, define that statement and get their toys. Be really excited about their play and they will quickly become distracted.

This pattern of arms outstretched, and kisses on the hands could become a routine in itself for your little one, which is fine for the waking routine but not okay for resettling. If they do this same behaviour at a time during the night when they need to resettle, then perhaps consider changing the pattern to just walking over to the cot and sitting on the floor so they are encouraged to sit to chat with you. Ask them to sit if they are trying to peep over the top of the cot by releasing their hands from the top of the cot bars and allowing them to plop onto their bottoms or by taking their hands through the bars and gently pulling them down to sitting. Follow through and ensure they sit, even if there is a protest, and then continue to get all excited about the play. Remember to always define what sitting down means. 'Sit down' does not mean 'try to stand up'.

Q Can I change their nappy during cot play?
A Unfortunately, if they do a poo in their nappy while in the cot it signifies the end of either that sleep or playtime. Obviously, you will need to get them up and change them but you should still complete your pack away (having a poo in their nappy for an extra minute won't make a difference). Once you are all packed away, play your wait game briefly before you say 'Up up' and then change their nappy.

Don't forget to use your pre-emptive language here. If you note that they have done a poo, then say 'Ok, Jack has done a poo, time to pack away, mummy change your nappy. Nearly time to lie down and wait for mummy.' Note the use of the regular streams of language for each of the usual events. 'Time to pack away' will be recognisable. They will also know 'lie down, wait for mummy'. So when using this style of communication with a baby, your little one will know that they are about to get up, and about to have their nappy changed. This is the benefit of having routine patterns at typical event times of the day. It's important to use your pre-emptive language here because lying down and getting a nappy change is generally not the most favourite thing to do when they first get out of bed.

Once a baby gets out of bed, they are generally not in favour of having to lie down again and have their nappy changed immediately. If you can, I generally suggest you take them out of their room for a little while and have a snuggle and a play before changing their nappy. If they have done a poo however, you will have to change their nappy as soon as you get them up so you will need to use lots of pre-emptive language while you tidy their cot before you get them up so they know to expect what is coming.

As I said, this means the end of playtime in the cot so do not put them back in the cot once you have changed their nappy, either for play or for sleep. Exception: if they poo before they fall asleep you can change their nappy then start your settling routine from 'lie down' again. Use your cue 'nearly time for sleep' as you change their nappy however, so they know you plan on putting them to bed once they are changed.

Q How do I fit cot play into the family timetable?

A Sometimes mornings are the only time when some mummies or daddies get to see their little baby. In these special cases you do not need to cot play at this time. Just go through the motions of a predictable pack-away routine before getting bubby up. I would suggest you use your normal waking routine with a brief two-minute play while you prepare their change table with clothes for the day. Once they have played for a minute or two and you have left a couple of times and returned, pack away as usual, then get them up to have special time with you before you go to work. I always suggest that if this is the only time a mum or dad has with your baby during the day, then be absolutely sure to be showered, dressed and have had breakfast by the time your baby gets up. This way you can both share some quality time together where you can focus your full attention on baby, and not feel rushed or like you need to watch the clock.

10
Playing in, out and about

The high chair, pram and shopping trolley are examples of times during the day when you will have great communication opportunities to teach your little one a skill vital for lying in their cot patiently while their body prepares to drift off to sleep. This skill of waiting and being patient, calmly challenging only the environment around them for entertainment helps them learn how to just be, comfortable in their own skin, and able to relax and enjoy the peace that comes with that skill. Here you will need to establish and confidently use your wait game (see page 74) and gradually improve your child's attention span through the use of your bag of tricks (see page 369).

Playing in the high chair at home

In all my routines I suggest you take the time to encourage your baby to have an extended quiet sit and play in their high chair at least once a day. For some, this is a simple task; for others, a little extra encouragement is required to help their babies relax and enjoy this time of the day. The reason it's important is that it gets your little one used to waiting until you have indicated to them that certain events have come to an end and this is, of course, paramount for sleep. In fact, it is the first skill required by your baby when it comes to feeling comfortable with you asking them to lie down happily in their cot and wait while they drift off to sleep chatting to themselves. High chair play offers them the opportunity to practise these skills in a non-confrontational environment: your home with you guiding them.

It has become almost the norm over the past five years for me to enter a home where the baby won't eat and the mother says to me, 'He really doesn't seem to like to eat his solids'. Is it often a surprise when I explain that the actual problem does not lie with the food or their ability to eat, but in their ability as parent's to guide their child to be a little patient and to sit patiently in their high chair. I often meet babies who have two spoonfuls of solid food after three minutes of fussing and then, just as their attention span wanes, they demand to get down. This always results in a grumpy and hungry baby within thirty minutes who is snacking on breast milk instead of developing a great appetite for their next nutritionally balanced solid-food meal.

A balanced eating plan for little ones is essential for them to reach optimum health, a good night's sleep, and a happy demeanour. It's also just as important to develop a child's ability to comfortably look to their mother and father for guidance around this area of health and safety. You always need to be able to make decisions for your baby based on their true needs, not just what they demand. If you know your baby needs to sit longer in the high chair so they will eat more effectively but they are unable to because she has become too demanding around high chair time, then you will need to implement a different strategy. High chair playing skills are also really important to develop if you wish to maintain the quality of your family life, and go out to restaurants or to visit friends or enjoy outings to the shops, that coincide with a meal time.

The foundation for healthy eating starts at six months. It is more difficult starting a family healthy eating plan when your child is three years old because they will have already developed poor habits. If you start healthy behavioural patterns around the task of eating from six months of age, you will have a child that has learnt to eat the right foods and behave in the right way. You will be free to enjoy the social occasions that naturally occur at every meal by the time they are three. As a parent, it's your duty to ensure you identify the things that may be impacting on your baby's ability to have a good meal, and this is most definitely one of the most common problems when it comes to meal time. The second most common problem is snacking. It's important to note here than once poor eating patterns have begun, usually due to the inability to sit for too long or excessive or inappropriate snacking, you may find that meal times for your baby become tied up with poor associations and almost always with rejection of food, which you will need to repair (see page 242).

To restore the balance around this daily event you need to look closely at developing refined communication with clear boundaries around positioning:

'Sit down, wait for mummy / daddy.' Remember to define that statement. Don't teach them that 'sit down, wait for mummy' means arch your back or hang off the side of the high chair, or pull your legs up and get your arms out of your buckles. 'Sit down and wait' needs to simply mean 'sit and focus on play', and *not* 'try the usual getting up from sitting tanties'.

The most appropriate time for high chair playtime is after dinner. The last solid meal of the day gets the strongest response from the babies as far as an energy boost goes, so this is when they are at their absolute best to play. Most people want to try and calm their babies down at this time of the day but it would be best to allow their food to settle while they have a fun little play in their chair. Once they have eaten ensure your baby is still comfortable, their buckles still nicely done up and firm and they are sitting forward with their little feet facing the front. If they cannot reach the tray because they are still a little short, pop a towel under their bottom before you buckle them in at the beginning of the meal, or a soft towel behind their back so they can sit forward comfortably. If they are older and try to shuffle around in their seat or arch their back, calmly and patiently reposition them using the clear and friendly verbal cue 'sit down and wait for mummy'. When they are sitting, grab a chair and sit in front of them if they are having difficulty and help maintain an appropriate sitting position that you would like to use to define the statement 'sit down and wait'. Remember that whatever you allow them to do after you have made the statement is what the statement means to them so be sure it's a position you would like them to always sit in at meal times.

> You always need to be able to make decisions for your baby based on their true needs, not just what they demand.

Stay really enthusiastic and confident, even if they are being a little stroppy with you. Bring out a toy that you know is a favourite and establish playtime. Ensure you offer toys where you have already helped them develop personal play strategies and lovely associations so they are really interested in what you are offering them. An example of this would be to role play playing with them. Say 'Mummy get the lion . . . roooaar . . . mummy play with it'. Get the toy and, if they are hesitant, initiate parallel playing in front of them (see page 131). Now that it's your toy, they cannot take it off you, or push it away. They may get cross but stay confident and make the play look really exciting without making it look like you want them to play. Follow your parallel play strategies until they are playing.

Now you have two choices depending on your baby's reaction to being kept in the high chair. If your baby starts playing happily in the high chair, then you can stand up and take their high chair with you over to the sink, where you will be tidying away after their meal or beginning to prepare your food for the evening meal with your partner. Chat away happily to your little one, talk about their toys and their play, about the day you have just had together and about what you're doing. As they get more involved in their play, you can gradually become less verbally interactive if you like.

If they are cross however, because you have not picked them up, you will need to stay where you are and help them move past this feeling so they can learn how to play. Don't be discouraged. It is common and quite normal for a baby to resist high chair play initially. If, however, you identify that this is hard for your baby then it is well worth investing a little time to help them feel comfortable with your simple loving guidance. It's a basic requirement for a balanced respectful style of family communication. If they refuse the toy by pushing it away, or by taking it off you and throwing it, then acknowledge what they have said: 'Okay, Charlie doesn't want that toy.' If they are still refusing to play after five minutes of trying to establish playtime in the high chair, you can decide it's time to carry on with your chores and simply bring their high chair into the kitchen anyway and

Good high chair play hints

- Be sure to use your flow of communication at all times of high chair play, particularly if you are going to duck out of their line of sight. Always be conscious of letting them know 'I'll be back' if you plan on going for a short period of time.
- Moving the high chair to a window or to a new section of the room may create a new feel to the play and keep them interested for a little longer.
- When you start play and they are about to cry, try to distract them quickly. Call out to your dog or cat, asking your baby 'Where has Jessy dog gone? Jeeeeessssy?' This should buy you some time and help your baby forget what they were going to start crying about so you can introduce a new toy and move them into the kitchen with you!
- If your partner comes home, it's natural to want to chat to them but be sure to stay emotionally available to your baby so you are conscious of what they are doing and saying to you or they will want to come and be with you rather than in their high chair.
- I also often notice dads come in, kiss their wife and, with the intention of getting changed for a fun play with their child, race off to their room without greeting bubba effectively. So dads, take a moment to go to your little one, get down on their level, greet them and have a quick chat about their toys then tell them what you are about to do: 'Daddy is going to get changed, I'll be back, nearly playtime!' This means your baby can start to anticipate this means they have one last little play before you always come back for a great fun nudie playtime (see page 209). Or you could sneak in and get changed without baby noticing before you enter the room to say hello and get them straight up.

carry on and they can sit and wait for a little while watching you. If baby is still cross at you when you do this, then follow the 'still having trouble' instructions below, only put more emphasis on happy singing to yourself and looking busy. The more enthusiastic you sound and pre-occupied you appear, the more likely they will become distracted.

About ten to 15 minutes of high chair play after a meal is a reasonable timeframe to work with for a six to nine month old and gradually this can be increased and you can expect about 20 minutes by the time they are 12 months old. Once high chair play is finished, use your wait game (see page 74) before getting them up for a bit of a rough-and-tumble, extra-fun, energy-burning play on your bed. This important burn-off time is highlighted further on in this chapter under 'Nudie playtime' (see page 209).

Still having trouble?

When helping a family suffering with sleep and daytime blues I find that if the babies haven't mastered what to do when playing in a high chair within a few minutes and persist with crying, the mums and dads always say 'Now what? Should we get him up?' It's really important to be conscious of the time it takes a little one to learn something new. The first time you do this, it may be entirely unfamiliar to them, and they will need to get used to not getting out of their chair the moment they have finished eating like they are used to. That takes time. You are changing their old self-instigated routine into a parent-guided positive routine and, like anything new, it may involve a few tears, but they are temporary. Babies usually learn a new routine in a day and settle in like it's been around forever when you are consistent and remain confident. This means, don't teach them to cry to get out of their high chair. Play with them and establish play until they are calm, then you can get them up using your wait game.

The most important thing to do now is be patient with them, persist, and practise. It doesn't happen immediately for all babies so if your little one is showing signs of getting really cross because you have not picked them up, just be patient, and stay confident and reassuring until they find the predictability in this new expectation and start to settle down. It may take a couple of days. Remember not to teach them to cry to be picked up.

Be cautious to not feel bad for asking them to have a play in their high chair. It's not mean and unfair, it's actually just a normal life skill and request. It's also the same thing you will need to be able to say when they wake at 2 a.m., having no concept of time, and they ask to get up for the day. You will need to have established times of the day where you say 'Not now bubby, mummy / daddy will tell you when it's time to get up', and they need to understand that, know how to cope with it and know what to do, and that starts here. If the first time you ask your child to accept that request is when they are in the cot at night, then you are guaranteed of sleep time stress, which is what we are always working to avoid.

Stick to the recommended timeframe and, if absolutely necessary, spend more time sitting with them playing than trying to move away to do your chores. By the time the play session is finished, always complete the task by packing away and using your wait game to create predictability. This ensures they don't learn that they need to cry to get up, and helps them trust that they can relax and you will always let them know when playtime is over. It also gives you the opportunity to govern the end of the event in a non-confrontational way. This makes you predictable and makes the routine of high chair play consistent and comforting for baby.

If your baby is under ten months, and starts a high-pitched scream between pauses and it doesn't sound like the usual happy squeals you hear, then you can be sure they are yelling at you. Make sure there is nothing wrong, that they are comfortable and they haven't done a poo in their nappy, then carry on with your initial request for playtime. If the screeching persists you can simply ignore these boisterous demands and expressions. You certainly don't give them attention at this time as you don't want to teach them to scream like this to get your attention, because that would be awful for them and unpleasant for you from that day forward.

Chat and sing to encourage busy playing, but stop singing and chatting momentarily to indicate you won't continue if they scream. Once the behaviour subsides, chat and sing again. Persist patiently with this until the pattern stops. This may take one to two play sessions but then it will be all over, and the patience (and perhaps ear muffs) that was required to help establish a more pleasant style of communication will be well worth it for both baby and you.

If your baby is ten months or over, it might be that you have a serious bossy boots on your hands (and they do get very, very bossy sometimes), so you will need to implement a new cue, 'too loud for mummy's ears'. Once you have said this, either turn baby's high chair around so it is facing away from you, making sure bubby can no longer see you even when they look around or turn away. Cease verbal interaction for about a minute as well. If you show them that the opposite of what they expected happens when they scream, they will quickly discover that your attention actually comes when they are interacting with you through chatter and happy sounds and not the other way around. After a minute has passed, turn them back towards you and greet them happily again and offer them an 'illegal toy' (something that is not one of their toys), perhaps something great off the bench like the whisk, the measuring cups, or a broken TV remote control or mobile phone, then carry on.

The daddy factor

As mentioned in the box on high chair hints, it can be disruptive to a new routine when daddy, or any member of the family, arrives home mid play. I think it is important to encourage a baby to play in their high chair for their daddy. If every time daddy walks in the room, even on a day when he stays home, your baby insists on being picked up by him, a routine pattern is being set up where baby thinks it is normal to always be picked up immediately by their daddy. That one expectation can be very confusing during any attempts to resettle baby back to sleep at night if they have woken, so you should aim to create a balanced and honest set of conditions for your little one through the day.

Start to change the way daddy (and other members of the family) respond to your baby when they enter the room at all times of the day, for instance, when baby is playing on the floor. Sometimes they might use the up cue and get them up, sometimes they could sit with bubba to play only, and sometimes they may just chat to the baby but carry on with their chores. Once the decision has been made (usually before you even enter the room) then you will need to follow through. It's important to sometimes choose your response play before entering the room so you don't fall into the trap of changing your mind every time they cry when you try to pursue any method other than picking them up on demand, which then only teaches baby to cry to be picked up. Once a blended style of requests from daddy is established during floor play and baby has learnt to wait for the cues as to what daddy will be doing that play session, you can use that same style of blended play at high chair playtime.

Stay really enthusiastic and confident, even if they are being a little stroppy with you.

Once your baby is better at playing, you can use your pre-emptive language to tell them daddy will be home soon, and they need to 'sit down and wait for daddy'. That means when daddy comes in, he can come and sit and play before following the pack away, wait game completion of routine, and up cue. Eventually daddy will be able to enter the room after baby has been given some simple pre-emptive language and your little one will smile and babble away happily but continue to play until everyone is ready for the next part of the day. This is harmony. This takes the burden off the baby, and helps the house flow more peacefully.

Playing in the high chair at a restaurant

Obviously, establishing a good pattern of expectation in the high chair needs to be worked on at home first. Once you have achieved this you will be ready to embark on a trip to a restaurant. If your baby is too little to sit in a high chair, which is rarely the case by six months, then it may be more difficult to encourage a long play in their pram. This is simply because they cannot see you as well when they are down in their pram and will quickly become a little frustrated with that arrangement. By six months of age however, a high chair (slightly reclined until seven months and upright thereafter) is generally a perfect location to encourage a fairly decent playtime in a restaurant.

There is generally a flow to the way your time in a restaurant unfolds. Here it is along with some hints to make the most of your time at the restaurant so everyone is happy:

- Don't forget your playtime bag of tricks.
- Try to choose a restaurant that is not terribly overcrowded.
- Try to pick a time that lines up with one of their meal times.
- Make sure they get a high chair to sit in or you will not be able to get a long enough playtime out of them to get through a whole meal.
- Once you arrive at the restaurant make sure you start using your clear language cues like 'Sit down, wait for mummy'.
- When you first sit baby in the high chair, just let them sit there with nothing. This way they will get a chance to take in all the sights and sounds of the restaurant.
- Get the menu immediately and order fairly efficiently. Longer more relaxed meals comes as a privilege when you don't take advantage of how obliging your baby is being on those first few trips to a restaurant.
- Ask the staff to heat up your baby's food, if it is not already warm, and while you wait for your meal to be served give your baby their dinner.
- After baby has eaten, your food will probably be served so give baby the spoon to play with and sit back and relax and enjoy your meal.
- If your baby is eight months plus they will be interested in what you are eating. This is when you could safely pull out a Cruskit or, if they are older, choose something off your plate that is appropriate for their age and allow them to have a munch. By now they will have something

to munch on, a spoon, and possibly a small lid from your baby-food container to keep them well and truly entertained as you all chat together and to baby.

- Don't leave baby out of the conversation; they enjoy the social interaction of a chat at a restaurant as much as you do.

- Once you see them starting to tire of the eating concept it's time to pull out your bag of tricks (see page 369) to extend their concentration span for a while longer. Gradually work through your bag of tricks while you wait for your dessert.

- When all the tricks in your bag have been used up, offer your little one some of the interesting and unique things from the table: a menu, napkin, etc. This is when you know their time in the high chair is fast drawing to a close. Once they grow tired of these objects, it will be the final stretch of your time in the restaurant. This is generally the time your dessert or a final drink has arrived and when most babies come out of the highchair (after a quick pack away, wait game and up cue). Baby can now sit on your lap until it's time to leave the restaurant.

- If you choose, you can set a boundary so that baby *never* gets out of the high chair for the first five visits to a restaurant, which often sets a tone for happy extended playing from then on, but it depends on how long you like to be there. Just be certain to never get them up because they are having a tantrum or they *will* tantrum every time they go to a restaurant.

Troubleshooting

Q If my baby is on a routine, when is the latest time we can get home?

A You will need to try and be home in time by 6.30 p.m., in time for the final milk feed of the day and the usual settling routine. Don't cut it too fine the first few times.

Q How long after I start my new routine can we start to go out to dinner?

A I usually say, try to make sure you give your baby at least a month to get comfortable with the new routine before you throw a curve ball at them and change the routine at the end of the day.

Q What happens to their normal routine while we are out at the restaurant?

A You can just reshuffle things. Give them a bath and pop them into their pyjamas early in the afternoon before you head to the restaurant. This way, when you get home they are right to go straight to bed.

Q When can we start to take them out and let them sleep while we have our dinner?

A Please go to SURE *sleep* on page 741.

Pram play

Going for a walk in your pram, with the sun shining and the birds floating around above your head is one of the most delightful parts of going on an adventure with your mum and dad. But the opportunity for a baby to relax and just lie back is slowly becoming a lost joy. A by-product of extreme parenting strategies is that children are burdened with guiding their parents and as a result lots of babies struggle with feeling comfortable when allowing someone to push them around for a relaxing stroll. It's a lovely time of their day, though, and you need to establish it or re-establish it to ensure your baby's delight in interesting adventures.

It's important to have established playtime in the pram for two main reasons. Firstly, it's nice for them to be able to have a relaxing outing to the shops without stress or the need to be carried everywhere and, secondly, it's another great opportunity to practise your sleep-time communication skills with them at a non-confrontational time of the day. If you cannot ask them to sit in the pram for an interesting social trip to the shops while you are present, then how can you ask them to lie in their bed when they are tired, it's dark, and you aren't with them? The whole idea of taking the opportunity to practise these listening skills through the day is to ensure they have experienced the emotions and feelings associated with you not always obliging their demands. Given the opportunity to practise this communication with you, your baby will identify a predictable pattern in your behaviour and happily accept your line of communication. To only expose them to a governing line of communication at night is unfair and is behind the reason babies cry—they have not had the opportunity to see that you are consistent and predictable once you have answered them through the day with a simple 'wait for mummy' cue.

When is it appropriate to ask your baby to sit in the pram? In all my routines, I suggest the mornings be predominantly reserved for physically demanding home and independent playtimes, whereas the afternoon is the best opportunity to provide a lovely wander in the pram. The reason for this is fairly simple. Your baby will be asleep at 7 p.m., and won't wake until 6 or 7 a.m., then they'll want a snuggle and breastfeed or to have breakfast in their high chair, then another sleep. Can you imagine how frustrating it would be after being physically inactive for 14 to 16 hours to be asked to sit patiently in a pram while your mum or dad does the shopping in the morning? After a long day of playing and growing and learning, the afternoon can become quite difficult for them from around 4 p.m. onwards, so this is an ideal opportunity for your little ones to put up their feet and happily watch the world go by as their energy levels drop off and their tolerance for playing and co-operating starts to diminish.

Does this mean you won't have to work through some old patterns of difficult behaviour that usually occur at all pram times? Not at all! Many babies settle into pram time immediately when the routine and communication skills are adjusted and they are no longer burdened with having to guide their parents; however, while we are targeting the best possible time for pram play, there is always a strong possibility that some fairly negative routine may have already been established. Because babies are creatures of habit, they will continue to exhibit their usual pattern of behaviour because it's all they know to do.

I always suggest you use your pre-emptive language, so they know that they are about to have a wander in their pram with you. Ensure you have implemented and have been practising your 'wait for mummy / daddy' cue at home so they will be able to look to you for guidance with ease from the moment you pop them into the pram. Then I'm cautious about a few basic things:

- Make sure they are comfortable—don't overdress them with bulky items that make it difficult to sit or move freely and equally don't leave them feeling so exposed and loose that they arch their back and slide around hoping someone will pick them up so they can feel more secure.
- Sit them upright, and be sure to have their buckles done up firmly so shoulder straps don't tease at their cheeks or slide off their arms. If they still need a little help sitting, have the pram slightly reclined, but by nine to ten months of age all babies respond positively to a clear message given when you sit them upright.
- Turn them so they can see the world. While it's lovely for us to watch our babies, it can be a whole lot more interesting for your little one if they have more to look at and are not travelling backwards.
- Do not start your pram journey with all their toys already in their lap. This is problematic because by the time their attention span has reached its limit, we have already used up all of our distractions. You are looking at providing a graded exposure to stimulation and distraction as you progress through your trip to the shops, so take your bag of tricks (see page 369) and only use it once they have had a lovely long wander admiring the view around them first.

It's always lovely to just allow your baby to sit without toys as they settle into their pram and take in the world around them. If they have the odd complaint, you can simply carry on with your journey without the need to intervene. If an older baby aged ten to 12 months is turning in their chair and this results in them crying as they reach up to you for your attention, help them turn around and sit facing the front and ensure their buckles are firm enough to prevent the pattern that created the tears in the first place. As you travel, take the time to stop and point out the balloons, signs and pictures of other children, and other babies in prams as you go. By taking their focus off demanding you pick them up to looking at the many things that will be of great interest around them, babies will often suddenly discover how interesting the shops or a walk in the park can be.

It's always lovely to just allow your baby to sit without toys as they settle into their pram and take in the world around them.

Once you can see that they are finding the chore of sitting for a prolonged period of time a little difficult, it's time to dip into your bag of tricks. Always ensure you have a selection of toys that ranges from some interesting ones, some favourite ones, and some 'illegal toys', like a out-of-use (but safe to play with) mobile phone, or that broken remote control that seems to be every baby's favourite. Slowly introduce your toys over the remainder of the excursion, ensuring you save the best toys for last.

This expectation that a child can play happily in their pram is fair and totally possible, even for those as young as six months. I have spent years in this business teaching and observing children develop this skill in a matter of days. They go from squirming, grumpy, crying little babies with their arms outstretched trying to get picked up, to relaxed, content, happy little people busily pointing to all the interesting things around them and, as the pram session continues, they focus on playing happily with one of their bag-of-tricks toys.

Still having trouble?

For those parents on full recovery, an unsettled baby in the pram is an extremely common problem that I encounter when I spend time with families. The following strategy will help your little one to establish a more positive association towards their pram and extend their patience when on an outing. If your baby is still finding this time a *real* challenge, then it's time to go into slow motion. Graded exposure to this event will ensure they can learn that these journeys can be short and achievable and will start to help them change their expectations of this time from negative to positive.

Start off with brief periods of time in the pram in your local neighbourhood. About 30 minutes before you head off get excited about going for a walk in the pram. This pre-emptive language will set the tone of your journey. If you are nervous, your baby will be nervous. When heading out it's important to follow through and define your original request to 'sit down and wait for mummy'. Be sure to keep your little one focused on what's ahead, like looking for a cat, or looking for a bird. Most babies will have encountered cats or birds by six months of age, and you will have taught them the sound they make, so when you say 'Where's the bird gone, tweet tweet?' you will catch their attention and have the opportunity to keep them calm. Continue to talk about everything you see around you, and sound happy and enthusiastic. This will distract your baby and they will start to calm immediately.

Food as a distraction

Whether to use food as a distraction when a baby is in the pram is a question that comes up all the time when I am visiting families. Here a battle occurs between encouraging effective coping skills in your child when it comes to entertaining themselves, and what has become quite the norm: giving children food so they don't complain when they start to get bored when you aren't entertaining them. My main concern with this distraction strategy is that you are essentially teaching your children to eat if they are bored or frustrated.

I am very conscious of not avoiding an easily resolved situation or avoiding a normal healthy interaction for the sake of short-term peace. I would prefer to work through some demanding behaviour and answer it appropriately and teach them a healthy coping skill than provide a short-term relief strategy like feeding that potentially teaches them poor emotional coping strategies for patience or boredom in the future. It is better that your baby learns that life is not always about being entertained because the true reality of it is that they have to learn that a lot of time is actually spent 'waiting'. Doctors run late, dentists can take forever, the queue at the checkout is usually long enough to send most new mums into a state of panic. We stand in endless lines to pay for products, and even a walk down the road involves your baby sitting and waiting at several sets of traffic lights. You need to teach your little one that sometimes they will need to entertain themselves in ways that don't involve food, and help them develop the essential life skills of patience and waiting.

Obviously, those parents on the full recovery program (see page 541) will have very specific meal plans so this will not be an option for you anyway. For everyone else, if you provide food simply to stop your baby from being bored it will not help your little one get back on track with healthy and more effective eating. Snacking in the pram would also be potentially very disruptive to their next meal time. Therefore, no food in the pram unless it is in a designated snack time is the rule for all.

As you are rounding the corner to go home, tell them 'nearly home, nearly time for up up'. This simple cue will become familiar and serve as an instant settler for a slightly impatient bubba. When the pram time is finished, complete it by using your wait game (see page 74).

Crying when you stop the pram

Good communication becomes vital in ensuring you are able to have a lovely trip in the pram, and the occasional and necessary stops don't open the floodgates of little baby fury. Let's be honest now, babies can be pretty impatient sometimes, and I have seen some poor mums and dads get told off royally by their delightfully soft, round little babies when they dare to stop pushing that pram for even a moment. It's important to introduce some of those new language streams you have been practising at home. Always keep your little one informed. So before we go on a shopping trip, where we may be stuck in a typical queue for up to five minutes at a time, you will have already started to play the wait game (see page 74).

When you walk around your neighbourhood introduce a new cue: 'stopping, wait for mummy'. When you say this pause the pram for a really brief time, and when they stop demanding you to move on, simply say 'Off we go'. If they start to cry and protest when you stop briefly, use your wait game and see if they will settle, then resume your walk. If they get very cross at you, go around to the front of the pram, get down on their level and ask them to wait. Try to distract them by pointing to some of the interesting things in the environment. When they stop fussing or crying say 'Good waiting, bubba, off we go' and head on your way quickly before they start to cry again.

Repeat the strategies above, extending the length of your pause as your baby gets better and better at this game. Remember it's a game, so create a fun feeling about stopping and waiting. If you create a fun association with stopping the pram, then your baby is more likely to smile and wait in anticipation of a fun take-off rather than complain about the fact that you have stopped.

Prams in a large shopping centre

Occasionally, a baby or toddler may find busy environments like those at a shopping centre significantly more stressful compared to an enjoyable pram trip to the local shops up the road. The reason for this may be varied but there are usually a couple of things to bear in mind. Don't generalise all unsettled pram behaviour into the category of stress. If they always battle with you about the pram, which they should be able to happily ride in until the age of two and a half, then their behaviour should be managed as mentioned in the above section of pram play. If, however, you find your little one is behaving in an unusual way in a larger shopping centre environment, you can take some steps to try and reduce stress.

I often find that providing a visual or physical security helps them feel less exposed and vulnerable as they surge through a large crowd. It can help them calm down almost immediately. Something as simple as a blanket or muslin over their knees and tummy and tucked around their back is often a comfort to a baby. Equally, placing a soft blanket or muslin around their shoulders can provide comfort. Attaching your little one to a comfort item like a teddy bear can be a great way to help them cope with the sensation of being vulnerable in a shopping centre (see pages 352 and 461). Alternatively, if you have a pram that reverses direction, it may be helpful to turn them around so they can face you. Ordinarily, facing the wrong way in the pram can cause tears and boredom when out and about but for a child showing sign of stress in a crowded environment, this may be helpful for a short period of time until this passes.

I tend to find these episodes rare and short lived, but the important thing to remember is that you are working to move your child through and past these kinds of concerns. You never stamp your child with a tag like 'they don't like crowds', or no longer expose them to that environment. Just be careful to reduce the stress of the situation until they become a little more comfortable within that environment (see page 122).

Hot Tip

One of the biggest accidental mistakes I see many people make, even though it is a lovely sweet and almost instinctive pattern, is to over rock or jiggle a baby in a pram when they stop it. Even when the baby is content to sit and wait happily, parents continue to rock them energetically. This can, for some babies, set them up to need constant rocking or movement to stay calm. In turn it will naturally create difficult expectations around play and, worse still, develop a dependency on rocking that could turn into a sleep solution for you and your little one that will need to be done over and over and over again all night, every night. This means that as they get older, you will have taught them that sitting still is not normal and this makes play and sleep a more difficult task. Simple solution: do not jiggle or rock the pram when you stop. When you're walking the pram moves. If you stop, let the pram be still.

Shopping trolley play

Just like an enjoyable pram play, getting a child to sit patiently in a shopping trolley can be challenging to achieve for some families. For all the same reasons that pram play is important, it is just as crucial to encourage your child to experience and adjust to sitting in the shopping trolley when you ask them to. While I find that an appropriately timed routine with consistent communication is generally enough to settle a baby down during a shopping trip, occasionally we may need to go that extra mile to ensure a successful and happy outing.

As discussed in the pram play strategy, you need to select your times for going supermarket shopping fairly carefully. Afternoons are always best for outings as quiet sitting in the morning is a challenge for a baby who has been asleep all night. Even if your baby is sleeping poorly at night, allowing them to be inactive all morning by being in a pram or shopping trolley to compensate for that poor night's sleep will actually either create or perpetuate cycles of poor

> Shopping time can be so much fun, and such a wonderfully rich communication opportunity.

sleep and early waking. Why would their little body ever need to change the poor pattern of sleep at night or early waking cycles at 4 to 5 a.m. when they get to sit all morning in a pram? So make the mornings physically active and the afternoons the time for pram and shopping trolley play.

This time can be so much fun, and such a wonderfully rich communication opportunity. Even though you are busy and trying to get your shopping done as quickly as possible, it's a great time to involve your child. Talk about all the things you are buying, point out pictures and colours on labels, give them special things to hold and stay happy. A happy mummy equals a happy baby.

Before you set out make sure the trolley is comfortable and predictable for your little one. A trolley mate by Clean Shopper (www.cleanshopper. com.au) is a wonderful idea to soften the hard edges of the trolley, keep germs at bay and help stop little toys or drinking cups from slipping down through the bars creating frustration for your baby. Watch for positioning problems that may create frustrations for your baby and keep them sitting forward with buckles firmly fastened.

All too often I watch a baby tell their mother they want to be picked up by raising their arms and, instead of answering them, the mother gets a little bit pink and launches into a frantic race to get her shopping finished before baby loses the plot. The best way to handle this effectively is to make sure you're not dawdling, so be organised before you even leave home. Have a list, and watch the time. Then it's really important to show your baby that you have heard their request to be picked up and intend to answer them. Your answer should be one of two things, and should be used equally. It's either a clear 'yes', or 'no'. My suggestion is that while you embark on a supermarket trip, it's not the best plan to establish a boundary of not being picked up unless you are happy to do it every time you go to the shops. It's not okay to say one week, 'Sure I'll pick you up', and then the next to get frustrated at them when they demand it every time. This is being unpredictable and inconsistent and always creates a clingy baby and unnecessary tears. You are best to establish a predictable rule that while you're in the supermarket, they don't get picked up.

Instead, when they ask you to pick them up, take their hands and say in a loving way 'Not time for up up now, hands down, wait for mummy'. You will have been practising this wait game and routine at home, so now it's time to implement the positioning request at playtime. Remember to define your statement—'sit down, wait for mummy' doesn't mean 'ask to be picked up'. Place your baby's arms down at their laps and say 'Hands down, wait for mummy' and reach for your bag of tricks and ask in an excited tone, 'Oh, where's your lion gone? Rroooooaaar.' This will give

Tips for trolley times

The same principles apply to high chair play before you attempt a restaurant visit as they do to a shopping trolly expedition.

- Don't forget how amazing the world is to your baby. There are thousands of things they have never seen before. Make your trips interesting and exciting.
- Always stay calm, happy and consistent even if they are becoming demanding or making a baby racket.
- The ability to stay emotionally available to your child, even while you are busy doing the weekly shop is a skill that will set you apart from the rest.
- Implement your new language stream of 'no touch' to your shopping trip and you will be able to safely guide your little one and ensure you don't have to continually take things off them once they have collected them off the shelf , thus reducing the trigger for tears (see page 324).
- Always be sure that you have given your baby the opportunity to learn new language cues and requests at home while you have time and patience to follow through to ensure you don't confuse them.

Remember, it's all about giving your baby the opportunity to learn before asking anything of them in a more challenging environment.

you ample opportunity to distract them, say you have heard them but you can't oblige their request right now, and show them a positive alternative for when they feel like this in the future.

What if it keeps happening? Consistency is the key. Stay calm, stay consistent and repeat yourself over and over until they understand that 'sit down wait for mummy' doesn't mean 'if you cry long enough, I will get you up'. Be careful to not accidentally teach your baby to cry for a long time before they get up. Once you have made your request to wait, follow through and complete your shopping trip with that same expectation in play. If you feel you are on the brink of giving in, it is better to finish up your shop early, pay and leave, then pick them up outside. This ensures you don't teach your baby they need to cry loud and strong for you to pick them up. Within one to two shopping trips, your baby will happily accept the predictable conditions of the trolley and all your shopping blues will be a thing of the past.

Nudie playtime

This is an extremely important part of your baby's day for a great number of reasons. As the day draws to a close, a child's body is fairly depleted of fuel and energy as sleep and food sources start to dwindle after the demands of a long day on a growing body. Because of this the final meal of the day, dinner, provides a sudden glucose high that promotes a naturally elevated mood. For years parents have been told to keep children calm for the last portion of the day and, while this is true to a certain extent, fighting their bodies' natural urge to use up the fuel just consumed creates one of two problems:

1. Your baby will be difficult to manage, often appearing grumpy and as you try desperately to calm them down and keep them quiet, you blame your husband or wife coming home from work for overexciting them.
2. It may promote night wakings because when food is consumed it converts to glucose, which is energy. If it is not used, it is stored as glycogen in the liver. This is energy storage. When it is needed again, it is used. Think 2 a.m. Need I say anything more?

The fuel from dinner is needed only to sustain them until it's time for a full night's sleep, so my advice is to burn off the excess with a quick active play before bath. If your child's natural energy levels remain low after a meal, it's important to try and pull on any fuel reserves they have in their body. To tap into this fuel reserve from dinner you can give them a final lasting burst of energy to make the last hour of the day enjoyable for them.

Change the tone at the end of the day

Often full-time working mums or dads miss out on having fun with their babies as they are encouraged to come home and be very quiet—the 'hush hush' zone. If a parent makes it home in time, nudie playtime is one of the most enjoyable one-on-one times of the day, and a wonderful way to close a busy day on a great note. It gives working parents a chance to come home and have a fun interaction with an excited, giggly baby who has just eaten.

In addition, by promoting rough-and-tumble play, your children become confident with their gross motor skills, develop spatial awareness, boldness, strength, and a love of high-output exercise. By promoting an open nudie playtime, when children have fun and feel confident within their own space, you can set normal healthy body boundaries that enable a child to learn from an early age what is and isn't normal physical contact. Because children are creatures of habit, a change to any kind of interaction at a nudie time will evoke a strong response and an initial resistance. This alone will act as a deterrent, making up one part of your child protection plan.

> If a parent makes it home in time, nudie playtime is one of the most enjoyable one-on-one times of the day, and a wonderful way to close a busy day on a great note.

Protection from predators

Sadly, we live in a world where innocent children are often the victims of predators. During nudie playtime you can instil two simple language cues as soon as your child can use the words 'stop' and 'no'. You do this by playing games that allow them to use these words. For instance, if they want you to stop tickling them they can say 'No' or 'Stop'. Empower your children with the ultimate control over their body with any 'no' then 'go', or 'stop' then 'go' games. Predators are notoriously cowards, thus preying on what they deem as helpless children. If a child was to say 'No' or 'Stop', an adult would perceive the child as having a logical concept of right and wrong which would more likely make them stop out of fear the child may tell. Also, by making this a normal response for you to stop when they request it, it is more likely that a child will accidentally say 'Uncle Rupert didn't stop', even if they have been told not to tell you. This two-step plan, hand in hand with parental vigilance will offer great protection for your children.

Instil an important expectation around their body even before they can talk. As you blow on their tummy, or tickle them you can end with a clear

'Stop mummy' and raise your hands up next to your head. Once you roll them over to daddy he can have a tickle and roll them around and then say 'No' before briefly raising his hands, and passing baby back to mum again. As they reach the age where they can use single words, you can say 'Mummy is going to tickle your tummy, say "stop" when you want me to stop'. Be careful to allow them the opportunity to say 'no' or 'stop' if they are laughing by not relentlessly tickling them, not that anyone really enjoys that anyway. So always pause in any tickle game to allow them time to catch their breathe and move away if they want, or if you can see they are trying to stop you. Encourage the words with the cue 'say stop / no'. The moment they say it, raise your hand off them and say 'Mummy / daddy stop'. If they want to keep going you can encourage them to say 'go'. A child who cannot say 'go' will come and lie in front of you ready for more tickles, and this is your cue to use the word 'go'.

Always respect the words 'stop' and 'no' the first time your child says them. Do not make them repeat it. Even if they say 'no' as soon as you go to start again, it must be respected. You can play it in reverse with older toddlers too. Daddy and toddler can tickle mummy until she says 'stop' or 'no', then everyone stops. It's a simple game that leaves your children empowered with control of their body.

Troubleshooting

Q Isn't it too soon after dinner to have a big rough-and-tumble play?

A Not at all. By the time you start your nudie playtime, their bodies are naturally energised and telling them to go wild for a little while anyway. You can't argue with nature. All the families I work with assume they can't play after a meal and are thrilled to find nudie playtime after dinner and before bath has nothing but positive benefits on their baby's body, mood and sleep.

Q Won't they get cold in winter?

A One of the reasons for the nudie aspect in this energy-burning time is to cool them down so they can burn more fuel. If it is winter-take the chill out of the air but by no means should you warm the room for nudie playtime. The active play will provide that opportunity.

Q Won't they wee on my bed if they have no nappy on?

A Only if they are kept still. If that isn't incentive to make this time constant rough and tumbling good fun, I don't know what is.

Q Do they have to have their nappy off?

A Not if they indicate that they don't want it off, or if you have people over. Just use your instincts.

Confidence building around gross motor skills

By providing a highly active, adventurous nudie playtime you promote jumping, rolling, climbing and confidence in big butterfly-mimicking moves that will build their confidence and prevent them from being nervous and fractious with their movements. Every day should have a silly time, when there is no intention other than fun, and they have your undivided attention. To provide this at the end of the day makes everyone look forward to this usually exhausting process by promoting laughter, togetherness and a final closeness before bed for the night. It ensures any last needed snuggles are had, everyone ends the day on a great note, and they are definitely ready for a relaxing bath, feed and kiss before getting tucked into bed pooped after such a fun day.

Teaching *them* when to stop

During nudie playtime toddlers, in particular, tend to get very excited. This is when they don't know how to express themselves and they may become rough in a way that we would deem as aggressive, like hitting, biting or pinching. It's the same sense of joy and excitement that comes when they are playing with their little friends or you pick them up to have a fun play and they whack you, or overexcitedly bite their friend lovingly on the cheek. Nudie playtime gives *you* a chance to say 'stop' when things go too far and so your baby learns what is and isn't good expressions of excitement.

Practise the 'lie down' game and cues

Where toddlers are concerned, the secret to teaching them to sleep often comes down to their ability to lie down. While some strategies suggest you lie them down a hundred times or more while they cry for hours on end in their cot, I think this is tormenting and unfair. I prefer to teach them what the term 'lie down' means by teaching them in a non-threatening way. By playing the 'lie down' game (see box) you create a positive association around the event of lying down, and enable them to accept this request at sleep time without stress.

Playing in the car seat

Difficulty around promoting playtime in the car can be a common problem. Unfortunately, when a little one is not at the size where their chair can be safely turned to face the front of the car, some babies find the process of going backwards in the car extremely uncomfortable, and often a long drive will have lingering effects. I tend to find that once an appropriate routine is established, where your child is sleeping well and a balance of communication is part of their lives, it becomes much easier to tackle this area.

While your child is very young and they have to travel backwards, it's important to make sure that any long trips are targeted around their usual sleep times. Ensure they have some toys attached to their seat, and make sure they are well hydrated before you leave. Keep your bag of tricks (see page 369) next to you on the car seat so you can access it at traffic lights and head off on your journey.

Once your little one is able to face forwards, things are less difficult and you will see an immediate turn around in their ability to cope with a longer car trip. Regardless of the direction their car seat is facing, graded exposure to toys is your best option to extend their attention span and ability to cope for longer periods in their car seat.

When you set out on your journey, it's always good to start with no toys at all. This will give your little one the opportunity to take in their surroundings. Please note: only if it is appropriate to your routine, would you allow them to fall asleep, otherwise car naps are a big no no! If they sleep whenever they like, it will make them more tired because it will disrupt their ability to sleep at the next designated sleep time, and that will ultimately make them unhappy. A misplaced nap, even as brief as five

The 'lie down' game

Keep this game a parent-governed line of communication. During your normal nudie playtime when you see your baby lie down say 'Awwww lie down' and lie your head on the bed. If the baby sits up, say 'Good sleeping'. Everyone should clap and cheer at this wonderful new game. You can encourage them with positive language like 'Good lying down'. Once this basic game has begun, repeat your cue, 'Okay, mummy / daddy lie down', and make sure the adults lie their heads on the bed and say 'Awwwwww lie down'. Pretend to sleep. Snore, and have your eyes closed (but keep them in your sights for safety reasons). Stay still for a moment then end the session with a big 'Good sleeping' and sit up. They will leap up with you and proudly clap themselves. Everyone clap and cheer again.

If your baby instigates more lying down, you can join then and repeat the game, but be careful about one thing: if they jump up, don't let them end the lying-down session after that initial start to the game. The completion to lying down should be retained as a parent-governed line of communication for sleep-training purposes, since that is the whole purpose of the game. Encourage them to lie down by either staying there sleeping, or telling them to lie down until you are ready, 'Quick lie down, wait'. They will quickly learn that when they lie down, you will call an end to the situation and they will wait grinning at you from their lying position. This means they are used to you governing the end of a lying-down session, and prevents confusion at sleep time.

minutes, in a baby with a low sleep requirement can detract up to two full hours of their precious sleep in a 24-hour period. This means your poor tired little baby cannot, no matter how much their little body wants them to, fall asleep or, worse, stay asleep longer than 20 to 30 minutes because their power nap has taken away their ability to do so.

If they are not at a designated sleep time when you need to travel in your car, then be careful to not dress them too warmly. Being warm will only make them sleepy. It's also important to ensure they are not wearing bulky, irritating items of clothing because that can make them feel restricted. This is a common cause of tears on a long car trip where every time they try to turn their head they get a fluffy collar in their mouth.

The general flow of a car trip, however, should be based around you gradually exposing them to their toys. But remember: safety first. I see too many mums reaching or looking back and taking all their attention off the road while they are driving. As most new mums are always tired, this is a recipe for disaster and you are better to just let your baby cry and stay focused on the road than run the risk of a car accident. There are mirrors that will help you see your baby while you are driving without the need to turn around, even if they are facing backwards, so consider tracking one of those down at a local baby store.

Unfortunately for some babies, long car trips will just not agree with them and you will have to plan your travel carefully. There are many children who suffer terribly from travel sickness, my beautiful little nephew Gage being one. If your little one throws up a lot during or after a long car trip, talk to your doctor about using something to help settle their tummy so they do not have to feel so uncomfortable. If your baby is not throwing up, and only showing clear signs of frustration, impatience and crying there is no magic wand I'm afraid. If your baby is still upset despite your bag of tricks you may have to look carefully at finding opportunities during the day when they sit with you and learn how to play in a stationary position. A good settling routine with books will help them start to enjoy quiet play and this should help your little one tremendously with car travel.

If your child generally does have a problem with sitting in one place, such as a pram or high chair, then you may have to wait until they grow out of it. In this case, lots of happy repetitive singing, a calm mummy, and perhaps something unusual to hold like your water bottle may help keep them occupied while you are driving. For the longer trip, when you might have the luxury of having two adults in the car at once, it is a sensible idea to sit someone in the back seat if your baby predictably finds travel difficult. Obviously, with a long car trip, regular breaks and time out of the car are essential to keep them fresh and happy. I always suggest you stop for all their normal feed times, and if you are in the car all the way up to and including one of their main sleeps of the day, you should stop, feed them, change their nappy, follow through on their settling routine before taking them to the car, buckling them in, covering them over with a cotton blanket and saying their sleep cues.

Try to remember, if the sensation of falling asleep has been uncomfortable for them, or only ever associated with you holding them to help them cope, then repairing their sleep issue will almost guarantee car travel issues will stop. This is simply because you have equipped them to cope independently with feeling tired, so even a drowsy car trip will no longer represent stress to them.

11
Nutrition and meal-time management

There are thousands of good books available that cover the natural transition from straight milk-fed babies into the world of solid foods. Each of them highlights the types of foods to start with, appropriate ages to introduce them, and which foods should be avoided and for how long. They give helpful recipe ideas, great cooking instructions and offer terrific time-saving suggestions. In this section, however, I am going back to basics to talk about aspects of meal-time planning, which is where most of the other books don't dare to go. In the next two chapters I'm going to talk to you about the practical side of feeding your baby:

- what position works best for feeding
- how food intake impacts on a baby's ability to sleep
- when it's appropriate to allow your baby to spoon-feed themselves
- how to manage the typical trouble areas of meal times, like throwing food, cups and spoons; grabbing bowls and spoons off you; covering their mouth with hands and little podgy arms; shaking their head to avoid spoons; flapping arms; pursing lips; turning in their chair so you can't feed them; and mouthing the high chair table or their seat rather than eating
- how to handle the sudden and notorious 'I've had enough, get me out of here *now*' stroppy moppy
- how to repair severe meal-time problems, where your child has developed a true aversion to meal times and is now virtually unable to eat

- how to provide respectful language around meal times so your child's needs are taken into consideration
- how to set those all-important boundaries around meal times to keep the tears away.

I will talk you through how to establish boundaries around meal times so it can be a pleasant and an enjoyable experience rather than an endless battle or a fruitless negotiation that often results in even less food going in your baby's mouth as the negotiation goes south. I will discuss how to introduce meat into their diet without having it cause gagging or damage to your baby's delicate trust relationship with eating vegetables, which you might have been spending weeks developing and fostering. I will talk about the role your attitude towards play during meals has, and of its importance in your little one's ability to relax and trust the meal-time process. I will discuss communication at meal times and how to ensure you don't make spoon-feeding a stressful event. I will talk about adopting humour with your toddler so they can work through and past existing difficult behavioural meal-time routines to find a better way. I will also discuss the two major causes of general meal-time disruption:

- poor appetite
- loss of trust or behavioural issues from imbalanced communication lines.

Positioning for feeding a fussy baby

When I arrive at a house for a homestay, I am always focused on the environment and what it has to offer first and foremost. As parents show me through my temporary home for the next week, my eyes are looking for anything that will be of use over that time, to help make their little one comfortable and assist them to settle down as quickly as possible. One of the most important things I look for is a good quality, comfortable and *practical* high chair. I cannot tell you how many times I have entered a house, knowing that we have a real troubled eater on our hands, and found either one of the oldest or the most impractical funky-looking high chairs sitting ominously in the kitchen.

I am going back to basics to talk about aspects of meal-time planning . . . to talk to you about the practical side of feeding your baby.

If your child is having a difficult time with solid meals, one of the most valuable and practical things you can do is invest in a good-quality high chair. There are many that look amazingly cool with sleek edges and designs to suit a modern home but they often offer little to no security for a baby as they embark on something quite new. The only high chair I recommend these days is the Peg Perego Prima Pappa because of its useful features which include:

- seven adjustable height positions for toddlers
- four reclining-seat adjustments
- nicely padded seat liner that can be removed for cleaning
- removable, dishwasher-safe dinner tray
- 5-point harness
- lap and shoulder harness to make transition to family dinner table easy
- large, mark-resistant castor wheels
- folding up easily and compactly for storage.

A chair like this helps prevent a baby from back arching, sliding down, hanging off the side and kicking off the foot rest. It helps a baby stay focused in the forward position rather than a distracting 360-degree angle. A good practical high chair with well-fitted buckles helps a child feel fully supported, helps parents keep them safe and in a good comfortable position for feeding and, through the 5-point harness and the seat safety bar, prevents your baby from sliding forward or getting themselves into a real pickle by going into a full back-arching tantrum.

When you use the 5-point harness, please ensure it is well fitted so it does not allow them to slide their arms out or become irritating if it rubs on their cheek or gets in the way of spoon-feeding. This is the same for a six month old as it is for a two year old. Just because a toddler may choose to not have the buckles on, it does not mean you do not pop them on them anyway. It is not safe, nor practical, to go without the buckle system, which has proven only to cause more problems.

This chair may be a little pricey for some people's budgets but it is a very good investment when it comes to helping your little one settle into meal times with ease. I have many clients who have managed to pick up second-hand ones quite cheaply, so take a good look around before you buy a new high chair if you are working on a shoestring budget. If you cannot afford one of these high chairs or have purchased another chair already, then you just need to remember the following things.

- Always install and do up the 5-point harness correctly—it is both unsafe and disruptive to meals to have your child in their chair without adequate safety devices in place or without them being fitted well.
- When you first introduce solids, or when you plan on trying to correct a disrupted meal-time behavioural pattern, it is important to remove

the high chair meal-tray altogether and recline your child so they can relax back into their seat. Make sure you tell them before you recline them, however, as this may make them feel a little uncertain about the chair and they will cry or become rigid. Always recline them slowly and if they do tend to get unsettled, hold their hands and make it a fun thing, a little like the way you would vocalise and smile as you slide them down a slippery dip. You can recline your child up to the age of 12 months.

- If your high chair does not recline, and you have a little baby under nine months of age, putting them into a bouncer / rocker chair for meal times is an important part of restoring meal-time harmony. Obviously, you will need to remove the toy bar first so it does not get covered in food but you can manage them during spoon-feeding in one of these without difficulty.

- Get yourself comfortable and prepared for a little bit, or a whole lot of mess. When I say mess, I mean don't worry on those first few days if you and they are beautifully spray-painted with food, if it ends up in their hair, or the chair looks like you need to take a fire hose to it. The mess thing does not last for long, and it is well worth the clean-up required for a day or two to achieve relaxed, settled meal times where your little one happily sits and eats while having a little chat and playing with their toys. To not address an existing poor meal-time routine because you don't want a little mess will ultimately result in ongoing meal-time battles.

After reclining your baby in their high chair, remove the tray and be sure that, if they try to sit upright by getting up on their elbows or pulling on the sides of their high chair, that you can help them to relax by putting their hands back into a comfortable position in front of them so they aren't trying to sit upright anymore. Yes, this means physically releasing their hands from the side of the chair as you gently say 'Lie down bubby, it's time for lunch'. Remember that you will have been managing this kind of behaviour during nappy change so they will have become accustomed to the request. As you do this make sure you use your clear language stream, 'lie down, wait for mummy / daddy'. By now, this cue should be recognised easily by your child and be something that they trust. Be sure to define that statement (see page 44) just as you would when you help them lie down for you on the change table, and physically help them to relax and lie down if they appear to be having difficulty.

I always remind parents that if there is going to be a little battle about who is governing the outcome of the meal-time events, it is better to have it during the process of putting on the bib (see box on page 220) or asking them to relax in the chair than when feeding them. It's important that you understand that after years of observing thousands of children it has become clear to me that a child will only try to retain the governing line and, therefore, the outcome of the situation at meal times, if they are not given clear communication and a predictable pattern to follow. A successful outcome requires a confident parent who is vocal, enthusiastic and persistent.

Always recline them slowly and if they do tend to get unsettled hold their hands and make it a fun thing, a little like the way you would vocalise and smile as you slide them down a slippery dip.

Positioning and strategy for bottle feeding

If you are needing to introduce a bottle, it should really happen in the early months of life, even if it is one containing expressed milk late at night so that daddy can feed the baby while mummy catches up on some much-needed rest. This ensures your baby is able to be fed from a bottle as they get older, which will help you keep them well hydrated with water as they grow.

Meal-time cue: 'bib on'

Place a bib on your baby by showing them the bib and saying 'Bib on' with a big smile on your face. Remember your inflection (see page 58). This is not a punishment. If they become upset, please remember the role you and your attitude play in helping them calm down and feel safe (see page 85). Make sure you put the bib on correctly, and then define what the statement 'bib on' actually means (see page 44).

If your little one tends to try to fight you putting it on or tries to remove the bib, then it's important that you take the bib out of their grasp and repeat the statement 'Bib on' patiently and gently. Tuck the ends in under their buckles or around their sides (it should be big enough), or hold the bib in place with your hand for older children so they cannot lift it or take it off. If they are protesting heavily about their bib don't even try to feed them at this point. 'Bib on, bubba' is a simple request you have made when you are governing the outcome of a situation (see page 29). If your little one fights you about something as simple as having their bib put on, you can be sure it is only a symptom of a more significant communication problem that is contributing to meal-time dramas and stress for them. It's so important that your child can relax and allow you to do things for them, like place their bib on them, so that the task of spoon-feeding them is *not* where your biggest battle takes place. This means persist until they stop trying to remove the bib, or at least can be managed more easily before you start to feed them.

If your baby is showing initial resistance to bottle feeding at six months, then it is a good idea to make sure you always inform them of the taste they expect to get when they do try and drink from it. It's also important to make sure that bottle sucking is not too difficult. This means having appropriate teats and making sure that the top is not fastened too tightly. Once the milk is warmed, replace the lid firmly and shake the bottle well. Once you have shaken the bottle, release the lid almost completely then fasten it gently until it just catches. When your little one starts to drink, you should see a steady flow of bubbles trickling into the bottle as they suckle. If the bubbles do not start within 30 to 60 seconds, then the lid is too tight. Without breaking the feed you can just slightly loosen it until you see the bottle is drawing in air. No bubbles streaming into the bottle is the number one cause of projectile vomiting in bottle-fed babies as they are forced to break the feed regularly. Do not break the feed to allow air in, and ensure your baby does not have to do the same. Simply allow air to flow freely into the bottle through the feed and enjoy the difference it makes to your bottle-fed baby.

Positioning is important, too, when feeding with a bottle. Once you have established the ability to guide your little one and ask them to sit still or lie still through your flow of communication, you are in a much better position to use your new language cues and ask your baby to lie down for their feed. This request will need to be defined so there is no confusion about what you mean. To position you and your baby, make yourself comfortable in the corner of a couch. Have a pillow under the arm that your baby is going to lie on for support. Say 'Lie down, wait for mummy' then lie your baby down so one of their arms is tucked securely down your side or behind you. Angle their body into yours and hold them firmly. If they are waving an arm in the air, use your non-feeding hand to hold on to their hand. Initially you may need to hold their hand quite firmly so they don't flap it about, but once the feeding has started, they will be more settled.

Establishing bottle feeding is similar to the first spoonful of food when feeding them solids. It's just a little glitch to get past and the feeding is established. It's important to watch how well you define your positioning request. All too often I go into a house where a child will sit up, get down, get back up, and crawl around the floor, then stand and bounce on their mum's knees before having a little suck again. When a parent sees the child is drinking, they then try to pick them up and lay them in their arms to feed, and the child back arches and gets cross. This is absolutely *not* what your baby should be learning about feeding times. It will never result in a good healthy feeding opportunity, and will make the time it takes to feed them too drawn out. Make sure that your baby stays on your lap for the entire feed and, unless you sit them up to wind them, which is not so vital by six months, they need to remain there until either the feed is finished or you are satisfied they have had enough and are full.

A baby does not have to drink all their milk; the suggested quantity is just a recommended amount. What I would target as an adequate quantity would be around two-thirds of the recommended quantity as a minimum all the way up to 240 millilitres maximum. Once your baby has decided they do not want any more, try to get them to lie still and offer them one last amount. If they refuse then that signifies the end of the feed. Do not go back and forth on feeds and make a normal ten to 15 minute feed last for 45 to 60 minutes. That is not balanced and would be the equivalent to excessive snacking as far as its impact on their appetite is concerned.

When helping them get used to a bottle, if your baby is finding it hard to take a bottle and keeps opting for a breastfeed, try to make sure that you offer the bottle feed when they are going to be quite hungry, perhaps the first feed of the day, and try to get daddy to give it. Be persistent and make sure you don't compensate by offering milk from another source if they have not taken their bottle feed, unless they have taken no milk at all.

If you have tried in earnest to give your baby the bottle at a particular feed for several days, and not compensated with a breastfeed when they haven't eaten, and have still achieved no results, then it is time to raise the white flag and move on. Your little one will need to graduate to a sippy cup for their milk feeds and water. While this is initially a little bit of a longer and more messy process, it is perfectly fine for them to graduate straight on to a cup from the breast. In fact, many prefer this. Whatever you choose to do is entirely a personal decision, and whether you transition to a bottle or a cup while still breastfeeding will not impact a well-breastfed baby's feeding routine, nor early weaning. Please know that I am in no way suggesting bottle over breast, or visa versa. This is simply a suggestion for the many that choose to, or have to introduce a bottle into their baby's day, for whatever personal reason.

Introducing solids

There are so many inflexible things I hear people being told that just don't seem terribly relevant, and are really not that big a deal at the end of the day. Things like 'they must be eating lumpy food by [. . .] months of age', or 'they need to learn how to sit with no distractions at meal times', or 'they must be self-feeding by [. . .] months'. Most of these statements are only ever intended to be suggestions or ballpark ideals to work towards, and should never take the place of your child's clear personal need or your consideration of their personality.

When it comes to meal times, I think there should be no hard and fast rules other than ensuring there is a good balance of food being eaten each day. There are some babies who find it virtually impossible to eat lumpy food as it appears to trigger or overstimulate their gag reflex and make them retch. Because of this I often see a child's personal preference is to go straight from pureed food on to finger foods. This can often mean there is a transitional period where your baby is spoon-fed their pureed food for longer, and then they have an opportunity to pick and choose from steamed vegetables or small shredded pieces of chicken or finely chopped pieces of meat off their tray. Once your little one becomes very efficient with finger-feeding themselves a large enough portion of food that is adequate for their age and stage of development, then you can relax about offering spoon-fed pureed food as well. This is obviously where you need to learn how to be flexible and discerning.

When introducing solids, sometimes your little one should have individual tastes of foods, such as pumpkin, then carrot, etc., in separate sections of the plate, but on other occasions they can enjoy their food blended together. Go with your little one's preferences here, you'll soon work it out, and know that over time they will be able to cope with the strong individual flavours of foods a little easier and their preferences may change. If your little one has a real sweet tooth and getting vegetables into them is proving to be quite a trick, then you can add some pureed fruit to the vegetables, or make a vegetable and protein mix until they become accustomed to the textures and flavour of the foods, and then gradually reduce the volume of pureed fruit to vegetables until it is eliminated.

Babies vary tremendously in the volume they need to eat. The best way to judge the right quantity of food for their age is to go by the supermarket pre-packaged jar sizes for their age group. Obviously, I am not suggesting you feed your children these food necessarily, although I am not opposed to jar food on occasions when it is more convenient or hygienic to do so. If you look at the size of the jars of solid food for six-, nine- and 12-month-old children, you will clearly work out a quantity suggestion that is fairly adequate. Again, however, I am loathe to give exact proportions because some children grow rapidly and need extra food, while other children are naturally petite and require smaller quantities. Always work on the premise that anything less than your child's age-group suggestion size is not adequate; for example, a 12 month old eating the equivalent of a nine month old's portion is not eating an adequate amount. Some babies are also hungry, and those jar sizes are not adequate for their individual body's needs as they grow. Be cautious to not give up on the solids and revert back to milk too quickly as your little one can get a little lazy and may always opt for what they know best and can do with the least amount of effort, which is the breastfeed or the bottle.

You'll also find that little ones vary greatly in their eating ability as well. Some little ones still need to be spoon-fed their vegetables up to two years of age and, not uncommonly, beyond that point to ensure there is an adequate quantity of vegetables and iron being consumed each day. Other children are happy to progress on to lumpy foods but prefer to eat only meat with their fingers and therefore may need feeding for a little longer to ensure they get a healthy portion of vegetables in their diet. Others still will eat a terrific quantity and healthy balance of finger foods from an early age and don't need to be fed via a spoon for long at all. In this case, however, a parent needs to retain the right to pop some food into their baby's mouth from time to time to make sure the pace of the meal is maintained in those first ten minutes. However it works for your baby, be flexible. There is enough to worry about in early childhood without thinking you have to meet deadlines on when they should be totally self-sufficient at meal time; that is really not so important in the grand scheme of things.

As a parent, you need to decide what and when are best for your child to eat. It is not appropriate to relinquish your common sense and knowledge on good health to an impulsive baby or toddler.

As a parent, you need to decide what and when are best for your child to eat. It is not appropriate to relinquish your common sense and knowledge on good health to an impulsive baby or toddler. This is where you need to teach them what is a healthy option for food or snacks, and make executive parenting decisions about the things that will damage their appetite for a healthy meal later in the day. If they refuse to eat anything but carbohydrates like bread all day, then reducing that particular carbohydrate in their diet dramatically will ensure they have an appetite for the other food you offer. Just because they ask for crackers all the time does not mean they should eat them all the time. Just because they can help themselves to food in the cupboard does not mean they should always be allowed to. Children should always ask their parents about food, and toddlers need good solid guidance about when and what they should and shouldn't eat.

Water is important, but when?

Hydration in the form of water is one of the most important aspects of helping your little one sleep well at night, and stay happy for the entire day. Some of the most obvious tantrum-style behaviours with 16 month olds plus can be put down to simply not drinking enough water. Sounds a little hard to believe it could be that simple, but when I was working with children in kindergartens I made a policy for all children to have multiple, good drink breaks throughout the day, and the impact it had on the group was quite profound. I have since observed fluid-intake levels during the day in the home environment with hundreds of children and then compared those observations with those taken once I have increased their water consumption. Again, the results have been quite profound.

Keep your children well watered. Keep suggesting they have drinks by sitting them down and holding the cup for them and guiding them in a confident parent-guided line of communication, so watch your inflection. Say 'Okay, bubba, have a drink for mummy please. C'mon quick sticks, one sip, two sips. Yeah! Another sip, another big one, and last one.' This style of 'quick sticks let's have a drink' communication in a fun and bubbly tone often gets effective results to help your little one's temperament and help reduce the frequency of night wakings. Please note, if your baby likes drinking water, there is no need to say 'quick sticks', it's only necessary if they are prone to try and negotiate out of having a drink every time.

Just as importantly, water should not take the place of good healthy foods. I have a policy of no drinks 30 minutes before a solid meal is due if you are trying to restore or repair meal times. Often, when your child starts to feel the natural and healthy sensation of hunger, they think they must be thirsty and subsequently ask for and gulp huge quantities of fluid. Obviously because of their age, they are unable to know what is best at this point of hunger, so it's important that you help them retain a healthy appetite for the thing their body is truly craving, which is solid nutritious food.

If your child would like a drink during the first ten minutes of a meal, try to only provide a sip so they do not fill their tummy and ruin their appetite. They are often desperate for a drink because they are very hungry and this is the fastest way they know to settle down that feeling, but as adults we know that the water will not keep that feeling at bay for long, and will sadly only quench their appetite, preventing them from eating effectively. This will ultimately result in a baby who is wanting snack foods before the next meal, which will impact also on their ability to eat. In order to restore a balance you must be careful to feed them food when their body needs it and offer adequate water between meals; give no snacks two hours before lunch or dinner; try and avoid water intake during the first five to ten minutes of any meal, and longer if they are not asking for it.

Spoon-feeding your little one

The flow of meal times should consistently follow the pattern of the spoon going into the bowl and scooping up a little bit of food, and then the spoon coming to their mouth, and the food going into their mouth. The spoon is then returned to the bowl and the predictable pattern repeats itself. There is one thing that is certain, though. You cannot govern what happens once the food goes in their mouth so you do not need to worry about that part other than managing their behaviours during meal times. The only part you want to master at this point, other than the basic meal-time boundaries, is the process of scooping up the food, and putting it in their mouth and showing them when they have finished.

It's also important to start to establish some language cues that will help your little one learn how to feed themselves. A simple 'scoop it up' as you put your spoon in the bowl and fill your spoon, then 'in your mouth' as you place the spoon in their mouth will make it much easier when you need to encourage them to feed themselves. Once you have repaired their meal times and they have been given a spoon of their own, while you feed them you can offer the bowl briefly, and say 'Scoop it up, Brooke' and wait for them to scoop the food up, then encourage them by saying 'In your mouth'. Clap and cheer as they go and before you know it you will have a little person feeding themselves beautifully!

Don't forget to reheat the food regularly if they are taking quite a while to eat so they are not being asked to eat stone-cold vegetables—yuck! Don't put too much in the bowl initially. Try to make the meal volume achievable, and limit the time it takes you to spoon-feed them to a maximum of ten minutes so meals don't become dreaded epic sagas of boredom.

When you are looking to start correcting your current meal-time fussiness, you need to be mindful of 'The communication learning ladder' (see page 67). Invest a few days in your future family's harmony to correct the current unpleasant meal-time routine. Follow the instructions outlined for spoon-feeding your baby, 'When spoon-feeding isn't happening naturally' (see below), but be prepared for a bit of mess. Your attitude towards their food and meal times is so important here. You must stay calm and enthusiastic, and have a little repertoire of songs and conversation ready to distract them and maybe even be prepared to have them protest louder than you can talk. This does not mean you increase your volume of singing or talking, however. The rule is that the more unsettled they become, the calmer and more soothing your tone becomes.

This is an important element to remember when trying to work through meal-time difficulties. There are also several other simple mistakes I hear people make. Comments like 'just one more' said over and over again to toddlers, or said after only two bites of dinner is not a helpful or productive strategy to adopt because you are encouraging protests to achieve a negotiation, which will ultimately cause the meal to end prematurely. Always target an achievable portion size you would like them to eat, and work through the meal enthusiastically. People give up well before I would ever give up and I have never had a poor end result to the meal-time repair strategies.

I've found that all the children I've worked with run to their high chair and happily climb in and wait for lunch and dinner within a few weeks. One thing I commonly hear when I am helping a family work through the meal-time difficulties is 'Oh my goodness, I can't believe they ate all of that, I would have given up ages ago'. My suggestion is: don't give up, keep going until the meal is complete but remember the first ten minutes are the most important, so keep your pace up.

When spoon-feeding isn't happening naturally

Because meal times with under-two year olds are one of the areas of the day that need to be governed by parents until they are correctly established, it is vitally important that you retain the capacity to feed your child all the way up to their second birthday or they may stop eating enough, resulting in multiple wakings for feeds through the night, which will ruin their appetite for daytime calorie intake. Bearing in mind that you need to predominantly govern the 'behaviours' at meal time, you should always retain or reclaim the capacity to spoon-feed your child to ensure that their food intake is adequate and there is a balance of control around healthy dietary intake. Please do not misunderstand this statement. I'm not talking about force-feeding, but about managing the behaviours that prevent you from being able to feed your child, such as covering their mouth, putting fingers in their mouth, snatching the spoon off you, mouthing the high chair or flapping their hands, or shaking or turning their head in refusal.

All of these behaviours require a two-pronged approach: a consistent language cue and your physical intervention to correct the problem. This way they will understand what the statement actually means and your expectation of their behaviour. Always praise good eating!

Being prepared

I always have my bag of tricks handy (see page 369), but I am careful to use a graded form of exposure to any distraction toys so I can still provide something of interest after five to six minutes of feeding. Often people say to me that they are concerned that meal times should be without toys or distraction, but the only thing I personally think should be a definite is that you need to do your best to ensure a balanced meal is provided at two out of every three meals of the day. If distraction helps your little one get through a meal time in those first few days of correcting poor meal-time habits, then I say 'Hurray for distractions'. I am really only concerned with establishing healthy, social meal-time boundaries for when they are over the age of two years, and even at that age certain distractions are fine for some meal times while other meal times should be had without them. This means that when a baby is at that age, parents are able to resume normal family activities and start to go out to cafés for lunch or dinner without stress.

I always suggest you have the entire meal, including any pureed food, finger foods, desserts, drinks and all utensils and plates you'll need, prepared and on the table so you aren't coming and going from the kitchen too much. I find the best spoons to use are the Tommy Tippee heat-sensitive ones for both the six to 12 months' and the 12 to 24 months' age groups. And always cut any meat portions that you offer as finger foods for older babies into very, very small pieces so they do not over chew larger pieces. The chewing can be too time consuming, and also often results in a child chewing the meat down to sinew or fibre before spitting it out. For older children, however, always have the drink cups and desserts tucked discretely behind an object so your child is not distracted by them, wanting them instead of what's on offer right now.

If you find your child's attention span is particularly short, you can give the meal in two parts. The first is the spoon-fed portions (everything else hidden away) followed by a finger food of vegetables, and protein or carbohydrates like pasta. The second section is like a shared plate where you prepare a dinner plate for yourself and sit down and start to eat and, when they ask, share it with them. Obviously, this is helpful at lunch as it can be a great way to encourage a little more time focused on food. Make sure you always make enough for yourself and your little one as it's important that you eat as well.

In addition to the preparation above, it's important with older children that they have all distractions removed, such as other food items that are on the bench tops. Often too much choice will result in your hungry little bubby putting in a mouthful of their food, only to spot something delicious on the bench, such as a block of cheese, and remove the food that is in their mouth so they can have a bit of what's on the bench. This can happen over and over again in the same meal time, resulting in almost all the food going in and coming out again before it is swallowed. This can also happen when you put too much in front of them at once. Always offer a small assortment of food nicely spaced out on their tray for them to choose from. Remember: too much choice and they can't make any choice at all. I rarely offer a plate of food unless they are super-efficient eaters.

What to feed your child

Many people get caught up in the idea that the final solid meal or milk feed of the day is the one that helps their baby sleep better at night, but this is actually not the case at all in my experience. It is the careful balance of nutritious calorie intake, as well as the balance of milk and fluid intake, throughout the 12 or so hours they are awake during the day that impacts on a baby's ability to sleep well at night. Ensuring you encourage good solid eating, good milk intake, and great water hydration during the day puts you in a far better position to help your little one achieve a great night's sleep.

While I don't believe all babies need to eat solids from six months of age, I certainly do believe that any child having a difficult time with sleep will need to have their food intake supplemented with solids by around six months of age to sustain sleep for the long night sleep. This means you need to balance your baby's intake of solids, milk, snacks and fluid intake for sleep repair.

Excessive milk intake will impact on a baby or toddler's ability to start eating solids, which can be the cause of sleep-time difficulties. Whether the milk intake is from the breast or bottle is up to you, but this is what I find is a good number of milk feeds per day for the different ages:

- at six to seven months of age, if they are not having meat in their diet or haven't started solids yet, they need four to five milk feeds
- six to ten months = four milk feeds
- ten to 12 months = three milk feeds
- 12 to 18 months = two milk feeds.

As they get older milk feeds can remain in breast or bottle form, or can be offered in a cup.

For balanced main meals throughout the day, make sure you offer good healthy-eating opportunities. These are the number of solid feeds I would recommend:

- six to seven months = two to three solid meals (two would be savoury—one with iron introduced at the lunch meal, and one vegetarian—the third would be sweet)
- seven to eight and a half months = three solids (two savories—one with meat, the other vegetarian—and one sweet).

Low-sleep-requirement babies (see page 534) over eight and a half months can also have fruit for morning tea if they appear hungry long before lunch plus a snack for afternoon tea (toast or Cruskit, or breadstick, or rice cake with spread plus yoghurt or cheese, or fruit). High-sleep-requirement babies (see page 534) from the age of ten months can also have fruit for morning tea if they appear hungry long before lunch and a snack for afternoon tea (toast or Cruskit, or breadstick, or rice cake with spread plus yoghurt or cheese, or fruit).

Excessive snacking is possibly one of the most disruptive elements to both a child's appetite, and their need for sleep. There are a few simple things to bear in mind when looking at how sleep or appetite is impacted by snacking:

- Healthy balanced meals provide longer energy sources and therefore often help a child stay calm and content.
- Snacks are often higher in calorie and lower in nutrition content than a healthy balanced meal and are therefore effective for short bursts of energy and designed to bridge the gap between good solid meals.
- Continued snacking and poorly balanced meal intake often result in behavioural difficulties as the day progresses.
- If a child snacks too often (more than twice a day) the snacks will impact on their ability to build an appetite for a healthy nutritionally rich meal, and a child who has a lower nutritional content through the day will wake more often at night.
- If a child sleeps poorly but compensates for this with excessive calorie intake through snacking often during the day, the snack then replaces the need for good quality sleep or continues to compensate for poor sleep, therefore perpetuating poor sleeping patterns.

Something to be cautious about when it comes to snack foods is the quantity of dried fruit your child consumes. While dried fruit is a healthy snack option, the energy, or sugar content, of such foods is high. Dried fruit is a whole food in a very concentrated form, less the water content. If you are offering fully hydrated apricots for instance, you would not offer them six to eat, plus a big bunch of grapes and half an apple as this would be too much. The same care with quantity needs to be taken with dried fruit. It is most definitely a healthy option, but please be mindful of the amount you offer your child.

Recipe suggestions for first spoon-fed meals

I often find that parents think they need to offer a new taste sensation at every meal, but babies respond so much better to the predictable when they are unsettled. You are best to stick to a few simple recipes until you have re-established trust with their meal times, and then look into broadening their food repertoire a little each week. Always begin with a repertoire of the puree meal suggestions in infant and toddler cookbooks and gradually progress from pureed foods to lumpy foods *if* your little one can tolerate them. If not, it is okay for your little one to go from purees straight to finger foods if that works best for them.

> Always offer a small assortment of food nicely spaced out on their tray for them to choose from.

The most common mistake I find with people blending meat and vegetables for their little one is that often the meat is very overcooked or does not bind effectively with the vegetables, resulting in the meat sticking to a baby's tongue and making them gag, cry or vomit. In order to avoid this for the fussy eaters I tend to start with three simple recipes and remain predictable and consistent until they settle down and start to trust the food you feed them again. Here are three simple recipes to get you started to ensure there is a good blend of vegetables and protein in their daily intake. These simple, smooth, creamy mixtures will help them get back into eating quite easily.

Mixed vegetables and pasta / rice
500 g pumpkin
2 large potatoes
3 large carrots
2 zucchini
1 cup mini pasta stars or rice
formula, breast or cows' milk (optional—see 'Notes')

Peel and chop the vegetables into similar-sized pieces and steam until tender. Place in a food processor and puree until creamy smooth and there are no lumps remaining.

Boil pasta or rice until very tender. Remove, drain and rinse thoroughly in cold water. Add to pureed vegetable and blend in the food processor until smooth and fluffy.

If you feel the blend is too sticky and needs to be fluffier add a little bit of milk (see 'Notes'), about 10 to 20 ml, which will help you achieve the right consistency.

Pureed vegetables and chicken

500 g pumpkin
4 to 5 red Delicious apples (optional)
2 large potatoes or half a sweet potato
3 large carrots
2 zucchini
½ to 1 small chicken breast (do not use mince)
formula or cows' milk (optional—see 'Notes')

Peel and chop the vegetables into similar-sized pieces and steam until tender. Place in a food processor and puree until creamy smooth with no lumps.

Cut the chicken breast into cubes of a similar size. Add chicken to a saucepan with 3 cm of boiling water and poach chicken until it *just* turns white all the way through. Do not overcook or it will not blend well. Once the chicken is white through (cut and check one of the larger pieces) remove immediately from the water with a slotted spoon and place in a small cereal bowl. Place a bread-and-butter plate over the top of the bowl containing the chicken and allow the chicken to steam in its own heat for a further five minutes.

Add the chicken to the pureed vegetables and blend until the chicken is completely mixed in with the puree. It should look like tiny white flecks in the vegetable mix and if you were to place some on your finger and smooth it between your thumb and first finger, you should not be able to feel the chicken. The entire mix should be fluffy and completely smooth.

If you feel the blend is too sticky and needs to be fluffier add a little bit of milk (see 'Notes'), about 10 to 20 ml, which will help you achieve the right consistency and ensure the chicken and vegetables remain blended together. Do not add water as the chicken and the vegetables can actually separate and you will end up with the chicken clinging to your baby's tongue.

Mixed vegetables and sirloin steak

500 g pumpkin
2 large potatoes or half a sweet potato
4-5 red Delicious apples (optional)
3 large carrots
2 zucchini
sirloin steak, about the size of the palm of your hand (do not use mince)
formula or cows' milk (optional—see 'Notes')

Peal and chop the vegetables into similar-sized pieces and steam until tender. Place in a food processor and puree until creamy smooth and there are no lumps remaining.

In a skillet, cook the steak on a low heat until it is cooked through, but not overcooked. Watch the meat carefully to ensure it is cooked so it is no longer pink, but remains moist and soft. Remove from the heat and place on a plate to settle for five minutes.

Cut the meat into cubes and add to the pureed vegetables, and blend until the two are well combined. It should look like a darker blend of vegetable mixed with tiny brown flecks and if you were to place some on your finger and smooth it between your thumb and first finger, you should not be able to feel the steak meat. The entire mix should be fluffy and completely smooth.

If you feel the blend is too sticky and needs to be fluffier add a little bit of milk (see 'Notes'), about 10 to 20 ml, which will help you achieve the right consistency and ensure the steak and vegetables remain blended together. Do not add water as the steak and the vegetables can actually separate and you will end up with the meat clinging to your baby's tongue.

Notes:
- Only if your little one eats just pureed fruit at this stage, add the one cup of stewed fruit (apple preferably, or pear) to the vegetable mix and blend until smooth. This is optional of course but can make the first few days much easier for baby. I know for a fact that this does not cause a baby to only eat sweet foods. If anything, it helps a sweet tooth adjust to the more savoury foods in a gradual way.
- Use cows' milk only if your baby is over 12 months; under this age use formula milk.
- Breast milk is effective when blending plain vegetables with rice or pasta.
- I do not find that breast milk binds the chicken and vegetables or steak and vegetables as well as formula or cows' milk. Therefore, for the purpose of repairing poor eating patterns with solid food, I do not recommend it.
- The added formula milk will not impact on a breastfed baby, and nor will it discourage them from taking their next milk feed. This recipe is a solid food so combining it with the vegetable and protein mix is perfectly fine.
- As there is often only a small portion of milk required, buy the formula in sticks if you do not already have formula in your house. That way you do not need to buy an entire can for such a minimal quantity of the product.
- If freezing a batch of the mix, add cows' milk first. If using formula milk, freeze without adding the milk; add it later to the thawed product on the day you serve it.

Troubleshooting

Q How can I wean my baby off the breast and on to a bottle?

A This is often a daunting process for parents, but the reality is far less challenging if you have a plan, and stick to it, no matter how challenging it may feel for two to three days. Firstly, you will need to establish bottle feeding (see page 220). Secondly, you will need to establish a balanced meal-time plan (see page 247). Finally, you will need to follow your plan, without compensation feeds for poor feeding, for three to five days straight. If you are experiencing difficulty with your baby's behaviour, you will be able to manage this by working with their body, as the body is less stubborn and determined than some little people; meaning, when the body is hungry, it will eat.

Q   Will I lose my milk supply when I introduce solids into my baby's diet?

A   This is a concern for many mums, but in all my years of working I've only come across one mother with a baby over six months of age who had a problem with milk supply. With careful management she was able to build up her milk supply again. This is a far more common problem for the under-six months' age group. You shouldn't experience full loss of milk if you are on a balanced meal plan and carefully manage the transition. If you have any doubts or concerns though, please monitor your progress carefully. If you feel this could be occurring, offer your baby more milk feeds and see a lactation consultant for a more closely monitored reduction program.

Q   On your program I will be weaning them from many feeds down to a few a day. How can I do this without becoming engorged or developing mastitis?

A   There are many mums I have on what is called 'mastitis watch' but with careful management I have had less than five mums develop mastitis over my 20 years, even if they dropped from 20 plus breastfeeds a day (this many feeds is more common than you will ever imagine so don't worry if this is your situation) to as little as three, all in 24 hours. There are a few areas that need to be considered. The first is the breasts becoming engorged, the second is becoming infected and, finally, the breast being correctly supported and cared for through the weaning process. My formula for this weaning process is really quite simple:

*   massage your breast regularly, using your thumb to disperse any firm lumps or pockets of milk that are developing
*   express off the top of your milk supply if your breasts are feeling very full
*   wear a firm (well-fitted, non-maternity) bra 24 hours a day for three to four weeks
*   drink lots of water, and eat healthy regular meals.

The amount of milk you express off should just be enough to make you feel comfortable again. If you are weaning your little one off night feeds you may need to express twice a night for between three and seven days, depending on how much milk you continue to produce. During the day, express off twice, once in the shower in the morning and once in the evening. Massage your breasts after each expression.

The right bra is essential to keep your breasts in an aesthetically firm, supported position to allow the fat deposits returning to your breasts to go back in a more firm position, helping retain the shapeliness of your original breast shape rather than depositing in the more relaxed position of a slightly emptier breast in a poor fitting bra. While this is predominantly for cosmetic purposes, it also helps enormously with comfort.

At no point are you to allow your breasts to become engorged. A light hand express to take the pressure off your breast will allow you to keep your breast and milk supply in good health. Be mindful of keeping good breast hygiene, with clean hands, clothing and bedding. If you develop a temperature, start to feel generally unwell, experience any unusual discharge from your nipples or experience intense tenderness in your breasts, chest or armpits, please see your doctor immediately.

Q When is it safe to start finger foods?

A Offer finger foods, like pieces of cooked vegetables and bread crusts or Cruskits from around seven to eight months onwards to encourage chewing and self-feeding. Encourage drinking from a cup from about seven to eight months of age. Progress from food that is pureed to food that is mashed then to food chopped into small pieces.

Q I'm frightened of them choking, so how can I avoid it?

A To reduce the chances of a child under two years of age choking at meal time, insist they eat at the table or in the high chair and that they are sitting down correctly and calmly. Watch young children while they eat. Encourage them to eat slowly and chew their food well. Cut up foods that are firm and round and can get stuck in your child's airway, such as sausages (lengthwise and then into small pieces), grapes (quarter) and raw vegetables (small strips or pieces, not round). Other foods that can pose a choking hazard are better avoided, and these include lollies, nuts and seeds (don't give peanuts to children under age seven), popcorn, marshmallows and spoonfuls of peanut butter (be wary of all nut-based products). As a precaution, I suggest you become fully aware of what to do in case your child starts to choke on their food. Or better still, do a St Johns Ambulance course (see www.stjohn.org.au) to learn about choking management and other first-aid measures before an incident arises so you know how to manage it in a crisis, and have an emergency plan should things ever go astray.

Q How will I know if he doesn't like a particular food when he protests about most foods?

A I usually suggest, initially, that you stick with the simple recipes listed above. Once your baby is eating well, then start to add variations to his diet. Always pre-warn your little one about any new tastes, and wipe some of the food on his bottom lip so he can get the taste first before you slowly offer more and more on each spoonful. If at that point when he is eating well you see him shudder, gag or physically react to the food, then you can be sure it may be a taste that you need to hold off on for a little while longer. Keep it simple. Variety is not always the spice of life for babies when it comes to anything, including food. Keep it predictable and you will have success. A word of warning however: do not mark his slate (see page 85) and tell him he doesn't like that flavour. Try to use more positive language and say 'Good trying new taste, let's have some water and get you [state alternative]'.

Q How will I know that they are ready for me to stop spoon-feeding them?

A When they can spoon-feed themselves efficiently and mostly complete a meal, or when they are able to eat quantities of food that sustain them to the next appropriate meal-time window without the need for snacks, and no longer have tantrums or wakeful nights.

Q How long is too long for a feed?

A By six months of age, once you are on a balanced feeding plan, most feeds should be a maximum of ten to 20 minutes. This feeding time only becomes more and more efficient between now and 12 months of age where a regular feed will be between five to 15 minutes long. This applies to both milk and solid feeds.

Q When are they ready to go on to a sippy cup?

A A sippy cup can be introduced from six months of age and it is a great way to give your child water. But, while I find that the spill-proof cups are good once a child has established the ability to drink from a cup, a child who does not realise there is water in it will often chew the cup, unaware of the need to suck. This can dramatically delay the process of them learning to use it, and can be confusing for a child. Therefore, I recommend that a child is offered a sippy cup with the spill-proof mechanism removed, or a non-spill-proof cup while they are learning. Once they understand that those cups are for water, they will be more likely to suck to get it out.

   If you plan on offering milk in a cup, please do not offer it in the same cup that you offer water in. This can trigger the same loss of trust in using a cup as not informing them of texture, taste or temperature changes with solids. Be respectful and always inform your little one if they can expect to taste milk or water from their cup. It is always useful to have two very different cups. One for milk, and one for water so your child can anticipate the taste change without always needing you to tell them.

Q How can I wean them off a bottle on to a cup?

A This is never as difficult as everyone thinks. I wean them from the bottle to a cup following a few simple steps. Firstly, always introduce a spout cup and establish good drinking first. Then I make sure I have a separate milk cup, and water cup. Never offer milk in a cup, or water in a cup, or juice in a cup without first warning your child or they may stop trusting the cup and refuse it altogether. It's important that when you want to wean them off the bottle and on to a cup that you first establish a balanced meal-time plan with your little one to stop them needing to ask for food 'after' they get hungry. By following a balanced meal plan you will then be able to govern when they feed, taking away the element of them asking for a bottle. If they are not asking for the bottle because they have become so hungry, then it is a much easier task for both you (to offer) and your baby (to accept).

   Over a period of time I usually try to start with the mid-afternoon feed. By eight to ten months you can literally replace the milk in a bottle feed, with milk in a cup feed during afternoon tea. They may not drink exactly the same amount, and may require a little more encouragement to drink their milk before you offer them their solid but they will soon get the hang of this. Then you can start to offer the milk in a cup for the final evening feed. This is ideally not until the twelfth to fifteenth month as a regular thing, but if work or lifestyle commitments deem it necessary then it is okay to start it sooner.

   Be careful to watch your motivation for changing from a bottle to a cup. If they are drinking well from their bottle and there is no real lifestyle need to transition from a bottle to a cup they should be allowed to keep their bottle for as long as they need in these first two years. There does seem to be a real aversion to bottle feeding in this country, but while I do suggest a child is breastfed, I have had enough experience to know that for a thousands reasons that is not always possible and a bottle can be a wonderful substitute for a breastfeed both position wise and comfort wise. Therefore, please be sure to not be trying to get rid of their bottle based on an ideology, or because you feel others are judging you as so many have tearfully shared with me. No one will ever know what your journey has been like. Trust in yourself, and your heart, knowing you love your baby and you have made the right choices for them based on *your* circumstances, and allow your own judgement to define you, and nothing or no one else. I usually say that the first and last feed of the day can remain in a bottle (if they are not breastfed) up until the age of two years, but by 15 months onwards, you can and should transition any other milk feed to a cup.

Q If my child has food allergies does this impact on their ability to eat?

A In short, no. If you eliminate the foods that your child has an intolerance to, then you are fine to follow through on your meal-time repair. If their food is not causing them discomfort anymore, then feeding difficulties can be re-established even after there has been a loss of trust in food. As most of what I suggest a child under two eats grows naturally, such as fruit, vegetables, rice and meat, you will find that this program will support their ability to eat, rather than complicate it.

Q My child eats better off our plates than their own. How can I encourage them to eat their own food?

A Let's face it, eating is most definitely a social event, and sharing food is a very natural and instinctive action. Role modelling good eating is a positive aspect in sharing meal times, and as children love to do whatever their mum and dad do (think car keys, remote control, mobile phone, hand bag, shoes, light switches—need I go on?) it is no surprise that a child wants to eat off that big plate just like you. In my mind this should be encouraged, but this should be a part of a balanced system of eating. As soon as the communication balance of healthy eating is shifted too far in one direction or the other, we start to experience some difficulties. Always try to remember that meal times and eating are an area of health and safety, therefore needing to be governed by an adult. If the governing line around meal times is entirely relinquished to a child they will start to refuse a balanced diet and only eat their favourite foods and then the ability to ask your baby to eat quickly diminishes. If this pattern of only eating off your plate has resulted in your child beginning to eat poorly, then it is time to make a change. I always say that if things have got out of hand, and not getting to eat exclusively off your plate results in huge tantrums and very low food consumption, then you will need to eliminate that element from the meal time altogether.

To do this try to spend a week eating at separate times. You need to be able to say 'no' to eating off your food plate if they have refused their food and subsequently feel hungry when you eat. It is okay to offer them food on a big plate, but be sure to set boundaries about the plate needing to be on their high chair tray, and only mummy, daddy or carer is to pick the plate up. If you do offer them a big plate, you are not to eat off that plate, and you need to be honest about the fact that this is their plate, and about your request for them to eat off their own plate. Don't just trick them into thinking they are eating off your plate and think this is success. You will make no progress if you simply offer them a plate of food that looks like your normal plate of food, and then eat off it yourself like normal. That is not a request to eat their own food. In fact, this to them is the same as always. You may as well keep allowing them to feed off your plate if this is your proposed strategy.

Don't be afraid to establish clear cues like 'no, bubba, mummy's food' and then define what that means 'Oscar needs to eat his food. Here is Oscar's food.' Maintain these new meal-time rules until your little one is able to eat off their own plate, and is able to accept the request to not eat off your plate. Be careful at this point. You can teach your child to continue crying by teaching them that if they cry extra loud, or for an extra long period of time, that then they can eat off your plate. This means your baby will think that you have said, 'If you really want to eat food off my plate you will need to cry extra loud for a really long period of time'. Once you have said 'No, bubba, mummy's food. Oscar needs to eat his food' do not change the defined meaning of that request (see page 44).

Once this has been established, you can then start to reintroduce sharing into meal time but, this time, you need to govern the sharing opportunities to make sure the balance to sometimes share, but always eat predominantly off our own plates, remains. This means you make a clear parent-guided statement like 'Here you are, Oscar, mummy is sharing her chicken, ta for Oscar'. If your baby were to then push away his plate and start demanding your food again, then you need to again say 'No, bubba, mummy's food, Oscar needs to eat his food' and define what that means. The whole purpose of eliminating all sharing for a week was to give your little one time to get used to the conditions and expectations around this statement so don't go and confuse them now by changing its meaning. See it through and see if you can re-establish their eating off their own plate. If they cannot, then your child in not ready to share food for a little while yet, and both you and your child need to spend a few more weeks on your communication before you try again.

Q How can I encourage them to eat fruit and vegetables on their own?

A All aspects of encouraging appetite are important: managing behaviour, providing the right textured foods, and being sure to respectfully warn them of changes to those tastes, temperatures and textures. While addressing your response to your child, balancing food and fluid intake, and making sure the environment is comfortable, it's also so important that you start to submerge yourself in the *concept* of food for a few weeks. Looking at, touching, smelling, thinking about and talking about the foods you wish to encourage are all good ways to entice a child to start to feel familiar and ultimately comfortable with something new. A study from a leading university suggested that a child would need to be exposed to a new food between seven and ten times before their bodies had assessed it to be safe for consumption.

With this in mind, it would be a helpful strategy to expose our little ones to these foods they are finding challenging many times prior to meal time. This can be done via very indirect methods like getting a food brochure and looking through it together like a book. This brochure can then be a tool of cross-reference and distraction for a parent when they are sitting and feeding their child. Doing 'cut out and stick on' activities with a toddler is a lovely way to enjoy these foods together without the stress of meal time. It also ensures that a good positive association is build around those foods and helps a child familiarise themselves with the food and see a parent's positive attitude towards that object.

Remember that a child tends to want to do whatever their parent does. Think about the things they are most attracted to like the keys, the remote, the mobile phone, the pots and pans, shoes, handbags, computer keyboards and, as you will have no doubt realised, the list goes on. Logic then tells us that if a parent spends a lot of time eating and dealing with fruit and vegetables personally, it is only natural for a child to follow suit. Always have bites of their fruit and vegetables, or spoonfuls of their mashed vegetables and be really positive about them. Please be careful to not make it an obvious 'look at me, yummy, now you eat' experience. I want you to genuinely want that food, and to genuinely enjoy it, and to not always do it in an effort to get them to eat. It's often the quiet observing moments a child participates in that establish new taught patterns.

Always bear in mind that they will mirror your behaviours so the constant action of offering them the food will usually yield the same results in return. This is when we see a child always offer you food and insist you eat it, rather than having a desire to consume it themselves. Obviously we need to offer them food, but just make sure that you also show a healthy example of eating yourself, without there always being an ulterior motive. Often a child will show an interest in eating whatever you are eating naturally, so this is a great, non-confrontational way to encourage them to eat healthy foods.

Often, while you are preparing food, chubby little fingers will make their way into the raw fruit or vegetables. This simple action of just touching food, and feeling their textures is a positive move in the right direction. You can casually snack on these foods yourself, and if you know your child enjoys certain dips (cream cheese, hummus, tzatziki) then provide these and allow them to lick or suck those dips off the vegetables. Eventually, encourage them to 'bite' and show them what 'bite' means by biting some off yourself. Show your child the bitten off piece in your mouth, and sound like it is really tasty. Show your child how you chew, and swallow, and then 'all gone'. Cheer. Be excited about this process and repeat it.

Take it slow. They might only touch the raw or steamed foods at first, then they might suck or lick it, then they might bite it and spit it out, then they might bite and chew and spit it out, then in time, they will swallow it. Encouraging the ability to feed themselves fruit and vegetables is important but does not stop the process of working through them learning how to be spoon-fed.

If all else fails, and your child eating fruit or vegetables independently becomes a challenge, the important thing to remember is to make sure they are still being offered the food and consuming it daily, even if it is against their better knowledge. While this is not always ideal, it is still more important to get them eating these nutrients in their rawest form. Finally, as I have highlighted many times before through this book, the use of role play cannot be under estimated. Grab your role-play teddy and sit him in the high chair, and put a bib on him, and spoon-feed him. Share this food with him and with you partner, and anyone else willing to try some of teddy's food. Work through some of the anticipated behaviours your child may use when feeding with teddy first. For example, teddy keeps putting his paws over his mouth, then we use out new cues 'hands down' while we correct his position. Lots of praising for teddy is really exciting, and demonstrates achievable expectations for them to attempt during meal time.

Q My baby really dislikes meat, so how can I get protein into them?

A Please see recipes above. If well pureed, the meat is almost undetectable. You can also add these purees to pasta dishes such as ravioli. It's important to encourage iron intake from a meat source as no other food even comes close. You will need to offer this until they start to eat protein. To get them to begin eating it independently, try to start by offering finger-food options of chicken off the bone that has been slow roasted or barbequed. The 'brown meat' or thigh and leg meat appears to be more enjoyable for a fussy baby. Role model positive eating with and for them. If you are not introducing meat for cultural or family-value reasons then you will likely need to maintain the dream feed (wake and feed them milk at 10 p.m.) until they are 12 to 18 months of age. Supplement their diet with natural alternatives for iron and consider a multi-vitamin if they appear tired, lethargic, get dark circles under their eyes or struggle to maintain sleep at night.

Q My child chews up food then spits it out again. Is this normal?

A Yes, it's quite normal. If they spit it out, look at it then pop it back in to complete the meal, that is fine and normal. That said, try to discourage forms of this behaviour that occur with every meal mouthful where they do not put the food back in. You do this by setting a boundary around no fingers in their mouth. Might be tricky for a couple of days, but well worth your effort and theirs. I usually grate harder foods like apple and offer the food in smaller portions to encourage swallowing. Do not place too much food on their tray and always encourage swallowing before more is offered. I always cut meat into very tiny pieces and make sure it is never overcooked. If your child spits and blows raspberries right through the meal, please see page 255 for more strategies on coping with this pattern of behaviour.

Q My baby is starting to poo more often through the day. Is this normal?

A Totally normal. They may open their bowels often when there are meal-time changes or daily schedule changes. It usually settles down after five days. Keep their bottom clean, provide a treatment cream first (such as pawpaw ointment or Bepanthen) and then smooth on a layer of protective barrier cream (such as zinc and caster oil). When you start your little one on a meal-time plan, or they suddenly start to eat solids or greater quantities of food, it is extremely normal for a baby's body to increase the frequency of bowel movements for a period of time until the body adjusts to this sudden influx of food. This frequency can be mild, one to two bowel movements a day, to extreme with a bowel movement for each meal time. One thing that is certain is that this does always settle down. The biggest concern with this sudden change in bowel movements, however, is the risk of nappy rash, and if you are in the middle of a sleep repair program it is absolutely vital that you avoid that from occurring as much as possible.

To do this I usually get pretty liberal with the barrier cream. I use a treatment cream (like pawpaw ointment or Bepanthen) over the entire bottom, including in the bottom crease and around the anus then smother them in a thin coating of barrier cream (like sudocream or zinc and caster oil). This makes sure that at no point is the skin at risk of getting burnt or inflamed. It's also important to note that you must clean their bottom thoroughly. I know this sounds obvious but during sleep training when their little body is going through so many changes even the slightest trace of poo left anywhere on their bottom can trigger a chain reaction that is very painful and subsequently disruptive to the sleeping and eating process.

If the poo appears or smells particularly acidic, try to watch their diet and try to eliminate the more acidic foods until things settle down. Keep them well hydrated.

12
The basic elements of meal-time repair

Throughout this book, the one thing I have been insistent about is communication. My program is language based. I believe this is respectful and is easy for a child to understand so long as your cues are consistent and, therefore, predictable. To put in place strategies to repair meal-time fussiness and / or behavioural problems that contribute to poor eating and, consequently, sleeping, you need to look at what is actually the cause of the issue and then respectfully put in place consistent language cues and your physical intervention to correct the problem.

A typical example of fussy feeding promoting poor sleeping and eating arose when I stayed in a house recently where the little baby was becoming a real fusspot on the breast. At the delicious age of just four months she liked to have a ten-minute feed, a 30-minute break, then maybe the 'rest' of her feed, which she would sometimes take when it was offered, or sometimes fuss and complain and sit up on her mum's lap to watch the world go by before eventually lying down for the final part of her feed, almost an hour after the feed had begun. Her mother reasoned 'but she is usually such a good feeder, this only started four weeks ago'. Well, when your baby is only 16 weeks, there is no such thing as 'usually'.

This fussy, new feeding routine baby Ally had developed meant she was starting to get tired soon after her feed ended because the feed had essentially taken over an hour, and she was invariably waking a lot sooner after going to bed because she hadn't had a really good solid feed to encourage a good solid sleep, more a series of little snacks encouraging a nap before invariably being hungry for another snack. So we set about putting a time limit on her feeds. Thirty minutes from start to finish was the new agenda. We didn't mind if she took her first ten minutes then needed a little break, but if she then refused the breast the next time it was offered the feed was considered officially over until her next feed was due.

Within 12 hours her feeding was re-established to a good solid feed from both sides that lasted the full 15 to 20 minutes with no need for breaks, and then good solid sleeps to her next feed as her big feed was tiding her over for much longer between feeds. While this approach is not for everybody, it certainly is for babies who have become super-fussy feeders, and as a consequence have begun catnapping. Demand feeding is not for every baby either. Remember that this book is about striking a balance. There is no one strategy that is perfect for every child in a uniform sense (no matter how much some people wish to insist on this). Look to your child for what effect your feeding techniques are having. If things are not running smoothly, then it is time to try something new. If they are sleeping well on fussy drawn-out feeds, and you are all happy with the way it's going, then don't try to fix what you don't think is broken.

> If things are not running smoothly, then it is time to try something new.

Managing a very hungry baby

If your little one appears to be feeling overwhelmed by their sensation of hunger, often indicated by strong crying or tired signs, then remain calm and get the food into them as quickly as possible. Even if they are crying and appear to be refusing food, the only way to help them settle is to increase their blood-sugar level quickly. So persist with the meal, even through the first couple of minutes when they are upset, by feeding them quickly. They are obviously unsure of why they feel this way and only your gentle reassurance, calmness and persistence will see them settle within ten minutes as the food starts to be absorbed. This is how you become a trustworthy and dependable guide, because you are able to lead them to a positive outcome, even when they do now know the way.

Watching the change come over your baby as the food converts to energy is one of the most amazing things that the parents I work with experience. They all say 'I would have thought they weren't hungry and given up but he was so hungry'. Once the turnaround happens, complete the spoon-fed portion of the meal quickly then your child can start to finger-feed themselves and will be back to their normal lovable selves.

Tired? Or hungry?

Tired signs and hunger signs do look almost identical. Your child will become fractious, jerky in their movements, rub their eyes, and get pink eyebrows, nose and pink-rimmed eyes. A toddler may become very upset 15 minutes before dinner time, and getting food into their little tummy is the only thing that will help the tears and tantrums pass, usually within five minutes of starting to eat. If they are very upset, explain to them that they are okay, remind them that they are very hungry and that when they have some food in their tummy they will feel better. As mentioned, it should only take about five to ten minutes for the effects of the food to start to work and everything will settle down quite quickly.

Watching the change come over your baby as the food converts to energy is one of the most amazing things that the parents I work with experience.

It's important you get the food into them promptly. Often people will not persist with the meal because their child is crying and will opt to either put them to bed or end the meal. But, be warned. This will either result in a grizzly baby for the better part of the morning or afternoon after this event, or promote frenetic behaviour. Get some food into their tummy and they will suddenly settle right down for you. Once they start to feel better let them know that the food helped them feel better, and praise them for letting mummy / daddy help them eat.

If you identify this pattern of excessive hunger right before or on meal time in your little one, it is a good sign that the previous afternoon- or morning-tea snack was not adequate enough and you will need to increase it the following day to avoid this same over-hungry pattern from occurring again. I also often suggest a ten- to 20-minute quiet time in the lead up to lunch and dinner so your child can settle calmly into the meal time rather than try to play or remain active as their body runs low on fuel.

Settling in to their high chair

If your little one is likely to become upset when put into their high chair (which is more common over eight months of age but can happen sooner) then it's a nice idea for them to have a little ten-minute quiet sit and play in their high chair after you have popped them in, before you start their meal time. This will help them settle down before they start to eat and should be used as a tool in the lead up to their two major solid meals of the day at lunch and dinner. Make sure everything is ready and on the table next to their high chair so you do not have to get up or move away from your little one, once you have started the feed, as this can often trigger tears and stress. It's obviously important that you plan ahead as asking them to play for ten minutes when they are already hungry is not appropriate. The idea is that you have established a healthy meal plan and can predict when they will be hungry, and can place them into their chair ten minutes prior to this anticipated hunger window.

You should always sit in a chair that has you on a similar eye level to them so you have good eye contact and can chat to them and make the meal time a social and positive experience. Sitting on a stool and towering over your baby is not appropriate when helping a little one learn how to eat.

Your child's concentration span for eating

Brace yourself, folks, this is one of the biggest shocks most people get: up until the age of two years, a baby's concentration span for eating lasts between three and eight minutes. You will see them predictably lose interest in the meal, and you will often need to call on your bag of tricks (see page 369) to string them out a little longer while you finish feeding the spoon-fed portion to them. The more efficient your feeding style, the better they will eat.

Forewarning about texture, taste and temperature change

When regaining a child's trust around being fed, it is so important that you are considerate when it comes to changing textures, taste and temperature. This is done quite simply. First of all, always tell an under-two year old what they are going to have for dinner before you plan on serving it. Why? Well, think about this. Imagine you want some grilled chicken and a jacket potato and some steamed vegetables for dinner. You get home, your body is hungry, you've been salivating on the idea of this meal, but when you get home someone serves you a green leafy salad. How would this make you feel? You can bet your life you would be looking at the fridge or cupboard wondering what else is in there. I see children do the same thing. They get hungry, their mum or dad say 'Nearly home, mate, and you can have some dinner', and the baby is excited at the concept yet when they sit down and get offered the food they look horrified, push it away, burst into tears and point to the kitchen.

To avoid this trigger for meal-time tears, please be sure to keep your baby informed about what you plan on making them for dinner. Be careful though to not get into heavy or heated negotiations with a fussy eater. If you are now governing food in order to correct poor eating patterns, that means you are deciding, based on your wisdom, what is healthy for them to eat, and you are respectfully informing them before you serve this meal, so there is no misunderstanding about what is for dinner.

Secondly, you should adopt a routine style of language around what they eat to keep it simple when you first start feeding them at six months of age. This would be 'cereal and fruit', 'vegies' or 'dessert'. Other key phrases would be 'cold', 'hot', 'smooth' or 'lumpy'.

Thirdly, show them what they are going to be eating before you sit them down. Always be enthusiastic about the meal, regardless of their reaction. Once they are sitting and comfortable. Dip the spoon on to the food and say 'New taste: vegetables and chicken, nice and warm' then wipe a little of the food on their bottom lip with the spoon. This will give them a chance to taste the food, and feel its temperature and texture before you place a small portion in their mouth with the spoon. Only once they have established all of the above would you then progress with the normal pace of meal time. Every time you plan on changing the texture, taste and temperature it is important to repeat the above process. Dip the spoon on to the food and say 'New taste: yoghurt, nice and cold, brrrrr', then wipe the spoon on their bottom lip.

> When regaining a child's trust around being fed, it is so important that you are considerate when it comes to changing textures, taste and temperature.

What to offer first

Watch the order of things with a toddler. If you present a meal to a toddler where they have sausages or chicken or something that requires a fair bit of chewing to get through, and you know that they are likely to opt for that before their vegetables, then only provide a small amount of the chewy item and ensure they have some of their vegetables in that first ten minutes before you offer any more meat or sausages. You have a very brief window of opportunity to feed your under-two year old and it is actually not in their best interests to only eat a sausage at a meal. You should always be looking for balance so be sure your little one is having vegetables as well as meat at each meal time.

Meal-time mess and flow

On the first meal you do with your new meal-time management in place, you may well be neatly spray-painted from head to toe with pureed vegetables, and your baby's beautiful face and once fluffy hair may well be caked in their lunch *and* you will remain positive about the process. When they have finished that meal you will show them the bowl and say 'All gone, bubby, good eating. Mummy get you some dessert / face washer to wipe your face.' It is during this messy process that most parents give up feeding their child, but if you remain positive and encouraging and follow the basic meal-time rules of 'hands down', and 'out of mouth', and 'sitting forward', etc., then you will quickly find they will start to accept the food, and the face painting and pumpkin hair will become a distant memory.

Distraction during meal times

All children adore singing and really respond well to active communication when they have a little task to do, like finding the dog, 'Where's that puppy dog of ours gone? Blicky, come and say hello to Sammy while she has her dinner.' For toddlers, sharing a meal with their favourite teddy, or showing their pet cat or dog how good they are at eating, is often a non-confrontational way of encouraging good eating. It is distracting, and while you are busy saying 'Look, Blicky, look at Brooke eat her vegetables, isn't she a great eater', before clapping and cheering, usually accompanied by your little one proudly joining in and looking around to see if teddy or puppy is as proud as you both are, they have finished their meal and haven't focused on anything but wanting to eat, rather that trying to avoid it.

Encouraging balanced eating

It is common knowledge amongst all those who work with little ones that the first spoonful is often the most difficult. Don't assume they don't want it. It is just a little warm-up process they go through, and I suspect that this occurs because of the lack of forewarning on taste, texture and temperature. If you make sure you always inform them respectfully as highlighted above, this first spoon battle will not last terribly long in your house.

Please remember that if your child has never been able to accept spoon-feeding, and is not eating adequate quantities, or has a severe aversion to food or your guidance at meal time, you should go right back to a very smooth puree for their meals and spoon-feed it to them. Not every baby is able to cope with lumps, and certainly not by a certain age. I know that there is a general school of thinking that recommends babies start eating lumpy food by a certain age, and I agree this is achievable in *most* cases, but when you come across a little one who, for sensory reasons, finds lumps in puree or mash absolutely vile, then it is okay for those little ones to eat purees. You only transition to more solid foods with finger foods. It's okay if some little people, who think lumpy puree is revolting, remain being spoon-fed their purees for a little longer while they establish good self-help skills around finger-feeding themselves, and just skip straight to solid finger foods when they are ready, bypassing the lumpy food they so passionately dislike.

Truth be known, some babies simply cannot tolerate the texture of lumpy mash, and there is actually nothing remotely surprising about this simple fact. It's not humanly possible that every single child could possibly like the same texture of food, just as all adults don't all enjoy the same textures of food. Therefore I believe it is far more important to look at your little one to determine what suits them best as individuals. Some babies do the 'text book' recommended thing and progress happily from puree, to fork mashed to finger foods without so much as batting an eyelid. Some babies take a little more time to get used to puree and find the concept of fork mash a slightly challenging one to get used to. Eventually, these babies will start to eat a more vigorously mashed version and eventually eat their finger foods better than their fork mash. Some babies will take time to settle into puree but gag, retch or vomit at even the slightest concept of lumps in their food. These babies never get used to lumps in their food and will move directly from puree only to puree and finger foods. These little ones tend to need to be spoon-fed their puree for a while longer until they are effective at eating their solid finger foods, at which point they start to eat finger foods having skipped the lumpy food process.

> It's not humanly possible that every single child could possibly like the same texture of food, just as all adults don't all enjoy the same textures of food.

None of these feeders is better or worse than the other, or should be defined as a 'good' or 'bad' eater based on this; they are just unique with individual likes and dislikes. At no point should there ever be a 'blanket' strategy for children under two years of age when it comes to feeding because it is not balanced and certainly does not take individual needs into consideration.

Pacing the meal well

When repairing stressful meal times with your little one it is so important to note that the pace of the meal must be increased to a fast progressing feed where the bulk of the meal is finished within three to five minutes. This is for a number of reasons. The first important reason is to ensure meals are achievable and over quickly for a child. The second is to align with their usual feeding patterns of suck–swallow, suck–swallow, and an immediate reward to the introduction of solids so they do not get frustrated. The third is to ensure that a hungry baby or toddler uncomfortable with the sensation of hunger can have their appetite satisfied quickly, thus preventing the child from associating the sensation of being extremely hungry with the scenario of being fed.

By making meal times fast paced you ensure your child learns that food solves the feeling of hunger and stress, not causes it. This literally translates to a process of fill the spoon, in their mouth, then immediately fill the spoon and bring it back to their mouth and tap their lip, and then spoon straight in their mouth, and repeat until the meal is over. When people watch me being able to feed their baby for the first time, they are staggered at my pace. This pace does slow down, but not until the meal times have been repaired and your child is enjoying their meal times.

Re-establishing feeding after a drink of water

This is actually a slightly tricky aspect of meal-time management with many babies. It is often a very misunderstood aspect of meal-time difficulties, however. If your little one absolutely needs to have a sip of water during a meal, I almost always find it difficult to re-establish the meal. It is a fact that some babies and toddlers, particularly the fussy kind, may stop eating and choose to end a meal with any mild indication of a transition. Each time this occurs you will need to re-establish the meal understanding that 'the first spoon' is always the hardest, and that you need to re-establish the taste, texture and temperature again all while watching your pattern of response to their behaviour around being offered the spoon.

Encouraging an appetite

When you need to repair meal-time difficulties, it is so vital for you to have first established a balance in their days' and nights' food and milk intake. This ensures an appetite that will help a child feed well. So often I have people say to me 'I was going to wait for them to start eating better during the day before I tried to drop the night feeds' but it is important to understand that the excessive night feeds are preventing the child from eating their solids through the day in the first place. This will become a vicious cycle. A child has an increased calorie intake through the night, usually through excessive milk feeds, and is therefore unable to eat effectively through the day. In order for them to need to eat more effectively through the day, you need to actively eliminate some of the night feeds in order to build their need for solids through the day.

Please bear in mind that it is normal for a newborn infant to need feeds every two to three hours, but as they grow and their capacity to consume higher volumes of milk increases, their need for feeding that regularly 'should' naturally decrease (unless milk feeding has become an association to go to sleep or you are on a snack cycle of demand feeding). By around six to seven months of age, with the introduction of solids, a baby's need for night feeds should diminish naturally. A baby should only develop a need for around two night feeds 'again' if solids have not been introduced by six to seven months, or one milk feed a night if solids have been introduced but no meat has been introduced, or no milk feeds through the nights if solids and meat have been introduced.

This need for night feeds is based on nutritional input only, and is not designed to be a guide regarding a settling or resettling association (see page 10). In these low, daytime, nutritional input cases this is corrected based on two key triggers of poor appetite:

- excessive calorie intake through the night disrupting daytime appetite—if your baby (six to 24 months of age) is needing excessive milk feeds through the night, defined by the need of more than one or two night feeds between the hours of 7 p.m. and 7 a.m., then you need to promote a better daytime appetite
- excessive snacking (on snack foods or excessive milk feeds) through the day disrupting the more highly nutritious meals and / or including excessive night feeding.

The above is repaired by stopping all night feeds from 2 a.m. onwards on the day you plan on starting your positive eating plan until 6.30 or 7 a.m. in the morning. Then you need to commence one of the balanced meal-time plans highlighted below. This can be done either within a full recovery routine (see page 541), or via a meal-time recovery routine listed below:

Low sleep requirement

6.30–7 a.m.   Milk feed (breast or bottle). This feed continues for your child from the age of six months until you can see it impacting on their ability to eat breakfast. This usually occurs between 18 and 24 months of age. At that point onwards, no milk is offered until after breakfast is eaten, at which point you can chose to offer milk in a cup, or not.

7.20   Breakfast. Cereal and fruit. By eight months toast can be offered. As your child gets older, variations such as eggs can be offered.

9.30   Milk feed (breast or bottle). This is a brief feed of ten to 20 minutes. It continues for your child from the age of six months through to around nine to ten months. By eight and a half to nine months, a morning tea is usually incorporated. Once your little one gets to nine months, you can offer the fruit first, then their milk. Within a short period of time, this milk feed will no longer be desired and you can drop it, naturally dropping their milk feeds down to three feeds by ten months of age.

11.20   Lunch feed (vegetables and protein) plus a dessert by eight to nine months. This solid lunch feed starts with a poor sleeper no later than six months of age, and within a two-week interval it's important to have introduced meat into that meal. Dessert does not come into the mix until around eight months of age, and no milk should be incorporated with this feed.

2.30 p.m.   Milk feed (breast or bottle). This milk feed lasts until around the age of 12 to 15 months of age and eventually turns into afternoon tea. At around eight to nine months of age you will need to incorporate a snack here as well as their milk. A Cruskit with avocado, or some toast with ricotta, and some yoghurt or cheese, etc., is an ideal snack. By 12 months you will need to offer the solids first, then finish with the milk feed. By around 12 to 15 months your child will not be terribly interested in taking the milk and this is the final transition into two milk feeds a day and solid foods as a primary source of nutrition. When you are ready, this milk is fine to be in a cup from 12 months of age onwards. This is a matter of personal choice, and necessity, particularly if a mother is going back to work, etc.

5:20   Dinner time (vegetable and carbohydrate). Many people think that this feed needs to be the biggest and best to get them to sleep through the night, but it's important that you understand that that is an old wives' tale. Sure, they need to have a good dinner, and it will help them to not wake early due to hunger *but* it is in a child's overall food, fluid and nourishment intake collectively through the day that contributes to a good night's sleep, rather than just the final meal of the day. This meal should be easier to digest, so I usually always suggest that the meat is offered at lunch time. A vegetable and pasta or rice dish, a good minestrone soup, a risotto dish, etc., are all good options for this time of the day. Some children ask for meat at this meal too, which is okay from time to time. Offering protein at this final meal as well as lunch is important for a child who is over ten months of age and has not been eating solids at all at this stage. This will be a part of your sleep repair program. This will ensure we can quickly build their iron stores before expecting them to sleep through the night. The need to offer two protein meals a day will diminish after around two weeks, and when you have seen good solid night sleeps with no wakings in the 'hunger windows' through the night (see page 253). There is no need for dessert at this meal. We do not want to offer excessive fuel to burn only a short time before bedtime.

6.30   Milk feed (breast or bottle). This milk feed is a lovely snuggly one and can be maintained as long as you like. This will not impact on a child's balanced food and solid intake, and is something that comes down to personal choice and family dynamics when it comes time to drop it or make this a milk feed in a cup. In my view, you can keep this feed for as long as you and your little one choose.

10.30   Dream feed for six month olds only, and only when a child is not on solids or has not been introduced to a source of iron from meat in their diet. The dream feed is to ensure that your baby is not waking though genuine hunger through the night. The reason I believe it is important to offer this as a dream feed when looking at sleep repair is to remember that we do not want to confuse our little ones about the conditions of sleep time once they wake through the night. You are better to ensure they are not waking from hunger as a preventative measure by offering this single night feed at this designated time for a period of two weeks while you work through your program. This way, when your baby wakes through the night, you can be sure it is not a genuine hunger-based issue and can therefore stop the guess work which ultimately leads to inconsistency and anxiety. When it comes time to drop that dream feed, you will know because they will sleep solidly from the 7 p.m. settling time, through until the following morning between 6 or 6.30 a.m., apart from the parent-instigated 10.30 p.m. dream feed. This means you can start to wean back that dream feed until it is eliminated. The best way to do this is to simply offer the feed 30 minutes earlier for a period of three nights running. For example, the 10.30 p.m. dream feed becomes a 10.00 p.m. dream feed. Once you see your baby continue to sleep effectively, then you can pull that feed back to a 9.30 p.m. dream feed. You baby may be less interested and only take a brief feed, but continue to sleep effectively for those three days. This is then your final transition and you pull the dream feed back to 9 p.m. Your baby will be predominantly uninterested and you will find that even on a brief snack of the feed, your little one will continue to sleep effectively. At this point, there is no need to dream-feed your baby anymore. Importantly, you cannot dream-feed and demand-feed your baby at once during sleep training. You either do one or the other. The significance of this comes when you look at the messages you deliver. A dream feed is parent-directed and designed to ensure that your baby is not hungry so you can teach them to settle without food as a solution for sleep. Demand feeding teaches a child to wake up and call out for a feed to resettle. As they have no concept of sleep or time lapsing you cannot say to a child that you will feed them at 10 p.m. when they ask, but not at 2 a.m. when they ask. For this dream-feed strategy, you need to ensure that you only offer the dream feed by going in before they wake and offering it without them needing to ask for it and incorporate a full settling, resettling and waking routine plan outside it that does not involve feeding.

High sleep requirement

Because the high-sleep-requirement routine need is varied, based on age, I suggest you move to the routine section of this book (see page 515), and develop your meal-time strategy based on the age appropriate suggestions for your little one. The LSR routine is very specific and easy to use as a single structure because these little ones are quite inflexible, but the HSR routine leaves much more scope for variability because these little ones are quite flexible.

Introducing iron in their food for sleep

The one thing that truly impacts on a baby's or toddler's ability to sleep through the night is almost always a lack of iron in their diet or registered low iron stores or absorption rate. In these cases you are more likely to see a baby or toddler wake between 11.30 p.m. and 1.30 a.m., or occasionally between 2.30 and 3.30 a.m. (based on a baby going to bed at 7 p.m.). Be sure to provide a good source of iron each day in the form of meat, so they can sleep peacefully. While they sleep they grow, so when their need for more fuel is triggered, because their daily intake was inadequate, the body encourages a baby to wake up for a feed. If your child will not eat for you then you will need to do something entirely different to achieve better eating.

When your baby is having trouble sleeping, be sure to introduce a meat at one meal of the day by six and a half to seven months of age. This meat is usually chicken and should be combined with vegetables and blended very well. If they are this young, have not been introduced to a meat yet, and you are planning on repairing their sleep, wait until they have had meat in their diet, as suggested above, for a full seven days prior to commencing your new daily routine and sleep repair program.

By seven to eight months of age, when your little one is on three meals a day, if they are still showing signs of hunger during the night and needing feeds, then for a week one meal in the day should be cereal and fruit, and two meals vegetables and protein in the form of meat. Once you have built up their iron stores, drop them back to a daily intake of one meal being cereal and fruit, one meal vegetables and protein in the form of meat, and one meal pureed vegetables and a carbohydrate like rice. This will seriously improve their chances of sleeping through if the need for feeds during the night is purely hunger based. You must eliminate or significantly reduce their milk feeds at night by the time they are around six months of age (unless otherwise instructed by your doctor) before they will have the appetite to eat their solids during the day.

d55esy

The most important meal for sleep

If you are having any problems with their evening sleep patterns or their behaviour in the late afternoon, then *do not* give them sandwiches for lunch until they are over two years of age and, even then, only if they can eat a good healthy salad and meat sandwich. The biggest meal of the day should be in the middle of the day, not at 5 p.m. This meal should always include a source of iron in the form of meat and a balance of vitamins and minerals. Two slices of bread with a lick of spread on it will provide none of the essentials for sleep under two years of age. This middle-of-the-day meal should also have the only dessert of the day.

Milk, solids and snacks

Solid meals and milk feeds should be separated, apart from breakfast. Low-sleep-requirement babies will need a morning- and afternoon-tea snack at a younger age than a higher sleep-requirement baby. I find by eight to nine months a lower sleep-requirement baby needs a Cruskit with avocado or something similar in the afternoon as well as their milk feed, and by around nine to ten months a light fruit snack is needed as well as their milk feed in the morning. Higher sleep-requirement babies will be burning less fuel during the day as they spend more time sleeping and therefore may not need morning or afternoon tea until they wean off their mid-morning and mid-afternoon milk feeds at around ten to twelve months.

The need to add a solid snack and weaning process is easy to identify: your child is not lasting terribly well to lunch or dinner. If you find they are hungry, grumpy or showing tired signs without the need to sleep well before a meal is due, then it is a clear sign that the milk is no longer sufficient as a mid-meal feed, and they will need something more to help sustain them in the long gaps between breakfast and lunch, and lunch and dinner. The need for solid afternoon tea to be introduced as well as their milk often occurs before the need for a morning tea. This is only a guide and your baby may need slightly more or slightly less than is suggested.

Snacking between meals

Excessive snack cravings for carbohydrates are often a child's way of sustaining themselves after poor sleep, so ensure you have well-spaced and planned meal times. To correct poor sleep cycles, do not provide additional feeds or snacks or you risk perpetuating the cycle of poor sleep. When food is restored to its rightful role of nourishing and strengthening a child rather than keeping them going simply because they are so low on fuel from poor sleep, your child's need for sleep suddenly increases again and we see the balance restored. The daily routines chapter provides more information on appropriate food intake and times (see page 515).

Setting meal-time boundaries

If your child has established a very poor association with feeding and will not even try eating food then you can be sure that, until you actually get them trying food and achieving at meal times, that feeling around meal times is not going to change any time soon. This is where you need to look at the way you are responding to their behavioural patterns; for example, if a baby habitually refuses food every time a parent offers it they will have established a series of behavioural responses to you offering them their food. These patterns would involve things like blowing raspberries, pursing lips, turning head from side to side, loud shouting.

Do not pull your hand away when they blow a raspberry, turn their head, make a crying sound or scream at you or the spoon. This will only encourage this behaviour to continue because you give it a valuable currency (scream / raspberry equals no feeding). It's important to keep the spoon at their mouth, chat to them and try to distract them but teach them that meal time always follows a flow, which is 'scoop it up, in your mouth' and when the meal is finished you say 'All finished, good eating bubba'. If you never make plans to change the current ineffective pattern of 'no spoon in their mouth' to a new and more effective plan of 'putting the spoon into their mouth', then you will never progress past the current ineffective routine of them refusing food.

Remember: you can't keep doing the same thing and expect a different result. It is here that a parent needs to manage their pattern of response to these behaviours. This is where I often see a child learn that:

    to blow a raspberry = spoon is removed
    to turn their head = spoon is removed
    to spit = spoon is withdrawn
    to scream = spoon is withdrawn

How will they ever learn to accept food if this is your communication with them? This is not a meal time governed by your wisdom; it is a meal time based on your baby's misunderstanding of food and what it represents. This parental pattern of response is naturally only going to sustain the child's refusal of food as feeding is never achieved; therefore, the child never gets the opportunity to learn differently about food and meal time.

Because of this, you will need to stop withdrawing the spoon. This will help the behaviour stop happening in the first place. This will assist you with feeding. This means, when your child blows a raspberry, keep the spoon at their mouth. If they turn their head, then keep your left hand gently on their right cheek (which will discourage them turning their face into your hand) and then you can follow their mouth with the spoon on the 90-degree angle. If they protest, pop a mouthful in, and continue to feed them, even if they are in their usual protest mode. Use distractions, offer toys, sings songs, remain happy but whatever you do, respond differently to how you normally respond to their meal-time behaviour once you introduce your new daily routine or meal-time plan.

To correct poor sleep cycles, do not provide additional feeds or snacks or you risk perpetuating the cycle of poor sleep.

Babies should not be able to take the spoon off their parents at nine months of age and in doing so say 'You're not allowed to feed me'. I can assure you that this always leads to meal-time blues, tears and frustration for all in the long term. They can have a spoon of their own by all means but a simple boundary of 'mummy's / daddy's spoon' should be retained, and it is important that theirs or 'baby's spoon' is given to them in a different way when reintroducing that spoon a few weeks into your meal-time repair. This is achieved simply by only ever offering a spoon in an upright position so it is pointing to the roof and the parent saying 'Ta for Simmy!' when they offer it to their child. This will make using a spoon to feed them a clearly different statement and there will be no confusion about when you are offering them a spoon to hold and when you are offering them a mouthful of food.

If your little one has a real issue with the spoon in general, it should be offered as a chewing object at many different times of the day whenever possible—while in the bath, car, during floor play, etc. This helps them get used to the object, and become accustomed to the texture, smell and feel of the product in their mouth so they can develop a new relaxed association with their spoon. Use your flow of communication to prepare them in a happy and enthusiastic tone that the meal time is coming up, and to tell them what they can expect to be eating. This is particularly important from eight months of age and most definitely a pivotal part of re-establishing feeding with the 12 months plus' age group.

Responding to their existing behavioural patterns during meal time

It is quite important that you are aware of a disruptive parenting-response pattern to break yourself when trying to repair poor eating. That parenting-response pattern is the currency or answer you give a certain behaviour from your child. Remember that you cannot keep doing the same thing and expect a different result. This means you need to start to respond differently to your child's behavioural response to being offered the spoon.

While we can't make a child eat, we can manage their behaviour at meal time.

Behaviour / boundary	Language cue	Physical intervention
Allowing mum and dad to wash hands and face	'Hands down, mummy do it.'	Don't allow them to grab the face washer or try to pull it from their face. Block their hands with your forearm. Wipe a cheek at a time, then their chin and nose consecutively.
No throwing food, cutlery, plates, etc.	'No throwing—plate on table'	Take their hands and help them place the plate back on the tray / table then make them let go. Hold the plate in place firmly if they refuse to have it on the tray and repeat your cue gently.
Always put cup down in a no-spill position	'Cup on table'	Use a sticker or drink coaster to show them where to put it. This is obviously more important for the 12 to 24 month old but should be encouraged with younger babies, too.
No fingers in mouth	'Fingers out of mouth'	Take their hands away from their mouth.
No covering mouth with hand	'Hands down'	Take their hands away from their mouth.
No leaning sideways off chair	'Sitting up, please'	Stand behind them when they get heavy, or from the front for younger babies and sit them upright. Tighten buckles if necessary.
No snatching spoon from mummy	'No, ta. Mummy do it.'	Avoid allowing them to get the spoon but, if they do, release their grip from it without giving them the spoon.
No mouthing high chair while being fed	'Sitting up, please'	Stand behind them and sit them upright. Tighten buckles if necessary.
No flapping hands around when being spoon-fed	'Hands down, mummy do it.'	Block their hands with your forearm as you feed them.

Only when your child gets better at allowing you to feed them, can you then introduce a spoon for you and a spoon for them, usually around 15 to 18 months of age if you have had a very stressed feeder. Until then you should be the only one to have a spoon at meal time. This takes the burden off them. If they are eating efficiently, you can start to allow them to feed themselves, but always retain the capacity to offer a spoonful now and then by following through with your management strategies. If their eating becomes poor again and they start to get bossy about you feeding them, you need to take the spoon off them and re-establish parent-feeding to stop the behaviour, and try again later. They will be far more unhappy, long-term day and night, from hunger than they would from not being able to have a spoon for a few more weeks. What you want to achieve is confident parenting, where your child understands that you expect them to eat for you as well as on their own, and if they are fussing or tantruming that you will assume the feeding role, and there is no need to get into a pickle negotiating because mummy / daddy have this one for them.

The reason I am so no-nonsense about this is simply because they can become so unhappy and so unsettled when they do not eat effectively. When you take the fussing part out of meal time they are usually busy playing and eating without the fighting and crying, as well and happy and content through the day, and sleeping better at night. To me, the idea of allowing fussing that is strictly behavioural to continue is not in any way helpful or fair to a child.

With the actual feeding process, there are a few vital things you need to address when they are just starting out with the eating process regardless of their age. Always remember that whether they start eating at six months of age, or 16 months of age, they still need to go through the same learning process. They don't have a concept of consequences, and they don't know their attention span is really short and that to refuse food now will disrupt their sleep or impact on their happiness later, so you are the one who has to speed up the process. You need to ensure that there are no great pauses between mouthfuls, and that will ensure that they don't store it in their cheeks, and that they understand that food keeps coming, so they can get an adequate portion of a nutritious meal into them.

It's important to have a repetitive pattern of feeding. Dip the spoon into their food so there is just a little bit on the spoon and proceed to tell your little one that it's dinner time and they are eating chicken and pumpkin. For the first mouthful, I always then wipe the spoon on their bottom lip and say 'New taste, chicken and pumpkin'. Your little one will lick their lips and this will give them a chance to taste the food they are about to have a fuller mouthful of. For the first few mouthfuls make sure you have just enough on the top of the spoon so they can gradually build up the size of the mouthfuls over the first minute.

Once they have the flavour in their mouth you can increase the quantity of each mouthful. This is the same when you are feeding a six month old as it is when you are preparing to help an 18 month old re-establish their meal time and eating. The most important bit of information I can remind you of right now is that right up until the age of two years, your baby's true attention span for eating will only be three to eight minutes long, right from the moment of their first taste. You should be feeding them consistently without pausing. While they are swallowing that mouthful, you should be preparing the next spoonful, encouraging them about their yummy meal, and remaining emotionally available and engaged with them. As soon as the spoon is filled, you should be tapping their bottom lip once then pulling the spoon back a little preparing them for their next mouthful.

The assisted portion of the meal should be for the first ten minutes of every meal, and then finger foods and self-feeding are appropriate after that point. Do not be distracted for that short window by an older child, the TV, telephone or by having a conversation with someone else. While you are feeding your little one for the first ten minutes of each meal time, stay focused and confident and happy about the meal. You need to make sure there is only enough food on the spoon to cover the base with a slight rise, and it's smoothed off on both sides. You need to make sure they keep their little hands down and away from the spoon and your hand by using the cue 'hands down, mummy do it' and defining that statement by showing them what hands down actually means by lowering their hands with your own. This should be a normal expectation at each meal time.

If you are having trouble with your little one storing food in their cheeks like a chipmunk, put the spoon side on to their lips and tap on their bottom lip to encourage swallowing. If they still won't swallow, a little massage under their chin should move the food and trigger the swallow reflex. Smile like you are tickling them, or like you would if you were squeezing their beautiful cheeks. Between mouthfuls, if they don't realise you need them to open their mouth on the first few days of teaching them effective eating (whether it's establishing feeding or repairing and re-establishing feeding) you need to use the side of the spoon to push down on their bottom gums to break the natural suction of their mouth, then quickly tip the spoon so it is angled slightly downwards (side on) but into their mouth and slide it in, then turn the spoon so it is on the correct forward-facing position quickly, then wipe the food off on their palate as you remove it.

Remove the spoon and prepare the spoon again immediately. Do not perpetually wipe their mouth with the spoon; it can be irritating for them. Only once every few mouthfuls, if it is necessary, should you wipe their mouth with the spoon or a cloth. Repeat process. The time that the spoon is actually in their mouth should be minimal. Please remember that the emphasis of the time with the spoon at their mouth should go into putting a little pressure on their bottom gums, and as soon as you break the natural baby suction of their closed mouth, quickly getting the food in and wiping the food off on to their palate. Remember, it doesn't matter what they do with the food at that point, so long as you maintain your boundaries and keep up the pace of the meal.

Use lots of smiles and chatter and praise while they get used to having things like a spoon or solids put into their mouth, even if they are not sure at all about the process. This may well be the case for a baby when they are first reintroduced to solids again, or for an older child who has never truly learnt how to take solids from a spoon before. Be prepared for the normal pattern of swallowing that occurs with very new eaters when they are introduced to solid food. In the early days you will note that some food comes out of their mouth as some is swallowed. So many parents have said to me, 'Look, they don't like it, they are spitting it out', but I want to reassure anyone who is curious about this pattern that this is perfectly normal. This is to do with the muscles in the tongue that are well developed for suckling milk. When they automatically suckle the food it will automatically roll on their tongue and some will come out of their mouth, and some will go down the back of their throat. These spills do not indicate dislike of food.

> Use lots of smiles and chatter and praise while they get used to having things like a spoon or solids put into their mouth, even if they are not sure at all about the process.

Some babies will enjoy suckling the food off the spoon after they are first introduced to solids which is also an effective feeding strategy. If, however, your little one has been having difficulties, you are best to follow a more confident parent-directed style of feeding to help guide your little one into a more predictable and pleasant meal time of spoonful in their mouth, and swallow.

The role you play in their attitudes towards meal time

The role you play in helping your little one feel positive about meal times is more crucial than you can imagine. I can turn a failure-to-thrive baby around in a matter of hours from a baby who was gagging at the sight of a spoon to loving their meal by dinner time on that first night for under-12 month olds, and in a matter of a couple of days in the 12- to 24-month age group almost solely by using my confident, encouraging and persistent approach to the meal time.

I appreciate that many parents say to me that it's easy to be confident when this is what you do for a career and you know you are good at it, but for them, first-time parents, it is a far more challenging and complicated process. They want to know how long is too long to persist. They are nervous that their child is going to develop poor associations with their meal time, and they doubt that a strategy that starts with a little bit of a battle could ever turn out so positively. I think it is important to highlight the fact that it took practice on my part too to find a way that was well balanced and practical, but it can also be achieved by anyone who is patient enough to work through meal-time dramas to reach a better place.

The main thing I need you to remember is that this entire strategy of learning how to eat from scratch again is designed to be a confident parent-directed and -governed style of communication so all your language needs to be in statements, and not in question format. Once you have mastered the confident, happy, enthusiastic tone around meal time, your child will adopt your same mannerisms. Remember your learning ladder of success if you are feeling uncertain (see page 67).

You must be ultra-cautious that you do not fill their little inner dialogue about meal time with comments like 'Oh, you don't like that', or 'You're not going to eat this for mummy are you', or 'Darling, this isn't going to work, he just won't eat', or 'Mummy's sorry, she is not very good at feeding you', etc. If you tell them these things, they will do and believe everything you say, and this is never more prevalent than when they are 12 months plus. This is not to say you must not be cautious of your language with the under-12-month age group because your expressions and tones say a lot while you talk, but over 12 month olds are particularly sensitive to language, inflection, tone, expression and your overall demeanour. If you approach every meal with a happy tone, positive language statements and an air of confidence, then your little ones will have the same attitude towards meal time in a matter of days.

If you dread meal times, they will become anxious of this time too, and if you get frustrated, angry or impatient they will not understand this and will become stressed at the thought of eating. Even something as simple as a huff, heavy sigh, eye roll, talking under your breath in an exasperated tone or through gritted teeth will frighten them. The key is to stay calm, be confident, have clear expectations of them, and don't teach them to use extreme behaviours to avoid meal times. Sit down with a happy confident disposition with the intention of feeding your baby, and follow through.

Meal time is a lovely time to sing songs, chat about the day's events, or talk about their favourite people or things. It's a great time to share food and your enthusiasm towards food. When you want to repair meal times with toddlers, it's so important to incorporate a healthy attitude to food right throughout the day. Involve them in the grocery shopping, have them hold fruit and veggies for you and don't worry if they lick, smell or try to bite the food. Incorporate pictures of food into their play by cutting pictures out and making a 'contact' collage or by having drawings of food you have sketched up with them at meal time.

> Meal time is a lovely time to sing songs, chat about the day's events, or talk about their favourite people or things.

Provide positive role-play opportunities for them to see you eating so when you make them some steamed vegetables, make sure you have made enough to join them, and make sure they see you 'bite' and 'chew' the food, which means that when they are learning to eat vegetables it is sometimes handy for them to see the food in your mouth as you chew, and see you really enjoying the food. Being enthusiastic is a very important and encouraging way to communicate with your child, and while some parents have said to me that they feel a little bit contrived or false when they are enthusiastic, I can assure you that enthusiasm and praise in the form of clapping and cheering and specific praise are so encouraging for your baby. Sometimes to communicate with a baby (which all children are until the age of two years at least) you almost need to think about the things that appeal to babies. They love to clap, love smiling, love bold vocal sounds and really enjoy one-on-one attention, all of which is achieved in an enthusiastic and honest meal time.

Many parents ask me, 'Do we still praise them even though they haven't actually eaten that much?' My answer is always a resounding 'yes'! They will respond better to encouragement, and to your belief in their ability and to positive input about meal times than they will to anything else. If you feel that they have eaten so poorly that you cannot even draw on a single mouthful of food to be positive about, it is worth acknowledging what they did do: 'Thank you for sitting in your high chair bubba, that was a little bit tricky but thank you for trying'.

Keep your cool

And this is a big one: don't have a tantrum yourself because you are frustrated, feeling like it is not working or because they are having a tantrum when you ask them to eat. Remember, the more unsettled they become, the more calm and soothing you should become. Drop your voice an octave or two, slow your speech right down and sound empathetic and loving but, most of all, confident and reassuring. Asking your child to co-operate with you or to eat their food in a parent-governing line of communication must not be confused with sounding harsh or demanding, *ever*. They will simply not understand a stern or exasperated expression, tone or statement; you will only unsettle or frighten them and you will most certainly achieve nothing taking that approach. Be consistent with your feeding plan, sound confident (even if you have to bluff), and be persistent with the feeding process: spoon in the bowl, scoop up the food, spoon in the mouth.

'Surely something is better than nothing'

While I know that one of the strongest natural instincts in a mother and father is to nourish their beautiful baby, this is often the anxious thinking that leads to a child appearing to want to eat nothing at meal times. Try and imagine what it would be like if you snacked all afternoon, and then tried to sit down to a good healthy meal at dinner time. How enthusiastic would you be when that plate was put in front of you if you weren't really that hungry? How much of that food do you think you might want to eat? How much of that food then could you eat before feeling satisfied?

Then imagine that you have been busy all afternoon, and have not snacked since a light afternoon tea. On the lead up to the meal your tummy starts to grumble and you officially feel hungry. Imagine that you then tried to sit down to a good healthy meal. How enthusiastic would you be when that plate was put in front of you if you were really hungry? How much of that food do you think you might want to eat? How much of that food then could you eat before feeling satisfied?

The same occurs with children who snack. If you do not overfeed them with snacks, they will actually start to eat effectively. A child will not starve themselves, and if you build an appetite in them for a healthy meal time, they will start to eat so much better than you ever imagined. For these reasons 'something is better than nothing' is absolutely a false statement because it's eating something at the wrong time that leads to them eating nothing at the right time.

Don't compensate for poor sleep with excessive food

This is an important topic to discuss. When you are balancing a child's meals to help repair sleep time, it is fairly common for the balanced feeding to promote sleep based on one simple principle: the food your child is consuming is a normal healthy amount required by the body as fuel to grow, heal and develop as well as to be active and energised throughout the day. As that fuel source starts to deplete, a child who resists sleep may appear to want food to correct the way they are feeling. When that food is not offered you will see a natural desire from the body, to sleep more effectively, being restored. This is how we repair sleep in a child who is fighting sleep and demanding food in its place, but your child may go through a day or two of hunger until their sleep is fully repaired.

Do not be tempted to compensate for poor sleep with additional food, or with additional sleep at other times. By doing this we are actually working with a baby's body and its need for sleep more than we are working with a child's temperament and their desire to stay awake. When your child starts to feel true tiredness from their poor sleep because food is not a compensation tool, you may see them appear more tired than you or they have experienced before. At this point, keep them awake until their normal sleep time is due, and let them know what they are feeling: 'It's okay, bubba, you are just tired, you can have a lovely sleep in your bed soon that will make you feel better'.

Equally, when your child becomes hungry because they are now having 'normal' and healthy gaps between meals instead of constantly grazing to keep their appetite subdued constantly, then they may not know that feeling of true hunger and may become very agitated. Again, it's important to tell them what they are feeling: 'It's okay, bubba, you are just hungry, mummy will get your dinner soon'. On those first few days, help them cope in the lead up to meals by keeping them still and distracted. A toddler may enjoy their favourite DVD, for instance, while sitting in their high chair for ten minutes before their meal. Just be careful that they don't fall asleep.

Be cautious of using food as an emotional solution

This is something that I see often. Snacking becomes essential because it becomes one of the 'only' tools for keeping a child quiet or content. Now while I agree that this is an effective tool 'sometimes', like if you are on a plane, or trying to keep a child calm and content in a doctor's surgery or in a restricted location where they cannot move around freely, I do not believe it should become a solution to all situations. That is a very unhealthy and unbalanced approach to emotions and can send a child unhealthy messages about emotions, and their ability to cope and about food.

A child learning how to be patient in their pram, or while you wash the dishes, or how to sit and look to the environment around them for interesting things to see rather than just eating all the time is working towards gaining vital skills. Being bored, or having to 'wait' is a normal everyday occurrence. We wait in the pram, bath, high chair, at traffic lights, for food to cook, for people to arrive, to pay at checkouts, to see doctors, for our turn, or to fall asleep. The list goes on forever. Telling a child that when they are bored at the shops, or sick of waiting that they should eat, or if they have to sit in the car for a time they should eat, or if they are feeling impatient they should eat, is actually setting them up for some significantly poor, emotional-coping mechanisms when they get older.

It's important to remember that your little one is learning about the world around them, themselves and how to deal with a multitude of situations they will experience every day, from you. What are you telling them about simple emotions? Which emotions are you telling them are normal, and don't require breastfeeding, or snacking, or bottles to resolve? And how does this translate into a long-term solution for your child?

What tools are you equipping them with in this first precious five years? Are you arming them with an emotional tool kit that they will be able to take with them everywhere? How have you started to equip your little so they can to cope when you are not there? This is where balance is important. We live in a society where many people struggle to cope with their emotions. We have people needing to numb their feelings through prescription or elicit drugs or alcohol, and we see more and more people developing addictions at a rapid pace. We see high stress rates in our society and we see many people unable to cope with that stress.

> A child learning how to be patient in their pram, or while you wash the dishes, or how to sit and look to the environment around them for interesting things to see rather than just eating all the time is working towards gaining vital skills.

Is it in a child's best interests to tell them that whenever they have a feeling that is even remotely uncomfortable (boredom, frustration, impatience, tiredness, anxiety, etc.) that the best way to cope is to stop it from occurring through snacking? Or should you assess what they are feeling and work on developing a series of healthy solutions? The pram, for instance. A child can learn to find interesting things in the environment to enjoy, can learn that stopping and waiting are normal and safe, and something they can cope with without the need for food or some kind of intervention to resolve that feeling. This way you equip your child with multiple tools for coping in a variety of situations in a more balanced and healthy way.

Repairing significant meal-time blues

I live by a simple principle: you can't keep doing the same thing and expect a different result. If your child already thinks meal times are a complete disaster, and food is the window to stress and anxiety, then sadly they have an incorrect view of food and meal times and you will need to correct that belief. When I enter a home where the baby or toddler and their parents are finding meal times extremely distressing, I cannot wait to show them that it is actually a time of the day that they can look forward to. I am excited to show parents that you can in fact work through and past even the most extreme anxieties around food and eating. More importantly, I am thrilled for the parents who, within two to three days, can sit down and spoon-feed their hungry little baby without a single tear or look of concern from the little one for the first time in their parenting lives. One of the strongest desires I find in parents is the desire to feed and nourish their baby. When they start to be able to feed them peacefully for the first time in their lives most parents can become teary while laughing, or even begin to cry.

The process that you need to go through for a day, or sometimes two or three days, to reach that place of peace at meal time, however, is often really messy and almost always involves a lot of bluffed confidence, persistence, singing, happy chatting and game playing, and distraction from you; at the same time you might encounter a fair bit of crying, resistance, spitting, food in hair and protests. I always take a peep at the parents' faces when I am working through a poor meal-time routine to re-establish a new eating pattern, and they usually always look a little surprised that I am persisting despite the failure to get much food into baby on the first attempt, and a quiet sense of relief that 'even Sheyne is finding it a messy challenge'. I assure them that the only reason I am ultimately successful, however, is because I have a plan, I have a goal and I am patient. It's important that people know that the end result is so wonderful for the child and the family that it makes the challenging part a very worthwhile venture.

When it comes to getting your head in the right space to work past your little one's meal-time stresses, it's important to always assess the environment and meal-time conditions from an adult's perspective. Is there any reason for them to be frightened of meal times, and should food be something that is truly stressful or unpleasant? If the answer is 'no', then they have a misunderstanding about an aspect of their life and it's your role to show them otherwise. If you never attempt to correct it, they will continue to feel that way about food and your house will always have meal-time blues. As their guides in life, you need to work past that association with them and help them move through the stress until they discover that food is actually predictable and enjoyable and something that they can look forward to.

The only time a process like this could be destructive to a child's association with food—in the cases I work with, it is already terribly destructive before we even begin—is to start, reach a peak of resistance, then quit and never see it through to a positive outcome. When you have a child who has previously had a difficult time with something like severe and painful reflux, then it is likely that meal times are associated with pain. While the pain part of the meal time is likely to have subsided by six months of age, the association with pain often remains long after the symptoms have gone. This is when you need to help them eat solidly and consistently while you stay positive and confidently reassuring. That way, they can see that while they feel uncomfortable with the new meal-time plan, their mummy and daddy

One of the strongest desires I find in parents is the desire to feed and nourish their baby.

are okay, which ultimately translates into a simple message that they are okay too. Ultimately, they start to see that meal times do not hurt them, and they can start to eat free of that anxiety, thus restoring pleasant meal times to the family dining room.

When your child does not have a history of pain with eating, however, they may still have developed distrust in their meal time through something as simple as many flavour, texture and temperature changes without warning. There are lots of reasons that meal-time plans can go astray. Often all the standard approaches, like 'let them eat what they want' and 'let them do it themselves', will do nothing other than keep you and your little one in the same place of poor eating and poor associations with eating. Why? Because you are not educating them with your wisdom to move them beyond that old pattern of association. When you need to restore a very disrupted style of feeding you will need to revert to the full spoon-feeding plan (see page 226). This means that meal times go back to being an entirely parent-governed part of the day for three full weeks until everything settles down, and they get familiar, comfortable and ultimately relaxed with and looking forward to meal times again.

Regardless of your little one's age, it's important to go back to their actual eating stage for their ability as opposed to trying to get them to eat like a child their age. This is particularly important for a child who has never really learnt how to eat correctly. This means that if your 16 months old has never learnt how to eat vegetables, that you should go right back to very pureed vegetables with no lumps at all. If they have never learnt how to eat meat or vegetables then you need to go back to basics and start from scratch (see recipes on page 231). It is unfair and unrealistic to expect a six month old to eat lumpy foods because they are only just being exposed to food for the first time, and if your child is still in that situation at 16 months, you need to go back to how you would feed a six month old if the meal disruption is significant enough. Equally, if they can eat solids but not nearly enough, then it's important to go back to pureed food that you feed them to ensure they are eating adequate quantities and then follow it with some finger foods that they feed themselves. Often they then progress very rapidly on to lumpy and then solids foods so do not feel anxious if you need to climb 'The learning ladder of success'.

Like I always say, there is no avoiding things with a child; you are just putting them off—so don't put it off any longer. Teach them how to eat. Equally however, if they can eat solid foods quite well but not nearly enough, then it's important to go back to pureed food that you feed them and then follow it with some finger foods that they feed themselves to ensure the right quantity and balance are provided.

Troubleshooting

Q What if they gag while I am feeding them?

A When you are repairing significant meal-time problems, this is not uncommon unfortunately. Often when I arrive at the house to help a little one who has developed a very poor association with feeding or food, they will cry, cough and gag when their parents so much as show them their spoon or the bowl, or place the bib on them. Often a child who has a real aversion to food has an 'incorrect perception' of what food is actually like, and due to the stress of having that incorrect perception has never had the opportunity to learn that food is actually not a bad or frightening thing and subsequently never had the opportunity to discover that eating is actually quite a pleasant experience. This is what you need your child to experience, so they can relearn what food actually means, rather than grow up with an untrue perception of food.

An example of this 'incorrect perception' of food developing and not being corrected would occur when a child has suffered from reflex or silent reflux and thinks that food equals pain. Once the reflux is corrected however, it is so important to actually expose your child to food again, even if they are fretful at first, so they can move past that fear (which is no longer true) and can start to enjoy food again. To not do this often results in a child remaining stuck in a fear (that is actually a misunderstanding) for many years to come.

Another example may come from a child who has lost trust in the feeding process because it took too long for them to be fed, usually because some parents misunderstand that crying means 'I'm hungry' not 'I don't want to eat' and instead of going faster, they either slow down or stop feeding the child altogether. Slow feeding could also be due to a parent being distracted. Both of these scenarios can result in the perception that food / feeding equals frustration.

Another typical example of loss of trust would be a child who was not warned before the food changed texture, flavour and temperature; like when a parent moves from warm pureed vegetables to cold yoghurt, to room-temperature mashed banana. The best way I can get you to imagine what this might be like for your child is to remember what it was like when you have picked up someone's else's drink by accident and taken a sip expecting it to be something else entirely. Even though the drink you have picked up is usually not repulsive, your body will react to that unexpected taste as though it were. This is what can happen with a child just learning to trust the process of being fed. This process usually results in food equalling something unpredictable and unpleasant.

When this is the case, you will need to only offer enough puree to cover the tip of the spoon and remain reassuring as you move past the old associations that have them stressed at meal time. Do not look or behave concerned, and continue on with the meal as you sing a happy song. Often, the faster you feed, the less the food is manipulated in their mouth, which reduces the incidence of gagging. Keep the pace up to quickly move past the gag reflex and you will see them eating without stress within a day or two. Remember to follow the feeding communication and behavioural-response chart (see page 257), and to be honest about flavour, texture and temperature changes, to encourage better eating.

Q My baby has finished their whole meal in two to three minutes. Is that going to teach them to not enjoy food?

A When you are repairing significant meal-time stress in a little one, the most important things to establish are quick, effective stress-free meal times. This will quickly take the stress out of meal time for your little one and the concept of eating stops being so daunting for them. Once your little one can see that meal times are not drawn-out stressful events then you will be able to slow them down a little and this will teach them to relax and enjoy their food, but that always comes in time. The fast pace is the best and most effective way that we repair the anxiety associated with meal times. As they begin to feel more comfortable with eating you can gradually slow down the pace of the meal, but only based on your child's preference. Do not leave them sitting there with their mouth open like a baby bird without filling it for them if they would like the next mouthful. It's important to remember that from the moment they are born they learn to fill their mouth and swallow, so their desire when they are hungry will always follow that same process when you start to feed your baby. If they are having a difficult time, or if you need to re-establish their meal time, you will need to feed them at a fairly rapid pace initially, until you see them relax about meal times.

Q My baby is biting my nipple while feeding. Is there anything I can do to stop this?

A It is a common problem unfortunately. While a child never does this with malicious intent, the injuries that a mother can suffer can be quite extreme. For this reason the pattern of behaviour does need to be halted quite quickly. Most mothers find that the natural response of a loud sharp 'ouch' is enough to give their little one enough of a fright to discourage the behaviour from happening too often. For others, however, this natural shout of pain does give their little one a fright but can trigger curiosity as well. Not unlike a child who accidentally bumps their head as they walk past a table then goes back and deliberately bumps their head to learn more about the event, a child may want to understand the sequence of events that led to a mother making a loud noise. Occasionally it appears that, when a child realises that they can actually trigger a predictable response from their mummy, it makes them giggle, but they do not understand that the noise you make is actually because you are hurting. This is no surprise because your baby plays peek-a-boo games designed around a repetitious action with a loud noise, so this might seem to be a similar game.

The best way to handle this is to take the game out of it for your child. Don't get angry, but make sure that when they do bite your nipple you remove their comforts for a minute or so. This is done by simply using a cue 'no biting' and an immediate action, which would be removing them from your breast and putting them on the ground for a minute. If they are able to get up, they must stay on the ground in a sitting position until that time has passed. Do not talk with them, or make eye contact. This essentially feels uncomfortable and means the results of biting are actually the opposite of the desired response.

Do not worry if your little one has a little cry and is not comfortable with the outcome. This helps discourage the action of biting. Maintain your 'out of arms' consequence for biting for a full minute before distracting them to stop the crying (we don't want to confuse them and have them think that they need to cry to get the feed back). Once they have stopped crying, use your up cue and then pick them up and lie them down for their feed again. As they start to feed, praise with 'good feeding' and request 'No biting mummy'. Distract them with a song or chatter and make sure that they don't feel they need to bite you to get your attention.

If they bite again, repeat the process. You may need to repeat your 'out of arms' strategy several times before your little one understands the link between biting and losing your attention. If the biting continues, cease feeding in that instance, then place them on the floor and walk away to do some chores in the kitchen. Do not feed them again until the next feed time is due. Do not get angry but be very clear about the outcome of continued biting, and do not change the outcome because they cry a lot. This will only draw the process out as a baby learns to cry to achieve their desired outcome, undermining the message your actions originally set out to establish. Simply end the feed and carry on with the day. This is where you will need to adhere to specific feeding-interval windows.

Nipple shields can provide some protection. However, they do not address the reason for the biting which is vital. Nipple shields are a useful aid to prevent serious injury while you teach your baby not to bite, but will not protect you fully from injury, thus they should only be seen and used as an aid. There is no reason to feel you need to wean your baby if you are addressing the biting correctly. Remember practice makes perfect, and you must be absolutely consistent. If you have attempted, using this strategy, to correct the biting problem but still achieved no relief, then you may need to consider the future of your feeding if the biting is significant and causing you injury. It is always best to seek some professional help with a behaviour management strategies first, before taking such drastic measures.

Q Pinching while feeding, how can I stop this?

A Another common problem. Two main things: develop a cue 'no pinching' and use the above strategy if the pinching is very bad. A sock on their hand will prevent you from being bruised badly but, much like the nipple shield, it does not address and correct the problem in the first place. A sock being placed on their hand can be a 'consequence' to their pinching, just as the 'out of arms' strategy can be, which means that even if they protest about the sock, it stays on for a set amount of time and you continue to persevere with the feed. If this does not help, then you will need to adopt the 'out of arms' strategy highlighted above. Do not get cross. Often a child pinching has absolutely no idea they are causing you discomfort and may require the repeated 'consequence' of the 'out of arms' strategy before they link the pinching with the consequence and stop pinching. This is the same for eight month olds as it is for 23 month olds.

Q My baby vomits after their evening bottle. Is there anything I can do to stop that from happening?

A Fortunately, there usually is. If this is the only feed where they have a bottle, or the only bottle that they regularly throw up on, it can usually be caused by the same problem the world over. The vomiting is almost always the result of the feed suction being regularly broken through the feed. This causes a build up of wind in the tummy. A simple burp sitting just below a portion of milk can trigger an avalanche of milk that just keeps coming and coming and coming in waves as the gag reflex is stimulated by the first, then subsequent, portions of milk. This can occur for two main reasons, both of which can be corrected if addressed:

- positioning problems or lack of boundaries where the child comes on and off the feed regularly
- bottle lid being done up too tightly.

To correct the positioning issues you will need to refer to page 220. The bottle lid being done up too tightly makes it impossible for the air to naturally run in through the caps. I hate to say it but often it's those super-helpful but slightly too-strong dads that get this bottle ready and fasten the cap so tightly that it makes this the one feed of the day that is usually 'return to sender'.

There are usually some really clear signs that your child's bottle lid has been done up too tightly. These include the teat of the bottle constantly being sucked together before eventually collapsing back into the bottle, or your child partially releasing their suction on the teat to allow air to flood back into the bottle through the teat. It can also take quite a while for your child to drink their milk despite constantly suckling. The final sign is that there are no bubbles feeding back into the bottle as your child suckles, and the only time bubbles feed into the bottle is when the suction is artificially broken by baby or parent. If you notice this occurring, then the solution is usually quite simple.

Firstly, make sure you have a correct speed flow teat so this is not causing frustratingly slow feed times for your baby, making them fuss. Then you need to address the way in which air travels into the bottle. As your child sucks the milk out of the bottle, the void that the missing milk once vacated will now need to be replaced by air, or the bottle will collapse in on itself. The way feeding bottles are designed is to allow air to trace back into the bottle along the threads on the plastic lids. If these lids are secured too tightly, the air is blocked from running along the thread into the bottle and your child will have a much more difficult task on their hands when drawing milk out of the bottle. This will cause the teat to collapse as the bottle empties, or force a baby to release their suction so the air can travel back into the teat holes.

If this is you, once the milk is warmed, replace the lid firmly, and shake the bottle well. Once you have shaken the bottle release the lid almost completely then fasten it gently until the thread just catches enough to keep the lid on. Remember that warm milk slowly cooling will naturally cause suction within the bottle as well so it's important to always release the lid a little to allow air in and do up again lightly just before you offer it to your baby.

Q   My baby refuses to drink milk of any kind. What can I do?

A   This is a condition I have encountered a few times in my career. It seems almost unimaginable that your baby would not want to drink milk when it is their life source, but there are some children who absolutely refuse point blank, so don't be frightened. If your little one is six to 12 months of age it is important to adapt a balanced eating plan immediately, as outlined above. If your baby is six to 12 months of age, then it is important that you have a lactation specialist come out to your house, or a specialist in feeding come to your house at your baby's designated milk-feed time to make sure that the reason your little one is refusing milk is not due to a position or environmental imbalance. If your baby is six to 12 months of age, then you can try a series of formulas, from lactose-free to soy to other alternative milk products.

If they still refuse to drink their milk, then look at making sure that their diet is as balanced as possible, but offer a mid-morning snack, and a mid-afternoon snack at this time. If you can make it milk based like a yoghurt or custard or smoothie-style snack, then that is great. Try to substitute the calcium lost by providing a form of calcium in each of their three solid feeds. By six months they can be on three solids and two snacks if you have tried all of the above suggestions and still have had no success with milk, and they will be okay.

Be inventive with their solid meals and snacks, however. Think of ways of hiding milk, if it is a taste-based refusal. Also, think of ways that your baby might just take it: frozen drinks, smoothie-type drinks, or perhaps by offering it from a normal drinking cup, or even from daddy's or mummy's favourite coffee mug. The excitement of such a grand offer might just be enough to convince even the most stubborn of little people to take a swig.

Most importantly, however, is that when your child is eating these three solid meals and taking two snacks as alternative options for this lost milk feed, that you keep your baby super hydrated. This means that as often as you can offer it and insist they take at least a few sips of water. They should be so well hydrated that they have that beautiful oily film on their eyes, their lips are glistening, their skin is plump and moist, and they are dribbly. This will ensure you avoid constipation from the solid diet, and that they are not low on water content due to the loss of milk feeds through their day.

It has only occurred once, however, that I have been unable to get a baby drinking milk again between the sixth and twelfth month. Interestingly enough, his baby brother did the same thing at the same age seven years later. It does happen rarely that milk cannot be re-establish and a solid diet needs to be fully established, however, I strongly recommend that you do everything you can, through persevering with the strategy above, before offering alternative snacking options between the sixth and ninth months, predominantly because their need for milk feeds remains very high.

If your little one is over 12 months of age however, while the loss of milk in their diet is not ideal, it is certainly less to be concerned about than it is when a baby is under twelve months. The above strategy can be followed entirely but you will only really need to be supplementing two milk feeds in their diet. I usually find that smoothies, or big boy / girl drinking cups are enough to encourage milk intake of sorts, but all is not lost if you need to supplement their diet in other ways.

Q My child sleep / eats much better at daycare, but not at home. Why and how could this be?

A This is almost certainly an indication of two things. One, your need to put your child on a meal-time and sleep-time plan that is slightly more rigid time wise. Use the centre's timeframes as a guide. They will happily share their daily routine with you if you explain the situation. Two, your meal-time difficulties are almost certainly behaviour-based and you will need to establish a meal-time mini routine, with some solid boundaries, which they would invariably have at daycare. If meal time is a challenge it is usually an indication that you need to work a little on your balanced lines of communication. I strongly recommend you read the communication section for a full understanding of this.

Q Is there a time for 'treats' that won't impact their sleeping or eating?

A This strategy is all about balance, so I acknowledge that treats do happen. I am of the school of thinking though, that as long as they don't know what they are missing out on, then why introduce junk food, but I know it's not always that easy. I am also of the mindset that it is often a parent's enthusiasm and excitement about a certain type of food (chocolate, for instance) that makes the food so appealing to a child. I think that a parent or carer should be as enthusiastic about fruit (nature's sweet) and vegetables as much as they are about biscuits and lolly treats. That said, I also know that those treats do taste yummy, are more-ish and many people see the act of offering a child a treat as kind and loving. So the question remains, how do we manage this?

Firstly, most people's first question is to know if these kinds of treats impact on their child's ability to sleep? The answer simply is 'yep'. Most treats are high in sugar or carbohydrates, which convert quickly to glucose in the blood stream. Now this is essentially energy. This energy needs to be burnt or it stays in the body. If this energy is not burnt off, and the child eats again, or perhaps goes to sleep, the body ingeniously converts this to something called glycogen. This ultimately remains as a stored fuel source, a little like a battery that is ready to be accessed at any time should the body need it. Now two things happen to this glycogen. It is either stored (in the form of fat) because the body has a new source of glucose surging through the blood stream therefore knows there is no need for it immediately, or it gets used as energy. This means that snacking on treats and sweets too close to a sleep time, particularly at night, can result in a very energised baby or, worse still, a baby with a little store of energy that they are ready to use at some ungodly hour in the middle of the night when they wake next.

How can you offer treats without making your life and theirs miserable? Easy! Offer them as much as possible during afternoon tea only. This window allows lots of time for the energy to be burnt off, and a child to enjoy them without any impact on a meal. It also allows grandparents, aunts, uncles, friends and sometimes mum and dad to enjoy offering these little treats. Please remember the size of your child, and the size of their little body. Offer small treats, not huge ones. Small bite-sized pieces rather than entire chocolate frogs.

It is really not at all healthy or appropriate for a baby to have sweets under 12 months of age in my view, and wherever possible I try to avoid a child having them under two years of age. This is obviously only a personal view, and many will vary in attitude to this topic so I am not proposing that my view where this is concerned is the right one. There are some who say no sweets ever, others who are completely relaxed about them and offer their child treats from a very early age, and others who try to avoid them wherever possible. This last is where I sit. I think it is dangerous to say never, and unhealthy to say whenever, so I feel it's ok to say 'sometimes, but not until they are x months of age, and they need to know it's a treat (so not a daily event) and it's only ever a small portion'.

Q My child throws their cup. How can I fix this?

A You know, this is so common, and I tend to not get too carried away with it unless it is really problematic. Some things are just not worth getting in a pickle about. If you would like to help them stop then you can start by using a clear language cue and defining it. 'Cup on tray' is clear enough, and you will need to accompany this request with a simple action of tapping the tray as you say it. If your little one looks like they are going to drop the cup over the side of the tray, then quickly hold their hand with the cup in it and direct it to the tray as you repeat your cue, then make them place it on the tray and help them release their grip. Clap and cheer and be all excited before repeating the action several times concurrently yourself as an example. 'Mummy take a sip' (pretend to take a sip), 'cup on tray' (place the cup on the tray). Clap and cheer and be all excited. Your baby will either think you are really funny, or really crazy but either way they will enjoy the experience and start to understand the meaning of this statement.

Each time they pick up their cup to take a sip remind them 'Cup on tray' and tap the tray. If they drop it over the side when you aren't watching, simply pick it up and place it on the tray saying 'Cup on tray'. If they try to then pick it up and throw it over the side because it appears to be a pretty great game or good way of getting your attention, then simply pick up the cup and say 'Cup all gone' and place it on another table where they cannot reach it. Do not return the cup even if they get very cross for a period of time until they stop asking for it.

Reintroduce the cup by holding it in front of your little one and saying 'Cup on tray' and placing it on the tray. Guide their hands carefully here and, if they then place the cup on the tray, give lots of praise. If they throw it, the cup should be removed for the rest of the meal time.

Q As I breastfeed / bottle-feed my child they start to fall asleep. Is this really a bad thing?

A This is a good question. If your baby has no problems eating enough before they fall asleep or sleep well afterwards, and do not wake up crying wondering where you have gone after you have put them to bed, then feed sleeps are okay. There are many children who are not in the least bit affected by sleep feeds, and equally as many parents who are not in the least bit affected by the impact the feed sleeps are having on their child's sleeping and eating. If everyone is happy, then don't fix what isn't broken. On the other hand, if you or your baby is having a difficult time with their sleeping or eating and you are trying to resolve it then the answer is an absolute 'yes'! Sleeping while feeding for a poor sleeper or eater is an absolute disaster in my books. A five-minute doze on a feed could cause up to 40 to 60 minutes' worth of crying when you next try to settle them and is a prime cause of the catnap.

It's important to keep a child who is having difficulty awake no matter what. People say to me, 'You don't know how hard that is Sheyne', but I actually do. The key lies in preventing them from falling into a surface sleep (see pages 403 and 412). This phase is recognised through their glassy eyes, staring, eyes rolling or a change in breathing and alertness during the feed. When this even starts to happen ring a little bell or rattle and talk to your baby, touch their body and tickle them sometimes, but not enough to have them break the feed, just to see them smile while they maintain their suction and move in anticipation of another little tickle. Talk a little louder and have some toys for them to play with.

If your baby is very likely to try and fall asleep on their feed then pull out the big guns. Get one of those pretty LED light-flashing badges, sticker or other equally distracting item, that you can attach to you as a brooch (but make sure they can't use their fingers to explore it) and turn it on to keep them awake. You may need to stop the feed and sit them up or take them for a little walk but don't allow their head to rest on your shoulder, or gently sway and pat them. This will only make it harder for them to stay awake because your actions will make them even more sleepy. Sit them on your hip and encourage them to support their own weight as much as possible by having your arm placed low around their hips and have an enthusiastic tone and be full of energy. This will help your baby pick up quickly so you can resume the feed.

Q What if they vomit when they eat?

A While this is never a desired outcome, some babies who have never really established the ability to eat before may have an over-responsive or oversensitive gag reflex. Unfortunately, if you are a mum or dad of a little one who has a tricky time eating solids, it is usually only through practice and stimulation that this trigger-happy gag reflex stops being so sensitive. Persevere if the gagging is not too prevalent. If you have been working on your meal times for several days and your little one is really having a difficult time, then it may be important to have baby checked out to make sure they do not have something else going on.

If this is a significant problem in your house then you will probably have to get some assistance and guidance from a reputable consultant rather than trying to do it on your own. It is a stressful event for a parent to witness, however children seem to be remarkably un-phased by vomiting. There are some typical things that almost always induce vomiting accidentally:

- baby putting too much food in their mouth at once
- baby placing their fingers in their mouth with their food
- bananas (whole or mashed)
- slimy or stringy foods, like mashed beans, zucchini or squash
- crying throughout a meal
- post-nasal drips.

If your baby has just accidentally vomited from one of the typical scenarios mentioned above, clear up the tray, wipe them down, offer a sip of water and carry on with the meal.

Q How will I know if they don't like a particular food when they protest about most foods?

A I usually find that, if you stick to simple food initially like those on the recipes in the previous chapter, then there will be a significant difference between their usual protesting cries about learning how to be fed and a genuine dislike of a texture or taste of a particular food. Something to look for is a quick gag reflex even on a small portion of that particular food. If they do that with all food then it has nothing to do with dislike.

Q How will I know that they are ready for me to stop spoon-feeding them?

A When they are eating adequate quantities of finger foods or spoon-fed food that they have been able to do themselves. A child refusing to allow you to feed them, when they are unable to consume adequate quantities on their own to promote good sleep and a happy demeanour, is not ready to have you stop feeding them.

Q Should I use a multi-vitamin with my baby because they are a poor eater?

A Always see your doctor, nutritionist or dietitian if they are eating very poorly, as you and your little one may need solid guidance beyond what a book can provide. While the jury is still out on the benefits of vitamin supplements, I have personally found them to be helpful in keeping the runny noses from daycare and kindergarten at bay. I do find this can be helpful if your child is a very poor eater. I have observed an improvement in the prevalence of runny noses with vitamin use when a child is eating very poorly. This of course is only a safe guard and can never take the place of good eating, therefore I highly recommend you correct the eating via the strategies suggested in this guide.

Q Toys during meal time, is this okay?

A I believe that there is nothing wrong with a child having a toy to play with during meal time when they are learning how to sleep. In fact, I almost insist on the use of a bag of tricks (see page 369) to help make the transition as easy as possible. Once you have established healthy eating through spoon-feeding, then you can go back to a form of graded exposure with toys through playtime. I do not find it necessary to eliminate toys from meal times under two years of age if they are an aid that assists a child to stay calm and relaxed. It does not stop a child from recognising that they are eating; it only assists the process to remain enjoyable.

Q TV during meal time, is this okay?

A Actually, this is quite different to toys at meal time. I have been invited into the home on many occasions where a child is only ever able to be fed if they are completely transfixed on the television. In a sense, they are so distracted that they appear to not even be aware of the fact that they are eating. If the parent attempts to establish the next meal time without the television on, the child is extremely distressed by the concept of food and eating, and the meal time is unpleasant for all. I tend to try to completely correct the meal-time difficulties through the use of all the strategies outlined in this section and try to do it without the use of the TV at all. The reason I believe it is important to try to replace TV with toys is that while they are playing with toys, they are still aware of the eating process and therefore able to start to accept this and become comfortable with it. However, when the television is on, the child often becomes completely unaware of the eating process which can result in fairly significant eating difficulties whenever your child needs to be 'present' at any other eating experience.

Towards the end of the day, if I become aware that they are finding it particularly difficult, I am happy to use the television so long as I can keep them relatively present and aware of the fact that I am feeding them. All of that said, if it was a matter of deciding between teaching my child to be present at meal times, or getting a good quantity and balance of food into my child when I was in the process of teaching them how to sleep, I believe that the food intake should take precedence over the meal-time presence. Therefore, either address this issue well before sleep repair begins, or wait until your child is sleeping well and then work on this issue. You may find that once they are sleeping better they respond fairly well to meal times with TV simply because they are not feeling so irritable from being tired.

Q My child eats better for me than for my partner and I was wondering how I could encourage him to eat for them?

A This is about creating a language-based predictable framework around the routine of meal times for your baby. When your child becomes inflexible and insists on only one person and one person's way, they are trying to create some predictability of their own. This means that their conditions for eating become environmental and another person feeding them, or feeding them elsewhere, becomes a challenge. In order for your little one to feel comfortable for your partner to feed them, create an entire meal-time flow. Sit them in their chair using the same language, and put on their bib the same way. Use the same language cues for introducing their food, and setting their meal-time boundaries. Have a feeding style and always end a meal, clean up and get up the same way. This then becomes a language-based routine, and allows you to transfer those condition, after allowing your partner to watch, and to hand over the feeding responsibility to daddy. Remember it may take a little time for your child to learn they can trust daddy so leave him to persist, and do not take over or rescue baby from a safe situation (see page 67).

For the purpose of this discussion, let's say that your child eats better for mum. This is a common problem and can occasionally come down to how consistent and predictable the primary carer is, and how much negotiating a parent offers at a meal time. The first thing to draw on when trying to develop a consistency in feeding between one carer and the next is that children love predictability in their day, and it is through this predictability that your child will feel a sense of control and, therefore, relax. Meal times are what I call a mini-routine opportunity. This means it is a time of the day that a parent should establish a governing line of communication, yet a sense of control should be returned to the child through the predictability of a mini routine.

You should have a set of conditions that depicts the beginning of a meal time, the boundaries and expectation of behaviour during meal time, and a way of letting your child know when meal time is over (see page 255). This language-based meal-time flow should first be established and locked in by the person who has the most success with meal times. Once this is established with the primary feeder, additional people can enter into the situation and use this same flow of communication and the child will be able to adjust quickly to the transition of carer.

Let's look at a brief example of this mini routine:

Pre-empting: 'Jake, it's nearly time for lunch, *nearly time* to sit down in your high chair and wait for mummy.'

Forewarning: 'Last one Jake, then *it's time* to sit down in your high chair and wait for mummy.' Remember to forewarn him about what he is going to be eating.

Stating event and expectation: 'Okay, Jake, it's time for lunch, sitting down, waiting for mummy.' Establish eating by using the strategies highlighted above then set the boundaries suggested above.

Completion: Wipe face and hands, wipe down tray and use wait game and cue.

This is a mini routine. It is consistent and allows a child to predict the events without having to become bossy and boisterous. This will help a child relax and accept yours and other people's guidance without stress. Please be aware that it is important to not accidentally undermine your partner by taking over and rescuing your child from their father and a safe situation.

It's important to remember balance if the eating challenge is quite intense. Make sure you allow your partner and your child plenty of opportunity together to do a typical daily routine, and not just playing. The reason this is important is that often during playing, a child is happily guiding a parent, whereas during nappy change, cot play, meal time and sleep time, a parent is guiding a child. If a parent only established a role of communication where the child only ever governs them, accepting a parent-governed line of communication at meal time can feel foreign and therefore uncomfortable.

Finally, when you are sticking to a solid meal-time plan, be cautious to not compensate for poor eating when daddy was feeding baby, to good demand feeding when he finally gets down from the high chair. Stick to the times of your meal plan, and if your child does not eat when daddy feeds him at this feed, don't compensate but wait until the next appropriate meal time and ask daddy to feed him again using your mini routine. It can be helpful to leave the room while your partner tries to feed your baby a good 15 minutes before the meal time is due using your long-term absence cue, and only return after daddy has completed the wait game and cue and taken baby out of the high chair. It can also be helpful to offer a child's favourite food for these first feed windows.

Always remember positive language. No negative statements should be used whatsoever during the learning process for eating. Always remember the role your confidence level plays in your child being able to accept this request with minimal stress the first time.

Q My child tries to stand in their high chair. Should I move them to a table and chair set?

A I would have to say 'not at all' to this. If you can't ask them to sit in their high chair, then you will have a real job on your hands trying to get them to sit at a table and chairs. Buckle them in, secure the buckles, and then follow the position strategy in the encyclopaedia (see page 313). Once they can accept the simple request to sit in their high chair without a battle, and sit on your lap for stories or lie still during dressing time, then you are ready to ask them to sit at a table and chairs.

Q My child pushes back on the legs of the table when they are sitting at the table. How can I stop this?

A A simple, well-defined cue of 'legs down' (See page 316). This is a communication issue and needs to be managed with communication more than simply taking them away from the table, or physically restraining them. To repair this kind of behaviour you need to adopt the same kind of management that you would see during nappy change repair, or sitting down in the cot or bath, only using a different cue 'feet down' and be sure to define that statement. Always remember that whenever you are discouraging a pattern of behaviour it's more important that you block them from doing the action (putting their feet on the table) than it is to correct it (take their feet off the table) because they learn the true definition of the statement 'no feet on table' as being 'don't even try and put them on the table', as opposed to the definition of the statement 'no feet on table' being misunderstood to mean 'put your feet on the table, then I'll take them off'.

Q My baby hates meat. How can I make sure his iron levels are adequate for sleep?

A If your little one wakes for night feeds, there is a chance that this is the reason. I have observed that a child who is lacking in iron from their daily food intake, who goes to bed at around 7 p.m., will usually wake between 11.30 p.m. and 1.30 a.m. or 2.30 to 3.30 a.m. If this is your child, then you will need to establish spoon-feeding again through the use of the recipes and the techniques highlighted in this section. You will need to ensure that your child is getting at least one serve of protein (meat) a day.

A multi-vitamin in the form of Penta-vite can be a little helpful, but nothing really comes close to the real deal when it comes to adequate iron stores from natural food. I have not observed a supplement prevent the night wakings. However, they can slightly lesson the frequency of the waking. If you feel that your child may be very low in iron, there is a history of anemia in your family or your baby has been deemed a failure-to-thrive baby then you may need to go to your doctor for blood tests, or may require a prescription iron supplement. This of course is to be determined by your doctor but if you are given iron supplements you should experience relief in the frequency of your child's night wakings.

Q If I cannot settle my baby without breastfeeding how can I follow this plan?

A This indicated that your child also has a clear settling and resettling association with feeding to go to sleep. This is not a simple hunger trigger for your child's night wakings and will need to be addressed. A full recovery routine will be required as there are now a series of areas making sleep time challenging and stressful for your little one. Your sleep repair will require a little more than just a simple flick through small sections of this book. Please go to page 20 for more information on how to use this book appropriately where your child's sleeping and eating are concerned. Regardless of the avenue you choose to go down, the repair of daytime meals needs to be corrected in the same way. No feeds from 2 a.m. onwards (even if your child doesn't know how to go back to sleep without their feeding association). I always say that, as this is the night before you plan on starting your new plan, you can actually do whatever it takes to get your little one back to sleep so long as it doesn't include feeding them in any way, shape or form from 2 a.m. onwards until you start your meal or daily routine plan the following morning. This is achievable, even if it means that you will all start your new day a little tired for the efforts, but this in fact often goes in your favour as your child is able to go to sleep quite quickly without needing to be fed because they are tired. One thing is certain: you cannot correct meal-time difficulties and still expect to be able to continue to use feeding as a method of settling and resettling your baby without it impacting on their appetite. This will need to be addressed via daily routine, as well as new settling, resettling and waking routines.

Q Can I feed my baby outside the feed-time windows in your routine plan?

A If your child is eating poorly, then it is not recommended. The only way to correct eating habits is to eliminate the snacking that impacts on their appetite in the first place, particularly as the consequence is poor food intake which in turn triggers the need for snacking outside normal meal times. This is a vicious cycle and to allow snacking will only perpetuate a cycle of poor eating. As it stands, I find most children who over snack rather than eat balanced meals are unsettled and have some difficult behaviours to manage as the day progresses as they are not able to consume enough nutrition to keep them in good stead. With that in mind I see it as an easy decision to work through one to two days of varied hunger responses in order to repair the poor eating. Be cautious that food is not being used as an emotional solution.

13
SURE communication, independence and play

What is *SURE*? Well, it stands for 'Sheyne's ultimate resource encyclopaedia'. You will probably find yourself turning to this section of the book constantly. Here I am going to cover a lot of the daily events and routines that can be typical tears-and-tantrum times for you and your little one if your baby is a sensitive type or your communication is slightly behind for their developmental needs. Each of these events can, in some homes, prove to be very difficult for baby and a real confidence destroyer for mums and dads. This stress for little ones is most commonly triggered around a transition from one event to the next, around something new or unfamiliar, around an area where they may need to wait, around an area where they may have lost trust, or around a time when a parent may need to guide them. This section is designed for those who struggle to help their under-two year old transition or cope with any of the many events peacefully.

Some people will be blessed to never need this section, while others will find it a lifesaver for their family. For each event routine I will provide the scenario that you are aiming to achieve within one to five days, then clear instructions on how to achieve it as well as some 'what if' scenario answers, so you can manage the event with your parent-governed line of communication and find your solution quickly. I have developed and used these routines over my 20-year career with children, and either use them myself or have taught others how to use them every day of my working life. But while *I* know the end result of working through a few tears or, indeed, some mighty tantrums, I do appreciate that you cannot see that far ahead. Let me reassure you that the outcomes of these strategies still amaze me, so while you might feel a little anxious about starting, know that you will get there in a surprisingly short time (even when it feels like you are going backwards on that first day or two as they resist the change) and you too will achieve a whole day's worth of a happy, content and relaxed baby as easily as I do, every day.

Obviously, this next section is designed to help you *correct* any areas of the day that you or your child may be having trouble with. Please just skip right past the routine ideas if your child and you have found a way to do any of these tasks where you are both happy, regardless of the strategy. I live by the common-sense rule of 'if it isn't broken, don't try to fix it'. That said, if it takes you half an hour, and way too much negotiating or tears to change your little one's nappy or you find yourself regularly frustrated by your child's behaviour during daily tasks, and it causes you or them stress at times, then it would be a great idea to change the governing line of communication back to you and teach them a better, more enjoyable and pleasant language experience than endlessly tiptoeing around what should be a simple task.

For each event routine I will provide the scenario that you are aiming to achieve within one to five days, then clear instructions on how to achieve it.

Finally, and most importantly before we begin, you must remember that you should always use your flow of communication (see page 40) as your first line of prevention against needing to address any stress or behavioural issues with your baby or toddler. Consistent communication is what helps prevent them from resisting guidance from others in the first place. Remember this entire balanced communication philosophy is about prevention, not providing yet another Band-Aid solution. Always try to avoid having to manage difficulties rather than having to repair them every time they come up.

SURE and steady as you go

These scenarios and repair strategies are designed to help you work past old poor patterns while you repair your communication and routines initially, so that there are no more problems or confusion around your language or expectation that causes the tears in the first place. If you do not see significant results within one to five days you will need to either review the strategy thoroughly to ensure you are defining your request correctly or stop implementing the strategy as something may still be unclear to your little one and be causing them difficulties in understanding you. Occasionally, as your child gets older, you might need to revisit some scenarios as your little one questions the boundaries to see if the safety nets are still predictably in place, but there is still no negotiation around those requests. This is a normal level of follow up and what I call maintenance. However, the following are only designed as short-term repair strategies to bring relief to a situation within a few days of beginning your new parenting approach. They are not meant to be used endlessly if you are not achieving positive results.

Using your flow of communication (see page 40) and the strategies outlined in this book, you and your little one will quickly get into the new swing of these event routines and will be able to enjoy every moment of your day together again, perhaps even for the first time, within a few short days. Remember, whether your baby is six months or 23 months old, the process of learning is achieved through a predictable event routine, where your child becomes familiar with the flow of any event of their day. Most people automatically create patterns of repetitious language and behaviour for children but rarely realise how powerful a tool these can be when used to also help babies and toddlers calm down and happily accept our loving guidance so we can teach them how to enjoy certain events in their day or sleep peacefully.

Please be patient with your baby or toddler as they learn each new routine. There is always an adjustment period (see page 67) as they learn the new flow. Remember, while they are experiencing the conditions and expectation of your governing line of communication around any new event for the first time, they will often continue to try and recreate the old patterns that they are more familiar with (even if that involves tears). This is why you must remain calm, consistent and reassuring and know that practise makes perfect.

It's not uncommon for them to feel a little uncomfortable with the unpredictability of the new events so while I want you to expect quick results, I also need you to be realistic and give them a little time to get used to something new if they are finding the changes to conditions tricky at first. It's vital that you remain aware that this reaction to the change is where they are saying to you 'This feels different, am I okay?' So make sure your answer is a confident 'yes, even though it's different, this is a good way to do this' by staying consistent, loving, patient and defining your statements clearly the first time so there is no confusion. This learning process could take as little as one nappy change or as long as two to five days where meal and sleep-time expectations are concerned. Remember, if you are calm, loving and confident and follow through with your plan consistently, then your baby will immediately start to relax and begin looking to you for guidance.

How to navigate this encyclopaedia

This section is broken loosely into four primary areas:

1. positioning your baby using your flow of communication
2. boundaries and events that are more challenging to deal with
3. difficult areas of management or behaviour repair
4. play strategies.

Here I've listed what routines and tasks fall into these areas so you can quickly find them when you need them—sort of like a mini index. You'll also find a reference to those strategies elsewhere in the book that complement these tasks.

1. Positioning using your flow of communication

Strategies elsewhere in the book to assist these positionings

2. Boundaries and events that are more challenging

Strategies elsewhere in the book to assist boundaries and events

3. Difficult areas of management or behaviour repair
Working past fears (see page 346)
Learning to love their sleep environment (see page 349)
Developing an attachment to a teddy (see page 352)
Working with harmful behaviours towards self and others (see page 354)

Strategies elsewhere in the book to assist these areas
Developing their emotional tool kit (see page 87)
Responding to existing meal-time behaviour (see page 256)

4. Play strategies
Using your bag of tricks (see page 369)
Teaching them to play through role play (see page 372)
Dealing with the old trouser tug! (see page 374)
Crying when put down to play (see page 377)
Safety proofing your play area (see page 380)
Play when moving house, renovating or going on holidays (see page 385)
Loud noises preventing play (see page 387)
Pets and play (see page 390)
Talking on the phone (see page 392)
Delivering a mixed message during playtime (see page 393)
Avoiding the tears and tantrums over rides at the shops (see page 395)

Strategies elsewhere in the book that assist these strategies
Cot play (see page 175)
High chair play (see page 192)
High chair play in restaurant (see page 199)
Pram play (see page 201)
Supermarket trolley play (see page 207).

1. Positioning using your flow of communication

Positioning is such an important skill for your little one to accept from you. At any given time of the day, you are communicating with your child even when you are simply holding them, or moving them from one location to another. You may position and reposition your little one hundreds of times a day and, while you may not always be articulating a request in words, you are very clearly asking them to do something every time you position them. For example, you might sit your baby on your hip so you can chat to the neighbour over the fence, or sit them in the high chair for their lunch, or lay them on the change table to get dressed, or place them in the bath to have a splash around and a clean up.

If each time you ask your baby to sit on your hip, in the bath, in their high chair or car seat and they say a clear 'no' by refusing to allow the positioning to occur, you are looking at a baby who is either not comfortable with your governing line of communication or does not understand you are communicating with them. This is your first point of communication, and one that is important for your baby so they can have a peaceful and relaxing day. It's also vital that you can ask these simple things of your little one without creating stress for them so you can then ask them to do more complex tasks, like go to sleep for you.

Nappy changing and getting dressed

This is the routine that should happen every time you or one of your baby's trusted primary carers change their nappy. Always remember to be respectful of your child's vulnerability and reluctance to allow someone they are less familiar with to change their nappy.

'Nappy change' communication broken down into component parts

Pre-empting: 'Charlie, mummy is just getting dressed but *soon* it will be time for nappy change. Nearly time to lie down and wait for mummy.'

Forewarning: 'Last one, Charlie, then it's time for nappy change, *nearly time* to lie down, wait for mummy.'

Stating event and expectation: '*It's time* to change your nappy, let's go.' Charlie looks up and you say 'Up up' and he raises his arms. You then carry him if he is still a crawler or say 'Let's go' and gesture to your toddler for them to follow you. Your toddler will grab a toy and run towards the room where the change table is and stand waiting for you. You pat the table and say 'Lie down, wait for mummy'. You lay your baby on the change table and say 'Lie down, wait for mummy' again. They lie comfortably and babble, chat or sing along with you while you change their nappy. As the nappy change draws to a close, you play a little game or do a little nursery rhyme much to your baby's delight.

Defining your statement: If they move to roll over or stand up, make the wait sign (see page 74) with your hand and say 'Wait'. Remember 'lie down, wait for mummy' means 'don't even try to reposition'.

Praise: If they are lying happily and don't look like they are going to challenge you, praise them: 'Good lying down, Charlie'; 'Good waiting for mummy, Charlie'. Praise and praise and praise good behaviour throughout.

Following through: To manage behaviour use your cues: 'Lie down', 'wait', 'legs down', 'hand out, mummy do it!' Add nursery rhymes, small toys and songs to hold their attention.

Completion: At the end of the nappy change, when *you* are ready, you get your baby up with your up cue (see page 76) or use the wait game. Give them a cuddle and kiss, then leave the room with a little ritual that could be closing the door or turning off the light or putting the nappy into the bin together and washing hands.

This entire nappy-changing routine is achievable through your flow of communication (see page 40). If, however, the concept of such a peaceful and relaxed response from your child sounds too good to be true, then you are one of many parents struggling with difficult and sometimes unpleasant negative routines at nappy change time. You will need to read through the simple rules I will give in this section and then implement the strategy to achieve these same results in as little as one nappy change time.

This management strategy can be used from the time your baby starts to challenge you on the change table, but the language structure can be implemented as early as you like. I personally communicate with a baby in a routinely predictable style through the use of defined cues from the moment they come home from hospital. I do not think it is appropriate to communicate with an infant like they are an adult, but the use of modified clear repetitious cues, and consistent associations to accompany those cues, creates an easy and effective style of communication that they can understand under the age of 12 months. When they are one year old, I continue to use the same language and routine but their ability to clearly understand your language starts to be more noticeable and you can form more complex and varied sentence structures. That said, if your 15 month old is only just learning to listen and understand you, then you need to start with the most basic, defined language cues and expectations, and gradually build your language from that point.

When re-establishing the ability to change your baby's nappy, or to dress them without the dreaded tantrums, corkscrews and flipping over, here are a couple of simple rules you need to follow:

- Always use your flow of communication.
- Go back to using the change table—gasp . . . yes, get it out of the garage and put it back in their room even if you were finding it too difficult to use. They are much easier to manage on the change table than the bed, floor or couch, and you have no choice but to be totally consistent so they don't roll over on you.
- While dressing them, do not treat them like a puppet and roll them, then sit them up, then lay them down multiple times, randomly. They

are not puppets and they tend to find it a very unpleasant experience when they are treated like one. Get effective with dressing them completely while they are lying down, and then sit them up for the final part of adjusting their cloths. Please note, I said 'sit', not stand. Once things have settled down to a lovely, calm nappy change and dressing routine, you can then stand them before you get them up. Also, please do not teach them to jump off the change table into your arms. They are so impulsive and egocentric at this young age that they will not stop to consider that, when you are bending over and reaching for a new bin liner, it is not a great time to take their little leap of faith.

- If you are unable to use their change table at certain times of the day, then have some kind of cloth that they always lie on to indicate that they are about to have a nappy change or be dressed. A cloth nappy provides a great visual association to help them understand that you are going to change their nappy or dress them now.

- Be considerate if you need to change their nappy somewhere entirely new, at a swimming centre, for example, where the change area is hard or loud, or incredibly busy. Your baby may find this extremely stressful. In these cases you are better to try and change their nappy in their pram so they don't feel so vulnerable.

Obviously, the use of your flow of communication suggests that if you plan on changing their nappy or dressing them for the day, at the very least you need to pre-empt the event for your little one. You then offer a final forewarning cue so they have an opportunity to warm up to the idea of the transition and your guidance of it, and they can finish what they are doing. Even if your baby looks like they are doing nothing, they may actually be extremely busy trying to grab a piece of lint out from between the floor boards. Your interruption can be equally frustrating and upsetting for them if you do not use your flow of communication.

Your pre-emptive language would comprise a familiar statement they associate with a particular event: a cue. The cue I use for dressing and nappy change is always 'lie down, wait for mummy / daddy'. This will have a strong association tied to it, and your baby will be aware of the upcoming event as soon as you use your cue. Therefore, you need to state the impending event, and use the cue that highlights your expectation of their behaviour: '*Soon* it will be time to change your nappy. Nearly time to lie down and wait for mummy!'

If they do not show a clear indication that they are ready to come with you, then you will use your final forewarning line so they know that

Mason, a bundle of energy

If you need more proof that getting your child to position calmly is a good idea then let me introduce Mason, a beautiful little boy who was the most physically mobile and active six month old I had ever come across in my entire career. His mother was desperate with exhaustion and had literally been everywhere to try and help her little boy sleep and eat. Both these tasks were extremely stressful for Mason and his mum and dad. As a result the entire family's future was at stake as Mason's parents' relationship was crumbling. They had been to three sleep schools, employed two private sleep consultants and visited various paediatricians and clinic sisters to seek advice and had been given a whole range of settling and feeding strategies, none of which had been successful. Mason's mum was absolutely convinced that no one could help her as all the other experts had told her that this was just the kind of baby Mason was, and it was better to adjust to that than to try to fix it. But she knew he needed to sleep and to eat.

Mason's mum told me she was frightened her little boy was hyperactive or had ADHD (though she didn't know it, it is absurd to even suggest such a thing at his age) as he was extremely active and others had suggested this to her. I wondered if positioning and really basic communication misses could be the main problem we had to deal with, so I decided to visit the family to see for myself. When I arrived I was a little taken back by how petite Mason was. He looked the size of your average four month old and was way off the bottom of the chart for height and weight. After dozens of tests with no results he was about to be medicated with a calorie booster. More shocking to me, however, was the fact that this tiny, teeny weeny little baby boy was standing independently and was cruising furniture confidently on his own and had been doing so for nearly seven weeks. When he wasn't standing and walking around he was crawling either commando-style or on his knees double time. He was like an Energizer rabbit, but faster.

I asked his mother to pick him up and hold him and, as I suspected, he would not stay still for even a single moment despite her most valiant efforts. He stood on her hip, moved himself from one hip to the other like a little orangutan, and then spent most of the time trying to push off her with his hands and feet while she clung on desperately. He was not wanting to get down, he was just enjoying the challenge this new physical situation presented him with. I asked to observe her breastfeeding him. This was equally as frantic with a counted 23 attachments in a three-minute window. He was up and down, and sitting, then squatting, then dancing with one foot twirling beautifully or jumping, all while feeding.

His poor mother burst into tears and my jaw was literally on the floor. She was completely exhausted and clearly a little bit frightened about his excessive physicality. And this was the

you are about to take them to get their nappy changed: 'Last song, nearly time to change your nappy. Last one, *nearly time* to lie down and wait for mummy!' As soon as that last stated event ends you change your language to a confident parent–governed line of communication: 'Okay, let's go, bubba, *it's time* to change your nappy, time to lie down and wait for mummy'.

At this stage, your baby can take a small object with him to hold while you change his nappy. Take him to his room and follow this same ritual root cause of Mason's sleeping and eating problem. It was not some random suggestion of ADHD—which almost implies permitting the behaviour—but simple positioning and communication like asking him to 'stop, and be still please'. While this might be a shocking suggestion to a number of people, it is an absolutely vital request and boundary that should be set for some, if not most, babies. Mason needed to learn how to sit still, and be still and to relax, and to start to observe the world around him sometime *before* he acted. So his frazzled mother and father needed to learn how to set new boundaries.

We set up a new positioning plan to tackle the main issue and then a week later we planned to start a sleeping and eating program. We decided on just one sitting position on an adult's lap, and eliminated all other sitting options for him for the short term. We decided on one comfortable breastfeeding position and eliminated all other options in the short term. We decided on one hip-carrying position and eliminated all other options in the short term. We locked in simple cues for these new positions: 'sit down, wait for mummy / daddy', and 'lie down, wait for mummy'. And I showed them how to define what those cues meant and how to be consistent until they achieved the results. Based on his response to my initial requests to sit still, it was going to be hard work.

I waved farewell, aware that even for me the next two days would be extremely tiring and challenging. However, within two days Mason was able to sit, to lie, to wait quietly on his parent's hips with no tears and no tantrums. He was able to eat, feed and play more effectively. He was starting to calm down. They were doing great. So it was time to start his new routine. Within two days of starting his new sleeping and eating program Mason was able to self-settle, and resettle independently (with the aid of a no-movement wrap creating a single sleeping position), eat solids in his high chair and relax and enjoy a complete unbroken breastfeed. His parents said their new baby was 'bliss and happy to boot'. The best of both worlds.

Were there tears when mum and dad put the new boundaries in place? Most certainly. He was furious in fact, and it took one and a half days for him to learn the new expectations of how to sit, lie and be carried in the new ways. There were lots of cranky baby moments, and lots of tears. Was it worth it? Well his weight increased within three weeks and he was no longer required to start a calorie booster. He was full, well rested and happy. His mother came off her antidepressants within three months, and his parents repaired their tattered relationship and are still together three years later. Mason still sleeps and eats beautifully and is a healthy, happy and bright little boy with a new baby brother. While he did learn some simple positioning boundaries, he always remained a vibrant and energetic little man, just in a more balanced and healthy way. I'd say that was a happy ending. Absolutely worth every moment required to correct his positioning issues.

each time you intend on changing or dressing him. Show him the change table, pat it, and say 'Time to lie down, wait for mummy' in a confident happy voice. Show him the wait sign (see page 74) and smile. Then proceed to lay him down slowly.

Offer him a toy by dangling it above his chest, and wait momentarily to see his reaction. If he is fine and accepts the toy then proceed with the nappy change and acknowledge his good listening with praise: 'Good listening, bubba, good lying down and waiting for mummy'. Be happy, and enjoy this lovely one-on-one time. Fun games like blowing raspberries, or singing little nursery rhymes are always a lovely way to make this time really special.

What if . . .

Well, *what if* it doesn't turn out so beautifully? Imagine, you lay him down and he starts to tantrum, arch his back, tries to roll over, grabs the side of the change table and tries to flip over and grab the tubes of cream. You struggle and struggle and eventually, because it is easier, you are tempted to just sit him up so you can dress him. To correct this, if he starts to fight, simply put your hand on his chest or nappy, and every time he goes to roll over, hold the hand of the arm he is rolling on and gently pull it up towards the ceiling repeating your 'lie down, wait for mummy' cue and flashing the wait sign again in front of his face. This gentle raising of his hand will replace him on his back and help him understand the line 'lie down and wait'. This is you defining your statement. He will probably (at first) continue to resist you and try to roll, or move your arms out of the way and you will continue to ask him to 'lie down and wait for mummy' with a repeated pattern of physical response and the language cue.

If your baby is challenging your request or simply doesn't understand it yet, and you are trying to define your statement, please do not even attempt to change their nappy yet. It's not the most pressing matter at hand. Focus on defining your communication first. Once they have stopped physically resisting you, then you are fine to carry on with the nappy change. It's okay for them to have a little cry while they get used to this clear request. Remember you're only asking them to lie down while you change their nappy and it's a perfectly reasonable request—so, no guilt. They will understand the routine within a day or even a single nappy change if you define it properly.

What if . . . he stays flat on his back but uses both arms and some pretty impressive tummy muscles to sit bolt upright? Use both your hands at once to quickly slip and release the grip of his hands off the change-table sides and then put your hand on his chest gently and say 'wait for mummy'. Show him the wait sign by flashing it in front of his face briefly: 'Wait!'

What if . . . he uses his legs and wraps them around the outside of your arms, then over the top and pushes down pinning you to the change table? Pull your arms free before he gets to put pressure down on them and hold his legs for five to ten seconds. Position them so they are flat on the change table and hold them down at his little knees and say 'Legs down, wait for mummy', and show him the wait sign again by flashing it quickly in his face. If he struggles or resists your firm hold then continue to hold his legs still, and repeat your verbal cue, 'Legs down, wait for mummy'. When he is still, release them saying 'Good listening, legs down, clever bubba!' before resuming your nappy change.

If he does it all again, repeat the entire steps above. Don't worry about how long those first few attempts take to complete a nappy change. If you are dealing with the leg trick, you need to ensure you tell him when you plan on raising his legs, so have a basic cue such as 'bottoms up' to define that position, just as 'legs down' defines the lying positions. This same principle applies if he is kicking you through a nappy change. However, the language changes to 'legs down, no kicking'.

If he continues to use his legs to pin your arms down or kick you, then simply move him down the change table so that his legs drape over the bottom of the change table from his knees down, and position yourself between his legs so he can no longer kick or fight using his feet. This way you can simply manage his hands. If he then tries to push you away with his hands while you are changing his nappy, confidently move his hands upwards saying 'Hands out, mummy do it', then hand him a toy with the 'ta' cue (see page 328). This may take some time and patience. At no point do you so much as sigh or roll your eyes, just calmly repeat your cue and manage his behaviour by correcting it to define your statements: 'Legs down', 'No kicking', 'Hands out', etc.

> To be consistent with your cues you *must* use the same pattern of speech and body language each and every time you use your parent-governed line of communication.

If he stops fighting or resisting you but keeps on crying, don't feel you need to resolve that emotion for him. This is an important thing for him to feel as well as for him to find his own self-soothing solutions. Unlike when you say 'No, I need you to go back to sleep' in the middle of the night and don't let him get up and come out and join you in the main living area, during the day you can actually stay with him and guide him through these emotions at routine events, making the need to help him cope with these emotions around your guidance at night less likely. By picking him up and hugging him etc., you are saying 'I'm the only one who can fix this feeling', or 'There is something terribly wrong when you feel like this'. We all know that this is a normal and safe emotion for him to feel when mummy or daddy patiently but clearly asks him to lie down so it's important that when he does stop fighting but has a cry that you then chat happily and empathetically to him, thank him for waiting for mummy and complete your task at a normal pace with confidence before you pick him up. He may fight again throughout that same nappy change and you will need to follow through again.

Completion

Play your wait game once his nappy change is finished, when *you* are ready to get him up. He has to stay lying down (with all your rules in play: 'Legs down', 'Lie down, wait for mummy', 'Hands out, mummy do it', 'Wait') until you use your up cue (see page 76). This is you governing the outcome of a particular situation, which is what you and he need to practise before sleep-time repair can begin. Once he is up, you can then let him guide you again. It's just a balanced communication style where you ensure you use the same communication you need to use at night during the day as well. You can apply this same principle to most of the event routines during the day where you use your parent-governed line of communication.

> It's okay for them to have a little cry while they get used to this clear request. Waiting is a safe and normal emotion to experience, and a skill they need to be able to fall asleep peacefully, or play harmoniously.

Be calm, he will get there

Repeat and repeat and repeat in a calm, confident, compassionate but persistent no-fuss manner until he sees the pattern, and understands the language, and stops resisting you or starts to understand. Remember to always assess the situation from an adult's perspective (see page 70). You have asked him to lie down while you change his nappy. This is definitely a reasonable request. Be patient and be consistent and your baby or toddler will learn to lie happily and play with a toy while you change their nappy.

Nappy change issues are always resolved in one to two nappy changes and it generally takes me just one nappy change and maybe five minutes to achieve this with a seven to 12 month old. It may be slightly more challenging with a toddler. If you follow these rules 100 per cent you will have achieved it by the end of your first day. The only thing left for you to do at that point is maintain it by being consistent. Try to remember it is a little bit of work for them to learn new expectations so, if you don't plan on being consistent, can I suggest you don't ask them to learn it in the first place as all the work will have been in vain.

Your baby will need to learn this expectation with each member of the family so be patient and make sure he knows well in advance who is going to change him and what their expectations of his behaviour are by following this routine and the flow of communication to a T.

Carrying your baby on your hip without a fight

If you have no reason for your child to stay on your hip and they have suggested they would like to get down, give their body language a verbal response / cue like 'Would you like to get down, Charlotte?' Allow them to get down with 'Okay, down you get'. This is a balanced style of communication where you continue to govern the line of communication (see page 29) even though it is the child's wish. It's called willing negotiation. This is one of many options available to you and your little one to make sure your day goes smoothly with as few tears as possible.

You can and should apply this principle to all times of the day where you have not made, or do not need to make, a clear request. This means when you initially pick them up, you make your suggestion that they come to you an option through the use of words such as 'do you want to come up?' or through upward inflection 'up for a cuddle with mummy?' (see page 58). Once you have said 'Okay, bubby, it's time to . . .', however, you do need to follow through or you risk teaching your baby to negotiate (see page 29)—aka crying or protesting—every time you ask them to do something, and that is not balanced.

If you need them to happily and calmly sit on your hip while you do your chores or talk with someone else, then you need to draw on your flow of communication (see page 40) to ensure your little one can predict and understand what you are asking of them. Here is how you do that:

'Carrying baby on hip' communication broken down into component parts

Pre-empting: As these moments are often spontaneous, there is rarely opportunity for pre-emptive communication. If this occurs it's okay to make a spontaneous request once you have practised the request and defined the statement at home for a couple of days first. If you do know you are going to visit someone in a shop or front garden, for instance, then you would say something like 'daddy is hosing the garden now, but *soon* we might go and see Jenny at the shops. Nearly time for up ups, and sitting still for daddy.'

Forewarning: 'Last one, baby. *Nearly time* for up up with daddy. *Nearly time* to sit still and wait.'

Stating event and expectation: '*It's time* for up up.' Child looks up and you pick them up using your up cue (see page 76), and pop them on your hip, making sure they are comfortable, and say 'Sitting still, waiting for daddy'.

Wait game: Make sign with hand and say 'Wait'.

Defining your statements: If they move, make eye contact with them and with a warm tone ask them to 'sit still, bubba, wait for daddy'. You may or may not choose to offer them something, such as a teddy bear, to hold.

Praise: If they are waiting happily and don't look like they are going to challenge you, praise them, 'Good sitting still, bubba', or 'Good waiting for daddy'. Praise and praise and praise good behaviour throughout.

Completion: When you are ready, say 'Good sitting still for daddy, Caleb. Daddy is so proud of you, time to go and . . .', then put them down or move on to next task.

What if . . .

But *what if*, like hundreds of other families I have worked with over the years, it doesn't ever go that smoothly at your house? How do you manage the situation to make it this simple within a couple of days then? Some of the more common things I see when a parent is having trouble with carrying their little one are when baby / toddler:

- uses a parent's hip as a step and hooks both feet on the pelvis and stands while the parent struggles to stand comfortably and hold their baby safely
- throws their head back and cries
- puts both their arms forward and leans forward with all their weight, putting a lot of pressure on the parent's back or shoulder
- pushes off the parent's body with their arms and feet, making it difficult for mum / dad to hold baby safely
- cries and becomes stressed or cross due to the above behaviours and hits, bites, scratches or pinches
- swaps from hip to hip.

What if . . . your baby / toddler uses your hip as a step and hooks both their feet on your pelvis to stand up and you struggle to stand comfortably? You need to say 'No climbing on daddy' and 'Sit down and wait for daddy'. Once a baby reaches 16 months of age, giving an explanation for your request is an important part of your cue. You can preface your cue with a clear reason like 'Careful, Charlotte, daddy's frightened he might drop you', or 'Ouch, Charlotte, daddy's back is sore'. The use of your language is extremely important in expressing a respectful request to your child.

If you find this pattern of behaviour from your baby unpleasant, and would like them to stop, remember to articulate that by creating the simple cue 'no climbing on daddy, please' and then define that statement. Most parents keep correcting the position without saying anything and wait until the child has already repeated the behaviour before repositioning them, but your child cannot read your mind and does not know the reason you keep moving them is because you do not wish for them to do it anymore. Subsequently they keep going back to the same pattern of behaviour, which in this case is standing on your hip. If you would like the behavioural pattern to stop altogether then you will need to be much more honest, verbal and careful with the definition you give your language.

Make sure they are sitting comfortably then hold them closely and firmly to your hip to prevent them from even trying to stand on your hip. If they raise their leg to stand, immediately pull it back into the normal sitting position with their feet hanging down and say 'Legs down, no climbing on daddy, sitting down please'. Each time you need to correct the leg position repeat that cue. If they stop trying to stand, give immediate and specific praise for their great listening, 'Oh thank you, bubba, no climbing on daddy, good listening'. Also offer a clear physical message by relaxing your embrace around their hips too.

As soon as you can, try to distract them during these transitioning periods by offering them something else to focus on like a toy or something to look for / at rather than just trying to stand up on you. If the behaviour starts again, however, repeat your cues and behaviour management strategies all over again. Always remember, the sooner you move on and try to distract them, the sooner the entire behavioural episode will come to an end. Get them positioned and quickly try to distract them before they start trying again.

What if . . . your baby throws their head back and cries when on your hip? Well, hold them firmly with your arm around their back up as high as possible and pull them close to you, saying 'Sitting up, bubba, no lying back'. Your little one may get cross that your position is preventing them from throwing themselves back, and only permitting their head to look up, but at this point I would just carry on and ignore the behaviour.

If you are finding them too strong and you have to use your own strength to keep them safely in your arms but still feel that you may drop them, turn them on your hips so they have their backs to you, and are sitting high up on your hip facing out, and tip them so they are leaning forward while holding them firmly low around their hips. You may find they continue to tantrum, in which case I would simply carry on and wait for the behaviour to subside if it is attention seeking (as if they don't want you to talk to daddy or mummy, for instance), or try to distract them if they are simply learning how to wait and sit still.

Equally, they may quite like the scenery when facing outwards and calm down quickly without the need for any further intervention from you. If they do calm down you can either bring them into a more upright position still facing out so they can see the world, or praise them and return them to the forward position on your hip using your cue. Don't forget to praise them when they are calm, 'Thank you for sitting up, Charlotte, good listening', and carry on. Get them positioned and quickly try to distract them before they start again.

What if . . . they are leaning forward and putting pressure on your back? You will need to have your arm that is holding them placed higher up around their rib cage and hold them close to you. Offer a clear verbal cue putting forward your expectation of their behaviour, 'Sitting up, wait for daddy'. Once you have used your cue you will need to define that statement with its true definition. Your main aim is to try to keep one of their arms around your back or shoulder and the other arm in front of you. To achieve this I hold the hand that is in front as a way of preventing them from leaning forward while they are actively trying to get down and I use my cue, 'Sitting up, bubba, wait for Sheyney'. Remember your calm patient tone here. I then hold them firmly so they remain close to my body and unable to lean forward easily and carry on with my chore and distraction with a happy tone and demeanour.

If they still manage to lean forward, even when you are holding their hand, then pop your hand under their arm at the front of your body and with a little jump reposition them correctly on your hip before holding them close to your body but firmer than before when they were able to lean. Hold their hand again, or hold under their armpit so they can't lean. As I reposition them, I use my calm, patient cue, 'Sitting up, bubba, wait for Sheyney'. As soon as you have them repositioned, try to distract them immediately. Don't forget to praise them when they are calm with 'Thank you for sitting up, Charlotte, good listening', and carry on. If they relax and start to show more interest in their environment or what you are showing them rather than challenging you, then you can relax your firm hold and allow them to sit back a little. Get them positioned and quickly try to distract them before they start again. If they have calmed down, place your arm around their waist again to allow more freedom of movement for them.

What if . . . your child tries to swap sides to sit on your other hip? This is common and requires you to be a little stronger than your baby. Some babies are amazingly strong, and so very quick. To address this behaviour, you need to adopt a basic language cue like 'no swapping sides, sitting still, wait for mummy'. Once you have done this, you will need to follow through with the strategies highlighted when they lean forward and put pressure on a parent's back. Always remember, the sooner you move on and try to distract them, the sooner the entire behavioural episode will come to an end. Get them positioned and quickly try to distract them before they start again.

What if . . . your child becomes limp and impossible to carry? This one is a little tricky and is definitely the domain of a toddler. If your toddler does turn into a little limp noodle on you—by completely relaxing their body and raising their arms high and slipping through your grip—when you have said you need to hold them for whatever reason, then you still need to follow through with your original request. Before you embark on your reposition, use your cue 'sitting up, wait for mummy' but add an 'Adam do it, or mummy do it?' I find once you have shown them the definition of this statement most toddlers choose to reposition themselves. If they do decide to stop being a noodle then praise them with 'Good listening, Adam, thank you for sitting for mummy'.

In order for that line to be effective, though, you will need to define 'or mummy do it' correctly, 100 per cent of the time, if they remain a noodle. Make them sit as you have requested through *you* repositioning them. To do this turn them to face away from you. Sit them on your right hip (or left hip if you're left handed) and lift their left leg so they are now in a semi-sitting position. Use your right arm to reach around and under their right arm, and across the front of their left leg and hold it just above the back of their knee. This will mean they are still sitting for you, and you will need to praise them for co-operating with you even if they are still trying to be a little limp noodle.

I often find that when they see you are not affected by the noodle attempt and are carrying on with your request and then starting to distract them with your conversation, that they quickly stop the behaviour. Just remember, the sooner you move on and try to distract them, the sooner the entire behavioural episode will come to an end. Get them positioned and quickly try to distract them before they start again.

> The sooner you move on and try to distract them, the sooner the entire behavioural episode will come to an end.

You can also place them so they have their back resting on your stomach. Grab each leg and make them comfortable in the sitting position. It will look like they are sitting in a chair. Again, once they are in this position, thank them for co-operating with your request even though you were the one to create the co-operation and try to distract them by moving on with tasks.

Putting baby down on the floor

Doing this might seem obvious and easy to some, but it can prove to be a perpetually challenging task for many parents and the cause of lots of tears for baby. When they are in your arms they might just not want to be put down . . . ever! But with a little bit of work, this is how it will start to happen:

Putting baby down on the floor

Pre-empting: 'Let's have a little dance now bubby, but *soon* it will be time play on the floor, soon it will be time to sit down and wait for mummy.'

Forewarning: 'Last one, Eliza, *nearly time* to sit down and wait for mummy. Where are those cars?'

Stating event and expectation: 'Ok, *it's time* to sit down, let's play with your red car.' Child looks at you and for the car. You squat down and sit them on your knee so they are facing away from you to prevent any monkey grip if they are prone to doing that. You point to the floor so your baby sees where you intend to put them. You show them the toy by playing with it but do not give it to your child just yet. When they show an interest in the activity, you say 'Sit down, wait for mummy' and quickly but gently pop them on the floor.

Wait game: Flash wait sign with hand and say 'Wait'.

Defining your statements: To lower them to the ground, you lean forward so your shoulder rests on their upper back and lift your baby off your knee by pulling their legs up slightly; raising them in a mid-air sitting position while your child leans on your shoulder, then put them on the ground. Place your hand on their upper back to support them in case your baby throws herself back. If they are new to sitting, pull their nappy up at the back a little so they are comfortably balanced on their bottom with a straight back. Then put their legs at gate position (slightly apart) to centre their weight and have a brief play with the toy that is in front of them. You are likely to be positioned behind them. Manage behaviour through troubleshooting strategies.

Praise: Be specific with your praise, 'Good sitting for mummy, thank you, bubby'.

Following through: Don't allow them to lie on you, lean on you, crawl and stand at your legs, etc. None of these is defining the term 'sit down' for them and you will confuse the meaning and they won't know what you need them to do. Finally, be cautious to not make the same mistake a lot of people make when they are learning to define statements by allowing them to do any of the above-mentioned behaviours *before* you correct them with your cue. If you do, your 'sit down' will mean they can also 'lie down', 'lean over', 'crawl away' or 'stand up' before they have to sit back down. You are asking them to sit and sit only. Be careful not to confuse them.

Completion: Wait game or up cue (see pages 74 and 76).

What if . . .

When you try to pop your little one on the floor *what if* they go as stiff as a board and throw their head back or walk backwards so you can't get them in the sitting position? Above I suggest you have their back resting on the front of your shoulder while you hold up their legs so they are in a sitting position before you put them down. But there is the chance that as soon as you go to put them down they will use their head on your shoulders for leverage and arch their back, making their tummy and face point skyward, and be difficult to sit down. In this case proceed with placing them on the floor but lie them down *then*, if they allow you to, sit them up at that point. Keep them facing away from you, however, and don't allow them to just stand straight up once you have said 'Sit down' or you confuse the meaning of your cue. They either remain lying down, or they allow you to sit them down or up. If they won't allow you to sit them down in the first place, and try to stand instead, then lie them back down and simply get on with playing with the toys yourself.

Do not allow them to climb all over you. They either sit down on the floor or they lie down on the floor. Distract them with a toy and carry on with defining your statement 'Sit down, wait for mummy'. They should be sitting on the floor and not on you but if they are in a full protest, you can sit with them, and have them sitting between your legs but still on the floor, with your arms wrapped around them and playing. If this is still not good enough for your little one and the only thing they will settle for is sitting on your lap, then they are being very bossy indeed. This would be sitting on *their* terms only and would not be something you could maintain as a long-term expectation for them every time you asked them to sit down on the floor for you. Therefore do not have them sit on your legs or they will expect that every time, and asking them to sit will remain an impossible task for your child and you. In this case, persist with sitting them between your legs but on the floor while you cuddle them but don't allow them to turn around, get up or do anything but sit down. Play with the toy until they calm down. It may take some time but stay strong, continue to position them to face away from you and, as mentioned above, don't allow them to stand, turn, lie on you, or lean back completely.

What if . . . they do the monkey grip when you are placing them down on the floor from a standing position after you have been carrying them? The monkey grip describes a child raising their legs and wrapping them firmly around you, making it impossible to put them down. In this case it's important to stand up again, and reposition them so they are facing away from you. Return to the identical strategy mentioned above where you face them away from you, place them on your knee, use your shoulder to support their back and place them in a sitting position with your hands before gently placing them on the floor.

What if . . . your toddler or baby goes stiff and won't settle into a sitting position or walks backwards preventing you from sitting them down? In this case you can get them to sit with a little swing. Anyone who has a toddler will know that as soon as you attempt to sit them down they walk backwards or go stiff so you cannot get them in the sitting position. And no matter how fast you move them back into the sitting position, they walk faster to prevent you from doing that as their little faces go pink with determination. In this case, you must still use your flow of communication to prevent them from resisting in the first place and give them some incentive to want to sit, like offering them a fun toy.

Remember you are always trying to avoid having to manage difficulties rather than always having to repair them with strategies such as these. This is why these scenarios are designed to help you work past old poor patterns to repair language and expectation so there are no more problems or confusions around your language or expectation. If you do run into these problems, despite the use of your flow of communication or if you are on the first week of the behaviour or communication learning and repair ladder, then you will need to pick them up under their arms, and give them a quick swing between your legs saying 'Weeeeeeeee, sitting down' so their heel lands on the floor in front of them. This way they will end up sitting before they can place the soles of the feet down to re-establish a standing position or start to walk backwards. They should be facing you when you do the little swing.

Toddlers, particularly at 18 months plus, are super quick so you will need to be super fast with your swing and bottoms-down strategy to achieve the desired outcome without stress or a battle. It may take a couple of goes but stay calm, defining your statement, sit them down, and thank them for listening: 'Good sitting, thank you, my darling'. If you do swing them and they arch their back, then simply lie them down on the floor instead of sitting them down and they will sit up when they are ready. Just be sure to follow through with your expectation that you would like to put them down. Obviously, a toddler or baby able to stand independently or holding onto objects is fine to be placed on their feet unless you have specifically asked them to sit down. Always balance your requests and make sure you can actually ask them to sit down, so don't stand them up simply because it appears easier.

Sitting and waiting patiently on your lap

Your ability to occasionally ask your child to sit still while you hold them is extremely important, and is often an unacknowledged contributing factor to sleep-time issues and the cause of other tears and tantrums throughout the day from an early age. The lack of development of a child's ability to do this will often be obvious; for example, when it's time for them to sit still while you read them a book, wait patiently in a doctor's surgery, be co-operative on an aeroplane while the seat-belt sign is on, on a long car trip, in the high chair, going shopping, or participating in group-learning opportunities like music or baby gym. It also significantly impacts on a child's ability to develop their concentration skills and attention span and, therefore, the skills they will need during playtime and other learning activities.

In the following section I will break the positioning request to sit on your lap into two simple scenarios. One will highlight a more specific request to sit on your lap while you read stories at home, when your child is allowing you to govern both the positioning request and the book reading. The second one is a more casual request to sit down and wait on your lap for times like when you are in a doctor's surgery waiting room, or on a plane. It's important to note, however, that the home story-time strategy is your first port of call to ensure your little one has developed the skills they need to cope with, understand and become confident in co-operating in the more public and casual sitting situations.

Positioning for sitting and reading during the settling routine

Pre-empting: 'Gage is getting all dressed and warm now, but *soon* it will be time for stories, nearly time to lie down and wait for mummy.'

Forewarning: 'Brushing hair, Gage, then it's time for stories. *Nearly time* to lie down wait for mummy.'

Stating event and expectations: 'Okay, little man, *it's time* for stories, time to sit down and wait for mummy.' Child looks up at you. You then use your wait game and cue (see page 74) and carry your child if they are immobile or a crawler, or pop them on the floor if they can walk and follow, while you say in an excited tone, 'Let's go find your books'. Your baby kicks in anticipation as you carry them to your reading environment. You point to their books saying 'Time for stories, time to sit down and wait for mummy'. You sit down and place your baby on your lap with their head on your chest as you repeat your cue to 'sit down and wait for mummy'. They happily oblige. If you have a toddler, they race along holding your hand or on their own to wherever you guide them or to your usual book-reading place and wait excitedly for you to sit down. You pat your legs and say 'C'mon then, sit down and wait for mummy'. They raise their little arms for you to lift them onto your lap and spy their favourite book. Once you have them on your lap, you confidently repeat 'Sit down, wait for mummy' and flash them your wait sign (see page 74).

Defining your statement: They sit comfortably and look to where the books are kept. If they are under 12 months old, you chose the book and begin reading. If they are over 12 months they can choose from your selection of two books before happily allowing you to begin reading. From six months of age onwards they can listen intently, point to pictures they recognise, turn the page when you ask using your cue, 'Turn the page', and lift the pop-up flaps when prompted using the cue, 'Gage do it'. By 12 months they will babble through a reading experience. By 18 months to two years they will try to articulate words and parrot your words and point out pictures and objects on request. During the reading they don't rush through the book, or try to get down.

Praise: If they are sitting and waiting and listening happily and don't look like they are going to challenge you, praise them, 'Good sitting, Gage', 'Good waiting for mummy, little fellow'. Praise and praise and praise good behaviour throughout.

Following through: If they try to get down at any point through the book reading, they will readily stop and wait when you politely ask them to 'sit down, wait for mummy' using your wait sign. If they try to get another book, you will tuck it behind your back and redirect their attention to the book in your hand with 'Not time for last book yet, wait for mummy'. If they try to wiggle free you will use the strategies highlighted in the *'What if . . .'* section of this strategy, and a simple 'sitting down, wait for mummy' cue, and you reposition them to help them sit calmly.

Completion: At the end you put the books away without any protests from your baby and they are happy to start snuggling in for the settling routine or the stated event you have been pre-empting during reading by saying, for example, *'It's time* for sleep'.

Positioning for sitting and waiting patiently in casual situations

Pre-empting: 'Gage, we're going to see the puppies in the shop now, *but soon* we will go to see the doctor. *Soon* it will be time to sit down and wait for mummy / daddy.'

Forewarning: 'Gage, time to wave bye bye to the puppies, we're going to see the doctor. *Nearly time* to sit down and wait for mummy.'

Stating event and expectation: Wave bye bye to the puppies and take your little one to the surgery, where you will sit with them while you wait. You follow through by entering the surgery even if they are challenging you. They are able to calm quickly. You point to where you plan on sitting, and if you anticipate a challenge from your child, then you also point to or show them the object they can have *once* they are sitting (like a book or comfort item). As you sit down you say 'Okay Gage, *it's time* to go sit down, wait for mummy'. They sit as requested.

Defining your statement: Use your cue, 'Time to sit down and wait for mummy'. You sit down regardless of any fussing and you place them in a sitting position on your lap.

Praise: If they do sit happily and don't look like they are going to challenge you, praise their great listening with a specific 'Good sitting for mummy, Gage, thank you, clever!' and carry on casually. If you feel it is appropriate, then offer them a toy, or if they are happy to sit there and hold or play with your necklace, then always allow them to explore their environment for entertainment first, rather than solving it for them by offering them a toy.

Following through: If they are moving around you use your cues 'legs down, wait for mummy', or 'sitting still, wait for mummy', or 'sitting up, wait for mummy', or 'good sitting / listening', or 'mummy get you a book / toy, sitting down, waiting please'. All your tones should be light and happy but confident with a clear downward inflection (see page 58). Remember the importance of defining each statement. To make sitting in the doctor's office less stressful for them try to make sure you have either talked through, or role played, or both at home beforehand so they know some of the things the doctor might do. Perhaps look in their ear while pulling down gently on their lobe like a doctor would saying 'Let's check those ears', or look in their mouth saying 'Where's that tongue', or by putting something on their chest or back just like a doctor would. I use my bag of tricks (see page 369) in the surgery if I know they are prone to becoming unsettled, or I simply use my cues to sit and wait as the doctor is distraction enough to keep them occupied.

Completion: When the sitting episode draws to a close, complete the event with a simple, 'Time to go. Let's go find mummy's car. Wave bye bye to the doctor.'

It's important to note that a casual sitting opportunity can also be at home at the dining table as they sit on your lap with toys, for instance, or on the floor on your lap with an activity or story. The above scenario is simply an example for you to base all other sitting events on. If you are at home and pursuing a sitting-down event it's important to complete that request differently to the way you would if you were somewhere like a doctor's surgery, on an aeroplane or at a café. Simply leaving those environments signify your request has come to an end. At home the wait game and cue are appropriate to conclude a positioning event on a positive note. To simply change the conditions, without saying your expectation for them to sit has ended, may confuse the definition of the last thing you said, or give currency or weight to the last thing they said or did.

Asking a child to sit still on your lap is actually not a complex task, and it is one that you should start to help them develop from the age of six months. At six months of age, their ability to sit and concentrate on a single task or activity lasts for around three to eight minutes, and will quickly proceed to ten minutes within a short period if you provide opportunities like this often, both during a play activity and story times. Try to remember that by the time they go to daycare or enter preschool at three years of age, your little one will be expected to have developed the listening and concentration skills to sit for around 15 to 20 minutes during a group time, meal time, play session or story. By the time they are school age, they are required to use this skill between the hours of 9 a.m. to 3 p.m., five days a week (excluding meal breaks) for the next 18 plus years of their lives. So let's get realistic. This skill is in fact a vital life skill, and vital for their education, and you are responsible for teaching it to them.

Some parents think that while their child is a baby they shouldn't have to do this, but I have to say, they really should. You need to be able to feed them, and put them into their bed without the need to hold them or stay with a thrashing baby, so they can learn how to relax and accept the sensation of tired peacefully. It's a basic life skill. Other occasions when you can expect your little one to use this skill, from the age of six months up to two years, include:

- lying in your arms or elsewhere while you bottle feed or breastfeed them until the meal is completed
- sitting on your lap for an enjoyable language-rich story session (for eight to ten minutes initially, for ten minutes within two weeks of active book-reading sessions, and 15 plus minutes by the time they reach 18 to 20 months of age)
- being put into and staying in their pram, car seat or high chair without a fight or struggle and remaining there for a reasonable amount of time without you needing to rock or entertain them perpetually
- sitting on your hip in one position without trying to stand up on you, or swap your hips, or squirm out of your arm, or insisting you sway, jiggle or rock, and without trying to leap out of your arms, all the while refusing to let you put them down
- being able to sit down on your lap without insisting you stand when holding them
- being able to take a plane flight without the dreaded screaming and stress that can accompany the 'fasten your seat belts' instruction (believe me, with the amount of flying I do, I so wish more people knew this skill so children weren't so stressed on flights . . . *really!*). There is a very clear difference between a child experiencing inner-ear discomfort on assent and descent and a child who has never been asked to sit down and wait before
- holding your hand patiently while you are walking (18 months plus)
- sitting quietly on the couch and waiting for you to get their milk, or feed their baby brother or sister (18 months plus).

So what's the secret, where's the magic wand? The answer is in your flow of communication and your ability to confidently ask them to do something for you, and your ability to define your statements or requests and, finally, in being consistent. This strategy is the fastest and most effective tool you have. Anything worthwhile doing usually takes a little bit of work to achieve and self-discipline to maintain. But if you need a baby or toddler to learn how to do something, then you need to be the one doing the work, and you're the one that needs to be disciplined enough to be consistent. If you would like things to stay really peaceful and pleasant once you have taught them these new boundaries, then you definitely need to be consistent. Your ongoing consistency is what I call maintenance and it's particularly important for sleep.

If you are not consistent and do not correctly define your statement (see page 44) then it will take your little one longer to learn the skill and they may become stressed from the confusion. You also risk a relapse into old behaviour and that's not fair because then your baby needs to learn all over again. The point of correcting the old poor routine is to teach them clearly how to do it and then it is done and you or they never need to go through that learning process again. They should master this positioning within one to three days. If you are behaving nervously, are frightened or upset, however, because they won't sit and you are losing your confidence, they will think there is something wrong with sitting and take much longer to relax, if at all. The key then, is confidence, so remain happy and relaxed at all times (even if you have to pretend a little), and be consistent and define your statements clearly.

Both of the above scenarios are realistic expectations of your child from six months of age once you have taught them the new routine and cues that go with the activity. It is an ideal form of communication and will help prevent tears for them and stress for you at a time when they have to sit and wait and calm down, particularly for sleep time. It's also a way of saying long before you ask them to go to sleep, 'Look to me for guidance', and any discussions that need to be had are then sorted out well before you reach their bedroom, guaranteeing you success.

This entire expectation to sit down calmly is achievable through your flow of communication (see page 40) and the simple 'sit down, wait for mummy' cue. One of the most important aspects here is the actual position you sit your little one in initially. You must not mislead them into believing they are going to have a breastfeed, or put them in a position that they think means they can turn around and stand up on your lap. When you plan on sitting them down and asking them to wait for you, it's important to encourage them to sit:

- upright on their bottom, not lying on you or turning to face you
- parallel to you, as in you both face the same direction with their legs out in front of them
- leaning slightly forward.

Make sure you have introduced the intended activity at the same time as your cue so they can clearly see the intention of this sitting activity before they have to sit on your lap. This gives them a little more incentive. Sitting down and waiting need to be defined with its true definition, which is sitting peacefully without them even *trying* to continually adjust that position. Be sure that you are well prepared for any event when you need to manage their positioning. You are not asking your child to sit and be bored, so have something for them to do, listen to, look at or play with. Be prepared for the event.

What if . . .

What if . . . they challenge you through this process? The more intense the response from your baby the more work you will need to do with your parent-governed lines of communication throughout all the other times of their day to help them through it quickly. In the following scenarios I will highlight the most extreme types of behaviour I have witnessed with some of my most unsettled children to make sure all the bases are covered. Some of this will not apply to you but for those of you who need it, I am with you all the way, having gone through it many, many times myself. You will get there and your baby will be able to sit calmly, but you must teach them how first. Consistent, calm, repetitious language-based routines around the request to sit down and wait *do* produce the most remarkable rate of behaviour turnaround. Within one to three days children are completely relaxed and happy to sit with no more tantrums or stress.

What if . . . you are experiencing real problems with guiding your sprightly little pickle? Don't fret, be confident and use the following management and language cues without losing your confidence and failing to complete the task through fear. You will find your child will quickly stop the old negative pattern of behaviour and relax into your new honest, well-defined language cues and routines almost immediately if you are confident with your request. But be under no illusion at this point: you might now be dealing with a fully fledged tantrum. If your child is saying a very definite 'NO' you need to be able to guide them and define your statement, so you have to follow through to achieve your goal. Remember to always assess the situation and request from an adult's perspective (see page 70).

> The number one reason for managing positioning: if you can't ask them to sit on your lap for a lovely story time, how can you ask them to go to sleep peacefully when you place them in their cot to lie patiently as they wait for the Sleep Bus to come?

The typical times you will need to use the 'sit down' language cue will be when you pop them on your lap, on the floor, in the high chair, in the car seat, in the pram or bath or cot. If they are reluctant to allow you to govern a situation, asking them to sit down will be a guaranteed tantrum zone, right from eight months of age. Obviously the older they get, the more difficult this situation can be to manage, but the suggestion that they are too strong is simply not true. You can easily manage this short-term challenge while your little one transitions from a poor style of behaviour during a routine that was making them and you miserable and stressed into a new more positive, co-operative and pleasant demeanour.

The most challenging behavioural responses I've commonly experienced when requesting a little one to sit down are back arching, going stiff or kicking; using their arms to try and turn around; and mistaking every sitting event as breastfeed time. These behaviours are rarely displayed but not unheard of in little ones under eight to ten months of age; they are more common between 12 and 24 months. Read and reread the following two behaviour strategies carefully before embarking on your repair. There's no rush. Better you do it correctly, than rush and use an incomplete strategy.

What if . . . your baby arches their back, goes stiff or kicks because of a tantrum, or as a clear way of saying they don't want to sit down? Try to sit them down and firmly and confidently use your language cues 'sitting up', or 'sit down, wait for mummy'. It's important to follow through until you achieve the result of them sitting down for you. You should sit them so their back is facing your stomach, they have one leg on either side of your legs, straddling you, and you are looking over their shoulder so if they throw their head back they don't hit your face accidentally—this could injure you both, so be mindful of it. Once sitting, if they continue to tantrum and arch their back, try to lean forward a little and bring their legs up (so their feet meet if they are a baby, or with both legs outstretched on both your legs) without allowing them to stand on your lap. This will help them to stop trying to thrash around. They may fight against this but it will prevent you or them from getting hurt and will bring the tantrum to an end quicker by giving them less leverage with which to throw themselves back.

Often the thrashing and arching are more upsetting for them than the original request to sit down. Always remember to assess that request from an adult's perspective. It's only sitting, so it's not an unreasonable request. Talk confidently and try to distract them with enthusiastic language about a book or toy. Stick with your story telling until the tantrum subsides and they start to calm down. Do not release the firm hold you have or allow them to be in any other position until they calm down. Your firm hold is what is comforting for them. Only when they are feeling far more at ease should you lessen this safety net for them. Periodically, repeat your cue in a calm and confident tone, 'Sit down, Gage, wait for mummy', then go back to your enthusiastic reading.

If they are sliding their bottom forward, try to hold them so they can't slide forward. Perhaps firmly place your hand in front of them on the leg they are sitting on so it acts as a barrier. At all times you will need to have your arm firmly around them. You will need to keep repositioning their arms at their side and not allow them to turn and grab your shoulders. You may feel a little awkward while you struggle to establish and maintain this position for a few minutes but stick with it and your baby will soon settle. Please remember, this form of intervention is rarely needed unless your little one is struggling with guidance, and should only last a day before significant improvement or complete relief is achieved for the child. Always remember that the sooner you move on and try to distract them, the sooner the entire behavioural episode will come to an end.

What if . . . your baby is using their arms to try and turn around? Again, your positioning is important here. Make sure you remember the basic rules of sitting them on your lap. You must not mislead them into thinking they can turn around and stand up on your lap. When you plan on sitting them down and asking them to wait for you it is important to have them sit upright and facing away from you; don't allow them to lie on you or turn to face you. Sitting down needs to be defined for its true meaning, which is sitting with their legs in front of them, sitting on their bottom, and sitting peacefully without trying to adjust that position. If they try to turn around, simply put their arms back at their sides and turn them to their original sitting position and repeat your .cue, 'Sit down, wait for mummy'. At no point should you allow them to grab your shoulder, or place an arm under yours. Just keep repositioning their arms and repeating your cue before it gets out of hand. Prevention rather than full correction is desired here so stop them before they lie down and nuzzle in for a feed etc.

After each reposition, they will be a little cross, but keep reading from your book enthusiastically and reposition them a couple of times while doing so. If this does not defuse the situation gradually and distract them; then repeat the cue and reposition them. The sooner you move on and try to distract them, the sooner the entire behavioural episode will come to an end.

What if . . . your baby is mistaking every sitting event as breastfeeding time? There is nothing wrong with breastfeeding on demand when it is balanced. When the breast, however, becomes the emotional solution to every single feeling outside being happy, I find this to be an extremely unbalanced and potentially confusing message for a little one learning how to deal with their complex responses to the world around them. Added to that, when a child mistakes every sitting opportunity as a breastfeeding opportunity, then they are simply demanding the feed because it has become a routine event on sitting. Let me tell you about the negative cycle of breastfeeding on demand on sitting when there are no boundaries.

If you know your little one has had enough food or is not due for a feed, but every time you sit with them they keep sliding into a breastfeeding position, you need to be aware of the way little people work. Like us, they are creatures of habit, so if you mainly sit with them to feed them, then they will automatically assume that is the only purpose of sitting and demand it every time you sit down with them, therefore you need to create two separate scenarios to help them understand the difference between a sitting request and a feeding opportunity. Also be aware that if you say 'yes' once when they 'demand' it upon sitting, then 'no' the next time they demand it upon sitting, you are being unpredictable. This will unsettle your baby, frustrate them, and possibly even encourage a battle for a feed every time you sit down. This means you have to be clear about your parent-governed lines of communication when it comes to sitting down with your little one. It is either time for a feed or it's not. You can say 'No, it's not time for milk, sitting on lap, wait for mummy' and correct their position and they will understand immediately once you have established your language for positioning and sitting calmly on your lap.

Breastfeeding on demand can also become a bit of a stumbling block when your breast has gone beyond the need for food and is now only for comforting. Comfort feeding is a useful tool if there is a *true need* to comfort a child—with deliberate emphasis on those words 'true need'. But be very cautious. This is like telling them that every time they experience something new or feel anything other than happy that they cannot cope without you, but here you are saying that they cannot cope without the need to suckle (which is eat and drink). By doing this you are not necessarily helping them to learn balanced coping skills or equipping their emotional tool kit (see page 87) with the variety of valuable skills they need in order to cope as they grow. I personally do not encourage feeding as an emotional solution to normal everyday situations and requests. I opt to let children experience new things, and choose to work through those new things confidently with them until they understand them and find comfort in their familiarity. I prefer to offer many opportunities for a child to learn how to cope when experiencing normal emotions. Breastfeeding should only be used where there is a true need for comfort to calm down from fear, discomfort, etc., so you can create a balance.

Why not just let your child experience the feelings they have when you ask them to sit on your lap? Anything new for a baby or toddler tends to make them feel uncomfortable, but by no means is this a situation where you want to reinforce the need to breastfeed as a coping strategy for something new. The way you respond to their learning process, no matter how vocal they become, and the things you can teach them to do to calm down without the need to eat or become clingy will empower them to cope with this same normal life experience every time this emotion comes up throughout each and every day.

If you know that it is not time for a breastfeed, then the most important thing to remember when you sit them down on your lap is to be conscious of how you are sitting them so you don't mislead them into believing it's milk time. Do *not*:

- sit them side on on your lap
- tuck your arm over their one little shoulder, which allows them to tuck one of their arms around you and lie back
- support their full weight in a cradle position.

Sit them down upright and leaning slightly forward with their back facing you and both their arms in front of them.

Once you are sure the cause of your child attempting to reposition themselves for a breastfeed has not been triggered by you, you need to use your language carefully. If they start to slide their back across your front and turn for a feed (usually because this is a habit in the case of a child taught to demand feed on sitting) then try to stop them from getting very far as quickly as you can and re-sit them upright, saying 'Sitting up, wait for mummy'. Lean forward slightly and keep reading their book to them with lots of animation and enthusiasm. The less progress they make in repositioning themselves, the fewer tears you will have to deal with. Every time your baby tries to slide, quickly block them with your arm and sit them back in position and say 'Sitting up, bubba, wait for mummy'. If the behaviour is repeated, be sure to answer their request with an honest answer: 'No milk now, bubba, sitting up, wait for mummy'. At this point, keep them sitting upright by wrapping your arms around their waist. Remember, the sooner you move on and try to distract them, the sooner the entire behavioural episode will come to an end.

The way you respond to their learning process, no matter how vocal they become, and the things you can teach them to do to calm down . . . will empower them to cope with normal life experiences.

Sitting calmly in their high chair

Yes, you can put your child in a high chair from the age of eight months without them dissolving into tears. Here's how it should happen:

'Sitting calmly in their high chair' communication broken down into component parts

Pre-empting: Campbell, mummy change your nappy, *soon* it's time for lunch. *Soon* it's time to sit down, wait for mummy.' Show the wait sign.

Forewarning: 'Okay, bubby, last song, *nearly time* to sit down and wait for mummy.' Flash wait sign. 'Lunch time, yummy chicken and vegetables.'

Stating event and expectation: You walk to the kitchen carrying your little one, or with your toddler walking with you, and go to the high chair together. You pat the high chair and say warmly '*It's time* to sit down and wait for mummy' and show them the wait sign. You then point at the high chair, then pat the seat so your baby sees where you intend to put them. You show them their pre-prepared lunch, and say 'Yummy lunch', then put it out of reach. You pick up your child if they are a toddler using your up cue and say 'Sitting down, wait for mummy', and pop baby / toddler into their high chair. At this point you do up and secure safety buckles and adjust tray table and put on bib. You then feed your child, perhaps singing songs and chatting to them as you do, bearing in mind that their concentration span is three to five minutes' long during a meal.

Wait game: As you clean up your baby and the high chair tray and surrounds and put utensils in the kitchen, use the wait cue and game. Say 'sit down and wait for mummy'.

Defining your statement: Manage behaviour by using your cues 'Sit down and wait for mummy', or 'wait', or 'hands out, mummy do it'. Add nursery rhymes and songs to keep their interest while they eat.

Praise: If they are sitting happily and eating the food given to them say 'Good sitting, bubba, thank you for listening'.

Following through: If they are moving around use your cues 'sitting down, wait for mummy', or 'legs down', or 'hands out', or 'face the front', or 'sitting up'. You need to manage their position in the chair and their eating behaviour through your flow of communication.

Completion: When you are ready use the wait game before unbuckling them and saying 'Up up'. Baby raises arms once the cue is said and you lift your child out of the high chair and give them a big hug and raspberry kisses with lots of praise for good sitting and listening.

I am called into many houses where the above scenario seems incredibly unlikely. The child and family are in significant distress or, at the very least, extremely unsettled. Within two days of consistent management, their little ones are almost jumping out of my arms to get into the chair for their lunch or a story, much to the stunned amazement of their parents. The entire purpose of this strategy is to stop the endless fighting that occurs in some houses around sitting in the high chair, or anywhere for that matter, when their parents ask them to. This comes back to you creating predictability for your child with your parent-governed line of communication. If they do not find you predictable enough, they will want to govern the situation so *they* can predict or control events. This feels safer to them if you won't provide the predictability they crave.

Often if you take the negotiation out of the sitting request, a child is happy to co-operate and sit because they learn that all they ever do when asked to sit is sit, taking the stress of who, when and how that is done out of the event. The problems around sitting only come up when a child thinks there is another option to negotiate through. Once your child realises that choices about whether to sit in their high chair or not are no longer available, you have established a clear boundary around that event, and you govern this line of communication with your single request, defined with it's true meaning: 'Sit down, and wait'. Only when they are able to cope with the responsibility of having multiple choices at sitting time, which is indicated by a lack of tantrums, you can consider offering other lines of communication at this time.

When you have them safely buckled in the high chair, get a chair for yourself and sit at their level. I do not recommend stools as you cannot have as rich a connection or as powerful a language experience as you would if you are at their eye level. Talk about their food, their day, and the sounds you can hear around you. Try to find the humour in your day. Use lots of repetitive cues to encourage strong language associations needed for self-feeding like 'scoop it up', or 'in your mouth'.

What if . . . you need to sit them into a high chair and they are fighting you? During this reaction from a child they are likely to try and kick off the chair with their feet, and throw their head back and arch their back. If you know they are likely to do this, then your work lies in preventing the old pattern from even starting with your flow of communication. You then do things a little differently. While standing at the side of the high chair holding them, place them in the sitting position in your arms first before attempting to put them in the seat feet first. Hold them in the sitting position firmly so they can't arch and move them into their seat efficiently. You should stand beside the high chair and their feet should never touch the seat as you put them in. This way you can put their feet in first, then quickly reach around under the tray and pull their feet through so they end up on their bottom. Be persistent.

If you have a toddler who is very strong both physically and in will, you will need to be just as strong to remain calm and repeat your cue reassuringly—'Sitting down, wait for mummy'—to achieve results as quickly as possible. Make sure you buckle them in firmly and quickly so they don't try to turn and stand up. If they try to get their arms out of the five-point harness you can simply tie a thick ribbon bow between the two shoulder straps at chest height. This will stop them sliding their arms out of their shoulder straps. Please supervise them at all times. Once their habit of taking their arms out of their shoulder strap stops, you can cease using the tie on their harness as they will have stopped trying to get out.

If trying to put them in feet first is too difficult, then stand them on the seat and reach under the tray and pull their feet through. I often prefer to remove the tray with a toddler if they are finding sitting in their chair stressful. This will help you make the sitting down process much faster. Once they are sitting, they may get very cross that you have followed through despite their most vocal protests. If this does happen, expect them to continue arching their back or trying to turn around by pulling one knee up in an attempt to stand. On both these occasions, you will need to be as quick as possible and very consistent until they are safely buckled in. If they try to lift their leg and turn around so they can get back up, pull that same leg gently back into sitting forward position and say 'Legs down, wait for mummy'. If they try to turn around to stand up, correct the legs and release their grip from whatever they are pulling on and repeat 'Legs down, sit down, wait for mummy', or 'Hands down, wait for mummy'.

You can attempt to enthusiastically offer a toy at this stage, staying 100 per cent focused on keeping them sitting however. More than likely they will throw it away or furiously sweep the tray to clear it of any toys. In this case, do not try to return the toy—they have made it very clear they don't want it and to force the issue would be adding insult to the injury they are feeling. This whole time you will need to be trying to get their buckles on so they can be safe. Stay calm, stay confident and loving, but be as quick as you can. Once the buckles are done up, thank them for sitting and be empathetic: 'Good sitting, Campbell, thank you for listening. Mummy knows it's a little tricky, you're okay.'

Replace the tray and carry on. If you are having trouble replacing the tray follow through by calmly saying 'Tray on' and using cues like 'hands down, mummy do it', 'feet down, mummy do it', until the tray is in place, even if it takes you quite some time. Stay calm, and be endlessly patient, even if you have broken into a bit of a sweat by this stage. Attempt to calm them down with parallel playing (see page 131) or reading a book without burdening them too heavily with lots of eye contact or statements like

'Look, Campbell, look, look at what mummy has'. You simply need to try and distract them while they adjust to the brand new boundary you are setting. Just calmly play with your toy or read the book in an enthusiastic tone without telling your child to do anything, or even making eye contact if it upsets them. Always remember, the sooner you move on confidently and happily and try to distract them, the sooner the entire behavioural episode will come to an end.

Carry on with your meal time as planned, and stay positive. Complete the entire meal in a way that you would like to on any normal day. Remember this management may only need to be used twice on one day then all the old fussing will be over and within three days getting in the high chair will be a relaxed event.

What if . . . they are kicking their legs furiously? Once you have used your cues, and are managing their back arching, their kicking is something that can be left unmanaged unless they are kicking you. If they are just cross and having a tantrum, stay calm, be reassuring with your language and try to distract them. They will settle down if they can see that you are okay and that you have moved on to something new.

> Often if you take the negotiation out of the sitting request, a child is happy to co-operate and sit because they learn that all they ever do when ask to sit is sit.

If they are kicking you, you will need to respond by removing yourself from the kicking range if possible. If you cannot remove yourself from harm's way, then you need to manage their legs in the same way you would manage their hands or in the same way you would manage their hands for hitting. Simply hold their feet firmly at the ankles and position them as you would like them to be. Confidently say 'No kicking, bubba, legs down' and hold them for around ten to 30 seconds. Repeat this pattern until they stop kicking.

If the kicking continues, repeat your request 'Sit down and wait', but try to reposition yourself, or hold them in a way that they can kick freely without kicking you, and carry on trying to distract them. Always remember that the sooner you move on and try to distract them, the sooner the entire behavioural episode will come to an end.

Putting baby / toddler into the car seat or pram without tears

Whether you are putting your baby or toddler in a car seat or pram, the strategy is the same. Your aim is to complete the task without tears and to do this you need to use your parent-governed lines of communication. This is the how it should pan out.

'Putting baby / toddler in car seat / pram' communication broken down into component parts

Pre-empting: 'Daisy, mummy change your nappy, *soon* it's time to go in mummy's car / pram. Nearly time to sit down, wait for mummy.' Show wait sign. Sing a little song as you change their nappy.

Forewarning: 'Okay, bubby, last song, *nearly time* to go and sit down in the pram / car and wait for mummy.' Show wait sign. 'We're going to drive in mummy's car . . . brrm brrm / going for walk in pram.'

Event and expectation: 'Okay, Daisy, *it's time* to go in mummy's car / your pram. Sit down, wait for mummy' and show wait sign. Child will look up at you and you say 'up up' and carry child to car or pram, or say 'Let's go' and gesture for them to come with you if you have a toddler able to walk to the car / pram holding your hand (see page 341). Open car door or pull pram into position and pat car seat or pram to show child where you intend to put them and warmly say 'Time to sit down and wait for mummy', flashing wait sign again. You can also show them their car or pram toy unless you are starting from scratch and teaching your child to sit patiently by introducing toys gradually using your bag of tricks (see page 369). Put your child into their seat, adjust their safety buckles and offer them their toy once they are sitting as requested, if appropriate. If car scenario, the parent then gets into the car while being conscious about letting the child know their movements: 'Mummy get into the car too, I'll be back' before parent walks around to other side of car. Parent hops in the car and says 'I'm back, mummy is sitting down too'. If pram scenario, parent says 'Mummy pushing pram, let's go'.

Defining your statement: Manage behaviour using your cues 'sit down and wait for mummy', 'wait'.

Praise: 'Good sitting, bubba, thank you for listening.'

Completion: When it's time to get them out of the car seat or pram, play the wait game and use your up cue.

The scenario is easy to achieve but it seems to be such a common problem in many households. It's also a problem in many of the homes I go into where the child and family are in significant distress or, at the very least, extremely unsettled. Within two days of consistent management, I find a child is almost jumping out of my arms to get into the car seat or pram to play with their toys, much to the astonishment of their parents.

What if . . .

What if . . . they arch their back, and sitting them in a pram or car seat is a far more challenging task because there is nothing to stop them sliding right out of their pram or car seat? If you have a little one who is very strong both physically and in will, you will need to be just as strong to keep them from sliding straight out. Put them in their seat by placing them into the sitting position in your arms first. Their feet should not touch the seat. Remember, to remain very calm and repeat your cue reassuringly, 'Sitting down, wait for mummy'. Make sure you are defining your statement quickly and without confusion to achieve results with as few tears as possible. This means don't put them back on your hip when they start to tantrum or you will be teaching them to tantrum if they don't want to get in the seat. Remember, this is a confident approach, so if you have said 'It's time to sit [anywhere]', then you need to follow through to completion until their tantrum disappears.

To help stop them from sliding out of the seat, it's so important to use your arm to keep them in place. Firmly push down on the seat between their legs. This will act as a block to stop them sliding but it won't stop their back arching. You will need to be patient and wait for that to subside. Be prepared, they will push against your arm with all their strength, so push down against the chair with all your strength. It might be easier if you close your fist tight so your fingers don't get hurt in the process. While they may well be very cross at your confident insistence that they are not to slide out of their chair as you will need to put their buckles on, at no point should you be frustrated or annoyed by them. The reason you are correcting this pattern is because they are stressed and confused and you need to lay a new predictable pattern so they can relax.

If they are having a big tantrum and really pushing hard against your hand that is preventing them from sliding down as they would like, then don't even bother trying to do up the buckles just yet. Just keep your arm firmly in place so they don't slide and wait for them to relax a little before you put one buckle over their shoulder. You may need to keep them from rolling and grabbing the side of the chair by putting their arm back at their side and repeating your cue 'Sitting down, bubby, waiting for mummy'. You need to be patient throughout the tantrum. Work right through it. Don't lose your cool or your confidence. Once they relax a little, you can get one buckle on, then the other.

Once the buckles are done up, thank them for sitting and appear as calm and unaffected by the tantrum as possible with 'Good sitting, Daisy, thank you for listening'. Unlike the bag-of-tricks strategy (see page 369), if they are unsettled, it's okay to offer them a toy for distraction. If they don't want to play with the toy you have offered, however, then accept their decision to not play with it as much as you would respect their request to play with a toy.

Offer them a drink of water and give them a reassuring kiss. Always remember, the sooner you move on and try to distract them, the sooner the entire behavioural episode will come to an end.

What if . . . they are kicking their legs furiously? Remember your cue, 'no kicking, legs down'. Once you have used your cue and are managing their back arching, their kicking is something that can be left unmanaged unless they are kicking you. If they are just cross and having a tantrum, stay calm, be reassuring with your language and try to distract them. They will settle down if they can see that you are okay. If they are kicking you, you will need to respond by removing yourself from the kicking range if possible. If you cannot remove yourself from harm's way, then you need to manage their legs in the same way you would manage their hands for hitting, by simply holding their feet firmly at the ankles and positioning them as you would like them to be.

Confidently say 'No kicking, bubba, legs down' and hold them for around ten to 30 seconds. Repeat this pattern until they stop kicking. If the kicking continues, please do not alter the request to 'sit down and wait', just try to reposition yourself out of their leg range, or hold them in a way that they can kick freely without kicking you, and carry on trying to distract them. Always remember, the sooner you move on and try to distract them, the sooner the entire behavioural episode will come to an end.

Sitting baby in the bath

Water play at bath time is a valuable developmental skill across the board, and a wonderfully soothing and relaxing wind down to the day. It is important for obvious safety reasons that you set a bath boundary of sitting while bathing. This is how a good bath session should go:

'Sitting baby in the bath' communication broken down into component parts

Pre-empting: 'Emily, it's time for nudie play, but *soon* we're having a bath. Nearly time to sit down, wait for mummy.'

Forewarning: 'Okay, bubby, last play, then it's time for bath. *Nearly time* to sit down and wait for mummy.'

Stating event and expectation: 'Time for bath, Emily, *it's time* to sit down and wait for mummy.' Your child will look at you and you will flash the wait sign again. You carry or lead your child into the bathroom and if your child is old enough they can choose some toys for the bath. You gently pop your child into the bath, and hold them until they are settled and balanced. During bath time you and your child can enjoy songs, rhymes and fun play together, and even practise pouring water over your baby's head in anticipation of shampooing times.

Defining your statement: You understand that at no point does 'sit down and wait for mummy' mean 'but you can stand up repeatedly if you like'. Each time they reach for the side of the bath with the intention of using it to try and stand, block their hand with a slow sweeping movement of your hand to prevent them from touching the wall altogether and repeat your cue, 'No standing, sit down'. They will happily return to playing. If they shift their body position on to one foot and one knee, you sit them back onto their bottom and remind them that this is sitting down. If they try to kneel or squat this can be also corrected using the same cue before they manage to position themselves: 'no kneeling / squatting / standing, sit down' as you correct their position physically. Always remain happy and distract them with songs, rhymes, and fun play, which they will enjoy.

Praise: 'Good sitting, Emily, thank you my darling.'

Following through: Say 'Sit down' if they attempt to stand, kneel, squat. Be consistent.

Completion: When you are ready, initiate the packing away of toys and use your 'ta for mummy' cue before pulling the plug. Use your wait game and up cue before you lift your child from the bath.

Exception: Lying down in the bath is fine and it can be suggested to them with a simple cue like 'lie down for mummy' while they are still learning to do it, or by asking 'Are you going to lie down? Good thinking', once they understand the boundaries of sitting down in the bath for you.

When your baby is old enough, allow them to choose toys from the toy bucket and pop them over the edge of the bath before they get in. Play with the toys for a moment then make clear eye contact with your baby and repeat your cue, 'Sit down, wait for mummy'. When in the bath, practise pouring water over your baby's head, using a simple 'ready for water, 1, 2, 3' cue before you pour. When you pour the water sound enthusiastic. As soon as you have poured the water, use a flat hand to wipe down their face to remove the water. You can gradually build up to this by just wetting the back of their head for a few days at first, then slowly incorporate more of their head until it also flows over their face.

Your main communication strategy at bath time is only to prevent your child from standing up in the tub. Your main objective is to block or quickly release their hands each time they go to grab the side of the bath to stand up or reposition their legs as they ready themselves to stand up. As you do this use your language cue 'no standing'. Remember, you need to work through your request patiently: 'Sit down, wait for mummy/daddy.' Remember to define that statement with its true definition. 'Sit down' does not mean 'stand up and I'll sit you back down', or 'squat', or 'sit on your knees', or 'stand to get your toy then sit down again'. It means 'sit down' only.

What if . . .

What if . . . your child just cries or tantrums about getting into the bath, and then about getting out again at the end of bath time, or bursts into tears when simply asked to sit down when asked? Then you are dealing with a little one who is having trouble with your guidance. This means you need to work on your parent-governed line of communication. You'll need to re-read the three lines of communication (see page 29) to understand more about your guiding line of communication. Before your child gets used to sitting down in the bath, it would be considerate to role play (see page 372) with teddy to show your child your expectations at bath time. Use your cues 'sit down, teddy, wait for mummy', and 'sitting on bottom please, teddy', and 'good sitting'.

The other obvious thing you need to think about is to make sure there is no reason for your baby to feel the need to stand up in the bath in the first place. Have their toys within reach. Also think about buying a bath mat for them to sit on so they can feel safe. I often find the slipperiness of their bottoms on the bath enamel makes them feel less secure than they feel when they are standing up. A bath mat or, better still, a bath seat for an under-one year old will prevent them from sliding around and help them feel less vulnerable when sitting.

If they continue to stand even once these measures are in place, however, then you need to be one step ahead of them, and know your baby well enough to pre-empt when they might be about to try and stand up. Try to play and keep them occupied so they don't think about standing up, and keep reinforcing the request through praise, 'Good sitting, Emily, no standing in the bath, thanks for sitting'. If they do manage to get on one knee, or turn their feet indicating they are about to get onto their knees, then you will need to correct their position so they are sitting back on their little bottom, with their feet out in front of them. If they manage to stand up, you will need to sit them down quite quickly. If you have a baby under 12 months, this is more easily achieved by holding them under the arms and walking them backwards fairly quickly so they sit. If you have a toddler, however, you need to define your statement with 'Sit down please, quick. Emily do it, or mummy do it.' If they co-operate then praise and thank them. If they refuse then pull down on their hands to get them to sit down.

If you have been unsuccessful getting them to sit down by gently pulling their hands down so they squat, then sitting them on their bottom quickly, then you can use the quick swing technique outlined in 'Putting baby down on the floor' (see page 300). But remember, the sooner you move on and try to distract them after they have been sat down, the sooner the entire behavioural episode will come to an end. Get them positioned and as quickly as possible try to distract them before they start again. If necessary, continue to distract them as you casually block any attempts to stand again. If they are very determined to stand then stop attempting to distract and go straight back to solid communication about your expectations and defining your statement so there is no confusion about what you might be meaning.

Dealing with an excessive need for movement

One of the biggest mistakes I witness some parents making with a baby from the very earliest of ages is getting them far too accustomed to excessive movement. Don't get me wrong here, this book is about balance. It is natural to rock, jiggle and sway with a baby who is crying. In fact, it's not that uncommon for anyone who has had a baby or spent a lot of time with a baby to automatically sway if they are talking with someone whose baby is crying even when they are not holding a child themselves. This almost instinctive tool has been used for generations and the sensation of rocking or swaying remains a relaxing pastime for many, well into adulthood, through the use of rocking chairs and hammocks. The problem is when the instinct to pat, jiggle a knee, bounce on the spot, rock the pram or sway is present when the baby is not crying or unsettled.

Water play and bath time is a valuable developmental skill across the board, and a wonderfully soothing and relaxing wind down to the day.

By creating an overstimulating physical environment when the baby is wide awake and happy, or falling asleep calmly, or already calmly asleep, you are inadvertently teaching your child a few unhelpful things:

- a message that being still is not normal
- strong associations with movement to fall asleep, stay asleep or stay calm and content.

In doing so you waste a tool that would be more effectively saved for when your baby is unsettled. You also make shopping extremely difficult: for your child, stopping will become unfamiliar and uncomfortable, and when you shop, you always need to stop and do things.

You need to foster your baby's natural ability to learn how to sit quietly and play with a toy (see page 302) to master a new skill. To deliver a message to them that they always need intervention to go to sleep does not encourage them to learn how to have a calm wind-down period before they drift off to sleep. Don't leave a child feeling they are unable to cope with simple emotions without adult intervention like jiggling. This only creates a learnt dependence on our intervention to cope with most normal situations that they should be starting to distinguish between by six months of age. Being bored, feeling impatient, being a little frustrated at your toy, or having to wait while mummy pays the man at the checkout are all normal feelings. Teach your child that they don't need to look to us to always resolve those feelings, otherwise you encourage crying and clinginess.

The most important thing to remember is to find a balance. When your baby is not crying, learn to be still. If your baby gets a little cross when you stop the pram, take the time to teach them a new way to be calm without the need for excessive movement. Give your baby a chance to feel a normal range of emotions, and give them a little space to start looking to themselves or their environment for ways to move on. Encourage them through praise, and be reassuring. Try to use as little movement as absolutely possible to resolve a situation, and look for ways to teach your baby what you would do to feel better, like having a drink of water, reading a book, finding a toy, looking out the window for birds, watching other babies in prams etc.

2. Boundaries and events that are more challenging

Let's face it, there are always some things in the day that appear to be almost too difficult when it comes to getting your child's co-operation or, indeed, permission to follow through with a request, and you start to question the point of even trying. While I do live by the principle of 'pick your battles', my personal definition for that is more to do with the question of whether your baby is at their best to face a slightly specific request to co-operate, and if you have the energy to remain confident and consistent enough to always correctly define your statements to ensure you never undermine yourself or confuse your little one. Ask yourself, 'Do I really need them to do this?' This is in stark contrast to the reality that there are times when your baby co-operating with you *does* really matter and should be pursued even if they don't agree.

It's always important to strike that balance during the day and work on your communication skills around challenging tasks to ensure your baby's emotional tool kit (see page 87) is fully equipped with the coping skills that enable them to feel relaxed when you do need to guide them at crucial times concerning health and safety, like sleeping, eating and staying safe. A baby being able to relax enough to accept a parent-governed line around something that is a little challenging during the day is ultimately the dream baby who is learning to be flexible and to trust in the wisdom of others, as well as being able to follow their natural impulsive desires.

Without working on creating a balance during the day, you naturally start to see the symptoms created by this lack of balance around crucial health and wellbeing areas, such as sleeping and eating, because those areas start to be the *only* areas in which people *think* it's important to be able to guide their baby. Try to remember that as you work on following through on some of these more challenging tasks during the day, your baby is learning the exact skills they need so they are not stressed at sleep and meal times, or when you do need to ask them to co-operate with you so they can be safe.

The 'no touch' strategy

This strategy becomes useful when your tiny vulnerable baby becomes mobile. To think they have access to any number of dangerous or precious or expensive breakable things from the tender age of six or ten months of age is a slightly scary concept, and one that means your house most definitely needs to be made baby safe. To strike the balance, look up Kidsafe Australia on the internet (www.kidsafe.com.au). They have valuable information on preparing your house for a mobile baby.

Your house should contain a normal level of tempting objects that they can't touch and that they are likely to encounter when they visit other houses and environments, so long as they are safe. Your role as a parent or primary carer now is to set normal boundaries by teaching them a basic form of listening and co-operation using a simple form of communication called the 'no touch' strategy. The example of Miss Melanie and the laptop (see box on page 325) highlights the deep level of understanding a ten month old can have around a simple, well-defined line of communication. At ten months of age, being able to accept a respectfully and politely made request is a simple concept, most of the time. Enjoying the journey your two-way line of communication will take you is where parenting can be so extraordinary.

Teaching the 'no touch' cue

It's vitally important to establish exactly what your baby can and can't touch in the house. From the age of eight to ten months most babies are able to grasp the concept. Obviously, a lot of time and patience on your part will be needed if your baby is under 15 months for them to truly understand the cue once it's established around an object. From 16 months onwards, your little one will definitely understand the language-cue boundary and learn it more quickly, but they will more than likely try and give things a little whirl when you're not looking. Temptation becomes more challenging to resist, and the more capable they are at doing the task, the more they'll be tempted.

The case of Miss Melanie and the laptop

To highlight the capacity of a mobile baby, and therefore a busy toddler, to learn and understand the simple 'no touch' language cue, I would like to share a story about a little girl and my laptop. I was fortunate enough to work with a family in Melbourne who had the most adorable little ten-month-old girl called Melanie. She was bright, inquisitive and delightful company despite her dreadful lack of sleep. Her mother and I giggled the week away as we watched the clever and cheeky antics of this sweet little baby girl. Melanie learnt very quickly how to not touch the kitchen oven, which was at her height, and within one day was able to crawl up to the door, put her hand up without touching it and blow while looking at her mummy. This was Melanie's way of confirming the item was still definitely a no-touch zone. When her mother said 'That's right bubba, no touch', Melanie would happily go on her merry way and find something else to do.

Within three days Melanie was so effective with understanding the basic cue of 'no touch' that her mummy could put a glass of water on the coffee table and if Melanie reached to grab it, a polite 'no touch, Melanie' would result in the little girl confirming she definitely couldn't touch the item with a little raised hand and a blow. All was going beautifully and Melanie was enjoying her new communication with her mummy and me. This was until I brought out my laptop and put it on the coffee table.

Melanie's little eyes lit up at the sight of a million buttons and she immediately stood up on the couch and admired the screen from a distance. Her eyes twinkled as she toddled her way over to my legs and turned to look at the laptop. I then did the unthinkable: I asked her to 'no touch, Melanie'. She looked up at me, held her hand up to the computer and blew a few times. I confirmed it was definitely a no-touch zone, which she accepted but couldn't help but look at the screen. It was almost too tempting to resist, so she checked with me one more time by raising her hand towards the item, looking at me and blowing. I again confirmed it was a no-touch zone and gave her a little cuddle. She laid her head on my lap . . . then tried once again. With an unstoppable smile I confirmed to her that, despite her lovely cuddle, it was still a no-touch zone. Melanie accepted this and decided to stand, holding the coffee table and looking at me while I worked.

After a few minutes she asked again, only this time her hand was almost touching the monitor. I gently brushed her hand away and repeated the cue with a smile, knowing she was finding it very hard to resist. I was just about to pack away my laptop as I could see it was too tricky for her when she picked up a coaster and asked me again, only this time she used the coaster as a way of almost touching my computer. I repeated the cue as I started to pack away. Finally, in a desperate bid, Melanie threw the coaster at the computer and, having finally touched it in the most indirect way, clapped her little hands with delight.

Your request cue will be 'no touch', and explanation cues will be 'hot', 'break' or 'mummy's / daddy's [name object]'. This is a progressive language–based process where you initially need to be far more physically involved in defining the language cue so they can actually understand, and then progress slowly through three more steps until they accept the basic language cue without the need for you to help them physically.

First step: You need to sit with them and physically intervene while you define the 'no touch' cue and they learn what 'no touch' actually means. This needs to be done with each new object you would like them to not touch.

Second step: You need to sit with them but do not need to physically intervene much at all while you define the 'no touch' cue. This is them being able to accept the cue and the wait sign near the object without the need for you to prevent them from touching the object. This is language-based communication and co-operation.

Third step: You no longer need to sit with them but you do need to sometimes start to come towards the area if they are wanting to touch a 'no touch' object. They accept the cue before you get there. This is language-based communication and co-operation.

Final step: They accept the cue when you deliver it from any place in the room without the need for you to come to them and intervene.

Be aware, that your child may be at the final step of the 'no touch' strategy with the TV equipment once you have taken the time to teach them, yet still be at the first step on a new boundary like the computer.

From 12 months of age, you should offer your child a brief explanation as to why they cannot touch the object. Simple words like 'hot' and 'break' are sufficient when you first teach them a new boundary. As their language develops you can build upon these simple explanations but always remember to keep it simple and do not turn this parent-governed line of communication into a long discussion or negotiation. Do not argue with them like a sibling if they say 'yes touch', etc. Stick to your basic cue, be patient and kind, and follow through until your little one understands that 'no touch' means 'no touch', no matter how much they challenge this boundary.

The main things you need when teaching your little one to not touch is time and patience. When you plan on teaching your baby to not touch an object, make sure you start at the beginning of an appropriately timed play session. Often your little one is more receptive and able to accept boundaries better in the morning. Be careful to not ask too much of them later in the afternoon. You are better to work on establishing boundaries in the morning, and removing temptation in the afternoon. That said, you should still be able to maintain previously established boundaries from the morning, and follow through with your request as usual at all times of the day. Just be conscious of not trying to establish a brand new boundary too late in the day. And ensure you have nothing special to do that morning so that you can patiently work on your new boundary and request to 'no touch'.

Step-by-step 'no touch'

Imagine there is a new pot plant filled with large shiny stones placed nicely at your front door. If you don't want your child to play with this new decoration in the house, you need to set your boundary clearly for your baby or toddler before they start to play in that area. Take them, carrying them if possible, to the pot and point at it without touching it. Say a clear 'no touch' and be very expressive. Be wide-eyed and repeat 'Oh, no touch'. Show them by reaching out with your hand towards the object, then pull away before you touch and repeat your cue 'no touch'.

Now your groundwork is established, take them back to their play station and establish play before heading off to do your chores. Once your little one has started playing, be sure to keep an eye on their play: be prepared to stop what you are doing at any moment to go and help your little one learn with time and patience what this new boundary and cue 'no touch' actually means. As soon as you spot them looking at the new pot, even if they aren't moving towards it, take the opportunity to remind them of the new boundary. This can be done through praising them—'Good listening bubba, no touch'—or though the use of your basic cue 'no touch'.

> Often your little one is more receptive and able to accept boundaries better in the morning.

As soon as they start to crawl or walk towards the object, walk at a pace that will ensure you reach it before them and say 'No touch'. You will need to get down on their level and if they try to touch it, block their hand from touching it *at all* with a gentle sweeping upward or downward waving movement of your hand. You will need to be fast to ensure you block their hand. You are not to grab their hand and restrain them; you are just blocking their hand from touching it. With each sweep, you need to repeat your 'no touch' cue. This may need to be repeated for quite some time. Stay patient. Try to enthusiastically redirect them verbally with an excited sounding little gasp and 'Where's your red car? . . . brrrrrm is that it over there?'

If they are entirely uninterested in your suggestion to do something else, then you will need to keep going until they stop trying to touch it and leave the area, or they acknowledge that you have said they cannot touch it, so you can take them back to playing elsewhere. The way an eight to ten month old will acknowledge your request is by getting cross at being prevented from touching it as they would like, or getting upset and having a little cry. This is different to not understanding you are making a request of them. When they don't understand what you are asking of them, they just busily repeat the same action over and over regardless of your intervention.

It's when they stop and look at you and get cross or cry that you know they have identified you are intervening.

Often they'll stop trying to touch the object, sit on their bottom and look at you and the object, and you again. They may hold their hand up towards the object without touching it and look at you to see if they understand the request is to not touch the pot. Then you say in a calm manner 'That's right, good listening, mummy said "no touch"'. You can then clap, or kiss them or just smile warmly. At this point, you can acknowledge them and say 'good listening', then repeat your statement 'No touch' and move them away and on to a new activity.

For an older child (18 months plus) recognition that you have asked them not to touch the object would be either the response above or a tantrum or frustration. However they react, once they have acknowledged that you are governing their actions around the pot, it's time to move them on, if you can. Pick them up and go to a new activity and play enthusiastically with them. If they refuse to play and want to go back to the pot, then don't stop them but maintain your request to 'no touch' and your management to ensure no touching. You will need to repeat the above process patiently.

When you first teach your child to not touch an object that they are used to being able to touch, you may need to prevent them from touching the object for a full five minutes, and occasionally longer per intervention. Be patient and be consistent, and soon your baby will understand your new request. Be conscious about defining the statement 'no touch' so that it means they actually do not touch. It does not mean 'don't touch sometimes' or 'you can touch it and then I'll remove your hand', it simply means don't touch at all. If you occasionally let them touch the object because you are busy then they will always attempt to touch it. Pick your boundaries wisely. If it is unrealistic, then either remove the object or border off the item with a child-proof gate or fencing until they are a little older. Do make sure you make the effort to establish a boundary around at least one or two objects in the house by the time they are 12 months of age. Once they turn one, grow your boundaries to include boundaries that will be expected of them in other environments.

Respectfully taking from or giving to a child—the 'ta' game

Many tears happen when you need to take an object off your baby / toddler. To develop a respectful and fun listening game around this simple task it is important to lock in a cue that you will use over and over again: 'Ta for [insert name].' Each time you give your child an object, start to use this basic cue to get them used to its meaning. During a high-chair play session, start the game by offering your flat, upturned hand and tap it with your other hand, saying, 'Ta for daddy'. You may need to tap the toy, then tap your hand while saying the cue. If they have problems understanding this request and tap your hand, then it is okay to guide their hand towards yours so they are placing it in your palm and gently take the toy as you repeat 'Ta for daddy'. They'll soon get it.

If they give you the toy then be really excited. Clap, cheer, smile and tell others around you as you show the toy to them: 'Look, ta for daddy. Lucy gave daddy the toy'. If your child does not want to give you the toy when you attempt to take it, you can say 'Okay, ta for Lucy' and suggest it's okay for them to keep the toy. This way you retain the governing line of communication. Remember, it is meant to be a fun game that will ultimately enable you to respectfully ask for an item without tears.

To help get the idea across, you can role play the 'ta' game between mum and dad, and then let your child join in when they show an interest. Role play is a great way of gently encouraging their participation. Once you have their interest, offer a variety of toys and continue playing the game.

Please note, if you look and sound nervous when you start the game then expect your baby to become uncomfortable with the task of giving you a toy because you are indicating that it might be a bad thing. Be enthusiastic and look happy, because that is the style of communication children under two relate to well. As your child starts to respond to the basic cue, pick up the speed a little and make the game faster. In your baby's mind it will become a funny game: 'Ta for mummy', clap and cheer; 'Ta for bubby', claps and cheer; 'Ta for daddy', clap and cheer. Once you have established your cue through the game, you can then incorporate it into your positive routine management whenever you need to give your child something or ask your child for something they can't have or you need to take something from them.

When you first teach your child to not touch an object that they are used to being able to touch, you may need to prevent them from touching the object for a full five minutes, and occasionally longer per intervention.

Imagine you are at a shop and your child has plucked a baby bottle off the shelf. Give them a little forewarning: 'Bubby, nearly time to leave the shop, nearly time for ta for mummy' and tap the bottle. Sound confident and sure of what you are saying. Within two to five minutes say 'Last one, nearly time for ta for mummy' and tap the bottle again, then offer something else instead: 'Mummy get you a special book'. State the event and your expectation of their behaviour: 'It's time to say bye bye to the bottle, ta for mummy'. Show them the book and say 'Ta for Lucy' and offer the book to your child, sounding enthusiastic about, for example, the picture on the book. Tap the bottle now and confidently say 'Ta for mummy', and take the object before praising your child and giving them the book. Remove the other object and place it out of sight and / or reach.

By now, after playing your fun 'ta' game at home, the feelings associated with handing you something around this statement should be very positive for your child. Thank them immediately when they give you the bottle, and then pop it back on the shelf. Say 'Bye bye bottle' then move them on to the next activity as quickly as possible. If they do protest, however, don't hesitate. You have been fair and asked nicely with plenty of warning and their cry could be something as simple as your baby trying to say 'Awww, do I have to?' Make sure your response remains a compassionate 'yes' and take the object, offering it's replacement, and move on quickly. Your baby will soon learn with one or two practises that 'ta for mummy' means just that and *not* 'ta for mummy, but negotiate if you don't want to give it to me'.

Packing away toys

Packing away toys at the end of a play session in the cot, on the floor, in a high chair or in the bath is a really important part of a little one's routine. It gives them a sense of responsibility and therefore a sense of real importance within the family. To encourage packing away also helps them to learn how to listen, how to care for their toys, and how to work as a team. It is a completion task that requires persistence and patience and great memory recall to just know where to put their toys, as well as excellent observational skills to spot them all scattered around the room. It's a language-rich opportunity for both parent and child to learn how to communicate and understand one another.

Packing away also offers the amazing opportunity for your baby to learn how to transition from one part of the day to the next. This ability empowers them with control over their day and, importantly, control over the most difficult portion of each day, transitioning. I use packing away as a clear indicator that one part of the day is drawing to a close and a new part is about to begin. The benefit of this style of daytime flow means that your little one does not learn to cry to be taken out of their high chair, or cry when you take them out of the bath, or demand to be lifted from their cot immediately, because they are always used to their packing-away routine first. So when your baby has had enough of a particular event, rather than feeling they need to cry, they will clearly indicate their desire to move on by offering you toys and starting to pack away.

By school age, this will be a natural routine of event completion, a great skill for them by this stage of their life as during that first year at school it will bring praise and confidence-building independence. A child who has not learnt how to complete and transition from one event to the next by then often requires more input from the teacher, and finds moving from one task to another more complex and unsettling. So the benefits of packing away are obvious but the ways to encourage this task clearly vary, based on your child's stage of development and their ability level.

'Packing away' communication broken down into component parts

Pre-empting: Thirty minutes in advance state what you are doing now and what will comes next, such as 'Holly, mummy is cooking now, good playing with your pots and spoons, *soon* it will be time to pack away'.

Forewarning: The final warning before the event goes something like 'Last play with your pots, Holly, *nearly time* to pack away'.

Stating event and expectation: A specific statement that is easy to define is '*Time* to pack away, Holly. Help mummy put the pots away.' Throughout, remember to tell them what they can look forward to next through the use of the flow of communication (see page 40).

Defining your statement: '*It's time* to pack away, Holly help mummy' does not mean 'Holly can play while mummy packs away'. Take your child's hand and break down the packing-away process into easy step-by-step instructions, even if you are pushed for time. 'Pick up the pot, Holly. Mummy pick one up too'; or 'Let's take it to the drawer, put it in the drawer'; or 'More pots'. All are good definers.

Praise: Walk to each area and be specific with not only your statements but with your praise. Packing away is a very clever thing to do, and something that should get lots of encouragement: 'Good packing away pots for mummy. Thank you for helping Holly.'

Following through: Regardless of their reaction to the request or statement made, you continue enthusiastically until the task is completed. Guide your little one while holding their hands through the pack-away process, encouraging them to bend over even if you have to help them pick up the items with their hands guided by yours. If they are happy to pack away you can move from task to task together, using language rather than carrying them, and as they reach the age of 18 months plus you can encourage them to pick up and move some of the larger objects without your physical help.

Completion: Wrap up the event with a clear statement that indicates it's all finished now and make sure you have a big cuddle and a reflection on what they did as you thank them—yes, even if they have been a little stroppy throughout the task: 'Look, Holly, all the pots are packed away, thank you so much for helping mummy'.

Packing away with a non-mobile but sitting baby

For a young baby who is able to sit, learning a basic pack-away game can be a really wonderful challenge for them. This is a simple game that will lay the foundations for packing away. Always use your PRM flow of communication (see page 40) to ensure you are using the right language to prevent tears. I always pack away to a song, using the words 'This is the way we pack away' to the tune of 'This is the way we clap out hands, clap our hands, clap our hands, this is the way we clap our hands on a cold and frosty morning'. I also use the basic cues 'it's time to pack away', 'pick it up' and 'in the box'. As I say my cues I demonstrate its simple action over and over again. I then offer the baby a block and say 'Ta for Charlotte' (see page 328) before pointing to the box and saying 'In the box' or 'Ta for box'.

As soon as the baby drops the object I clap and cheer then repeat the game. If they do not drop the object, I guide their hand to the box and help them drop it so I can clearly define the statement for them, and then clap and cheer. I then say 'More' and offer them another block, 'Ta for Charlotte' and point to the box, repeating the lines 'In the box' or 'Ta for box'. As soon as the baby drops the object I clap and cheer every time. This then becomes a fun game. As they get better and better at this game, I can move them from one spot to another, point to the new toys to be packed away and say 'More, in the box' and point to the box. Before I know it, the baby is proudly participating in a game of pack away and cheering on.

I do this until they are competent with the game and the pack-away song. This will take a few days of focused play and practise for a child under 12 months to get really familiar with the routine. Within the week, I am able to forewarn them that 'soon it will be pack-away time, and time to sing the song', and the clever little baby will then be actively participating in completing one part of their day and transitioning into the next.

Packing away for crawlers

The process for crawlers is identical to that for a less mobile baby. The only point of difference comes in defining your statement 'it's time to pack away'. Always use the PRM flow of communication (see page 40) to ensure you are using the right language to prevent tears. When you have a busy little crawler, there is obviously a fairly decent chance that they will crawl off as you pack away and, maybe, if you're unlucky, helpfully unpack the toy box as you encourage the pack-away game. Be patient; this age group is beautiful, inquisitive, and extremely busy.

Before you start, always sort the room into a few neat piles ready to tidy away. For each area have a little crate and completely pack away one area before moving on to the next. Once you have said 'It's time to pack away' and gone to the area to pack away, it's time to help them understand what that means and what you need from them by defining that statement.

You can try and say 'Come over to mummy / daddy' and 'Wait', but as soon as your little one doesn't respond, they are showing a sign that they don't understand you would like them to join you. Simply get up and go over to your busy little baby and repeat your statement and follow through with its defined meaning 'Come over to mummy / daddy, it's time to pack away'. Take them to the pack-away area where you were originally sitting as you repeat your cues.

Once in that area, you can follow the routine for non-mobile babies above. Make sure you discourage unpacking with a simple 'toys away, time to pack away' and prevent them from taking the toys out. Again, please remember they are not doing this to be cheeky, they just don't know the boundaries of packing away, and will not until you clearly state them and follow through. Each time they go to crawl away, bring them back, and encourage them to pack away using the strategy highlighted in packing away with immobile but sitting babies above. Occasionally you may need to sit them on your lap as you pack away.

> Before you start, always sort the room into a few neat piles ready to tidy away.

This should be a fun game, with clear boundaries. Always be aware to complete your task, even if there is a little protest but be cautious to not teach your baby to tantrum if they don't want to do something (see page 73). If you know there are days when your baby is too tired, or not in the best form to pack away, do not even ask them to get involved in the task. A simple 'mummy pack away the toys today' will suffice. At the same time, this is about balance so make sure you make the effort with this age group at least a few times a week.

Packing away with toddlers

As I write this section, I have an image clearly visible in my mind. It's of a very serious little person squatting by their pack-away crate and busily filling it. What a delightful sight it is to see a little toddler so engaged in such a familiar, well-mastered task. Packing away represents one of those times in the day when a child is so competent with the skill set required that the task has become a fun activity, and this concept is not isolated to just packing-away time as they seem to enjoy the effort of any responsibility at which they have become efficient.

At the same time, this can be a challenging time for some parents as they battle with a toddler who finds this a completely annoying thing to have to do. More often than not, though, it's not the packing away that is problematic for the child, it is the task of being guided by mummy or daddy that they are finding so unsettling. If this is your little one's problem area, it's important to have established the crucial balance of communication (see page 38). In order to be able to guide your child despite their tears and tantrums, you must understand the importance of your language. If you cannot guide your toddler through a simple pack-away game, putting them to bed and expecting them to learn how to go to sleep on their own is extremely unfair.

One of the first things I like to do when working with an older toddler (18 months plus) is to set up a great toy storage area (see box on page 172). This helps them and you pack away, and makes it easy for your toddler to learn how to pack away without too much intervention. A good toy storage area empowers your child with being able to go and access specific tasks with little difficulty making play more interesting, and packing away a fun problem-solving task.

Avoiding toy-box disasters

To help you understand why it's important to set up a simple toy storage area it's important to look at the function of toys at this age. Most toys designed for a child 18 months and older have a specific problem to solve or sequence of events to process through or hold an interesting role-play (Duplo and the Fisher-Price Little People range come to mind here) opportunity for them to work through. The desire to spend time with an activity comes from a place of real interest and challenge in that toy. If that toy is always incomplete however, the child will often never learn how to finish a task unless guided by an adult and will be more likely to demand to watch television or wander around after mum or dad bored—or, as many parents put it, 'whinging'. This can often lead to a child disliking indoor time and always wanting to play outside, or make a parent want to spend more time out of home.

The desire to play with a toy often comes from a child's feelings of enjoyment when they master the activity, and the ability to concentrate comes from the desire to master an activity they feel confident they can complete. When toys are just thrown into a toy box, however, it often takes me up to an hour to find a series of complete activities which is, therefore, an impossible task for your toddler. So the small amount of time invested in packing away into a great toy storage system has lasting benefits.

In order to establish effective play and easy packing away with this age group I have developed a simple system. There are no stackable crates, no huge toy boxes unless they are only for cars, dolls or dress ups, which is a complete task isolated to one area. Instead I have a series of four small, removable, lightweight drawers in a light plastic frame on casters. These drawers are available from hardware and storage shops and they provide the perfect means to circulate the toys you provide your child to keep play fresh and exciting. Each drawer can be allocated to a particular type of toy. Simply pop a picture of your child playing with that toy on the front of the drawer to suit the toys inside, such as:

- Duplo
- puzzles
- cooking
- cars
- Fisher-Price Little People range
- animals and small life accessories (trees, rocks, floor mats)
- language (books, felt board, magnetic stories)
- music
- balls
- dolls
- and, yes, there is always a random drawer with the oddest but most enjoyable objects that your little one has taken a real shine to.

Now, before you get too excited thinking about those pretty wicker pull-out drawers in wooden shelves instead, consider the weight of those drawers (wicker baskets versus plastic ones) as the removal of them from the shelving unit might need your constant intervention, and so defeats the purpose of a self-help play area. Also, it's not so easy to attach a visual prompt on the front of the wicker box, so your child knows where to go to either find or pack away their toys.

For the labels, I try to make it easy for little ones to recognise what is in the drawer. I set up each area of play items so it looks nice then take a photograph of it. The picture is then stuck on the front of that particular toy's storage area and your little one then knows what the complete play station is for setting up, and the right drawer for packing it away again afterwards.

Keeping their hat on

If you were told tomorrow that a single sunburn increases your child's likelihood of developing leukaemia by the time they reach their twenties, there is no way you would expose them to the harmful rays of the sun. Well, research shows that exposure to the sun at an early age causes painful sunburns, cataracts (clouding of the eye lens), and immune system damage. It contributes to skin cancer, namely melanoma, the most dangerous form of skin cancer, as well as premature skin aging and wrinkling. Your child wearing a hat is not an option. Your duty of care towards your child is to set a boundary of 'hat on'.

Wearing a hat should not be a negotiation under the age of three. They can choose to stay indoors rather than wear a hat, but once outdoors, whether they are in the shade or not, a hat is an absolute must. Research indicates that exposure to sun in the first 18 years of a child's life accounts for between 50 and a staggering 80 per cent of a person's lifetime sun exposure. This puts the responsibility squarely on you to protect your children from the damaging effects of the sun.

Consider this! The sun produces three kind of ultraviolet rays: UVC, which is absorbed by the ozone layer, and UVA and UVB, which filter

Troubleshooting

Q 'I'm finding it really hard to get my toddler to help me pack away?'

A In the beginning, this is nothing particularly unusual. When I'm establishing packing away I don't do it every day, and I don't always ask them to help me do more than one or two small areas of the packing-away tasks with me. You are better to start small by packing away after playtime in the cot, high chair or bath. This will help build their autonomy with their skills and their understanding of the routine, and develop your confidence and patience with this request. Once you are able to ask your little one to help you pack away at these smaller, easier playtimes, you can then invest a little time in teaching them how to pack away their floor play area with you.

Q 'He just keeps unpacking the toys as I pack them away. How can I get him to understand the point of packing away?'

A They are so little and inquisitive at this age, and mummy plus toy box usually sparks great exploration ideas. Think about it, whenever you sit at a toy box with them you usually pull toys out and start to play with them so they are only doing what they know. Make sure you develop a basic language cue like 'toys in the crate, time to pack away' and define that statement by preventing them from taking them out again. It's important to not confuse them by thinking 'oh, he can have that one', when you have asked him to pack away. Sitting and playing with a toy while you pack the others away is not the true definition of the statement 'pack away'. To help your little one quickly learn how to pack away, it's important to be clear with your statements and to prevent them from taking any toys out at all, but encourage them to put toys away with you, even if you need to place the objects in their hands, and guide them if need be to place the toys in the crate for you.

Q 'When should we be packing away?'

A PRM is about balance so becoming too focused on a tidy clear environment is not the intention here. Try to pack away twice a day; once after their home independent play session (see page 143), and once at the end of the day before you start your dinner, bath and bed routine.

through the ozone and can burn our skin. UVA rays are responsible for causing skin aging and wrinkling and contribute to skin cancers. UVB rays contribute to skin cancer, in particular, melanoma, the most dangerous form of skin cancer, which is thought to be associated with severe sunburns that occur before the age of 20. When these ultraviolet rays enter children's skin, they react with a chemical called melanin. Melanin absorbs the dangerous rays before they do serious damage. A sunburn develops when the amount of ultraviolet exposure is greater than what can be protected against by the skin's melanin.

Unprotected sun exposure is most dangerous for children with:

- moles on their skin (or whose parents have a tendency to develop moles)
- very fair skin and hair
- a family history of skin cancer, including melanoma.

You should be especially careful about sun protection if your child has one or more of these high-risk characteristics. But both dark- and light-skinned children need protection from UV rays because any tanning or burning causes skin damage. To protect them:

- avoid the strongest UV rays of the day, normally from 10 a.m. until 4 p.m.
- cover up: slip on a shirt, slop on some sunscreen and slap on a hat!
- put an umbrella or a tent over them when they are playing outdoors for any length of time
- use sunscreen constantly—for kids aged six months or older, select an SPF of 15 or higher to prevent both sunburn and tanning and select a sunscreen that states on the label that it protects against both UVA and UVB rays. (To avoid possible skin allergy, avoid sunscreens with PABA, and if your child has sensitive skin look for a product with the active ingredient titanium dioxide, a chemical-free blockout.)

For a child who burns after 20 minutes of sun exposure, applying a sunscreen with an SPF of 15 gives him or her 15 times more protection from harmful rays. Wearing a hat increases that protection many fold.

I cannot begin to tell you how many parents with children under the age of two years of age who say to me, 'They just won't keep it on, so I just gave up'. It staggers me how quickly a parent will give up when their child protests about something, even about something as important as this. (Remember the section 'Parenting from a place of love' (see page 91) and assessing a child's true needs versus their short-term demands (see page 91) The only answer I have to parents who give up is, 'Well, you weren't patient enough and they may not thank you for it later'. Teaching your baby to wear a hat and not take it off from the age of six months is a simple task that takes a couple of days of hard work, and a few little battles. This means, you persist until their true need is met.

'Teaching baby how to keep their hat' on communication broken down into component parts

Pre-empting: 'Mummy is having her breakfast now, but *soon* we can go out for a play. Nearly time for hat on.'

Forewarning: 'Last one, bubby. Mummy is going to wash her plate, then it's time to go to the sandpit, *nearly time* for hats on.'

Stating event and expectation: 'Oh, bubby, *it's time* for hat on, hand down, mummy do it, where's that spade?'

Defining your statement: As you place your baby's hat on their head prevent their hand from reaching up to take it off, 'Hands down, bubby, hat on'. Prevent them from reaching their hat by blocking them from raising their hand. Do not physically hold their hand but block them from raising it to their hat. If they do manage to get their hand on their hat and start to pull it off you will need to be lightning fast and put the hat back in place by taking their hands and releasing their grip on the hat by sliding your thumb into their closed hand and saying 'Letting go, bubby, hat on'. Repeat this action while trying to distract them until they stop trying to take their hat off. You will need to be patient here. It could take some time. The most important point here is that you don't teach them that 'hat on' means 'take it off and I'll put it back on'. This means they should not get it off in the first place to accurately define the statement 'hat on'. Try to start your new boundary at home or on a local walk so you can focus on your new task without the disruption of public humiliation. Distraction is an important tool here to try to take their mind off trying to remove the hat. Toys or looking for birds, cats or dogs are all equally effective. A outside activity that is a favourite will encourage them to want to play more than want to take the hat off and may aid in making this first discussion quick and efficient.

Praise: Do this immediately when they accept 'hat on'. 'Good listening, bubby, hat on, look, just like mummy, yeah! Yeah for mummy, yeah for Melinda.'

Following through: Every time you put a hat on your baby follow the instructions above. Make sure anyone else taking your little one outside is aware of the hat boundary so your child is not confused with a mixed message of sometimes being allowed to not wear their hat.

Completion: Play the wait game. 'Wait . . . wait . . . okay, hat off.' If they are under 16 months you should always be the one to remove the hat even if they understand what 'hat off' means as you need to govern hat wearing completely until this age. At that point, if they are good with the 'hat on' request, and great with the waiting game, you can allow them to take their hat off with the addition of a simple cue: 'Melinda do it, hat off'.

It's important to note that all hats need to have the same boundary and language set as they do not know a dress hat from a sun hat.

When establishing a hat boundary, the best advice is to be a good role model. *You* need to wear a hat whenever you go outside. The above strategy is ideal for an under-two year old but as they start to get closer to two you may find their resistance becomes very strong and you may need to establish a firm boundary over a couple of days at home. That boundary is simply 'no hat on, no outside'. To implement this strategy you need to make sure everyone has hats to wear for playing outside.

Verbally talk through your expectation of 'outside, hats on please' right from the first meal time of the day. I always find high chair time a great chatting time as they are focused on your conversations with them. When you state your cue 'outside, hats on please', touch your head or place a hat on yourself then clap and cheer. Make this a fun game and, when they are laughing at your 'hats on' antics, involve them in the game by placing the hat on their head too. Next, talk through the consequences of not wearing your hat to your 20 to 24 months old by saying 'No hat on, no outside, oh dear' and looking a little disappointed. As the day progresses, use your flow of communication to build them up to the request '*Soon* it will be time for hats on, then outside', 'Last one, *nearly time* for hats on, then outside' and '*It's time* for hats on, then outside'.

Consider this! The sun produces three kind of ultraviolet rays.

Stand at the door using your wait game and cue then start with yourself. Say 'Okay, mummy first, hat on' and place the hat on your head. Clap and cheer yourself, 'Good job, mummy, hat on, outside', and step out the doorway and repeat 'Mummy's hat is on, outside, yeah'. Then move to your baby. 'Okay, Oscar next, hat on' and place the hat on their head. Clap and cheer them and say 'Good job, Oscar, hat on, outside' and walk them out of the doorway and repeat 'Oscar's hat is on, outside, yeah'.

Once outside, immediately point to the things they can play with to take their focus off the hat. If there is no resistance then move on and have lots of fun. Please be sure to have already put your blockout sun cream on your child *before* you start your 'hat on' game. If, however, your baby removes the hat, then take them straight back inside and repeat your consequence cue 'No hat on, no outside, oh dear'. (This strategy is reserved for children without significant tantrum capacity and specifically for 20 to 24 month olds with more even, co-operative temperaments.) Wait for a reaction and ask them 'Would you like to go outside?' as you point to their sandpit or something equally as inviting. 'We can play in your sandpit,

Melinda and the dreaded sunhat

Melinda was a beautiful 13-month-old with a lovely home play environment, including Melinda's most prized possession, a big blue sandpit in the backyard. The pit was filled with her favourite toys and she regularly gazed down from the balcony at its splendour. On the morning I arrived, Melinda's mother filled me in on all of her little bunny's sleep-time dramas and daytime difficulties, but commented that the one thing that was guaranteed to make her happy was the sandpit.

As the first morning progressed, Melinda became tired, which is normal when working to correct sleep-time problems, so we ventured down to the sandpit. I popped my hat on, her mother put her hat on, and we headed for the door.

'Where's Melinda's hat?' I asked.

Her mother laughed. 'You'll be lucky if you get within 100 yards of her with the thing.'

With that response, I instigated a new important communication boundary: 'Sheyney says hats on', and that's just that. This is when I am absolutely no-nonsense. I used my flow of communication to put the hat on but immediately she took it off. I repeated the 'hat on' cue and action all the way to the sandpit. Melinda continued to remove it. I put her hat on again and with lightning speed (which you need to have) I stopped Melinda's hands from even reaching her hat. Every time she would try, I would block her hand and repeat my cue 'hat on'. It didn't take long for Melinda to get frustrated with me.

'How long is this going to last?' her mother asked anxiously.

'Until she stops taking it off,' I confidently replied.

'We could be here a long time, Sheyne,' she gulped.

She was right. For 25 minutes her little girl absolutely battled to take her hat off, and I would not let her. I stayed calm, and either blocked her hands, or held the hat on her head

would you like to go outside?' If they indicate 'yes' then enthusiastically start again from the point where you said 'Okay, Oscar's turn, hat on' and place the hat on their head. Clap and cheer them quickly as you say 'Good job, Oscar, hat on, outside' and walk them out the doorway and immediately redirect them.

If they go to raise their hand remind them, 'Hat on or no outside', and physically block them while you try to distract them and get them to focus on play. If they remove their hat again, repeat your cue and take them back inside. Repeat this management until they are willing to keep their hat on. If it goes on for too long then you end the opportunity to play outside for the next 30 minutes and start again at that point. Stay consistent with your flow of communication leading up to each attempt.

If you are struggling with this process, then please revert to the strategy for younger babies as highlighted for Melinda.

while I released her hands as she tried desperately to remove it. On the rare instance that she did get it off, I would pop it back on immediately. Needless to say, she got very upset with me. She rolled over because she was kicking her feet, so I sat her up, replaced the hat, and carried on. The whole time we intermittently tried to distract her with the sandpit, but she was one determined little button. We praised her, reassured her, but stuck 100 per cent to defining the statement 'hat on'.

Could we not have just gone inside? Sure, but she would have learnt nothing, and it would have all been in vain. Melinda was definitely going to spend more time outside over the next four years of her life, particularly as she loved her sandpit so much, so leaving her hat on was a long overdue boundary that needed to be set, so I decided to work right through it until she stopped fussing and left it on.

Finally, far more tired than when she started, she picked up her spade and started to play. I adjusted her hat, praised her, and we had a lovely play. She would occasionally reach for her hat, but a simple 'hat on' would remind her, and after a brief 'waaaaah' as she dropped her hand again she would resume playing.

That afternoon, we headed out for a walk down the street and her mother and I used the PRM flow of communication to keep the established 'hat on' boundary in place, and guess what . . . instant success. No tears, no tantrums, no attempts to even touch the hat and no skin damage. Her mother sent me an e-mail when she was almost three saying, 'Melinda has never taken her hat off again, nor cared about her hat going on since that first day in the sandpit. Now, if we want to go out to the sandpit, she reminds *me* to get the hats.'

Make your decision about a certain boundary, and stick to it. Your child will only need to be exposed to it once or twice to understand there is no offer of a negotiation when it comes to wearing their sun hat. Their skin is far too precious a commodity to just 'give up' on!

Holding hands

Asking your 18 to 24 month old to hold your hand is extremely important for safety reasons alone. Whenever you are at a busy shopping centre, in a large crowd, at a train station or near a road, even in a cul-de-sac, you will need to be mindful of knowing your own and your child's ability to achieve this outcome, particularly near a road. You will perceive a threat but your child doesn't think of it as a road where cars travel; they will simply treat it as they would any pathway, for running along. Similarly, a cul-de-sac may not appear a major threat to you but to a child it's a road and if one road is okay to walk on, then all roads are okay as far as they are concerned—so treat all roads the same, please. In any environment where they are free to run like the wind they are at risk but particularly within the street environment. You need to make sure your children are always within your sight and will always come and hold your hand when asked in case you perceive a danger or need. To do this, you must always be practising hand holding with your toddler.

'Holding hands' communication broken down into component parts

Pre-empting: 'We can play with your blocks, Olivia, but *soon* we need to walk to the shops. Nearly time to hold mummy's hand.'

Forewarning: 'Last tower, Olivia, then it's time to go to the shops. *Nearly time* to hold mummy's hand! Let's build it together.'

Stating event and expectation: 'Okay, all finished, *it's time* to go to the shops. It's time to hold mummy's hand.' You suggest she comes and offer an outstretched hand and a big smile 'Let's go, yeah, a walk to the shops. Mummy loves holding Olivia's hand.' With this, your little one happily stands and comes to take your hand. You walk together holding hands and if you need to stop and lock the door with both your hands, you ask your little one to hold on to your trousers and they happily oblige. You walk to the shops, and can change between the cue 'hold mummy's hand' and 'letting go' with ease as you determine the need to hold their hand in certain location.

Defining your statement: 'Holding hands' and 'walking' are both simple statements and should be easy to define. If they try to pull away you ensure you continue holding their hand and wrist despite their efforts to release until they are happily allowing you to hold their hand. We don't want to teach them that tantrums or crying will make you let go, therefore do not let go when they do this during the learning period of defining this request. Equally, when you ask them to walk, that request does not mean 'but tantrum if I want to be carried'. This means they walk for the duration of the trip. Please be realistic as you are teaching them and make any trips brief; perhaps ten minutes each way and gradually build up as they become more confident with their ability to enjoy the event. You can swap hands using simple language that you govern: 'Swapping hands', 'Holding hands'. As you walk, if you deem it safe for them to let go of hands, and they are not protesting or demanding you let go, you can say 'Okay, letting go' but make sure they remain walking. Equally when you deem it's time to hold hands again you simply say 'Okay, bubba, holding hands' and follow through.

Praising: 'Good holding hands, Olivia', and 'Good listening, thank you'.

Completion: Once you return home, you say your final 'letting go' and your child can toddle back inside having had a lovely time.

Even when your child reaches the age of eight to ten years of age, there is still a need for them to hold your hand near roads and when crossing roads. This is why you have to establish this basic safety boundary and language cue now, and define it, and remain consistent with your cues and management of this behaviour.

I hold a child's wrist and place my thumb in the palm of their hand for them to hold. This ensures that if they are their typical toddler self and act impulsively and want to head off and chase a bird without even thinking about it (which is vastly different from them deliberately challenging you when you ask them to hold your hand), then I have a safety grip on them to prevent them from letting go and start running. If they are challenging me I will hold their hand firmly so they cannot pull away, or I hold it as mentioned above for safety if they are relaxed and happy to hold my hand.

Make sure you stay close to home on the first few attempts of holding hands, and gradually build up to the time that you would normally walk for doing this. You want to make sure they have an opportunity to see these trips are short and achievable, and can be enjoyable. Once they are autonomous with their ability to achieve this, you can gradually increase the length of time you spend out with them within reason.

At no point should you carry them on a walking adventure during the training period. Practise makes perfect. Initially, ask them to hold your hand as you walk from one room to the next at home. You should not introduce the option for 'letting go' until you have successfully taught them 'holding hands' first. When ready, you can progress to swapping hands if yours or their hands get hot or clammy with a simple cue, 'swapping hands'. Once they are effective at all of the above, then you can offer to carry them if you think they look tired or hot etc.

Even when your child reaches the age of eight to ten years of age, there is still a need for them to hold your hand near roads when crossing roads.

What if . . .

What if . . . you are having trouble getting your little one to hold your hand? Use your cues: 'hold mummy's hand', 'holding hands', 'no letting go' or 'letting go', 'walking', 'faster, bubby', 'swap hands', and 'hold daddy's trousers, wait for daddy'. Again, positioning and the way you hold their hand is very helpful. Be ready to anticipate that they may run as soon as you start to suggest it's time to hold hands, so stop them before they even get started. You should be fast enough to only need to take one step at the most before catching a little arm and stopping them from running off when you request they come to hold your hand. Repeat your request that they hold your hand while you position yourself for correct hand holding. Stay confident, relaxed and patient. Please see above suggestion for holding their hand and wrist for comfort, control for the child and safety.

Start to walk at a fairly solid pace to help stop them fussing because they will be busy focusing on their busy walking. Try to distract them by sounding excited about finding a cat or spotting a bird etc.—'Where's the cat gone, did you see the cat, meow?'—if they start looking with you, stay very vocal. Do lots of talking about all the things around them and repeatedly praise them and repeat your cue. While they are learning, you will need to sound like an over-enthusiastic, broken record. Children respond so well to genuine enthusiasm about the world around them, events and, of course, to repetition.

What if . . . they turn into a limp noodle or hang off you like a monkey? If your child drops and goes like a limp noodle and refuses to stand on their feet or they lift their legs up and hover above the ground hanging off your hand, you need to use and define your language cues and add a new one to mix: 'standing up, walking.' Both of those actions are pretty typical, a bit cute but sometimes frustrating and need to be managed in a similar fashion. You can manage this behaviour with a simple two-step process.

Firstly take both their hands in yours and say 'Standing' and raise them up just above the ground and lower them quickly, like a little mid-air jump. The movement will make them instinctively put their feet on the floor. Secondly, and you need to be very fast with this step, once they put their feet down release one of their hands and lower the second hand to normal hand-holding height as you quickly start walking in a forward motion to discourage a second attempt at the limp noodle or monkey hang while you try to distract them and redirect them. Stay very focused on trying to redirect their attention towards looking for something like a bird or a cat. As they become distracted you can slow down your pace again.

If this doesn't work and you are unable to get them back on their feet despite a fairly persistent effort on your part and multiple attempts to get them back on their feet, then you may need to let them lie on the ground. In this case, just lie them down and stand and wait. They won't stay there for long. They will start to stand up, at which point you will start all over again. Hold their wrist and place your thumb in the palm of their hand to hold their hand firmly so they cannot pull away if they are fighting. Repeat your request, 'Holding hands', and hold their arm while you position yourself for correct hand holding. Stay confident, relaxed and patient. Start to walk as soon as possible and at a pace that will stop them fussing, and try to distract them by sounding excited about finding a cat or spotting a bird: 'Where's that cat gone, did you see the cat, meow?'

If they drop again, then lay them down and wait until they stand and repeat your request. Be patient, they will soon understand the rules of walking mean they need to hold your hand or they won't be going anywhere. They are not to crawl or move off the spot you lie them down on, other than to sit up or stand up. If they want to get up, then say 'Okay, standing up, holding mummy's hand' and be ready for them to run. Catch them before they have even raised a foot off the ground and carry on with your strategy above. Practise makes perfect. Make your first hand-holding walks close to home at a time when you don't feel rushed, and make them brief to begin with so they have a great chance of success before building up the time spent out for your walk.

What if . . . they keep running in front and grabbing your legs? Holding your hand but running in front of you, then turning to hug your legs so you can't walk forward, is a fairly predictable little technique children use to ask to be picked up. It is clear language and something that needs to be acknowledged and answered clearly so they do not become agitated because they think you don't understand them. Either say 'Okay, mummy carry you' or 'No up ups, Megan, walking'. Once you have answered their request with a clear 'no up ups', you need to continue holding their original hand, then release the hand that is hugging your legs. As you move forward, turn them back so they are facing the front and walking alongside of you. Repeat your cue of 'holding hands, walking' then start to distract them. Offer specific praise, 'Good walking, Megan, mummy is so proud you', when they are walking well. You will need to keep up your pace, so they can't get in front of you too easily and can also use your hand to stop them getting around in front of you as you continue to walk forward. This behaviour usually turns into a limp noodle position if they are very determined and you will need to use your noodle management PRM to achieve your outcome.

Be careful what you are teaching them. Once you have said 'no up ups, walking' do not then change your mind because they are tantruming. You do not want to teach them 'no up ups, Megan, walking' means 'but if you tantrum I will pick you up'. Think carefully what you say before you say it, then follow through. You should be balanced here, though. No avoiding it: sometimes, 'yes, I'm happy to carry you', and sometimes 'no, I'd like you to walk please'.

3. Difficult areas of management or behaviour repair

This section of the encyclopaedia addresses some of the areas that the many families I have worked with find the most frightening or have the most confusion around how to handle. It is obviously difficult to cater for everyone's needs in this section so the first thing I would suggest is to use your instincts if you feel your child is profoundly distressed and not coping. If, having read through this section, you still feel your baby's situation is more fragile, then please look into getting one-on-one assistance through a trained early childhood worker or teacher, or a specialist such as a psychologist or the like. Do try to find someone who specialises in emotional development and strategy, however, rather than anything else.

For everyone else, this section is for you. While some of the behaviours you are experiencing might concern you, there is a reason why they are outlined in this book: they are fairly common things to experience with little ones who are having a little trouble adjusting to the world around them.

Working past fears

Our influence on children is tremendous, and many parents would be horrified to think that their personal fears, those that have haunted them for half their lives, may also soon become a burden for their children for the rest of their lives. A child's attitude to the world around them and the objects in it is strongly influenced by their parents' responses to those same things. If parents wish to encourage their child to feel safe and secure in a particular environment, or around a particular object, thing or event then they must look carefully at the way they respond to that environment, object or event themselves.

The ability of a parent to assess a situation from an adult's perspective (see page 70) is the only way to appropriately assess and therefore respond to an environment or situation that may be frightening your child. By reassuring your little one that you are not concerned for yours or your child's safety in this particular situation, you employ one of the best tools you have to soothe their concerns and help them learn to accept that situation without stress in the future. This principle applies to any fear that a child may develop.

I find there are two kinds of fears that occur in under-two year olds. The first is a frightening experience from a personal encounter. Generally a very loud or unidentifiable source of noise such as a thunderstorm, dog barking behind a fence, vacuum turning on near them unexpectedly or water draining loudly from a bath can trigger these fears. These sudden and often loud noises are alarming and can frighten a child when there is no predictable pattern to them (such as in the case of a thunderstorm). They just suddenly occur, scaring the child, and creating in the future a fear response associated with that noise and the object that made it. This response may or may not occur again the next time they are exposed to even an indication of that sound, such as the sight of the vacuum or a bath plug about to be pulled. These fears are not isolated to noise, however. The unpredictability of an excited puppy, a lizard that runs under their shoes or a balloon popping can also leave a child feeling fretful of a situation that may contain those events.

The second is a learnt fear. These are the fears that literally run in the family. This is a very real and common phenomena in many houses I visit.

A parent has a significant fear, and then expresses that fear in front of the child either obviously or subtly. That situation or object is then identified to the child as something they must be wary off. If your fear is cockroaches, spiders or lightning, your children will quickly find these things and events stressful purely because you have taught them that you are frightened of that thing, meaning they are in imminent danger when exposed to that same situation.

Fears are generally called irrational when they involve objects or situations that do not represent a true threat, but the time in which these fears are formed is an extremely important time in early childhood. As I have stated before, it is thought that by the age of 16 years, over 80 per cent of our opinions about the world have been formed, and few people ever revisit and reassess the events, opinions or attitudes from their childhood from their adult perspective. When looking at addressing your child's fears, you need to examine closely your attitudes to the events that cause your child's concern, and be absolutely certain that you are not creating or perpetuating an irrational fear.

While you may not be responsible for the fear itself, in the case of loud noises or a sudden and unpredictable event, your reaction to your little one becoming frightened is just as influential. By responding in a panicked way to your child's sudden fear in a non-threatening situation, you reinforce that their feelings are warranted. To always avoid a situation that you know stirs emotions in them is to never give them the opportunity to experience and, through your gentle guidance, move past that fear to discover that the noise, object or situation is actually nothing to be concerned about. To never expose them to that opportunity means you allow them to stagnate in a fear that is irrational and they become burdened with something that needn't even be a part of their world.

Let's look at fear of the dark for instance. The lights go out, and the sensation of not being able to see is occasionally startling but usually only uncomfortable to a child. They cry, and instead of reassuring them, staying calm and carrying on, you hold them tight, yell at your partner to turn the light back on, then sit shushing and rocking your child for ten minutes. The child's reaction to the event frightened you, so you automatically become reluctant to expose them to this situation again. You then go out and buy a night light, and officially 'decide' that your child is scared of the dark or, should I say, is going to be scared of the dark indefinitely.

When your child is scared of the dark, what images do you think they have? Monsters under the bed, a bogeyman in the cupboard? Or do you just think that they don't like not being able to see? Until your child has developed an imagination, usually from three years onwards, the only images they can conjure up are what they have experienced in real life. If you are careful about the media they are exposed to, and the books you read to them, the concept of frightening things do not exist for them, and therefore the fear is actually a sense of discomfort when they cannot suddenly see. This is where you need to assess the situation from an adult's perspective (see page 70). Remember, it's dark for half our lives and it's normal for lights to go out in every house every night.

By correctly assessing the situation and its true threat, and then being absolutely relaxed and reassuring about the event, you can slowly, through graded exposure with games, build up your child's confidence around this normal life event and condition, and help them work all the way through the fear to resolve it. This means your child does not have to be burdened by a fear that was established at the age of 18 months of age.

Another common fear-based scenario occurs when your child has shown no fear to a certain situation, yet you never expose them to that situation because you didn't like it as a child yourself. So you are again placing your child in a situation where they may learn, through your constant avoidance of that situation, that this is something they should not experience.

I once spent time with a delightful family whose nine-month-old boy was quite the handful. His mother, however—bless her—was an even bigger handful. Out of pure love for her son, she spent half the day avoiding all the things that she didn't like when she was a child in an effort to not expose her child to those fears. The problem was, he was a confident little boy who loved to explore. He wanted to pull the plug out of the bath, but she would panic when he did. He didn't care about thunderstorms but she ran and grabbed him to reassure him every time the sky crackled, and she crossed the road mumbling and concerned to avoid a dog and their owner coming down the street towards them. She never closed his bedroom door, even though their movements at night disturbed him regularly, because she perceived that as a form of punishment when in fact it should have been perceived as an act of courtesy.

She was assuming fear for her child. At no point is this a healthy or balanced strategy. This creates an irrational learnt fear. You teach your child what is and isn't safe, and by never exposing them to perfectly safe events means they will never learn to distinguish the difference between your fears of them touching a hot oven door, which is a dangerous thing that they should be cautious of, and pulling the plug from a bathtub, which is a safe thing and something they should not be cautious about. To put this another way, to create an attitude of fear around non-threatening events can mean your child will not understand what a true threat actually is. The plug in the bath may be fun for a child, despite the parent's insistence otherwise, so when the parent reacts the same way in a situation of real danger, such as walking on the road, then their child may not register that the road is a real threat.

This book is all about balance, so you need to help and reassure your child when they are exposed to a true threat and respond appropriately. Explaining to your child that the road is dangerous and them playing near it makes you nervous instils a healthy fear of that situation. To grab your child and leave the immediate vicinity of a snake or unfamiliar growling dog is teaching your child to not trust that situation. On the other hand, to help them become comfortable with the dark, with a thunderstorm, with the loud noise of water going down a plughole or passing dogs on leads in the street, you ensure you do not burden your child with, or stagnate them in, these unnecessary fears.

To help them work past fears, you expose them gradually to the event or thing and maintain a confident attitude as you do so. When introducing your child to dark environments it's important to make a game out of it, and slowly increase the level of darkness as you do. This is when an attachment to a teddy (see page 352) and playing 'where's teddy' (see page 649) in their bedroom comes in handy.

Learning to love their sleep environment

If a parent wishes to encourage their child to feel safe and secure in a particular environment, they must look carefully at the way they, as parents, respond to that environment. If your child has lost trust in their sleep environment or cot room, it is important to show them that there is no need to be fearful in that space. Remember to assess this situation from an adult's perspective (see page 70). This is their room that you lovingly decorated and prepared for them; there is no risk to their safety in this room, and at no point will they be in harm's way. Based on this, you should not to be fearful of bringing your child into this environment, even if your child feels unsure initially.

When a child loses trust in an environment, they will often cry when reintroduced to that same place later. If every time your child cries, however, and you assesses the situation from the child's perspective and remove them from the room, then the child will stagnate in that state of not trusting that space rather than moving through their feelings and regaining trust. It's important to remember that if you walk away from the room every time the child cries, you reinforce those feelings as being accurate and justified and that they should not be exposed to that environment or the emotions that are stirred by it. This is simply not the case and should not be reinforced.

In order to change this cycle of distrust it is important to reintroduce your child to the environment with as much enthusiasm and confidence as you can muster. Make sure you have an enjoyable activity for your little one to look forward to when entering the room. Establish a really fun association around this new activity by having great one-on-one play experiences (see page 131) in their normal play environment with that activity.

Be prepared to stay close to your little one on those first few visits to the room, without setting off alarm bells. We do this by ensuring you are holding them close and firm *before* you enter the room in an excited and enthusiastic way, and be mindful that you don't use body language (see page 60) that may suggest you are concerned for them. By pulling them tightly when they cry, or behaving in a way where you are using the same physical response—rubbing their back, frowning and saying 'Awww'—you would normally use in a situation that was actually troubling, you deliver a message that you are concerned and that this environment

A child's attitude to the world around them and the objects in it is strongly influenced by their parent's responses to those same things.

is also troubling, making their concerns warranted. Keep them close, keep their attention on the activity you are going to be involved in, and perhaps don't consider putting them down for the first few visits.

Throughout this remain confident and happy and stay focused on the interesting activity, even if they remain feeling unsure. It is your response to the environment that will ultimately help them feel safe. If your little one has had a particularly difficult time in their room or in their cot and you need to re-establish trust, it's important to just gradually get them used to the idea of that environment again. Over my career I have sadly encountered many families who have endured hours and hours of control crying, or painfully long, repeated lying-down sessions in the cot. These have only resulted in a stressed baby every time they need to go near the room, and no sleep. If someone advocates seven or eight hours of crying as normal, or the need to do control crying for weeks or even months on end, then you need to seek advice from elsewhere! If you do not see significant results within three days of starting any crying management program you should stop immediately. There will be a bit of crying while your child is learning something new, this is to be expected, but if your baby needs to cry for endless hours while being laid down hundreds of times, then the cause of their sleep-time disruption is not being resolved respectfully.

To slowly build your child's confidence, it's helpful to develop positive language around their bedroom without venturing into it during those first few visits. Place a nametag on their door and enjoy the process of reading through each letter to create an attachment to the room. It will help your child to get close to the room and show them that they don't need to become stressed every time you go near it. This helps you to eliminate the trigger of the tears and develop a new more positive association with approaching their room.

Looking for, finding, then waving at a carefully placed teddy (see page 649) in their cot without entering their room is a far more pleasant and indirect way to get a child comfortable with the idea of their room without actually exposing them to the stress of entering it. Spending time playing on the floor outside their room can help change their response to approaching their room from concern and stress to a calm interest. A parent slowly venturing into the room to retrieve a lost ball or a well-placed car under the cot will enable the child to experience any concerns they have about entering the room indirectly as they observe you do it. This way you get the opportunity to reinforce that you are happy and secure in that environment before they have to enter it themselves.

Gradually incorporating play around the cot environment will build up their confidence. Place some of their favourite toys in their cot, and play with them yourself. If your little one indicates that they would like a toy, you can allow them to sit in the cot to play with the toy. If they choose to get out, you can immediately remove them, but the toy must remain in that environment. Continue to play either through the bars or over the top of the bars to build up their confidence. Eventually, as they see that you will take them out if they request it, your little one will start to play with the toys that are in the cot.

No matter what their reaction is, stay calm, reassuring and confident and spend as much energy on using your flow of communication to keep them occupied and distracted from the way they may be feeling when you initially re-enter the environment. Having their teddy to hold as you talk about how lovely all the toys in the room are, and all the colours, sounds and things to do, will take your child's focus off the room and place it on the bear and the toys you are describing.

Remember, practise makes perfect. The more often you can expose your child to this situation and re-establish good associations with their cot room, the sooner your child will feel safe and secure in their sleep environment.

Once you have re-established your little one's trust around the room and their cot, it's important to keep them well informed of the new settling routine and sleep conditions they will encounter through role play. A loss of trust in an environment comes from the unpredictability of an event, and a sense of confusion that arises from that event. So before you embark on your new settling routine, role play the new sleep-time conditions (see page 631) and carefully prepare them by building their emotional tool kit. This way, by the time your child starts their new sleeping journey, they will have regained their trust in the room and the cot and they will know the exact process involved in going to bed, including where you will be and exactly what you will and won't do.

Developing an attachment with teddy

Encouraging your child's attachment to a comfort item is an important management strategy for you, particularly for role playing to teach your child a new sleep-time routine (see page 631). It's a lovely comfort item too when you need to leave them to go to work, or would like them to have some company at sleep time as they transition into their new independent settling routine. The way to do this is far simpler than you could imagine.

The two important tools to encourage an attachment to an item are role playing and association. Through role playing, *you* 'develop an attachment' with the bear, first, by including him in many aspects of your day. The bear is given the same respect and love as you would give your own child, and this helps your little one develop a strong sense of attachment and belonging with the teddy because you have.

The association method involves using the teddy around important soothing times, such as when you are cuddling your child. Introduce teddy when your child needs soothing and during relaxing times of the day, like when reading a book, having quiet cuddles on the couch, enjoying a walk in the pram, and as a way of developing a strong sense of comfort in your child when they are near the bear. You also interact with the bear in fun and enjoyable times of the day, encouraging an association of warmth and friendliness around the teddy.

Combined, these two strategies help your little one feel a sense of warmth, comfort and affection towards the bear, and help your child to feel safe and loved as all the interactions with the bear are strongly associated with affection from or with mummy and daddy. A child's attitude to the world around them and the objects in it is strongly influenced by their parents' responses to the same things.

If you wish to encourage your child to attach to a toy, do not directly and continuously offer it to them as this will only encourage your child to constantly offer it back to you or push it away as you are doing. You need to be quite in love with and attached to the item yourself. This means that every time you see the desired teddy, be happy to see it. Pause for a moment and give it a little pat on the head and lovingly greet it by saying 'Awww, hello teddy, mummy loves you'. Give teddy cuddles and give that activity of wanting a cuddle a name: 'awww cuddles for teddy'. Once your baby shows a similar response to teddy you can then offer cuddles to your child with a similar cue, 'awww cuddles for Oscar'.

When daddy comes home, make sure he greets teddy and has a little cuddle too. As you move from room to room, take teddy with you, saying 'C'mon, teddy, let's go and find Oscar's new drum'. Allow teddy to join in with the play, and give teddy the chance to bang the drum too. Use teddy as a play friend. Read a book to your baby / toddler and to teddy. Make sure you take the time to kiss your baby, and kiss your teddy. Stroke teddy lovingly, and keep it nearby.

To slowly build your child's confidence, it's helpful to develop positive language around their bedroom without venturing into it during those first few visits.

When it comes time to role play your sleep routine with your child, use this teddy, and lovingly settle it into the cot for its sleep first. When it's meal time, share food with teddy and always remember to have important conversations about how clever your little one is with teddy. Praising your toddler by encouraging teddy to watch how they can eat off the spoon, pack away or clap their hands, for instance, is a wonderful way for your child to engage and interact with the bear. Make teddy clap his hands or jump in surprise and you will be delighted at how funny your child finds teddy's antics.

Teaching your child how to be soft through 'bear being soft' is another wonderful role-play example for helping them understand new language and expectations of behaviour. For toddlers, teaching them how to look after bear and how to sit bear down, and give bear books or toys is a lovely way to bring their little bear friend into your child's life, and give your child a sense of ownership towards their little friend. If your baby / toddler is upset, pick them up and reassure them as you would normally do, and when they are calm incorporate teddy into the cuddle but don't make too big a deal out of cuddling teddy at this time. Just put teddy in your arms close to your baby as you soothe your little one.

Once your child has become attached to the teddy bear, then the teddy needs to stay in the cot until sleep time if your intention is to develop it as a cot comfort item. This can be done through a role-playing settling routine with teddy bear and leaving it in there for extended periods of time. This gives your little one something really special to look forward to at sleep time.

Working with harmful behaviours towards self and others

Behaviour that is harmful, such as headbutting, biting and aggressive behaviour towards themselves or others, is quite possibly one of the most unsettling things parents have to cope with. Their precious little baby hurting themselves or others is what most parents become extremely distressed about when calling me for assistance. I have seen many forms of this kind of concerning behaviour but the cause of such actions can be varied.

Some of the worst cases I have ever encountered have been the result of profound emotional distress of both the parents and children. Once things start to spiral out of control within a household and everyone feels helpless, a child can display severe forms of headbutting and biting themselves. It is rare to see such extreme behaviours, but they do happen from time to time, and if they do they should not be ignored. If you feel you are experiencing this level of distress and it is triggering in your little one negative behavioural episodes, seek a referral from your family doctor to consult an early childhood psychologist or visit a reputable family therapist that specialises in early childhood development. You will also likely need professional support to resolve sleep-time or daytime difficulties.

Allow teddy to join in with the play, and give teddy the chance to bang the drum too.

If your household is emotionally stable despite the unsettling element a sleepless baby has brought into your world, but your child is showing signs of headbutting or aggressive behaviour towards self and others, then you are *probably* dealing with your average, garden-variety, stroppy / frustrated or attention-seeking baby. This is far more common and nothing to be frightened about. Babies have many ways of communicating, and expressing themselves, and in this instance you will need to work through the possible causes to find the best way to manage these episodes effectively.

If your child is showing a tendency to headbutt, bite or hit then starting any form of routine and communication management may trigger a few days of increased incidences of this behaviour. The reason for this is that you may be exposing them further to the triggers of such behaviours, such as frustration or the desire to retain the governing line of communication. Do not be fretful as this does happen occasionally. Sometimes you need to stir the pot to make things better rather than desperately try to keep a lid on things when it will inevitably boil over. Be reassured, I have seen these types of behaviour equally in houses where the child is both co-sleeping and completely guiding a day, and in a house with strict boundaries, so the likelihood that different parenting styles increase the chance of this behaviour is extremely low. It's just something that happens with a few little people, so if they are prone to using it as a way of expressing themselves, you need to work through the triggers first, and *then* past the behaviour to help your baby find a better way to express themselves, or to soothe any stresses that are likely to trigger such patterns.

Some children simply become more frustrated than others, while others learn how to use and vent through this form of expression by accident or through observing other children. Discovering what is normal childhood behaviour, what is attention seeking or which behaviours are borne out of true stress or frustration will enable you to develop a management plan to eliminate or, at the very least, significantly relieve the stresses triggering these episodes for your little one.

Babies have many ways of communicating, and expressing themselves, and in this instance you will need to work through the possible causes to find the best way to manage these episodes effectively.

Normal childhood behaviour—body bumping

It is quite normal to expect your little one as they learn spatial awareness to body bump. Children develop an understanding about the parts of their body and how they fit in the world around them through accidental bumps, such as hitting their back on an object as they turn around or their head on something outside their immediate range of vision. When a child bumps themselves in an area that they had not understood was a part of their personal space, they often become fascinated. So repeating a little bump on the table with their head several times confirms to them the space their body takes up. Equally, you may notice a crawling baby sit back and lean against a wall accidentally. This can be a surprise to them and you will see them rocking back repeatedly and bumping against the wall to get a sense of their body and where it fits in the world around them.

These forms of body bumping are a normal part of development and most certainly don't need to be managed. They rarely make a child cry, but can take them by surprise as they reach up to their head or face to discover what just happened. You can communicate the situation to your little one by touching their head and touching the table and saying 'You bumped your head'. You can touch the same spot on your head and say 'Mummy's head' and then touch their head saying 'Joshie's head'. This will help them understand the event a little better. Once you have explained the situation, if you feel you need to remove them from harm's way, simply take them to a new area.

All these steps are not always necessary. You can be a silent witness to your baby's self-discovery. Do not, however, hit an object or call the object 'bad', such as 'bad table', if a child walks into it. Your child needs to know that sometimes we accidentally walk into things and that it was their actions that caused the bump—the inanimate object did not thoughtlessly jump out and knock them on the noggin. We don't want them to become anxious about furniture etc., as this will disrupt their happy play.

Attention-seeking behavioural triggers

While some attention-seeking behaviour is from frustration, the intention is still attention seeking. It's easy to identify such an event: often, your child will be close to you and looking at you and for your response to the event, or already be having a confrontation with you at the time. They may drop to the floor and headbutt it, or headbutt a wall or even you if they are upset with you, and sometimes even when they are not upset with you but would still like you to stop doing something, or start doing something. If you do not come to assist them, they will look at you and become more active with the behaviour or start to cry until you do attend to them. Occasionally, if they can see you are not coming over to them, they will come closer to you and repeat the action. This generally encourages concern from you, you intervene and fussing ensues and, hey presto, your little one, through somewhat uncomfortable means has got your attention. Whether you respond to their attention-seeking behaviour in a positive or negative manner, the outcome is the same—they get your attention.

Good or bad currency triggers for headbutting

To understand the process of attention-seeking behaviours, you need to understand the currency you can give certain behaviours displayed by your child. Good currency should be given to the kind of behaviour you want to teach your child to use if they would like your undivided attention. Poor currency should be given to the kind of behaviour you want to teach your child to *not* use if they would like your undivided attention. So your attention to poor behaviour gives it a good currency, whether you mean to or not, or your lack of attention to good behaviour gives it poor currency.

Your child will learn to only use behaviours that hold good currency to get your attention, and more often than not, these can be the very disruptive, loud or particularly demanding behaviours. Think about these following behaviours and the kind of currency you give to them in your household:

- crying to get something
- screaming to be picked up
- playing quietly
- lying still on the change table
- eating well
- babbling
- self-discovery by, say, exploring a hand
- hitting anything or anyone
- biting anything or anyone
- headbutting
- smiling.

If you always race to pick your baby up when they scream in the high chair, that gives that behaviour good currency and your child will either think you would like them to behave this way when they want to be picked up, or use that behaviour as a means of getting your attention. If you run to them when they are headbutting the floor in a temper, that also becomes a good currency behaviour with similar results. If you don't dare to disturb them while they are playing quietly, then this behaviour is given poor currency, and it is not valuable if they would like your attention.

What you may work out from the above, is that it is vitally important to notice and respond positively to all the little things your baby is doing when they are happy, and not just when they are stroppy, being impatient or demanding. This is where you become involved, not because they have asked you to, but because you like the behaviour they are displaying, and you would like to reward that behaviour which gives it a good currency. This encourages more episodes of good (positive) behaviour. When they smile, giggle, babble, play well, explore their toys or concentrate on their task, take the time to join them in those events occasionally. If they are vocal in a delightful way, stop what you are doing momentarily and respond with clear eye contact and great verbal feedback. If they are busy playing or exploring, simply go and join in with as much concentration towards the event as they are displaying. Stay for a little while, kiss their cheek and go back to your chores.

It's equally as important to not notice some of the less desirable behaviours, so they achieve little attention from you, and are therefore given by your child poor currency for achieving your attention. Picking up a child from their high chair because they are screaming at you from impatience would only encourage the screaming behaviour every time they get bored with being in their high chair. Sitting down immediately and waiting until they stop, however, teaches them a new higher currency for not crying. Rushing through a nappy change because they are cross and crying at you because they are bored with waiting will become a useful currency for them if they do not want their nappy changed or are impatient during any task in the future, and therefore quietly playing while you change their nappy or getting involved in other tasks will never be achieved.

Always try to replace an inappropriate behaviour currency with an appropriate behaviour currency. For instance, if they are screaming during a nappy change and you get them up quickly, this only encourages screaming to get up. What you need to do is not get them up until they stop screaming. Use distraction, and be patient. Only pick them up when they stop the less desirable behaviour, and are lying still in a manner you would like them to achieve at each nappy change for both your comfort levels. Your child then learns that screaming means they have to stay there, and being more relaxed and playing with a toy or watching you for cues that the event is drawing to a close, results in them being picked up. Always end every event with a wait game (see page 74) or the up cue (see page 76) and praise if they are prone to be impatient, stroppy or demanding.

It's important that, where appropriate, you attempt to not respond to the less desirable attention-seeking behaviours—crying / screaming / head butting (attention-seeking triggers only), or smacking / pinching / scratching you because they want to be put down, for instance—and wait until it ceases before you carry on and oblige their request by governing the end of the event with a completion routine like the wait game, rather than asking them to tell you it's over. Distraction and ignoring the behaviour are both appropriate tools here, as well as clear requests from you to not hurt themselves, you or others (please see page 354). Once the behaviour has stopped or been stopped, and you are seeing a more agreeable behaviour, then you should respond favourably to that better behaviour to give it a valuable currency for your child by obliging their original request.

What if . . .
What if . . . your child hits, bites, pinches, scratches themselves? You will need to go back and carefully consider the possible triggers, whether they

are normal, attention seeking or from frustration or emotional distress, before moving forward.

What if . . . your child behaves aggressively in any way towards you or others, including growling, scowling, baring teeth and threatening to hit or kick? The answer is often easily discovered. It usually comes down to two main causes: learnt behaviour or simple frustration at your unwillingness to meet a demand / request. These learnt or simple frustration-triggered events need to be managed in much the same way as those of the attention-seeking range and are fairly normal and common occurrences in early childhood.

I often find that these behaviours can be easily learnt by the child through the observation of others. This could be happening at home from watching sibling, the TV, from their parents or from any daycare, park or playgroup situation. If you know it is a behaviour they are witnessing at home then it's important you remove these examples from their day before you ever consider addressing the behaviour in them. It is not okay for a child to witness behaviour like this or for you to expect them to not do it when others around them do it.

Address the behaviour of older siblings or adults first—even the family pet if its something done in fun, like play growling. If it is behaviour they are witnessing in a group situation, then consider removing them from that group if the culture is significant, or stay close to them to work through teaching them to not use the behaviour despite what they are seeing, or talk through it and teach them the 'no' and 'stop' game (see page 210).

The management of these kinds of learnt, simple frustration-triggered or attention-seeking behaviours is threefold: laying the foundation for desirable behaviour, communicating honestly, and responding appropriately.

Lay the foundation for desirable behaviour

Always take the time to develop good currency around desirable child activity throughout the day at other times. This entire philosophy advocates prevention first rather than management after the incident has occurred. We do this by stopping and having a little cuddle and play if they are busy exploring the room, or stopping whatever you're doing and responding to their babbles or giggles so they learn to communicate through babble and sound, not just crying. Make an effort to turn every nappy change, meal time, and transition in the day into a happy, language-rich, and tickling-good-fun opportunity to enjoy each other, while you also take the time to teach them how you talk and communicate with them, and what you would like from them as far as communication is concerned.

Do not run to them every time your child makes a noise of complaint. If they are frustrated at their toy, or trying to do something that is making them a little cross, just wait a few moments to see if they can resolve it themselves. If they are struggling with the task then casually respond by showing them how to fix the situation appropriately. Use their hand and show them how to lift, turn off or move the object themselves. Do not do it for them, however; teach them how to fix it themselves for next time where appropriate, then carry on with what you were doing. Make any needed responses to less desirable behaviour low key and fairly light on with attention. Don't move faster because they are crying and demanding you do something quickly. Wait until they have stopped fussing before you pick them up or give them what they are demanding, even if you need to use distraction through parallel play (see page 131), or ignore attention-seeking behaviour to ensure they calm down first.

Communicate honestly

Tell them you do not want them to do those specific behaviours. For biting, say 'No biting mummy / daddy' and tap your teeth. Tell them that teeth are for food. For head banging, touch your head and say 'No banging your head, soft to your head, bubby' and show them how to stroke their hair. For hitting say 'No hitting' and imitate the behaviour in the air and frown, saying in a deep, concerned voice 'Oh no, no hitting, soft to mummy' then demonstrate the action of being soft to you / themselves using either your hand or theirs.

Respond appropriately

For headbutting on a hard surface, have a thin pillow on hand to place under their head beforehand if your strategy is to ignore the behaviour, such as around attention-seeking triggers. Even an easily moved mat can be quickly placed in position to lessen the impact of their banging. If they move away from the mat or pillow, then you can do nothing more, and must ignore the behaviour by exiting the room without further ado. I would rather deal with a few short events ended quickly because they are watching you leave the room and working out how to manage that, than deal with worsening headbutting over months.

The first place to attempt to manage these behaviours is at home. When it is resolved at home you will see a reduction in the need to manage the behaviours elsewhere. Once you have started to change the currency of attention-seeking events in your house, it's important to completely discourage the more concerning forms of attention seeking by giving them the completely opposite response to the one the child is expecting. If your child hits, bites or pinches you, headbutts the floor, wall or others, then your immediate response should be to follow right through this sequence of events:

- (if you're holding the baby / toddler) put them down immediately without saying anything, or after a simple and clear 'no biting / hitting' etc.
- walk out of the room, as does everyone else
- remain absent for up to a minute
- return to the room, but do not carry them in with you if they have tried to follow you, even if they request it, as you are still ignoring them until this sequence of events is complete
- do your chores for one to two minutes
- return to the activity you were originally doing when they first did the behaviour, and wait for them to come to you before you give them attention
- assess the original situation honestly and ensure it was nothing you were doing to trigger the episode (such as teasing or tormenting). If it was you who triggered the episode, then rectify that situation immediately, and apologise if necessary. These do not include you not responding to demanding behaviour.

Until that process is fully completed, they do not get your attention at all.

When you leave the room, everyone else in the room should also leave, using the closest exit available to them. Stay out of the room for 30 seconds to a minute, or until your baby comes looking for you, but pay them no attention yet. Return to the room and walk past your baby as though nothing has happened. Busy yourself with chores for a further minute or two. If your child attempts the behaviour again, then leave again. If they follow you into another room, walk back to the original room quickly before addressing them but act as though nothing has happened.

Once you are sitting back in the room again, you can give your little one your full attention but do not behave as though anything has happened. Do not go back to any of the resolutions you used to do previously when this behaviour was exhibited, like rubbing their head, breastfeeding, looking concerned, ice packing, sitting and rocking them in your lap etc. It's important that you ignore the fact that they were headbutting and carry on happily playing, even if they are seeking your old response to the headbutting behaviour. Position and sit your baby on the floor to establish play (see page 161).

To sit down, pick them up, sound and look concerned, and rub their head will not resolve the situation. Because that old response didn't work you are now trying a new one. Always remember, nothing changes if nothing changes. Only ignoring their attention-seeking behaviour entirely, which means acting as though it did not happen and playing with them and encouraging them to play with the toys also, will completely stop the behaviour and achieve a quick resolution to this situation for your baby and you.

You may find your child will want to explore this new response from you and may drop or repeat the pattern to see what you will do. Just walk straight out of the room and remain out for 30 to 60 seconds again. When you return and have completed a few basic chores around the room, regardless of their tears at your feet, you can then say 'Let's go and find something to play with'. Do not pick them up, however, just encourage them to follow you to an activity by walking over and sitting straight down and starting to play. They may be cross at this request but it is all a part of the completion of this response to their behaviour.

Whenever they headbutt, bite, pinch or hurt you, themselves or anyone, always respond in the same way immediately, and provide no currency to that behaviour. You should see significant results, if not a complete halt to the behaviour within the first or second day of this PRM strategy. In rare cases you will have the occasional episodes on the third and fourth day, but you will still be experiencing significant improvement from the episodes you were enduring originally. Remember this strategy takes practise. If you were experiencing many episodes of poor behaviour then it's reasonable to expect them to take a couple of days of consistent PRM on your part to discover that those behaviours result in a lack of attention from you. If you see no improvement or worsening symptoms over a two- to three-day period, however, stop immediately and consult an early childhood behavioural specialist for one-on-one observation, assessment and assistance.

> If they are frustrated with their toy, or trying to do something that is making them a little cross, just wait a few moments to see if they can resolve it themselves.

This is a delicate area and not everyone will be fixed through a book. Some people simply need more solid one-on-one advice.

Aggressive behaviour due to emotions

Managing actions due to being overwhelmed or stressed or frustrated is actually quite different to managing, say, attention-seeking headbutting. When your child is using this as a coping mechanism or an expression of their emotions, you can often see that they are clearly not looking to you for attention and are rarely comforted by you during an episode. While I find these cases to be extremely rare, they do still occasionally happen, and can be resolved through simple communication unless the symptoms are extremely severe.

If you are experiencing severe symptoms of chronic headbutting over a prolonged period of time, you are NOT to follow the advice of anyone who tells you to ignore this behaviour. If your child headbutts in a repetitive rocking motion as a strategy to go to sleep, to block out excess stimulation or stress, as a way of coping with feeling overwhelmed, or because they are developing calcium build-up on their skull, then they are in real need of assistance and quickly.

If your little one is emotionally stressed or frustrated they will often be insistent on pursuing the behaviour despite your best efforts to stop them. In this case—and I have only experienced one severe case in my career—you must seek the advice of a fully accredited early childhood practitioner to explore the origins and triggers of your child's stress. A referral from your general practitioner will be required.

In all other cases however, where you *are* able to comfort and distract them, there are three simple steps to use to help settle and eventually stop the behaviour from occurring:

1. prevention by pre-empting the behaviour
2. through communication—asking them to stop
3. by intervention—physically preventing them from repeating the behaviour until they understand your request to stop.

If you know the things that trigger events of headbutting, hitting etc., then the best plan is to avoid them, or to teach your child the skill sets they need to not feel that way the next time they encounter the same situation—you can equip their emotional tool kit all through their day (see page 87). In other cases, see if you can just predict their response to what you are about to ask them to do. Most parents know their baby very well, and knowing what they might do is actually a fairly simple thing to work out.

For instance, if you know your baby dislikes coming inside after being outside, and is likely to do the classic double-hand smack on your face, then you will need to plan ahead. If you know there is a typical trouble time ahead, plan for it, put things in place so you can actually move your child past the things they don't like to do and have them focus on something of interest in the new destination. This takes their mind off what they are losing (which is what triggers the smack they give you) and puts their attention squarely on what they are about to do or get. This is always a great way to transition from an exciting event to something slightly less fun.

Try to remember that children are spontaneous and have the blessed gift of being able to be present in the moment and just enjoy that moment for what it is. They see no reason to change from one environment to another if they are happy, so it's common for them to need some incentive to leave one situation to go to another, without getting a little annoyed at you for spoiling their fun.

An example of this would be to choose a special toy for the next event. Take the time to play excitedly with it for a minute or two before you head

Troubleshooting

Q 'What if they just chase after me out of the room?'

A If your child is old enough to just stand up and follow you when you leave the room, go into another room altogether and, each time they enter that space, continue to busy yourself with chores in each new environment. Ignore their behaviour and do not allow them to hang off you. The idea of this strategy is to eliminate your attention, so you will need to achieve that via leaving their sight altogether and not communicating with them temporarily. In this case, you will need to state a clear explanation as you leave the room: 'No biting, too rough.'

Q 'Will leaving the room without saying my short-term absence cue affect their trust in me?'

A Not if you always use this same response sequence of events to these particular behaviours after offering a simple statement like 'no biting, too rough'. The idea is not to leave them, but to give them absolutely no attention. When walking away from them, even if they are following you to get your attention, move fast so they can't grab you and look busy doing something. Carry a washing basket or a pile of towels and, if they do stand in front of you and block your path, either walk around them or move them and walk on without even making eye contact.

Occasionally you may need to sit them down on the floor and walk out of the room if they are tantruming, but this is also done without eye contact or communication. Once you have done this for a minute, return to the original room of the behaviour and follow on with your predictable sequence of events mentioned earlier. Your lack of attention is the consequence of their attention-seeking behaviour. This then means that their old attention-seeking behaviour (headbutting, kicking, biting, etc.) holds no currency and is therefore redundant, meaning it will no longer be used to get your attention.

Q 'What if they continue to headbutt whether I'm in the room or not?'

A If your exits and casual returns make no difference to their behaviour, then this is not attention-seeking behaviour and it needs to be managed differently according to the emotionally overwhelmed or distress management plan (see page 354).

Q 'What if my under-two year old is still hurting their older brother even though they have stopped hurting me?'

A Your older child will need to be told what to do when their younger sibling hurts them, or you will need to help the older child do this. Explain that you are going to walk away and outside, then leave it behind with the intention of coming back to see it soon. The experience should be really fun, and try to make Taylor laugh with your best tricks. Make sure you name the toy / game so you can refer to it when you need to come back inside or to the car. For instance, our new friend is called 'Froggie'. Place Froggie somewhere special inside the house or car where you need to return after your play outside or at the park. Say 'Bye bye, Froggie' after your fun play, and then redirect Taylor's attention on to the exciting task outside or at the park.

not play when baby is being rough, and you will both come back when the baby is being softer. Explain to them that they can take any toy they were playing with out of the room with them too. If the older child is still quite young and needs your help, then you can pick them up and take them out of the room with you upon your exit. This would only be necessary in the case of twins, or children very close together in age.

Q 'What if they are biting me during a breastfeed?'

A This is a slightly different scenario. Depending on the age of your baby, this does happen but is rarely attention seeking. I often find a mother's natural response of a loud sharp 'ouch' and immediately pulling the baby off the breast is an adequate and honest response to biting the breast during feeding. If the child continues to bite your breast, however, taking them completely off the feed and placing them on the floor for one full minute each time they do it will stop the pattern of behaviour quickly. If they continue to bite, you may need to consider whether they are terribly interested in the feed and are simply playing. In this case, stop feeding and do not feed again until they are due for their next milk feed as per your normal routine.

Q 'What do I do? As soon as I sit down, they headbutt the floor or hit / scratch me again.'

A Repeat your management plan by standing up and leaving the room again. Be absolutely consistent, and do it as many times as it takes for them to stop this pattern of behaviour. Please read the management for emotionally overwhelming triggers (see page 354) to ensure you are using the right technique and this is definitely only attention seeking, though them doing the behaviour every time you sit down would suggest this is attention seeking.

Q 'When I ask him to follow me back into play, he gets upset and starts the behaviour again. Can I just carry him?'

A You need to be careful what you tell him is appropriate behaviour. If he headbutts the floor, and you say 'Okay then, I'll carry you', you are giving the behaviour a valuable currency and encouraging it rather than discouraging it. This pattern of them following you back to the original play area ensures you are guiding them until this consequential sequence of events comes to an end. So don't confuse them and give currency to any demanding behaviour accidentally. If they headbutt the floor because you will not do as they insist (which was usually your old pattern of response), then you will need to repeat this new strategy by standing up and leaving the room again. Be absolutely consistent, and do it as many times as it takes for them to stop this pattern of behaviour.

While you are having a lovely play, every now and again remind him that soon it will be time to go and see Froggie, and be really excited about the idea of that. Try to keep him playing outside by distracting him again and carry on. Then when it's time to go inside or head to the car, be really excited about going to see that funny Froggie that makes us laugh. Say 'Wave bye bye to the park / flowers / hose' and call out to Froggie. You child will be as excited as you are to go and find him, and may even try to help you remember where you left him. By the time your little one has left the park or come through the door or is sitting in the car seat, they won't have even noticed the transition that took place because you placed their attention on Froggie and not on leaving. Have a lovely play with him and Froggie in that new environment, then offer your baby Froggie to play with and simply get on with your day.

The idea is to leapfrog (no pun intended) the actual problem area by giving him a reason to come inside rather than focus on what he is about to stop doing or lose. This is a positive spin on something that can be quite hard for a baby. If he still fusses, then there is nothing more you can do. You have used your flow of communication and respectfully offered a positive alternative but sometimes your little widget will just be tricky about saying goodbye. In this case he will need to have a little tantrum as the emotions will be too hard for him to cope with. This is when you need to be prepared as well. Be prepared for a hit but try to pre-empt it and stop him before he even does it by holding his hand and using your cue or by positioning him so he cannot hit you. If he does, follow through with your hitting management plan and flow of communication.

You will need to express an expectation of his behaviour: 'Time to go inside, no smacking daddy, soft to daddy, where's that Froggie gone?' This ensures your little one knows you do not want them to hit you. You will need to physically intervene to prevent him from hitting you. As he raises his hand take it in your hand and repeat your cue, 'Time to go inside, no smacking daddy, soft to daddy, where's that Froggie gone?' Encourage him to be soft to you by holding his hand and making him gently stroke your face and praise him, then be excited about finding Froggie. If he relaxes then release his hand, but if he keeps trying then stay focused on your language and request as you hold his hand.

If your child headbutts the floor, wall or door etc., put forward an expectation of behaviour by pre-empting their action and preventing them from actually banging their head in the first place. Try to look at the typical triggers of the event and either avoid putting your baby in that position again or equip them with the tools to be able to cope better when faced with a situation that may cause frustration (see page 87). At the next available opportunity you will need to actually show them how to fix this problem by guiding them through the steps they need to go through the fix it. Say to them, 'No banging, bubba' to ensure your little one knows you do not want them to bang their head.

Everyone's natural instinct to prevent their child from actually banging their head, once an episode is about to begin or has begun, is to pick the baby up, but this is not a clear enough message. It is more important that you allow them to stay in the position and you remain calm and reassuring but stop them from being able to carry out the behaviour. This means physically stop their head from hitting the object without picking them up or repositioning them. To stop them from banging their head on an object, place your hand over the area of their head which they are trying to bang, then hold their head with that hand to prevent them from making contact with the ground. It's okay if your hand makes contact with the object, so long as their head does not and they are unsuccessful at banging their own head. As you do this say your cue again, 'No banging, bubba'.

> Try to remember that children are spontaneous and have the blessed gift of being able to be present in the moment and just enjoy that moment for what it is.

Your baby may try to move to a new location so they can continue to bang, and you will need to stay with them to prevent them from doing so. This usually means you have to be quite fast. Try to offer distractions but, if they are not listening, stay with them. Once they have acknowledged that you do not intend to allow them to bang their little head (by trying to push you away or by looking at you or your hand), that's when you should pick them up and reassure them, and move on to a new activity to try and distract them. This will need to be done every time they attempt to head bang. They will quickly learn it is something they cannot do and the behaviour should stop.

4. Independent play strategies

Playtime is a wonderful part of a baby's life, or it should be. Sadly, many babies are finding this once-simple task too complex, due to the many complications arising from lack of predictability in parents because of busy non-stop coming-and-going lifestyles, loss of independence development and the lost art of communicating with a non-verbal child. When correcting playtime difficulties, you need to put many different environmental strategies into place. You could provide all the beautiful toys a baby could ever wish for, develop the best and clearest lines of communication, and set out with the most patient, enthusiastic attitude but it won't necessarily guarantee that a child's old patterns of behaviour will not continue for the first few days after you implement your new strategy. In this next section, we look at patterns of behaviour that actually create problems and investigate ways of eliminating them so that your precious baby can play happily without the need for tears and drama.

Troubleshooting

Q 'What if she manages to hit / scratch / pinch me before I can stop them her?'

A Use the cues 'no hitting / scratching / biting' and 'show me how you can be soft'. For any actions that require their hands, you will need to take the hand they used to hit, scratch etc., and hold it firmly out from their body at arm's length and pause while still holding it out. Remain calm and patient but say in a confident tone with clear eye contact, 'No hitting mummy' and continue to hold their hand for 30 seconds. They will naturally try to pull away and you will need to hold their hand and not release it until the full 30 seconds is over. If they are trying to remove your hand from theirs repeat your cue, 'No hitting mummy'. Once you plan on releasing their hand say 'Show me how you can be soft' and make them stroke your face. Say 'Awww, soft for mummy, thank you for being soft' and then carry on in a happy tone with 'Where's that Froggie? Frooooooggie, where are you?' Once the behaviour is over it's over, but if they hit you again, repeat your strategy exactly as above.

Q 'He hits, pinches and scratches me with the other hand while I am holding one of his hands. How do I handle that?'

A Try to remember he is only little and is smacking you because he is feeling overwhelmed that he has to do something he doesn't want to do. He might want to stay in the park after dark or do any number of things that seem like a good idea to him, or you just might not be reading him right . . . and let's face it, adults are pretty annoying sometimes. In this case you will actually need to turn him on your hip so he is facing away from you. Hold him low on your hip so you can lean him forward. As you reposition him, state your cue 'No hitting mummy'. Hold this position for 30 seconds to a minute without walking. It is not terribly comfortable for them and there is not much they can do from that position but the currency response is clear and the request is simple. If you are unable to put them down, you will still need to respond to the behaviour. They will either look around, or try to fight you and turn back. If they are fighting the outward position, repeat your cue periodically while you define your cue, 'No hitting mummy'. Remember, you should not sound cross or even remotely upset with them as what you are doing is taking the value out of the behaviour and discouraging it from being a useful tool in the future. Once the time has elapsed say to him, 'Show me how you can be soft' and turn him and encourage

Using your bag of tricks

When a baby is sitting for a prolonged period of time in the car, pram, a high chair in a restaurant or in a supermarket trolley, you want them to be content. For this to happen you need clear and concise strategies to teach your little one how to achieve this skill. I'm sure I don't need to remind you how it feels when faced with a screaming baby in a public place. It's good to have a plan in place for these situations so you can focus your attention on helping your baby have a more relaxed time, rather than you

him to be soft by making him stroke your face. Say 'Awww, soft for mummy, thank you for being soft' and then carry on in happy tones, 'Where's that Froggie? Frooooooggie, where are you?' If they hit you again, repeat your management strategy.

Q 'What if they are biting their toys out of frustration?'

A In most cases, it's important to allow this behaviour to pass but think about what exactly happened with the toy to bring them to that point. Was it that the truck got stuck on the wall, or their push-along cart got halted at the bump from wooden floor to carpet? At the next available opportunity (perhaps their next one-on-one play session) you will need to show them how to fix this problem by guiding them through the steps they need to go through to fix it themselves. Show them the wall, or the bump in the floor, then get their hands and show them how to turn the truck or lift the cart so the next time they are faced with this same situation they are equipped with the tools they need to not feel so frustrated.

Q 'We have been doing this management consistently for two days and are seeing no significant results?'

A Stop all management and just pick them up when the behaviour starts. You will need to seek a referral from your general practitioner for an early childhood psychologist or contact a consultant like myself, who has training in early childhood development, for personalised care so they can help you identify and eliminate the triggers of the behaviour. There is absolutely nothing wrong with asking a trained professional for their opinion because sometimes a more objective and trained eye will see more clearly. Do ensure the person you seek help from is trained in early childhood development—unfortunately it seems anyone can call themselves a specialist these days—and do carefully question their qualifications, experience and ability to help you.

Q 'My baby headbutts in her cot to fall asleep. If I try to stop her she fights and struggles to get back into the cot to continue the behaviour. What do I do?'

A This can be managed through environmental aids but the cause of the behaviour needs to be closely examined as well. A consultation with a qualified childcare professional with training in early childhood development would be a wise step to take in resolving your baby's sleep-time issues. In the mean time, a SafeT Sleep and a leg wrap could help resolve or lessen the occurrence at home.

fretting about the seemingly thousand judgemental eyes watching you and your very upset baby. This is where your bag of tricks comes into play.

Your bag of tricks will contain a variety of toys. As you won't want to carry around huge toys when you're out and about, choose appropriate-sized travel toys. The bag of tricks is a graded exposure experience. That means you bring out the toys gradually and as needed, when your little one's attention span for a particular toy is waning. The toys will range from simple ones that you know they like playing with, such as small hard books, Fisher-Price Little People textured animals, through slightly more challenging objects that catch their attention, such as a small Tupperware pot with no lid, to 'illegal toys'. These illegal toys are the kind of things you know they love to play with but don't for obvious reasons, objects like a TV remote (obviously one that is broken or unused), a set of washed, safely secured but not necessary (in case they lose them) keys, some photographs of loved ones, an empty, washed nappy-rash cream pot or tube or even an old mobile phone (off, of course). They are generally interesting to a child for the most part because they like to do what you do, and they learn from role modelling. You often hold small containers to feed them with, or chat on a mobile phone or race about with interesting jingling keys, and these are the items that fascinate little ones. Be sure not to be tempted to take too many toys or you may inadvertently plough through your toys and not develop the more calm and prolonged kind of play this graded exposure experience is aiming to achieve. Ten items are more than enough to keep a baby content for a shopping trip two to three hours long.

Once you've got your bag of tricks ready, it's best to practise this means of extending the time your child will happily stay in one place away from public glare, in the privacy of your own home or your neighbourhood. To begin, remove all toys from the environment; that is, either in the room you are in, the pram or the car seat, or wherever you are when you are teaching your child. One of the biggest mistakes you can make is to offer your child all their toys right at the beginning of any play session. Having no toys at all gives you the opportunity to teach your baby to look around their environment while it is new and fresh for them, so they can notice all the wonderful things there are to see in our colourful world. If you are at home, stop to point out the things outside the windows, sing songs with them while you busy yourself around the room, or simply chat and show them things around the room or in the car or outside the car window. If you are washing dishes, pop some suds on the highchair table so they can enjoy the sensation and experience of bubbles popping as they touch them, or make a funny game out of blowing the dishwashing bubbles in the air.

Most babies will blink, jump a little, then chuckle merrily if you act surprised and add an enthusiastic high pitched 'ohh' each time you repeat this action.

Singing or telling interesting stories, talking to the pet cat or dog, or listening and imitating sounds you can hear around the house are lovely ways to start a play session that encourages your baby to look and listen to the world around them for stimulation rather than expect to be given a brightly coloured, extra-stimulating and entertaining toy. When you are at a shopping centre, stop and take the time to point out the smiling faces on large posters around the walkways, balloons you may pass, other babies in prams, the Wiggles car and the Thomas train (without feeling the need to offer them a ride), and show them how to wave hello and goodbye to these things (see page 109). If you are out and about, point out the birds, the cars and the big trucks, and flowers, or stop and feel a dry crunchy leaf, or look at a spider's web sparkling in a tree. Listen to a dog barking at a fence and imitate the dog (if it is safe to do so) before moving on.

Try to allow them time to enjoy these new things with just occasional interactions from you. If they are quite happy to sit there and take it all in, let them. Can you see how this will encourage your little one to sit for a longer period in the one location? Once your baby starts to show signs of becoming restless, chat to them more often and redirect their attention to their surroundings several times until it becomes clear that they may need something new to hold their attention. By now, depending on where you are, a good 20 to 45 minutes will have passed, you may even have been able to get them to sit happily for up to an hour or longer. Then it will time to dip into your bag of tricks.

Always start with the most simple toy, then as the adventure continues and their attention span wanes on each object, simply pull out another toy until it's time to bring out the illegal toys. Along the way your baby's eyes will sparkle with delight at each new item to emerge. Once you've exhausted the toys in the bag of tricks their little hands will stretch out for you to pick them up and the mood may change to grizzly. This is a strong indication that it's time to head home.

If you are at a restaurant this will happen about the time you have completed your meal but you might just want to stay for a final chat or even the odd dessert. It's okay to pack away the toys, play the wait game before offering the 'up up' cue and play 'pass the baby around' with the guests at the dinner table. This way, your baby can start to play in a whole new environment, on your lap. (For more tips on going to restaurant with baby, please go to page 199.)

Teaching them to play through role play

So often I hear a parent say to me that their children 'don't seem to like their toys', 'they don't really play with them', 'they only throw their toys', or 'they only suck their toys'. Just because a toy looks obvious to us, does not automatically make it obvious to a child. A series of coloured blocks are nice to look at, and warrants exploration through oral examination for a young baby and even some toddlers, but rarely looks like something that would make a great tower to a baby. They explore their new toy, and when it does something pleasing, they repeat that pattern. In the case of colourful blocks, throwing them and hearing them bounce as they scoot across the floor appears to be the obvious thing to do for a toddler. It's interesting to a point, and who cares if they are all across the room. A huge crate of Duplo may be construction heaven to a dad or mum, but when presented to a toddler, the idea of tipping the crate and watching and listening to the wonderful event that follows appears more obvious.

> If you are out and about, point out the birds, the cars and the big trucks, a flower or stop and feel a crunchy dry leaf, or look at a spider's web sparkling in a tree.

If you think about the way children respond to their environment, you will realise that they are strongly influenced by your own patterns of behaviour. The idea of playing with the box you battled with for 30 minutes to get their new toy out of looks far more inviting than the toy itself because they want to do what you did. Your mobile phone or set of car keys looks far more inviting than the large plastic toy version you bought them, because those are the objects you play with, and they want to do what you do. Even climbing into your bed, and tucking themselves under the sheets beautifully holds huge appeal for a toddler because that's what you do, and they want to be just like you. Parents often say to me that they 'bought them a queen-sized bed because they like ours so much but they still won't go to sleep. Why? Well, you are their life role models. Every thing you do, they will want to try. They don't want a queen-sized bed of their own, they want yours.

Based on this basic instinct to do as you do, it makes perfect sense that if you would like them to enjoy their toys, and play with the toys in the manner they were intended, then *you* first must enjoy their toys, and play with them in the manner they were intended. Every time your child is presented with a new activity, or new routine or task, role play and learning through example are the most effective tools you can provide to help them easily learn about, get the most out of or adjust to any new scenario or activity.

This is easier said than done as each time you pick up an object your baby says 'Me too' and takes it straight off you. Your attempts to take it back as they mouth it furiously are likely to be met with a less than impressive response. How then, can you show a baby how to get the most out of their new toy? This is where you need to use your communication skills. Before you offer it to them for the first time, take the time to play with it in front of them. This can be done by playing with the activity while your partner holds them, or playing with the activity on the kitchen table while your baby sits in the high chair, or while you play on the floor with them. The idea that you are the first to play with it essentially represents a rare opportunity for you to play with it like you are reading a book. Because your child will have had no previous experience with the toy being in their regular possession, they are more likely to watch as you put on a show of sorts than they would if you were to ask to play with it while it is in their possession.

If they do show a desire to play, gently say 'Mummy's turn, wait for mummy' and then play with it enthusiastically. Your wait game cue (see page 74) will be effective and well received if you have been reading and practising your governing lines of communication. If they attempt to touch the toy, gently brush their hand away and repeat 'Wait for mummy' but feel free to offer them something from the activity if it has multiple pieces. Run through the mechanics of the toy, but not in the same way you would explain it to your wife or husband. Play with it like you are a child. In fact, play with it like you are your child. Open the doors, turn the wheels, build the tower and clap when it falls, or push and pull it along the ground, and make all the appropriate noises.

It's important to highlight, then experience and work through the normal complications your child will experience in the activity. If it is a puzzle, for instance, have difficulty placing a piece in its slot. If it is a shape sorter, try multiple holes before you find the right one. Essentially explore the toy in the same way as your baby will be exploring it. Discover and work through the same learning opportunities that they will discover. Play with the toy as though it is the best toy you have ever played with. You are now actively playing with the toy which is exactly how a child under the age of two best responds and learns.

Once you have finished playing with the toy, place it in front of them and then play with it together. If it is necessary to help them as they try one of the many things they saw you do, because they are having difficultly, then it's fine to use your cue 'ta, wait for mummy' and quickly show them, before offering the activity back to them 'ta for Lucy, Lucy do it'. Each time you introduce a new toy to their collection, make sure you spend time role playing how to use that toy, and then actively engaging in play with your child and the toy after that. Even at the age of six months, simple forms of play, touch, movement and exploration can be role played with their environment and the toys around them.

Continue to provide new examples of how they can extend and challenge their activities through role play as they master each stage of play that the toy represents. If you identify your child struggling with a particular concept, make sure you take the time at your next one-on-one play session (see page 131) to teach them that skill. Try to also find other ways to develop that skill through different forms of play. For example, if they are having difficultly understanding the concept of a basic puzzle, provide opportunities to practise this skill through nesting cups, sequence rings, posting boxes and shape sorters. Create a cardboard box with multiple-sized holes to fit certain large shapes and create an environment rich in the concepts required to solve a simple puzzle problem.

Please note: if your little one does not play with it like you, it does not matter. The idea here is to simply expose them to the toy in a positive way. After that, they are free to play with it any way they like, unless you are attempting to stop them doing something in particular. For example, if your child prefers to post their blocks into the video recorder then you will need to use your no-touch boundary line of communication (see page 324) to explain that is not the way you would like them to play with their toys.

Dealing with the old trouser tug!

Who on earth has not had a crawling or toddling child tug their trousers? Some may experience it occasionally but baby more often than not settles quickly and crawls off to find a new challenge. For others, it becomes a guaranteed tears zone. Does this sound familiar?

Your beautiful baby comes crawling, hands slapping rapidly on the kitchen tiles, occasionally growling or grumbling, but always head down on a mission straight for your legs. It feels so lovely to see them come to you, and makes you proud as you watch them use every muscle in their tiny body to co-ordinate the strategic move to stand up holding your legs. Finally they stand and try to balance themselves holding on to your trousers, skirt or shorts but, very predictably, wobble precariously as the material of your clothing moves. You freeze, wanting to bend and grab them so they don't fall but knowing that one wrong move could send them flying. You know it and so do they. Instantly, they burst into tears, closing their eyes, and if you don't dry your hands double quick and pick them up, they will land on their bottoms or worse, with their little heart racing at a million miles an hour, having given themselves the same predictable fright. If they do manage to steady themselves, they usually squish between your legs and the bench and, with routine precision, gaze up at you, little arms craning as high as they can reach, groaning and grumbling to be picked up.

You happily pick them up each time for the first ten days, until a little alarm bell starts to go off in your head as you realise your baby is learning to ask to be picked up constantly, and it's getting more and more difficult to do anything without your baby on your hip. The more they are on your hip, the more bored they become, and the more unsettled their behaviour continues to be, but it's too late: the pattern is already well established, and now you don't know what to do to help change this negative child-directed routine that has developed.

The idea of playing with the box you battled with for 30 minutes to get their new toy out of looks far more inviting than the toy itself because they want to do what you did.

If this sounds familiar, then you are one of the families where, if I were to come to visit, you would be told that the leg tug was no longer a pattern you were going to allow your baby to perpetuate because, when the pattern becomes the same as it is above, nothing positive eventuates from the routine. All babies do in this situation is cry once they stand and ask to be picked up because it's a routine for them now and they know nothing else.

Firstly, look at your communication streams. Your baby has no idea how to articulate what they would like without the use of crying and body language. Both these styles of communication are their way of talking. If your baby stands and cries at your legs and your immediate response is to pick them up, regardless of your reasons, you have just informed them that if they would like to be picked up, they need to stand at your legs and cry. If this is not the stream of communication that you would like to establish you need to create some new boundaries around this behaviour. Until this pattern of crying stops, you are going to eliminate standing at your legs from being an option all together so you don't confuse them.

Firstly you need to learn how to be very quick and always aware of your baby's movements so you can pre-empt them climbing up on your legs. Then you will need to establish the sit down cue (see page 375). Once your little one has had a day to practice and understand your request to sit down, you can then begin to implement your new play strategy. This is where you have three options available to you and each one should be used in equal proportion on a daily basis with no one particular option used more, particularly if your motivation is because it seems 'easier'.

Option 1

If you hear them coming over to you and you don't mind having a chat and a cuddle with them, then offer a parent-directed line of communication that clearly indicates your willingness to talk and snuggle with them without them feeling the need to cry and fuss to achieve that outcome. Turn to face them well in advance of their arrival, and if you can see they are coming to you, get down on their level by squatting and offering them your hands to climb up on. You can chat or cuddle from this position for any period of time, before using your 'sit down, wait for mummy' cue. Once you have asked them to sit down, remember to define your statement by following through (see 'Flow of communication', page 40). Offer your baby a toy like a ball or toy car and roll it a short distance before standing and going back to your chores.

Option 2

If you are busy or you know they should be in an active, independent play session then you'll need a collection of interesting things for them to play with at the entrance to the kitchen. This is designed to distract baby as they make their way to you. In addition to their toys, have a fun selection of 'illegal' play things sitting on the bench ready for your quick access. As they make their way to you, you need to say 'No climbing on mummy's legs' and 'Sit down, wait for mummy'. This needs to be done well before they reach your legs. This way you have clearly and honestly expressed your expectations before they attempt to try and express anything with the old crying pattern. When they get closer to your legs, be ready. Offer them a toy and say again 'Sit down, wait for mummy'. Then sidestep their efforts to grab your legs. Continue to sidestep by shifting away to create a distance between you and your baby while you continue your chores. If they are very persistent then moving from one bench top to another will be more effective and send a clear message. Offer toys by placing them in the distance between your baby and your legs. Following through and defining this request on the first day of implementing the new strategy are the most important aspects of establishing any new stream of communication. Will they still get cross at you? Quite possibly, until they understand the new request you are expressing to them. Within a day or so, they will happily come and sit by you to play without demanding you pick them up, instead waiting for your cue that it's time to have a snuggle, clearly indicated by your squatting down and offering your hands. Obviously, none of this applies if they are coming to you because they have had a fright or feel in any way vulnerable.

Option 3

The third choice is designed as a back-up. I call it the 'uh-oh . . . what-now?' strategy. When your baby's lightning speed takes you by surprise and they manage to grab on to or climb up your legs, despite your best efforts, you need a plan that is consistent with your original request. Once your baby has climbed up on your legs, you simply need to take their little hands happily and say one of two things: either 'Sit down' or 'Wait for mummy'. My personal favourite, however, is to place their hands on the cupboard or wall and allow them to remain standing, but not holding on to your legs. Here the statement 'no climbing on mummy's legs' means that you will teach them it's okay to climb on the front of cupboards, but it will enable you to step away if they are screeching and demanding to be picked up. When they are playing and chatting happily, then you need to be more responsive and acknowledge that with a 'lovely playing, bubba' before redirecting their attention to their toy, or stopping for a cuddle and redirecting them back to their play.

Above all, you need to try really hard for your bubby's sake not to allow confusing mixed messages to occur. Parents can often become completely relaxed about their request to their child when a phone call comes in. They allow the baby to stand against them, wobble and cry before picking them up, and don't even notice what they've done until it is too late. They then ask me why it's taking more than a day to correct their child's old patterns. If you are on the phone and you know you get completely distracted, then it's important to just sit on the floor and allow your baby to climb all over you if you are not going to follow through with your actual strategy. This ensures your baby does not get confused with inconsistent communication. The reason it is important to be consistent goes back to the definition you give a statement (see page 44). To occasionally allow climbing on legs and crying to be picked up means you actually teach your baby that the statement 'no climbing on mummy's legs' means 'every now and again I'll let you climb on my legs so always give it a try'. If you want to eliminate this pattern of behaviour from occurring, then you need to be totally and utterly consistent.

Crying when put down to play

Helping your baby through a teary or stroppy transition may be a natural part of correcting the situation, particularly if your little one requires more intensive behavioural changes, or is quite a spirited and determined little creature. You don't want to squash that natural spunk or boisterous confidence; you just want to channel it into a more positive direction. Understanding your motivation here is so important.

Remember, it is not neglectful or harsh to realign an existing poor communication stream with a more positive and peaceful communication stream and, as a parent, if you see your little one struggling or confused about how to communicate better with you, then it is your duty to guide them to a better way. Once this new system is established, an indication that your baby may want to have a snuggle will come in the manner of them crawling to your feet, maybe touching your leg, and sitting down and looking up at you while holding a toy. This will mean you have the opportunity to say 'Hello, bubby, let's have a snuggle', or 'Time to sit down, where's your [insert toy suggestion here]'. By being able to properly answer your child and taking the time to help them understand that both answers are okay, you eliminate tears, and create harmony in your home.

Let's look at crying from the three management angles we are working with. Any change from a predictable pattern will trigger upset, but you can imagine that if you ask them to 'not do' the only thing they 'know to do' they can initially be left feeling unsettled and unsure of what to do instead. This unpredictable response from you may make them feel uncomfortable, and even a little lost. As a result, they will often ask you to fix the way they feel by allowing them to follow through on their old self-directed routine, no matter how negative it has become. Because the old pattern of behaviour already involves a grouchy baby who cries, there is much to be gained by investing a little time working through the crying that occurs when you establish this new positive communication stream.

There are three things you need to remember when following through and defining the new statement 'no climbing on mummy's legs'. The first is patience, the second is persistence and the third is that the tricky transitional period does not last long at all. Stay calm, do not be impatient or get frustrated, and keep in mind this is a brand new request. At the same time, the way you react to them crying will tell them if the way they are feeling is valid and something that they need rescuing from, or if it is just new but they are okay. If you look at them in a panic or with an 'oh you poor thing' tone and a miserable-looking expression, then they will think there is something dreadfully wrong when, in fact, that is not the case at all.

Stay confident, reassuring and consistent. You should persist with offering them toys and stepping back repeatedly. If they refuse and push the toys away, then just avoid their little hands by staying busy and moving around the kitchen while repeating your cue 'no climbing on mummy's legs'. They are likely to cry and follow you on your first attempt. Perhaps sing a happy song in a bid to distract them from being cross. Remember that when you stop moving around, if they come over to you, you need to repeat your cue before taking a step to the side so you are out of reach each time they go to try and grab your trouser pants.

If your baby is persistently following you and getting more upset by your excessive movement you may need to follow through with a sit down strategy rather than walking away (see 'No touch' on page 324). Try to remember this is a reasonable and fairly simple request that needs to be put into perspective. You have only said you can't pick them up now while you are right next to them, and you are reassuring them by offering toys and staying patient, calm and confident. The request to not climb on your legs is not an unreasonable boundary to set, particularly considering the only result from standing at your legs is crying.

If your baby becomes very cross at you and has a big cry about the request, offer them one of the special toys off the bench and give them a gentle stroke as you praise them for 'good trying, bubba'. Empathising with the situation often encourages a reassuring tone when you say 'Mummy knows it's a bit tricky learning something new. You're okay, mummy's here', and then trying to redirect them. Often, trying to draw their attention to a pet or favourite animal like a bird by saying 'Where's that Jessy cat / birdy gone?' with an excited look on your face is a great way to quickly take their focus away from what they are crying about.

Work hard to try to achieve a full five-minute interval of no standing on your legs if you can. If you can't, then wait three minutes. At the end of the period, get down to their level and distract them with toys until they stop crying or calm down significantly. Once your baby is calm, offer your hands and say 'Good playing, up up' and help them get to their feet. Give them a big cuddle without picking them up, and stay happy and confident for them. Spend a few minutes playing with your baby before starting again.

Don't over-linger with the cuddles and end up solving it for them as you've just spent a full five minutes working hard to support them while they tried to settle themselves down. This would only teach them to cry until you solve simple problems for them that they are capable of doing themselves (and I'm talking simple things here only), which defeats the purpose of the exercise. Remember, you are looking to teach them that some boundaries and subsequent emotions are normal and healthy, and the feelings that go with these simple requests are able to be resolved in ways other than just being picked up. This is where you need to look at the emotional tool kit you are equipping your baby with when it comes to dealing with a normal range of human emotions (see page 87). In other words, just because it makes them feel cross or frustrated, doesn't mean they should not experience it. Remember the point to all of this. If they are in their cot and wake at 2 a.m, with no concept of time, how will they cope then if they have not accepted a 'not time to pick you up' response from you? They need to have experienced this through the day to be equipped with the skills they need to adjust peacefully to this request at night. It is all designed carefully to ensure no tears at sleep time, and an ongoing maintenance program to maintain healthy sleep no matter where you are.

Safety proofing your play area

When setting boundaries around your house when your baby starts to become mobile, there are three distinct things that you need to take into consideration to ensure you are maintaining a balanced approach with your communication:

1. safety
2. removal of real temptations for them that will cause you stress
3. establishment of clear verbal cues to not touch or setting of boundaries.

Safety proofing your house is obviously a must when your little one becomes mobile. I rarely enter a house where safety has not been made the highest priority. That said, you should always make sure you have gone through a safety checklist regarding your house as, occasionally, I find parents have implemented the obvious light-switch, power-point safety tips but are unaware of the many other hidden dangers that lurk in their home. There is always free advice available at your local clinic or through organisations like Kidsafe Australia.

In every home there are real temptations that you really don't want your baby to play with but no matter how many times you say 'No touch, bubby' or remove them from the situation, the temptation remains too great for them. A great example of this was when I went to a house where the baby regularly played in the dirt of her favourite pot plant. The mother said she had tried everything to stop her tiny baby from touching it, even getting a bit cross at her, but nothing worked. In this case, getting cross with your baby or, in some extreme cases, smacking a tiny baby's hand is such a negative and unproductive strategy that you must look at what it is they are trying to touch. In this case, we needed to be fair to the baby and remove the temptation from her reach. If you are at the point of getting cross, or even considering smacking your little baby as a teaching tool over an easily removable object, then place it in another room or put a gate around it so the baby no longer has access.

When establishing a verbal request to not touch, think about it. You have a fireplace or a low oven, and because you are so nervous of your baby being injured you have made it very clear that those two places are an absolute no-go zone for your little bubba. As a result your baby doesn't even consider touching the objects because you have been consistent with never allowing your baby to touch them. This is you defining your statement and teaching your baby safety boundaries (see 'Defining your statements' page 44). This same principle of consistent communication should also apply to other areas and objects in the main living area. This is not too complex a task for a little one to achieve as I do it in every house I go into with children as young as ten to 12 months. The importance of this basic boundary setting goes beyond a simple request as it applies to other social boundaries, such as other people's houses.

The story of Charlie (see box on page 382) highlights the need to establish normal boundaries when babies start out on their adventures when newly mobile. To wait could be extremely confusing and stressful for your baby. The areas that you may wish to establish a no-touch boundary around could be a low oven door, the dog, low art work on the walls or tabletops, a case of wine bottles by the fridge, and any television or hi-fi equipment, including the CDs and DVDs. Setting a no-touch boundary requires consistency, calmness, a keen eye, but most important of all, patience.

When I decide it's time to work on this strategy for a family I choose a day where they all have the time for that particular play session. I make sure there is nothing pressing that needs to get finished so at no point will the parent run the risk of getting frustrated or impatient, and I make sure the play environment is at its best. Any unsafe areas will have been corrected, any temptation that is just too hard to not touch will have been put away, out of reach or blocked with a gate, and the areas they can't touch will have been decided upon. It is pretty simple. Just decide which things are no longer play zones and write a little list and put it on the fridge. This ensures that when your partner comes home they can be consistent and follow through with your request so bubba doesn't get confused about the boundaries.

Once they have had their afternoon or morning tea it is usually a good time to take them from play station to play station, highlighting all the lovely toys they have available to them (see 'Getting organised for play' page 143). Take the time to point out any no-touch zone. This can be done simply with the 'wait' hand gesture put close to the object then pulled back towards your chest and a clear statement 'no touch'. If you create an additional action of a sucking motion through your lips your baby is likely to approach this object

The case of Charlie's baby-proof world

I met Charlie, a beautiful little 18 month old, when his parents were finding it more and more difficult to get him to do anything without a massive tantrum. Things hit a crescendo when he became so distressed he cried for over 24 hours straight. This is a crisis- or critical-care case, so I dropped everything and arrived on their doorstep in another Australian state just over six hours after talking to the parents on the phone. I was greeted by his crying but also by a grateful mum and dad. Both mum and dad hugged me in relief and I went to sit next to their very distant-looking baby boy.

Charlie was sitting in front of the television sobbing, a little more settled than earlier when I was on the phone, but totally tuned out. I just sat quietly next to him watching his favourite episode of 'The Wiggles' and observed the environment. The whole house was bare. The TV cabinet was emptied of any adult items and filled with toys and the doors were taped closed. There were no bookcases and every single cupboard and door was sealed shut. The kitchen was blocked off with a gate, the coffee table was removed and the room was literally pared down to its bare walls, a couch, a baby seat, a television and toys. Charlie was living in a world where he never had to experience the normal request to not touch certain things. His parents, in their desire to make his life easier, had actually made it so foreign for him to need guidance that he became the ruler of his own domain.

As he got older, it became less and less possible to guide him at all until ultimately the concept of being guided by his parents became something that evoked foreign uncomfortable feelings inside him. In the end, his parents were resigned to doing whatever it took to make him happy, until suddenly their tiny little boy who desperately needed guidance was being burdened with the task of guiding his parents to raise him. This finally became too much and he was no longer able to cope, let alone guide them. This meant all three family members had no one to guide them and didn't know what to do.

That night, once Charlie was asleep, I sat down with mum and dad. 'What is it you are wanting from me?' I started.

'Help,' they replied. 'Help us, just tell us what to do, we just don't know any more.' My heart broke for them.

'So what you are wanting from me is exactly what your baby is wanting from you: some guidance, the burden lifted off him, some good ideas from your pool of wisdom.' Both parents looked at me glassy-eyed.

'Yes please,' they sighed. 'Our poor little man,' his mother sobbed, 'we thought this would make him happy but he just got so stressed.'

The three of us set off on a five-day mission to turn their lives around. I gave them the ability to be the same lifeline to their son that I was to them. As confident, guiding parents with a balanced set of communication streams in a house with a normal amount of things he had access to, some of which he could touch, and some of which he couldn't touch, Charlie became happy and settled. He suddenly began to talk and participate in a huge range of normal, healthy listening tasks.

and look at you and, without touching it, to imitate your reaction to these items by sucking and blowing through their own lips. Your mouth will almost look like you are whistling while you make this sound.

Always finish your introduction to their play stations with showing them the play station they can start at so their mind is on an activity. Put them down and step away as thought you are going to do your chores, but wait. You need to stay busy as usual so they actually focus on play and not you, so fold some of that giant pile of laundry gathering dust while you wait for an opportunity to show your little one what 'no touch' means. When your baby starts to approach the object they are not to touch, calmly walk over, making sure you are there before they can touch it, and bend over. Use your hand gesture for wait and your voice 'no touch' to help them learn what it means to not touch something.

At this point, most people make the mistake of physically removing the child from the situation or holding their baby's hand so they can't touch it. This is the wrong thing to do. You are going to help them understand what you are saying without physically doing it for them. If you physically do it for them, then they *never* learn how to not touch, because they don't have the option to try and learn: they are not being allowed to. 'Blocking' is a little gentle sweep of their hand as they reach for the object to prevent their hand from touching it. By following through on a request to not touch and blocking them from actually touching the object you are now able to see if they understand you.

Use one, and if necessary two hands, to sweep their hand upwards or downwards each time they reach out. As you prevent them from touching it, repeat your cue 'no touch'. This needs to be patiently repeated over and over and over again until one of two things happen. Either they don't touch or they get frustrated and start to cry, in which case you would end the session and pick them up saying 'Good boy, no touch'.

When you have picked them up, repeat your hand gesture for wait and the no-touch cue with the withdrawal of your hands a few times so they can see that you don't touch it either, then take them to a new play station and start your play over again. This is where your patience is needed. Most babies will find the idea of a boundary fascinating and want to find out what it is all about, and if there are any options around that boundary. Because of this, having to repeat confirmations that they can't touch an item is normal at this early age.

Another thing that could occur would be that they sit down and look at you and the item, but may be cross and crying as they don't yet understand why you won't let them touch it. This is where you need to talk with them.

Repeat your action of 'no touch' and blow and give a reason why like 'Mummy's one', or 'Daddy's toys', or 'Uh-oh, might break'. At this point you may find them asking you through an outstretched hand or blow if they can touch it. If they ask you without touching it, there is no need to brush their hand away, just repeat the cue 'no touch' and be ready just in case they try to touch it. Remember to define your statement. Think about what you are teaching them that this new statement actually means. 'No touch' doesn't mean 'touch it with your fingertips', so don't even allow one little podgy finger to touch the item or you will confuse them and wonder why they continue to touch things when you have asked them not to.

Finally, they may need a little cuddle for reassurance just to know that even though you are acting a little differently and it makes them feel funny or uncomfortable, you are still both great friends. If your baby asks for a cuddle, have a quick happy snuggle then redirect them to a new activity. You are the one who will inform your baby if this new expectation is normal or awful by the way you act. If you feel guilty and horrible, what do you think you baby will learn about a normal healthy boundary being set? Have your snuggle, remember your motivation around balanced communication and move on.

Once they are playing again, go back to your chores and look busy, but keep an eye out. If they approach a new no-touch zone, you will need to go there and start all over again. At this age a baby does not have the ability to transfer the understanding that comes with learning about one item to another, so you may have to start from scratch. Within a day, they will have a good grasp of the language cue and, once fully understood, it becomes a basic concept that will enable you to teach them to transfer expectations from one object to another.

If, however, they approach the same object you have established a boundary around within one or two sessions of 'no touch', you should ensure your language is effective. Occasionally, when you have a very spirited baby, they will need a little extra encouragement, but the general plan is to not do the listening for them by actually moving them about like a puppet. Within a day or two, a simple, politely put, 'no touch bubba' should be enough to have them sit on their bottom, perhaps have a little protest cry about the way this makes them feel, then carry on with something new. Sometimes they might confirm with you that it's 'no touch', and you need to watch and interact with them until you are sure they understand the boundaries are not negotiable. If you need to go over and start again, then go for it. At no point through this entire process should you get impatient and look exasperated, angry, frustrated or intolerant of the time a little baby needs to develop this skill.

Play, when moving house, renovating or going on holidays

All three of these events are difficult for a baby, and play is always impacted. When you look at the world from a baby's perspective, predictable and consistent surroundings and people are what make it possible for a baby to trust that they are safe enough to take their gaze off their primary carers (their only means of survival) and look down and focus on their toys. If something happens to change their surrounding, the unpredictability of the environment makes it challenging for them to feel secure enough to focus on play.

When moving house, there are a few simple rules you should follow to help them settle into their new play environment. Where possible, take them up to the new house often before you move in to give them a chance to become familiar with these different surroundings. If they are happy to let you, and you are able to, take one of their favourite play rugs from home and place it on the floor with some of their best-loved toys and encourage play while you sit with them. This enables you to transfer a trusting and predictable environment from home to this new unpredictable and therefore untrustworthy environment.

Don't walk away from them so they can't see you, or they won't allow you to put them down to play next time because they won't trust you will stay within eyeshot or at a safe distance. This will make them clingy. Give the new home a name like 'the big house' and talk about it positively and excitedly every day. When you arrive at 'the big house' be really happy and keep saying its name in a positive tone, no matter what their reaction is.

When you first move in, set up their main areas of living first. Their bedroom should be put together, and then their primary play areas should be established before reintroducing them to play or sleep in both those environments. Obviously sleep will need to be role played multiple times before you even ask them to sleep independently in a foreign room, but play is best re-established by actually sitting and playing with them until they are comfortable enough to allow you to step back. (Follow the gradual step-back process provided with the cot play strategy on page 176.)

Renovating is almost always disruptive to a baby in the area of sleep and play. Here are a few simple rules to help make this time less stressful for your baby:

- Be respectful of your baby's boundaries around their personal space, particularly where strangers and workmen are concerned, asking them to keep a distance.

- If there are days when the noise will be particularly loud, please remove your little one completely from the environment as this could cause them to become stressed and untrusting in their usual play environment.
- If you cannot leave the house for the day, then keep your baby with you and play down loud sounds with a confident mimic of the noise to turn this slightly frightening event into a funny routine—your ham acting and laughing off any noises that make them jump will be great defusers.
- If they become very frightened, remove them from the environment and reassure them with cuddles until they settle down.
- When it comes time to re-enter an environment that has been frightening, it's important to stay confident and slowly make your way back in by redirecting their focus to a favourite toy with which you have already established play strategies. Diverting their attention away from the thing they feel fretful about and redirecting their attention on to something they can look forward to works wonders.
- Where possible try to move out whenever major renovations are taking place to minimise stress to your baby.
- When reintroducing them to a dramatically different-looking interior, use the strategies outlined for moving house.

When going on holidays, play is ironically rarely affected. I tend to find that sleep is severely affected whereas play doesn't suffer so badly. Whether this is because parents tend to be down on the floor and playing more often with their baby, or everyone is in such a great mood, I'm not sure, but I tend to find that a baby feels safe and confident to play in most cases. Just to ensure your baby has a great time on their holiday I always suggest a few things:

- Take some of their favourite home toys with you and ensure you take their familiar play rugs.
- Don't allow your child to be over handled by loving but overzealous family members if it is stressing them. This only caters for the adult's desire for a cuddle and not for the baby's need to feel in control in an unfamiliar environment.
- On the first day in the new holiday accommodation, be sure to sit on the floor and have a really fun and exciting first play with them as this will help develop strong, happy associations with play in the new environment.
- For the first few days don't stray too far from their line of sight without at least one parent remaining present.

- Always use your short- and long-term absence cues when walking out of the room so they can predict your movements.
- Whoever puts an unsettled baby down for sleep should be there when they wake up.

When following a routine but on a holiday, only allocate the times suggested for play if you are planning on staying in, otherwise, just do as you would choose on your busy holiday. If you notice that a morning sitting in a pram causes regular early morning waking and you wish to eliminate this, you will need to ensure your baby spends some time playing, exploring and challenging their environment each morning.

Loud noises preventing play

One thing that is guaranteed to disrupt a baby's ability to play is when their play environment is frequently disrupted by loud noises that startle them. If you know your little one dislikes the sound of the blender, the cappuccino machine, the vacuum cleaner or loud bangs that happen during cooking or unpacking the dishwasher, you need to take the time to introduce them to the objects and the actions that cause those noises. Often, I find parents avoid even using the objects around their baby again after an initial negative reaction scares them into thinking that it's too much for their baby. To not re-establish the object that makes the noise is to confirm to the baby that their fear is justified and any loud noise is bad or dangerous or something to be truly frightened of.

If you know that your baby is nervous about a normal household sound, it's really important that you take the time to show them that there is actually nothing to be frightened about. This is important as it facilitates healthy transitioning through and out of their fears and helps your baby find strategies to work through things rather than run away from them. A baby left to stagnate in a fear based on their lack of experience is so unfortunate. You have years of wisdom to impart on to your little one, and a confident mum and dad will be able to show them that they are okay to trust those noises.

It's important to look carefully at how you introduce or handle loud noises around your little one if they are sensitive. The first thing that needs to be done to help your baby to learn to cope with the normal flow of noises that occur in your house is to introduce them to the objects that make the noise, and then, before even turning the appliances on in their company, imitate the noises they make yourself. Once you have imitated the noises several times, you will see your child settle down. Remember to stay confident even if they are feeling anxious. This is important because if you are okay, it means that they are okay.

This is about you being a reliable emotional foundation that they can depend on for security, even when they feel unsettled. If you become involved in their emotional head space and become as stressed as them, then they will not feel safe because you are both frightened. Be strong, assess the environment from an adult's perspective, and if you know there is no real danger, reflect that in the way you respond to the noise.

This strategy relies on a confident respectful form of forewarning that gives your little one the time they need to get used to the fact that they are going to hear the sound. It also ensures your baby is empowered with the ability to know what is making the sound, and have a positive feeling about the sound because you have stayed confident while exposing them to it.

A pretend surprise or a little jump may make then giggle, and suddenly you have turned a frightening sound into something that they discover is safe, and even a little funny.

When it is time to turn on the noise, do so for as brief a time as possible. Make the noise with your own mouth first. Turn on the machine briefly, and then switch it off and be excited. Repeat the noise yourself and try to have a little fun around it. A pretend surprise or a little jump may make them giggle, and suddenly you have turned a frightening sound into something that they discover is safe, and even a little funny. Repeat this several times until your baby finds it funny. Once this happens you can leave them sitting down, and repeat the above process. When your little one has developed a positive association with the sound, then you will be able to use it for longer periods of time.

The important thing to remember is that you must always use forewarning to tell them what is coming, and show them the object before imitating the sound. Always stay confident and reassuring. If your funny surprise game at the sound makes them laugh, then play that without picking them up unless it is absolutely necessary. This simple flow of communication tells your baby that you don't think the noise is something dangerous because you not only highlight the way it may make you feel, like a surprise, but you also laugh about the way it makes you feel. Not rescuing a baby from a mix master shows the baby that the mix master is not something you see as dangerous to them, which of course it isn't.

Routines around noises that are too exciting can become disruptive, and so they can create a fear response to a specific noise, as the story of Jed (see box on page 434) clearly shows. This was not only impacting on his ability to play, but had spilled through and was now impacting his ability to sleep effectively.

The case of Alex and the Mack truck

I met the lovely Alex when I visited his family in the south of Sydney. Alex was 11 months old and had developed a really profound fear of the sound of truck engines. This was not just your usual reaction by a baby: it was near hysteria that would often take him between one and two hours to recover from. Most people would think that while this was unfortunate, it was okay: how often does your child encounter a truck when playing at home? Sadly, though, in Alex's case the neighbour was a truck driver and he owned a giant Mack truck. Much to Alex's horror the truck would rumble into life right next to his house at all hours of the day and night.

In this scenario we needed to help Alex overcome his fear and become more relaxed about the noise made by the truck. Initially, we used the 'white noise' setting on a sound therapy spa to eliminate the noise for his environment altogether as his reaction was one of significant distress. We needed to take this measure because trying to teach him to get used to the noise when we didn't have the opportunity to give him some forewarning was clearly going to be too difficult for him, and for us. Instead, we went to the neighbour and recorded the sound of the truck on to a digital recorder and made a CD. In addition to the truck sound, we recorded a series of normal household sounds and created a loop of the six different sounds, one of which was the truck. We then made picture cards to match each sound.

On the first day we sat down with our CD and picture cards and worked through each sound. We made sure the volume was set to low and, knowing the truck was coming next, we would pause the CD, show him the picture of the truck and make the sound with our mouths. This would initially evoke a reaction of real fear in little Alex but we would stay calm and confident for him. Slowly, one loop at a time, Alex became more and more used to the fact that the truck sound was coming. After playing the game four times the first day Alex was getting better and better about hearing the sound.

We repeated this same strategy on day two and as he got more and more used to the sound loop he began to show a desire to play elsewhere and lost interest in the CD. This was a great sign for us. The next part would be easy. We simply left the CD playing and went to a new area of play. As the day progressed, we increased the volume of the CD until it was quite loud. We would carry on as usual and occasionally see him hear the truck and look up at us. As he crawled towards us, we would smile, reassure him and make the truck sound with our mouth while handing him the picture card, then offer him a toy. The truck sound would end its cycle and he would go back to what he was doing. In just two days he went from near hysteria to a whole new level of coping.

We played this CD every day for a week for between one and two hours after an initial sitting-down game. By the third day, the sound of the truck starting up was no longer something that even drew his attention. His mother and I were delighted for him and he has never had a problem with the sound of trucks since.

The story of Alex and the Mack truck (see box on page 389) shows the value of graded exposure through play to things that evoke a response of fear in a child. This same principle can be applied with older children who develop a fear of thunder. The results are just as fast and just as effective.

Pets and play

Pets can often create disruption around baby's playtime, particularly the noisy, licking, yappy kind. I'm talking about a cheeky puppy, the only pet that causes real drama in your average home. I always say, if you can't communicate with a simple creature like a dog, and set basic boundaries around your infant child for the pet to follow, how on earth will you manage the complex, sophisticated and intelligent communication needed to guide your baby? Just as with everything, babies learn from their surrounding and if your dog doesn't have to listen to you, can jump all over you, can snatch your baby's toys and can generally have full run of the house, how could you expect anything different from your child?

Your communication streams with your other children, your husband or wife and *even* your pets make up a complex repertoire of definitions to statements and words, and can impact on your baby's understanding of your language. In addition to a poorly behaved and overbearing dog creating confusing language streams in the house, the pet can also cause real stress to your baby as far as unpredictability goes. Babies are not keen on unpredictable patterns of behaviour and if your dog's tail occasionally, without warning, wacks them over the head, or your baby is nervous they will be bowled over when the doorbell rings as your dogs flies past them at 100 kilometres an hour, then you have a real problem on your hands.

> Pets offer a beautiful form of loving company to a family, and often loyal and steadfast protection for the baby.

Added to the mix is the fact that poorly disciplined pets create a couple of responses from you: yelling or neglecting your pet-owner duties. Things can quickly go from bad to worse. If you are yelling, your baby may be on tenterhooks as they will have absolutely no idea you are not yelling at them, and this might just frighten or disrupt them. You may find baby yelling (in the form of crying) right back at you whenever they feel frustrated. This is because you are teaching them that this is how you respond to these emotions. You are their social role model. Think about what your interactions with your pet are teaching your little one about communication, compassion for animals and general behaviour.

Just as bad, and sadly a common occurrence: if you are neglecting your pet by leaving it in the back yard the whole time and never spending any time with it you are quite possibly making its behaviour worse, not to mention being unfair to the pet. I am a firm believer that respect and compassion for all living things start at home with a pet. I am surprised how often parents tell me they have had their beloved pet destroyed because they just couldn't trust it around the baby, rather than taking the more sensible approach of desexing and training the dog. Of course, if your pet shows even the slightest threat to any child, then I would recommend you sell the dog to a loving home, but if the problem is a simple boisterous, bouncy dog issue, these problems are easily fixed.

Pets offer a beautiful form of loving company to a family, and often loyal and steadfast protection for the baby. Here are my hints for managing pets when you have a baby:

- Your dog must be disciplined correctly through group dog obedience classes or through personal sessions with a trainer in your house.
- Dogs are not allowed to take baby's toys.
- Dogs are not allowed to lick baby.
- Your dog must stay away from baby until you give it permission to come over and interact with the baby.
- Do not yell, hit or act aggressively towards the animal. It sets a bad example and encourages aggressive defensive behaviour from the dog, and in many cases is imitated by your child.
- A poorly behaving dog should be made to leave the room.
- Set clear, separate times of the day where the dog must play outside while your baby engages in independent playtime inside.
- If your dog barks loudly when the door bell rings, or frightens your baby when it responds to certain things, then this must be firmly but fairly trained out of the dog. Speak to your local vet for more information on local resources to help you here.
- Your dog must not have access to the baby's room, and is not permitted to be present while you change baby's nappy. These are both times when your child must have respectful boundaries set around their personal space.
- Be consistent with your dog. Don't set confusing inconsistent language streams.
- If your dog in an inside dog, always use the dog's name as the first word when communicating with your pet so your baby does not feel the need to look up when you speak.

- Baby is not permitted to pull a tail, hair, ears or fur, regardless of how good your pet is about it. It's cruel to the animal and a dangerous practice to teach your baby. If they encounter a strange dog and do the same thing they run the risk of being bitten or worse.
- No rough play that encourages play biting or aggressive play behaviour with the dog is permitted. Opt for great walks, runs or ball / stick chasing in the park.

Talking on the phone

Mums or dads talking on the phone is a problem in just about every single house I go into. Look at it from your baby's perspective:

> You play with me and chat with me all day. You almost always look at me when you talk, and you smile and sometimes even walk towards me, and when I want to talk back with you, I crawl over, while you're chatting, making lovely clear eye contact with me and you pick me up most of the time. This is usually followed by half an hour of my favourite things . . . kisses, tickles, the odd raspberry and a whole lot of loving. Then, all of a sudden, for no apparent reason you start to act strangely when you talk. You use a different tone of voice to normal, you rarely make eye contact with me, and if you do it's a little inconsistent with the way you are talking, and sometimes you even look sad or cross. When I come over to you, you sigh and look exasperated and you always have that thing stuck to your head! Is that what we do now, mummy? Hold something on our head? Perhaps I should do it too! Since you seem to think it's a good idea. Here, hand it to me, I'll do it just like you.

Mummy suddenly frowns, signs, and becomes exasperated, wondering why she has no time to even make a simple phone call:

'James, stop it, mummy is on the phone!'

'Wwwhhaaaaaaaaaaaaaaaaaaaaaaa!'

Sadly, your baby does not understand that the thing stuck to your ear is a way of communicating with others and thinks you are talking to them. Stop and think about a conversation you have had today on the phone and the body language used while you were talking. It is vastly different to the way you usually interact with your baby so is it any wonder they feel uncomfortable and ask to be picked up? You're just acting oddly as far as they are concerned.

Trying to work through these telephone dramas is a little tricky while they are so little. If your baby becomes upset when you talk on the phone, try to go over to them and sit with them while you talk on the phone. Offer them a toy, smile at them and make eye contact and within a short period of time they will settle. Watch out if you're talking through things with your caller about matters that evoke a strong emotional reaction from you. If your conversation is destined to evoke tears or make you growl as you recall an event that has made you feel that way, reserve the call for the times when your baby is asleep.

Be careful to only initiate time for the baby to talk on the phone on your terms. This might sound harsh but it will actually save a lot of tears and stress for your baby. If you tell them that they can ask to talk on the phone whenever they like, but the reality is that this is not a possibility all of the time, you are being inconsistent and may frustrate or upset your baby. You need to ensure your baby learns quickly that if it is mum, dad, nan, pa, sis, aunty, cousin or [insert other really important people in their lives here] then you will let them know when they can have a talk on the phone. Develop a cue like 'Jamie's talk time now' and offer the phone, still holding it.

If you are going to allow them to talk on your terms, you will need to be clear with your language and tell them when it's 'nearly time for saying bye bye' as a way of pre-empting the fact that you are going to take the phone back soon. Finally, when it's time to hand the phone back, you will need to get them to 'wave bye bye phone, mummy's turn' and quickly offer them a toy to distract them. If they cry, it does not change the conditions of taking the phone back. Always be careful about the meaning you give some of their cries. If you want to teach your baby to cry to get the phone back, then hand it back again when they cry. If, on the other hand, you want to teach your baby to accept that 'bye bye' means 'no more, you have to go play now', then do not give it back.

You can practise this new game and new set of conditions when there is no one on the phone so they can get used to the new language and start to feel comfortable about the expectation while there isn't an adoring granny waiting patiently on the other end of the line.

Delivering a mixed message during playtime

There is no argument from me: watching a baby play is quite possibly one of the loveliest things I can think to do. They are beautiful, funny, clever and irresistible. They have a magnetic quality that makes it almost impossible, through no conscious effort, to not stand right next to them and watch their every move. But it makes getting things done notoriously difficult and it can also make play for them a bit of a challenge. It also impacts quite significantly on some babies' ability to play.

This is more about body language than anything else. It's about ensuring that in your delight at watching them play your actions are not confusing them by saying 'do you want me to pick you up, play with you, or entertain you?' If you have clearly asked them to play on their own for a little while, you need to be sure you don't say two things at once by contradicting your verbal language with conflicting body language. Like everything else, you just need to be consistent so it is clear that this is an independent playtime of the day. You don't want to be hovering over your little adventurous baby so much that they can't focus on their toys and end up thinking they should be carried instead.

Try to be conscious of your movements, and if you catch yourself sneaking over to admire the way their eyelashes rest on their cheek as they try to look at their toes then make sure you are a little subtle. Sit on the couch perhaps, or stand side on at the kitchen bench and peep over your shoulder. I am not saying that you shouldn't watch your baby because there is barely a home I enter where I am not mesmerised by their absolutely perfect child. I'm just saying that while watching might be really enjoyable for you, when was the last time you enjoyed your mother / husband / friend walking over to you and just staring at you without speaking. If they did do that, you would almost immediately stop what you were doing and try to engage them in conversation. If they then did not answer you, you would probably feel a little uncomfortable.

Follow these simple tips to ensure your baby doesn't receive a mixed message, even if you can't help yourself and need to sit and watch them during their playtime:

- Don't forget independent playtime only lasts for one hour in every 24 so try really hard to give them the space they need to practise and grow confident with the skills they need for going to sleep and staying asleep happily.
- Stand side on to your bub so they don't think you're about to come over to them.
- Try to keep your hands busy so they think you are occupied doing something else.
- Don't stand front on, feet astride, hands on hips as I see most lovely starry-eyed daddies do.
- Try not to move around the room too much while they are playing. It might make them a little unsure of your location so they will be inclined to watch you, which means play won't happen. They will then get bored and will ask to be picked up.

- Stay happy and reassuring if they have misunderstood your actions and immediately correct your posture.
- When approaching a lying baby to offer new toys, most people straddle the baby and hang over the top of them. Try squatting side on to the baby, so your body is side on to theirs. Only use one hand at a time when offering toys then turn away before you stand up.
- Baby proof your house, put up gates, or close doors so you don't feel you have to follow them all over the house. Remember, their comfort level around happily crawling away from you and going on an adventure is great, and perfect for developing and maintaining the skills they need for sleep. So make the environment safe so you don't have to go with them, even if you want to keep watching them. Imagine the message you deliver if you always follow them: 'you shouldn't be on your own'. How different is this to the message you need to deliver at sleep time?
- Often happily chatting to someone else in the room when the baby starts to fuss, if they think you were about to pick them up, is enough to help them settle down.

Avoiding tears and tantrums over the rides at the shops

I find that very young babies rarely demand to sit on the rides at the shops, but coming off them and getting back into the pram can still be quite a problem. Most people are so nervous of their children getting upset that they try to avoid the tears by removing their child from a situation with as little warning as humanly possible. Their little person is bobbing happily up and down on this great fun Wiggles car at the supermarket. Then, with a knowing look of fear to one another, the parent grabs their child and physically battles the somewhat-shocked little one into a pram before running off to the nearest exit. The whole time the child is saying 'Hey, I was just playing on that car if you hadn't noticed and I hadn't quite finished yet'.

Well, that course of action, taken to try and avoid tears and tantrums, is actually the number one cause of all those tears and tantrums. What you need to do is to create a respectful flow of communication (see page 40), where you warn your baby that the fun ride is soon drawing to a close. Always begin by simply forewarning your baby: 'Jet, soon it will be time to say bye bye red car'. Then tell him what it is you are doing next so he knows what's coming up, so he isn't focused just on what he is losing. Use a well-rehearsed stream of communication that you know your little one understands along with some clear visual cues.

This simple pre-emptive style of communication involves patting his pram and saying, 'Jet, soon it will be time to sit down in your pram, and wait for mummy. Say bye bye to Wiggles car.' Then keep reminding him, 'Nearly time to _____. Okay last one, then it's time to sit down in your pram, wait for mummy.'

Once the ride has come to an end, with a big smile say 'Okay time to say bye bye to Wiggles car. Wave, bubba.' At this point, you will need to guide him confidently, offer a clap and show of hands and your up cue (see page 76). This will have him ready to come to you so you can pick him up confidently. Then follow through with your original statement, 'sitting down, wait for mummy', before you sit him in the pram confidently.

> Once the ride has come to an end, with a big smile say 'Okay time to say bye bye to Wiggles car. Wave, bubba.'

Then it's time to redirect or divert his attention quite quickly: 'Ooooh, where's that balloon?' Point to it and say, 'Look let's go see the balloon. Off we goooo.' This will move him on to the next part of his shopping adventure immediately, and as you go on your way talk to him about the new target to keep his attention diverted from the activity he has just left. Once the previous activity is out of his line of sight, he should settle straight away.

Part 2
Sleeping well
for peaceful nights

14
Sleep—the basics

Learning how to help your baby / toddler to sleep correctly can be one of the most eye-opening and personality-revealing journeys you embark on during the first precious years of their life. To truly understand your child's needs at sleep time, you must get to know your little one on a very deep level at non-sleep time, to learn about all the things that make them tick. To try and fix your child's sleep-time problems only at bedtime means you are ignoring who your child is and what makes them that way. Problems at sleep time are merely a symptom of an imbalance elsewhere, so our aim must be to correct the imbalance as a way of taking away the cause, and *only then* do you aim to correct any of the existing poor, confusing or disruptive patterns of communication and expectation that are causing all the fuss and bother at sleep time.

To address the whole cause of sleep-time problems you need to work with your child's little body's needs, and with them on a psychological level to ensure you provide a balanced learning opportunity that is neither confusing nor short-term with regards results. While doing so, you need to cater for your child's strengths and weaknesses. This is respectfully teaching your little one how to sleep and ensures that, once they have become proficient in how to sleep, it remains a pleasant area of bonding for both you and your child.

Everyone knows that putting a baby or toddler down to sleep can be a stressful event, so you need to be certain that the way you guide them is focused on empowering them, not just demanding that they co-operate. For you, this means putting in a short-term investment of time and energy so you can discover how to respectfully and honestly communicate with your child to help them learn to sleep independently for the long term. All of this will have an impact on their entire life in a positive way. Achieving an all-encompassing approach to sleep may require a little bit of extra work on your part, but it is the way to a complete parenting philosophy that should be, in my personal opinion, developed from the very earliest age of life to ensure your family has a healthy, open and respectful style of communication. Just as importantly it will ensure your journey as a parent is joyful, and every challenge is exciting rather than frightening or frustrating, by encouraging a confident style of parenting in you. This is both wonderful for baby, and therefore wonderful for you.

> To truly understand your child's needs at sleep time, you must get to know your little one on a very deep level at non-sleep time, to learn about all the things that make them tick.

This healthy style of parenting and balanced communication is often neglected for the first three to four years of a child's life, but to establish it from the beginning will influence the entire future for your child and family in an extremely constructive and positive way. A respectful sleep-time strategy is dependent on three key factors:

- physiology of sleep
- biology of sleep
- psychology of sleep.

These three key factors make up a child's world of sleep, and they comprise the many things that can affect, both positively and negatively, their ability to actually fall asleep and stay asleep. This chapter will provide you with a much greater understanding of the things that are causing your little one's sleep-time difficulties, enabling you to repair it respectfully. But before we explore these three important elements of sleep, let's take a little look at the world of sleep from your baby's perspective.

A child's-eye view of the field of dreams

Your child knows nothing about the concept of sleep. They only have associations linked with the sensations leading up to being asleep. These associations are your baby's personal coping strategies for when they feel tired. They develop these associations by simply looking to you for guidance about what to do when they start to feel tired. For this reason these coping strategies are either a learnt *dependent* pattern of association, such as patting, breastfeeding, rocking, or suckling a dummy for instance, or a learnt *independent* pattern of association like sucking their thumb, playing with a satin-edged sheet or a tag on their teddy, twirling or rubbing their hair or playing with an ear.

Your child also has no concept of time lapsing. This is a vital point to consider because, as you will soon discover, your child will naturally stir or come to a partial waking multiple times through any sleep cycle prior to the sleep session being naturally completed. This means that, when they fall asleep after feeling the sensations of being tired and wake some time later, they do not know they have been asleep or that time has passed. All they know is that when they open their eyes again, if they still feel the sensation of being tired, that everything should still be the same as it was when they first had the feeling of being tired. Even after hours have passed, they expect to still have their usual sleep associations available to them and to be in the same place as they were before they went to sleep. If those associations have changed after they have gone to sleep, like their dummy has fallen out, their breastfeed has ended, or they are no longer in your arms, you risk creating three separate sleep-time complications.

Your child knows nothing about the concept of sleep. They only have associations linked with the sensation of feeling tired.

Firstly, if the change is dramatic, such as a parent has left the room or has put them down in their cot after they have fallen asleep elsewhere, they will be startled when they wake up because as far as they are concerned someone has just vanished, literally, in the blink of an eye. Because of this they may lose trust in the sensation of feeling tired at sleep time and start to fight going to sleep in general. I have had so many parents ask me 'Sheyne, my baby is just so tired but they fight their sleep so much, why?' Well, a change of sleep conditions is your number one culprit.

Secondly, when they do partially wake up in mid sleep, still feeling tired, they will need to recreate their sleep conditions (coping strategies for feeling tired). They do this by either using their independent associations (sucking thumb etc.), or will call out for assistance through crying as a means of asking for their usual dependent associations (breastfeed etc.) to be recreated by you. If these associations involve your intervention, such as learnt dependent associations, then they will need to cry out to get you to come in again and again, and repeat the process they have learnt to rely upon to cope with the feeling of being tired, and to go back to sleep. Logically then, the only difference between a child who can sleep through the night and a child who cannot sleep through the night is actually a matter of one child having independent associations to cope with sleep, meaning they don't cry out, and the other child having learnt dependent associations, meaning they do need to cry out each time they partially wake during their sleep cycle. It is not a matter of one waking up and the other not waking up, because all children do wake up naturally multiple times mid sleep.

Thirdly, if all the above fuss and crying out and stress happen in their cot, then they start to develop a poor association or bad feelings around their cot environment. You will see them become reluctant to go into it, or indeed anywhere near it, thus creating a high likelihood that your baby will develop a strong, learnt, dependent set of associations to go to sleep, perpetuating the cycle of crying out at night and through day sleeps.

Knowing this, think about what tools you have given your child to cope with the sensation of being tired and therefore going to sleep. Are you their only strategy for this feeling, or can they be in their cot alone as they drift off to sleep? If you are their only method for going to sleep, then this is such an enormous burden on your baby and on you, and unnecessarily so. You have taught them that they can't or shouldn't feel comfortable about going to sleep without you. But they *can* and *should* feel comfortable to go to sleep without you. It's all in the messages you send to your child about the situation. You need to use your confident, loving and reassuring tones, verbal expressions and body language to tell them that their cot is safe and that feeling tired is normal, and that they are okay when they feel tired and are going to sleep.

A child is perfectly capable of developing their own coping strategies if you give them some time and space to do so. But why would they even think to try if you are always there fussing with them? It is important to have a parent-governed sleep environment and there is absolutely a need for consistency in that strategy to prevent tears and stress for your baby. If you are to use a parent-governed line of communication to ask your children to look to you for guidance when it comes time to go to sleep and go back to sleep (which you are about to learn how to do), then you *must* also ask them to look to you for guidance when sleep time is over. You must not confuse them by teaching them a different style of communication upon waking by looking to them for guidance, through any child-directed waking communication such as crying to get up. This would be a contradiction in communication terms to the governing line you use during the night and only serve to confuse your baby, causing tears. Allow me to explain.

In your new sleep routines that you are about to learn, if your child cries when you put them to bed, you will reassure them through the use of your new settling routine and cues that they are okay, and that mummy is there and has heard them. Bu they still need to go to sleep and you can't do that for them, and they will be asked to listen to your guidance and to go to sleep independently. This will mean that you have defined your new settling cues clearly with their true meaning and given your child the time and space needed to develop independent settling associations to go to sleep in a supportive and language-rich way.

Your new routine then ensures the conditions they originally went to sleep with (in their room, with no one else in the room with them, going to sleep after mummy requested it) will be identical to the conditions they will experience at all partial wakings during the night, which will be, in their room, with no one in the room with them and going to sleep by themselves as requested. This means that your child will start to sleep through the night without the need to call out because nothing will have changed from when they initially fell asleep to when they come to any of their partial wakings during the night. However, on those first few nights of learning to sleep independently under your guidance, your initial parent-governed line of request to go to sleep will set you up to be able to help them to go back to sleep in the night, should they wake and cry, using communication in the same way that you did when initially putting them to bed. So while your child is first learning to sleep through the night, if they do wake and cry out, you will again be asking them to look to you for guidance to go back to sleep by using the same flow of communication from your settling routine. You will say 'There is no need to fuss and demand, mummy and daddy will tell you if it's time to get up'. They will then be able to understand your request because you defined it at the settling routine, and will go back to sleep. This is also a parent-governed line of communication.

> Don't get me wrong, I would expect a child to let you know when they are awake, but it's your response to that crying that will teach them that crying is not necessary because that is not what instigates their waking-up time.

Now remember, to be truly fair to them you will need to be honest about the sleeping environment they will encounter when they wake briefly during the night by providing identical conditions to when they initially go to sleep each night. You need to create conditions where they can self-resettle without you being there initially, and that they are comfortable with those circumstances, meaning that during any partial wakings in their sleep session they will remain comfortable and familiar with the conditions present.

Having worked hard and been consistent all night by asking your baby to not cry and fuss at sleep time and to try to go to sleep on their own, be careful not to make the biggest error of all when morning comes. You check your clock in response to your baby's cries of 'I'm awake, can you come and pick me up' with an 'okay, just cry and I'll come in and pick you up'. Can you see how this will be inconsistent and confusing for your baby and will encourage them to cry through the night the following night? How will your baby know 2 a.m. from 4 a.m. from 7 a.m.? This is where many sleep-solution strategies available to families today are entirely inconsistent and confusing for a baby from a communication standpoint.

Because your baby has no concept of time lapsing, all they know is how you respond to them. Looking to their cries in the morning to let you know they are awake and responding to those cries by getting them up will undo all your work and their learning to look to you for guidance and not cry through the settling and resettling process. To be truly consistent then, you need to ask your child to look to you for guidance around all three areas of sleep: going to sleep, going back to sleep, *and* when it's time to get up, by providing them with a settling routine, a resettling routine *and* a waking routine.

Don't get me wrong, I would expect a child to let you know when they are awake, but it's your response to that crying that will teach them that crying is not necessary because that is not what instigates their waking-up time. Instead, you develop a set of language cues and a little waking ritual that indicate the time to get up has arrived. Then your baby will not need to cry and will learn to wake and play in their cot and wait for you to instigate their usual waking conditions. This is peaceful for not only your child, but for your entire family. This is a healthy sleep process.

The physiology of sleep

As mentioned, there are three distinct processes to what I call the physiology of sleep that I work with when it comes to sleep:

* going to sleep (settling)
* going back to sleep (resettling)
* waking up (waking).

Each is interlinked and each one relies heavily on the continuity between all three to maintain good sleeping.

Going to sleep is the function of settling yourself to sleep from a stage of consciousness. The settling conditions you provide for your baby when they initially go to sleep, and how you manage them during their partial waking, will impact on your child' s ability to resettle during a sleep session.

Going back to sleep is the function of resettling yourself back to sleep from a state of semi-consciousness, and I call this 'surface sleep'. Surface-sleep windows last around three to eight minutes, and it is when a baby's brainwave activity indicates a transitional sleep–wave pattern. While they are partially aware of their surrounding, they are not fully conscious of it. A child can easily have a habitualised pattern of expectation for your intervention in their surface sleep if you usually rush in to try and get them back to sleep quickly. If you can give them enough space, they will become more conscious of their environment, see everything is as it was when they were first willingly drifting off to sleep after you requested it, and then relax and willingly go back to sleep again.

Waking up is the function of coming to a full state of consciousness from a sleep state. The waking conditions you provide your child can impact on their ability to resettle through a sleep session elsewhere in the day.

Your child's ability to sleep relies on all three stages being predictable and consistent. Based on an inconsistency in your approach to the physiology of sleep you will see two different kinds of settling problems occur: settling and resettling difficulties; or just resettling difficulties.

A child who can't self-settle when they are going to sleep will generally not be able to self-resettle back to sleep either. This is when parents end up having to put their baby to sleep, and back to sleep, at all times of the night and / or day. Occasionally your child may not be able self-settle but does not wake during the night. This is a rare circumstance, however, and be aware that here there is a high risk that this pattern is unlikely to last long term. It's common to also encounter a child who may be able to self-settle during the day but not at night. This is classed as a 'routine association problem'. Your child is still considered unable to self-settle despite any daytime success because the governing line of communication falls on them, making sleep unpredictable at best.

> Your child's ability to sleep relies on all three stages—going to sleep (settling), going back to sleep (resettling), and waking up (waking)—being predictable and consistent.

The far more common scenario is the second problem mentioned above: a child self-settling when *going* to sleep but finding it difficultly to self-resettle when *going back* to sleep. Here the child is functioning on an entirely different state of consciousness when they wake during the night or during day sleep cycles. They are in a surface or transitional sleep pattern for three to eight minutes. Due to this, the child can learn patterns of dependency around resettling on a subconscious level. A parent might be able to put their baby to bed and request they go to sleep on a conscious level, but will need to assist their baby to go back to sleep during the night and day on a subconscious level. Typically, parents who experience this problem know that if they enter the room fast enough they can prevent their baby from waking up fully and get them off to sleep within minutes. This 'if I'm quick' approach appears to be a good idea in the short term, but long term it is the cause of night time wakings that will need to be addressed or the child and the parents will become exhausted with such disrupted sleep sessions.

The biology of sleep

Every baby has a certain amount of sleep they need to consume in a 24-hour period. Every baby's sleep requirement is different (see box on page 407). You cannot expect them to sleep more than their body actually needs. An average baby between six and 12 months of age will have a daily sleep requirement of between 13 and 17 hours. A baby / toddler between 12 and 24 months of age will have a daily sleep requirement of between 13 and 16 hours. You can break that sleep requirement into two distinct portions of the 24-hour cycle:

- day—7 a.m. to 7 p.m.
- night—7 p.m. to 7 a.m.

Why 7 to 7? For two very simple but related facts: the mean time the sun comes up in the morning, and because the largest portion of solid sleep needs to be achieved during the night when it's dark. Nature's and your home environment's alarm clocks—sunlight, birds chirping or squawking, traffic rumbling, increased room temperature and the house creaking into life as people get up and get ready for the day ahead—will, on average, be around 7 a.m. for most of the year, so you will need to put your little one to bed by 7 p.m. the night before to ensure they achieve their night sleep quota. As baby's night sleep is always 11 to 11½ hours long—and there is no need for them to have night feeds from six months if solids are introduced into their diet (unless instructed otherwise by your medical practitioner)—their day sleeps are then arranged around the remainder of their sleep requirement.

Establishing a healthy night-time body clock, or 'circadian rhythm', is achieved in the first five years of life; that is, the night sleep pattern established when a child is young remains with them for the rest their life and the 7 a.m. waking time will not alter for the best part of their entire adult life. To try and get your child to wake at this time only when they reach preschool or school age significantly impacts on their entire day, every day, and they will not be at their absolute best during the day. You need to make a 7 a.m. rising the normal and natural time so that their energy peaks between the hours of 9 a.m. to 5 p.m. Either side of these hours is the essential wind up and the wind down to and from the day. Both the wind up and the wind down are essential to a balanced healthy day.

This is an important point. All our bodies are tuned to respond to the sun naturally. Learning to work in a balanced and harmonious way with nature is crucial when it comes to good sleep. You rise and warm-up with the sun. Your energy and activity levels are highest when the sun is brightest. You wind down and cool down with the sun. You have low to no energy levels when the sun is not present because, as darkness falls, enzymes in the brain stimulate the release of melatonin from the pineal gland. Melatonin induces sleep by influencing the suprachiasmatic nucleus. The release of melatonin is halted when daylight arrives, and you experience wakefulness as a direct result. So you are meant to sleep through the night, and be awake during the day.

Your body's circadian rhythm should work in perfect harmony with nature. As a fresh new life your baby is not meant to go to sleep five hours after the sun goes down and wake up five hours after it rises or, worse still, go to sleep hours after it sets and wake up when it first rises in the morning. Nature has it right and we have, sadly, almost always got it wrong in our modern-day lifestyles.

Nature produces foods that are healthy, balanced and nutritious for our body to promote optimum growth and development. Our society produces food that is often unhealthy and unbalanced with flavour taking priority over nutritional benefits. Nature provides a system of resources that we can use and dispose of that will break down into nature yet again, thus creating harmony and balance. We produce systems that we use and discard aimlessly into the environment and atmosphere that cannot break down into nature again, thus creating an imbalance. Is it any wonder that lifestyles today see us staying up well into the night, lessening our sleep intake, lessening our activity levels during the day, and creating a depressed system, both on an immunological and an emotional and physical level? When you take your cues from nature, which is a perfectly balanced working system, then you know you will be finding the harmonious balance you need for optimum health and wellbeing.

> Your body's circadian rhythm should work in perfect harmony with nature.

Signs of sleep imbalance

Because you need to lock in the night sleep first (11–11½ hrs of your child's full sleep-requirement quota), you then only need to work on balancing their *remaining* day sleep requirement from 7 a.m. to 7 p.m. You do this by working with two distinct sleep windows during the day to correct any remaining sleep-time imbalances. To understand this general principle, which applies to all children, morning sleeps happen any time between 7 a.m. and 12 p.m. and will impact on your child's waking time between 6 and 7 a.m. the *following* morning as well as how long they can sleep at the next sleeping window for the remainder of *this* day. Equally, the afternoon sleep between 2 and 7 p.m. will impact on your child's settling time each night between 7 and 8 p.m. and will affect the length of time they could stay asleep in the midsection of the day (12 to 2 p.m.) the *following* day. Sleep taken between 12 and 2 p.m., however, will generally not effect their 7 p.m. settling time of *this* day or their 6 to 7 a.m. waking time the *following* morning.

If your child has a higher sleep requirement, they will generally be able to sleep for longer periods of time during both day sleep sections (7 a.m. to 12 p.m. and 2 to 7 p.m.) without it affecting the other sleep window of the day, their 7 to 8 p.m. settling time each night, or their 6 to 7 a.m. waking time the following morning, which is the opposite for lower sleep requirement babies. This is why 'what works for one, does not necessarily work for another', and why you cannot apply the same routine to every child. It means that both your child's sleep requirement and the times they sleep during the day are most often the causes of reoccurring sleep inconsistencies. For example, a typical routine miscalculation for a lower sleep-requirement baby can occur when their 24-hour sleep requirement (14 hours) is used up between the hours of 7 p.m. one night and 11 a.m. the next morning because a parent provides one large morning sleep between 7 a.m. and 12 p.m. after a full night's sleep. This makes it difficult for baby to achieve a second sleep during that day if their sleep requirement is low. They may have already slept 11½ hours at night and a further 2½

How many hours makes what?
If your child's daily (24-hourly) sleep intake, averaged over a week is:

- 8 to 14½ hours, they have a low sleep requirement (LSR)
- 14½ to 15½ hours, they have an average sleep requirement (ASR)
- 15½ to 16½ hours, they have a high sleep requirement (HSR).

Knowing your child's average daily sleep requirement will help you work out their day sleep routines so that their night sleeps are unaffected and remain steady. To work out your child's current average sleep requirement, please go to the 'Sleep diary' section on page 534.

hours somewhere between 7 a.m. and 12 p.m., totalling 14 hours. So any additional sleeps that day will be difficult for bubby to achieve.

Once the night cycle has been achieved (in this case, 11½ hours) you have only a certain amount of sleep to work with for that child through the remainder of their day, which needs to be either divided up between the two windows of the day (7 a.m. to 12 p.m. and 2 to 7 p.m.), or provided in the midsection of the day (12 to 2.30 p.m.). For a 14-hour sleep-requirement baby you would calculate the day sleep as follows:

Total hours required   = 14
Minus overnight sleep = 11½
Leaving   = 2½ hours for a full 7 a.m. to 7 p.m. day.

If all that sleep is used up in the morning, leaving no sustainable sleep cycles available for the rest of the afternoon, the child will typically have only a brief catnap or no sleep at all in the second window of the day (2 to 7 p.m.).

Once this miscalculation cycle starts to happen, babies get very overtired by the end of the day and need help to go to sleep, creating dependent settling association. This is when a parent with a baby who has a lower sleep requirement can easily fall into the cycle of teaching their babies learnt dependent associations for the sensation of feeling tired (see page 399), and why some children find it so hard to self-settle at night compared with the rest of their day. Imagine, after a poor night's sleep due to the need for regular assistance to resettle, a child will be naturally more prone to needing to a longer sleep in the morning to compensate, which perpetuates the cycle of poor afternoon sleep and an overtired baby needing assistance at 7 p.m. again.

You also need to be careful with a low sleep-requirement baby's day sleeps to ensure they don't oversleep during the day, leaving them struggling to achieve a full night's sleep. As soon as you allow 9 hours' sleep at night in order to achieve longer day sleeps that you might have been told they need, you run the risk of shifting their body clocks and damaging their important full-night sleep quota of 11 to 11½ hours. This often happens in the case of a low sleep-requirement baby when they are expected to take a big sleep in the morning and a big sleep in the afternoon, as babies with a high sleep requirement do, despite it not suiting the low sleep-requirement baby's true need. You would never steal sleep from the nights to achieve a particular day quota of sleep. You always establish their nights (11 to 11½ hrs) first, and if they cannot take the routine amount of sleep suggested after a full night's sleep, then chances are, the routine quota is too high for them and they need a different routine.

The early and late shift

If your baby goes down too late at night (between, say, 9 and 10 p.m.), and wakes up late the next morning (between, say, 8 to 9 a.m.), their day sleeps are shifted to later in the morning and later into the afternoon, which perpetuates a cycle of late settling at night. Equally, but in the opposite direction, if your baby goes down too early at night (between 5 and 6 p.m.) and subsequently wakes up early the next day (4 to 5 a.m.), their day sleeps are shifted to earlier in the mornings and earlier in the afternoon, perpetuating a cycle of early settling at night time. Both these patterns over a long period of time affect their body clocks.

Stolen partial-night cycles

When a portion of their 11 to 11½–hour night sleep is stolen and used as a day sleep, three typical scenarios are played out:

- morning sleep-cycle thief—baby wakes at 5 a.m. and stays awake for two hours, then sleeps between 7 and 9 a.m., which means two hours have been stolen from the night sleep, so the sleep between 7 and 9 a.m. is actually stolen from 5 to 7 a.m., and needs to be restored
- afternoon sleep-cycle thief—child goes to bed at 5 p.m. and sleeps until 7 p.m., then wakes and plays until 9 p.m. before settling for the night, so the sleep between 5 and 7 p.m. then is actually stolen from 7 to 9 p.m., and needs to be restored
- evening sleep-cycle thief—baby has a prolonged waking of perhaps two hours somewhere between 11.30 p.m. and 3.30 a.m. then goes back to sleep for the remainder of the night. The following day they then need longer day sleeps to compensate for the broken night sleep. These longer day sleeps are both compensation sleeps, only achieved because of their poor night sleep the night before *and* excessive accumulated daytime sleep, which then steals sleep again from this coming night, resulting in another prolonged waking between 11.30 p.m. and 3.30 a.m.

Catnapping

If your baby sleeps for 30 to 40 minutes and is then impossible to resettle it is a good sign of a routine miscalculation. When a baby's sleep times become imbalanced, then only looking for tired signs, as some sleep programs would suggest, becomes an ineffective tool that almost perpetuates the cycle of catnapping. A child who has short sleeps is often tired again within a short period of time. Generally, this means they are put down after a short period of time and subsequently they are unable to sleep for a substantial period of time again. This promotes multiple short sleeps, short intervals apart, and the parent is destined to have failed attempts at resettling. I always say if you snack too often you are never hungry for a full meal, and if you nap too often, you are never tired enough to take a good sleep.

Upside-down days

We have all heard this said at least a hundred times: 'Your child needs to know day from night!' It's almost a generic statement with no true understanding of why it is being suggested. You are told to ensure their sleep environment is different from the night by allowing sun in the room, but why and who decided this was a good idea, and how could it ever apply to every child? It doesn't apply to every child, just to some. The importance of knowing day from night only applies to one group of children. That group is made up of the little ones who like to sleep the day away.

I find this sleeping-the-day-away phenomenon happens very rarely yet we hear people rabbit on about it like it's some vital pearl of wisdom that will fix everything. Well, it is actually the cause of more sleep problems than the solution. While I do agree with the concept of allowing a baby to sleep in a slightly lighter environment during the day if the child appropriately fits the group prone to oversleeping during the day, I do not subscribe to the school of blanket thinking that 'they must *all* sleep in brightly sun-drenched rooms through the day', particularly if they are overtired, simply so 'they can know day from night'. If your baby is waking multiple times through each day sleep cycle or can only catnap, then knowing day from night is not the problem in your house and you need to consider tapping into the goldmine that is melatonin production by darkening your baby's room (see pages 428).

If, on the other hand, your baby is one of those rare beings who does take two or three excessively long day sleeps, of between three and five hours in length, and then struggles to sleep at night, then, by all means, the statement 'your baby needs to know day from night' applies directly to your child. They do then need to sleep in a lighter environment during the day to ensure they don't fall into a pattern of big day sleeps and poor night sleeps from excessive daytime melatonin production. This is where you could get into a pattern of upside-down days and nights which results in only brief sleep periods at night, or full wakefulness through the night and massive quantities of sleep happening during the day. This is more common in tiny babies under four months of age.

High caloric / fluid intake at night
If your baby takes the bulk of their calorie consumption or fluid intake during the night, they will inevitably eat poorly throughout the day. This is obviously destructive to a baby's ability to eat solid foods or drink their milk during the day, or drink water through the day, and it also affects their sleep patterns. An appropriate day meal plan is important to ensure you discourage the wakings for feeds at night, before you entirely eliminate them.

The biological clock

Here, I am going to share with you what I have observed and recorded while working with thousands of babies and the findings from my research into sleep cycles. There are many stages of brain activity while a child is asleep and each has a different function. However, there are really only four basic stages during sleep that you need to be concerned with:

- stage 1: surface sleep
- stage 2: power sleep
- stage 3: healthy sleep
- stage 4: dreamy sleep.

These will help you understand the importance of correctly assessing your child's need for intervention at sleep time to ensure as few crying sessions as possible throughout the night and day while your baby is learning to sleep undisturbed. But first, let's start with a baby who is wide awake.

Fully conscious
Fully conscious is being awake and alert. This is the state your baby needs to be in when you leave them to go to sleep. If you would like them to be able to self-resettle when they stir during the normal transitional stages of sleep (see page 412) without calling out (crying), you need to remember that they have no concept of sleep or time lapsing so they must go to sleep initially in the same environment they will encounter in the middle of the night or in the middle of their sleep cycle. If, like many other babies, they have their own room, then this will be in their cot, in their room, on their own after you have said goodnight and left, and when they are relaxed about and accepting of the sensation of being tired independently. For this reason I always aim to keep a child fully conscious throughout the entire settling routine, right up until I say goodnight and leave them in their room to drift off to sleep peacefully.

During their settling routine, despite their obvious alertness, their tired body is busy preparing them for sleep. The normal body reactions aiding your child's natural progression into the stages of sleep will occur when your baby starts to relax. They close their mouth and start breathing predominantly through their nose. One nostril will close, lessening the oxygen supply to the brain, and they will begin to breathe shallowly. This triggers a drop in body temperature and hormones, which helps prepare them for the process of going to sleep.

During their settling routine, despite their obvious alertness, their tired body is busy preparing them for sleep.

When you are tired tonight, take notice of what is happening to your body. Be aware of whether you have closed your mouth and are breathing through your nose only with no real desire to mouth breathe. Be mindful of your nostrils and whether one is closed. Notice how you might be starting to feel cold and move to pull a covering over yourself. These are the same things your baby will feel when they are tired, but still fully conscious. Once you begin falling asleep, you enter the realm of the four sleep stages.

Stage 1: Surface sleep

This is a transitional stage of consciousness. I call this 'surface sleeping' and it is the shift between being awake and being asleep, or being asleep and waking up again, or between being asleep, rolling over and getting comfy and going back to sleep. This transitional stage lasts for between three and eight minutes. During this time, short dream snippets may occur, usually involving recall memory and depicting images from the day. To be technical, the brain's electrical activity slows as exhibited by beta-rhythms on the EEG, a brainwave test. This is classically known as a k-complex brainwave pattern.

I am extremely careful about attending to a child during surface-sleep windows, when they first start to fall asleep and when they first wake up from being asleep, particularly in the middle of the night. To over fuss, or to not give your child and their body the vital sleep they need, is not catering for their needs.

Stage 2: Power sleep

This is where you have fully drifted into a sleep cycle. You are well on your way to the deeper stages of sleep, and you are likely to stay asleep for a prolonged period of time. This occurs about five to ten minutes into a sleep cycle. This is that stage of sleep where, after around five to ten minutes of snoozing, your breathing slows down and your heart rate drops. If you are holding your baby, this is when they become limp and heavy in your arms and you are safe to move them if you need to because they are less likely to stir. To be technical, this is when the brain shows slow beta-rhythms interspersed with periods of fast alpha-rhythms, called 'sleep spindles', and some delta-rhythms. About 50 per cent of night sleep is dedicated to this stage.

Stage 3: Healthy sleep

After around 20 to 30 minutes in the first two stages of sleep, the body drops into a deeper stage of sleep that I call 'healthy sleep'. This is where the body maintains and restores itself: it grows and heals. This is when growth hormone secretions are at their highest. This stage is not about dreaming, it is about the body. When a baby first goes to bed at night, this stage of sleep is at its longest but gradually shortens as the night progresses. This appears to be why the first sleep of the night is always the best. To be technical, this is the deepest level of sleep and it is when the brain measures its slowest waves, its theta and delta rhythms.

Stage 4: Dreamy sleep

This is when the body and brain become active during sleep. The heart rate increases and the eyes flutter back and forth. It is suggested that the brain is as active, if not more so, during this stage than when your little cherub is awake. Imagine that . . . sleep being an exhausting task. In stark contrast to the fluctuations in body metabolism, muscle activity is almost nonexistent, and the body is virtually in a paralysed state. This is called 'REM' (rapid eye movement) sleep.

Children have a higher incidence of REM sleep than adults. The function of this sleep is still being understood but research has identified this portion of sleep with the inner workings of the brain, compared to healthy sleep which is about the body. So while healthy sleep still functions to replenish the brain, there is speculation by researchers that information learnt during the day may be processed by our brains during REM sleep. Other brain functions may also be mediated during REM sleep, such as problem solving, memory consolidation and creativity. This stage forms the last part of a full sleep cycle before the brain goes back to the start. This is when your baby comes back to a surface sleep, and the whole sleep cycle starts again.

How long do these sleep cycles last in children?

Each complete sleep cycle lasts around 40 to 45 minutes in total but can be as short as 20 and, more commonly, 30 minutes. The reason the shorter length cycles occur is still a mystery to me, but the impact these brief sleep cycles has on a baby's day is quite profound. At the point where the baby's sleep cycle completes it's four stages and they return to the first stage of sleep, surface sleep, to repeat the process, your baby or toddler needs the environment to be the same as it was when they first started the sleep cycle to be able to go back to sleep in this second surface sleep.

Now, while I have made it clear that there is a very real need for the same environment each time a child transitions from one full sleep cycle into the next full sleep cycle, this is only one aspect to uncovering the variety of things that may affect a child's ability to sleep. It is now that I need to make it abundantly clear that you also need to consider sleep requirement, distance between naps, food intake and frequency of food intake, as well as physical factors like warmth, comfort, light, noise and movement. Then look at how you communicate your need for them to go to sleep independently and define that request accurately on the first few days of your new sleeping journey while everything corrects itself.

What causes catnapping?

In observing and analysing so many babies—logging their days including sleep times and length, environmental factors, communication, physical needs and emotional factors—as a way of trying to discover the facts behind catnaps, I have found that there are four main reasons babies and toddlers under two years of age adopt this pattern of sleeping:

1. overtired or overstimulated baby or toddler
2. sleep debt or routine miscalculation
3. for physical comfort—they are cold or moving excessively
4. associations and communication difficulties.

It's obviously not an easy question to answer. If I could give you one in a single paragraph, there would not be an epidemic of sleep problems. Some babies simply need a better routine that suits them to eliminate catnapping, but if you have already tried routines and your little one continues to catnap despite your best efforts, then you will need to look elsewhere to help you work through the problem.

As pesky as they are, catnaps actually have a useful application for those babies with a low sleep requirement. Catnaps can recharge a baby, giving them up to 2–2½ hours of alertness. If you look carefully at your child's sleep requirement and consider them low, you might find they need around 13–13½ hours of sleep per 24-hour day. When you break that down into day and night, they need 11–11½ hours during the night and so they are left with a ridiculously minimal 1½–2½ hours sleep requirement to use in a massive 12½-hour long day. These babies tend to take three 30-minute catnaps, leaving them tired and, if you're unlucky, grumpy. Often these babies are placed on to a standard routine for the age group and it is a little like trying to fit a square peg in a round hole. With two big sleeps a day, one of two things starts to happen. You get your days right but your nights go out the window with later settling times and early wakings, or you experience prolonged wakings during the night, or you get your nights right but you can't make them sleep for the required two longer sleeps each day, no matter how hard you try.

If you would like to increase and balance the amount of daytime sleep a LSR baby can take, then use the catnap cycles, or 'bridging naps' as I call them, to your advantage. By providing a bridging nap of a certain length in the morning and afternoon, you can actually achieve a full one and a half to two and a half hours sleep at one time, during one nap, in the middle of the day.

If your little one is taking a 30-minute catnap, multiple times a day, and they are likely to only achieve one or two more sleeps of 30 minutes duration, you can achieve their full one and a half to two and a half hours sleep requirement once later in the day if you allow them only the shortest possible sleep-cycle length of just 20 minutes. By trimming back the 30-minute catnap by ten minutes, you can actually dramatically change the sleep intake of your baby during the day. Most people baulk at this ten-minute trim, even if its application results in a dramatically improved sleep pattern on the next sleep, but put aside the old 'never wake a sleeping baby' generalisation and work with your child's needs. This will create a well-rested and far happier baby, and mummy and daddy. Let me show you how waking a catnapper actually works to their advantage.

Catnappers who wake naturally will usually cycle through the day in the following way:

   30-minute sleep in the morning
   30-minute sleep in the middle of the day
   30-minute sleep late afternoon.

This achieves a total of 1 hour, 30 minutes day sleep.

By contrast, catnappers who are woken earlier usually cycle through the day in the following way:

   20-minute sleep in the morning
   1½ to 2½–hour sleep in the middle of the day
   20-minute sleep late afternoon.

This comes to a total of between 2 hours, 10 minutes and 3 hours, 10 minutes. As you can see, waking them a mere ten minutes earlier than they would naturally wake during that morning bridging nap can gain between an extra 40 minutes to 1 hour, 40 minutes sleep during the day. So it's easy to justify waking them just 10 minutes earlier.

Your baby's sleep requirement will also increase with the new, routine sleep format, and while the sleep is not being taken in the conventional 'two big sleeps a day' format, they are still able to achieve almost an identical amount of sleep, if not more in some cases, than babies on the 'two big sleeps a day' routine, just by providing it in a different way.

There is no way that every baby could ever possibly suit the same routine suggestion. Do away with the one-size-fits-all mentality, which actually causes sleep problems, and look at all the options available to your baby and their sleep needs.

The psychology of sleep

As discussed, children learn a set of predictable conditions which they then rely on when going to sleep. These are called sleep associations. During all sleep cycles a child comes to brief periods of semi-consciousness, surface sleep, where they are only slightly aware of their surroundings. They stir, make sure the environment is the same as it was when they first fell asleep and their associations are still available to them and, if unchanged, they go back to sleep without help. If, however, the associations they went to sleep with have changed, they will need to recreate those conditions before they feel comfortable enough to go back to sleep.

If the associations they required to go to sleep with originally involved your intervention, then your baby will need you to recreate them in order to go back to sleep again. This will happen over and over and over during each sleep session throughout the night and the day sleeps. A typical association involving a parent's intervention includes feeding, patting, rocking, putting to sleep with motion like in a pram or car, sleeping upright on your shoulder, lying in your bed, sleeping in your arms, on the couch next to you, holding hands with them, playing with their hair, or putting the dummy in their mouth. In order to be honest about the environment they will encounter when they wake during the night, you need to allow your baby to learn to be in the environment they will encounter in the middle of the night when they first fall asleep. This is generally in their cot, awake, in a dark room, without you present. This scenario is achievable for all babies without profound sight or hearing loss, or without profound intellectual delays.

As a child has no concept of sleep or time lapsing, if they originally go to sleep in their cot, in a dark room, without you there, then once they have been taught to self-resettle they will feel comfortable to look around briefly before drifting off back to sleep in the middle of the night because everything is as it was. Go a step beyond this process of associations into the psychology of sleep, and imagine the feelings linked with that tired sensation if you were to be holding them and telling them it was safe to accept that feeling of sleep because you were there and holding them, but when they stirred a little while later they were suddenly in a cot, on their own in a dark room. This startles them, and they will automatically call out (cry) to you to try to recreate their normal sleep conditions.

Two things happen in this process. The first is the trust they have when the sensation of being tired is compromised. If your child associates the feeling of being tired with you disappearing, then they will start to fight sleep. The second is the messages you send to your baby about their cot. If you never put them in their cot while they are awake or leave them in their cot awake, and if they do wake during the night they are taught that you always take them out immediately, or stay with them until they are asleep again, then the messages you deliver to them about the cot are: you should not be in your cot when you are awake, and you should not be in your cot alone. It's important to remember your child's cot, or your child feeling tired, are not things they need rescuing from. To repeatedly do this means you are teaching your baby that their cot is not a safe place to be and that being tired is not a safe feeling to have. This is simply not true if they are in a house where they are loved and their room is safe and their cot is warm and comfortable. And while it is never a parent's intention, it's extremely important that you are mindful to never burden a child with this concern.

Obviously, the very first thing a child needs to be comfortable with and relaxed about when going to sleep and going back to sleep is to be comfortable about being in their cot awake. The second thing a child needs to be comfortable with when it comes to going to sleep peacefully is being able to cope with you leaving the room. Because of these two things, whenever you set out to repair any sleep-time issues, be considerate and work on these basic skills first. Anyone who does not work through these basic needs first is being extremely demanding of a child, and not taking their child's actual needs into consideration.

To do this you need to teach your baby how to play in their cot (see page 175), and develop short-term absence cues to use through the day and night (see page 94). To address associations and deliver the right messages to your baby about the process of going to sleep so they are empowered to go back to sleep, you need to develop a new settling, resettling and waking routine (see page 605). Before you ask them to sleep under the new routine conditions you set up for them, though, you will need to ensure they will be able to understand you in the first place by providing language-rich opportunities at non-sleep times of the day; for example, lying down for you at nappy change time is one opportunity I can think of out of 20 typical daytime events where you need to guide your baby and help them understand you, and feel comfortable with you guiding them at sleep time.

Your child will then need to be given opportunities to get to know the new sleep-time routines though role playing before you introduce them personally to those conditions and expectations at their sleep time. Even once this is done, however, you may still need to provide temporary physical comfort if your baby is only just learning how to sleep on their own for the first time until they feel autonomous with the task of self-settling and self-resettling without the need to be held. This is usually in the form of a wrap (see page 439) or tuck-in technique (see page 453) for a baby under the age of 12 months, or a comfort item (see page 461) for older children. Once you have catered for these needs, make sure their sleep requirement (see page 534) has been taken into consideration before choosing your routine or implementing a sleep adjustment. Then, and only then, should you move forward to correct any learnt, habitualised or behavioural problems through interpretation and responding to their cries.

> Your child will then need to be given opportunities to get to know the new sleep-time routines though role playing before you introduce them personally to those conditions and expectations at their sleep time.

Myth busting

True or false? A child who sleeps through the night is at a higher risk of SIDS (sudden infant death syndrome) because they sleep too deeply?

A This is absolutely not the case. They still surface sleep just like everyone else, but they have self-resettling associations they rely on to go back to sleep, so therefore do not need to call out.

Signs of association problems triggering sleep disruptions

Unlike the sleep imbalances discussed in 'The biology of sleep', sleep disruptions caused by an association dependent upon a parent's intervention will follow a fairly predictable timetable during the night. If a child goes to sleep at 7 p.m., they will stir (come to surface sleep) and require you to provide those same conditions or a different set of typical resettling conditions between 10 and 11 p.m., around 2 a.m., and again between 4 and 5 a.m. They will then wake between 6 and 7 a.m., ready for the day—that's if you were able to settle them at their 4 to 5 a.m. waking, which can often be a challenge after 10 hours of sleep. If your child goes to bed earlier or later than 7 p.m., then simply adjust the time windows to quickly see if your little one's sleep-time dramas are the result of an association requiring your intervention to resettle.

The other clear sign is when your child cannot settle or go back to sleep without your presence or attendance, even if it's only for a moment to, for example, touch their tummy, to pop a dummy in their mouth, or to quickly lie them down. You need to help your child develop independent settling and resettling associations (see page 399) in order to resolve this problem.

Communication and the psychology of sleep

Without the ability to guide your baby or toddler during the day at non-sleep times, you will have no possible chance of respectfully guiding your baby at sleep time. These two are linked and make up the need for balance during the day in order to achieve sleep through communication. Anyone offering you advice on sleep must understand this, and be able to advise on developing respectful boundaries around clear and trustworthy communication at non-sleep times *before ever* offering suggestions of sleep-time management strategies. This need to have experienced, balanced, guiding lines of communication through the day once a child reaches six months of age is high, but absolutely necessary by 12 months of age. It is most common to experience some difficulties in managing your baby during the day if you have not yet developed some consistent, respectful, guiding lines of communication for them by the time they have reached around eight months old.

Going to sleep independently means they do not rely on parental intervention, and it is a skill developed by your child through listening to you and trusting you at all times of the day, not just at sleep time. If you have not exposed your child to the normal circumstances of being guided using parent-governed lines of communication during the day while they are awake and at their best, to start a sleep-training exercise where you use this line for the first time when they are tired, and you are trying to ask them to try and be on their own, is destined to be extremely stressful for your child and result in a lot of unnecessary tears. An example of this parent-governed line of communication is when you change your baby's nappy. If you cannot ask them to simply 'lie down and wait for mummy' while you change them, then how can you possibly ask them to lie down when you put them into the cot and wait patiently while you leave the room and they drift off to sleep?

Some other examples of areas in which you may be experiencing daytime communication blues that are affecting your ability to settle your little one to sleep could appear around typical times of the day when you ask them to do something for you, such as during the following events of the day:

- getting dressed
- getting in the pram, high chair or car seat
- staying in the pram, high chair or car seat
- getting them to wait on your hip or lap without fussing
- feeding them
- playing on the floor without always demanding you pick them up
- coming inside from out
- going to sleep
- going back to sleep.

If you are experiencing these typical daytime communication blues, then it is so important you reread the first part of this book to understand the importance of communication and how it effects a baby's ability to sleep, and learn how to use the respectful flow of communication (see page 40).

Once you have established the ability to guide your little one through the day, teaching them to go to sleep on their own is a quick learning process that is resolved once and for all the first time you *teach* them how to sleep using your new, correctly 'defined' routines and cues. There are many times in the day when your little one needs to be guided from one event to the next—this is called 'a transition'. Babies under two years of age often find this a difficult task because they do not particularly like unpredictability, and even the slightest change in routine represents that for them resulting in stress. As a result, they will challenge this by trying to change the condition back by crying and attempting to create a predictable set of conditions that they are governing, such as you picking them up, in order to feel less vulnerable.

In order for your little one to learn how to cope with a parent-governing line of communication at sleep time, however, you need to take the time during the day when they are not tired and depleted to practise guiding them respectfully. To do this you use the flow of communication (see page 40). This is where you equip their emotional tool kit with vital life skills that will help them in every area of their life, not just sleep.

When you practise your flow of communication and define your statements (see page 44) and expectations of behaviour (see page 44) with their true definition, you help your child to work through the sensations associated with being guided, and build their trust through predictable cues and reassuring feedback. In doing so, your baby learns that sometimes you guide them and, while their short-term demands will not always be met, you will always keep them informed through your communication with them. This is when you teach them that they are safe, and it is okay to feel a little cross or unsettled while mummy or daddy guides them around certain events that they know how to do better than their baby does. By remaining confident and following through, your child learns to trust and cope with the sensation of being guided because it always leads to a positive outcome (because you follow through), and also indirectly learns the vital skills required for learning how to go to sleep with your guidance.

Predictability and the psychology of sleep

Let's get something straight. Once you have identified that your baby is having a hard time in the area of sleep, it's time to fully guide them to a better way. You cannot look to your child for guidance about how you should put them to bed, because they just don't know. It is too much of a burden to place on a tired child and it's your role, if not your duty, to take that stress out of the day for them. Once this need for guidance has been determined, you know it's time to confidently and lovingly take charge of the situation.

Assuming control of a situation does not give you the right to be controlling, however. This is about balance, so you always need to look at how to re-establish a better way of doing things, correcting a situation lovingly, and then returning control of that new healthy set of conditions for sleep back to the child. This is a win—win situation. This is where your wisdom and their need for freedom to grow and become autonomous and confident come together in harmony.

The way we do this is in a four-step process:

1. plan new settling, resettling and waking routines for your baby just as you would like to see them happen

2. role play those routines with them to help them become familiar with the process before you use them with your baby
3. begin the new routines and reassuringly and confidently define them with their desired outcome—going to sleep and back to sleep independently
4. reinstate the feeling of governing the sleep-time routines back to the baby simply through their predictability of those events, thus allowing them to start guiding the new appropriate parent-established flow of sleep time.

This is officially a win–win situation. You establish the new conditions of sleep, yet your little one feels in control because they know exactly what to expect.

Mikaela and her sleep-time blues

I met baby Mikaela when she was nine months old. Sleep time for her mummy, daddy and herself was an extremely stressful and unpleasant event. At night her mother would rock her for hours before she would fall asleep, then carefully put her in her cot, and leave her to sleep. Mikaela would wake up shortly after, discover her mother had vanished and she was in her cot, all by herself, and so would cry out.

Her mother would then return to the room and pick her up. Then she would do one of two things. She would firstly attempt to rock Mikaela back to sleep, but by now Mikaela was nervous her mother would disappear again, so this would often take hours. Or her mother would take Mikaela to the master bedroom to sleep with her and her husband. Mikaela would crawl all over them, play, poke their eyes and, eventually, lying over her mother's head (to make sure she didn't disappear when she felt that funny sleepy feeling approach again) she would fall asleep for brief periods of time. As a result, their days were a mess. Mikaela was overtired and taking three 30-minute catnaps during the day. Her mum, unable to settle her, was utterly exhausted and questioning her ability to be a good mother to her baby.

So we set about establishing a new routine. Mikaela was clearly a baby with a lower sleep requirement so we created new sleep routines and role played them for Mikaela. From then on, Mikaela would always go to sleep with the same set of conditions: two books read beforehand, wrapped with one arm out so she could get her dummy if she wished (something she was particularly efficient at), then a final snuggle and sing-song before being tucked into bed with a 'nigh' nigh'' from her mother as she left Mikaela in her cot still awake.

On the first day Mikaela was not impressed. It was all very new to be in her cot alone. We kept reassuring her. It took her 20 minutes to go to sleep, but her new wrap and the new timing of her routine meant she could now sleep for over two hours during her day sleep. We were making progress.

On the second day, she complained heavily about going to bed while we read the stories, because she was now able to understand the sequence of events that told her it was almost sleep time. But by sleep time, she was ready to go to sleep all by herself after a brief minute or two crying. She was doing great. It was brand new, and she was learning the sequence of events perfectly.

On the third day it was her mum's turn to put her to bed for the first time in this routine, and without me in the room with her. She followed the new routine and Mikaela loved it because it was mummy and she knew the sequence of events. Mikaela did not cry at all but when her mother walked back into the room where I was waiting, I could see Mikaela's mum was crying. I assumed it was the relief of being able to put her baby down so peacefully but she informed me it was more than that. It was relief to her that her little girl felt so empowered by her new routine. But, she explained, Mikaela had not only been happy with her new routine, which was amazing to her, she had actually pre-empted the whole thing.

At just nine months of age Mikaela had looked towards the room she was usually wrapped in, had tried to lie herself down on the bed to be wrapped, and after the singing portion of the routine, had given her mummy a sloppy kiss (or rather a lick) on the cheek then reached in towards the cot to be put to bed. As her mother tucked her in firmly Mikaela got her dummy and popped it in her mouth, then turned her head to the side and closed her eyes. This was Mikaela being in control of a routine that we had established, and highlights the importance of developing a parent-directed flow of communication within a routine-based predictable format, and sticking with it until you achieve your results.

15
Creating the right sleep environment

There are many vital elements when it comes to respectfully correcting your little one's sleep disruptions, and they can be broken down easily into two distinct areas of repair. The first is your homework or the preparation that goes into skilling your child emotionally and nutritionally for the task of being asked to go to sleep independently and to sleep contently all night without cause to cry out. The second is your action plan (see page 5). In this chapter, you will learn how to thoughtfully put your action plan into place by providing a lot of the environment support you'll need to consider to implement changes to your routine.

The suggestions below are designed as temporary measures and will dramatically help reduce the need for tears while your child first learns to sleep under the new conditions. This is the one area that, when managed well, can be the key factor in reducing, if not eliminating, tears when initially helping your baby work past their old, poor, habitualised behavioural patterns at sleep time. The one thing I say to *all* my clients is that, once you have done all your preparation homework through encouraging communication, role play, confident independent play and balancing their meal plan, then all you have left to do is to implement the new routine and work through your little one's response to the changed conditions. At that time, the most powerful tools you have to comfort them and the *biggest* reducer of tears are the environmental aids mentioned below.

If you get your environment right, your child will settle very quickly for you from the very first attempt, and the number of times they wake will be instantly reduced by up to 90 per cent. So armed with that new knowledge, please read this chapter carefully, dismissing no section, regardless of what you think your baby likes and doesn't like, to learn how you can establish your transitional sleep-time environment to help support your little one as they learn how to sleep independently.

Your baby's ability to cope with environmental stimulus

When a baby becomes overtired they become what is commonly known as 'overstimulated'. This means they are over-responsive to elements in their environment around them, and so you will find them more reactive to any light, movement or noise than your average well-slept baby. This makes them over-sensitive and in some cases frenetic (appearing more alert and responsive than your average baby), making the task of going to sleep difficult, and going back to sleep, when they naturally transition from one sleep cycle to the next, almost impossible if they can hear you pottering around in the next room. Because of this, you must first correct the environment to reduce those things that keep them alert so you can repair their sleep quickly. You do this by removing light, sound and, in many cases, movement around them. This will help them learn how to go to sleep quickly, and being consistently well-slept will reduce the incidence of them being overtired. Once your little one stops being overtired, noise, light and movement will no longer be so disruptive and can be gradually reintroduced to their sleep environment.

When guiding your little baby while they are learning to sleep, there are many pieces of generic advice you are going to hear: a baby must learn to sleep in the light to know the difference between day and night, or a baby must be able to sleep in noisy surroundings, etc. Most of these will be based on the notion of a 'logical' sleeping environment, but all too often these are placed in an illogical order and are hugely overgeneralised. When looking at repairing broken sleep, disrupted eating habits, or an inability to play, you need to start with the basics. Learning how to do something always follows a process—no one can start school in grade six because the basic foundations learnt in the earlier years have not been established. We all need to start with the basics in any new endeavour and then build up to higher levels of capability and increased skill sets as we grow, understand and become confident in the task.

All too often I see a baby at ten months of age or a toddler 23 months old, who has never actually learnt how to go to sleep in the first place, suddenly being expected to go to sleep in a manner and environment that I consider requires a top-rung ability level—being able to settle themselves with ease, resettle themselves with ease, and where environmental factors such as light and noise have no impact on them. They are also expected to go to sleep without fuss at other people's houses or in the pram in extremely noisy venues, all the while being flexible and relaxed. The bottom rung in these situations is when a baby is not at ease when going to sleep. They tend to not be able to settle themselves without significant difficulty, or resettle themselves without the need for help from an adult carer, and are extremely sensitive to things like light and noise and comfort levels. These are two very different stages of development in the field of sleep when talking about a child's ability level and must be considered.

It's perfectly fine to expect a baby or toddler who has already learnt how to go to sleep to not be bothered by noise or light. It is perfectly unreasonable and inconsiderate to expect a baby who has not learnt how to sleep and is struggling with overtiredness or overstimulation to be able to cope with the same level of light and activity around them. While it may be possible for some babies to learn to sleep well in a noisy and light environment where well-slept babies can usually cope, to even suggest that it makes no difference to an unsettled baby's ability to sleep better and faster on those first few days of sleep training is completely inaccurate. When teaching your little one to sleep, you need to set up the right conditions in a supportive environment so the process of learning to sleep on those first few days is made as easy as it can possibly be.

The reason I started to develop my strategies many years ago was to make the process of learning how to sleep for the first time, or again, as supportive of and sensitive to the needs of all those tiny little babies under two years being asked to go to sleep for me in an entirely new way. I wanted to avoid tears or stress to the child because I'm not a fan of crying, as my comprehensive strategies suggest. It doesn't mean I don't expect some tears, and certainly does not mean I won't allow a child to express their concerns about a new set of conditions for an event, like sleeping independently. It just means I have gone out of my way to make the first couple of days as easy and stress free as possible to promote the least amount of crying as possible.

Most unsettled babies will respond almost immediately when you start their sleeping program with very basic environmental help; this means them being in their room, in their cot and with light and noise in the room restricted or fully eliminated. If they are under 12 months of age and have been struggling with either going to sleep or going back to sleep, or multiple or premature wakings, it will also mean providing physical comfort aids, like firm Houdini-proof swaddling wraps, such as those used when a newborn baby is wrapped and put down to help them settle and feel warm and like they are being held. While the technique for swaddling is very different at this older age, the point is still the same—to provide security and help them settle as quickly as possible. It's also useful to stop them from startling themselves awake with sudden limb movements.

For older babies who are just getting too big to be wrapped (13 to 16 months and upwards), firmly and securely tucking them in with the use of a SafeT Sleep or clear boundaries around the request to lie down are required. In babies six to 12 months old though, firm swaddling not only allows them to feel safe and secure and comfortable, it also helps those babies in the habit of automatically sitting or standing up, before they have even woken up fully, but who are still developmentally unable to lie down again. How many seven, eight or nine month olds are good at lying themselves down? They all learn how to sit up and stand up long before they learn how to sit back down or lie back down gracefully without the risk of taking a little tumble.

A small anecdote: almost every baby I have wrapped, and that is a lot of babies, has had parents who have said to me 'They hated being wrapped' or 'they can get out of every wrap'. I have to say, this is where my life is very Groundhog Day in its repetitiveness. They will stay in and *love* their wrap when your new PRM program is underway if you follow my instructions. The biggest issue you will have is keeping them awake while you wrap them. And this is where my life is a little repetitive again, because all those same parents say after the program starts to work: 'I had no idea they would love the wrap so much, I thought they would hate it'. If your baby is under 12 months do *not* dismiss the wrap, because even an extremely unsettled 14 to 16 month old can be seriously comforted with a leg wrap, SafeT Sleep and the tuck-in techniques provided in this chapter.

By providing an environment free of stimulus like light, noise or movement for a baby who is just starting to learn how to sleep well for the first time in their life means you are ensuring you are making it as easy as it can possibly be for your child to adjust to this whole new way of going to sleep, thus reducing the trigger of premature waking and, therefore, tears. So steer clear of people who make the blanket statement that *all* babies should be able to sleep in light or noise or without a swaddle, because that's unfair and unrealistic. If you were tired, could you go to sleep with a lot of noise and expect to not be disturbed? Even if you could, we all know that there are *some days* when hearing noise as you are trying to sleep is just downright irritating.

Taking that a step further, remember those wonderful pyjama parties of your youth. In every group there were always one or two children who could not cope with the excessive noise or chatter and would get grumpy or burst into tears, or those who caused mischief through sheer tiredness. The parents of the house would complain as *they* couldn't get any sleep because there was too much chattering or other noises being made by those children who couldn't sleep and who were disturbing those who could. The adults subsequently stomped down the hallways insisting on quiet time. So tell me, why should babies be any different? Why should they *all* be able to sleep in a noisy or light environment when clearly not everyone can do that even once they reach middle childhood or adulthood? When you only work by a set of ideals or a blanket statement like '*all* babies should be able to sleep in light or noise', I question whether you are taking each child's individual needs into account.

Before I start any form of PRM plan I always remove anything from the environment that could possibly make the process of going to sleep or going back to sleep take longer, and make sure I remove anything that could possibly contribute to more tears. This is just a temporary strategy and lasts for between one and six months, depending on each child's ability to cope with the gradual reintroduction to extra stimuli. By adopting these simple practices you will make it much easier for your little one to be able to learn how to sleep. Those things that might contribute to tears always come down to excess stimulation and they are:

- light
- noise
- temperature
- movement
- toys in the cot at sleep time.

Reducing the stimulation of light

As previously discussed, our bodies are designed to respond to the sun (see page 406). When darkness falls, enzymes in the brain stimulate the release of melatonin, which induces sleep. When light hits the back of the eye's retina, the release of melatonin is halted and we experience wakefulness as a result. As sunlight affects this sleep hormone production, artificial lights, particularly the popular and extremely bright downlights that babies merrily stare into, influence the brain much in the same way. While most people would expect that it would take bright light to cause such a reaction, once a child becomes overstimulated, even the slightest amount of light can affect them because they are now sensitive to light. This, in addition to any association that comes with being able to make out shapes in their room during a partial-waking phase of their sleep, will be enough to cause them to wake up. When helping a baby to learn how to sleep past 5 a.m., or to sleep past a pattern of catnaps, make it as easy for them to resettle on those first few days as possible by taking advantage of the wonderful sleep-inducing hormone by eliminating light in the room.

The reason I started to develop my strategies many years ago was to make the process of learning how to sleep for the first time, or again, as supportive of and sensitive to the needs of all those tiny little babies being asked to sleep for me in an entirely new way.

I measure the windows in a child's room, taking into account the entire frame that the window fits into. Then I visit my local haberdashery store and purchase curtain backing that provides 100 per cent light block out. This is call P3 curtain backing. P3 refers to the level of light protection, in this case 100 per cent. Using thumb-tacks, I secure it to the outer edges of the window frame to make sure there are no rays of light peeping around the top or the sides. Once this is done, the room will be almost pitch black. (And before you ask, no, cardboard does not do the same job.) Then disconnect, turn off or cover with duct tape any night lights, clock displays, stereo systems or LED lights on monitors. Roll up a towel and place it on the floor outside their door to prevent light filtering in under the door. Ensure all lights are off and doors in the hallway are closed initially. You are now ready to role play your sleeping routine (see page 631) and play 'Where's Teddy' (see page 649) with your little one.

If you wish to put up permanent curtains, ensure they have a block-out backing. I always suggest you make the curtains ceiling-to-floor, and allow a lot of extra width so light doesn't come in from the sides of the window. I also suggest you make them as flush to the wall as possible but, if that is not possible, have a pelmet over the top of the curtains so light doesn't shine up over the top. It's also a good idea to have a blind that also is 100 per cent block out behind the curtains so you can open the curtains and, if it suits them, gradually reintroduce a lighter environment as they get older.

While I don't usually suggest outside awnings and roller blinds for the purpose of temporary light reduction during sleep training, they can be very useful if your child has a particularly hot room. While costly, they are an alternative to air conditioning, which may be helpful for some children prone to irritated airways and repeated conditions of ear, nose and throat infection that can possibly arise from sleeping in air conditioning.

Reducing noise from the cot room

There are certain things that you can do with children only as the result of being able to achieve great sleep at home first. I call this a parent's privilege for working hard to establish good sleeping patterns. For some people with higher sleep-requirement babies, or with very mellow bubbies, this privilege comes easily; for others, it is a well-earned honour. An example of this is the ability of a baby to sleep in brighter environments such as at other people's houses, in the pram or car, and at restaurants. Sleeping in situations where there is a reasonable amount of noise is another area of privilege.

But if noise is causing or contributing to your child's sleep problem then you can't keep doing the same thing and expect a different result. It's important to give your little one the chance to recover their sleep disruption without noise before you even consider trying to get them to sleep in a noisy environment. This is because they will remain over-sensitive to noise as long as they stay overtired. By eliminating noise when you are teaching

Troubleshooting

Q But how will my child know day from night?

A If your baby isn't sleeping terribly well, it's not the predominant concern here. For some families, by settling a baby to sleep in an extremely dark environment from an early age, the environment does what it is intended to do. The dark encourages great sleep because it triggers melatonin. Some babies are tremendous daytime sleepers and, as a result, can start to sleep in blocks of up to four to five hours at a time. This is extremely rare beyond a certain age, but the impact of such lengthy daytime sleeps could be quite disastrous on a child's ability to sleep at night. For this reason be cautious with big daytime sleepers and provide a lighter daytime sleep environment to help prevent a baby from oversleeping. The lighter environment promotes less sleep and this is what I suspect motivates the adage 'a child needs to know day from night'. However, when you are trying to help your baby or toddler to learn how to sleep you could battle it out and struggle with resettling, or try and resettle them in the pram or car to achieve a longer sleep, or you could, more effectively, work with your child's natural response to light and dark as well as to noise and movement. You simply make it so much easier through this latter method by preventing wakings in the first place so you don't even need to try and resettle them.

Q Why can my baby sleep in the light when in the pram or the car but not in their cot?

A Most babies are lulled off to sleep easily with the perpetual motion of the pram or car and are exposed to a level of natural white noise (see page 430) as you potter through the shops or neighbourhood. The motion and unchanged sleeping conditions (in the pram or car seat) make it easy for a baby to drift from one cycle of sleep to the next. These help them to sleep, you decrease the chances that you will accidently wake them—believe me, you do not want to be responsible for waking them—and you ensure you can correct the sleeplessness that is causing their over-sensitivity to noise.

Now it's obviously not reasonable for you or your entire family to be completely silent. Nor can you avoid the normal sounds that happen outside the house. So another solution is needed. In my search to find something to help babies supersensitive to noise when sleeping, I discovered a company in New York that made a sound machine that played a constant pattern of white noise. I bought one and tested it to see if it would produce any results. It far exceeded my expectations and brought so much to the process of teaching a baby how to sleep.

What is white noise and how does it work? White noise is equivalent to silence. Scientifically, it's not considered to be noise at all (even though we can hear it). It is a sound consisting of all audible frequencies with equal intensity. It's the aural equivalent of white light in optics—the simultaneous

them maintain a longer sleep because they don't need to even open their eyes to see that the environment is still the same and mum is still there because everything feels as it was when they fell asleep in the first place. The comfort and natural reduction in ability for them to be able to physically move when in their pram or car seat provide the minimal movement I aim to achieve in the cot by offering an elevated level of warmth and stillness, such as when we provide the wrap and the cot tuck-in (see page 439). All this means noise, light and movement are generally not an issue when they are sleeping in the pram and car. If you have never been able to get your baby to sleep in the pram, however, you may then need to take their needs into account. You must temporarily reduce the excess stimulation in that sleeping environment so they can get the sleep they so desperately need to grow and be healthy, whether they know it or not. Once they have learnt the cues and requests around going to sleep in their cot and are able to do that with relative ease, you can then try and slowly reintroduce the more challenging sleep environments like their pram and the car seat. Eventually, when they are sleeping well when you mention the cues in their pram, you can slowly offer a little more movement or light to that environment.

Q What if my baby is frightened of the dark?

A This is an important point because no matter what age they are under two years, many people will put an adult concept of fear of the dark on to a child who may simply feel momentarily uncomfortable with the inability to see. There is one thing you must always remember: it is dark for half of our lives, for all of our lives. You need to understand the importance of not burdening your child with an unnecessary fear of a normal life condition, or lovingly and confidently help them move past any initial discomfort in a darker environment.

presence of the wavelengths of the visible spectrum. White light is not a colour and yet it contains all colours. White noise is not noise and yet it contains all sound. White noise creates a constant background 'noise' which the brain gets used to so it doesn't register it. The mind blocks it out, and you can sleep without noticing it. This means that any noise in the house is subsequently blocked out.

If you consider that this is what you need for your child, there are several machines and CDs on the market. Do your research first to make sure whatever you buy will do what they say it will (buyer beware). If you buy a CD it must be played on repeat all night, so make sure the tracks last for at least an hour. Also, if you run any equipment like a CD player in your child's room throughout the night, install a smoke detector in that room. If you buy a white noise machine, ensure it is only true white noise you are getting and not just the ocean 'sounds' or a heart beat. Do not buy a white noise machine that has ceiling projectors or bright digital displays as you create another problem.

Once you have brought your white noise home always introduce it to your child's play environment first. I do not tend to allow a child to be a part of that process. I just quietly tuck it up high where they can't see it and initially turn it on fairly low. You will be able to hear it when you turn it on, it's not silent, and it's the consistency of the sound that encourages the brain to tune out, and you do stop hearing it after a while. To understand this, think about when you get a blackout in your house and suddenly the fridge goes quiet, the lights stop humming, the fish-tank filter stops bubbling and the computer fan stops blowing in the background. Until the power went out, your brain had actually tuned out these sounds because they were consistent and your brain determined them to be unimportant. This is how white noise works.

When you turn on the machine or CD while your little one is playing you may see them react to the sound and look around. Try not to respond in any way other than to carry on as if it isn't there. It's not something you will want them to play with, so do not react to it. When they see you don't notice the sound, they will quickly tune out to the noise. If you have a toddler, and they look outside thinking it's raining, or are a little unsure of the sound, you can acknowledge their curiosity or concern and imitate the sound and comment that 'ttttccccchhhhhhhhhh, it sounds like rain' and ask 'shall we look outside and see if it's raining?' Once you get to the window, say 'No rain' and immediately distract them with a simple 'Is that a butterfly in the garden? Quick wave, hello butterfly.' Once you have moved on direct them back into play and carry on as though it's not there.

Gradually, as the morning progresses, turn the volume up. Leave it on for a couple of hours and get them used to the sound before you introduce it to their sleeping environment. I usually turn it on and pop it under the cot and leave it running for the entire day, so it's on when I change their nappy, after bath, or if we walk past their room. This means it becomes a normal sound in their room and it is something they do not even think about when it comes time to put them to bed. Eventually you won't need to leave it on all day, you can just switch it on and off for sleep times.

I tested this product myself for a period of eight weeks before I tried it out on any of the babies and toddlers. I had it on the highest volume and admit that at first when I turned it on I thought it was absolutely impossible I would tune it out. It sounded like a jet engine. I went to sleep, though, without any more difficulty than I would normally have. I was amazed to wake several times having not heard it or anything else for hours and hours at a time. Within a week I would roll over and have to check if the jet engine was actually on.

I was aware of one thing though. As my brain started to slow down and drift to sleep, I suspect it was trying to make sense of or decode the noise it was hearing. As a result I would regularly hear rhythmic sound patterns that were my brain's attempts to interpret the white noise. These patterns were quite soothing and tended to be a therapeutic distraction as I drifted off to sleep. If you do hear these sounds yourself, please know that the therapy machine in not creating these patterns of sound, it is only your brain trying to decipher the noise and this will either change or pass in a short period of time.

I'm now a huge fan of this clever little gadget. It not only helps babies cope with the task of learning how to sleep but, if you can find a machine, it is also portable so you can take it on holidays, to dinner parties, restaurants, etc. You can use it when you have a dinner party, play the stereo system on your home theatre at a reasonable volume, or simply when people come knocking on your door while your baby is sleeping. The one-hour white-noise CDs are not as portable but do the trick for any environment for which you have a power source.

Once your little one starts to sleep better, you can then gradually introduce sounds at a reasonable volume to test your child's threshold for noise tolerance. You do this by gradually reducing the volume of the machine. I tend to reduce it down slowly to a fairly low volume, and eventually turn it off completely. I do not pack it away, however, because by turning it on during your little one's sleep every few days or so means you can keep it as an option for other times when you may really need to have it on, such as on holidays or during a dinner party.

The case of Jed and his train

I once travelled for an hour by car, two hours by plane, an hour on a bus, four hours on a train and an hour in a car again to discover the cause behind the mysterious frequent wakings of a baby who seemed to be on just the right routine. Generally, I can identify fairly quickly what the cause of most sleep problems are by just chatting over the phone, but occasionally a baby like Jed will turn up and, no matter how much I investigate, I just cannot put my finger on the cause.

When I arrived, they showed me to my room and apologised for the fact that the house was right on the railroad tracks. Within a few minutes, a train tooted as it approached and the entire house went into a flat spin. Jed became frantic. Dad ran for Jed with great excitement, mum ran for the door keys, and baby Jed squirmed excitedly as mum fumbled to get the door unlocked in time. When the door was opened we all ran to the back fence. I looked on with great interest as Jed and daddy waved to each one of the 35 carriages before heading back inside.

'Does that happen every time the train goes by?' I asked in amazement.

'Yep,' the dad said proudly, 'he sure loves his trains: he is such a little boy!'

Needless to say, this was the source of the problems. Twenty-four hours a day that train rumbled by and Jed had become so used to running for the door than even when he was asleep he would hear it a mile away and panic, calling urgently to be picked up day and night. He had become so unsettled at sleep time by this that we had to take drastic measures. We quickly stopped responding to the train altogether and, within two days, I was able to happily wave goodbye to begin my marathon journey back home. The moral of the story is, 'Beware of the habits you create for your child.'

Making the temperature just right

There are so many variables when it comes to room temperature that it is a little tricky to give precise advice. A baby cannot sleep effectively below 16 degrees or above 24 degrees so you will need to seriously consider your child's room temperature before you embark on any sleep repair program. The ideal room temperature for sleeping is considered to be 19 to 20 degrees. In this temperature, you can safely pop your baby into a cotton long-sleeved and full-legged outfit. This can also be in the form of a safe, baby sleeping bag and long-sleeved top, or a full-body swaddle with a singlet and nappy, or a singlet, with long, cotton pyjama top and pants plus socks.

It is actually far more common for me to encounter a baby or toddler experiencing sleep-time problems during the day because they are too cold rather that too warm. So while it is important that you don't overheat your children, you need to be aware that a baby will often sleep poorly when they are cold. As a first step to solving a little one's daytime sleeping problem if the temperature is ideal, try adding an extra layer of clothing to their torso and arms for the day sleep sessions before you go any further. A child will also always need long sleeves at night, but may actually need an additional layer for the days compared with the early portion of their night sleep.

There are also some slight body-temperature fluctuations that occur as a result of hormones and the body's natural biochemical response to tiredness. In my experience, the most obvious times that a child aged six months to two years wakes from being cold is during the longer daytime sleeps where there is a far higher chance of their body temperature dropping too low, despite the room temperature, waking them early as a result. For this reason I always dress babies more warmly for the longer daytime sleeps. This might include always ensuring they have a long-sleeve top on.

The other most common body-temperature fluctuation occurs when a baby first goes to bed at the end of the day. At this stage they are actually more inclined to be warmer than usual. I always reserve any warm layers of clothing such as sleeping bags, long-sleeved tops, or swaddles until just before it's time to go to bed and ensure they go to bed at a cooler temperature and allow the environment to gradually warm them. If your baby is a warm baby naturally, then cool their room for 30 minutes before you put them down at night in the warmer months, or turn off central heating to their room in the cooler months to ensure they don't overheat in that first few hours of the evening sleep. I tend to ensure they have a cooler bath at the end of the day, and their room stays at around 20 degrees until around 10 pm. During the cooler months, I only place blankets on babies at around 10 p.m. after the first portion of their night sleep has passed and they have naturally cooled. I will also not turn on heating to their room until closer to this time in the cooler months unless the room is 18 degrees or below, at which point I will take the chill out of their air, being careful to not make the room hot initially.

In addition to the body-temperature fluctuations there are a couple of normal house temperature fluctuations that you should be aware of. The house temperature usually drops quite dramatically by about 4 or 5 a.m., just as your baby will be approaching the final stage of their night sleep. As a baby cannot regulate their temperature by pulling coverings on or off for quite some time, they have to rely quite heavily on the warmth / cool of the environment around them to keep them at a comfortable temperature. If they become too cold, their body will wake them and they will instinctively cry to warm up.

When you first put them to bed at night they are warmer than they will be later and it's obviously not really possible to physically dress them in preparation for 4 a.m. without running the risk of making them too warm when they first go to sleep. Equally, you can't rely on them being able to stay under the blanket you put on them before you go to bed, so there's a little dilemma here. How do you cater for their warmth in the first part of the night, but still cater for the cold at 4 a.m., especially in the cooler months of the year?

The only answer is to dress your little one to cope with the first part of the night (as suggested earlier), and then work with the room temperature in the early morning hours to prevent them from getting too cool. You do this by using an oil heater with a thermostat and preferably an in-built timer. If your oil heater does not come with a timer, you can easily buy a portable one, to be slotted into the power point that the heater is plugged into. Make sure you pre-empt the 4 a.m. house-temperature drop by setting the heater's timer so that it comes on and regulates the room by around 3.30 a.m. This ensures the room is at the right temperature when your baby's body comes to the next light stage of the sleeping pattern, making drifting back to sleep for that final stage of the night a much easier task.

If your little one is prone to getting very warm or is in the first couple of days of learning how to self-settle and you anticipate that they may have a cry and get a little hot, then you should use a free-standing fan for the early part of the night in your baby's room. Run an extension lead out to the hallway so you can turn it on and off easily without the risk of waking your baby. Set the fan to medium and place it on oscillate. This is particularly valuable during those early days of your new settling conditions as it means you can offer a cool down if you are concerned about their warmth, without disturbing them. Point the fan at a wall so the air flow bounces off the wall and runs down over the top of the baby's head lightly into the tuck-in to keep air flow around them without drying out their nose or lips. Turn it off at the wall switch in the hallway and only put it on when they first go to bed, or if they are crying and need your assistance. Always turn off the fan after 11 p.m. if your baby's room is a healthy 19 to 22 degrees unless you have a particularly warm baby.

Air conditioners can be helpful in very hot climates or houses where the baby's room is far too warm to sleep in. As indicated earlier, anything above 24 degrees is difficult to achieve sleep in, particularly sleep repair where a swaddle may be necessary. In this case a room needs to be around 19 to 21 degrees. Try to get an air conditioner that has a temperature control on it but, if needs be, you may have to be responsible for turning it on and off manually. If you have difficultly gauging your child's room temperature you can easily purchase an all-weather-system house thermometer which has a portable main-base station, and then one or two separate thermometers. You can then keep the main-base station with you in the living area or your bedroom and place one of the thermometers near your baby's cot and check it at any time of the day or night without even entering their room.

Always cool a room half an hour before you put a baby to bed rather that start to cool it once they go to bed. Otherwise they may become too hot before the room cools and wake up quickly as a result. Always use your instincts. If you are sleeping under covers at night and kicking them off because you are too hot, there is a pretty good chance that your baby will feel the same way. This is when it can be valuable to have a fan plugged in that you can switch on and off from the hallway.

Equally, if you are freezing cold, and looking for extra layers at night, or putting on the heater, your baby's room should have some form of warming device (heater) to prevent them from getting too cold and needing to roll on to their tummy and curl up in a ball to stay warm, which is obviously a high-risk factor for SIDS. I always say that you should ask yourself: 'Could I sleep with the same amount of clothing on without any covers on during the day or night?' If you couldn't, then add some more. If you could and may still feel hot, then offer some cooling device in their room.

Always bear in mind the safety aspect of heaters, including the following:

- never allow anything to lean on or touch the heater when it is on, and never leave it within reach of your baby
- when using an oil heater use a humidifier to help prevent your baby's mouth, lips, nose or airways drying out—in my experience this can prevent many of winter's snuffles, sneezes and wheezes
- do not use a glowing bar heater or any heater that does not have an automatic switch-off device incorporated into their design so that they switch off if they fall over
- keep all heaters, fans and air conditioners well dusted, and clean the air conditioner filter regularly in hot water, allowing it to dry in the hot sun for a few hours
- always have smoke detectors installed correctly throughout your house, including baby's room, and always check them regularly.

Comfortable sleepwear to encourage good sleeping

If your baby does not need swaddling, then I always recommend the use of sleeping bags, both summer and winter weight. These discourage standing up, keep your baby at just the right warmth, help prevent climbing out of the cot and act as a lovely pre-sleep cue. I use these with all babies 12 months of age and over. There are good sleeping bags, and there are bad sleeping bags, as in most things in this diverse world of ours. I do not recommend sleeping bags that have a removable lower button-on foot portion. Apart from the obvious inherent dangers associated with the buttons, they can get their feet caught outside the sleeping bags, defeating the entire purpose of wearing one.

In winter I suggest warm long sleeves under a sleeveless sleeping bag as a baby's arms will get cold and they tend to have more difficulty sleeping if their torso or arms are cold. You might find a baby over six months of age roll over on to their tummy, tuck their knees up high, and tuck both arms under their body. Instinctively, they are warming their torso and arms, which helps them sleep more soundly. For this reason, regulating their torso and arm warmth is important.

In summer, a lightweight, cotton, sleeveless sleeping bag will enable a baby to sleep soundly with a light, long-sleeved cotton t-shirt under their cotton sleeping bag. Only in extremely hot environments would I ever suggest an under-two year old sleep in anything less that a lightweight cotton t-shirt (long or short sleeves). Only when sleeping out and about in hot weather, such as in a pram would I suggest they sleep in just a singlet.

So, in summary, use your instincts when it comes to winter and summer wear for your baby. Always try to regulate the room temperature to 19 to 20 degrees with heating or cooling devices so you don't have to constantly try to figure out 'what to dress them in today'. If you use heating, always use a humidifier. The use of a portable free-standing fan is fine, but do not aim it directly on to a baby's face as a general rule of thumb. It is okay to have

Troubleshooting

Q Does air flow affect their sleeping?

A Keeping a room well aired each day by opening windows and leaving doors open between sleeps is adequate enough to keep your baby's room fresh. If you have block-out material up on your window temporarily, while you are teaching your little one to sleep, simply release a corner and open the window that way. On slightly warmer days the use of a free-standing fan is a nice way to keep the air moving around your sleeping child.

a fan run air down over the crown of their head towards their toes, but be mindful of wind blowing on faces and drying out little lips and eyes.

A surrogate cuddle—swaddling

If there was just one piece of advice I could give parents when they ask me how to help teach their little ones to sleep—as quickly and with as few tears and as little stress as possible, with the least amount of wakings during those sleeps—what I tell them is not such a big secret as they have most likely heard about it already. Think about this, from the moment your baby is born, the first thing you do if they are unsettled or unsure of the world around them is hold them in your loving arms to make them feel safe again. You might even hold their face up close to your neck to block out excess stimulation so they can focus on the comfort you are providing. And you might even 'sssshhhhhhhhhhhhh' them to block out excess stimulation in the form of external noise.

You instinctively hold them firm and close to help them calm down.

You instinctively limit their visual stimulation of the world to help them calm down.

You instinctively block out excess noise by creating your own white noise of sorts with the classic 'shhh' to help them calm down.

So what have you taught them by using these innately instinctive calming tools? You have *taught* them that being held firmly is comforting. That when they are held firmly, they are okay. Because of this, one of the most important temporary comforting tools that I advise parents to use, my magic wand of sorts, is the swaddle. I call it the 'surrogate cuddle in the cot'.

Now stay with me here. Even for children as old as 12 months, who 'hated' being wrapped as a tiny baby or prefer to sleep on their tummy or like to move around in the cot, the swaddle can make the difference between crying and barely crying or not crying at all. I have literally seen hundreds and hundreds of parents who have done sleep training elsewhere, for hours at a time, for periods lasting days, weeks or even, in some cases, months, that has only slightly improved the situation or provided just short-term relief. These same parents have been able to put their babies to bed for the first time using their new PRM approach, the right routine and the swaddle, and seen almost instant recovery in their child's sleep problems.

The swaddle is important for children who have trouble settling and resettling without the need for dependent associations and is also extremely important for babies who can self-settle but have significant problems with short sleep cycles or regular wakings that require intervention from a parent or carer.

It takes just one or two sleep sessions, often within the first 12 to 24 hours, for most babies to adjust to the swaddle and they can then go to sleep without crying and stay asleep for periods of 11 plus hours, even those children who have been unable to sleep for longer than 30 minutes to one hour at a time prior to wrapping. It *is* a bit like a magic wand and parents are staggered at the level of comfort it actually provides for their child, despite their assumptions to the contrary.

In nearly all the families where I have recommended they swaddle their baby, the most usual comments I get from parents at my suggestion are: 'But he hated being swaddled as a baby', or 'He will hate that', etc. I ask then how they know this, and they would explain that they tried swaddling, and then their baby would wiggle out of it and cry, and they would have to go in and cuddle them to sleep. To me, this is a simple example that their babies just wanted to be held firmly, and the swaddle they had was not providing the security they were looking for. If your swaddle does not make them feel safe, then they won't like it. Another comment parents make is that 'as soon as I lay them down to wrap them they just really started to cry and fight'. The interesting thing about this point is that often a wrap is a strong indicator that 'it's time to go to sleep' and like a lot of children I have met, they do have a tendency to say 'I don't want to go to bed'. In this case, it's not the wrap that is the problem, but the request to go to bed that is causing the reaction. A sign that your baby doesn't actually like the wrap is when they wiggle out of it and stop crying and sleep better for the freedom.

Bear in mind when you are working on introducing a swaddle to repair sleep, that a baby needs their sleeping environment to remain the same from settling through till the morning, so if they go to bed swaddled they need to stay swaddled for the entire night. You could spend days trying to get them to sleep, and have floods of tears, or you could provide a firm, snugly comfort item like a swaddle and have them sleeping in as little as 12 to 24 hours, and long term. I usually have to explain all of these aspects to a parent when I suggest swaddling, and that it is a *temporary* surrogate firm cuddle in their cot to make them feel safe while they are *learning* how to go to sleep in an environment that is brand new to them. Your flow of communication and appropriate daily routine will ensure ongoing sleep when your baby transitions out of the swaddle. Going to sleep will by then have become an easy and enjoyable time of the day for them. In as little as three weeks your baby's need to feel held will probably pass and they will be able to sleep with or without the swaddle.

Do not put adult concepts on the swaddle. You are not a baby. When your child becomes very upset, and you hold them to calm them down, you don't do that with the mindset of restraining them. You hold them because you know you are providing serious comfort to your child. You did not teach them that cuddles represent restraint or any other adult style of imagery that your mind might conjure up about the swaddle. And remember, swaddling has long been a normal part of a baby's life in every culture and country of the world. Whether a baby is in a pouch, a sling on a mother's back in rice fields or on long treks, a cotton blanket at birth or in muslin in their cot, swaddling is the best and most effective comfort and sleep-inducing device available and has been used for centuries.

If your baby is needing to be held, is in your bed, won't sleep in their cot, is standing and screaming in their cot to be picked up, or wakes over and over and over again unable to sustain sleep, then firmly swaddling them *will* be the quickest way to help your baby get to sleep and stay asleep.

Who should be fully swaddled?

I tend to swaddle any babies from six to 16 months who are:

- transitioning from being totally dependent on contact with others to help them fall asleep to self-settling and self-resetting for the first time in their life —primarily because feeling comfortable with anything new comes with time. This can be up to 12, and in some special cases 16, months of age—remember this is all about taking each child's individual needs into account
- under 12 months and who cannot sleep for more than 30 to 40 minutes at a time through the day, or who wake up repeatedly during the night
- constantly calling out to be held to go to, or go back to sleep
- wanting regular feeds and snuggles to go back to sleep—they are often a little cool and the warmth of the swaddle is the same as a cuddle with a toasty warm mummy or daddy
- between six and 12 months and who constantly stand up at sleep time, and are unable to lie themselves down again, including those babies who stand up automatically before they have even opened their eyes when they reach the semi-conscious state of surface sleep.

You won't need to swaddle your baby when they are comfortable with putting themselves to sleep and back to sleep (independent settling and resetting associations), but are sleeping at odd times of the day and night.

In that case you just need to adjust their sleep times by adopting an appropriate routine to suit their daily sleep requirement (see page 534). You don't need a swaddle if your little one is 12 months or over and just wants you to pop a dummy in their mouth so they can happily put themselves to sleep. In this case you can teach them how to get it themselves (please see page 467). You also won't need to swaddle them forever. This is a temporary comforting aid to be used until they are used to your new sleep-time routines, and feel autonomous with the task of going to sleep and love their bed. Then you wean them off the swaddle or wait until they gradually progress out of the wrap at their own pace (see page 456).

Troubleshooting

Q What about safety when swaddling?

A Obviously you want your baby to stay on their backs while sleeping in a swaddle. While a six month old will be strong enough to lift their head and free their airways, swaddles prevent excessive movement of the hands and this will mean it is important to keep them on their back when swaddled, and the swaddle will need to be done firmly to maintain both the consistent sleep environment and to ensure your baby doesn't get tangled up in it. There is a great product to help keep babies safe on their backs when used in conjunction with the swaddle and a good tuck-in, or when used with just a good tuck-in. This product is called a 'SafeT Sleep'. The old idea that a child is unsafe in a swaddle after around four months of age is no longer a concern with this product and techniques to keep them safely in their wrap and on their back: catering for a baby's individual needs becomes far more realistic.

Q Does the swaddle mean there will be no tears?

A Not necessarily. As with anything new, there will be an adjustment period while your baby gets used to not being able to do what they used to do, such as move freely, but this is always a short-lived learning window. If you think about it, any change would cause some tears, so even if you went from holding your baby over your shoulder to lying them down in your arms they are still likely to have an adjustment window where they will cry with the unfamiliarity (see page 67). This means your baby may need a little bit of time to adjust. The benefits of a swaddle, however, are tremendous. There is less crying simply because there are fewer wakings than there are with other forms of independent settling teaching strategies. Any waking is generally briefer than experienced without the swaddle. Be patient, and give them a little time to get used to the new sleep conditions for the first day or two, and you will see them settle down quickly. If you know that they would have cried when you asked them to try and put themselves to sleep after you left the room, then they will still need to learn how to cope with this, but the swaddle will truly make it easier.

Q What is the most important thing I need to know about the surrogate hug—the swaddle?

As far as all babies are concerned, there are a few simple and basic guidelines you must take into consideration:

- turn the mattress over so your baby is sleeping on the material side of your mattress if it has a plastic side to it (see also box on page 454)
- make sure your baby's bath isn't too hot, as they will not sleep if overheated at the end of the day and we are keen for the wrap to warm them, rather than having them too warm when initially wrapped causing overheating

A Do it correctly. That means do it firmly so it stays on for the night. There is no point putting them into a sleeping environment that will alter as the night progresses. Depending on the swaddle you use, there should be either no movement of the arms and legs, or no movement of one arm and their legs, or no movement of their legs only, or no movement of both their arms and legs as well as a firm tuck-in. Like holding a baby firmly to get them to sleep, you would achieve results if you are consistent and continue to hold them firmly. So that's what the swaddle needs to be like.

Q My toddler rocks on his hands and knees while still asleep and wakes himself up. How can I stop this?

A Episodes like this are rare. You can try to help alleviate the situation first by placing your little one in a sleeping bag and a SafeT Sleep or a firm leg swaddle with a SafeT Sleep. This may stop the cycle of him automatically getting on to his knees, and may just halt the behavioural pattern before it begins. A swaddle will help your baby learn it's normal to lie down while he goes to sleep. Personally, I've only had to deal with it a small number of occasions and the parents found that once their baby was put on one of my routines, and the environment was altered with a leg swaddle and SafeT Sleep the problem completely stopped. If you do not create a settling routine for your baby he will create his own, however inappropriate, and rocking on his knees or even headbutting the cot bars may well be a self-settling association of sorts and needs to be corrected with a safe, comforting, environmental addition like this. Babies who fall asleep in a folded position, the result of them accidentally falling asleep while sitting up and usually crying, can also be helped using the swaddle. This is also a good reason to ensure your baby understands your request for him to lie down to go to sleep. If your baby has fallen asleep sitting up, he is probably very confused and does not understand that he needs to lie down to sleep. I would always swaddle a little one rather than have this happen. If your child has significant headbutting episodes to go to sleep, where he 'wants' to headbutt and will struggle to get out of your arms to continue to pursue this activity, he may need to be checked by a paediatrician to ensure there is nothing medically triggering the episodes. In the interim, however, whenever I have encountered this situation the child has responded beautifully and immediately to the introduction of the SafeT Sleep and leg swaddle.

- if your baby is in a sleeping bag, ensure you dress your baby in the right thickness of pyjamas so they don't get too hot or too cold (see page 438)—check sleeping-bag instructions for appropriate size and thickness
- a wrapped baby must be safely positioned on their back for the night with a SafeT Sleep and tuck-in in place—a singlet, nappy and light muslin swaddle for summer or winter if they are in a full wrap or a nappy and a light long-sleeved top in a one-arm wrap or leg wrap; you can also use heating or cooling regulators in the room to moderate the room temperature (see page 434)
- be cautious about putting too many covers on them when they first go down for the night after their long day, even on cooler nights, as they are naturally warm when they first go to sleep at night but cool down as the night progresses. This is because their bodies sustain their increasingly tired little beings with adrenalin and hormones as the day progresses and these act as natural body warmers.

'As snug as a bug in a rug'—how to wrap

As in all my strategies, I prefer to swaddle using a clear and honest approach:

- I only ask a baby to go to sleep in the environment they will wake up in during the middle of the night
- I tell them that I am going to step out of the room so they can go to sleep all by themselves, but if they need me I will come in
- I use communication that is consistent with its true definition to encourage all of these things
- I role play so they understand what is going to be asked of them, to ensure they understand the sequence of events that will be their settling routine—this gives them realistic expectations, and all this is done before they are exposed to the swaddle the first time
- I give them a chance to practise and develop some of the more challenging new expectations at a non-sleep time, such as during cot playtime, so they can be comfortable with the two basic elements of sleep—to be in their cot awake, and to be comfortable with you leaving the room while they are awake in their cot
- I offer significant comfort in the form of a swaddle or, as I like to call it, 'the surrogate cuddle' in their cot to help the initial process move quickly and help bubby resolve their sleep-time difficulties with as little stress or confusion.

I do all of this because any change to any regular expectation that a child has will usually cause a little upset, so it's vital you try to take the time to make them familiar with, or skill them with, all the new skills and expectations before you start your new routine and sleep repair.

Because your baby will not be a newborn, this swaddle is done differently to those provided for tiny babies, as they are less wriggly at that age. When swaddling an older baby, you need to ensure the wrap stays in place all night and is a no-movement wrap. I find that a baby likes to either be fully able to move, or fully still, but nothing in between, so all the wraps are no-movement wraps, that are very firmly done. It's important that when you do swaddle this age group, to make it firm to discourage them from struggling to see if they can squirm free. I am a pretty good wrapper, but they can still wiggle free of mine if I'm not careful, so I do mean nice and firm.

If you are concerned that they will get their arms free no matter what you do, I've made a 'wiggly worm arm pockets' wrap insert that you can purchase (see my website), or a double swaddle may assist you in getting your swaddle just right to help bubby get sleeping as quickly as possible. I have found that the best wraps to swaddle with are the fine muslin, as large as or larger than a cot sheet and preferably the lightest and thinnest muslin you can find. The ashleyO wrap (www.ashleyo.com.au) provides a product like this. You are best to have two wraps available at all times so you can wash one and use one, or move to a double wrap if this is required.

The various styles of swaddles and tuck-ins I use with babies under the age of one year, four months to provide comfort and to speed up the process of your baby learning how to sleep peacefully all night every night, and through each day, every day, are:

- full surrogate hug
- one-arm wrap
- leg wrap
- the firm tuck-in.

It is important to practise and become fluent with your swaddle method before you start to try and wrap your baby so you can make the steps smooth and concentrate on sounding confident and reassuring. Use a teddy or a doll to practise over and over until you are extremely good at getting your wrapping firm enough to keep them still for eleven or more hours. I'll describe each of the four swaddle methods using a baby boy in my examples.

Full surrogate hug

The wrap is for his arms and legs and designed to prevent a baby from startling himself to a full waking during a sudden partial waking (between 10 and 11 p.m., at around 2 a.m., and between 4 and 5 a.m. if your baby goes to bed at 7 p.m.) or getting distracted from the task of falling asleep by rolling, kicking his little legs into the air, flapping his hands or standing and being unable to lie down or just generally fussing too much. It is designed to provide the same security that the car seat, the pram, a sling, hammock, pouch or a cuddle offers by holding him still so he can fall asleep in the first place. It is a temporary strategy to help him learn how to sleep with as few tears as possible during the transition, and in as short a period as possible. Once his confidence, in being able to fall asleep under these new independent sleep conditions all by himself in his cot, has built up, he won't need the added security of a firm snuggle and you can start to do the wrap up loosely, and just enjoy the security of the SafeT Sleep (see www.safetsleep.com).

I use the supersize ashleyO muslin wrap, a long rectangular sheet with the top folded down slightly (10 centimetres) for extra strength. You lay your baby head to toe on the shortest width, positioned slightly right of centre, so he has a long portion of sheet on either side of his body. In other words, he is not lying on the sheet like you lie on a beach towel, but the other way, across the sheet.

The steps to wrap are in four parts, each involving the four corners: the top-right portion, the bottom-right portion, the entire left side of the muslin wrapped around their body once, then the final leg wrap from the remaining muslin on the bottom left side of the wrap.

1. The top-right portion

Place baby on the wrap so the top of the muslin is at the bottom of his ears. Hold his little arm (his left one) down by his side against the mattress so it is close to his body, with his thumb facing up. Make sure you hold his arm straight and keep it by his side while you gather the muslin, all the way from his shoulder to his nappy—if you are having trouble keeping his arm in place while you do the first tuck-in, simply tuck his arm into a 'wiggly worm arm pockets' wrap insert first.

Once you have gathered the length of the muslin in your right hand from his shoulder, all the way down to his nappy, firmly pull the gathered material in your right hand towards the ceiling, then firmly across his body ensuring his little arm is still locked securely into place. After you have pulled it across his body using your right hand, firmly hold the piece of material you have just pulled across his body down against the mattress with your left hand, ready to tuck it under his back and bottom but not just yet. Only when the sheet is firmly held down against the mattress with your left hand ready to be tucked under him, are you safe to release the gather of material from the grip of your right hand. This ensures you don't lose any firmness holding his arm in place.

To get leverage to tuck-in this first side of material, reach over him with your now-free right hand and place it on the left side of the sheet that is still lying flat on the bed. Holding that flat left side of the sheet on the bed with your right hand, firmly tuck the gathered sheet from the right side under his bottom and back using your left hand. Please note, his right arm is not included in this tuck-in, but remains lying free beside him. In addition to tucking the sheet under him, try to push his body further into the wrap. This will ensure he is even more firmly locked in and prevent him from wiggling free while you wrap him.

2. The bottom-right portion
Find the furthest point on the folded lower right side of the sheet and pull it up and over his legs firmly and tuck under the same point of his lower back (if it can reach) as the first tuck-in you just completed. Again push him into the tuck-in firmly so the sheet becomes tight all the way down his body and his little legs are now moving within a pocket. Don't worry if his knee bends up; this is generally what happens with a wrap until the final wrap around is complete. Just try to make sure his legs are straight and together when you start this move.

3. The entire left side of the wrap
Do the same with the left side of the sheet. Hold his right arm down by his side so it is close to his body, against the mattress, with his thumb facing up. Make sure you hold his arm straight and keep it by his side while you gather up the muslin. In your left hand, firmly gather the muslin all the way down from his shoulder to his nappy. Now lift this gather of material firmly towards the ceiling, then across his body towards his left side.

With his right side held firmly in place by the gather of material in your left hand, pull all the sheet across the top of his body ensuring it stays above his feet, not below them. Using your right hand and arm, firmly sweep the rest of the sheet under his body from right back to the left side and promptly pull on the sheet very firmly to tighten it from the top, all the way down the length of the body, so he becomes well secured and unable to move his arms and legs. This needs to be done quickly and firmly to prevent him from wriggling free if you are not using the 'wiggly worm arm pocket' wrap insert.

4. The final leg wrap from the bottom (your left side)

Once you have firmly wrapped the sheet around him as discussed above, the long portion of sheet remaining on the lower left side is the final part of the wrap and it goes around his legs. In a broad sash, lift the sheet up and over his legs and back under his legs again, pulling really firmly to ensure his knees come together. When you have just wrapped the final piece of material around his legs simply pull it tight and tuck the end into the wrap. It should be tucked into a place where it is tight so it can be held firmly in place.

Just before you pick your baby up, tighten up the loose piece of material on your top left and ensure it doesn't come loose when you carry him to his room.

One of the most important pieces of advice I can give you at this point is to make sure you have practised the wrap on a large teddy bear or doll many times before you start your sleep repair program. If your baby learns they can get out of the swaddle the first time, then it becomes a challenge as they will try every time you put them down. If this does happen you can manage it, but your target is for it to not happen on the first wrap and never afterwards. You want to make sure you get it right the first time so they can stay focused on the task of going to sleep. They will settle quickly if you get this right. Always use a SafeT Sleep and the recommended tuck-in when using the full swaddle.

Always ask yourself whether they are sleeping better on the third day and third night after being swaddled to see if you are progressing. Try to remember that often the wrap is an indicator that it's time to go to bed, and more often that not, this cue is the cause of complaint from your little one when you first lie them down to swaddle them rather than the swaddle itself. Occasionally, if I come across a baby who doesn't cope so well with the sensation of tired they may have a few tears when you first start to wrap them for a little while longer than other babies, even though they will settle and resettle well and are happy through the day. Don't worry about this too much; it's okay if they are tired. You will usually find that once they are snuggled in place and you are singing 'Twinkle twinkle little star' they will be relaxing and getting ready to fall asleep.

One-arm wrap—variation for ten to 12 month old

The full swaddle is best but some older babies have self-settling comfort items, like thumb sucking, a cuddly toy or rag or some other tool to help them go to sleep so they need a hand free to do this. It is designed only for those babies who are already good at using an effective tool to settle and resettle themselves. Unless your baby is very effective with these tools do not use this variation if they are under 12 months but use the full swaddle. This swaddle leaves room for any established comfort device to be used, or to teach your little one to access their dummy during sleep times. The 'wiggly worm arm pocket' wrap insert can still be used for their one enclosed arm to help keep the wrap in place.

Designed to emulate the same feelings and limited movement a parent provides when they cradle their baby in their arms, one arm is generally free to move around while the other arm is tucked away, as it would be under mum's or dad's armpit. This wrap is for their legs and one arm. This should prevent them from startling themselves to a full waking during their partial wakings (at 11 p.m. and 2 a.m. and between 4 and 5 a.m.) or getting distracted from the task of falling asleep by rolling, playing and kicking their little legs into the air or fussing too much. It provides the same sort of feeling of security that a cradle in a parent's or carer's arm would provide so they can fall asleep in the first place. It is a temporary strategy to help your baby learn how to sleep with as few tears as possible, and in as short a period as possible. Once their confidence in being able to fall asleep has been built, they won't need the added security of the firm cot snuggle and you can start to do the wrap up loosely, and just enjoy the comfort of the SafeT Sleep.

This wrap is done almost exactly the same as the full surrogate hug with a single exception: part 3, the left-side section.

1. The top-right portion

Place baby on the wrap so the top of the muslin is at the bottom of his ears. Hold his little arm (his left one) down by his side against the mattress so it is close to his body, with his thumb facing up. Make sure you hold his arm straight and keep it by his side while you gather the muslin, all the way from his shoulder to his nappy—if you are having trouble keeping his arm in place while you do the first tuck-in, simply tuck his arm into the 'wiggly worm arm pockets' wrap insert first.

Once you have gathered the length of the muslin in your right hand from his shoulder, all the way down to his nappy, firmly pull the gathered material in your right hand towards the ceiling, then firmly across his body ensuring his little arm is still locked securely into place. After you have pulled it across his body using your right hand, firmly hold the piece of material you have just pulled across his body down against the mattress with your left hand, ready to tuck it under his back and bottom but not just yet. But only when the sheet is firmly held down against the mattress with your left hand ready to be tucked under him, are you safe to release the gather of material from the grip of your right hand. This ensures you don't lose any firmness holding his arm in place.

To get leverage to tuck-in this first side of material, reach over him with your now free right hand and place it on the left side of the sheet that is still lying flat on the bed. Holding that flat left side of sheet on the bed with your right hand, firmly tuck the gathered sheet from the right side under his bottom and back using your left hand. Please note, his right arm is not included in this tuck-in, but remains lying free beside him. In addition to tucking the sheet under him, try to push his body further into the wrap. This will ensure he is even more firmly locked in and prevent him from wiggling free while you wrap him.

2. The bottom-right portion

Find the furthest point on the folded lower right side of the sheet and pull it up and over his legs firmly and tuck under the same point of his lower back (if it can reach) as the first tuck-in you just completed. Again push him into the tuck-in firmly so the sheet becomes tight all the way down his body and his little legs are now moving within a pocket. Don't worry if his knees bend up; this is generally what happens with a wrap until the final wrap around is complete. Just try to make sure his legs are straight and together when you start this move.

3. The entire left side of the wrap

Do the same with the left side of the sheet. Only this time raise his right arm and gather the material from his armpit down. In your left hand, firmly gather the muslin all the way down from his armpit to his nappy. Now lift this gather of material firmly towards the ceiling, then across his body towards his left side.

With his right hand free, pull the sheet across the top of his body ensuring it goes above his feet, not below them. Using your right hand and arm, firmly sweep the rest of the sheet under his body from right back to the left side and promptly pull on the sheet very firmly to tighten it from his armpit, all the way down the length of the body, so he becomes well secured and unable to move his left arm and legs. This needs to be done quickly and firmly to prevent him from wriggling free if you are not using the 'wiggly worm arm pockets' wrap insert.

4. The final leg wrap from the bottom

Once you have firmly wrapped the sheet around him as discussed above, the long portion of sheet remaining is this final portion of the wrap to go around his legs one last time. In a broad sash, lift the sheet up and over his legs and back under his legs again, pulling really firmly to ensure his knees come together. Now you have just wrapped the final piece of material around his legs, simply pull it tight and tuck the end into the wrap around you have just done. It should be tucked into a place where it is tight so this loose end can be held firmly in place.

Just before you pick your baby up, tighten up the loose piece of material on your top left and ensure it doesn't come loose when you carry him to his room.

One of the most important pieces of advice I can give you at this point is to make sure you have practised the wrap on a large teddy bear or doll many times before you start your sleep repair program. If your baby learns they can get out of the swaddle the first time, then it becomes a challenge as they will try every time you put them down. If this does happen you can manage it, but your target is for it to not happen on the first wrap and never afterwards. You want to make sure you get it right the first time so they can stay focused on the task of going to sleep. They will settle quickly if you get this right. Always use a SafeT Sleep and the recommended tuck-in when using the full swaddle.

Leg wrap—variation for ten to 16 month old

Older babies tend to stand and cry if left and have the ability to be very persistent with their crying as the situation is stressful to them. They should still be provided with the security of a one-armed or full wrap if they are prone to becoming upset at sleep time up to 12 months if they have no sleep comfort items they need to get with their hand or hands, or if they are prone to flapping or startling easily on waking. Alternatively this firm leg wrap, SafeT Sleep and tuck-in is a great comfort for babies who can self-settle using a comfort item but are prone to multiple waking. This particular wrap is for baby's legs only and designed to prevent him from startling themselves to a full waking during a sudden partial waking (at 11 p.m. and 2 a.m., and between 4 and 5 a.m.) or getting distracted from the task of falling asleep by rolling, playing and kicking their little legs into the air about or fussing too much. It is also designed to emulate the same feeling and limited movement a pram or car seat provides, which is effective in helping little ones settle down and drift off to sleep quickly, as well as the same security a car seat offers by holding your baby still so they can fall asleep in the first place. It is a temporary strategy to help your baby to learn how to sleep with as few tears as possible, and in as short a period as possible. Once their confidence in being able to fall asleep has been built, they won't need the added comfort of the wrap so you can start to do the wrap up loosely, and just enjoy the security and comfort of the SafeT Sleep.

1. The top-right portion
Place your baby on the wrap so the top of the muslin comes up to his armpits. Raise up his left arm so it is out of the way. Then gather with your right hand the length of muslin from his armpit, all the way down to his nappy. Firmly pull the gathered material in your right hand towards the ceiling, then firmly across his body.

Once you have pulled it across his body, use your left hand to firmly hold the piece of material against the mattress, ready to be tucked under him, but not just yet. When you have the sheet firmly in your left hand, release the grip of your right hand. To get leverage to tuck-in, reach over your baby with your now-free right hand and place it on the left side of the sheet that is still lying flat on the bed. Pressing down on that part of sheet, firmly tuck the gathered portion of the sheet in your left hand under his bottom and back. At the same time, try to push him into the sheet. This will ensure your baby is even more firmly locked in to prevent him from wiggling out.

2. The bottom-right portion
Find the furthest point on the folded lower right side of the sheet and pull up and over his legs firmly and tuck it under his lower back at the same place as the previous tuck-in (if the muslin reaches), otherwise just tuck it where you can, perhaps behind their knees. Again push him into the tuck-in firmly so the sheet becomes tight all the way down his legs and body. Don't worry if his knees bend up; this is generally what happens with a wrap until the final wrap around. Just try to make sure his legs are straight and together when you start this move.

3. The left side
Raise his little right arm out of the way. Firmly gather the muslin on the left side with your left hand from his armpit all the way down to his nappy. Lift this gather of material firmly towards the ceiling, then across his body towards his right side. Now that you have his right side held firmly in place with the gathered material, pull the rest of the sheet from

the left side across the top of his body ensuring the sheet goes above his feet, not below them.

Using your right hand and arm, firmly sweep all the sheet under his body from right back to the left side, and promptly pull very firmly on the sheet to tighten it from the top down the length of the body so he becomes well secured and unable to move his legs at all. This needs to be done quickly and firmly to prevent him from wriggling free.

4. The final leg wrap from the bottom-left side of the wrap

You will notice that on the bottom left, once you have firmly pulled the sheet that you have wrapped around him, that you have a long portion of sheet remaining. This is the final portion of the wrap. In a broad sash, lift the sheet up and over his legs and back under, pulling really firmly to ensure his knees come together firmly.

Now you have just wrapped the final piece of material around his legs simply pull it tight and tuck the end into the wrap around you have just done. It should be tucked into a place where it is tight so this loose end can be held firmly in place. Just before you pick him up, tighten up the loose piece of material on the top left and ensure it doesn't come loose when you carry him to his room.

One of the most important pieces of advice I can give you at this point is to make sure you have practised the wrap on a large teddy bear or doll many times before you start your sleep repair program. If your baby learns they can get out of the swaddle the first time, then it becomes a challenge as they will try every time you put them down. If this does happen you can manage it, but your target is for it to not happen on the first wrap and never afterwards. You want to make sure you get it right the first time so they can stay focused on the task of going to sleep. They will settle quickly if you get this right. Always use a SafeT Sleep and the recommended tuck-in when using the full swaddle.

The firm tuck-in

This is designed for those little people who can sometimes self-settle and self-resettle, but may also stand and protest for a very long time if the mood strikes them and they are displeased with the current request to go to sleep. These babies tend to have a fairly comfortable positioning method already and only need the security of a SafeT Sleep and a firm tuck-in to assist them in lying down and feeling secure. This often corrects wakings through the night immediately by allowing them to feel as though they are being held when they surface briefly in the middle of the night.

It's *very* important that this strategy is always used in conjunction with consistent settling, resettling and waking routines. These routines should be role played before incorporating them into your baby's sleep–time strategy. You place your baby down on their back in the SafeT Sleep device, allow them to assume their favourite position and do it up firmly. Follow the instruction in the information provided with the SafeT Sleep. After that you tuck them in using 'The art of tucking in' (see page 453).

The art of tucking in

When tucking in a baby, there is actually an art to making the bed, and getting it just right so they can feel 'as snug as a bug in a rug'. One of my

Safe cot environments

When checking your nursery is safe to pursue independent sleeping for your baby, you should always utilise the latest information and research available to you. The reduction in the incidence of cot death over the past 16 years since the commencement of the SIDS and Kids public education campaign has been a staggering 70 per cent. For the latest information please see their website (www.sidsandkids.org). When shopping for a cot, if the product does not have a label or information indicating it has passed the basic safety standards test as set by Standards Australia for cots (see their website www.standards.org.au) then do not purchase the product. Some other basic hints and tips include:

- always place your baby on their back to sleep
- keep their environment smoke free, meaning 100 per cent smoke free always
- do not overheat your baby with excessive bedding or headwear
- do not leave hats, bonnets or other headwear such as hooded tops on your baby while they sleep as they need to cool themselves through their heads
- when tucking in your baby, lay them down towards the bottom end of the mattress to ensure they don't wriggle down below tucked-in bedding and risk sleeping with their heads covered
- securely tuck-in all bedding so it does not come loose through the night
- do not use electric blankets, hot-water bottles or heated wheat bags as a means of keeping a baby under two years of age warm
- keep the cot away from any curtains or dangling curtain / blind cords as these represent a significant accidental asphyxiation risk if the child gets the cord or connectors caught around their neck
- unless you are deliberately tucking them into their beds securely, a baby under two years of age should be wearing nightwear that will keep them warm rather than trying to cover them with loose blankets—sleeping bags represent excellent sleepwear for the cooler months, rather than blankets
- ensure your baby does not have access to uncovered power points, or power leads coming from those points

favourite times as a little girl was when I could hear my mum (the original baby whisperer) saying goodnight to my sister up the hall. She developed a routine for all of us that involved a song called 'Go to sleep and goodnight', and then she would tuck us in 'snug as a bug'. I clearly remember lying in my cot as she bounced my mattress tucking all the sheets in firmly. I loved, loved, loved that feeling. As we got older, it became a fun game as she bounced our bed mattress at our 'do it again' insistence, until she decided enough was enough and it was time to say nigh' nigh'.

After she left, I would lie there as still as I could so the bedding would stay all firm, just as my mum had made it. So when I tuck-in babies now, I am inspired by this lovely bed routine my parents successfully used on

- there should be absolutely no pillow or cushions, regardless of your child's age or whether they are sleeping or not, while they are in the cot as the risk of overheating or asphyxiation is far too great—pillows can be introduced after your child turns two and they are moved to a bed environment.

Hand-me-down / second-hand cot safety

If you have been given a cot that is older than four years, I would personally recommend you do not use it. If you have a family cot that has been passed down through the years, I usually recommend you put it in a safe place as a keepsake only and do not use it as a sleeping environment for your baby. If you have been given a cot that is not too old, you must ensure it is safe and meets current safety standards set out by Standards Australia for cots, and you must always replace any mattress with a well-fitted, standards-approved mattress. If you are setting up a cot you used with your first child, I always recommend purchasing a new well-fitted, safety-standards-approved mattress as well.

If you are unsure, the following basic common sense guides will help you:

- cot bars are no less than 5.5 centimetres apart and no more than 8.5 centimetres apart
- there are no broken, loose or missing elements to the cot
- the cot mattress should be brand new and safety standards approved; if not; you will need to purchase one
- the cot mattress fits the cot well, bearing in mind that gaps larger than 2.5 centimetres between the cot bars and the mattress represent a hazardous sleeping environment
- any mattress protector is well fitted and breathable—I personally resist the use of these as they overheat children and the mattresses are durable and can survive for two years easily without protectors
- the cot paint is not toxic lead based
- nothing at all can catch on your baby's clothing and trap or hook them if they lose their footing
- nothing can catch, trap, or hurt little fingers when they explore the cot.

all three of their children, born thirteen years apart. And we were all excellent sleepers.

Though this might appear obvious there is actually a real method to getting the bedding nice and firm so your baby can feel safe and snuggled each night. I use the length of the flat cot sheets across the width of the cot. Lay down the sheet so there is a lot of length under the mattress on the opposite side to you. Lay any extra coverings you need over the sheet and fix them in place on the opposite side of the mattress then push cloth nappies or a towel firmly down the gap between the tucked-in sheets in the mattress and the cot side to prevent the sheets coming loose during the night, so your baby can't get tangled if they do move about. Then lift the near side of the mattress and pull everything from the opposite side of the cot's tuck-in firmly so it is deeply anchored underneath the mattress and the weight of your baby and the mattress lock these in place when your baby is in bed. Then, firmly tuck-in the near side of the mattress with the bedding just as you did on the opposite side with locking it in place with the towel rolls. Now your bed is fully made. Now you will need to prepare it for tucking in your baby. Pull back the near top corner of the bedding and open up the SafeT Sleep if you are using one, ready for baby to be tucked snugly into their bed.

When you are ready to tuck-in your baby, with the cot side down, you will need to lay your little one at the top of the cot on the fitted sheet, then gently slide their legs under the neatly made sheets. When they are in the right position, do up the SafeT Sleep if you have put one in the bed or just smooth out their sleeping bag if they are in one of those before you start the process of tucking back in the near top corner of the bedding you had loosened earlier. Lift the cot side before you lock their sheet extra firmly into place by slightly lifting the mattress on your side and pulling and tucking the sheets firmly and deeply under the mattress. Now as a final step, push cloth nappies or a towel down the gap between the tucked-in sheets and the cot bars, all the way down the length of his body. Sliding the nappy rolls down the side on the mattress will be a little challenging, as it should be. It should be pretty hard for you to get them out again also, meaning they are safely secured.

Your little one is now officially 'as snug as a bug in a rug'.

Weaning your baby off the wrap

Weaning your baby off something implies that *you* have decided they should no longer have a particular thing as it is now detrimental to their development. If your baby is content in the wrap and sleeping well for the first time in their life, and you are using a SafeT Sleep and a good tuck-in, then it is clearly not detrimental to them. When you use a temporary wrap, and you suddenly find your baby sleeping all night every night peacefully, don't then be in such a rush to get rid of the one thing that your baby has found so relieving. Remember to throw away any preconceived adult concepts you might have about a swaddle. The idea that you have decided that you would like them to give it up is not how I assess a child's readiness to be without this comfort device.

I look for signs from them, rather than working with what I or the parents would prefer. Readiness to start to transition out of the wrap should come from your baby. Keep it in place firmly for as long as you like and do not attempt to loosen it until they start to show signs. Alternatively, if you are really keen to do away with it, wait a minimum of three to six weeks before you start to look for signs. If they come out of it and keep sleeping, then they are self-weaning and you can gradually provide a looser wrap for them to wiggle free of and sleep without before eventually no longer wrapping them. If they do start to wiggle free, however, and cry and need to be re-wrapped, then they are not ready yet and you should firm up the wrap again. Always maintain the SafeT Sleep even as you are loosening the wrap, and even once they have self-weaned, as their old sleep patterns will still definitely be prevalent for the first three full weeks, but potentially for the first three months before a new solid sleep pattern replaces it. Once they do start to wiggle free, if they are truly ready, you may find that the wrap will remain like a little cocoon in the SafeT Sleep. If they do wiggle free of it and they are ready to be without the wrap it will not unsettle them. If in that time, their sleep deteriorates again, then they must be wrapped firmly again and they are not to be given the opportunity to self-wean for a further three to six weeks. You will see them sleeping solidly again once you re-do the wrap.

This means that if they are doing really well then you can consider weaning them only after three to six weeks, and only if you feel confident to do so—otherwise your little one can keep it until they are ready—should you consider slowly, one step at a time, reducing the level of comfort they receive from the wrap. The last thing you will remove is always the SafeT Sleep. This remains the staple until the very last part of the process and will remain valuable to you and your baby when you take them to sleep in foreign environments as a form of comfort. The SafeT Sleep is one of the most comforting sleep aids I have found on the market to date and helps many babies and toddlers sleep more soundly than they ever have before.

Troubleshooting

Q Where should I wrap them?

A Not in their cot or on their change table. It won't be big enough to do the wrap correctly. Ideally, if there is a single bed or large sofa in their room then that would be perfect. Otherwise, wrap them on a nearby bed so you have lots of room. Avoid your bed though as this may be linked to nudie playtime (see page 209) or may lead them to believe they are going to sleep in your bed if that is your usual ritual. If your bed is the only bed in the house, then it is fine to use this bed, just be sure to have the lights off, use your cues well and point to the wrap before you say 'Lie down'. Make sure you have role played this with a teddy for your baby first (see page 631).

Q Won't they get uncomfortable sleeping on their back, or in the same position all night?

A On the contrary, once your baby is used to these sleeping conditions, they sleep more soundly and peacefully than they have ever done in their entire lives. This indicates they are comfortable. If they were not, they would remain unsettled or cry. Give yourself time to repair their sleep disruption first, however. I have been using this strategy for years, in fact, it's one of the main reasons I have such a strong reputation for fast success with minimal tears—and I can assure you, they love their wraps.

Q Won't she get flat head syndrome if she lies on her back?

A Plagiocephaly is the medical term for this. As this condition commonly occurs in the first few months of life, the likelihood of it developing over the age of six months when a child naturally and frequently moves their head from side to side, is zero. I have not had a single case of this developing since my program began. While I have encountered plagiocephaly several times in my career, it developed in children who had not been good sleepers. In my hundreds of cases of a baby needing the security of a wrap I have never once had a single round little head change shape.

Q How long will it take him to get used to the wrap?

A That depends on the temperament of your baby, how confident and happy you appear while you are wrapping them, how much role play you have done, and how good you are at making the wrap consistently firm. Some babies laugh the first time if I am smiling and saying the cues and bouncing them about trying to get the wrap all firm, and they only complain at the changed sleep conditions the first time they are asked to put themselves to sleep. Others are furious about the concept on and off for the first 24 hours, then love it to bits from then on. There have been three occasions where the baby protested about the wrap and the idea of going to bed for a full week, but never cried once we left the room. This could have been because they were tired, it may have been their own little pre-sleep contribution to the routine, or they could have preferred to be without the wrap—it's hard to tell. The one thing I do know, is that these protesters, who often complain about the idea of even lying on the nappy change table—so it's no wonder this evokes some crying—are ten times more upset without the swaddle. Either way, they are sleeping better and are less stressed by the swaddle than they would be if they were expected to cope with the sleeping environment without it. These are the babies who cry whether they are in their mother's or father's arms or not.

Q I have just put my baby down, but she has got out of the wrap and SafeT Sleep. Should I rewrap her?

A If they have done a little Houdini and wiggled free, don't worry, it happens. I wrap them really firmly and, if they really want to, they can still get out. You will need to rewrap them though. Before you get them up, place one of your spare large muslins out on your usually wrapping bed. Turn off all the lights, leaving only the dimmest of lights on for safety reasons. Make sure everyone in the household is out of sight. Go into their room, say 'Time for sleep, mummy swaddle bubby, up up' before you lift them up. Lay them in your arms in the cradle position immediately so there is no confusion about your intention. Shelter their eyes as you take them to the next room, quietly repeating your cues 'Time for sleep, mummy and daddy love you, nigh' nigh''. Point to the wrap and say 'Lie down'. Then get it right this time, or do a double wrap. A double wrap is usually only needed for the first 24 hours if your baby is a real Houdini. Do one complete wrap, then wrap your little person once again firmly a second time. Then just follow your normal resettling routine from the point of saying 'Time for sleep, lie down', making sure they are firmly snuggled into their cot with a good tuck-in and their SafeT Sleep.

Q What about wrapping in summer? Won't it be too warm?

A I have had to do this in the past. I had one job on the first of January on a cane farm in Cairns and, believe me, it was definitely warm and steamy. In this case, when it is this hot, and the baby's room is shooting anything above 25 to 30 degrees, it is just way too hot to encourage good sleep anyway. I usually suggest you invest in an air conditioner as, swaddled or not, sleep is going to be almost impossible to achieve if baby gets too hot. If you do not wish to or cannot afford to purchase an air conditioner, you can hire them at a reasonable price per weeks, which will suit your short-term needs of your baby to be swaddled. More often than not, if a baby gets too hot or too cold they will either wake up to cry to sweat so they can cool down, or wake up and cry to get a cuddle to warm up. A child getting too hot or too cold is said to increase their chances of SIDS so I usually always recommend you find a way to cool the room (see page 434).

Q What should he wear with the swaddle in the winter?

A Use your instincts, but I often find that the wrap and SafeT Sleep are warm enough for them to just wear a light short-sleeved singlet underneath if both their arms are tucked in. As the night progresses, you can add a layer of cotton blanket around 10 p.m. If they have one arm out, then a long-sleeved warm pyjama top or long-sleeved singlet will keep them warm. You are better to try and keep the room temperature regulated through the use of a thermostat on an oil heater (see page 434). This means you dress him to a level where he appears comfortable (as suggested in above answer regarding ideal room temperature and clothing) and only worry about keeping the room temperature regulated (see page 434).

Q My baby has eczema. Can I still wrap her?

A This can be an extremely challenging thing to deal with, particularly in its most severe forms. If your baby is suffering terribly from eczema, then you will need to find a way to settle down the symptoms before you embark on any kind of sleep-training episode because it is quite possibly the eczema that is causing the sleep disruption in the first place. When I say severe, these children do not just have the usual patches in their creases, they also have it spread across their body and are prone to regular flairs that often require hydrocortisone ointment to sooth the symptoms. The need to repair your little one's sleep is an absolute priority if you want to help reduce or lesson the stress on your baby's system, because poor sleep and stress can contribute to eczema in the first place. It can be a little bit of a vicious circle when this occurs. Once you have seen an improvement, use a wrap that is 100 per cent cotton in place of nightwear, as it is no different to normal sleepwear. Keep all baths prior to bedtime cool. Keep your baby well moisturised. Dress her in light clothing during the settling routine so her body can stay cool until it is wrapped, then be lightly warmed by the swaddle rather than have the swaddle trap heat against her skin. Skin-on-skin contact tends to trigger the itches even more, so dressing her in a cotton, well-fitted short-sleeved cotton all-in-one will keep any redness at bay for the short window you may need to swaddle your little one. A slight increase in redness may occur temporarily during sleep training as a baby finds any change in their tiny lives a little stressful. This redness occurs occasionally and is the same in those who are swaddled or not swaddled. Try to stay on top of it by using your hydrocortisone as soon as you note an area of irritation and always sorbolene her after bath. Keep a free-standing fan angled to blow air on her cot to keep the air circulating around the swaddle. Remember, the purpose of helping babies with eczema sleep better is to reduce the symptoms, so a little bit of management of her symptoms for a few days is more effective than long-term treatment because your baby being overtired makes her prone to more flairs.

To gradually see if they are ready to come out of their wrap, make it a little looser on one hand at a time. If they have an arm or both in the 'wiggly worm arm pockets' wrap insert, then stop using the pockets one at a time, but continue to wrap them as firmly as always. Don't loosen their little legs just yet. Just start with the arms and go from there. This is when your little one will tell you if they are ready to sleep without this added security or not. A great indication is that you go into them the next morning, and they have one or both arms out of the wrap and have continued sleeping anyway.

If they are in the wrap-weaning process, make sure they are wearing longer sleeves of an appropriate thickness on the top half of their body. Once out of their swaddle, I always transition them into a child-safe sleeping bag. In this initial self-weaning process, you should still, as always, be maintaining your surface-sleep window pause (see page 674) and appropriate responses to crying before attending to them. Apart from ensuring you do not trigger episodes of wild thrashing by waking them accidentally, you are also making sure you don't interfere with the natural process of them needing a little space on those first few occasions to move about and have a little grizzle and a grumble under the new conditions before drifting back off to sleep.

Once this process has begun and your little one is starting to sleep with their arms out each night you can either do the wrap loosely around their arms, or not wrap their arms at all. Remember to put them in a light long-sleeved t-shirt, and consider turning the cooling down or off if they are wiggling partially free early in the night. If they have difficulty falling asleep or they start waking up during the night again, then they are not quite ready and you need to take it slower and re-wrap them. Just please don't rush the process. You baby will eventually, when they are ready, stop needing to be wrapped.

I find that boys want and need to keep the wrap a little longer than girls, but will show clear signs when they are ready to be out of their wraps by wiggling hands out and sleeping on happily. Once they are in the leg wrap only, with the SafeT Sleep and sleeping well, maintain a firm leg wrap until you can come in the next morning and see that they have been able to kick it loose, and are able to move their little legs about inside the swaddle freely but still sleep happily. This means they are ready to sleep completely without their wrap and you can just provide a pretend leg swaddle, to maintain the predictability of the settling process. Once they are happy with this, just bypass the wrapping process all together and pop them into a sleeping bag instead, then the SafeT Sleep, which babies do find very comforting, and it protects them from the risks of tummy sleeping and climbing out of the cot.

Comfort items

This section deals with two types of comfort item: cuddly toys and the dummy. When I am dealing with a baby aged six to 12 months of age, unless they have naturally developed an attachment to a safe comfort item like a muslin toy or muslin cloth on their own, I never deliberately encourage one. It often takes longer to encourage a comfort item leaving room for crying and stress, so it is simply easier to just swaddle the baby to repair the sleep very quickly instead. Over 12 months of age, however, it's a different story. If they have a regular snugly comfort item they enjoy in their cot or through the day, then I am happy to encourage that attachment to a comfort item as it helps us tremendously with the settling process. If a child over 12 months is transitioning from co-sleeping to their own independent sleeping environment, then I will actually deliberately develop a comfort item association around a safe teddy bear (see page 352).

If your little one is still under 12 months and has developed a strong attachment to a comfort item, and still falls into the group of unsettled babies that needs to be wrapped to help them feel secure and comforted while they learn how to sleep, then I suggest the one-arm wrap. In extremely unsettled babies, you may need to eliminate the comfort item and replace it with the temporary comfort of the surrogate cuddle provided by the full swaddle (see page 439). As this is only a temporary measure, within a few weeks to months, when your baby has been sleeping well and is enjoying going to bed and sleeping through the night, then you can move to a one-arm wrap and reintroduce the comfort item. Gradually over the next couple of weeks your little one will begin to sleep without the wrap as they will then be very comfortable with the conditions of sleeping in their cot.

When choosing a comfort item, bear in mind that teddy bears need to be well sewn and be a good high-quality toy. It is easy to recognise a poor-quality novelty bear. You should choose a bear that has stitched cotton eyes, nose and mouth, and is free of buttons, or long ribbons. Read all tags carefully and always remove any non-essential tag, like the sachet pouch containing extra cotton or the bear birth certificate, and examine the bear carefully for any potential choking hazards. Remove any ribbons that are not firmly stitched to the bear, and avoid any bear that contains stuffing like beads or straw. If the bear starts to come apart at the seams, always have it professionally restored to ensure your baby cannot choke on any filling that may come loose. If the bear's fur shows signs of easily coming away from the product, then this is not an appropriate comfort item. It's normal for bears to wear down and become bald from excessive loving, but it should be a gradual process. Always try to buy a duplicate teddy if they are desperately in love with their bear so you can wash it regularly to keep it dust-mite free and hygienic.

Toys made of muslin are the safest form of comfort item for little ones over six months of age to have in their cot. This means bubby can still breathe if it happens to go near their mouth. Muslin-based comfort-snuggle rabbits and bears are widely available on the market but again, looking for a good-quality version is essential.

Dummies

Debate about dummies is a hot subject in the field of parenting. However, judging a parent for the choices they make is far more destructive than any dummy could ever be. While I try to eliminate dummies from a child's day once they are about six months old (see box on page 469), I admit they do have their place in the very early stages of a baby's life if the baby is having a difficult time with reflux or you would like to stretch out the time just a little between feeds without your baby becoming stressed. With reflux, the suckling and subsequent swallowing helps keep the peristaltic action of the oesophagus flowing downwards, thus reducing the stomach acids from tracking up and irritating. Because of this, it is perfectly understandable that a parent may have found a dummy to be extremely soothing for their baby and decided to adopt the practice.

By six months of age, however, if you have not resolved your infant's reflux at your family doctors, then you must do so immediately. I personally find that dummies are only ever associations and are never a relief for physical symptoms by this age. This means that your baby has a habit of sucking the dummy, not a need for it. The dummy is a solution to certain conditions or feelings they have. Ask yourself, what does your child use their dummy for? It can be their solution for coping with being tired, for boredom, for dealing with emotions like feeling grumpy, frustrated or angry, or when impatient on a car or pram trip.

Dummies can affect sleep in two ways. Firstly, if your baby does not know how to put the dummy in their own mouth, it means they will never ever be able to put themselves to sleep or back to sleep without your intervention. This is where the dummy is the problem, not the solution. This is a learnt pattern of dependent associations (see page 399) in order to sleep. These children will need help two to three times a night at a minimum, and if the constant need to call out makes them overtired, they can wake even more often. In a worst-case scenario, they can wake as often as every 20 to 40 minutes, 24 hours a day.

Secondly, by always solving their emotions with a dummy you teach them three things: to never express themselves, to always resolve emotions by putting something in their mouth, and to not learn to feel the range of normal emotion they would naturally experience at sleep time, like being a little grumpy perhaps, or having to be patient and quiet at sleep time. When you can see that your little one has become over dependent on this device throughout the day, and it is preventing them from learning through experience to feel and know how to cope with the range of normal emotions, it's definitely time to get rid of it. Please note, the overuse of suckling on the breast can create the same pattern as a dummy can.

If I am resolving significant sleep-time problems with a child age six to 12 months, I completely remove the dummy from their world. I tend to help little ones resolve this in a two-step process. The first step I take in the lead up to introducing my new daily routine is to make the dummy a sleep-time-only comforter. This means in the few days before I actually start any new routine I do not allow them to have it when they are out of their cot. This means that during the homework phase of your PRM you need to make your little one's dummy a sleep-time-only comforter. Most people gasp at this concept. 'But my baby will cry', they all seem to say. This may indeed be the case because their baby has not yet learnt that having to wait in the pram, or feel a little frustrated or grumpy on occasions during the day, is actually something they can cope with and recover from without this aid. Be patient, sometimes it takes a day, sometimes two, and sometimes, they don't even bat a beautiful eyelash. Just don't go back to the dummy as a solution once your remove it from their daytime. It's important to note that if they have not had the opportunity to practise feeling their emotions and resolving them without the dummy during the day, then it is hardly fair to ask them to cope without it at night yet.

Be cautious to not replace one oral emotional solution to the range of normal emotions with another (like offering snacks to your baby). Be reassuring, and comforting and use the strategies highlighted in this book's encyclopaedia and its communication sections as well as, or instead of distractions to help them get used to feeling those emotions without using a dummy or filling their mouth to resolve it. Remember to be consistent with this process; don't confuse your baby or teach them to cry by sometimes giving them the dummy at a non-sleep time if they *really* cry, or you literally teach your baby that 'if you really want the dummy, you need to really cry!'

Once you eliminate the dummy from daytime use, stick to your plan and help your baby firstly experience, then work through, new ways to cope with those emotions. Show them how books can be soothing for instance. Find a safe comfort bear, muslin or snugly toy to cuddle, or sit down and play together until they feel better. They will quickly learn that the emotions are okay, and they will be able to cope without the dummy. Within two days, it will no longer be an issue. This means you are ready for step two, which is embarking on your new daily routine, sleep repair program without the dummy and full PRM approach. By now, your baby will have had the chance to be exposed to their emotions during the day and, more importantly, to have had the opportunity to learn how to cope with them better for having the dummy removed at sleep time.

Please note, if your ten to 12 month old is not suffering significant sleep-time problems and you only need to pop the dummy in their mouth once in a blue moon when they wake, then you are best to work with the dummy game (see page 464) designed for 12 to 24 month olds, than to remove it.

The dummy and sleep time for 12 to 24 month olds

At this age you actually have an option about whether or not the dummy stays or goes at sleep time. When you look at true needs versus short-term demands (see page 91) you can see that your baby's sleep will not be disrupted if you teach them how to get the dummy themselves. If your little one has significant sleep-time problems to resolve, I tend to not take the dummy away from them as it can act as a real comforter when they go through a big change. I always say, if they have had it this long you may as well use it to their advantage. Then when they are more comfortable with their new self-settling routines you can consider removing it from sleep time altogether *if* and *when* it is necessary.

I have to admit that while I would not introduce a dummy personally to a child of my own unless it was for temporary reflux or feed-stretching purposes, and nor would I sustain the use of a dummy after six months of age, there is no way I would suddenly decide when they were 12 months old that because it now suited me, they could no longer have it. If they have had their dummy that long, making it a cot-only sleeping aid and teaching them how to get it themselves are not damaging to them in any way shape or form, so I would question my motivation for suddenly deciding to get rid of it.

If a baby was absolutely struggling with independence and the dummy pot game (see box on page 467), or the dummy was never really that big a deal to the child at sleep time when I entered a house to help a family resolve their sleep-time issues, then this would be my motivation to take it away at all sleep and non-sleep times without a problem. If you decide to keep the dummy as a sleep aid however, and wish to help them become more independent, then you can establish independence through the dummy pot game. I would still work on the principle that you eliminate the dummy

Troubleshooting

Q Does this mean there will be no tears at bed time?

A Not necessarily. As I have mentioned many times through this book, babies are creatures of habit and do not cope terribly well with change. This is why you need to carefully design settling, resettling and waking routines (see page 605), and reassuring management strategies to help them work through this brand new set of conditions at sleep time. You need to be a confident parent and correctly assess your little one's true needs versus their short-term demands. If your baby's need is to sleep, but their short-term demand is to have their dummy back but it is disrupting their ability to sleep, then their true need is to no longer have the dummy as a vice for falling asleep.

(see box on page 469) at all non-sleep time portions of the day. For this, I use the same strategy as I used for eliminating the dummy for six to 12 month olds. And be honest. Answer their request for a dummy with 'Dummy is all gone. Dummy is for nigh' nigh' time only.' Make sure you have removed it from their sight and from where they can get it, and work through their reaction without giving in and giving it to them.

Don't replace one oral solution with another, like a dummy with a biscuit or rusk. Remember, this strategy is designed to help them at sleep time so if you can't offer that solution at sleep time, you should not be teaching them it is the new solution at non-sleep time. Support them through the emotions of the situation with confident tones and body language and positive feedback. Showing them another way to make themselves feel better, like cuddling a teddy or muslin snugly toy for instance, which might be useful for them in the cot environment. Be consistent and remember to define what 'dummy all gone' means, so don't say it's gone then bring it out. That will confuse them and you will not be able to eliminate it quickly or without significant tears.

As mentioned earlier however, at this age, if the dummy is something they rely on heavily for sleep time, there is no need to actually take it away at sleep time. The main aim is to ensure they know that they are the ones that can put it into their mouth, that they know where they can find that dummy, even in the dark, and that they are empowered with the understanding that you would like them to do that for themselves. Empowering your baby with the ability to get their own dummy at sleep time eliminates the need to take it away from them altogether or constantly do the dummy run through the night. You do this in two ways: by the use of language cues within a routine, and the use of dummy pots.

The language cue is simply 'get your dummy'. The concept for the dummy pot is also simple: your baby has two centralised location, soft material pots, in the cot where they can go, even in the dark, and always find a dummy. You place several or all of their dummies in the two pots, which need to be safely secured to the top corners of their cot. You then need to teach your baby how to get their own dummy by playing the dummy pot game (see box on page 467) and show them where those pots are when it's time to go to sleep. You then establish a settling and resettling routine that incorporates them always getting their own dummy to go to sleep, and to go back to sleep. This teaches your child to automatically reach out and find their own dummy when they wake during the night, and eliminates their need to cry because they no longer need you to come in and find it for them.

You will need to play the dummy pot game first at non–sleep times so you can practise the new language and create a positive association around the use of the dummy pot. Before you start, always use your flow of communication to prepare them that soon you are going to play the dummy pot game (see box on page 467) while showing them the pot. When it's time to play, be enthusiastic about the concept. You will need to ask them to wait by using your wait cue (see page 74) so they don't just grab the dummies and put them straight in their mouth. While this is the ultimate

The dummy pot game

Sit your baby down on the floor, in their high chair, on the couch or wherever you are comfortable and show them their new dummy pot. If they are prone to crawling off, then you are better to play this game in the high chair, or on the couch where they are between your legs, etc. First you say 'Wait for mummy' and then show them their dummies and put them in the pot, still encouraging them to wait. When you ask them to wait, block their hands if you need to and have that enthusiastic look on your face that indicates waiting is fun, not a punishment or demand, and follow through.

Once they are waiting say 'Get your dummy' and remove your hands to allow them to get their dummy and pop it in their mouth. If they grab it, get excited. Clap and cheer, and repeat the cue 'Good getting your dummy' before saying 'Ta for mummy / pop' and quickly slipping the dummy out of their mouth and back in their pot. If you do all this with a sense of humour, they will laugh at your antics and you will be able to start the game again. Each time you pop the dummy out of their mouth, always say 'Pop . . . ohhh' and do a little surprise look and jump. If you are repetitious with this, they will think you are pretty funny.

If they are not sure if they are meant to grab the dummy, you are teaching them what 'get your dummy' actually means. The entire purpose of asking them to wait is to get them to respond specifically to the language cue 'get your dummy'. If they are not sure if they should reach in and get their dummy, you can repeat your cue 'Get your dummy, Blake' and point to the pot and touch the dummies. If they are still not sure whether they should get the dummies, repeat 'Get your dummy, ta for Blake'. You can guide their hand into the dummy pot, or pick up the dummy pot and offer the whole pot to them. Only let your baby take the dummies, and not the pot. They can take as many as they like when you say your cue, but when it's time to put the dummies back in the pot, you need to help your baby put them all back.

Repeat this game until they are familiar with the cue 'get your dummy' and know what to do when you say that. This usually takes five minutes, ten minutes maximum for a 12 to 24 month old. If they are enjoying the game, though, you can keep playing it for a little while longer before completing your packing-away routine. The more challenging they find this game, the more you should repeat the cues per game, and the more often you should play the actual dummy pot game through the day. It should only take one day for your baby to learn this new game.

aim of the game, you want to establish the language cue 'get your dummy' so you can incorporate it into their sleep-time ritual so they must wait.

Once they have been introduced to the new language cue of the dummy pot game, you can firmly fix the two dummy pots to their cot, with their bases resting on the mattress so they can reach in and get them without standing up. If they move all over the cot through their sleep I tend to have one pot at each end, or have two pots at the top end in each corner. I put all the dummies they own in the two pots. If they are going to have a dummy, they need to be able to find them at all times during the night, so there is no point in having only one or two dummies.

I make sure I show them the two filled dummy pots before I begin their settling routine. The dummies must stay in the cot however, so there can be no dummies during story time, even if they ask. The reason there are no dummies during stories is because it is just too confusing for little ones to not be allowed dummies outside the cot as a general rule, but then have a different set of rules when it suits us. It also discourages active communication during story reading, and makes it difficult to teach them how to cope without a dummy when going to sleep as they become older. By not allowing them dummies during stories, you encourage them to feel comfortable with the tired sensation without the need for a dummy, making transitioning into self-settling in their cot without the dummy as they get older an achievable goal. Finally, by leaving the dummies in the cot, you make it so they are excited to go to bed because they have something to look forward to.

If they ask for a dummy, simply say 'Soon, but let's have stories first' and head to the couch. You can incorporate the cue 'nearly time to get your dummy' into your settling routine pre-emptive language. Follow your settling-routine position and management if your little one protests about not being given their dummy for stories. Once you have finished your settling routine you can head into their room and continue your routine with their settling song and a snuggle in your arms without giving them the dummy. When it's time to pop them into their bed, remember to say the cues 'time for sleep, mummy and daddy love you' and 'nigh' nigh', lie down, get your dummy'. At this point, there are two simply non-confusing boundaries: they must lie down before they get their dummy and, if at any point during the sleep-time process they stand up, you take it out of their mouth and put it back in their pot until they are lying down again.

They must lie down (with or without your help) before they can have their dummy back. You can assist them to reach into their pot once they are lying down if they can't find it, but do not give it to them. They can take as many dummies as they like. Don't be alarmed if it is a large number of dummies initially; they will soon discover it's a little challenging to work out how to put so many of their favourite things to good use at one time. It's okay for them to hold some and swap them around and try a couple at once on those first days. It will all settle down soon, and they will go back to just enjoying one at a time.

If you dislike the idea of giving them more than one dummy because you would just rather they not have any at all, then it's time to take the dummy away altogether at sleep time. There is no point in doing the dummy game half-heartedly because you are reluctant to give them the dummy in the first place. They will need multiple dummies if you want to make sure they don't lose them in the middle of the night and don't need to call out to get you to help them.

On those first few days they do not have to take a dummy if they do not want to, but the request to lie down still remains. During resettling times, your routine should remain the same with a slight variation that is consistent with your original settling process. Once you enter their room to resettle them, you need to ask them to lie down if they are standing, and you will remove the dummies from their mouth or hands or both and put them back in the pot before assisting them or asking them to lie down again. I tend to have a quick feel around the cot and pop all the dummies back in the pots on those first few days. Continue on with your settling routine and when they are lying down as requested you can point to the pot, or rattle the dummies in the pot, or guide their hand to the pot again when you say 'Get your dummy'. Please remember you cannot put the dummy in their hand or in their mouth. The dummy pot should not be removed from its original position as it's important to teach them how and

Eliminating the dummy completely

It is best to eliminate the dummy from all non-sleep parts of the day first, and then lock in your honest answer and cue 'dummy is all gone' and define that statement. Remember, you do not want to make this a confusing statement when you first introduce it because when you eventually use this cue at night when they ask for their dummy the first time, you need to make sure they know what this statement means and that it is not a negotiation. It's also important for them to have the opportunity to experience the feelings that come up when they do not get the dummy, and find new ways to resolve those feelings and learn that they are still okay without it before you introduce the same conditions into their cot environment. When they are comfortable with the daytime conditions of no dummy, then it's time to implement your new daily routine and full PRM. Follow on as suggested in the settling, resettling and waking routine (see page 605).

where to reach out to find their dummies so they can become self-sufficient.

Monitors

Monitors are seriously overused in my personal opinion. I believe that everyone can benefit from having a monitor as a device to alert them that their baby is awake, crying or coughing. They can be useful if you are outside hanging out washing or taking a quick swim in the backyard pool, etc., or when you have a two-storey or large house where your child's cries are out of normal hearing range.

If you can hear your baby clearly from your bedroom when they cry out at night, then there is no real reason to use the monitor in your room unless you are an extremely deep sleeper. I find that parents with children who have trouble sleeping are never deep sleepers. They tend to be listening to their child's every move, and any natural stirring through the night encourages them to over-interfere during their baby's healthy sleeping cycles. This is a key cause of some of the more obvious resettling associations.

Equally, if you can hear your baby when you are in the main living area of the house, then you do not need to have a monitor on. If you do have a large house, or there is a genuine need to use a monitor to hear your child when they wake, then do so, but once you have heard your child, turn off the monitor, or turn it down to a low level. There is a natural chemical reaction a mother experiences when they hear their baby cry, and if you are already feeling anxious about their waking, the monitor will only exacerbate your levels of anxiety, or make you misread your child's partial waking (simply because the monitor is set at an unnaturally loud level), and could make your day more difficult that it needs to be.

If you can hear your child from your room and the living area, but still *need* to have it on for a sense of comfort, you should plug the monitor's receiving end into the hallway right outside your child's room. This means you will only hear any genuine crying and not rush in when they are just moving a little bit and having a little grumble as they get comfortable between sleep cycles.

16
Solving sleep-time blues

In this chapter you will find a broad selection of problem-solving tools to help you resolve some of your little one's sleep-time issues. After carefully reading this section, you can then decide the best course of action to help your family overcome any hurdles. Hopefully the information will empower you with a deeper understanding of your child's sleep to help you avoid running into any of the typical troubles with the little one you are now helping and any children you may be blessed to have in the years to come.

The reason I'm giving you these lists of dilemmas and resolutions is because I do not believe that every single child should be on a strict daily routine (see page 515). That is unbalanced. Only some of the more unsettled children or exhausted or stressed parents will need the guaranteed relief that comes from having a balanced routine. I also believe that a lot of sleep-time problems and unsettled behaviour can be predominantly solved through investigation and appropriate adjustments to routine and daytime communication to *remove the reason* for any unsettled behaviour, rather than adopt a crying management-only approach to the tears once they appear. This is about avoiding unsettled behaviour, rather than trying to manage it once it begins.

I always advocate a balanced approach first and foremost, so I firmly believe that armed with the right information there is a good proportion of parents whose children have relatively simple sleep miscalculations or basic association problems that can be corrected quickly with just a little sleep-time tweaking and a more consistent approach to managing your little one's daytimes and any teary or protesting wakeful times. While some sleep-time issues are fairly simple to work through, any changes should *always* be incorporated with basic and respectful communication strategies to ensure your child is able to cope with your requests to sleep, and the changes you will be making. No matter how simple your sleep-time miscalculations appear, your child will still need:

- a consistent settling, resettling and waking routine (see pages 609, 617 and 622)
- the opportunity to experience these new conditions first through role play (see page 631)
- to learn how to be awake in their cot and playing happily (see page 175)
- to be able to trust your movements and be comfortable with you leaving the room (see page 93)
- a *fair* amount of sleep—you should not expect them to take a quantity of sleep that is just too much for them (see page 534)
- good clear communication throughout the day so they are used to your guidance.

These basic, respectful tools and adjustments should provide tremendous improvements in your child's and your family's sleep in a short period of time. However, once a family has used this information to try to work through their sleep-time problems and feel they have not been able to strike the right balance for their little one within three days, then they should stop and adopt one of the balanced, pre-designed and well-refined PRM routines provided in the routines chapter (see page 515).

I don't think any particular problem-solving strategy suits everyone. That would not be balanced. A child and their family's needs vary from house to house and some families need a loose framework for their day while others need a precise routine in order for baby to be happy and content and the parents to recover from any problems they have been experiencing. I think you must carefully assess your child's and family's needs before planning a course of action. If a parent or a child is experiencing the following signs, whether mild or severe, the sleep problems should be quickly resolved with the correct PRM routine to reduce stress as quickly as possible:

- a child needs assistance to go to sleep and go back to sleep all the time
- a child is not sleeping adequately during the day or night or both
- it is taking hours of combined breastfeeding or bottle feeding each day to get a child to go to and stay asleep
- a parent with a six month old plus is feeling their life or they are out of control

- a parent with a six month old plus is feeling as though they or their child can't enjoy their day because baby / toddler is so unsettled
- a parent has completely lost their confidence, or can't even think about where to start to correct their child's sleep-time problem
- a child is showing signs of being particularly unsettled at sleep time or during their waking time, or both
- a mother has been diagnosed with postnatal depression
- you have previously been to sleep school and it has not resolved your sleep-time problem
- you have previously tried control crying or other routines or other 'sleep time-only' solutions and not achieved long-term sleep through your efforts
- you are too tired to even think about trying to work it all out.

If this is you and your child is over six months, don't try to work out what is wrong, simply go immediately to the corrective routine for your child's age group in the routines chapter (see page 541) and then, if it is appropriate or necessary, you can build up their sleep intake once harmony has been established in you house again.

When working through any sleep-time imbalance, it's important to read the 'Sleep—the basics' chapter (see page 398) first and foremost so you can understand sleep from your child's perspective and the many elements that make sleep achievable for your child. You should also take note of:

- assessing your baby's sleep requirement (see page 534)
- signs of sleep imbalance (see page 406)
- crying interpretation (see page 654)
- crying support and repair (see page 694).

What's normal and common

Before I discuss what could be causing your child's sleep-time problems, let's take a look at what's fairly normal so you can be certain you are not expecting too much of your little one. Compensation patterns of sleeping or eating will perpetuate poor sleeping or eating. For example, if they don't eat breakfast, but snack on biscuits, fruit juice and crackers throughout the morning, they will always refuse breakfast. If they sleep poorly at night so you allow them to sleep in until 9 a.m., they will continue to have unsettled nights. So the lists that follows gives you some ideas of the sorts of things that can affect your child's sleeping patterns and really only need an adjustment in order for you to find a solution.

When and how sleep times affect overall ability to sleep

Sleep intake (per 24 hours) is set per child, and it appears you can increase their need by providing more stimulation (not just physical). Day sleep affects night sleep and night sleep affects day sleep. Too much accumulated day sleep can cause prolonged wakings through the night. Too much accumulated night sleep can cause prolonged wakings through the day. A child can be tired but unable to sleep if you have used up their sleep requirement in one chunk, that is 13½ hours between 7 p.m. and 11 a.m.

Night sleeps should always be 11 to 12 hours long from six months of age onwards. Babies can get in the habit of sleeping shorter times at nights (nine to ten hours) but will then need more sleep through the day as a result. The nights can to be reset by their parents by adjusting (limiting) the amount of sleep offered during the day. If your baby has been very unsettled through the night and needed to be attended to often, their need to sleep in later in the morning or have a big morning sleep may suddenly disappear when you correct their sleep patterns and they begin to sleep solidly through the night. Don't expect them to need as much day sleep when they sleep solidly and peacefully all night as they needed when they were waking very often and exhausted after an unsettled night.

A child and their family's needs vary from house to house and some families need a loose framework for their day while others need a precise routine in order for baby to be happy and content and the parents to recover from any problems they have been experiencing.

Some babies don't sleep well for the rest of the day when they are given the opportunity to take a longer nap or too much sleep in the morning between 7 a.m. and 12 p.m., even if they have a moderate sleep requirement. A large morning sleep may encourage early morning wakings. A large morning nap may discourage a significant second sleep of the day. Some babies and toddlers over the age of 12 months need only one large sleep of two to two and a half hours a day, rather than two average sleeps of one to one and a half hours, to be able maintain good night sleep. A late afternoon nap (past 5 p.m.) will encourage late settling times at night.

An overtired child who is in a pattern of catnapping will show tired signs more frequently—often parents report their seven, nine, 12 or 18 month old can't stay awake for longer than one and a half hours in the morning. A five-minute power nap on the breast or in the car is equivalent to a 20- or 40-minute bridging sleep, even when you wake them after five minutes of sleep. This could keep your baby awake for an additional two to three hours.

Babies come to several brief windows of semi-consciousness during sleep sessions as they naturally progress from one sleep cycle to the next. These semi-conscious stages of sleep are called surface sleeps (see page 412) and they typically last for between three to eight minutes. If you intervene and assist a child to sleep within this eight-minute window, you can teach them to need your intervention on a subconscious level, or trigger a session of 'wild thrashing', when they appear incoherent and inconsolable for up to 20 to 40 minutes.

Babies / toddlers will generally only sleep half to three-quarters of their normal at-home, in-cot sleep when sleeping in the pram, in another sleeping environment or at daycare. Babies and toddler can also suddenly lose sleep and become unsettled when there is significant changes to their life that make it unpredictable and therefore difficult to trust that they can predict further changes. These include the arrival of a new baby, moving house, separation of parents, someone new moving in or temporary house guests—in some more sensitive babies even a brief visitor house guest can disrupt them, even if they love the visitor—holidays, grief in the family, mum / dad or both going away for work / holiday.

How and when you feed your baby affects their sleep

Calorie intake is set per child, and your child's calorie intake can be consumed either through the night or through the day. It appears that you can:

- increase a child's calorie intake need by providing less sleep
- decrease a child's calorie intake need by providing more sleep.

The need for night feeds beyond six months once solids have been introduced has two causes: hunger (not enough food, not enough protein, not enough solids through the day) and association (learnt pattern of dependence feeding / suckling to go to, or go back to sleep). Children also have growth spurts that impact on their need to sleep for up to five to ten days at a time. This pattern usually follows a sudden decrease in sleep need (and elevated hunger), followed closely by a sudden increase in sleep need (and decreased hunger).

Your baby may or may not need one or two night feeds until they are six months old. After that age, babies who are hungry during the night need to start solids. Once you introduce solids to their diet, they should be okay to sleep through the night. If you do not introduce meat into their diet by seven to eight months, they may go back to requiring one night feed between 11.30 p.m. and 1.30 a.m. until the protein source is introduced.

Often the only way to encourage the intake of solids during the day is via a reduction or elimination of milk feeds through the night.

If a baby or toddler needs multiple feeds during the night it may only be a sleep association, and it is likely to have nothing to do with hunger (though it will impact their ability to eat during the day). Associations are more likely to be the problem if your child is going to bed around 7 p.m. and wakes typically between 10 and 11 p.m., around 2 a.m. and again between 4 and 5 a.m., requiring your help to go back to sleep.

If babies over six months have a feed after 4 a.m. and then go back to sleep, this is considered the beginning of their day and the time will be stolen from their day sleep and food intake opportunities. Forty minutes before the day's usual first feed a baby's body may start to prepare for that feed. If you feed them at 6 a.m., they may start to stir from 5.20 the next morning. Then, if you feed them at 5.20, they are likely to stir at 4.40 a.m. the next day, and so on.

Hunger signs look extremely similar to tired signs after the age of six months (yawning, red eyes and brows, irritability). A baby can appear to need more sleep if their calorie and food fuel intake is too low, or a baby can appear to need less sleep if their calorie and food fuel intake is too high. Be aware that excessive milk feeds will create poor solid intake and affects sleep, and excessive solid intake will create poor milk intake and equally affect sleep. Excessive night calorie intake will detract from daytime calorie intake causing cycles of night wakings for food. Over snacking on whole foods (solids or milk are considered a whole food) in the morning can have the same impact on sleep that allowing excess sleep in the morning would have on sleep (encourage early wakings and a short second sleep of the day).

The associations your baby has affect their sleep

Babies can have a set of associations to go to sleep that require your intervention (patting, rocking, feeding, your bed, cuddles). Babies can have a set of associations to go to sleep that do not require your intervention (babbling, rolling, moving head from side to side, playing with ear, sucking thumb). Whatever you have taught them, they will use. Babies can put themselves to sleep with a set of associations that *do not* require your intervention, but may still have a set of associations that *do* involve your intervention to go 'back to' sleep.

Babies do not understand the concept of sleep or time lapsing. They only know feelings, and have associations attached to those feelings. If you stay in the room with a baby when they are going to sleep, and then sneak off, they will start to fight the feeling of tired as it becomes associated with you disappearing. This is what causes a tired baby to fight sleep. If they have had severe reflux as a little baby, and have associated the sensation of lying down with pain, then this is a 'learnt' loss of trust in the process of lying down beyond the actual experience of pain, and a new association and trust will need to be regained through your loving encouragement.

The environment in which your baby sleeps affects their sleep

Babies move around in their cot. Babies that are cold will often try to roll onto their tummy and tuck their arms under their bodies to stay warm. Babies will often lie against the sides of the cot for comfort.

Sudden night wakings

Babies often experience a phenomenon called a 'sudden partial waking', where they wake suddenly and scream a frightening cry. Many parents report this sounding like their baby has been bitten by a spider or an ant and they often strip their baby and the cot to check their bed. During sudden partial wakings babies can sit or stand up, and still be considered asleep, and can cry and still be asleep. This brief waking passes quickly if you do not rush in and disturb them in the first five minutes, which disorientates them. It is more common in overtired babies.

All sleep resolution strategies must be used in conjunction with a consistent settling, resettling and waking routine. And these routines should be role-played before being incorporated into your baby's sleep time.

Routine miscalculations—signs, symptoms and solutions

As you have read in 'Sleep—the basics' (see page 398), the origins of sleep problems in children between six and 24 months are extremely varied. Almost all the sleep solutions available in this country, however, seem to deal exclusively with sleeping and feeding times and sadly neglect the actual cognitive, emotional and communication needs of little ones. While some of these strategies may produce results, to truly help a baby learn how to sleep independently with less confusion or stress to them, and in a way that will actually empower them with the ability to understand, learn and feel confident with the skills needed to go to sleep and back to sleep, you must take 'all' their needs mentioned in sleep basics into consideration.

In 'Signs of sleep imbalance' (see page 406) and this following section we are going to explore some classic sleep-time imbalances that are predominantly timing based, which I call 'routine miscalculations'. You need to always lock in the night sleep first, then work in the two distinct portions of the daylight hours—the morning and the afternoon—to assess sleep-time imbalance.

As discussed, the morning sleep is between 7 a.m. and 12 p.m. and impacts on your child's:

- waking-up time between 6 and 7 a.m. the following day
- subsequent sleeping potential for the remainder of the current day
- ability to sleep solidly between 4 and 7 a.m. the following morning.

The afternoon sleeps between 2 and 7 p.m. impacts on your child's:

- settling time that night between 7 and 9 p.m.
- the length of time they will stay asleep during the previous sleep session that day (as in, is the big mid-afternoon sleep only a compensation for a poor mid-morning sleep and, if so, is this a regular pattern?)
- ability to sleep well that night between 7 p.m. and 12 a.m.

It is important that you balance day sleeps so your baby can make the most of the long 12 to 13 hours ahead of them in which they are predominantly awake. If you use up their entire day sleep requirement with one single large two-and-a-half-hour mid-morning sleep by 11 a.m., then your child has a huge eight- to nine-hour day ahead of them, when they could only possibly take a brief catnap if their sleep requirement is low. This will leave them exhausted and overtired by the end of the day, and create a situation where they are more likely to require intervention to go to sleep at night. This can be the beginning of a cycle of a learnt pattern of dependent associations to go to sleep, which will make it difficult for them to sleep through the night without crying out for your help. An overtired child has a higher potential of waking multiple times between 7 and 10 p.m.

What Sheyne says . . .

These suggestion, or any suggestion about caring for a child, should not become blanket one-size-fits-all rules. There is no one right way to raise a child! You should never make a disparaging statement to a parent whose baby is experiencing no sleep-time problems if they are putting their baby down for their usual 8 a.m. sleep, particularly along the lines that 'Sheyne Rowley says you shouldn't put a baby down before 8.45 a.m.' Sheyne Rowley would say, 'Lovely, your baby loves his sleep, how refreshing', not 'Oh well, even if that 8 a.m. sleep is working for your baby, I don't think he should take it because that's my rule'. That's not how this works. Balance is how these strategies work. Don't fix what isn't broken. Only when things aren't working out for baby should you then try to find a better way to do something.

While finding a solution to your child's possible routine miscalculation, we are going to break it down into two clear areas:

1. basic sleep miscalculations
2. solutions.

Shifted body clock (see also page 409)

When your baby / toddler goes down too late at night (say, between 9 and 10 p.m.) and wakes up late (between 8 and 9 a.m.), their day sleeps are shifted to later in the morning and later in the afternoon. This late shift perpetuates a cycle of late settlings at night. When your baby / toddler goes down too early at night (say at 5 to 6 p.m.), and wakes up early the next day (between 4 and 5 a.m.), their day sleeps are shifted forward to earlier in the morning and earlier in the afternoon. This early shift perpetuates a cycle of early settling at night time.

The late shift

Wake them at 6.30 a.m. and balance your day sleeps either by copying the timings of their existing sleep routine but just in a new time zone (e.g. if they always went back to sleep after three hours of being awake and have slept for one and a half hours, then wake them at 6.30 a.m. and don't put them down until 9.30 a.m., and allow only one and a half hours sleep), or as described in the PRM routines, after you have assessed their sleep requirement. This encourages daytime sleeps at appropriate times, and promotes a healthy 7 p.m. bedtime.

The early shift

Keep them up until the first appropriate nap time of the day, which is never before 8.45 a.m., from six months onwards and move forward with your day as per your routine. This encourages daytime sleeps at appropriate times, and promotes a healthy 7 p.m. bed time, which promotes a healthy 6 to 7 a.m. rising.

Stolen partial night time sleep cycles

This occurs when a portion of a child's 11 to 11½-hour night sleep between 7 p.m. and 6.30 a.m. is stolen and used as a day sleep. Here are three typical examples.

1. Morning sleep cycle thief—when your baby wakes at 5 a.m. and stays awake for two hours until 7 a.m. and then sleeps between 7 and 9 a.m.

This is two hours of sleep shifted from the night into later in the morning.

2. Afternoon sleep cycle thief—shifted sleep can happen in the evening when your child goes to sleep at 5 p.m. and sleeps until 7 p.m. then wakes and plays until 10 p.m. before settling for the night. This is two hours of sleep shifted from the night into earlier in the afternoon.

3. Evening sleep cycle thief—this happens in the middle of the night, when your baby wakes for two hours between 12 and 2 a.m., for example, and then goes back to sleep for the remainder of the night. The following day your child needs longer day sleeps to compensate for the broken sleep they experienced the night before. Excessive accumulated daytime sleep steals sleep cycles at night.

To correct any *significant* sleep imbalances with almost guaranteed immediate success a child should be put onto a defined age-appropriate PRM daily routine (see page 515). Here I will highlight the structure of the routine changes needed to correct such problems. In all instances, correctly assess your child's sleep requirement (see page 534) and then make adjustment to their sleep times.

Morning sleep cycle thief

For the morning sleep cycle thief, do not provide a 7 a.m. nap time even if they wake at 5 a.m. Put them down no earlier than 8.45 a.m. and do not allow them to oversleep at this time. Maintain this for a few days and their shifted night pattern will return to its rightful place of 4 to 6 a.m. rather than 7 to 9 a.m. In cases of a well-established pattern of early waking and early feeding it may be necessary for you to provide a temporary sleeping swaddle or firm tuck-in at all sleep times in addition to the settling routines to help them go back to sleep during their surface sleep as it prevents them from sitting or standing up, which makes resettling difficult for them. If they stir at that time but remain still, you have an 80 to 90 per cent higher chance of them self-resettling without the need for your intervention.

Afternoon sleep cycle thief

For the afternoon sleep cycle thief, do not provide any naps after 5 p.m. The length of their afternoon sleeps will need to be assessed carefully. A late afternoon bridging nap closer to 4 p.m. should be a brief sleep, rarely exceeding 20 to 30 minutes. This is a case where your child may be better suited to a different routine.

Evening sleep cycle thief

This advice is really relevant for people who have babies taking a couple of pretty decent-sized sleeps during the day. This is when parents say to me 'They are great sleepers through the day, but terrible at night'. If you have a night sleep thief on your hands, and the amount of sleep your child appears to need to take during the day is incorrect. They are oversleeping through the day. If your child were to sleep the solid 11 to 11½ hours required through the night cycle, you will find that your baby would no longer sleep as long during the day. You can't have your cake and eat it too.

Assess your child's sleep requirement for day sleeps carefully, and correct the amount they are allowed to take through the day and your nights will be quickly restored. When I suggest this, the response is usually 'I'm so tired, I need them to sleep that much through the day', or 'they are so tired, they need to sleep that much during the day'. Well, you need to bear in mind two important factors when it comes to adjusting day sleep consumption:

1. you and they won't be so exhausted when they are sleeping right through the night
2. the day sleeps are going to dwindle anyway eventually as they get older, but prolonged wakings at night will remain because you have nothing to work with through the days.

Correct your days now, and your peaceful nights will make the slightly more active days lots more fun and a lot less exhausting.

Catnapping (see page 409)

This is when your baby takes multiple 30 or 40 minute sleeps through the day and resettling is impossible. To correct this sleep imbalance with almost guaranteed immediate success, a child should be put onto a routine (see page 515). While the suggestions below may not be the complete resolution for some experiencing catnapping, I will highlight the general structure of the routine changes needed to correct such problems.

Keep them awake for longer periods between sleep. They are already overtired by now so the whole fear of them becoming overtired is null and void over the age of six months. You just need to take measures to correct the situation quickly and looking for tired signs or being concerned about them becoming overtired is no longer an appropriate way to deal with the problem. This is also a sign of a potential environmental imbalance (see page 424). Perhaps they are not warm enough—being cold will always wake a baby sooner. Perhaps you are inadvertently breaking their trust by changing the environment once they have gone to sleep—maybe holding or feeding them to sleep then putting them down. Perhaps they are in an overstimulating environment—too much light or noise, for instance. All of these will impact on a baby's ability to recover from catnapping.

Upside down days (see page 410)

This is when your baby takes two or three excessively long sleeps through the day of between three and five hours in length. This results in only brief sleep periods at night, or full wakefulness through the night. You need to wake your baby up from a daytime sleep after an appropriate amount of time. Yes, gasp, wake a sleeping baby. To do this your little one will have to make a quick transition and you will need the assistance of routine (see page 515). Your baby will most certainly be 'jetlagged' as you reset their body clock, but it will only last for one to three days and then they will only experience the same level of tiredness as any baby in the first three days of establishing a new pattern to their circadian rhythm.

High caloric / fluid intake at night

This is where your child consumes more calories (via milk or food) or fluids through the night, than they do during the day. Always use a routine (see page 515) to help fix this problem. On the day of commencing your PRM, I always suggest the baby has no food at all from 2 a.m. on the morning you are due to start until the first designated feed time of 7 a.m. You then get a head start on feeding for the next two days. Stick to the routine for your feeding and sleeping windows 100 per cent through the day and your baby's body's need for food will automatically shift to the daytime.

There is no time like the present when their circadian rhythm is imbalanced. You cannot increase daily food intake without first decreasing, or eliminating, night food intake. You cannot hope for different results when you continue to do the same thing. Even if their calorie intake is low in the first day, maintain your evening cycle of resettling without offering food and your little one's calorie intake imbalance will correct by the next day. Do ensure you offer more food at each meal than you would normally offer, because they need to eat more through the day to stop their hunger patterns from continuing through the night.

You cannot increase daily fluid intake without first decreasing, then eliminating, night fluid intake. Again, no fluid from 2 a.m. on the morning your new routine starts. Introduce lots of opportunities to drink water through the day (see page 225). And remember, milk is a whole food, not just a drink, so assess your baby's needs correctly.

False sleep

If your child has a milk feed every morning at 5 a.m., sleeps till 6.30 / 7 a.m., and then sleeps well throughout the day, your ability to maintain this level of sleep without the milk feed at 5 a.m. is reduced. This early morning sleep is a false sleep because, without the milk, their little body would rarely be able to naturally take this sleep. And this sleep will not count in their general daily sleep quota. For example, if your baby slept from 7 p.m. to 5 a.m. and you had to feed your child to achieve a one hour sleep to 6.30 / 7 a.m., and then you added that one-hour to a second day sleep of two hours, their sleep requirement averaged over seven days of consistent sleep would be 14½ to 15 hours a day. If you then corrected their sleep patterns so they no longer needed a 5 a.m. milk feed to sleep till 6.30 / 7 a.m., their average daily sleep intake may actually drop down a little as the extra sleep they used to achieve between 5 and 6.30 was not a naturally occurring sleep needed in their sleep requirement.

Progressive decline in sleep

This is when your child peaks in sleep requirement one day, sleeping between 16 and 17 hours, then suddenly drop down to only 11 hours of sleep intake the next day. Gradually over a couple of days, your child tries to recover from the very low sleep intake by increasing their intake to between 13 and 14 hours one day, then 14 and 15 the next day before peaking again at that glorious 'I think all our sleep problems have suddenly corrected themselves' 16 to 17 hours sleep again. Sadly, your hopes are dashed when the next day their sleep consumption plummets to a miserable 11 hours again.

This progressive decline in sleep is a clear sign of an imbalance, and it can manifest in many ways. Sometimes your baby will have one good day of 15 hours then one poor day of 13 hours, before going back to 15 hours one day and 13 hours the next. I call that the yo-yo routine. Other times they will sleep a consistently higher amount each day for a four-day window, then a consistently lower amount each day for a four-day window (see box on page 537). By allowing your baby to take however much sleep they like the day after a very poor sleep, you perpetuate a cycle of poor sleep, rather than balance it.

Keep a sleep diary (see page 534) for seven days and calculate their daily intake each day, excluding any prolonged wakings of 20 minutes or more they experience through the day or night sleeps. Add the seven-day totals up, and divide that total by seven to work out your baby's average 24-hour sleep requirement. You will then need to put your child on a routine (see page 515) and fix in their true 24-hour sleep requirement to that routine.

Taking the time to keep a diary may feel frustrating, but if you would like to do this correctly, you really need to know your baby's true intake rather than just an assumption or, worse, rely on wishful thinking. Not every baby is the same. I always say to parents, 'You have been without sleep for this long, you may as well invest a full week or two into developing a resolution that is permanent so it no longer has to consume another moment of your child's or your energy'.

Diversity in sleep requirement

The parents of seven-month-old Mia came to me for assistance. Mia would wake more than ten times a night and would sleep only in her mother's arms during the day. Despite this, Mia's average sleep requirement, calculated through a sleep diary done over a seven-day period, was 15 hours, 45 minutes. I placed Mia on a high sleep requirement routine, but put an emphasis on a PRM that concentrated on communication, environmental factors—such as a need to be wrapped—and routines for predictable settling, resettling and waking.

Through this management, Mia's sleep in her cot was quickly restored and she could self-settle, self-resettle, and was content to be in her cot awake. It took Mia just three days to learn how to go to sleep and stay asleep peacefully at all times. After that her parents were very careful and consistent for three full weeks for Mia to feel safe in her new routine because her sleep disruption triggers were difficult to work through. Mia had to learn how to be in her cot awake and put herself to sleep, and her parents had to learn *not* to rescue her from that normal and safe environment.

Classic sleep-time blues—signs, symptoms and solutions

This section is full of typical sleep-time problems in general and designed to help you assess your own stumbling blocks so you can decide on the best way to help your precious baby / toddler learn how to sleep better. Some of these questions will be of interest to you, some won't as they are not applicable to your situation, but I hope they are all enlightening in that they make you think a little more about the way you and your child communicate and your relationship grows.

Q1   My baby wakes at 5 a.m., so how do I get them to sleep longer?
Possible causes:
- Too early or too long a morning nap time the day before, for example before 8.45 a.m. for a six to 12 month old with low sleep requirement,

or before 9.30 or 10.00 a.m. for a 12 month old plus with average to high sleep requirement.
- The first feed of the day is too early or too big.
- They went to bed too early the night before, such as 6 p.m.
- Environmental reasons—daylight, birds, traffic, other household members disturbing them.
- Learnt hunger pattern—false sleep.

To fix:
- When you base a six- to 12-month-old baby's first sleep of the day on their waking time, you can easily perpetuate an early morning waking every day by putting them down too early the evening before to compensate. The only way to correct this pattern is to have a 'no-sleep before 8.45 a.m.' policy for a LSR baby 6 to 12 months old, or a 'no-sleep before 12 p.m.' policy for a LSR baby 12 months plus. Equally, have a 'no-sleep before 9 / 9.30 a.m.' policy for a HSR baby six to 12 months, or a 'no-sleep before 10 / 10.30 a.m.' policy for a baby 12 months plus.
- If your little one wakes very early, and is then allowed to have a great big sleep because they are tired from their early waking, their body will wake early every morning because it is now programmed to wake early and have a big mid-morning nap instead of sleeping in to 6 to 7 a.m. and having an appropriate sleep based on that good waking time mid morning. The only way to balance this is to work out their sleep requirement (see page 534) and taper your morning sleep down to an appropriate length while still maintaining your 'no sleep before _____' policy, depending on your child's sleep needs.
- The time of the first feed of the day is an important consideration. In all the years I have been working with babies, one of the most noticeable triggers for their morning waking time is the first feed time registered by their body's biological clock. If you usually feed your baby their first milk feed of the day at 7 a.m., their body will actually anticipate that feed and start to prepare for it 40 minutes before they are due to have it. An early milk feed at 6 a.m., for instance, may promote stirring and possibly even a bowel movement by 5.20 a.m. If you then feed them at 5.20, you may well see your little one become unsettled at 4.40 the next morning. So stick to a 'no feeds before 7 a.m.' policy for six month olds plus as much as possible. It's also important to note that excessive food can often replace good sleep as a form of sustainable energy, so providing extra feeds or snacks because they are tired and grouchy will only continue to promote wakefulness.

- Put your baby to bed at 7 p.m. Don't put them down earlier, for obvious reasons, or later. Later will cause shorter night sleep patterns, promoting a long day (for example, ten-hour nights mean 14-hour days) and this makes a baby or toddler overtired and promotes early morning wakings.
- If the problem is noise, light or someone disturbing them, then eliminate light by blacking out the room (see page 428) until the sleep repairs itself, close the door and do not disturb them by turning on lights or rattling around if you get up early, and consider getting a white noise machine if you would like to not worry about what noise you or others in the house are making.
- If it is none of the above environmental reasons (as in, it's still dark and quiet) then check if the room is too cold. Your child should be wearing appropriate clothing (see page 438). Try to regulate the room temperature before you try to change the amount of layers a sleeping baby is wearing.
- Re-read the section about false sleep (see page 483).
- If you have worked through the above points and you are still experiencing problems, then your baby is likely to be a low sleep requirement baby and you may need to go onto a routine (see page 534) to resolve the sleep problems.

Q2   My baby has 30- or 40-minute catnaps several times throughout the day. Can I do something to fix this?
Possible causes:
- Routine miscalculation.
- Being put down too early in the morning if they are six to 12 months old.
- Napping too often if in the six to 24 months plus age range.
- Milk feeds too close together.
- The 5 a.m. feed is creating false sleep.
- Too long a night sleep pattern because you are compensating for their frequent wakings—for instance 6 p.m. to bed, then five to ten wakings during the night, making them and you tired and causing them to wake naturally at 8.30 a.m.
- Dependent associations.
- Environment.
To fix:
- Ensure they are ready for a good sleep when you put them down. By putting a catnapper down when they show tired signs, they will always only take catnaps because they will constantly feel tired sooner because

their naps are too short. You need to push past this to find an appropriate length of time to keep them awake *before* you put them down to sleep, which will encourage better sleep. This is where looking for tired signs only as a way of resolving sleep problems can be ineffective from six months of age.

- Place them on a modified routine (LSR or ASR) if over 12 months old and it will correct the problem immediately and encourage up to two and a half hours sleep through the day and 11 to 11½ hours at night.
- Correctly assess your child's sleep requirement (see page 534). By assessing your child's true sleep needs correctly you encourage a catnapper to double the length of their day sleep with a simple routine adjustment. They may only need one sleep a day or no nap before 8.45 or 9.30 a.m., depending on sleep requirement, or no nap before 12 p.m. if they are 12 months plus.
- Ensure the night sleeps are no longer than 11 to 11½ hours long until you resolve the sleep disruption. To allow a night sleep session to go for longer than this could be eating into your baby's valuable day sleep allocation.
- Ensure they are not cold (see page 434) or that other environmental conditions are causing problems.
- Implement a full repair PRM Routine 1.

Q3   How can I stop my baby from waking early on her second sleep of the day (mid afternoon), after having just one big sleep in the morning, or not taking another sleep all day or, when she does, it is short? She is grumpy and ready for bed by 5 p.m.
Possible cause:
A classic symptom of a low sleep requirement child.
To fix:
You will need to put her on a routine to suit her sleep requirement and age group (see page 534).

Q4   My baby / toddler barely even naps or doesn't take any sleep all day but seems to be really happy and full of energy. Is it possible that he doesn't need sleep?
Possible causes:
- Even if your baby is really happy and full of energy, he will most likely be overtired and running on excessive adrenalin and hormones. Sometimes overtired, wired little pocket rockets get labelled as hyperactive, or incorrectly tagged as ADD or ADHD. Sadly, while they appear really energetic and super happy, these bsbies are highly strung, overstimulated,

have trouble sitting still and taking information in, or concentrating. They are happy but can have a short fuse and become suddenly unsettled late afternoon, only to pep right up to the point of frenetic after dinner. This can manifest in hysterical laughter at even the most simple things, and while it is amazingly beautiful to see a little person so full of beans and energy, it's not balanced if there are no shades of tired or placid moments to their day. You don't want to stop them, wouldn't want to, and, in most cases, couldn't stop that buzzy, super-energetic element of their little nature, but you do need to find harmony and some middle ground for their health and wellbeing.

- Excessive food intake to compensate for poor sleep can promote no sleep as well.
- Vacant staring episodes (glassy or glazed over eyes) or five-minute power dozes in the car, pram or during a breastfeed could prevent an extremely overtired pocket rocket from taking any sleep during the day.

To fix:

- Low sleep requirement routine based on appropriate age group suggestions (see page 515). There is no need to even assess their sleep requirement if your child is this overtired. Just concentrate on getting them sleeping better. The low sleep requirement routine offers opportunities to take great sleep (14 hours plus in a 24-hour day), and can increase their sleep intake by as much as five hours a day.
- Full recovery program (see page 541) is very important in these cases.
- You will need to work very hard on communication and positioning (see page 286) and the wait game (see page 74) through the day first to help them stop and accept the feeling of tired in an appropriate way.

Q5   What do I do? I can't resettle my baby when they wake up after a short sleep?

Possible causes:

- If they are ultimately only sleeping 30 to 40 minutes before you experience failed attempts at resettling, then please see question 2.
- You may be asking them to take a long sleep and their body simply doesn't need it because of too short a period between sleeps or they have a low sleep requirement (see page 534).
- If an overtired baby is overstimulated during a natural peak in a sleep cycles (every 20, 30 or 40 minutes) they can come to a full waking and be physically unable to resettle. A classic example would be excess light hitting the back of the retina, halting their melatonin production. This will cause them to wake up and they will find it extremely difficult to resettle.

- Excessive movement startling them to a full waking, or standing / sitting in a baby under 12 months before they are even awake, and subsequently being unable to lie themselves down without your intervention, may all make resettling next to impossible.
- Some babies over 12 months still need two to two and a half hours sleep a day, but need it in one large sleep cycle rather than two shorter sleeps. These are typically LSR and ASR babies.
- You may have established a set of confusing environment-based getting up routines. Sometimes your baby gets picked up straight away when you come in, sometimes they have to cry before you pick them up, and sometimes they have to go back to sleep. This ultimately encourages crying and confusion upon their waking because they can't predict you and this can trigger early wakings and difficult resettling efforts.
- You may not have established the ability to guide your little one respectfully as yet, making asking them to lie down and try to go to sleep for you a very difficult task. Please see communication (page 24).

To fix:
- Catnappers generally require a full PRM Routine 1 (see page 534).
- For confusing messages, it's important to establish a language-based set of routines around sleep time events such as settling, resettling and waking routines (see page 605) plus playtime in the cot (see page 175) and the up cue (see page 76) before you pick them up, so when you don't pick them up, it does not seem unusual.
- Manage the transition in sleep cycles (see page 412) and interpret their crying (see page 654) correctly.

Q6 My baby wakes up at 8 p.m. every night and is happily awake until 10, then goes down for the night. How can I get him to sleep through this time?
Possible causes / fixes:
- If six to 12 months old, their late afternoon sleep pattern is excessive or too late. No napping past 4 p.m. for those babies on two larger sleeps per day, not past 5 p.m. for those LSR babies on bridging sleeps (please see page 541 for age variations).
- Too much day sleep for a six-month-old, high sleep requirement baby still taking a third brief late afternoon doze in addition to their two larger daytime sleeps. This may be a sign that the late afternoon nap is no longer appropriate for them.
- If 12 to 24 months old, any sleep after 4 p.m. for those children taking two, one- to one-and-a-half-hour sleeps a day or any sleep taken after 2.30 p.m. for those taking a single larger two- to two-and-a-half-hour sleep.

- It could be a shifted night pattern (see page 479).
- Feed snoozing? Don't allow them to doze on any feeds through the day.

Q7   My baby wakes several times during the night but only needs me to attend quickly (often only a minute or less) to go back to sleep. What can I do to change this pattern?
Possible causes:
- Sleep association (see page 399).
- Subconscious (surface sleep wakings—see page 412).
- They may be cold (see page 434).
- Their need to feel secure and held when under 12 months of age is not being met.
- Lost dummy.

To fix:
- Make sure they are warm enough and feel secure if they are under 12 months, particularly if they are asking to be held to go back to sleep. They may need to be wrapped (see page 439) while you establish a new self-resettling association with going to sleep, and staying asleep.
- Establish new settling, resettling and waking cues (see page 605) through role play (see page 631) and communication, and manage environmental factors for the transition (see page 424).
- If you are feeding briefly, then you need to assess meal-time intake during the day by looking at their meal-time windows and food intake to remove the night feeds.
- Be sure to look closely at and correct your settling, resettling and waking routines before you attempt any form of change.
- Manage any crying confidently and remain reassuring, while being 100 per cent consistent with the definitions you give the cues (see page 44).
- Stop using the dummy (see page 461) or teach them the dummy pot game (see page 467).

Q8   My baby will sleep through the night and have two sleeps (up to one and a half to two hours each) during the day, but I then need to resettle him multiple times via patting, rocking or dummies during these sleeps. How can I correct this?
Possible causes:
- Associations making settling and resettling impossible without you.
- Possible loss of trust because the sleep environment changes once he goes to sleep, so you put him to sleep, and then he requires this to go back to sleep. Babies naturally become partially aware of their environment multiple times each sleep session (typically at the 20-, 30- or 40-minute

mark). If you don't plan on being there when he becomes partially aware of his sleep environment, then you should not be there when he first goes to sleep. This is being honest, and it is being careful to not damage the delicate balance of trust a baby needs to be able to go to sleep, and stay asleep without stress every time.

To fix:

- For multiple wakings you will need a full routine management for a high sleep requirement child appropriate for their age group (see page 569).
- Otherwise, correct this problem with balanced parent-governed lines of communication (see page 29) during the day. Incorporate sleep-time routines like settling, resettling and waking cues (see page 605). Role play (see page 633) to develop your baby's trust in the process, and assess possible environmental conditions (see page 424), particularly if he is asking to be held to go to or back to sleep. He may be cold or needs the extra comfort of a firm wrap to emulate a cuddle while he learns how to sleep though the surface sleeps he will naturally cycle through. Be sure to adhere to the normal surface sleep pause (see page 674) before attending to any crying so you don't startle him, wake him or trigger episodes of 'thrashing'.
- Manage the transition for a couple of day (please see 694).

Q9 My baby will sleep through the night and take two day sleeps (up to one and a half to two hours each), but I need to resettle him multiple times through these day sleeps via feeding. What do I do?

Possible causes:

- His surface sleep associations, generally environmental needs, are not being catered for, including the need to feel held.
- Possible loss of trust because the sleep environment changes once he goes to sleep, so you put him to sleep, and then he requires this to go back to sleep. Babies naturally wake multiple times through the night.
- Possible false sleep (see page 483) as the result of breastfeeds, causing routine miscalculation. This means that he is only staying asleep thanks to the sedating effect of the hormones during breastfeeding.

To fix:

- Assess daily sleep requirement (see page 534).
- Full routine management (see page 541).

Q10 Could it be possible that my baby only needs two 30 minutes sleep all day?

Possible causes:

Not at all possible. Never in my entire career have I not been able to help a baby who appears to sleep next to nothing each day to learn how to sleep effectively. The smallest amount of daytime sleep I have seen a child from the six- to 24-month age bracket take after being put on a PRM and having 11 to 11½ hours night sleep is between one and a half to two hours through the day. The cause of low sleep here is a combination of unassessed sleep requirement, overtired body responses and a need to refine environment, routines and communication strategies a little.

To fix:

Full repair PRM routine 1 will have your little one sleeping right through the night, and up to two to three hours during the day in as little as one to three days, even if they have never previously been able to sleep. In this latter case, when you have tried many other sleep training strategies or tried other routines and your baby is just wide awake and wired all day after one 30-minute sleep during the day, then you should bypass the sleep requirement section of this book and lock them straight into the low sleep requirement routine suggestion for your child's age group (see page 541). It will change your life.

Q11 My baby will only sleep lying on me. What do I do to get her to sleep in her cot?

Possible causes:

This is a combination of a few key areas:

- associations—she has learnt that she can't go to sleep without you there
- trust—she is wanting to make sure you don't disappear on her which makes her very unsettled if you try to move her
- positioning—learning to sleep on her tummy, and upright on your body can make lying on her back, reclined, a difficult task
- communication—allowing your child to govern sleep-time suggestions, even when she is not in a healthy sleeping routine for your whole family is not the right balance of communication. As parents, there are times when you will need to be confident and help them find a better way
- independence—not feeling comfortable to be on her own, or in her own space, or able to trust that your absences are not so unpredictable in length and frequency makes it very hard for a child to feel comfortable about her parents being out of her sight. So she can experience just being in her own space or feeling confident enough to explore her world around her, let her alone to be able to go to sleep on her own.

To fix:

This is a significant sleep situation to resolve if you want to achieve consistent, stress-free sleep for your little one, and regain a healthy balance in your life. There is nothing healthy about an adult being stationary for the amount of hours a baby needs to sleep for in a 24-hour day. There is nothing healthy about neglecting your dietary and fitness needs. There is nothing healthy about neglecting your marriage. If you are in this situation, then whatever school of parenting that appealed to you to get you in this situation is not appropriate for your baby or your needs. This is not a sustainable situation. You will need to embark on a PRM (see page 515), paying very close attention to:

- the environmental needs of your child—I strongly recommend wrapping (see page 439) any child under 12 months of age until they are comfortable with and used to their new sleeping environment as this acts as a surrogate cuddle and helps them transition off you with less stress
- adopting a confident parent-directed daily routine to take the burden of running your family off your child. It's important you learn about your child and understand their motivation for occasional crying. If you have adopted the approach of not letting them cry with the loving intention of sparing them any upset then, while I admire your intentions, you have a mighty job on your hands. You are essentially stopping your little one from feeling anything but happy. This is not always possible or healthy. It's important to introduce your little one to a normal range of daily events and guide them through it with patience and compassion so that when it comes time for them to step out into the big wide world without you there to make everything better, they know how to cope. Mummy and daddy have told them it is okay, and normal, to feel a little uncomfortable with change, but trust that it always gets better in time, or to feel a little grumpy when they are tired is normal, and it can be resolved with some quiet relaxing, some healthy food, or a good-old fashion snuggle in their bed and a big sleep.

Q12   My partner can settle my baby but I cannot. Why and how can I help my baby be comfortable with both of us?
Possible causes:
When it comes to babies I find this tends to be because of three things:

- mum does not attempt to settle without feeding them, making it hard for dad to settle them
- dads naturally hold their little one a little more firmly either in their arms or in the cot, which stops fussing and enables baby to drift off quickly. This then becomes a comforter for baby, and a clear set of no negotiation cues to settle, and they happily accept this as a normal

settling routine and go to sleep quickly. I often find that once a dad realises that baby will settle quickly when held firmly, they tend to be a little more patient and follow through until baby is asleep. This means baby knows that daddy means business and that they should sleep and nothing else. When daddy gets confident, then so does baby and, suddenly, going to sleep for their dad is associated with good feelings of reassurance and confidence

• one parent unknowingly undermines the other's attempts because they know baby can go to sleep quicker for them. This is often accidentally done by the primary carer (the person who stays home with them through the day), traditionally mum. It's never intentional but the message it sends to baby undermines the other parent's ability to settle them and the primary carer becomes the only one who can do it. Some fathers then don't attempt to settle baby to sleep, assuming that unless the baby is fed, they will be unsuccessful.

To fix:
• Environmental comforters (see page 461).
• Positioning (see page 286).
• Communication (see page 24).
• Trust (see page 77).
• Independence (see page 16).
• Settling, resettling and waking routines (see page 605).

All these equal positive routine management. As one parent may have an inconsistent style of settling to the other parent, you will need to establish full settling, resettling and waking routines, as well as look at environmental comforters like wrapping an under-12 month old, and tucking them in firmly. Then you will need to role play. When you need to incorporate this many changes, it is easier to just follow the positive routine management plan for your child's sleep requirement (see page 534).

Q13 My baby will not go to sleep in the morning at all. What do I do?
Possible causes:
• Too long a night sleep session.
• Shifted body clock / false sleep after early a.m. feed.
• No longer needing a morning sleep once over 12 months of age.
To fix:
• I find this to be extremely rare in a baby under 12 months if they are waking at a reasonable time, like 6 to 6.30 a.m. If you are experiencing significant sleep problems in the morning under the age of 12 months

of age, I suggest positive routine management (see page 515) with an emphasis on eliminating environmental factors that could be making it difficult for your little one to sleep, such as light, noise and movement (see page 424).

- If they are over 12 months of age, take a peek at my 12 months plus LSR routine and you may find that your clever little one year old is doing what is naturally right for her body's needs. You can still achieve a HSR sleep routine of two sleeps per day but each sleep is generally around one to one and a half hours long, a format that clearly suits your little one's needs. If you have tried to encourage sleep in the morning and they are just not interested, then shift them straight into the 12 months plus LSR routine.

Q14 My baby will only sleep in the car, pram, or in a sling or hammock. How do I get them to sleep in the cot?
Possible causes:
- Associations with perpetual motion for sleep.
- Positioning.

To fix:
- Address positioning issues (see page 286).
- Wrap and use SafeT Sleep for an under-12 month old to emulate the security of the cot environment for each of these mobile sleep environments.
- Use a sleeping bag and tuck-in for an over 12 month old.

Q15 My baby sleeps well during the day, but not at night. What do I do?
Possible cause:
This is a classic low-sleep-requirement symptom called sleep debt. It is a common phenomenon with lower sleep requirement babies. Your little one sleeps well during the day (in the same routine as a higher sleep requirement baby does with two large sleeps) *only* because they are sleeping poorly at night. Once a child starts to sleep effectively through the night, they can no longer sustain the longer sleeps during the day. Your baby is far better suited to either the low sleep requirement routine or modified HSR routine with ASR sleep-time suggestions.

To fix:
Correctly assess your child's sleep requirement (see page 534) based on their age and implement an appropriate daytime routine to suit their daytime sleep needs. Keep in mind that they should have a full 11 to 11½ hours of sleep through the night.

Q16 My baby sleeps well at night, but not during the day. Can this be fixed?

Possible causes:

- Classic low sleep requirement symptom.
- Possibly different settling routine used for day sleep.
- The sleeping environment is too stimulating.

To fix:

- Assess your child's daily sleep requirement and choose an appropriate routine. I generally find that when day sleeps are extremely low (40 minutes or less all day) the child almost always has a low or average sleep requirement and responds extremely quickly to the new daily plan.
- A PRM will ensure you have consistent day and night routines so your baby is able to sleep effectively at all sleep times.
- You will need to carefully assess your child's sleep environment to consider what short-term aids you can put in place or overstimulating conditions (light, noise, movement) you can temporarily remove to help make the learning process much faster. Once their sleep is resolved, you can gradually eliminate the aids, and re-introduce the usual conditions of light and noise.

Q17 My baby goes to sleep in his cot but always ends up in our bed. I'd like to get her to sleep in her bed all night. Can you help?

Possible causes:

- This is a resettling association. It often happens when your child has been taught on a subconscious level during their brief surface sleep that to go back to sleep they need an entirely different set of conditions to the ones they have for settling.
- They may be cold (see page 434).

To fix:

- You will need to carefully re-establish consistent settling, resettling and waking routines (see page 605), and you will need to role play these (see page 631).
- You will need to learn how to manage the surface sleep phase of sleep (see page 674).
- You will need to learn how to manage their crying (see page 654) carefully.
- Assess their room temperature (see page 434).

Because of all these possibilities, I suggest you establish an appropriate routine to ensure there is no other reason for the night waking.

Q18 We tried to get our little boy to sleep in our bed, but he just doesn't sleep. How can I achieve this?

Possible cause:

It either doesn't suit him or you need to work on your communication skills and, in particular, your positioning requests through the day. This means you need to set fairly clear boundaries around the task of going to sleep in your bed.

To fix:

If it is clear that sleep is a significant problem for your baby and you to achieve then you may need to consider another method. Alternatively, work on your ability to position him through the day for nappy changing, sitting and reading stories and lying down for milk feeds, etc. Establish your settling, resettling and waking routines and set boundaries in your bed much like you would for the cot. For example, once you start your settling routine he cannot sit up or stand up, and you should not talk to him other than to say your cues. Once your settling routine is complete, set boundaries around his positioning and what he is allowed to do, that is, he can roll only and cannot poke you, etc. Develop cues for each boundary—'no touch eyes', etc. or 'lie down'—and define those statements. If he cries, pause and lie still with your eyes closed and periodically repeat your resettling cues. Repeat management for resettling routine and implement a waking routine and playtime in the bed when he is allowed to sit up after your waking cue, 'Good sleep, time to sit up'.

It is important to remember that your choice of sleeping arrangement has to suit your baby's needs as much as yours. If he is trying to sleep but whimpers or excessively wrestles through the night, it may be very possible that it's not comfortable or peaceful situation for him to try and sleep between two grown-ups that move a lot and make noise. In this case, I suggest you adopt a settling routine for his cot routine and move on. Co-sleeping definitely does not suit every baby, even if it's what you want.

Q19 My baby sleeps in their cot at night, but will only sleep in my arms during the day. So how can I get her to not do this?

Possible causes:

- A daytime settling association. This occurs often when a child has been taught that during the daylight hours they need an entirely different set of condition to the ones they have for settling after bath at night.
- They may be overtired, causing them to become easily overstimulated by light and noise through the day. If they are unsettled about sleeping in their cot, the change of conditions will cause them to open their

eyes, which will immediately trigger a chemical reaction in their brain that may halt the hormones responsible to sleep.

To fix:

- Assess their sleep requirement and adopt an appropriate routine to suit their needs.
- You will need to carefully re-establish consistent settling, resettling and waking routines, and you will need to role play them. You will need to learn how to manage the surface sleep part of their sleep cycle. You will need to learn how to manage their crying carefully while they learn to self-settle (see pages 694 and 609).
- Eliminate light in their room during the day until you have repaired the sleep. Once they are sleeping, and they are no longer overtired, reintroduce light back into their daytime home sleep scenario slowly (see page 434).

Q20 My baby will only sleep in their pram during the day. I'd like to get him to sleep in his cot. How can I do this?

Possible causes:

The same causes and fixes as per question 19 apply here. Remember, if you cannot guide them successfully through the day with events like changing their nappy, feeding them or asking them to sit still on your lap or in the pram, then I strongly suggest you read through the communication sections to learn about the three lines of communication (see page 29).

Q21 My baby has reflux. Can this affect her sleeping?

It most certainly does make a difference if not treated, or the dose of medication prescribed by the doctor has not alleviated the symptoms within three weeks of starting treatment. In this case, you will need to go back to the doctor. When a baby lies down, stomach acid tracks back up their oesophagus and irritates the tissue. When this happens repeatedly the tissues of the oesophagus becomes inflamed and lying down becomes a painful ordeal. This is problematic on two levels. It obviously makes going to sleep very difficult for the baby because they are experiencing pain. And as children rely heavily on associations with the events surrounding going to bed, a child may learn to fear lying down, anticipating the pain.

To fix:

This should be dealt with in two ways:

1. make sure their symptoms are relieved by receiving proper medical advice from your doctor or paediatrician

2. once the discomfort has been dealt with, be sure to move your baby past the learnt pattern of fear of lying down by resolving the sleep-time issues with a full positive routine management (see page 515).

They will soon learn that going to sleep is no longer painful, but you will need to be patient and consistent to make this learning window as fast as possible. Some parents might wish to not expose their child to a situation again because their baby is so fretful about it, but I do not agree with leaving a child burdened with a fear that is no longer something they should be concerned about. I would prefer to show them that they are okay now, and that mummy and daddy have helped them feel better so sleep time does not have to remain something that evoke unpleasant feeling unnecessarily.

Q22 My baby / toddler seems to be cutting teeth. Could this be impacting their sleep?

Absolutely. It could be impacting on their ability to go to sleep, or to stay asleep. Regardless of what anyone tells you, teething is clearly uncomfortable and in some cases clearly distressing for babies. When they are in a good routine, the bulk of their growing should occur while they sleep, but when they having higgledy-piggledy days, where sleep is difficult, then teething is most definitely going to impact on their entire day.

To fix:

If you know your baby is suffering from very sore or uncomfortable teeth, then it's important to offer eight-hour pain relief if possible close to sleep times rather than when they are awake. Your little one's ability to cope with the discomfort will be higher when they are awake and with you, than when they are tired and on their own during sleep time. I reserve (whenever possible) the use of these pain relievers to around 30 minutes before their bedtime. Maintain pain relief through the night as discomfort windows are often between 11.30 p.m. and 3.30 a.m.

For those children on a PRM, it is extremely common for any typical sleep-time teething symptoms to either appear for the first time or reappear between 11.30 p.m. and 1.30 a.m (see page 556). In this case, offer another dose of medication (as per manufacturer's instructions) and then follow through with your crying management (see pages 694 and 734) for appropriate ways to help your child through the night when they are not feeling well or experiencing discomfort.

Q23 My baby needs to burp before they go to sleep. How can I help them and could this be causing problems?

I hear about this occasionally, but rarely when a baby is over six months, unless your child suffers severe reflux. I have dealt with thousands and thousands of extremely unsettled babies and one of the first things a parent tells me about is their infant's need to either burp or break wind before they can settle off to sleep. When a baby cries and fusses because they are protesting or upset they have a tendency to gulp air and this makes their tummy rumble and move about. When you pick them up, air naturally rises and shifts and they have a tendency to burp and break wind. They often settle because they were asking to be picked up at this time and you have obliged, so the cycle of winding starts at sleep time. This in itself becomes a routine or an association of sorts that is governed by your baby.

To fix:

If picking them up is what makes them happy, why not just do it? The answer to that is simple: because it is actually not making them happy! They are having to cry when you first put them down and, on some occasions, at multiple times during the night every single time they go to bed. Look at assessing true need versus their short-term demand (see page 91), and don't be so frightened of a little transitional window as this will never free them of this disruptive sleep routine. Why not teach them a whole new enjoyable settling routine (see page 609) that doesn't involve this cycle of crying, being picked up, and burping. Why not teach them how to fall asleep peacefully. That is what they would really like. Obviously though, they do not have the life experience to know this, and that is why adopting a confident parenting approach, where you are able to assess their true needs, is a balanced system. When you establish your new routine management, do not perpetuate the cycle of picking up and winding your baby to sleep, or this will need to be done over and over again through the night.

Q24 My baby snuffles and vocalises a lot during the night, but doesn't really cry. Can I do something to help them sleep more soundly?

Yes, you can leave them be, and turn down your monitor. Most of the time babies are oblivious to their own snuffling and movement and, even if they were aware of it, they are clearly not bothered by it. Infrared imagining of babies sleeping through the night clearly shows them cycling through different stages of sleep and, on some occasions, waking, happily snuffling and squirming around their cot for up to 40 minutes, then drifting back off to sleep.

To fix:
- The best thing you can do for them is to leave them alone. Imagine how it would feel if every time you rolled over during the night someone came and patted you and asked if you were okay. It would disrupt you, and you would likely wake up.
- If your child making noise means it difficult for you to sleep yourself, then you need to place the receiving end of the monitor outside their door so you only hear them if they cry. If they are close enough to your room though, and you can hear them crying without the monitor, ditch the monitor altogether. If they are in the next room a monitor should not be something you even have to think about—unless they live in a cone of silence or the wall between your room is reinforced steal or double brick, then you don't need a monitor.

Q25 My baby always wakes up when we go to bed. How can I stop this?
Possible causes:
- Change in sleep conditions.
- Sensitivity to noise.
- You are going to bed at a time when they hit a surface sleep phase, which is typically between 10 and 11 p.m.

To fix:
- Close their door.
- Get a white noise machine or white noise CD.
- Be conscious of the time you go to bed. Please read about the 'Sleep Bus' (see page 675) and 'The physiology of sleep' (see page 403).
- Check the settling environment conditions near their room—lights, noise, etc. (see page 424).
- Also consider your resettling associations—do you pause before you attend to them (see page 674)?

Q26 Is it possible for my baby to have nightmares?
Not in an under-two year old, unless they are exposed to frightening or confusing concepts on television, or your house is experiencing significant unrest with older siblings fighting, parental fighting or strong emotional unrest like grief or divorce, for instance. A child's capacity to have a nightmare as we know it is reduced by the lack of development in their imagination. Over two, this is a far more prevalent problem and it is common that a preschooler will experience clear instances of nightmare dreams.

When an under-two year old wakes screaming at night, it is far more likely to be caused by a phenomenon called a sudden partial waking (see page 700). Night terrors have been highlighted as a problem in the under-two age bracket in the past, but in my personal opinion these completely disappear when you adhere to the surface sleep pause (see page 674) and do not accidentally disturb them before they have come to a full state of consciousness from sleep. When you disturb them before this you can cause what is commonly known as 'wild thrashing'.

Because of this, I believe that only the night terrors little people experience are more in line with the information and behavioural patterns described by sleep clinics as *true* night terror phenomenon, and this is far more prevalent in my opinion and experience after the child has reached around two and a half years of age. Even in these instances, the episodes of night terrors appear to completely vanish when a routine is established. By three years of age, I see children who have developed an imagination start to have what appear to be nightmares with clear dream recall immediately after the event in some cases.

To fix:

I personally believe you should only be concerned with adhering to your surface sleep pause (see page 674) before attending to a child under two years of age to be certain that you are not actually disorientating them by attending to them while they are not fully awake.

Q27 When my baby wakes up she is not hungry so what could be causing this?

Possible causes:

There are two reason why you would be getting consistent night waking that don't include a need for feeding. Both are environmental factors:

1. temperature / comfort
2. associations.

- Night wakings that are not feed related are generally always about the environment. There are obvious problems like temperature, and it is usually because they are too hot when you first go to bed between 7 and 10 p.m., or too cold as their body temperature and the night temperature drops. During day sleep sessions it appears they are prone to becoming particularly cold, even on a mild to warm day.
- The associations your child initially went to sleep with may have changed, or they have developed a set of resettling associations that require your intervention in order for them to go back to sleep. You will know it is an association because you will consistently have to help them go back to sleep. Being too cold may be what originally caused them to call out to you for a cuddle to warm up, though, so make sure

you assess their environment to ensure they aren't getting cold, or consider wrapping them until they are older.

To fix:

- You may need to wrap your baby (see page 439) and regulate the room temperature (see page 434).
- Check their clothing is appropriate, and consider a tuck-in for a 12-month old plus.
- If your child is expecting you to repeatedly help them back to sleep, you will need to read the information contained in 'The psychology of sleep' (see page 416) and about associations (see page 419) to understand the origins of their sleep problem.
- Seriously consider a full PRM routine (see page 515).

Q28 My baby goes to bed at 10 and wakes around 8 or 9 a.m. Is this okay?
Possible cause:
Your baby has a shifted body clock. I call this the 'late shift' (see page 479).
To fix:
It's actually really quite simple to repair this sleep pattern with this age group. If your baby can self-settle and self-resettle and the only problem you have is the times they chose to sleep, then you simply need to read about the late shift and the body's circadian rhythms (see page 405).

Q29 I want my baby, who is under 12 months, to sleep in as I'm not much of an early person. If I put them down later in the evening will I achieve a later waking time?
This is an unrealistic expectation of a baby in the six- to 12-month age group. It is not so unrealistic for a child 12 months plus. Babies rise with the world; 6 to 6.30 a.m. is generally a pretty good sleep-in for a baby that goes to bed at 7 p.m., as they should. Perhaps you are going to bed too late, or you need to give your body a chance to recover from the terrible sleep disruption you have experienced over the last few months since your little bundle of sleepless joy graced your life with their presence. You need to correct your baby's sleep-time problems so you are not so exhausted in the morning.

To fix:

- It is quite possible you can encourage a 12 month old plus to sleep in a little later if they are on a solid midday sleep from the LSR routine, but you must be sure they are taking adequate sleep during the day to help them enjoy the second half of the day and cope well until they are due to go to sleep 7 p.m. These children, once they are taking a minimum of two hours of solid sleep at lunch and sleeping right through the night from 7 p.m., can gradually, in 20-minute windows, a week at a time per increase, be offered a later sleep in. Stop increasing the windows when they start to wake naturally either in the morning or at the lunch sleep or in the morning. If they stop sleeping so well at lunch, then you are altering their sleep need to suit your sleep-in desires. While this is tempting, it will make your little one overtired by 7 p.m., and cause them to wake through the night because they are overtired.

- Be aware, putting a baby or toddler to bed later will generally encourage an earlier wake-up time. Read 'Biology of sleep' (see page 405) for more.

Q30 My child fights sleep and I can't work out why. What do I do?
Possible causes:

- The most common reasons I find babies fight sleep is because of changes in their sleeping conditions. When a parent or carer puts a baby to sleep a certain way, be that in their arms, or by staying in the room with them with a hand on their back, and then sneaks off, the baby will wake up and, having no concept of sleep or time lapsing, will startle and call out to their parent / carer. This in turn makes them associate the sensation of feeling tired with their loved one suddenly disappearing. This is inadvertently breaking their trust, and it creates a situation where the child fights the feelings associated with going to sleep because they are concerned you may disappear.
- Other reasons can be through failed attempts at control crying or 'pick up / put down' strategies, or multiple lie down strategies, and the baby is unable to understand the new inconsistent conditions of sleep and are not empowered with the skills they need to cope with that request. These inconsistent approaches, with no predictable strategies incorporated around resettling *and*, most importantly, waking-up time, result in either a short-term success, or no success and a loss of trust. The child then becomes fretful about their sleeping environment and the process of sleep.

To fix:

- Read the 'Basics of sleep' (see page 398).
- Assess the most appropriate routine for your baby.
- Implement the environmental changes (see page 424) they may need to learn how to sleep.

Q31 My baby seems to be sleeping fine and I don't want to lose that. Do you think I should shift to a routine just in case?
Not at all! If you are in a good routine, and by that I mean a consistent 24-hour day where your baby is sleeping well at night and well through

the days, regardless if it fits with anyone else's suggestions or not, then you should never try to fix something that isn't broken. In your case, a new daily routine will *not* help you maintain your good sleep, *but* consistent settling, resettling and waking routines (see page 605) and excellent, balanced communication will help you maintain sleep. But be aware of your child's changing sleep needs as your child grows. Expect their need for sleep to change and change. You cannot expect them to need as much sleep at ten, 12 or 18 months as they needed at seven months (if they have been sleeping well). Be prepared to change as they show signs that a regular sleep time is starting to make it hard for them to sleep at another time.

Q32 My baby sleeps well some days, and bad on others. Why?

Possible cause:

This is actually a common problem. It comes down to sleep requirement. I often find parents *want* their baby to sleep their 'best' day sleep every day, when the reality is their baby's sleep requirement means they actually need to sleep the average between their best and worst days for a realistic and consistent daily routine to be locked in.

To fix:

* You need to keep a sleep diary to work out your little one's average daily sleep requirement (see page 534).
* Please read about progressive sleep decline.

Q33 I'm really worried about waking my family—my husband and other children—when my baby cries in the middle of the night. Can you advise me how to best handle this?

You are not alone. This is everyone's biggest concern when they have other children. The problem is, because you have been rushing into your baby in the first place and creating patterns of subconscious sleep associations during their surface sleep, your baby is crying out for you as a routine.

To fix:

There is only one true solution to this: eliminate the crying out by putting your baby's needs first. There are a couple of ways you can do this:

* ship the older children and husband off for the weekend and resolve the problem over this two-day window, when you don't have to be concerned about disrupting the others, or
* consider a white noise machine for your older child.

Talk with your partner about investing a weekend to help your baby sleep through without the need to call out so everyone, including you—you have an extremely important job that requires you to be alert and on your toes all day, too—and your baby can also get a good night's sleep. Always start at a time when you can all rest more during the day. While I usually suggest you start any routine management on a Monday so you can focus on having calm quiet days, this would be the exception to the rule if you are very concerned about others becoming tired for the two days it takes to correct the sleep patterns. In this case, start on Saturday. Establish your new routine and follow it carefully.

Q34 Are music CDs just as helpful as white noise?

If your baby is sleeping well with a music CD playing in their room, then there is no problems using it. It can be wonderfully soothing for some babies, and some parents have managed to establish a lovely sleep time association with a CD. I always warn, though, that if you need to continuously go in during the night to switch it back on when your baby wakes, then you have developed a resettling association for your baby that requires your intervention.

To fix any possible problems:

- Consider putting the CD on repeat so the conditions you have made available to your baby when they first went to sleep do not suddenly change on them. While some babies will absolutely love their lullaby CD at sleep time, there can obviously be inherent problems when you create an environment-based association around sleep, which is what a music CD does. Some babies will then be unable to sleep without it further more. If this occurs, you are limited to sleeping in a room in the house where they can hear the CD playing. If this is not possible, as it generally isn't, then you will need to re-establish a new association with sleep.
- If you want to correct a significant sleep-time problem I always try to encourage parents to work with products that either do not cause sleep associations or that can be used everywhere. I am big fan of white noise CDs for settling. These CDs contain white noise, which is essentially 'silence', and you do not run the risk of establishing an association, and you still get the added benefits of eliminating the noises that wake up babies.

Q35 My older child keeps accidentally waking my baby during the day when they are a little loud during play. I don't want to ask her to be quiet. Is there anything else I can do?

This is a great question. It's hardly fair, with all the changes that happened in an older child's life, to ask them to be really quiet while their new baby brother or sister sleeps.

To fix:
- Setting appropriate boundaries is reasonable, like no banging on baby's door, or shouting baby's name to deliberately wake them up, and it is not okay for your older child to just wander into baby's room whenever it suits them. But playing and chatting happily at a normal everyday volume is something every toddler should be able to do.
- As mentioned in the previous question, I am big fan of white noise CDs and it might eliminate the noises that wake your baby up. By placing this in your baby's room, your older child can play and chat freely, you can relax and stop feeling so tense about your older child being a normal chatty, noisy kid, and your baby can sleep on oblivious to the ruckus their big brother or sister is causing.

Q36   My baby boy was sleeping fine until two months ago and now he is not coping at all. What happened?

Possible causes:

I tend to find there are a few typical triggers for these sudden changes in sleeping habits:

- You may not be keeping up with their changing sleep needs, and may be holding on to a sleeping routine that they have grown out of. While it's hard to accept sometimes, and it's not unusual to secretly wish for an extra hour in the day to do some of those things on the 'to do' list, the ability to stay a step ahead of your child's changing sleep needs ensures you don't suddenly have to deal with significant sleep disruptions that sees you lose a large portion or all of your day and subsequent night sleep. Remember, just because they may no longer need to sleep the old pattern of two one- to one-and-a-half-hour sleep sessions during the day, it does not mean that cannot still achieve up to two and a half hours of sleep either at one session, or with supporting bridges, regardless of their age group.
- Your communication may have become a little imbalanced. This can often happen when a child starts to build their confident child-directed line of communication and you do not sustain a balance with a parent-governed line. When this occurs your child starts to create predictable sets of conditions around environments in order to feel a little more in control of a day that is always changing without warning. You then find your little one resisting your guidance through the day at times like nappy change, getting dressed, getting into the high chair, car seat, or pram, resisting you feeding them and resisting your guidance at sleep time.

- Conditions in the sleeping environment may have changed.
- Emotional changes, such as a sudden loss of trust in their world, can happen when big changes make things feel unpredictable. These changes could include a new sister or brother arriving into their lives, moving house, going on a holiday or someone moving in, or moving out. Perhaps there is a divorce, sudden bickering, a change in nanny or teacher in their daycare, or there is a grief in the family. During these changes a child has every right to feel uncertain.

To fix:
- Assess your child's sleep needs (see page 534) and re-establish your daily routine.
- It' important to read about communication (see pages 24) to understand the importance of establishing a balance and how to achieve that respectfully.
- Environmental changes could be when you stop wrapping them, change their room around, introduce a night light, take away a sleeping bag, or changes in season. Try to observe their behaviour. If you introduced a light, remove it. If you eliminated a wrap, introduce a sleeping bag and firm tuck-in (for an over 12 months) or a wrap again until they are ready to get rid of it. Consider the change in temperature and adjust accordingly.
- When emotional changes happen, support your baby, keep them close, and communicate with them all day using your flow of communication (see page 40) to keep them informed of any impending changes to help them settle down. Avoid fighting in front of your child, and try really hard to have an air of reassurance around you so they can feel confident that while things are different they are still safe. Always have consistent predictable settling, resettling and waking routines (see page 605) at sleep time so they can feel in control of the event, but if there are significant traumas happening in their or your world, you may need to keep them close and just get through this current season in your life before asking them to sleep away from you.

Q37 We have tried everything but my baby girl has never been a good sleeper. Can you help me?

If your baby has always been an unsettled sleeper, then don't despair, even the most unsettled baby has been able to learn how to sleep. In full recovery, they can be sleeping within 12 to 36 hours.

To fix:

When I meet a little one that is that unsettled, I immediately put them on the full recovery program (see page 541).

Q38 Can my baby have a cup or bottle in their bed?

I generally do not recommend a cup or a bottle in their bed under the age of 24 months. It's important to provide fluid intake (in the form of water—see page 225) regularly throughout the day, when they are *not* in their bed. Only once have I felt there was a genuine thirst during the night in a boy who was 21 months of age, so I provided him with a spill-proof cup in the dummy pot, and treated it in the same way I did the dummy (see page 467). I showed him the cup and reminded him to 'get your cup' when I attended to him if he was calling out on the first night of his new self-settling sleep routine. By the following day he was entirely self-sufficient with his cup through the night and no longer need to call out. If you do need to offer them a drink at night, and this would be a rare occasion, only ever offer water in their cup.

Q39 My baby was premature. Does this make a difference to their sleeping ability?

It does until they reach around eight to ten months of age if they were born more than a four to six weeks premature; otherwise, by twelve months of age, there is no need to keep adjusting a baby born four weeks premature for sleep purposes. In this case if your baby is only six to seven months old when their age is adjusted (see page 540), you can follow the normal routine suggestion for positive routine management for their adjusted age, not their age from birth.

Q40 I have a baby with profound hearing impairment. What adjustments do I need to make to help him sleep well?

This actually makes a significant difference. In the case of a deaf child, their ability to predict their environment is very dependent on watching those around them. You would need to be extremely careful and be sure to introduce full visual cues, much the same as signing, when it comes to leaving the room with the intention of allowing them to go to sleep. These would act in the same way as verbal sleep-time cues. This 'signing' could be in both a visual style and a contact / physical sense, in much the same way you would sign directly onto a child's hand if they were visually and hearing impaired. So, in the middle of the night when baby is needing to go back to sleep, you can use your sign on their hand to suggest you would like them to go to sleep and you are about to leave and they will be able to understand this request. The same principle would need to be adopted for their waking routine.

To help:

- I would be certainly encourage them to develop an attachment to a comfort item for sleep time only (see page 461).
- In a child six to eight months of age, pursuing sleep *should* be easier if you wrap a baby firmly (see page 439) and pop them in the comfort of a SafeT Sleep. If they are just having a little grumble and protest on those first few days, then leave them be.
- If they are having a more difficult time, or they are older, you will need to take more time when helping them sleep. Always keep doors open, come in and out of their room regularly without fussing with them, and tidy cloths or toys away to tell them you are nearby and they can relax.
- A visual hand gesture and physical on-hand signing cue to be used each time you plan stepping out of the room for a moment tells them you would like them to sleep if you always stick to your request of sleep on those first few days. It may take them a while to go to sleep but if you always make the outcome of your little sleep-time ritual, then the time it takes for your little one to go to sleep will become shorter and shorter.
- Taking it very slowly when encouraging them to try to self-settle will be important. Work hard on playtime in the cot strategies, and a visual short-term absence cue to build their confidence in that environment and help them become comfortable with you leaving the room.
- Pursuing sleep should still be maintained, and clear boundaries around not standing in the cot while you are in the room should be maintained with all children. Asking them to stay lying down and following through with your bedtime ritual, which should still follow the same format as my settling, resettling and waking routines (bearing in mind that a hearing impaired child should be able to clearly see you and your face while you are reading them books), is still important. If you need to stay near their room and potter in and out as you put washing away, and continually ask them to lie down until they eventually fall asleep, then that is your best plan.
- Leaving a night light in the hall if they are older and their door open if you feel it is stressful for them to have it closed will help them become comfortable with this consistent environment.
- For more information, talk with an organisation who deals with these common question in more detail. They will have many, many practical suggestion to help your little one sleep.

Q41 My baby has profound sight impairment. I know I need to do things differently, but how and what?

Because this is a language-based framework, it should be extremely helpful to your little one. It is suggested that when one of the five senses is lacking or missing entirely, the other senses may strengthen to compensate. It would be wonderful to think that your child's world being predominantly auditory based would encourage the language centre of his brain to develop and adapt quickly to new routine styles of communication, so the use of routine styles of settling, resettling and waking routines should be quickly adjusted to, particularly if you role play.

To help:

- I would be certainly encourage them to develop an attachment to a comfort item for sleep time only (see page 461).
- I would ensure there were strong smell association with their mummy and daddy in their cot. To do this I would place a well-used pillowcase (unwashed) under their fitted cot sheet so the smell of mum and dad stays in their cot. I would give their comfort item a good rub on mum and dad's hair, neck and even down mum's top if she is still breastfeeding. I would then not hesitate to pursue the appropriate PRM for their age and sleep requirement.
- For more information, talk with organisations who deal with these impairments in more detail. They will have many, many suggestion to help your little one sleep.

Q42 I don't think my toddler, who is over 18 months, wants his day sleep any more. How can I tell?

Possible cause:

With this under-two age group, I have never yet met a 12- to 24-month old in my entire career that has not been able to take a day sleep on my LSR Routine 1, 12 months-plus age variation repair plan. A 13- to 14-hour-long night could be causing problems with your toddler's ability to take a day sleep, even if they are awake through the night regularly. I never recommend such long nights when it takes away from their ability to take a daytime nap for one very good reason: they are simply too young and are growing and learning too rapidly to successfully get through an 11-hour day when they are only 12 to 24 months old and be in their best form to learn, grow and enjoy the last half of their day without a daytime sleep.

To fix:

- If your little one is sleeping too long at night, simply follow the PRM Routine 1 (see page 541) suggestion for age variation 12 months plus (see page 552) and your little one will start to sleep again during the day.

- If on the other hand, your child is not sleeping for a long time at night, and is full of beans and excited all day, then your child is likely to be overtired, and you will need to look carefully at the meal plan of the above-mentioned routine. I would adopt the full recovery program (see page 541), paying careful attention to the meal-time windows to correct their sleep-time problems.

- If your little one truly does not need a daytime sleep under the age of two years, you will see clear signsof this. These include:
  - a solid night's sleep with no fussing upon going to bed each night— hours of fussing at a 7 p.m. bedtime can be a clear indication that your child has become overtired, and is having trouble winding down, so does need a day sleep
  - willing to go in to their cot for a midday rest, and chat quietly through the day nap time for up to an hour without going to sleep—if your child is fighting going in their cot, their reluctance to take a daytime sleep is actually a communication-based problem rather than a true need for no sleep. Develop balanced, respectful, two-way streams of communication with your toddler through the day.
  - able to cope at 5 p.m. and are not tantruming or hard to manage leading up to this meal, and equally do not become *too* overexcited after dinner—a normal level of elevated energy is always present after the last meal of the day, but excessive frenetic behavioural patterns after 5.30 p.m. is indicative of overtiredness

If it is clear your baby is not tired, based on this list of signs, then maintain their quiet rest time in their cot so they can have a period of between one and two hours where there is reduced stimulation (and no, television is a poor option for quiet time). This will give them a chance to have a quiet wind down, and it will refresh them for the second portion of the day, and it makes sure mum and dad stay well rested and have a little wind-down time, too, to have a healthy lunch and recharge their batteries so they can be in top form for the second half of the day.

Q43 My little boy (over 18 months) talks for up to an hour when I first put him to bed at 7 p.m. Is it time to drop his daytime nap?

I always say 'no' when asked this about an under-two year old. It is quite a common situation for a toddler to have a little debrief about their day. You will hear them rattle off all their experiences almost systematically, and process all the different expressions and emotions they felt and witnessed throughout the day. I think this is a healthy part of early childhood and is perfectly fine to allow it to just run its course without interference. It should not go for more than an hour, and does not change the routine waking time you provide each morning, or for each day sleep. To allow them to sleep-in the next morning will simply cause a shifted sleep cycle, and perpetuate the pattern. If they chat for an hour and finally go to sleep at 8 p.m. and you compensate by letting them sleep in till 7 or 7.30 a.m., it means they can't fall asleep until 1 p.m. after lunch, which impacts on their settling time that night. This makes getting them into bed before 8 p.m. a difficult task, and they then still need to have their little debrief. A later debrief will obviously stop them from dozing off to sleep until closer to 9 p.m., and so a vicious cycle begins.

To fix if causing a problem:
- If you are having trouble with their ability to sleep beyond the age of 12 months, either at night or during the day, they will need to be on the PRM Routine 1 with the 12-month variation (see page 552).
- I would not allow for any daytime sleep to be over two hours if this is a common night-time occurrence, and their midday sleep must be from 12 to 2 p.m. and no later.

By allowing them to have a little debrief every night, and still working within your timeframe, you will discourage routine miscalculations, and encourage better sleep. If they are chatting, there is no need for you to interfere with that natural healthy settling process. We spend a lot of time encouraging confidence and independence in their cot environment, and chatting busily to themselves about their day is a beautiful sign of this being established. There are times when you should just leave well enough alone.

Q44 At what age can I give my toddler a pillow to sleep on?

If they are under two years, you should not introduce pillows to the cot for any reasons at all. They are unsafe, and your baby is perfectly capable of sleeping flat on their tummy, back and side without one. In fact their little bodies are designed to sleep flat to keep their airway nice and clear. If anyone suggests the use of pillows or cushions in the cot for any other purpose (to cuddle for instance), then you need to be extremely careful about the choices you make here. There is no reason to introduce a pillow other than to allow them to sleep on it because that is the purpose of pillows, and as it is a health risk and actually not appropriate for an under-two year old's body at sleep time anyway. I would be extremely reluctant to even consider them an option until they are two years of age.

Q45 When can I transfer my toddler to a bed?

I do not suggest anyone introduces a bed for a child under the age of two years. It is the kind of milestone that you want them to achieve around their second birthday and prepare them for carefully. Moving from a cot to bed can be the trigger of some extremely troubling episodes of settling problems and night wanderings, so you will need to prepare them for the excitement of the situation, and the boundaries of being in a bed.

I believe that if a child under two has demonstrated a tendency to find settling or resettling a little challenging, they will not be able to cope with the responsibility of their big bed and all that it entails just yet. To move them into a bed too soon may actually be a negative process to the introduction of the 'big bed' process and may therefore make it something that becomes a less that pleasant experience rather than an exciting new opportunity that is pleasing to both them and you, and fills them with a sense of achievement rather than anxiety or confusion.

17
SURE routines—daily routines to repair sleep

In this section of the book I am going to give you complete, almost minute-by-minute daily routines to get your little one settled into your new PRM quickly. You *must not* even consider starting any daily routine or sleep repair until you have done your homework and fully prepared and skilled your baby for the new expectations of sleep time (see page 20). Up until now I have concentrated on your homework to prepare your babies and the *event* routines around parent-governed lines of communication and play; that is, nappy changing, playing in the cot, sitting happily in a high chair, to name only a few. The chapters in the sleep section (see page 737) provide more of these event routines and, most importantly provide you with your new settling, resettling and waking cues and routines. These new routines must not be tainted or defined to mean anything but sleep, so please be sure to read the sleep section carefully *before* you embark on any new sleep routine. Once you have read the book and done your homework and feel ready to fully repair your baby's sleep, it's time to see how all these event routines fit together in a 24-hour cycle to make your baby's (and your) days happy and nights peaceful.

As I've said often, you cannot hope to repair sleep respectfully until you have practised and established your communication, independence and play event routines. It's all these event routines and skills together that lead to permanently peaceful, sleeping babies day and nights—the subject of Part 2 of this book. Remember there are two kinds of routine: environmental and language based. You are aiming to develop a language-based routine that you can pick up and take anywhere, making your baby's sleep transportable from one environment to the next and sleep routines transferable from one person to the next.

As you know, the best thing about my routines is that they are language based, which means they allow flexibility of environment and settler. As your child's comfort with their event routines is not dependent on a particular room or person—say, your child's bedroom or the breast and mummy only—you can literally take the routines anywhere and ask anyone to follow your plan: you and your child can go anywhere and follow through with your PRM. It also allows you to entrust other people who understand your child's routines, which are not hard for them to learn. You can wake up in the morning, pack a bag and drop them at their grandparents for the day, or go on a holiday with them, or sleep elsewhere, and can even change times zones with ease.

There is, however, a hitch—most good things come with a little hitch. You must invest three solid weeks into locking the daily routine in place first, and to do this you must remain consistent with your flow of communication and event-routine management at home. This is only to be started, however, after you have done your homework so you can clearly see there is a slight time investment in permanently repairing sleep and making baby happy. After you have given your baby / toddler the time to become completely familiar with, and therefore feel in control of and trust, the whole daily routine, you can start to slowly get adventurous about where you take your child within your little one's comfort levels.

This strategy is designed to provide predictability to both your child and you, so neither of you becomes a prisoner of a routine. But when you first start their new routine and they start sleeping well for the first time, just be careful about working *with* their body clocks. This means the time you do something should be bang on a certain time suggested in the program, so you can actually work with their body rather than just their temperament. Eventually these times will be ballpark because the language and skill will be set, making asking them to go to sleep a simple task. But, initially, when the language is not as well established, you may want to take advantage of a locked-in need for sleep or food at certain windows to help you achieve your goals quickly. If your child does not respond rapidly to the shift in the timetable and takes a little bit longer to settle in, then tone

You *must not* even consider starting any daily routine or sleep repair until you have done your homework and fully prepared and skilled your baby for the new expectations of sleep time.

down the amount of movement you are making within the routine times until you find your baby's and your comfort zones.

For babies under six months of age

Some of you will be wondering why there are no specific routines for under-six month olds in this section. The reason I predominantly focus on routines for six months to two year olds in this book is that there is simply not enough room in one book to put all the standard-routine suggestions that a rapidly changing baby's little body needs. Since the 1960s there have been standard high and average routine suggestions available for babies in the nought to six months group which can be found in most books and sourced from most early childhood clinics, so I feel no need to repeat them at this stage. It is when someone finds they do not fall into a natural flow with their baby, or that those standard routines do not fit their baby's individual sleep needs, that I suggest you investigate their sleep requirement further and adopt an appropriate routine to cater for their true sleep requirement. That usually needs to happen by six months of age. At that point it is extremely hard to find anyone who doesn't use a one-size-fits-all approach and that's where positive routine management comes in.

Babies are also so extremely precious when they are under six months that the communication style must be carefully examined before implementing any form of solid routine for this age group so you do not confuse them. You see, I am predominantly in the business of sleep repair and establishing communication. So although a good proportion of new families will find their way by using the communication, independence and play event routines outlined in this book, while incorporating the settling, resettling and waking routines there will be a large group who, having tried the standard suggestions and found no significant flow, will need to then adopt a more solid routine format to find sleep repair.

You can find your way for a newborn by either adopting a casual flow, such as the loose suggestion highlighted below which will suit many babies or, in the case of a fussy unsettled baby, by following a more specific routine suggestion found at your local baby health care centre or clinic. This will give you and your little one time to settle into the world, and give you time to identify and resolve any issues such as reflux before they reach six months. If at that point, however, you are still unable to find resolution to sleep-time difficulties using the tools in this book, then you can be sure that you will need to adopt a PRM routine from this book to end any ongoing fussiness and settle your baby into their new world of peaceful nights and happy days. Remember: it's okay to have a little 'getting to know your baby' stage when they are first born and not rush frantically into a one-size-fits-all feeding and sleeping regime the moment they arrive. This will mean many babies will find their way naturally when a parent understands communication and the need for predictability and sleep associations.

My casual flow suggestion for new babies

It's important to note that at this very early stage of development, just being awake and feeding are hugely exhausting tasks for a baby. Add to that nappy changes, getting dressed, being picked up and put down, and having very important conversations with mummy, daddy and granny, and it's just all a little bit overwhelming for the little possum. I have a few standard things that I am always conscious of when I meet a little one having a tricky time.

Firstly, please don't feel you need to stop breastfeeding. This is always a mother's first area of doubt but is generally never the actual issue. If you are concerned about your milk supply or the effectiveness of your feeding I strongly recommend you see a good lactation specialist who can come to your home and help you develop a good breastfeeding strategy and plan so you can put your mind at ease.

Babies are also so extremely precious when they are under six months that the communication style must be carefully examined before implementing any form of solid routine for this age group so you do not confuse them.

Good solid breastfeeds need good solid winding. This is really, really important. Go out of your way to ensure that your baby girl has no wind at all after her feed. I generally say that after that initial burp, keep going until you can get another burp up. I do this for each side of a breastfeed just to make sure you don't develop layers of milk and air trapped in the tummy.

Try not to allow your baby to break her feeds too often as this can be a key contributor to vomiting. The more she detaches, the more likely she is to throw up after the feed is through.

Be conscious of not allowing your baby to nap too heavily during her feed as well. I know this seems like a huge task when she is still little but it will impact on her ability to sleep solidly at her next in-cot nap time.

Watch out also for little snacking feeds impacting on her ability to feed well enough at a more regular feed time, as this will in turn impact on her ability to stay asleep for a prolonged period of time. This is an area of great debate amongst many different parenting groups, and what you choose to do as a mother is entirely up to you and should be respected. Do what you feel is right for your baby based on your observations of her needs because no one can know your baby like you. Don't do what you think will appeal to general schools of thought because other people tell you they believe strongly in that style of feeding / parenting. What I mean by this is: you must be careful that if your little one is having several little feeds between the big feeds that this could definitely, no matter what anyone tells you, impact on her ability to take a full feed later.

For some babies, this doesn't seem to matter and they still manage to sleep well. However, for other babies, this equally does matter and they don't manage to sleep well because they get hungry sooner. If your baby is one of those who do not respond terribly well to this style of snacking demand feeding, it will tire her out to feed too frequently. Feeding every 40 minutes to an hour will absolutely affect the length of time she will be able to sleep.

In conclusion, try to find a way to soothe her without always relying on a breastfeed as this will only perpetuate a cycle of shorter sleeps, which will create an unsettled little one who needs help to calm down, which in turn continues to perpetuate that cycle of snacking demand feeding.

Watch for early positioning issues

I have many new mums and dads who come to me saying 'My baby won't sleep anywhere but on me'. Often this means that you are appealing to a baby's natural desire to sleep on their belly. This ensures they stay warm, and limits stimulants like light and movement. However, this is an incredibly dangerous practice based on all the research you have been given, and cannot be used as a settling strategy. It also means that your little one is not learning how to cope with the vital positioning required to settle in their cot on their own, which is on their back, flat and still.

The other positioning problem that can occur early is when your baby will not lie down anywhere, whether it is in your arms, on the floor or in the cot, and you end up having to hold them upright the whole time. This is problematic for a couple of obvious reasons:

1. If you want your baby to be able to go to sleep in their cot, they need to be comfortable with lying down. This is something some parents need to work harder on than others, but it is an important skill for your little one to gain. I generally say then when your baby refuses to be in any position other than upright on your shoulder then I limit any upright

positioning completely for two full weeks. I find the first couple of days can be a little challenging but as they become used to the new position, they settle quickly and sleep starts to improve immediately. Always check for reflux first, however, if they appear in discomfort.

2. If you want your baby to be able to resettle at a waking, it's important that the conditions they will encounter at the 40-minute mark are the same as the conditions they initially fall asleep with. This is called a 'sleeping association'. If your baby is falling asleep on the breast or falling asleep in your arms, you are destined to need to recreate those associations at each 40-minute mark so your baby can go back to sleep. Obviously this only creates a tired baby and tired parents. A tired baby wakes more often naturally, and a tired parent becomes stressed. A parent's stress is transferred on to a baby and this creates an unsettled baby. So be careful to not fall into the trap of assisted settles in your arms or on your breast only to then put them in their cot and leave.

Making a sleep environment that caters for your baby's needs right now

If your little one is clearly overwhelmed, you need to cater for that. Some experts believe that a child definitely needs to get used to noise and light and movement—which I agree with—but in my view, when they are very tiny and just getting used to her new surroundings, you should make things as calm, quiet and as dimly lit as possible. I would tend to close blinds in the house 20 minutes before sleep for a week or two until she settles down. Make the room as dark as possible (see page 428) until good sleep is established, and then you can think about introducing light back into her sleep environment. I don't have overhead downlights on as babies' eyes are naturally drawn to these bright lights; I tend to favour the use of lamps.

Your little baby needs to be swaddled (see page 439) really, really well. When I say really well I mean so that there is no movement at all in her arms or legs. If she has her hands up by her face, and it is confusing her to nuzzle her fist like she is about to be fed and this is only proving to be frustrating, then I strongly recommend you wrap her with her arms firmly by her side or across her body. When I tuck babies into bed I ensure they are wrapped firmly. Then I get a sheet and cotton blanket and firmly tuck-in down the sides of the crib so baby feels snuggled and warm. If it is a cool day the day sleeps are when babies get cold quickly so the need for extra layers may become obvious when you have multiple wakings and you need to snuggle them or they need to cry to warm up before they can fall asleep again.

Create a cyclic routine. This is not necessarily time based but more routine based. You create a predictable, safe cycle of behaviour so your little one can settle into a flow. She will find this comforting and it will help her to relax. An example would be:

- baby wakes for feed
- go in, turn on lamp and unwrap her, let her have a little stretch and quiet time in her cot while you prepare her change table and room for the next part of her day—cloths and wraps out ready for next sleep, put any washing away, get nappy ready, etc.
- get her up, change her nappy
- take her to your feeding couch and sit down to feed her and try to keep her awake during feed
- wind well at the end of feeding on one breast or mid feed, then feed her the other side or complete feed and wind after that also
- have a little quiet one-on-one focus time, chat quietly to her, touch her, massage her tummy while you chat, stroke her little face, hold her hands
- offer a little quiet playtime on the floor on a soft base like a sheep skin
- look for tired signs, and wait for a couple of clear ones—I suspect she will have about one or one and a half hours in her from the time of waking up as a newborn
- be careful that you don't misread a dislike for lying down as a tired sign, or light in her eyes as a tired sign, or a rather loud and active sibling unsettling her as a tired sign; keep an eye on what is going on around her to ensure that you are spotting true tired signs
- tell her 'It's time for sleep, mummy loves you'
- take her to her room, change her nappy as needed
- wrap her firmly and turn off lights in the room while she is cradled in your arm
- close the door and sing 'Twinkle twinkle little star' slowly and quietly while rocking her in your arms as she accepts the sensation of feeling tired
- hold her tight if she is fighting the feeling of being tired until she calms
- watch that she isn't thinking you are about to feed her; watch her face and make sure she isn't over nuzzling into you—this will only frustrate her and create tears
- give her a little kiss and say 'Lie down'
- slowly lower her into her crib and tuck her in firmly—babies love the firmness and weight
- stop to stroke her face from the crown downwards so you brush over her eyes, and your fingers meet under her chin; repeat this action as

you quietly repeat 'Time for sleep, mummy loves you, nigh', nigh',' but try to stay out of the line of sight so there are no mixed messages—stand side on to the cot, one hand in, bent over. Repeat three or four times then step back.

You little one should sleep to the next feed. Once she wakes, repeat this pattern.

General flow with most babies

I find after a full night's sleep most babies don't last terribly well on that first waking of the day and you will find they need to go back to bed sooner rather than later. After the first sleep of the day the next two waking periods will be your little girl's longest before you need to put her down in her cot. As the afternoon approaches I tend to do the second-last sleep in the pram while out shopping or on a walk (good for fitness and a healthy way to keep those baby blues at bay as walking releases natural serotonin in the brain that is responsible for happy mood cycles). I always suggest when your baby is little and unsettled that the final sleep of the day be on you in a baby sling. She is overtired by now and in need of a nice doze so she doesn't run the risk of becoming so overtired she screams at night.

After the final feed of the day I generally suggest she has a lovely bath and massage then has a final top-up feed before being put down for the night at around 8ish. I always suggest a rollover feed, and the possibility of two more night feeds at, say, 2 a.m. and between 4 and 5 a.m. if she needs them. Between these feeds you can assist her to settle using your resettling stroking and cues and occasional cuddle to calm her before trying again.

No matter how long she sleeps or how many feeds she has at night, I always, always start the day at the same time every day, the following morning, including waking time and feeding time. This way you can create a pattern that is consistent for you and your baby each day. This may mean you need to wake your baby . . . Yes, gasp, wake a sleeping baby—whoever made up the rule to never wake a sleeping baby was far too much of a generalist. If she is sleeping poorly at night and sleeping in to make up for it, it will only perpetuate a cycle of poor sleep the following night, so the whole idea of not waking sleeping babies is flawed because to not wake them can often lead to a baby that is so unsettled they cannot sleep any more anyway.

A note on settling and resettling

You must always put your baby in the cot awake, and she must know you have left so she can self-settle or she will wake regularly because her sleep environment has changed. If you choose to stay in the room, make sure she thinks you've left and doesn't work out where you are. Get out of her line of sight so she can focus on the job at hand: going to sleep, and not what you are going to do next.

Give her a minute to try and calm herself. You are stepping back to firstly listen to what she is trying to tell you via a cry, and secondly to give her the opportunity to have that natural little cry as she first falls asleep (which enables her body to release endorphins that help a baby go into a deeper sleep). If, however, she is having a hard time and not able to calm down a little, then repeat your pattern of cues and strokes and ensure you sound reassuring and calm.

Step back again, out of her line of sight, to give her the chance to try and settle. Her being fussed with will not permit this. Repeat these steps until she settles. If she is becoming very upset and you have tried to settle her down several times then, after a few attempts to calm her with gentle stroking and cues, you are fine to give her a cuddle to reassure her. She may just need that soothing cuddle before you try again. Don't put her to sleep in your arms, however, unless you are willing to continue holding her while she sleeps. If the only reward is that you disappear after she falls asleep it will make her try and fight sleep. You want your child to trust you and to be able to predict you. Changing the conditions of when she goes to sleep will do the opposite.

I do not advocate leaving young infants under six months to just cry and cry without assistance ever. It may mean they cry a little more if you attend to them but you are ensuring that trust is not compromised as they are in a vital stage of psycho-social development called 'trust versus mistrust'. This is where they learn to trust their needs will be met by a carer or will not. I would prefer to attend and resettle young babies regularly until they settle, than to just leave them without attendance. They are too tiny for this, particularly at this young age. Your baby is far, far, far too young to be left when feeling overwhelmed.

That said, there are some settling cries that are perfectly normal and healthy and should not be interfered with. Any cries where bubby has breaks in between the cries of 30 seconds or more should be left or, at the very least, your baby given more time to settle down. If she continues to have longer breaks and progresses in settling down, then it is fine to leave her be, in fact, you should leave her be. Just being awake and having the odd call-out cry between settling cycles, like 'cry cry hic . . . cry cry hic' or 'cry hic, cry hic, hic cry, hic' (which is a baby's way of creating a rhythmic settling pattern) should be given more space as a baby can fall asleep with a three- to eight-minute window of these cries beginning if not overstimulated.

It's so important to put aside fear and actually listen carefully to what your baby is saying. Is she saying 'Help mummy I can't cope', or 'Boy oh boy am I tired and it feels a little bit uncomfortable'. If it is the latter, give her a chance to try and calm herself down and settle off to sleep with as little intervention and therefore overstimulation as possible. If it is more serious than that, then go back to your cues and stroking and occasional hugs until she starts to go into that settling cry, then step back for longer until she settles.

As far as routines go for this age, a baby doesn't even have a circadian rhythm to speak of until they are four months old, meaning you can't necessarily lock in a strict routine, but working to a loose schedule is great for many mums and bubs. Over the coming five to six months, milk feeding will and should become more efficient, and the amount of milk consumed by your baby at each feed will naturally increase. The ability of your little one to consume larger amounts in more efficient timeframes will have a flow-on effect to the length of time your baby can stay awake, and will also impact on the length of time they can stay asleep. Ultimately, this will gradually lower the number of feeds needed to sustain your little one through the night and effective feeding will also lower the number of sleeps they need during daylight hours.

Hot tips for feeding

Pay attention to your little one's feeding habits and their positioning as mentioned earlier (see page 217). As your baby get older encourage more efficient feeding, and don't allow feeds to be played out over an hour or two because of fussiness or snoozing. By eight weeks most babies are feeding effectively for about 20 minutes on each side, and they gradually become more and more efficient as they grow older. Do note, though, that some babies are far more effective than this, while others may need a little longer. If they start to fuss after a healthy amount of feeding time, simply finish the feed and wait until the next appropriate feed window. If your little one has become fussy, encouraging a longer gap between feeds by ending a feed session after a normal amount of time will encourage better feeding and less fussing at the next feed, and help change the cycle of sluggish to more effective feeds.

Initially, your baby will be having roughly eight feeds over a 24-hour period. During the next five months, as their intake per feed increases and the amount of time it takes them to drink it decreases, they will naturally reduce the number of feeds they need down to five to six feeds per day. The feeds that will increase in volume consumed will be those during the daylight hours, resulting in the feeds after their 10 to 10.30 p.m. dream feed becoming more and more redundant for nutritional and hydration needs. Your local baby health clinic will be able to supply you with the recommended amounts of consumption for both breast- and bottle-fed babies to help you ensure your baby's intake is adequate.

As the quantity and efficiency of the feeds increase, your little one will start to stay awake for longer periods between feeds during the day. This will see them progress from requiring up to four sleeps during daylight hours over the first month of life to roughly three sleeps during daylight hours over the second month. After that, between the second and the third month, it will start to become apparent what their sleep requirement is. Then, they will need for:

- an average to high sleep requirement baby, roughly two longer sleeps a day—one mid morning and one early afternoon (both up to two hours long)—and a late afternoon bridging nap (between 4 and 5 p.m.) of between 40 minutes to an hour. This requirement will kick in by around three months of age and last until closer to five months, when their late afternoon bridging nap will either naturally become, or need to be made, a little shorter (between 20 and 40 minutes) to sustain a healthy 7 p.m. bedtime.
- a low sleep requirement baby, roughly one short mid-morning bridging nap (gradually decreasing in length from one hour down to 30 to 40 minutes by around five months of age), one long midday sleep (of roughly two hours, give or take, depending on the amount of sleep they are allowed to, or naturally sleep for during their mid-morning and late-afternoon bridging naps), followed by another short afternoon bridging nap (gradually decreasing in length from one hour down to 30 to 40 minutes by around five months of age).

For babies over six month of age, refer to the sleep sections of this book.

Locking in times to prevent poor sleep cycles

A great tip I can give you while you find your way through these first few months is to lock in some basic times in your routine. The most important times are your little one's night sleep settling time and morning wake-up time, and the start and end times for the first and last sleeps of the daylight hours. Each of these latter times will complement the other and lock in good sleeping for both the early morning waking time and 7 p.m. settling time.

Nights and mornings first

The nights are the foundation of all your daytime sleeping and feeding patterns. A realistic expectation is to settle your little one in the first month between 7 and 8 p.m. and always wake them, regardless of the progress of their night, to start their day by 7 a.m. All day sleeps are then worked into the routine around this basic framework. By the fourth week, aim to always settle them by 7 p.m., so you will need to monitor the time they go to sleep in the late afternoon and its length. Never offer any additional day sleeps if it detracts from night sleep.

First day sleep

The first sleep of the day helps you manage the remainder of the day so be mindful of the time you put them down. For the first one to two months this should be roughly one hour and 15 to 30 minutes after your target wake-up time of 7 a.m. This means that even on the days they wake a little earlier, always aim to settle them no earlier than 8.15 to 8.30 a.m. This discourages perpetual cycles of early morning wakings. From the eighth to tenth week and onwards, try to keep them up each morning until roughly 8.30 a.m. and gradually, by the twelfth week, push that out to:

- 8.45 to 9 a.m. for high sleep requirement babies—these little ones will go down again for their second day sleep a little later than low sleep requirement babies and therefore go down a little later on this first sleep, and for a longer period of time
- 8.30 to 8.45 a.m. for low sleep requirement babies—these little ones will go down again for their second day sleep sooner than high sleep requirement babies and therefore go down a little sooner on this first sleep, and for a shorter period of time.

Always encourage good efficient feeding with no dozing and a substantial alert period before putting them down for their second sleep of the day. Remember to space the day well.

Final sleep time of the day

The last sleep or nap your baby takes during the daylight portion of their 24-hour day will need to be monitored carefully to ensure they do not sleep so late or for so long that they cannot fall asleep again by around 7 p.m. They are supposed to be tired enough to need to sleep for 11 or 12 consecutive hour at the end of the day (with or without the need for feeds), so it's normal for them to be fairly tired and grouchy after their bath. In those first precious six to eight weeks this last nap of the day will usually need to be assisted (with a sling, etc.) and be shorter than their normal day sleeps. The latest wake-up time is 5.30 p.m. in those first few weeks. Eventually, their late afternoon sleeps will be one and half then two hours prior to the 7 p.m. night sleep.

By the time your little one starts to demonstrate a propensity towards having a higher or lower sleep requirement during the day, the late afternoon sleep will start to vary between the two groups. The high sleep requirement babies will tend to sleep a little longer and will need to be put down and woken earlier in order the maintain their 7 p.m. settling time. The low sleep requirement babies will sleep a little less and will therefore need to be settled and woken a little later in the day. Experiment with your little one's wake-up times and length of sleep to meet their needs while aiming to achieve a 7 p.m. settling time at night. It's okay to wake your baby as you can reduce or eliminate tears at the 7 p.m. settling time each night by being strategic about the timing and quantity of sleep at this last daytime sleep.

The progression of night feeds over the first six months will see your baby develop from needing regular three-hourly feeds throughout a 24-hour period to a dream feed at around 10 p.m. and then sleeping through and not feeding until 7 a.m. the next morning by the time they are five to six months old. Initially, the dream feed will be around at 9.30 p.m. and will slowly progress to 10.30 over the first eight weeks of their life. During the first few weeks of life, your baby will wake roughly every three hours after this dream feed for more feeds, meaning there will be two late night feeds after their dream feed until their 7 a.m. morning feed. As they grow, the dream feed remains between 10 and 10.30 p.m. and they will start to sleep through till 2, then 3, then 4 and eventually 5 to 7 a.m. before requiring another feed. This is natural and perfectly safe and healthy so long as you are not having difficulty with your milk supply (at which point you may need to consult with a lactation consultant who looks at both better sleeping patterns and feeding patterns). Once you have identified a pattern of your baby sleeping to a certain time for three or more days in a row, try to maintain the night feed schedule and resettle them without feeding between their feed windows whenever possible.

It's fairly common for a little one who was once sleeping through the night to 7 a.m. after their dream feed to suddenly develop a hunger at night again around the fifth month, when their body's need for higher calorie intake encourages them to source solids. Until those solids are introduced, your baby may start to show genuine hunger through the night once more and require an additional night feed until both solids and an iron source have been introduced into their diet.

Please try to remember that a baby's circadian rhythm does not develop until around the fourth month, so you must rely heavily on the sleep and feeding you provide throughout the day to help keep them regulated and balanced, well slept and well fed. Once your baby is five months of age, you can then begin to use the more detailed tools outlined in the sleep section of this book to tweak their routine, develop their sleep skills, or adopt a healthy routine.

Finally, if your baby is suffering from reflux, and has needed medication, I generally always provide a dummy for short-term relief. With severe reflux, the stomach acid tracking back up a baby's oesophagus can often irritate and inflame the area. Obviously the more it happens, the more inflamed the area becomes until eventually any reflux causes significant pain. A dummy in the interim can help your baby keep the peristaltic action flowing downwards, which generally prevents too much reflux and stops the acid from burning the oesophagus. Therefore, if you feel the short-term use of a dummy is necessary, then by all means cater for your baby's needs, but be conscious of saving its use for when bubby is lying down, and only use it if they are having a tricky time.

Once your doctors have found a balance with their medication, your little one's discomfort will have passed and you may simply be left with the task of re-establishing a more positive association with lying down. Often, if a baby has had very bad reflux, the sensation of lying on their backs is generally associated with the sensation of pain as this is when reflux is most often noticeable. Once their medication has got the problem under control, your little one may still be very nervous of the impending discomfort and may cry in anticipation of an event that will no longer happen. This is when it is important to get rid of the dummy, and gently work through it with them until they regain trust in that particular environment.

Trust your instincts and you can always make a confident parenting decision to help them regain trust in an environment that was once uncomfortable.

It's important to always help your little ones move forward, and you, as their patient and loving parents, are the best equipped to do that with them. Don't avoid something because it used to be a problem or the baby will never learn that it is no longer a problem. When babies develop this learnt pattern of response to a particular event and are not helped past it—because the parents are too nervous to revisit it because baby cries each time they go near their cot—I see far, far too many parents having to attend places or seek advice from those strategists that just do control crying to resolve this issue. Can you imagine how unsuccessful a method like control crying in a completely unfamiliar environment, with a completely unfamiliar carer, can be to correcting a trust issue? Crying is still normal while your baby learns to trust this new environment with your loving guidance and reassurance. Help them through it gently with assistance in cot settling until they are better about being in that environment again, then quickly transition to the above systematic approach to sleep and settling.

Trust your instincts and you can always make a confident parenting decision to help them regain trust in an environment that had once been uncomfortable. I do this full time as a career and the one thing that I know is, if you truly believe and know you are doing the right thing in your heart, then they will trust you and settle very quickly. I always assume a confident carer's role and guide children consistently and compassionately until they calm. If a baby cries, it does not frighten me. I understand it's tricky for them and I allow them to rely on me. If I were doubtful, they would have no solid ground to stand on. Be a rock by being consistent and reassuring and your baby will settle down quickly.

Before you begin your new routine for babies over the age of six months

Once you have read the book, be sure to follow the structure outlined in the introduction carefully (see page 20). When you have finally done your homework and your baby is skilled and prepared for their new routine and sleep-time repair to begin, you must choose a time to start your PRM carefully. The following will help you do that:

- For one to three weeks leading up to beginning your new daily routine and sleep strategies, keep them away from places likely to cause illness, like public swimming pools and parties.
- Make sure they are physically well, and all medical issues (reflux, eczema etc) are well under control before you begin.
- Go for a final check-up at your doctor's to make sure they have clear lungs and ears.
- Try and have the grocery shopping done with easy meal plans in mind to take the pressure off yourself and ensure you continue to eat well on those first few busy days.

- Make sure you have pre-cooked and frozen food for baby so you are not trying to cook or you will feel overwhelmed and may run behind on those first few days.
- Always ensure all environmental changes to your baby's rooms are ready at least a day before you begin.
- Do not immunise your baby three weeks prior to starting your program, or for three weeks after the program has commenced.
- Please ensure their nutritional needs are catered for before you start (iron, vitamins and minerals) and ensure they are well hydrated in the days leading up to beginning, particularly if they are big milk drinkers through the night.
- The night before you begin, for example on Sunday night if you plan to start your program on the Monday morning at 6.30 a.m., stop all feeds from 2 a.m. onwards until 6.30 to 7 a.m. the next day and resettle them any way you can (nil by mouth though) to try and get them to take more sleep (do not use your new resettling routine until tomorrow however).
- They must be awake by 6.30 a.m. no matter what kind of a night they have had.
- Once 6.30 a.m. arrives, follow your routine exactly and keep your little one awake until their designated sleep time is due. Do not allow more sleep than is suggested. Do not offer it early.
- Only one person should be managing baby for the first five days of your new plan. You never play tag team. Whoever puts baby down manages the baby and gets the baby up after sleep time is completed. This makes you trustworthy for baby.
- Do not have guests over, or go too far afield for the first few days. Stay close to home and stay 100 per cent available to your baby's new needs. Don't be distracted. Don't go too far in a car if they are prone to get tired outside their sleep routines until they have recovered their sleep (usually about five days).
- You may need to temporarily or permanently reshuffle some of their activities to fit in their sleep and meal-time needs.
- Never use your settling or resettling routine and cues without starting your corrected daily routine, carefully defining what your cues mean. Only begin when you are fully ready to repair your baby's sleep quickly, completely and permanently by maintaining everything for a solid three weeks from the morning you start.
- Try to start on Monday so there is not too much movement in or around the house.

- Try to have older siblings cared for, and see if people can help you out with school drop-offs for the first few days.

Once you have determined that you will need a daily routine, you will need to work out what routine is best for your child. There are a few simple steps to do this:

- assess whether your child is an urgent repair case or not
- assess your child's sleep requirements
- choose the routine that suits your child's needs based on whether they are an urgent repair case or based on their individual sleep requirement.

Children who I classify as urgent repair cases need the full recovery program. These are profoundly overtired or unsettled babies and toddlers. The aim here is to take the pressure off exhausted parents by providing a well-established and refined daily routine and PRM program that ensures an extremely quick resolution to their child's sleep problems through balanced and respectful communication. Each plan is carefully designed to minimise the need for crying during sleep time and achieve dramatic results within 12 to 56 hours. It ensures a child can achieve upwards of 14 hours sleep a day, even if they had previously been taking as little as eight hours per 24-hour cycle. Once trust in the routine is established and sleep is repaired, these children can move on to a new routine based on their new recovered sleep requirement.

To assess sleep requirement, parents need to record the results of their child's sleeping pattern. This enables parents to take advantage of the all the strategies available in this book based on their own child's individual, daily sleep requirement; that is, low, average or high sleep requirement (see page 534). A seven-day sleep diary will help you calculate your little one's individual sleep requirement so you can implement the appropriate routine for them. When choosing an appropriate routine for your child's sleep needs you can take advantage of a 'modified' routine if you have older children. All too often school runs and extracurricular activities tax family lifestyles and do not fit in with the standard 'one longer morning nap and one longer afternoon nap' routine of other programs. So my routines are designed for you to adjust to suit your family needs while still providing the right amount of sleep.

As stated above, the daily routine comprises your communication, meal time, playtime and independence event routines. In the next chapter I will give you further event routines, specifically related to sleep, and these are settling, resettling and waking routines, which form a vital part of your new daily routine. The chapters that follow all relate to sleep-time issues including the typical triggers for a baby waking during the night and solutions to those triggers. But first things first: does your child fall into the urgent repair category?

Urgent repair cases

Now I'm in the business of sleep repair. It's my whole life, and there is one thing that is absolutely certain when I'm repairing sleep-time problems: those children and families who are having the most difficult time must be identified and helped promptly to repair their situation with as little fuss as possible. If you think sleep is very messy in your house, read on. If you think that you and your baby are coping pretty well for the most part but would like things to run a little smoother, bypass the full recovery section and begin reading the section on sleep requirement assessment (go to page 534).

Once I have identified families who are urgent repair cases, I place the babies / toddlers on to a full recovery program, and I intend on doing that here. To do that, a parent needs to take a week to read the whole book, do their homework, and then implement their new routine without the stress of trying to fix it when they don't know what's wrong. I have provided a checklist (see box on page 533) for those who think their entire days are out of control so you can assess whether you need to be fast-tracked to starting a full recovery routine within the next few days (assuming you have read all the book up to this point and been making inroads with your communication, independence and playtime strategies).

As you know, the best thing about my routines is that they are language based, which means they allow flexibility of environment and carer.

To make this as easy as possible, I have a fail-safe full recovery system that I work with that allows you to offer a sensible amount of sleep to help a profoundly unsettled baby / toddler recover quickly without the need to try and assess their sleep requirement. It is a fail-safe routine that has been refined over many years, so please don't try and add in your variation. If you fit into the categories on the checklist, please move immediately to the PRM suggestions for your little one's age group in the full recovery program (see page 541) and follow the instructions carefully. You should see an almost complete recovery within one to three days of starting the routine and a full recovery from sleep-time issues within around five days.

As mentioned above, you will need to allow a three-week settling window where you will lock in your new solid sleep by maintaining all the environmental aids and by following your routine carefully. Once your child's trust in the process of sleep has been repaired you can then move on to the next phase with ease, if it is necessary, to maintain healthy sleep

Full recovery routine checklist

Has your baby become profoundly overtired, indicated by:

- being unable to sleep for more than one, two or a maximum of three daytime catnaps of between ten and 30 minutes in length
- sleeping less than 12 hours in every 24 hours
- requiring excessive amounts of breastfeeding, or needing to feed for excessive lengths of time to cope with their day
- being unsettled during the night with prolonged wakings in excess of an hour at a time, regularly
- being unable to fall asleep without significant or lengthy intervention
- being unable to go back to sleep without significant or lengthy intervention
- being unable to stay asleep for more than two to three hours at a time at night
- being unable to be placed in their cot without displaying significant distress
- being extremely clingy, and you are unable to put them down
- being distressed and cries for prolonged periods during the day or night both during sleep and non-sleep times of the day, regularly
- not accepting solids or sleep without a big fight?

Have you:

- previously done control crying for more than a three-day window and had no success
- been following a 'classic' routine of two longer sleeps a day carefully, trying to allow your child to self-settle and been unsuccessful
- failed any kind of sleep training that was either designed by or managed personally by a 'professional' sleep consultant even when you stuck 100 per cent to the plan
- been unable to be helped at sleep school, and have been sent home with a 'we are sorry, we can't help you' farewell?

Has the mother of the child:

- been diagnosed with postnatal depression and is not coping terribly well
- feelings that she is not coping or not understanding her baby's needs and is feeling like a failure?

If you are experiencing a combination of some or all of the above symptoms and have a very overtired and unsettled little one with significant stress being experienced by the mother and father, then it's time to quickly repair your sleep through the use of full recovery PRM (go to page 541).

for everyone. At the next phase of the recovery process you can *consider* putting them on to the high-sleep-requirement routine, which comprises two large day sleeps if, and only if, it is appropriate for your child's individual sleep-requirement needs. Or you can simply look at how you can reintroduce normal levels of stimulation in their room during sleep time and be confident your little one will become more flexible with sleep when you are out or away from home. Remember, though, don't be in too much of a rush to make changes when things are working. They are working for a reason. So if you feel like sitting pretty for as long as your baby is happy then by all means you are very welcome to do so.

Sleep-requirement assessment

To assess your baby's actual sleep requirement, keep a solid record, a sleep diary, of your child's sleep intake for a full seven days in the following manner:

- Choose a day to start and record their sleep times per 24 hours from their official wake-up time on day one to their official wake-up time on day two, and so on
- Note the exact time they go to sleep and wake up again. If they wake during the day or night and you need to resettle them, note the time they wake and when they go back to sleep again.
- Add up your child's sleep requirement over the full 24 hours, being sure to calculate only the sleep they have actually had. If they have any night or day wakings of 20 minutes or longer, be sure to deduct that waking from their total sleep intake.
- If they have any milk after 5 a.m. to go back to sleep, deduct all sleep taken, after that milk feed until their day begins again, from their daily sleep needs (see page 483).
- Calculate the sleep they take from their waking start time in the morning on the first day (less false sleep), to their waking start time in the morning on the second day.

An example of a sleep diary would be:

7.15 a.m.	Awake (note: the hours prior to this waking are added to previous day's total)
10.12	Asleep (2 hours, 10 minutes)
12.22 p.m.	Awake
3.54	Asleep (31 minutes)
4.25	Awake
7.15	Asleep (3 hours, 39 minutes)

10.54	Awake
11.35	Asleep (7 hours, 40 minutes)
Next day	
7.15 a.m.	Awake

Total daytime sleep = 2 hours, 41 minutes (calculated up to 7 p.m.)
Total night-time sleep = 11 hours, 49 minutes
Total 24-hour sleep intake = 14 hours and 30 minutes.

Do this for each day of your sleep dairy, then add together the totals of all the days in the week and divide that by seven. This will give you your child's average sleep requirement.

Working with your sleep diary results

If your child's average daily sleep intake over a seven-day week is:

• 8 to 14½ hours, they have a lower sleep requirement (LSR)
• 14½ to 15½ hours, they have an average sleep requirement (ASR)
• 15½ to 16½+ hours, they have a higher sleep requirement (HSR).

Understanding your child's sleep requirement

When your child presents with a **low sleep requirement** (LSR) it generally means one of two things. Firstly, they are extremely overtired from getting such a poor quantity of sleep, and secondly, that you need to repair their sleep with a fail-safe routine, providing a minimum 14 hours sleep in a 24-hour period, as quickly as possible. Once that is done, you can reassess their response to the LSR routine to determine if it is appropriate for them to remain on it or not. The answer will be a clear 'yes' or 'no', and if needs be, whether they are coping and sleeping or not (remember you aren't being unrealistic here about how much sleep they can take, you just want a happy baby) you can shift on to the ASR routine with ease if they appear to need more sleep. This means that just because your child initially presents with a LSR, it does not mean they are a true lower sleep-requirement baby, it just means you need to correct their sleep problem promptly and then reassess within three weeks. That said, a good proportion of babies who present with LSR absolutely thrive on their new LSR routine and still achieve the same amount of daily sleep intake that many babies on the ASR routines achieve, so like I always say: 'Why fix what isn't broken?'

When your baby presents with an **average sleep requirement** (ASR) you are in a fairly privileged position. You get the best of both worlds by being able to choose which routine you believe would suit both your child's individual needs, and your family's needs. You can either slot your baby into the LSR routine and they can achieve up to 14½ hours sleep in a 24-hour period and in some cases more, or you can choose to use the adapted sleep on the HSR routine. Not all average-sleep-requirement babies respond well to the typical 'two longer sleeps a day' routine offered for higher sleep requirement children. A sign that they may respond better to the LSR-routine option is often indicated by their tendency to be an early riser, or the tendency to only take one good day sleep, and only a poor or no second day sleep.

Also, the LSR-routine option is also suitable for ASR babies who are second children and have to be a part of the typical kindergarten run or have an older sibling taking a midday nap. Adapting to this ASR routine would create a lovely daytime flow where all the children go down at the same time through the day. Alternatively, you can opt to place your baby on to the HSR-routine format (modified to accommodate their *slightly* lower sleep need). This is a lovely option for many babies who enjoy taking their two big day sleeps. It is also a favourite with many mums and dads because it gives them two solid breaks in the day and allows a carer to head out the door for some much-needed social contact right on lunch time. It's also a very common routine style recommended since the 1960s, so many mums say it is nice to share similar routines as their friends' and mothers' group families. Either way, your choice will promote the exact same amount of sleep, just in slightly different timetables. Please note, if your baby is ASR but in need of full recovery, then you must follow the full recovery routine suggestion for your child's age group.

If your child has a **high sleep requirement** (HSR), lucky you! This sleep requirement usually means you have a sleepyhead on your hands and that's always a joy. Generally, when a HSR baby runs into trouble sleeping, it is often association based rather than miscalculation based. While there is always a risk of behavioural difficulties due to communication misunderstandings, environmental miscalculations and independence skills being a little under explored, I tend to find that more often than not, these little sleepheads just need some time and space to find their way at sleep time. Follow your routine suggestions for your baby's age group and transition on to one sleep a day anywhere from 18 months to the second year of age. Once you have done your homework, simply set a date and create harmony by implementing your program and assisting them while they adjust to the new request and guidance. Within a couple of days your little one will be sleeping like a dream right through the night.

Lily's sleep diary

Lily was seven months old. She had previously been to sleep school. After she was still experiencing very unsettled sleep her parents sought assistance from a consultant who suggested Lily be placed on the standard '2 hours up, 2 hours down' daily routine and a 12-hour night pattern. Despite the parents' best efforts over a two-month period, Lily did not settle into this pattern but she did learn how to self-settle and self-resettle. When I met Lily it was clear she was a very overtired little girl. I asked her parents to keep a sleep diary and this is part of that record:

Day 1		Day 2	
6.34 a.m.	Awake	7.15 a.m.	Awake
9.30	Asleep	10.12	Asleep
10	Awake	12.22 p.m.	Awake
2.47 p.m.	Asleep	3.54	Asleep
3.17	Awake	4.25	Awake
7.15	Asleep	7.15	Asleep
11.30	Awake	10.54	Awake
2 a.m.	Asleep	11.05	Asleep
4	Awake	7.15 a.m.	Awake
4.07	Asleep		
7.15	Awake		

Total daytime sleep = 1 hour
Total night-time sleep = 7 hours, 30 minutes
Total 24-hour sleep = 8 hours, 30 minutes

Total daytime sleep = 2 hours, 41 minutes
Total night-time sleep = 11 hours, 45 minutes
Total 24-hour sleep = 14 hours, 16 minutes

Day 3
Total daytime sleep = 2 hours, 21 minutes
Total night-time sleep = 9 hours, 37 minutes
Total 24-hour sleep = 11 hours, 58 minutes

Day 4
Total daytime sleep = 58 minutes
Total night-time sleep = 10 hours, 45 minutes
Total 24-hour sleep = 11 hours, 43 minutes

Lily's sleep diary was kept for eight days. Looking at the figures it was apparent she had a sliding pattern of sleep intake—she would peak at around 14½ hours and then slowly decrease her sleep time to around 8½ hours before peaking at 14½ hours again some days later. To correct this sleep pattern, we needed to work out her average daily sleep requirement and determine the best course of action.

Lily's average daily sleep requirement was 12 hours and 5 minutes. This meant she fell into the category of requiring a full recovery for a six- to ten-month-old's daily routine. On this routine, Lily was able to sleep 14 hours, 30 minutes every 24 hours, with a consistent and uninterrupted 11½ hours at night and one full 2½ hours day sleep plus two additional bridging naps. It took Lily two days to settle into her new pattern and it resulted in her being well rested and happy. Lily's sleep disruption was sleep-requirement based. A carefully timed routine was all she needed to restore her sleep.

About the PRM routines

There are two basic routines for babies in the six- to 24-month age bracket. PRM Routine 1 (see page 541) is designed:

- for babies needing the full recovery program
- for LSR babies
- as an option for ASR babies
- as a HSR-single-sleep routine when they are 16 to 18 months or older.

Appropriate foods for your baby's age

As you know, when your baby starts to eat solid foods you need to be careful about what you give them. Below are the foods you can introduce at appropriate ages, how much of them they can eat together with some warnings about foods that might cause a reaction and recommendations on what to avoid in your baby's diet.

For a six to nine month old
Fruit: apple, avocado, banana, cooked apricot, mango, peach, pear
Vegetables: carrot, cauliflower, green beans, lentils (watch in case of reaction), potato, pumpkin, sweet potato, turnip, zucchini
Protein: chicken, egg yolk (reaction watch), fish (reaction watch), lamb
Portion size: between 110 and 170 grams (between the size of a four to six months or seven to nine months jar of bought baby food), some may want a little more, some may want a little less.

For a ten to 12 month old, in addition to above
Fruit: dried fruit—prune
Vegetables: Brussels sprouts, cabbage, leek, mushroom, onion, parsnip, pulse beans, rhubarb, beetroot, eggplant, garlic (small portions initially) tomato (watch for rash on face or bottom)
Protein: beef, cheese including cream and ricotta (watch for dairy reaction), liver
Portion size 130–180 grams, some may want a little more, some may want a little less.

For a 12 month plus, in addition to above
Fruit: berries (reaction watch strawberries), melon, plum
Vegetables: bean sprouts, cucumber, celery (once they have enough molars to chew it), lettuce
Protein: custard, regular milk, shellfish (watch for reaction—introduce from 18 months plus)
Portion size: 150–200 grams, some may want a little more, some may want a little less.
Water: You have *no* idea how important water is from six months of age or when a baby starts to take solids. When I conduct my workshops, the last thing I tell everyone before I send them home is that I want to see their babies beautifully hydrated. I want to see glistening lips and perfect, oily-slick, beautiful big eyes. I want drool and plump hydrated little faces, arms and legs. The level of water each baby will need to achieve this varies according to

PRM Routine 2 (see page 569) is designed:

- as an option for ASR babies aged six to 14 or 16 months.
- for HSR babies aged six to 16 or 18 months.

You will need to read through the whole of your chosen routine's information before embarking on your sleep repair PRM, so go and get your note pad and pen and start your sleep diary today while still reading on to learn more about your baby's sleep repair.

how active the child is and their diet and their climate, but the most important thing to be mindful of is to just offer your baby several good sips of water often throughout the day. Even if they push it away, try a couple more times. Offer no water 30 minutes before breakfast, lunch or dinner for fussy eaters until the meal is completed. For more information on fussy feeders and water intake through meals please see 'Meal-time management and repair' (see page 216)

Notes:
- Be mindful of foods that might cause choking. Grapes are not appropriate until around 12 months of age and then they should always be cut in half or quartered, as should berries, to avoid choking.
- No child under two years of age should have a sandwich for lunch unless they can consume a healthy portion of vegetables and iron within that sandwich in addition to at least half the bread. Bear in mind, the content of a sandwich should have a nutritional value vastly higher than the bread. Bread with a spread—vegemite, cheese, etc.—is not a nutritionally balanced meal. As lunch is the most important meal for sleep, this meal must provide a good balance of vitamins, minerals and iron.
- As iron absorption and stores play such a crucial role in sleep, if you feel that your baby is not eating an adequate quantity of their lunch's meat source, then be sure to offer an evening vegetable meal containing meat as well. Once they are eating effectively at lunch, dinner can become predominantly vegetarian.

Warnings:
- Foods to avoid until a child's third to fifth year include honey, kiwi fruit and nut products.
- Honey is definitely not appropriate until a child is 12 months old, although I would be extremely cautious when introducing it to your little one's diet at any age.
- Avoid *all* nut-based products due to the high risk of the potentially fatal allergic reaction called 'nut anaphylaxis'. Do not cross contaminate butter containers or food items by even using a knife that has been in the peanut butter or Nutella jar. Having a nephew who almost lost his life at nine months of age to his nut allergy, I cannot stress the importance of your vigilance where this is concerned. Even a seemingly untraceable quantity of nut product can prove fatal to a child suffering this form of allergic reaction.

Before you start reading about the routines . . .

When you are following your daily routine plan for your little one's age group, I always suggest you type or write up the routine in a brief, time layout form and pop it on your fridge or make a handy laminated bench-top version to use as a quick reference guide. You can then occasionally refer to the detailed timetable and management suggestions provided in this book for clearer directions if you hit any stumbling blocks along the way, which will be particularly handy during the first week of your new PRM while you are correcting your little one's sleep disruptions. As variations are made to the timing of events, due to your child growing older or to fit in family commitments (always being sensitive to your baby's ability to make these adjustments) or to tighten up the lunch-time sleep (from two hours, 30 minutes to two hours, ten minutes to encourage the afternoon bridging nap for instance), you simply insert your new sleep- and meal-time variations that suit your baby into your written / typed framework. This is how it becomes a personalised routine management, tailored exactly to your baby's needs.

During the day, refer to the box on foods appropriate for your baby's age (see page 538). This list is good for all the routines, tailored or otherwise, as it meets every baby's true dietary-intake needs. You will also find in the box those foods that could cause a reaction in your child so you can carefully monitor their intake of these items, and those foods to avoid in your little one's diet altogether. This is not a definitive list. It goes without saying that young children under two years should not be offered foods that offer no nutritional value, such as lollies, chocolates, chips, or sweetened drinks. Nor should your child have too much of one single kind of food (where your mind set has become 'well anything is better than nothing' as this is the key cause of fussy feeders). At this age you are creating responsible eating habits for your child both on a behavioural and neurological level where a baby and a baby's body are learning to *crave* certain types of food and fluids to respond to their hunger and thirst needs, so be responsible in what you feed them.

A note about premature babies

If your baby was born *four or more* weeks prematurely and is currently six to seven months old, please adjust their age so it reflects what was to have been their actual due date, rather than their premature birth day. After ten months, it is unnecessary to adjust back to due date unless they were eight or more weeks premature. A baby born eight weeks or more premature will need their age adjusted to their due date up until the age of 12 months.

PRM Routine 1

This positive routine management is for those children who:

- need full recovery
- are six to 24 months old and have a LSR
- have ASR, offered as a choice (see Routine 2 on page 569 for alternative).

The routine covers all ages up to two years but, for simplicity's sake, it is written as a single broad document, with meal and sleep variations for babies aged six to nine months and ten to 12 months. Changes to the routine for those older than 12 months have been added as a reference guide. Simply adjust your written / typed version according to your baby's age and need. As you are aiming for 'full recovery' here, which means ensuring your baby understands and follows the routine and is happy during the day and night, stick to the timetable rigorously for the first three weeks. Once your baby successfully follows the routine and sleeps to their natural sleep requirement you can introduce adjustments to fit in with your family needs so long as they do not cause confusion for your baby.

6–6.30 a.m.	Natural waking. Any wakings before 5.30 a.m. are managed with crying interpretation and support (see page 654).
	Waking routine (see page 609) and playtime in cot (see page 175) for 15 to 20 minutes. Throughout the day remember your wait game and cue (see page 74).
6.30–7	Breast / bottle feed (baby does not snooze). By nine months you should aim to have this feed no earlier than 7 a.m.
	Change nappy (see page 287), then free playtime.
7.15	Prepare baby's breakfast. Use pre-emptive and forewarning language (see page 43): 'nearly time for breakfast', 'nearly time to sit down and wait for mummy, yummy apple and oatmeal'.
7.20–40	Baby's breakfast. Difficult to feed (see page 255), use meal-time routine (see page 217).
7.50	Dress for day (see page 287) and then free playtime (they'll usually want to help you but allow them to be free to venture off if they wish). Prepare cot room for morning bridge, if necessary. Remember to use your flow of communication (see page 40): 'nearly time for stories, nearly time for nigh' nigh's'.
8.30	Nappy change, if necessary, then sitting room for settling routine (see page 609).
	By 12 months morning-bridging nap will have naturally been phased out, so use this time as a quiet time for baby until 9.30 and don't do settling routine.

8.45	Bridging nap (strictly 19–20 minutes only) until twelve months of age. Waking routine (see page 622), then cot play until 9.30 while you set up play stations.
	For children twelve months and older at 9.10 allow ten minutes quiet time for baby in the high chair with either books, toys or a favourite DVD or to watch you do your final morning-tea preparations if they appear grizzly.
9.30	Latest time for waking from bridging nap, even if under 20 minutes.
	Morning tea. By nine months you can add fruit puree (see box page 538) to determine this feed.
9.45	Independent playtime at play stations (see page 148). This is baby's most active, energy-burning session, so avoid the car or pram at this time if possible. This is also the time to help them become comfortable with being put down to play independently, a skill they need for sleep—think of it as sleep-earning play. It is also the best opportunity for you to do housework and / or cooking (this is when you need to do the whole day's cooking to get it out of the way). The busier you are the happier your baby will be to play independently. If they are not settling down to play remember your flow of communication and follow through (see page 47 and also page 374). If you leave the room, remember your short-term absence cue 'I'll be back' (see page 94).
10.30	Be prepared: this is a typical ten-minute tired window for LSR babies. It passes within ten minutes but in the early days of your new routine (maybe five to ten days of the new strategy) if your baby is getting weary and showing it, then a play outside or a little cuddle time (not the kind that might make them more tired) while you play with their favourite toy for a few minutes will help. But put them down again once they calm down.
10.45	Focus one-on-one play (see page 131) for 15 minutes. Give them your undivided attention and don't answer the phones. Remember to use your cue, 'nearly time to pack away' (see page 43).
11	Pack away toys completely, prepare cot room and wrap for lunch sleep while baby keeps you company and 'helps'. Allow ten minutes quiet time for baby in the high chair with either books, toys or a favourite DVD or to watch you do your final lunch preparations. They will be having a little blood-sugar drop here and their hunger signs may look like tired signs but don't be fooled: they need to eat here. Remember to use your cue 'nearly time for lunch, yummy chicken and vegetables'.
11.20	Lunch of vegetables with a protein (see box on page 538) every day; by eight to nine months they can be offered a dessert (fruit puree or the like). Follow your routine (see page 217) when feeding them and use your cues if there are problems (see page 40).

11.40	Wait game and cue (see page 74) while you clean up. Change nappy using cue for sleep: 'nearly time for sleep, let's go find our books'.
11.45	Begin settling routine (see page 609).
11.55	Final page and pack away, using sleep cues.
12 p.m.	Sleep (one and a half to two and a half hours)
1.30–2.10	Natural waking time. Leave baby in cot as long as you can, allowing them to self-resettle if need be. If they wake before 1 p.m., use your resettling routine (see page 617) all the way until 2.30. Once they have had a minimum of one-and-a-half hours' sleep and are fully awake, use your waking routine and cues (see page 622). Allow them independent play in cot up till 2.30 or for 20 minutes. Hint: if you haven't had a chance during their independent playtime, then cook up and freeze a large batch of food during sleep time once or twice a week. By the time 5 p.m. arrives, when all children are tired and hungry, it's a dreadful time to try and cook, so I don't allow for it in the routine.
2.30	Breast/bottle feed plus snack by nine months.
	This milk feed will naturally go between the age of 12 and 15 months and your child will just have the snack, but you can offer milk in a cup if they are interested.
	Adventure. Time to enjoy the great outdoors in car or pram. No napping allowed unless within afternoon bridging-nap time. Remember your cues for bridging nap.
4.15	Bridging nap (strictly 20 minutes) in pram or car. Six to nine months only
4.45–5	Latest time to wake from bridging nap, using waking cues, regardless of time it took them to fall asleep. At six months of age they could take their 19 minutes right up to 5 p.m., but as they start to get older, you tighten the afternoon bridge window to close at 4.45 p.m. This way you are sure to not offer sleep where it is not needed as it can create problems at other sleep times. This afternoon bridge phases itself out by the ninth to tenth month.
5–5.10	At this time you need to be at home for the first three weeks of recovery. Use this time to do your final pack away for the day, using cues, 'time to pack away', 'nearly time for dinner . . .'
5.10	Allow ten minutes' quiet time while you warm dinner. This can be in the high chair with books toys or their favourite DVD, or while watching you warm their food depending on their mood at this stage of the day. This is another blood-sugar drop window so prepare to see hunger signs that may look like tired signs. As mentioned earlier, don't be fooled: they need to eat here, not sleep.
5.20	Dinner then playtime in high chair (see page 192) as you prepare their bedroom and tidy kitchen and organise your own evening meal for when

	your baby goes to bed at 7 p.m. (NB: You must eat a healthy meal to stave off depression and poor sleep, plus it's a good time to connect with other members of your family. So, don't neglect this.)
6	Nudie playtime (see page 209), using pre-emptive cues for bath.
6.10	Bath time. You need to watch baby the whole time. Remember your pre-emptive cues as you head towards 6.30, 'nearly time to pack away', 'nearly time to get out of bath'.
6.30	Baby out of bath (not before). Household should start to become calm and lights dimed in preparation for bed. Dry and dress baby (see page 287) quickly but calmly. As they will be tired you might need to reassure them, 'It's okay, bubba, you're just tired. Nearly time for milk and nigh' nigh's.' Be patient; they should be tired enough to sleep for 11 to 12 hours.
6.35	Breast/bottle feed, ten minutes only. Baby must not doze at all as it will interrupt your settling routine and just five minutes' doze on this feed could result in 40 minutes' crying on settling. So avoid tears then by keeping them awake now.
6.45–50	Begin settling routine at 6.50 at the latest. Pre-emptive language all through book reading (see page 42).
6.55	Final cue, 'last page, then nigh' nigh's', and pack away. Enjoy a last cuddle and complete settling routine.
7	Bed. If baby cries, assess the situation from an adult's perspective (see page 70) and interpret the cries (see pages 654) before you go in to resettle. Remember your cues and resettling routines (see page 617).

Milk and food intake per day

There is no night feeding once baby is on solids. Some six month olds will not be on solids yet, although they have usually been introduced by now, so they may require a single parent-guided night feed at around 10 p.m. but be careful not to teach your baby to mistake the night feed as anything else. It is not waking-up time or playtime. It is simply a night feed where you go into them and offer it, and not the other way around where they wake and demand it. Don't confuse your cues and definitions (see page 44). A word of warning however: by six months, I strongly recommend you adopt the routine and food suggestions and drop all night feeds immediately unless directed otherwise by your general practitioner.

A six to nine month old has four breast / bottle feeds of milk and three solid meals each day. By nine months the need for the morning-tea breastfeed starts to lessen in preparation for the natural weaning process by ten months. So a ten to 12 month old has three breast / bottle feeds of milk plus three solid feeds and two snacks. By 12 months a child will naturally start to drop the afternoon breast / bottle feed, so they will have two to three breast / bottle feeds of milk, three solid feeds and two snacks.

At around eight to nine months of age children are introduced to pureed fruit after their 9.30 a.m. milk feed is offered. Past ten months all children have three solid meals and two snacks along with their three breast / bottle feeds. It is best to offer the solids and snacks before the breast /bottle feed to encourage healthy eating. The three solid meals should consist of breakfast—rice cereal and fruit, lunch—vegetable and protein plus dessert (fruit or yoghurt), dinner—vegetable and carbohydrate, or similar (see box on page 538).

Focus on giving your child extra water during morning playtime, from 9.45 to 11 a.m., and during the afternoon, between 2.30 and 5 p.m. Do not give them water 30 minutes before breakfast, lunch or dinner as this will make them want to eat less because they feel full.

For those on full recovery, LSR or ASR variation routine 1

Those children who fall into the low-sleep-requirement (LSR) group need a very specific style of routine to encourage more sleep. It's important to mention that many of the babies who need this corrective or alternative routine will be unable to sleep at midday for more than an hour if you allow them to sleep even a minute over their 20-minute bridging sleep at 8.45 a.m. in the morning. The lunch sleep success is very much hinged on you being vigilant with that bridge sleep. If they do wake from their lunch sleep in less than one hour and 20 minutes, then always attempt to resettle them using the resettling routine (see page 617) and careful interpretation and support of crying (see page 694) until 2.30 p.m. If they do not resettle, then enter the room using your waking cues and routine (see page 622) and carry on as normal with playtime in the cot (see page 175).

If your attempts to resettle them when they wake early are unsuccessful within the first couple of days, only try to resettle them if they wake under an hour. There is no point even attempting to resettle if it's not working as you will only end up teaching your baby to cry for prolonged periods before you get them up. As you all want sleep to be a positive, achievable experience for your baby on those first few days, it's important you do not pursue it too rigorously but just follow the routine sleep times to continue encouraging better sleeping. The problem does tend to sort itself out after the first two to three days and you'll find they sleep soundly after this time. I am only preparing you here for the possibility of more difficult scenarios because I know you will be anxious if they don't sleep the required time at first.

If you do have to resettle them remember to remain consistent and not confuse your baby / toddler by giving up and just getting them up when they demand it. You need to ensure your main aim is to help them understand the cue, and not taint it by changing its definition (see page 100). In the end, on that first resettling attempt, it may not even be about the amount of sleep they ultimately achieve, but rather about ensuring they are not confused about the definition of the cues. You will need to be aware of the Sleep Bus (see page 675) and carefully listen to what your little one is saying while you help them go back to sleep. Once they have gone to sleep, if they wake a second time after accepting your guidance once, it would signify the end of sleep time so please do not try to resettle them at that point.

Please stick to your daily routine-time framework like glue. Never alter the times, regardless of the progress of the day. All you'll achieve by altering the times is prolonged tiredness and more days of your child waking early and crying. Move on to the next stage of the routine when required. You'll get stunning results if you adhere to the timeframes when correcting sleep-time difficulties in a baby. You do not allow extra sleep, nor do you adjust their routine if they are not taking the sleep as suggested in the routine. You will simply wait for the cyclic effect of tiredness to encourage better sleep next time. If one sleep doesn't work out, the next sleep window remains the same as on their routine. Stay confident, and move forward with clear direction, instead of procrastinating and stressing through doubt and fear.

Also note that LSR babies and those on a modified routine will naturally have a higher need for calorie intake, thus the difference in frequency of feeding and amount of food consumed per age group between the low- and high-sleep-requirement routines.

LSR variation for 6 to 9 months old

Breakfast: Rice, barley or oat cereal and pureed fruit (see box page 538).
Morning bridge: Bridging-nap length is 19 to 20 minutes total. Do not allow sleep beyond this point. Not even a minute. This is literally your key to success for the rest of the day with this routine. Excess sleep here will ensure crying and short sleeps elsewhere during the day, so please be mindful of the significance of the length of this bridging nap. Set an alarm clock to ensure your little one is woken before they drop into too deep a sleep cycle beyond this 20-minute power zone. You are best to enter your child's room at 19 minutes and give your little one a minute to wake up. This will ensure you enter the room when they

would naturally be in a light phase, which prevents them from being grizzly when they wake up. If you miss your 20-minute window, they could be grizzly for a further 20 minutes while their systems try to take a full 40-minute REM cycle even once woken. Enter the room using your waking routine and stay happy and confident even if they are not too impressed at being woken on the first two days of your new plan. Establish playtime in the cot (see page 175), and allow them to play until 9.25 a.m. While they are taking their nap and playing in their cot, you can set up their play stations in the main living area, and make morning tea ready for a fun morning of exploring their world. At 9.25 a.m. pack away toys in the cot and take them out for the morning-tea feed.

Morning tea: For six to eight months old: breast / bottle feed only. This feeding window is 15 to 20 minutes long max. and designed to ensure they have a lovely snuggle and drink of milk before starting a busy play session. On the first day, your baby may not be used to this frequency of feeds and may only need a little feed, but their intake will naturally increase within one week of starting the program. Once the allocated time has passed, end the feed if it is not already ended, and carry on with your routine.

For nine months old: after their milk feed offer some pureed fruit. Between the ninth and tenth month, your baby may no longer be terribly interested in their milk feed. This is natural and your baby will start to transition from four daily milk feeds a day down to three by around the age of ten months. This is why you start to add fruit and water for morning tea. By ten months, they will have fruit and water only for morning tea.

Lunch: Vegetables (see box page 538), rice cereal, rice, meat
Lunch sleep: This sleep can be up to two hours, 30 minutes long if they wish. For babies whose sleep requirement is lowest, often indicated by an inability to take the afternoon bridge after a two-and-a-half-hour lunch sleep, you will need to cap their midday sleep at 2.10 p.m. (two hours, ten minutes) until their afternoon bridge is dropped at nine to ten months. Only then will you allow them to take the full allocation, lunch sleep time. When a baby has a very well established, existing catnap cycle of ten to 30 minutes for their day sleeps before they start the new routine, they *may* need assistance to resettle past this on the first three days but, if they are swaddled, this will be rare. Avoid resettling if they have had a fairly reasonable amount of sleep. The ideal outcome on the first couple of days would be a minimum of

one hour, 20 minutes. If that occurs, be satisfied and try to leave them for as long as you can before going in to encourage them with your waking routine and have a longer playtime in the cot. Their body's need to pick up the sleep the next day will happen if you remain consistent with your routine times. It's really a waste of your baby's energy and yours if you know you will be unsuccessful at resettling them and could inadvertently teach them to cry until you pick them up. I tend to try and avoid resettling during the day and wait for the cyclic effect of the routine to work rather than battle with baby. Only if their main sleep is too short would I feel it necessary to resettle on those first few days.

Afternoon tea: For a six to eight months old: breast / bottle feed. This milk feed will remain for quite some time to come; perhaps well beyond their first birthday. Some children opt to keep up this feed until mummy decides it's time to have milk in a cup with their afternoon tea instead.

For a nine month old, offer breast / bottle feed and a snuggle, then pop them into their high chair for a little snack. It is a long time between their solid lunch feed at 11.20 a.m. and their solid dinner feed at 5.20 p.m. so they will need a substantial snack in addition to their milk to sustain them. This can be fruit, yoghurt or finger foods like a Cruskit with avocado, cream cheese or ricotta (watch for dairy reactions), or cheese or homemade smoothies or a biscuit (see box on page 538).

Afternoon bridge: A six to eight month old has a sleep window from 4.10 to 5 p.m.; a nine month old from 4.15 to 4.45 p.m. but the nap is only 19 to 20 minutes long. Do not allow your baby to sleep beyond this point. Keep peeping at your baby every three to five minutes so you know the time they drift off to sleep, and then wake them either when their allocated nap time ends, or when their sleep window ends, whichever comes first. If they don't fall asleep early enough and don't nap the whole allocated time, wake them by 4.45 or 5 p.m. depending on their age anyway and carry on with your routine.

This is a good sleep for them to have in the pram whenever possible. Most babies have had enough of their cot by this time, and will need this sleep but will require some assistance to take it. As you cannot assist them in their cot, you should only help them in an honest assisting environment like the pram. So get it out and go for a stroll. If it is warm, stay in the shade. If it is hot, raining or blowing a gale, head to a local shopping mall. If you cannot do either of these, then push your baby in the pram at home briefly until they drift off to sleep, or they can try and have another sleep in their cot. This is also a good sleep for them to have on a car run if you need to pick up and transport older children. Your little one needs this sleep at this age so be careful to try and make it easy for them.

If your six- to eight-month-old baby has difficulty going to sleep at 7 p.m. on both nights one and two of your new routine, and they are taking their bridge sleep right up until 5 p.m., then you will need to taper it back to 4.45 to ensure they do not have difficulty falling asleep at 7 p.m. on subsequent nights. This may mean that you need to tighten their midday sleep back a little (to 2 / 2.10 p.m.) to help them fall asleep earlier on the bridging sleep. Their night sleep is the most important sleep to lock in first, and then you adjust their days depending just on how much sleep they have left to take. Never steal from the nights to achieve better days.

By the ninth or tenth month, your child's need to take this sleep may be beginning to diminish. Before making any decisions about day sleeps, wait for a pattern, which means two to three days in a row before you take action. Continue to swaddle them and lie them down. If they are happily lying there and looking around contently all snuggled into their swaddle but unable to drift off, then it is clear that your little one is transitioning out of the afternoon bridge. Continue to offer it until they are ten months if you like. As their need for the afternoon nap lessens, you can allow them to sleep as long as they like at the midday sleep, providing they still sleep through till 6.30 a.m. for their night sleep. This way, if they no longer wish to take their late afternoon bridging nap they have still achieved a good number of hours day's sleep and a solid night's sleep, around 13½ to 15 hours. This is more than adequate and for many little ones who have come from a place of very poor sleep intake, it is quite possibly more sleep than they have ever been able to achieve in their short little lives.

If you find that after a few days of good sleep and no afternoon bridge that they initially go to sleep at 7 p.m. with no problems but wake 40 minutes later and need help to go back to sleep again, it could mean they have become a little overtired and you will need to encourage the afternoon sleep. To do this, tighten up their midday sleep again (back to two hours, ten minutes) so they can take the afternoon bridge. Keep to the afternoon-bridge routine and wake them when the window comes to an end or they reach their 19-minute mark. If after attempting to encourage this afternoon-bridge sleep for a couple of days you are unsuccessful, then do not wake them from

	the lunch sleep at all anymore. Just allow them to sleep until they wake up and carry on with the routine. The evening overtired, partial-waking cycle will resolve itself over the next day or so. Do not alter your routine.
Dinner:	Vegetables, rice cereal / rice (see box on page 538)—this meal is similar to lunch but, however, does not include meat (see iron warning in box).

LSR / ASR variation for 10 to 12 month old

Breakfast:	Rice / barley / Oat / Weet-Bix / oats / semolina or baby's muesli cereal and stewed or mashed fruit or toast fingers (see info on spreads in box on page 538).
Morning bridge:	Refer to information in six to nine month old's section (see page 546). Bridging-nap length is 19 to 20 minutes only. Do not allow sleep beyond this point. Not even a minute over—I'd prefer 18 minutes to 21—or you risk compromising their lunch sleep.
Morning tea:	Between the ninth and tenth month, your baby may no longer be terribly interested in their milk feed. This is natural and your baby will start to transition from four daily milk feeds a day down to three by around the age of ten months. This is why you started to add fruit and water for morning tea. By ten months, unless they are still very keen on milk, they will have fruit and water only for morning tea. This can be pureed fruit or some finger-food pieces of banana, peach and pear, etc. (see box on page 538).
Lunch:	Vegetables, pasta / rice / couscous, meat (see box on page 538).
Lunch sleep:	This sleep can be up to two hours, 30 minutes long if they wish, even three hours if they are sleeping up to and beyond 6 a.m. each morning and settling well at 7 p.m. Start out at just two hours, ten minutes if they have been a troubled sleeper though. In a few weeks you can start to build on the solid framework of good sleep, if they indicate they may want to sleep longer now, by allowing them to sleep until 2.30 p.m. Some children do not have that requirement in them and do not mind if they wake at 1.30 or 2 p.m. A good indication that they are satisfied with their quantity of sleep is if they are happy and coping during the afternoon. It's normal for them have a little blood-sugar drop around 5 p.m. as their body prepares for dinner, which is why a quiet time then is good as you prepare their meal to prevent tantrums and tears from a hungry baby. But if they cope well at all other times of the afternoon and go to bed tired but sleep solidly, then your baby is not overtired and has met their natural lunch-time sleep

requirement. This should never be about fixing a baby to make them take some spectacular amount of sleep. It is about finding a way to have a happy baby all day, and one who sleeps beautifully all night.

Avoid resettling if they have had a fairly reasonable amount of sleep. The ideal outcome on the first couple of days would be a minimum of one hour, 20 minutes. If that occurs be satisfied and encourage them with your waking routine (see page 622) and have a longer playtime in the cot (see page 175). Their body's need to pick up the sleep the next day will happen if you remain consistent with your routine times. It's really a waste of your baby's energy and yours if you know you will be unsuccessful at resettling them and could inadvertently teach them to cry until you pick them up.

If they do wake within one hour, then always attempt to resettle them using the resettling routine (see page 617) and careful management of crying (see page 694) until 2.30 p.m. If they do not resettle by 2.30, then enter the room using your waking cues and routine and carry on as normal with playtime in the cot. If they do go back to sleep, even if it takes them quite some time to fall asleep on those first few days, the next waking, no matter how soon, signifies the end of this sleep time. The latest waking time is 2.30 p.m. It's more important to not confuse the language at this point, as you will only perpetuate a cycle of poor sleep the next day if you allow compensation sleep beyond the designated sleep repair windows.

If you continue to be unsuccessful at resettling them after a few days of them waking before 1.20 p.m., you might then decide to only try to resettle them if they wake under an hour. This is never usually a problem after the first two to three days as they sleep soundly after this time. If lunch sleeps continue to be a problem, please adjust to the six to ten months' variation (see page 547). I always try to encourage them to lie there by themselves for as long as possible before I enter the room once they wake up, before using my waking cue and routine, even if they are having the odd call out or a even a bit of a protest, so long as there are pauses in the behaviour area of crying. Lying happily in their cot is such an important thing for them to become comfortable with, predominantly because all of us have nights in our lives where you wake up and it takes a little time and work to drift back to sleep. To rescue your baby from simply being awake in their bed risks delivering a very poor message to them. Leave them to chat and play in their cot before you go in for as long as your can, even if they are wrapped. It is ideal for your little one to have a restful, reduced stimulation time for up to two hours to be in their best form for the rest of the day. Once you go in and use your waking routine, then establish their usual playtime in the cot that will lead them up to as close to 2.30 p.m. as possible.

Afternoon tea: Offer breast / bottle milk feed and a snuggle, then pop them into their high chair for a little snack. It is a long time between their solid lunch feed at 11.20 a.m. and their solid dinner feed at 5.20 p.m. so they will need a snack in addition to their milk to sustain them. This can be fruit, yoghurt or finger foods like a Cruskit with avocado, cream cheese or ricotta (see box on page 538). They can eat this while you are out and about for your afternoon adventure they but should still only eat it in the afternoon-tea window suggested until 3.00 p.m., and not as comfort food as a way of managing behaviour (see page 247 and page 255).

Afternoon bridge: Usually after ten months this sleep peters out if they are sleeping well at their lunch sleep. This bridge should not be offered to babies after they are 11 months old. I only occasionally offer it to ten month olds for the first two to three days only of implementing a new routine to help them settle into the new pattern, particularly if they are having trouble with the length of sleep they are taking at lunch. The sleep window is from 4.15 p.m. to 4.45 p.m. and is strictly only 19 to 20 minutes long. You lie your baby down and keep peeping to know the time they drift off to sleep, and then wake them after 19 minutes or when their sleep window comes to an end, whichever occurs first. Even if they don't take their whole allocated nap time, wake them and carry on with the routine. If the lunch sleep does not lengthen in those first two to three days naturally, then this sleep must no longer be offered. Stopping it will encourage a better lunch sleep over the next few days.

Dinner: Vegetables, pasta / rice / couscous (see box on page 538)—this meal is similar to lunch but, however, does not include meat (see iron warning in box).

LSR variation for 12 to 24 months old

Breakfast: Rice, barley, Oat / Weet-Bix / oats / semolina or baby muesli cereal and stewed or mashed fruit or toast fingers (see info on spreads in box on page 538).

Morning tea: Morning tea is a snack of only fruit and water (see box on page 538). No other style of food should be offered here.

Lunch: Vegetables, pasta / rice / couscous, meat.

Lunch sleep:	This sleep is as per ten to 12 month olds (see page 550).
Afternoon tea:	Between the twelfth and fifteenth month your baby will still be enjoying this breastfeed, but you will see that it may no longer be a primary dietary need as solids start to occupy much of their daily calorie intake. If they choose to take it or not, it will not impact on their sleep or happiness. Offer the breast / bottle milk feed and a snuggle, and if they say 'yes please', then go right ahead, but if they say 'no thank you', don't force it. If they don't want it, then they should not have to have it. They will need to have an afternoon-tea solid snack first, however, and it will need to be more than just fruit—it is a long time between their solid lunch feed at 11.20 a.m. and their solid dinner feed at 5.20 p.m. Include yoghurt or finger foods like a Cruskit with avocado, cream cheese or ricotta (see box on page 538). They can eat this while you are out and about for your afternoon adventure but it should only be eaten in the afternoon-tea window.
	If the milk feed makes it impossible for them to eat some solids at afternoon tea, then they must have their solids first, before milk is offered. This is vital to help prevent tears, tantrums or stress to your little one. They will not be sustained by milk alone between lunch and dinner. Remember this is about balance, so ensure they have a good snack to get them through. Do not feed them outside the meal-time windows on the recovery plan. Food intake and sleep intake are closely linked and these plans are carefully refined to make sure sleep is achieved as easily as possible.
Dinner:	Vegetables, pasta / rice / couscous (see box on page 538)—this meal is similar to lunch but, however, it does not include meat (see iron warning in box).

Typical triggers for night wakings

Once your child is established on PRM Routine 1, there should be few night wakings. But over the years, one thing has become very clear to me: any imbalance in the day will show up in the night-time sleep cycle of babies on a solid routine. They also have common time windows that indicate behavioural wakings, discomfort, illness, hunger and dehydration, and routine miscalculations (see page 477). While I have never had this officially studied, and therefore confirmed as a science, it occurs so consistently that I have adopted a method of identification to help me accurately finetune routines. This method of deduction has helped me over the years to determine, with tremendous success, what's happening in the most challenging, unsolvable cases.

There is a list of possible triggers for night-time wakings, including depression and anxiety in one or both parents (see box on page 000). If you have difficulty with your child's sleeping during the following times, these will help you work through the problem to quickly eliminate the cause of the waking by the following day, rather than only deal with the crying on an ongoing basis. The following information is to be used for a baby who is on PRM, whose sleep issues have already been successfully solved, and who is sleeping well. This is designed as a way of determining why a child might suddenly experience a disruption at night. You can then work on it the next day to avoid it occurring again, rather than work with the mentality that 'if they cry, this is how I have to manage it'. My strategies encourage you work out why your baby wakes, to resolve that so it doesn't happen again, and only then to deal with any communication or confusion issues that remain after such episodes.

At night, babies should only come to significant partial wakings between 10 and 11 p.m., at around 2 a.m., and between 4 and 5 a.m. All other wakings between these windows are a disruption where they are pulled out of their sleep cycle for one reason or another, and their normal, solid three-to-four-hour window of block sleep is disrupted. Here I highlight the most common triggers that I have observed causing disruption to each solid block of night sleep.

Trouble going to sleep initially at 7 p.m.
This is a classic behavioral / association window. They may be having too much of or too late an afternoon sleep. Shorten the afternoon sleep, or make it earlier. If it continues, it's one of two things:

1. wrong daily routine—reassess their daily sleep-routine needs and be careful to adopt a routine that suits their *actual* needs, and not necessarily your desire for them to sleep at certain times
2. daytime communication is not balanced—if you know they are able to self-settle ordinarily, then it may be that you have not been using balanced lines of communication during the day to ensure they are comfortable with you guiding them.

Wakings between 7 and 10 / 11 p.m.
If they are having trouble after they initially go to sleep:

- They were already asleep when you left—which means you were not honest with them and they were startled when they woke to find you gone. Always let them know by leaving the room before they fall asleep.

- They are too hot—as this is the hottest time in their 24-hour day, it's important to keep them cooler though the first part of their night. A fan or air conditioning is helpful but there is no need to cool them after 10 or 11 p.m. It is most important to be aware of this for babies who are swaddled. Babies who are uncomfortably warm in this first portion of the night are likely to fall asleep and then wake up for short periods of time frequently (around every 40 minutes) between 7 and 10 p.m. Babies who are extremely hot are more likely to wake up and stay awake for prolonged periods between 7 and 10 p.m.
- They are non symptomatic but may be starting to get ill—it's common for a baby to feel unwell and be uncomfortable before they show symptoms of an illness. Often, they will wake momentarily, frequently, without needing intervention. This is when I believe whatever illness they have caught (cold or 'flu perhaps) is taking a hold at the end of the day: their resistance is lower at the end of a long day. If you offer a paracetamol-based analgesic designed specially for their age group and they settle within 20 minutes, or stop waking, you can be sure they are feeling unwell, and that perhaps tomorrow you might have to look a little further into the cause. Always ensure their ears are clear when they are on sleep training.

After the initial settling-in period of any PRM is over (after the first three weeks) it would be highly unlikely that your little one will continue to wake for prolonged periods at night without it being a clear routine miscalculation (if they are able to self-settle and self-resettle ordinarily). In this case I would strongly suggest you reconsider your sleep-routine times and, in particular, look closely at your afternoon sleep, and the length of sleep they are taking through your entire day. When your afternoon sleeps are to blame for prolonged waking in this first windows of the night, they are either too long, and may need to be a bridging nap only, suggesting the low or modified routine may be more appropriate or, in rarer cases, may be the exact opposite, too short and they have become overtired. If they are overtired they are more likely to wake frequently for short periods of time. If you suspect they may be overtired, offer more sleep during the afternoon sleep for ASR and HSR babies, or try to encourage an afternoon bridge for a LSR baby.

Wakings between 10 and 11 p.m.
This is a classic behavioral / association window. The daytime communication between you and your child is not balanced. If you know they are able to

self-settle ordinarily, then it may be that you have not been using balanced lines of communication during the day to ensure they are comfortable with you guiding them.

Wakings between 11.30 p.m. and 1.30 a.m.
This is a classic illness or discomfort window. A prolonged waking in this window may be because your child is already experiencing symptoms of an illness, unlike the 7-to-10 p.m. forewarning of an impending illness. During this window it is very typical to hear from your little one when they are definitely unwell. If you have seen them teething through the day, or they have a cold, or are clearly suffering from an ear infection, tummy bug, etc., they are more likely to run a temperature at this time and be clearly uncomfortable, if not in pain. In this case I try to pre-empt the discomfort they start to feel at this window when the body goes to work healing, growing and fighting illness, and offer pain relief at 10 p.m. so they can peacefully sleep through their body's busy work.

If they have a food intolerance, as far as gut response to wheat, dairy, etc., it will show up at this time. If you introduced a new food the day before or that day and they are suddenly unsettled here, then remove the food from their diet and trial it again in another week's time. If it occurs again, remove that food from their diet for six months before trying again. If it occurs again at your next trial, do not introduce that food until they are at least two years old.

If they are low in iron or, in a more subtle way, not eating enough meat, then they are more likely to have prolonged wakings at this time. If their food intake is unbalanced, their body will wake them to feed here, to supplement the poor nutritional balance from the day (see page 247). If they are not drinking enough water through the day from six months of age and onwards, then you will suffer from a waking here. In this case you must ensure you are balancing their diet, incorporating meat once a day until the prolonged wakings settle down, and make sure they are getting a good blend of vegetables and fruit. Do not replace solids feeds with milk as their bodies will not be sustained by it through this growth window at night and you will continue to suffer from prolonged waking.

If you know that they are physically well, and you have catered for their dietary and hydration needs, a clear pattern of prolonged wakings at night at this time (three times or more is a pattern) is then a clear sign of excessive accumulated day sleep. Reassess your child's daily sleep requirement, over a five-day window, removing the lost sleep from the middle of the night to determine their true sleep need.

Wakings at or near 2 a.m.

This is a classic behavioral / association window—daytime communication is not balanced. If you know they are able to self-settle ordinarily, then it may be that you have not been using balanced lines of communication during the day to ensure they are comfortable with you guiding them.

Wakings between 2.30 and 3.30 a.m.

This is another classic illness or discomfort continuation window, although it appears to indicate a lesser level of discomfort or dietary imbalance: the tail end of an illness, or the last days of teething or earaches will commonly occur here as opposed to the 11.30 p.m. to 1.30 a.m. window, where a child may still be feeling unwell. See 11.30 p.m. to 1.30 a.m. wakings for guidance. Again, ensure they have a discomfort relief to cover them from 11.30 p.m. to 3.30 a.m. if you know they have been unwell and symptomatic and, therefore, prone to waking for a few days.

Wakings between 4 and 5 a.m. (more commonly 5 a.m.)

This is a classical behavioral / association window—daytime communication is not balanced. If you know your child is able to self-settle ordinarily, then it may be that you have not been using balanced lines of communication during the day to ensure they are comfortable with you guiding them.

Wakings between 5 and 6.30 a.m.

This is when they are waking early and are unable to go back to sleep and there are a number of reasons for this:

- Their morning sleep the day before was either too early or too long.
- Your baby is very hungry so their calorie consumption the day before was too low and you need to increase the overall quantity and quality of food you offer at the three main meals of the day (see page 247)—if they are fussy at the meal times, reduce the morning and afternoon snacks to ensure you are not overfeeding them then. Never give them snacks of food of low nutritional value outside the meal-time windows suggested, because it will always detract from their ability to eat meals of a higher nutritional value at their meal times. Believing that 'something is better than nothing' and allowing snacking on biscuits, milk and snack foods are absolute healthy food-intake destroyers. Don't give them snack foods between suggested meal-time windows and they *will* eat the healthy food you offer them.
- They may not have had enough balanced independent playtime the day before, which is when they are developmentally challenged across the board and become tired.

- The first feed of the day, the day before, was given too early, or was too long, too big or a combination of all three.
- They are overeating in the morning in general but, in particular, the food taken the previous morning between 7 a.m. and 12 p.m. could be impacting on their ability to sleep in. They don't need three breakfasts, or a large morning tea. Remember food is fuel, and sleep provides fuel; if you offer extra food, it's the same as offering extra sleep.

Moving forward and maintaining your LSR or ASR routines

There will be slight adjustments that will need to be made to any routine as your little one grows up and their daily sleep requirement naturally increases then decreases. For example, their daily sleep requirement will shift slightly and they may still need two to two and a half hours during the day but only in one solid block. So the 19- to 20-minute bridging naps naturally transition into one longer sleep in the day. The afternoon nap will naturally, with no intervention from you, phase itself out by the time your child is nine to ten months old. You will lie them down for their sleep and they will lie there happily, but not fall asleep.

Eventually your little one will take maybe three afternoon bridges out of the seven you offer them, or perhaps only take the odd bridge here and there. You may choose at this time to not continue the routine of lying them down and covering them over, sure in the fact that if their body needs it they will drift off independently. If they do fall asleep naturally during an afternoon-bridge window, even if you haven't laid them down, only allow it to be a 19- to 20-minute sleep or wake them by 4.45 and 5.00 p.m. (depending on their age group), whichever comes first. Remember this can only happen in the set afternoon-bridge window until your child is ten months of age, after that they are not allowed to drift off as it will cause tears at bedtime at 7 p.m.

It will be slightly more challenging to identify when the morning nap's usefulness is over and consequently it may require a little observation work on your part. Your child will not naturally drop this sleep but it will need to be gone by the time they reach around 12 months of age for most low-sleep-requirement babies, and by 12 to 15 months for most average sleep requirements. The following may be signs that the morning nap is no longer appropriate and you will need to eliminate it:

- he grizzles for long periods of time before he manages to fall asleep at that 8.45 a.m. bridging nap

- he is starting to wake predictably earlier in the morning; for example, his normal waking time is 6 a.m. and he starts to wake at 5.30 a.m. each day
- he begins to have disrupted midday sleep patterns; that is, he wakes after 40 minutes and needs to be managed for 20 plus-ish minutes before he sleeps for another 40 minutes
- it takes him longer to fall asleep at lunch time each day.

If you see a pattern, that means you see this occurring for more than three days in a row, and your baby is the right age with the appropriate sleep requirement to be growing out of this sleep, the best plan is to just drop this morning-bridge sleep immediately. Make a point of doing something extra busy at that time to help them move through the ten-minute tired period they may have for the following week. After they recover (within ten to 20 minutes) resume your day as normal. After a week there will be no need to try and keep them busy as the old rhythm should be starting to diminish.

At this point your little one is now officially on a single, solid, midday sleep, a solid and consistent night sleep pattern, and they can maintain their day meal plan and sleep times until they are heading to kindergarten. The midday sleep will ultimately become a quiet rest time in their bed by the time they are three years old until they go to school at five years of age.

By their very nature, high- and most average-sleep-requirement babies are, or should be, far more flexible with their sleep times as they grow, though they will still need all the other precautions taken when 'doing your homework' and 'creating harmony' to become independent with their settling and resettling skills. For this reason, anyone using these HSR routines will note that their little one is not anywhere near as sensitive as their lower sleep-requirement playmates when it comes to managing their actual routine per age group.

Troubleshooting for PRM Routine 1

Q Why is the first feed at 6.30 to 7 a.m.?

A It affects the time your little one wakes up. It appears that a baby starts to prepare for this feed during the final 40 REM cycle before waking. If you watch them you will see they squirm and get restless and may even soil their nappies then. If your habit is to feed your child at 6.30 a.m. then they will likely start to stir at 5.50 the following day, and if you then feed them at 6 a.m., they are likely to stir at 5.20 a.m. the next day. So 40 minutes before their first milk feed they can start to wake the following morning.

This is how you can often end up backtracking time on feeding schedules and have earlier waking times periodically. If you can hold out on that first feed till 7 a.m., the better they will sleep up to that time the next day.

Q How do I get them to hold out for the first feed if they wake at 6 a.m.?

A If they are six months old and wake at 6 on the first few days of your schedule you may not be able to hold out past 6.30 a.m. From 6 to 6.30 let them play in the cot, do a nappy change, have a little wander with them while you make a cup of tea or feed the puppy dogs or collect the newspaper just to keep them distracted. If you can, hold out to 7 a.m. The closer to 7 the better. It will only take a couple of days for bubby to settle into the new pattern. If, after a week on your routine you find your six to seven month old is sleeping really well, and sleeping to a reasonable time each morning and is very hungry and not coping terribly well with the wait in the morning, then you can feed them at 6.30 a.m. and watch carefully to see if it impacts on their waking time the following morning. If it has no effect, then carry on, but if they are starting to wake earlier, and that makes them tired and unhappy, you may need to work harder on distracting them in the morning.

Q Can my baby sleep till 7 a.m.?

A Not in the early stages of trying to help your little one repair their sleep. The morning bridging nap is a very important sleep to achieve when setting up a successful day. Extra sleep in the early morning may impact their ability to take the morning bridge, and therefore impact their entire day. Eleven to 11½ hours of undisturbed sleep is an excellent amount of sleep at night, and a minimum need for healthy growth and development from six months of age. Don't feel that you should let them sleep in either on those first few days if you had some prolonged wakings to work through on those first few days or you simply encourage more poor night sleep by compensating for the poor night. To help you cope with this waking time, make sure you get to bed early for a couple of weeks while you adjust to not sleeping in like you did when your baby was sleeping poorly. Eventually you will be able to let your baby wake whenever they like so long as it does not impact on the balance of their day or damage their day sleeps again.

Q I feed on demand and on this routine I've suddenly dropped from ten to 20 plus breast-feeds a day to just four. Is there anything I should do to prevent lactating problems?

A I suggest you do two full expresses during the night. It will be hard to wake yourself up because you will just be starting to get your sleep back, but you risk becoming engorged and getting mastitis if you don't. For the first few nights express at 10 p.m. and 2 a.m. For the first three days massage your breasts regularly, loosening up any lumps and keep any milk ducts from becoming engorged or infected. If necessary, you can also express in the shower, after your baby's feed, or if you are feeling particularly full. The use of cool packs on your breast is also helpful on the first three days to help things settle down. I have suggested this as a rule of thumb for the last 12 years and have not had a single problem with a mother getting mastitis (even in women prone to the condition) nor any issues with milk-supply problems for babies over six to 24 months of age. Make sure you wear a well-fitted bra for cosmetic purposes as well. As your body prepares to breastfeed, fat stores leave the breast leaving room for the milk ducts to fill so when the demand and supply drops, the fat stores start to come back to the breast. At this time, if your bra is not supportive, you may experience some drop. Wear your bra day and night for the first few weeks, and ensure you remain comfortable but firmly supported at all times.

Q Isn't breakfast too close to the first feed of the day?

A Remember, their last solid feed was at 5.20 p.m. the night before. The first milk feed will only take the edge off their hunger but their body will need this feed to prevent your little one becoming over hungry. If you miss the hunger window first thing in the morning, they will become uninterested in eating and your baby will want to sleep to cope with their low fuel levels. Hunger signs are almost identical to tired signs so thinking they need a nap is misreading their body's needs. I have worked hard on these routines with thousands of babies to achieve the best possible outcome, so follow through with the meal-time windows, even if you can't imagine it will work, and just watch your little one settle into the program with stunning ease.

Q There seems to be a lot of feeds close together in the morning. Is this right?

A You're right. If you compare the average- to high-sleep-requirement meal-time routines with the low-sleep-requirement routines, you will see a difference in feed quantities and frequency, particularly during the morning portion of the routine. This is for a simple reason: a LSR child's need for ingested fuel increases with the reduced sleep they take in the morning. As their sleep requirement is naturally lower, you cater for that within the routine and ensure they start their day with appropriate windows for feeding and milk intake so they can be at their very best. After nearly 20 years working through these routines, the LSR routine has the most positive impact of any routine I have ever seen on an unsettled child.

Q I'm having trouble with showering and keeping them safe. Do you have any suggestions?

A For the first week of your new management plan I suggest you try and shower in the evening for ease sake. Otherwise, for babies under 12 months I always recommend you pop your little one into a play gym Exosaucer or their high chair for peace of mind (see Sheyne's favourite products page 154). For older children, set your boundaries using your flow of communication. Tell them (if you would like them to *not* come in the shower) that 'mummy is having a shower, no opening the door', and provide some play stations to occupy them. Define that statement by not buckling and occasionally letting them get in or they will learn to protest until you let them in. If you are happy for them to have a shower with you on some days, tell them before you start getting ready for the shower. If they are not showering with you, tell them that before you start getting ready. If they are going to be in the bathroom while you shower always safety proof the area so they can't get into any mischief while you do so, and make sure the floor is free of water so they can't slip. If your bathroom is unsafe, you can pop a gate up to keep them from coming in and having toys set up at the gate. You can also set them up to play in an adjoining safety-proofed bedroom so long as the door out of the bedroom is closed. Always chat and sing to your little one, and play fun little games while staying happy so they learn that you are still accessible, even when you're encased in a little glass cube. Alternatively, playtime in the high chair (see page 192) may be a safe and less stressful option. Always practise playtime in the high chair once a day so this option remains available to you.

Q I'm concerned they won't take the morning bridge. What happens then?

A I have never had this happen to me, and it rarely happens with clients unless they have not catered for their baby's need to be wrapped (see page 439). If your little one is under ten months and you are seriously concerned that this could happen, swaddle them. If they are older and no longer need full swaddling, and they resist the morning bridge when you have catered for all environmental needs carefully—through the use of the leg wrap, SafeT Sleep and tuck-in or otherwise—then get them up at 9.30 using the waking routine and carry on with the routine as normal. Remember: you do not compensate for poor sleep at the right time with good sleep at the wrong time. Their body will pick up on the need to take the sleep by tomorrow, so just keep going. They may be tired but generally by the time they are waking multiple times through the night and catnapping through the day they are already overtired anyway, so you cannot keep doing the same old things and expect a different result. Move forward and wait until their next, routine sleep time is scheduled before putting them down to sleep. If they don't take that morning-bridge sleep, then just busy yourself keeping them distracted and entertained on this first day.

Q My baby didn't fall asleep for the morning bridge until 9.20, so do I have to wake them at 9.30?

A On the first week you can let them take more of their 19-20 minute sleep but no later than 9.45. After the first couple of days this won't be a problem as they will settle quickly, so it's okay on those first couple of days to allow them to doze outside their window to a certain extent. Continue to work with the basic principle that you don't compensate for poor sleep at the right time with good sleep at the wrong time or you will perpetuate poor sleep at the right time. In other words, after the first week, no matter what, wake them by 9.30.

Q My baby doesn't want their morning-tea milk feed. What should I do?

A Offer the feed, and if they are absolutely uninterested then listen to them. It's normal for them to drop this milk feed between nine and 11 months. Even if they are younger, if they don't want it on those first few days, don't force it. Pop them in their high chair and offer some pureed fruit if they are over eight months then get on with your day as per the routine. Don't try and offer it later as it will effect their lunch feed, which is the most important meal of their day. Also, stick to your baby's water-intake windows carefully as taking in water 30 minutes before a feed will make them feel full so they are less likely to want the feed. If they are under nine months, however, and you continue to have difficulty getting them to take this feed, slightly lower the quantity of their breakfast solid feed.

Q My baby / toddler doesn't want their morning-tea fruit. Should I offer it later?

A No, stick to your solid-intake windows only and let your baby / toddler tell you if they are interested. It's not a problem if they make it to lunch on their breastfeed and they are okay. It is a problem if you have a cranky baby mid-morning, or they are not making it to lunch before they want a feed. In this case I would definitely encourage their morning fruit if their breakfast intake was poor. I would also strongly consider offering it before their milk feed as by nine to ten months, milk will not fully sustain them to lunch. Remember, solids first, then all the milk they like after. Once the window is closed at 9.45 a.m. though, pack away and carry on with your day.

Q I'm having trouble getting them to play. What should I do?

A Reread the chapters on play and on how to encourage it (see page 180). If your child has never played or you have always had to stay with them while they do, then this is just a new pattern you are introducing. It's important to set boundaries and be patient as they learn. Make sure they are able to see you at all times, and you stay happy, reassuring and patient. Take it slow and don't move from room to room too often during the first week of their learning. This takes time, and it's the area that has the slowest turnaround time of them all. It can take a good week, even up to a month, of gentle encouragement to build up their trust. Eighty per cent of parents note an immediate improvement but, if things have been really difficult in your house before you start the program, then it should be no surprise that it will take a little longer for your child to completely relax with the new routine. Remember to stay busy, don't hover and watch your body language so that it is not confusing them.

Q Packing away takes a long time. Do you have to do it together?

A I would say in those first couple of weeks it is really the last thing I am worried about with the flow of the day. If it is too much effort, just do it yourself and focus on getting them to help you once you have established the rest of your routine. It is important to pack away as it helps them transition from one part of the day to another, such as playing to eating, or eating to sleeping. Most older children really love packing away and during their toddler stage will proudly race around gathering up all their toys and busily throw them in their toy box. Just make sure you aren't assuming that packing away is a chore to your child, and definitely avoid introducing it based on that premise. All children should learn to pack away their toys, whether they are theirs or not. It's an important part of being a contributing member of a family.

Q She didn't eat much lunch so should I persist or offer her a milk feed instead?

A No, milk is not on the menu for this feed on this routine. Offer her a good lunch and some dessert, and if her intake of savoury foods is low during those first few days, then add rice cereal to the fruit or dessert to make sure she doesn't have an empty tummy and feel hungry half an hour later or through her midday sleep. Your child should be offered her favourite foods on the first days of the program and, if she is a toddler, she can be offered an assortment of foods to ensure she gets a good meal. You can deal with food texture or flavour fussing a little later, the priority now is a good solid lunch. While it's vital you manage her behaviour at meal time, it's not crucial that she eats particularly lumpy or specific foods. Once the meal-time window is closed, end the feed. Don't offer milk, just carry on with your routine and her body will pick up on the need for a more solid-sized lunch the next day.

Q He is becoming very tired during lunch, sometimes making it hard to keep him awake or feed him. Is this normal?

A Yes, it is. Babies who are tired before they start the new routine can experience an elevated level of tiredness initially until their body adjusts to the new flow of their day. There are a few things to remember. When a child starts to sleep more, they tend to become very tired. The more sleep you take the more your body wants. He may have been used to having a big sleep in the morning or catnapping whenever it suited him but that was not ultimately good for him or the needs of your family. The other common thing that happens prior to starting the program, when a baby is fed to sleep as a settling or resettling strategy, is they can develop an association of swallowing with going to sleep (particularly obvious in those children who are breastfed / given a bottle to sleep). In both cases there is going to be an adjustment period, so keep them awake, no matter what, with enthusiastic tones and interesting feeding environments, and be patient.

Q My baby is used to going to sleep after a milk feed, so can I offer it anyway?

A Most of the time, this is half the problem with resettling during the night. Your child won't know how to sleep without the taste of milk in their mouth or a milk-filled tummy, or without the sedating hormones they receive through a breastfeed. It's important to change the conditions of sleep so they can cope with settling without these associations. It's about balance. Some feeds are before sleep, some are after (please see your routine). The feed should not be the only reason they can go to sleep. By providing a language-based settling routine, where sleep is not dependent of milk, you and your baby can enjoy your feed times without having them be a disruptive element to your baby's or, indeed, your entire family's sleep. The one exception here is to offer a feed if they are particularly unwell or you have been instructed to do so by your doctor or paediatrician.

Q My baby seems to be opening her bowels more than normal, is this to be expected?

A When there is a significant change in fuel intake and / or sleep, the body will often have a change in rhythm. This can result in multiple bowel motions for a day or even a week. Don't fret. It will settle down as their body adjusts to their new routine. Keep their bottom very clean, use lots of barrier and protective creams to prevent chafing, and change their nappy regularly as an increase in fruit may make their motions a little more acidic than normal.

Q Can I give him his 2.30 p.m. milk feed early if he has woken early from his midday sleep, or do I still have to wait?

A No, you can't feed him early. The same principles apply for waking times at this main sleep of the day as the morning waking time. If you instil a 2 p.m. feed time in his body he will always have trouble sleeping past that time, and may begin to stir 40 minutes earlier each day in anticipation of this feed. Over the years I have noted the most effective windows for food and sleep intake to complement one another and promote better sleeping and eating as a result so stick to the plan. Be aware also that there is quite a gap between afternoon tea and dinner and if you offer afternoon tea too early you might have problems leading up to dinner time. To help him wait, encourage quiet time in the cot before you enter the room initially, then playtime in the cot, and then fill in the time with distraction until afternoon tea is ready. Don't compensate for poor eating at the right time with good eating at the wrong time or you will perpetuate poor eating at the wrong time.

Q I wrap my baby for cot sleeps so do I need to wrap her for a pram sleep as well?

A For the most part, yes. If your little one has a history of not sleeping in the pram, then you will definitely need to wrap her. You will also need to be considerate and block out any excess stimulation when you put her in the pram. A dark piece of navy-blue muslin draped over the pram while she is reclined inside will have her asleep in a jiffy. If she has a habit of drifting off to sleep easily in the pram then simply use your pre-emptive language, 'nearly time for nigh' nigh's, nearly time to lie down', five minutes before you recline her, and say your sleep-time cues and offer her wrap as a tuck-in only or to hold, or offer her any other sleep-time comfort items to hold that she used to have.

Q Can my baby sleep at home for the afternoon sleep?

A As this sleep is the last one of the day before night, I sometimes find it is a little more difficult for a few babies to achieve in their cot. They will happily drift off in the pram or car, but find the cot environment a bit boring by the end of the day. I tend to take cues from each individual baby to decide if they can actually take that nap at home or not. Always give it a try after the first few days and, if they are having a difficult time, then offer this sleep while you are out and about for a little while. A simple change of scenery and a little bit of help are often enough to prevent tears. If they are happy to just lie in their pram and drift off without the movement of the pram, then you can tuck them into their pram and park them in their room or, if it's cool and safe enough, under a shady tree in the back garden.

Q What if it's hot, freezing cold or wet, do you still have to go out then?

A If it is too hot or wet at this time then you may well want them to sleep in their cot. I lived in London for many years so I'm afraid the 'too cold' to take the baby out doesn't wash well with me. Snuggle them in a snow suit or a firm wrap and blanket, then cover them over with the dark muslin and they will sleep beautifully. Equally, rain never stopped a walk in good old Great Britain, but I know you can be a little more precious about getting soggy here—the prospect of an adult wearing rain protection gear and a pair of Wellingtons is a little unheard of—but break the mould. Gear up and invest in a proper pram rain cover for a light drizzle. If you're not convinced about the joys of a walk in drizzle then head for a local shopping mall. Take them for a quick walk around the shops while they drift off to sleep, then step into the supermarket and do the shopping or whatever suits you best—there's nothing like a little retail therapy. If you don't have access to a cool and dry shopping mall, then you may need to pop them in their cot. If they won't have a bar of their cot, however (no pun intended), rock them in their pram around the house until they fall asleep; it shouldn't take long at all.

Q I thought they needed to learn to drift off to sleep on their own. Isn't it creating a parent-governed association if I walk my baby to sleep in the pram?

A Good question. The pram is one of those places where it is okay for your baby to expect someone to push them when they feel tired, and a good place for them to learn how to go to sleep. That means that it is a realistic and maintainable association between sleep and the pram. It is however, not balanced to have your baby get used to needing to being rocked every time they need a sleep. Always aim for either one or three sleeps a day in the pram, or practise one day sleep a week in the pram for children on one sleep to make sure they stay flexible and capable of this task.

Q What if they don't take the afternoon bridge?

A At some point between the ninth and tenth months of age they will drop this sleep. If you have laid them down and they have not taken it, don't fret. Complete the attempted sleep session with your normal, positive, waking cues and routine and carry on with your day. Do not feed them earlier, or put them down to bed earlier that night. Do not compensate for poor sleep at the right time with good sleep at the wrong time as that perpetuates poor sleep. To correct a significant sleep-time issue for a baby you must always move forward. You do this by maintaining your routine and that will encourage better sleep the next day.

Q Do I need to do the settling routine when I'm out with the pram?

A No, just use your cues and then follow on with your pram sleep management.

Q Do I need to use the settling routine when they sleep at another house?

A Yes, more than ever. This is what tells them it's sleep time. This will be their security in a completely foreign environment. Not only should you do your routine but you should role play with teddy so they understand that you will be asking them to sleep in 'that' cot in 'that' room and you will be just outside the door and will come in if they need you.

Q Do we have to go out every afternoon for the whole afternoon?

A No, you can stay at home if you like, but if they get a little weary and unsettled by 4.30 p.m. then go for a little walk with them in the pram whether they are due for a bridge nap or not. I recommend you reserve any short outings for later in the afternoon. They are at their best when they first wake after their midday sleep, and are more content to play and have a lovely time at home, but tend to get a little less willing to do so by later in the afternoon. Try to stay out until 5 p.m. if they are weary as this will make the transition to quiet time then dinner easier and help you avoid the late afternoon grizzles.

Q They don't want their dinner so what should I do?

A Don't fret. This is a lighter meal on purpose. Most babies are really fussy by dinner time because they are a little worn out. I usually make sure it's their favourite meal, and it is easy to eat. You have extra time here to encourage eating, and there can be a longer window for finger-feeding themselves after the initial spoon-fed portion of the meal is done. If they are not terribly interested in the savoury items despite your best efforts, then you offer a savoury dessert or finger food. Pull the pin at 5.45 to 6 p.m. if they are just playing and then carry on with your day as usual. Do always make sure you are managing their behaviour at meal times, however (see page 255)

Q Does dinner have to be at 5.20 as we all like to eat together at 6?

A I'm afraid so. Your baby will be on their home stretch to sleep time by 6 p.m. They will be too hungry, which could cause serious crying or tired symptoms at this time as they will not cope. Either that or you will miss their hunger window and they will not eat, and you also risk fueling them too close to bed time making settling a more challenging task for baby. At their dinner time they need your full attention, so if you are trying to eat and they are needing to eat, neither you, your partner or your other children will have a peaceful, quiet reflective meal together. Because of this I find adults eat poorly, are impatient and find this time a rushed and, on most occasions, less than enjoyable event. It's also not exactly the most positive example of a healthy meal time to role play for your baby. As adults you are the ones who have to compromise. They can't eat later to suit your needs so you either eat at 5.30, after they have had their spoon-fed portion and are now finger-feeding themselves, or you wait until baby / toddler has gone to bed at 7 p.m.

Q He is tired by 6.30 p.m., so can I put him down a little early?

A They are meant to be tired at this time. They are supposed to be ready to sleep for the next 11 to 11½ hours. Many people have never seen their baby ready for an 11½ hour sleep until they get on to these routines, so it's important to let go of the old tired-sign suggestions. That strategy does not work for every baby, particularly those over six months of age and most certainly not for the bulk of unsettled children aged ten to 24 months. If they are very, very floppy during stories, try to get them to sit more upright and support their weight. Don't allow them to get overly warm or hold them in any position that may indicate they can go to sleep. Keep the story time active and excited sounding, and try to maintain their participation by getting them to turn the pages and lift the flaps and point to the pictures, even if you need to assist them. Most importantly, from 6 p.m. onwards, stick to the flow of the day, particularly when they should get out of the bath. Getting them out of the bath early always leads to tears before bed.

Q She doesn't look even the tiniest bit tired so should I wait until she does?

A Not at all. You are locking in sleep times very carefully. It's also not uncommon at the end of the day for them to appear quite alert. The body has a wonderful way of sustaining our most tiny of people but, I can assure you, their body is in fact extremely tired. At the end of a long, busy and wonderful day the only possible reason a child on a good routine would not look even the least bit tired is due to their body trying to sustain them with adrenalin and hormones because they are very tired indeed. Put them to bed on time and you will be surprised how quickly they drift off.

Q He really complains when I wrap him. Is this normal?

A Anything totally new or different can be met with serious protest. A new routine may well create passionate protest from babies developing a trust in the sleep process, wrapped or not. You will usually see this during role play, so be sure to practise this lots and lots with a teddy first so they become comfortable with the sleep-time conditions. Make sure you also get them familiar with your cues during role playing.

Q She falls asleep while I wrap or sing to her, so what should I do to keep her awake until I leave the room?

A This usually ends up being the biggest problem people encounter with the wrapping process after the initial transitional learning window. The wrap is a clear message that it's sleep time. Babies know nothing else but sleep happens when they are wrapped and they feel comfortable and safe. If she turns her head and closes her eyes as soon as you lay her down, try to wrap her quickly and say your cues in a way that keeps her a little alert without startling her. Keep your voice at a level that is audible as you repeat your cues and give her tummy a little rub before you pick her up to take her into her room. Once in her room, close the door and get through the settling routine quickly. Just sing one line of 'Twinkle twinkle little star' and kiss her a few times on the cheeks so she is aware of you saying 'Lie down'. Say your cues, pat her a little more firmly than usual so she can hear the process unfolding, say your cue once before shuffling out of the room, and click the door firmly closed so she can hear you leave. She must not go into a deep sleep in your arms or while you are in the room or she will definitely wake and cry during the night because the conditions of going to sleep have changed.

Q He is still crying when I finish singing to him, so do I still put him into bed?

A Yes, follow through with your settling routine as you aren't putting him to sleep, you are helping him learn how to do it by himself. He won't know to try if you are there. He will just wonder why you aren't doing what they are used to. Just follow the settling routine precisely, tuck him in and say your cues, then leave. If he continues to cry, please see 'Crying interpretation and assistance' (page 654).

Q She seems happy to roll on to her tummy to go to sleep. Is this safe?

A If you have not wrapped her, or she is over 12 months of age, then there is not much you can do about her preferred sleeping position. Always put her down on her back and if she rolls over and doesn't try to get up, then leave her in that position. It is always best to try and pursue sleeping on her back though, and a SafeT Sleep and firm tuck-in can help you achieve this for longer if you would like.

Q He is trying to stand up when I lie him down. What do I do?

A I am extremely particular about not confusing a child by defining a statement with the wrong definition. 'Lie down' only means 'lie down', not 'try to stand up' or 'get on your knees' or 'stand up'. When I ask the baby / toddler I am teaching to lie down, it usually takes one to two settling routines to define the statement with its true meaning. I lie them on their backs and, just as I do during nappy change and getting dressed times, I define that statement. I don't allow them to grab the bars or roll over or even *try* to get up. I calmly hold their little hand or both hands if I need to, keep my hand firmly on their nappy to prevent movement, and stay confident and reassuring as I repeat 'Lie down, bubba' once, then say my settling or resettling cues before turning and leaving. Once I turn to leave, however, I don't mind if they stand up and I definitely do not turn back and try to lie them down again. This means standing up does not receive attention or change the outcome and your child is not confused. By the second or third sleep time, they tend to lie down without even the slightest concern because they understand what that means and the boundary I have placed around that request. It takes the stress and confusion out of the settling process, and without a doubt stops tears and tantrums.

Q How do I get them to find their dummy on their own?

A If you have followed the guidelines outlined in the dummy pot game in the sleep environment chapter, then there is nothing more you can do. Do not hand it to them. It's important they are empowered with the ability to get it themselves so they can sleep through the night with it or, if they choose, without it! They will not be able to get it themselves during the night if you don't allow them to do it when you first put them to bed. They may also just not want it at that time. You can get their hand and guide it to the dummy and say 'Get your dummy', but if they refuse to take it, or do not take it for whatever reason, just carry on seamlessly as there is nothing more to be done. Simply say your cues calmly and confidently and leave them for a little while to try and settle. Repeat this process as you interpret their cries and assist them to settle on those first few days.

PRM Routine 2

Babies go through typical transitional milk feed and sleep changes during their first two years of life and these affect their routines. The changes in sleep patterns occur whether the child has a low (LSR), average (ASR) or high (HSR) sleep requirement (see page 534). They happen at particular age brackets and result in changing or lowering sleep and milk intake once solid food has being introduced into a baby's diet. The following are the ages when changes in milk feeding times and sleep transitions occur:

- at five and half to six and half months solids are being established and milk feed begin to reduce
- at six to eight months solids have been established and milk intake has been reduced to four full feeds per day
- at nine months milk feeds begin to reduce to three full feeds by the tenth month
- at 12 months LSR babies need to move to one sleep a day
- at 14 to 15 months milk feeds have reduced to two full feeds per day and most ASR babies need to move to one sleep a day

- at 16 to 18 months milk feeds are reduced to a final night feed before bed, which is dropped at everyone's leisure, and most HSR babies need to move to one sleep a day.

Even with these natural changes, your aim should be for your baby to have a balanced and healthy 7 p.m. settling time and 6 to 7 a.m. waking time the following morning, so their routines will need to be adjusted as they transition to the next age group to achieve this.

The following routines are suggested for ASR and HSR babies who are establishing solids (from around the fifth month and onwards). Prior to that, variations between the sleep requirement groups and age transitions are extremely vast and their changing needs are rapid, and I'm sure you can appreciate would require another carefully and respectfully detailed complete book of its own to fully cater for their varied needs. Once your baby's night sleep is repaired to the minimum sleep suggestion for each routine, you can begin building up your baby's daytime sleep intake (see page 594). And remember to always keep your baby well hydrated throughout the day, but do not offer water 30 minutes before solids are due as water will make them feel full and impede eating.

While solids are being introduced (at 5½ to 6½ months)

The following routine is the classic '2-hours-up, 2-hours-down' format that has been around for decades, with some mild variations to cater for both the average and high sleep requirement babies' needs. The variation in the routine between the babies still establishing solids and those who are established on solids is due to lower calorie / fuel intake and lower iron intake, which creates a need for more regular sleep opportunities and more milk feeds. The dream feed is occasionally necessary when food is not adequate due to a growing hunger and need for iron in their diet. Until these elements are provided a dream feed is appropriate for this transitioning age group.

The reason you need to wake your child for a feed rather than wait for them to wake up is twofold. The first is to ensure you don't teach your baby to wake up and call out for a feed to go back to sleep. This would develop a dependent set of resettling associations and will contradict your normal communication style—obviously a child doesn't know 10 p.m. from 2 a.m. or 5 a.m., so obliging one request to feed to go back to sleep, yet not obliging any subsequent requests is guaranteed to create tears. By waking your baby and feeding them before they stir and call out you eliminate the pattern of them calling out for milk to go back to sleep.

The second reason is to try to prevent tears rather than manage them. As true hunger will typically (in my experience) occur between 11.30 p.m. and 1.30 a.m. and again between 2.30 and 3.30 a.m., you need to pre-empt their body's hunger and cater for that before they feel a need to cry out in hunger. All that said, by the time you start this program it is better to have established your solids rather than introduce or sustain a dream feed in order to avoid creating a learnt hunger pattern in your baby's circadian rhythm (which could cause them to learn to wake naturally then for a feed) or detract from your baby's daytime calorie intake as this can create a fussy feeder.

Daily routine outline

6.30–7 a.m.	Natural waking
7	Latest waking. Milk feed
8	Breakfast
9	Mid-morning nap: ASR babies takes one hour, 15 minutes; HSR babies one hour, 30 minutes
11	Morning tea: milk feed
12 p.m.	Lunch: vegetables and protein, plus dessert by eight months
1	Mid-afternoon nap: ASR babies take one hour, 30 minutes; HSR babies one hour, 45 minutes
3–3.30	Afternoon tea: milk feed
5	Dinner: vegetables with or without rice cereal
6.30	Milk feed
7	Bedtime for 11 to 12 hours
10.30	Dream feed

Daily routine in detail

6–6.30 a.m.	Natural waking. Manage any wakings before 6.00 a.m. with your crying interpretation and support (see page 654) and read about how to increase their sleep intake to encourage a later waking (see page 594). Use your waking routine (see page 622) and allow playtime in cot (see page 609) for 15 to 20 minutes. Before getting them up remember to pack away (see page 330) and use your wait game and cue (see page 74).
7	Latest waking time—use your waking routine and cue and allow a brief play and pack away. Breast or bottle feed—do not allow baby to snooze. Change nappy (see page 287), then allow free playtime.
7.50	Prepare baby's breakfast. Use pre-emptive and forewarning language—'nearly time for breakfast', 'nearly time to sit down and wait for mummy, yummy apple and oatmeal'—(see page 538).

8	Baby's breakfast. Manage their feeding (if their behaviour is difficult see page 255) and use your meal-time routine (see page 226). Then dress baby for day (see page 287) and allow free playtime. They'll usually want to spend time with you but allow them to be free to safely explore their environment if they so wish. This is the time you might need to drop off older children to preschools or schools. If you are in the car don't let your little one fall asleep. They need to stay awake until the morning sleep at nine o'clock. Prepare cot room for morning sleep. Remember to use your flow of communication—'nearly time for stories, nearly time for nigh' nigh's'—(see page 40).
8.45	Nappy change before beginning settling routine (see page 609).
8.55	Say goodnight to anyone in the room, then complete settling routine.
9	Morning sleep. See sleep requirement variations (see page 569). Set up play stations (see page 148) while baby sleeps. When baby wakes allow brief playtime in cot, then pack away. If baby wakes early, a longer playtime in cot is encouraged. Latest waking time is 11 a.m. Change nappy.
11.00	Morning tea: breast or bottle feed. Independent playtime opportunity. This is the time to help them become comfortable with being put down to play independently, a skill they need for sleep—think of it as sleep-earning play. If they are not settling down to play remember your flow of communication and follow through (see page 47). If you leave the room, remember your short-term absence cue 'I'll be back' (see page 94).
12 p.m.	Lunch: vegetables, with or without rice cereal, and protein, which is introduced as soon as they are comfortable with vegetables (see box on page 538), no desserts or fruit required here. Follow your meal-time routine (see page 226) when feeding them and use your cues if there are problems (see page 255). After lunch is complete, use the wait game and cue (see page 74) then get them up for a little one-on-one playtime (see page 131). Give your baby your undivided attention for around 15 minutes—don't even answer the phones. Remember your pre-empting cues, 'nearly time to pack away' (see page 42) towards the end of playtime.
12.40	Pack away toys completely, and prepare cot room and wrap for mid-afternoon sleep while baby keeps you company and 'helps'. Change nappy and use your pre-emptive cues for sleep—'nearly time for sleep, let's go find our books'.
12.45	Begin settling routine (see page 609).
12.55	Final book pack away and say goodnight to everyone in the room. Complete settling routine.
1	Mid-afternoon sleep—check sleep requirement suggestions above.

2.30–3	Natural waking time. Leave baby in cot as long as you can if they need to or naturally wake earlier. Once they have woken, use your waking routine and cues. Allow them independent play in the cot up until afternoon milk feed is due or for 20 minutes.
3	Afternoon tea: breast / bottle milk feed only. This milk feed will remain for quite some time to come, up to and in some cases well beyond their first birthday. Some children opt to keep this until mummy decides its time to have milk in a cup with their afternoon tea instead.
4.15–5	Afternoon bridging nap for six month olds if their food is still insufficient and they appear to want the nap. This nap is strictly 20 minutes. Do not allow your baby to sleep beyond 20 minutes. Keep peeping at your baby (if walking in the pram) every three to five minutes so you know the time they drift off to sleep, and then wake them either when their allocated nap time ends, or when this sleep window ends at 5 p.m., whichever occurs first. This is a good sleep for them to have in the pram whenever possible, or in the car if you are picking up older children. Most babies have had enough of their cot by this time, and will need this sleep but will most likely need some assistance to take it. As you cannot assist them in their cot, you should only help them in an honest assisting environment like the pram. If it is warm, walk the pram in the shade. If it is hot, raining or blowing a gale head to a local shopping mall. If you cannot do either of these, then push your baby in the pram at home briefly until they drift off to sleep, or they can have another sleep in their cot. If they don't fall asleep early enough and don't nap the whole allocated time of 20 minutes, still wake them by 5 p.m.

If your little one needs this sleep at this age, indicated by them not coping when they miss it, try and make it easy for them—you'll need to know your baby's sleep requirement. If they are sleeping for two hours at their mid-afternoon sleep and therefore unable to take this bridging nap but becoming overtired by 7 p.m. after the first three days of your new routine, then you will need to wake them after one hour, 15 minutes (ASR) or one hour, 30 minutes (HSR) after the mid-afternoon sleep to encourage this nap until they turn seven months of age and are ready to drop this bridge nap because they start to eat better, which will make it easier to cope with the longer afternoon. If your six-month-old baby has difficulty going to sleep at 7 p.m. after a few consistent days on this routine, and they are taking their bridge sleep right up until 5 p.m., then you will need to taper the latest sleep time for this bridge nap back to 4.45 p.m. to ensure they do not continue to have difficulty falling asleep at 7 p.m. This may mean that you need to tighten their mid-afternoon sleep back a little to one hour, 15 minutes (ASR) or one hour, 30 minutes (HSR) to help them fall asleep on the bridge earlier. Their night sleep is the most important sleep to lock in first, then you adjust their days, depending on how much sleep they have left to take. You never steal from the nights to achieve better days. Alternatively, if they are not taking the afternoon bridge nap and are still having trouble falling asleep at 7 p.m. because they are appearing overtired, then you will need to increase their mid-afternoon sleep by limiting their mid-morning sleep slightly to one hour, 15 minutes (ASR) or one hour, 30 minutes (HSR) and not waking them at the mid-afternoon sleep, or re-assess their sleep requirement after five days of solid routine management to ensure this routine actually suits your baby's individual needs. Always allow three to five days minimum of solid routine management before you make any major changes as your baby needs to work through their new settling request and develop new independent associations with sleep first.

4.15–5	Use this time to do your final pack away for the day, and prepare for dinner, using your pre-emptive cues if they are awake.
5	Latest time to wake from bridging nap, using waking cues. Please ensure you have read the details of this bridging nap carefully.
	Dinner: vegetables with or without rice cereal (see box on page 538), then playtime in high chair (see page 192) as you prepare their bedroom and tidy kitchen and organise your own evening meal for when the baby goes to bed at 7 p.m. Do not neglect yourself. It is very important you eat a healthy meal at the end of your day to stave off depression and poor sleep, plus it's a good time to connect with other members of your family.
6	Nudie playtime (see page 209), using cues for bath.
6.15	Bath time. You need to watch baby the whole time. Remember your cues as you get towards 6.30—'nearly time to pack away, nearly time to get out of bath'.
6.30	Baby out of bath (not before). Household should start to become calm and lights dimmed in preparation for bed. Dry and dress baby (see page 287) quickly but calmly. As they will be tired you might need to reassure them—'it's okay, bubba, you're just tired. Nearly time for milk and nigh' nigh's'.
6.35	Breast or bottle feed, ten to 15 minutes only. Baby must not doze or even zone out during this feed as it will interrupt the settling routine. To avoid tears then, you must keep them awake now.
6.45–50	Begin settling routine, by 6.50 at the latest.
6.55	Final cue—'last page, then nigh' nigh's'—and pack away. Enjoy a last cuddle and complete settling routine.

| 7 | Bedtime. If baby cries assess the situation from an adult's perspective (see page 70) and interpret the cries (see pages 654), being mindful of their sleep bus timetable (see page 675) before you go in to resettle. Remember your cues and resettling routines (see page 617). |
| 10.30 | Possible dream feed. As you attempt to increase their solid intake during the day you will start to wean them off this dream feed. |

Once solids have been established (at six to eight months)

By the sixth month on, all the routines assume you have started solids and introduced iron into your baby's diet via a protein with their lunch-time vegetable meal (see page 538). The 10.30 p.m. dream feed will now not be necessary if your baby is eating adequate solids and getting iron in their diet. If not, it's time to reassess your baby's solid intake before starting this routine as iron is essential for sleep between 11.30 p.m. and 3.30 a.m.

You may opt or find it more convenient to provide your baby independent play opportunity at 11 a.m. instead of after their mid-afternoon sleep. This may vary depending on your daily activities. I've indicated both times as independent play opportunity, simply choose one time to suit your day's activities. I usually suggest around 45 minutes to an hour of requested independent play followed by a solid 15 minutes of focus play.

Daily routine outline

7 a.m.	Latest waking. Milk feed
8	Breakfast
9.30	Mid-morning nap: ASR babies take one hour, 15 minutes; HSR babies one hour, 30 minutes
11	Morning tea: milk feed
12 p.m.	Lunch: vegetables and protein, plus dessert by eight months
1.30	Mid-afternoon nap: ASR babies take one hour, 15 minutes; HSR babies one hour, 30 minutes
3–3.30	Afternoon tea: milk feed (see hungry baby box page 578)
5	Dinner: vegetables with or without carbohydrates (rice, pasta)
6.30	Milk feed
7	Bedtime for 11 to 12 hours

Daily routine in detail

| 6–6.30 a.m. | Natural waking. Manage any wakings before 5.50 a.m. with your crying interpretation and support (see page 694) and read about how to increase |

their sleep to encourage a later waking (see page 594). Once they have woken leave them as long as you can before entering the room using your waking routine (see page 622) and allow playtime in cot (see page 609) for 15 to 20 minutes. Before getting them up remember to pack away and use your wait game and cue (see page 74).

7   Latest waking time—use your waking routine and cue to wake them up if necessary. Allow a brief play and pack away. Breast or bottle feed—do not allow baby to snooze. Change nappy (see page 287), then allow free playtime.

7.50   Prepare baby's breakfast. Use your pre-emptive and forewarning language—'nearly time for breakfast', 'nearly time to sit down and wait for mummy, yummy apple and oatmeal'—(see page 538).

8   Baby's breakfast. Manage their feeding (if their behaviour is difficult see page 255), and use your meal-time routine (see page 226). After breakfast, dress baby for day (see page 287) and then allow free playtime. They'll usually want to help you but allow them to be free to venture off safely once they are mobile if they wish. This might be the time you need to drop off older children to preschools or schools. If you are in the car don't let your little one fall asleep. They need to stay awake until the morning sleep at 9.30 a.m. Before 9.15, prepare cot room for morning sleep. Remember to use your flow of communication (see page 40)—'nearly time for stories, nearly time for nigh' nigh's'—in the lead up to the settling routine (see page 609).

9.15   Nappy change, before beginning settling routine.

9.25   Say goodnight to everyone, then complete settling routine.

9.30   Morning sleep—allow for any sleep requirement variations (see page 569). Set up play stations (see page 148) while baby sleeps. If baby wakes early, allow playtime in cot for a minimum of 20 minutes. If offering independent playtime when they wake up, set up play stations (see page 148) while they are sleeping.

11.00   Latest waking time; allow brief playtime in cot if they wake at 11 a.m. Pack away cot. Change nappy. Supply morning tea as soon as they get up (see page 538). Independent playtime opportunity. This is the time to help them become comfortable with being put down to play independently, a skill they need for sleep—think of it as sleep-earning play. If they are not settling down to play remember your flow of communication and follow through (see page 47) and positioning for play (see page 157). If you leave the room, remember your short-term absence cue 'I'll be back' (see page 94).

12.00 p.m.	Lunch: vegetables and protein everyday (see box on page 538), and by eight months they should also be offered a dessert (fruit pureed with or without rice cereal, etc.). Follow your meal-time management routine (see page 226) when feeding them and use your cues if there are problems (see page 255). After lunch is complete use your wait game and cue (see page 74). Get them up for a little more independent playtime then complete their play session with some one-on-one playtime (see page 131).
1.10	Pack away toys completely, prepare cot room and wrap for mid-afternoon sleep while baby keeps you company and 'helps'. Change nappy and use your pre-emptive cues for sleep—'nearly time for sleep, let's go find our books'.
1.15	Begin settling routine (see page 609).
1.25	Pack away of books, say goodnight to everyone in the room and complete settling routine.
1.30	Mid-afternoon sleep. Check sleep requirement suggestions for natural waking windows and latest waking times. Leave baby in cot as long as you can if they need to or naturally wake earlier. Once they have woken, use your waking routine and cues (see page 622). Allow them independent play in the cot up until afternoon milk feed is due or for 20 minutes, whichever comes first.
3–3.30	Afternoon tea. For a six to nine month olds this is a breast / bottle milk feed only. The milk feed will remain for quite some time to come, up to and well beyond their first birthday. Some children opt to keep this until mummy decides it's time to have milk in a cup with their afternoon tea instead. If you take up independent playtime opportunity here rather than after mid-morning sleep, your timings will look something like 3.45 to 4.30 p.m. independent playtime, then 4.30 to 4.45 p.m. one-on-one playtime.
4.45	Time for final pack away for the day, and remember to use your cues—'time to pack away, nearly time for dinner'. Pop them in to their high chair for a quiet time while you warm their dinner. This time may include their favourite Baby Einstein DVD on TV or books on their tray table in the kitchen while you warm their food.
5.00	Dinner time (see box on page 538): vegetables with or without rice cereal. Then playtime in high chair (see page 192) as you tidy kitchen, organise your own and the rest of the family's evening meal to be taken after baby goes to bed and prepare their bedroom. Remember, you must eat a healthy meal at the end of your day to stave off depression and poor sleep, plus it's a good time to connect with other members of your family, so don't neglect this.
6	Nudie playtime (see page 209), and use your pre-emptive cues for bath time.

6.15   Bath time. You need to watch baby the whole time. Remember your cues as you get towards 6.30—'nearly time to pack away, nearly time to get out of bath'.

6.30   Baby out of bath (not before). Everyone in the household should start to become calm with the lights dimmed in preparation for baby's bed time. Dry and dress baby (see page 287), quickly but calmly. As they will be tired you might need to reassure them—'it's okay, bubba, you're just tired. Nearly time for milk and nigh' nigh's'.

6.35   Breast or bottle feed, ten minutes only. Baby must not doze or even zone out at this time as it will interrupt their settling ability at 7 p.m. To avoid tears then, you must keep them awake now.

6.45–50   Begin settling routine. This must start at 6.50 at the latest.

6.55   Final cue—'last page, then nigh' nigh's'—and pack away. Enjoy a last cuddle and complete your settling routine.

7   Bedtime. If your baby cries assess the situation from an adult's perspective (see page 70) and interpret the cries (see pages 654) before you go in to resettle. Remember your cues and resettling routines (see page 617).

Sustaining the gap between afternoon tea and dinner

If you appear to have a very hungry baby who is not coping until 5 p.m. on just milk, offer a light snack (half a Cruskit, or some cheese, or half a piece of fruit) in addition to their 3 p.m. milk feed, and give them their solids closer to 5.20 p.m. Be mindful however of not filling them up so they cannot eat dinner. Dinner must be maintained. Gauge their response to the additional afternoon-tea calorie intake by their ability to eat their dinner and decrease or increase their afternoon tea accordingly. Keep them well hydrated all day before you offer additional food, but do not give water 30 minutes before solids are due as this will impede their appetite.

Nine to 11 month olds

At nine months milk feeds begin to reduce and by the tenth month your baby will need only three milk feeds per day, dropping the mid-morning milk feed. If your baby is still transitioning (typically more common in nine month olds) and is tired despite having eaten efficiently at their lunch feed and taken their mid-morning sleep intake correctly, then you can put them down for their mid-afternoon sleep anywhere from 2 p.m. onwards. In this case simply offer them water before their sleep and feed them their milk feed and afternoon snack when they wake up to help sustain them for the longer afternoon. You can then offer dinner at 5.20 p.m. instead of 5. If this becomes your baby's natural need for a short time, ensure you feed them their lunch closer to 12 p.m. most days. As they get older remember to progress this second sleep to later in the afternoon, and alter their afternoon tea and dinner windows back to suggested times in this routine.

There is an option for when you offer independent playtime opportunity to your child. Depending on your activities for the day, you may opt or find it more convenient to provide play opportunity after their lunch or after their mid-afternoon sleep. This is the time to help them become comfortable with being put down to play independently, a skill they need for sleep—think of it as sleep-earning play. If they are not settling down to play remember your flow of communication and follow through (see page 47 and also trouser tug page 374). If you leave the room, remember your short-term absence cue 'I'll be back' (see page 94). I usually suggest around 45 minutes to an hour of requested independent play followed by a solid 15 minutes of focus play.

Daily routine outline

6–6.30 a.m.	Natural waking
7	Latest waking. Milk feed
7.20	Breakfast
9.30	Morning tea: fruit and water
10	Mid-morning nap: ASR babies take one hour, 15 minutes; HSR one hour, 30 minutes
11.30–12 p.m.	Lunch: vegetables and protein, plus dessert
2–2.15	Afternoon tea: milk feed and snack
2.15–2.30	Mid-afternoon nap. Option: at 2.15 p.m. ASR babies take one hour, 15 minutes; at 2.30 p.m. HSR babies take one hour, 30 minutes. Offer water when they wake up.
5.20	Dinner: vegetables with or without carbohydrates
6.30	Milk feed
7.00	Bedtime for 11 to 12 hours

Daily routine in detail

6–6.30 a.m.	Natural waking. Manage any wakings before 5.30 a.m. with crying interpretation and support (see page 654) and read about how to increase their sleep (see page 594). If your baby is not awake by 6.30 p.m. on the first ten days, wake them. Use your waking routine (see page 622) and allow playtime in cot (see page 609) for 15 to 20 minutes. Before getting them up remember to pack away and use your wait game and cue (see page 74).
7 a.m.	Breast or bottle feed, but do not allow baby to snooze. Change nappy (see page 287), then allow free playtime.

7.15	Prepare baby's breakfast. Use your pre-emptive and forewarning language (see page 43)—'nearly time for breakfast', 'nearly time to sit down and wait for mummy, yummy apple and oatmeal'.
7.20	Baby's breakfast. Manage their feed (see page 255) and your use meal-time routine (see page 226). After breakfast, dress them for day (see page 287) and then allow free playtime. They'll usually want to help you but allow them to be free to safely venture off once mobile if they wish. This might be the time you need to drop off older children to preschools or schools. If you are in the car try to not let your little one fall asleep. They need to stay awake until the morning sleep at 9.30 a.m. Prepare cot room for morning sleep and remember to use your flow of communication (see page 40)—'nearly time for stories, nearly time for nigh' nigh's'.
9.30	Morning tea: fruit and water. During the ninth month you can offer milk *after* their fruit if they are interested. By the tenth month, this milk feed is naturally dropped and your baby will be taking only three milk feeds a day.
9.45	Nappy change, then begin settling routine (see page 609).
9.55	Say goodnight to everyone, then complete settling routine.
10.00	Morning sleep begins: ASR babies take one hour, 15 minutes: HSR babies take one hour, 30 minutes. If your baby wakes early encourage playtime in the cot until 11.30 a.m. While baby sleeps, set up play stations (see page 148) if you are going to offer independent playtime after lunch.
11.30–12 p.m.	Lunch: vegetables, and protein every day (see box on page 538), and they should also be offered a dessert (fruit puree with or without rice cereal, yoghurt etc.). Serve this meal as close to 11.30 as your baby wakes, and no later than 12 p.m. Follow your meal-time management routine (see page 226) when feeding them and use your cues if there are problems (see page 255). After lunch is completed use your wait game and cue (see page 74). This is a good independent playtime opportunity if not offered after lunch (see above).
1.50–2.10	Afternoon tea: milk feed and snack. The time of afternoon tea can be between 1.50 and 2.10 p.m., depending on when your baby woke and had their lunch. For example, if your ASR baby woke at 11.15 and ate lunch at 11.30 they can have their afternoon tea at 1.50 p.m. and go down for their mid-afternoon nap around 2.15 p.m. The settling routine for this afternoon nap will begin at 2.05 p.m. But if your HSR baby woke at 11.30 a.m. and ate lunch closer to 12 p.m. they can have their afternoon tea at 2.05 p.m and go down for their mid-afternoon nap around 2.30 p.m. Settling routine will begin at 2.20 p.m.
2.15 / 2.30	Mid-afternoon sleep: ASR babies take one hour, 15 minutes; HSR babies take one hour, 30 minutes. If your baby wakes earlier than suggested, leave

them in their cot as long as you can before attending to either resettle for wakings under 40 minutes or, once they have fully woken, use your waking routine and cues (see page 622). Allow them independent play in cot up until the designated waking time is due or for 20 minutes, whichever occurs first. Offer them water when they wake.

4.15 Latest sleep time allowed when building your child's daily sleep intake (see page 594). Wake your baby now if they are not already awake.

This is a good independent playtime opportunity if not offered after lunch (see above).

4.45 Use this time to do your final pack away for the day, using your cues—'time to pack away, nearly time for dinner'—then pop them into their high chair for a quiet time while you prepare their dinner. High-chair time may include their favourite Baby Einstein DVD on TV or books on their tray table in the kitchen.

5 Dinner: vegetables with or without rice cereal (see box on page 538). Then playtime in high chair (see page 192) as you tidy kitchen, organise your own and the rest of the family's evening meal to be taken after baby goes to bed and prepare their bedroom for the evening. Remember, you must eat a healthy meal at the end of your day to stave off depression and poor sleep, plus it's a good time to connect with other members of your family, so don't neglect this.

6 Nudie playtime (see page 209), using cues for bath.

6.15 Bath time. You need to watch baby the whole time. Remember your cues as you get towards 6.30—'nearly time to pack away, nearly time to get out of bath'.

6.30 Baby out of bath (not before). Everyone in the household should start to calm down with the lights dimmed in preparation for baby's bed time. Dry and dress baby (see page 287), quickly but calmly. As they will be tired you might need to reassure them—'it's okay, bubba, you're just tired. Nearly time for milk and nigh' nigh's'.

6.35 Breast or bottle feed, ten minutes only. Baby must not doze or even zone out at this time as it will interrupt their settling ability at 7 p.m. To avoid tears then, you must keep them awake now.

6.45–50 Begin settling routine. This must start at 6.50 at the latest.

6.55 Final cue—'last page, then nigh' nigh's'—and pack away. Enjoy a final cuddle and complete your settling routine.

7 Bedtime. If your baby cries assess the situation from an adult's perspective (see page 70) and interpret the cries (see pages 654) before you go in to resettle. Remember your cues and resettling routines (see page 617).

12 to 13 month olds

If your baby (typically more common in 12 month olds) is still transitioning to this reduced sleep and feeding routine, and is particularly tired despite having taken their mid-morning sleep intake correctly and eaten efficiently at lunch time then you can put them down for their mid-afternoon sleep anywhere from 2.15 p.m. onwards. In this case either bring their afternoon tea forward earlier or simply offer them water before their sleep and feed them their milk feed only when they wake to help sustain them for the longer afternoon. In these cases, you can continue to offer dinner at 5.20 p.m. As they get older remember to progress this second sleep to later in the afternoon, and alter their afternoon tea and dinner windows back to suggested program.

There is an option for when you offer independent playtime opportunity to your child. Depending on your activities for the day, you may opt or find it more convenient to provide play opportunity after their lunch or after their mid-afternoon sleep. This is the time to help them become comfortable with being put down to play independently, a skill they need for sleep—think of it as sleep-earning play. If they are not settling down to play remember your flow of communication and follow through (see page 47 and also trouser tug page 374). If you leave the room, remember your short-term absence cue 'I'll be back' (see page 94).

Daily routine outline

6–6.30 a.m.	Natural waking
7	Latest waking. Milk feed
7.30	Breakfast
9.30	Morning tea: fruit and water
10.15	Mid-morning nap: ASR babies take one hour, 15 minutes; HSR babies one hour, 30 minutes—once you have built their sleep up to this level, feed you baby when they wake up
11.30–12 p.m.	Lunch: vegetables and protein, plus dessert
2–2.30	Afternoon tea: milk feed and snack
2.30–3	Mid-afternoon sleep: ASR babies take one hour, 15 minutes; HSR one hour, 30 minutes. The latest time that sleep can be built up to is 4.15 p.m.
5.20	Dinner: vegetables with or without carbohydrates
6.30	Milk feed
7	Bedtime for 11 to 12 hours

Daily routine in detail

6–6.30 a.m.   Natural waking. Manage any wakings before 5.30 a.m. with crying interpretation and support (see page 694) and read about how to build their sleep (see page 594). If they are not awake by 6.30 on the first ten days of the routine, wake them. Use your waking routine (see page 622) and offer playtime in cot (see page 609) for 15 to 20 minutes. Before getting them up remember to pack away and use your wait game and cue (see page 74).

7	Breast or bottle feed but do not allow your baby to snooze. Change their nappy (see page 287) and then offer free playtime.
7.10	Prepare baby's breakfast and use pre-emptive and forewarning language (see page 43)—'nearly time for breakfast', 'nearly time to sit down and wait for mummy, yummy apple and oatmeal'.
7.20	Baby's breakfast. Use your meal-time routine (see page 226) and manage their behaviour if they are difficult to feed (see page 255). After breakfast is finished, dress them for day (see page 287) and then offer free playtime. They'll usually want to 'help' you but allow them to be free to safely venture off once they are mobile if they wish. This might be the time you need to drop off older children to preschools or schools. If you are in the car do not let your little one fall asleep. They need to stay awake until the morning sleep at 10.15 a.m. Prepare cot room for the morning sleep and remember to use your flow of communication (see page 40)—'nearly time for stories, nearly time for nigh' nigh's'.
9.30	Morning tea: fruit and water only.
10.00	Nappy change, then begin settling routine (see page 287).
10.10	Say goodnight to everyone and complete settling routine.
10.15	Morning sleep: ASR babies take one hour, 15 minutes; HSR babies one hour, 30 minutes. If baby wakes early encourage playtime in the cot until 11.30. Once you have built their sleep up to the time recommended, feed your baby when they wake up. If your baby sleeps for only 40 minutes or less when your first start your program or in the long term you will need to build up their sleep (see Q&A following). While baby is asleep, set-up play stations if you plan on offering independent play at this time.
11.30–12 p.m.	Lunch: vegetables, and protein every day, and they should also be offered a dessert (fruit puree with or without rice cereal, or yoghurt etc.) (see box on page 538). This should be served as close to 11.30 as they wake. Follow your meal-time management routine (see page 226) and use your cues if there are problems (see page 255 chart hands down). After lunch is completed use your wait game and cue (see page 74).
	This is a good independent playtime opportunity if you decide not to offer it later after mid-afternoon nap (see above).
1.35	Final opportunity for a great one-on-one play with your baby (see page 131).

1.50	Pack away toys completely, prepare cot room and wrap for mid-afternoon sleep while baby keeps you company and 'helps'.
2.00	Afternoon tea: light snack and milk feed.
2.15	Begin settling routine (see page 609).
2.25	Final goodnight to everyone in the room and complete settling routine.
2.30–3	Mid-afternoon sleep: ASR babies take one hour, 15 minutes; HSR babies one hour 30 minutes. If your baby wakes earlier than suggested, leave them in their cot as long as you can before attending to either resettle (for wakings under 40 minutes) or once they have fully woken, use your waking routine and cues (see page 622). Allow them play in cot up until the designated waking time is due or for 20 minutes, whichever comes first.
	Offer water when they get up.
	This is a good independent playtime opportunity if not offered after lunch (see above).
5	Use this time to do your final pack away for the day, saying your cues—'time to pack away, nearly time for dinner'. Pop them into their high chair for a quiet time while you prepare their dinner. This may involve their favourite Baby Einstein DVD on TV or books on their tray table in the kitchen while you warm food.
5.20	Dinner: vegetables with or without rice cereal (see box on page 538). Then playtime in high chair (see page 192) as you tidy kitchen, organise your own and the rest of the family's evening meal to be taken after baby goes to bed and prepare their bedroom for the evening. Remember, you must eat a healthy meal at the end of your day to stave off depression and poor sleep, plus it's a good time to connect with other members of your family, so don't neglect this.
6	Nudie playtime (see page 209), using cues for bath.
6.15	Bath time. You need to watch baby the whole time. Remember your cues as you get towards 6.30—'nearly time to pack away, nearly time to get out of bath'.
6.30	Baby out of bath (not before). Everyone in the household should start to calm down with the lights dimmed in preparation for baby's bed time. Dry and dress baby (see page 287), quickly but calmly. As they will be tired you might need to reassure them—'it's okay, bubba, you're just tired. Nearly time for milk and nigh' nigh's'.
6.35	Breast or bottle feed, ten minutes only. Baby must not doze or even zone out at this time as it will interrupt their settling ability at 7 p.m. To avoid tears then, you must keep them awake now.
6.45–50	Begin settling routine. This must start at 6.50 at the latest.

6.55   Final cue—'last page, then nigh' nigh's'—and pack away. Enjoy a final cuddle and complete your settling routine.

7   Bedtime. If your baby cries assess the situation from an adult's perspective (see page 70) and interpret the cries (see pages 654) before you go in to resettle. Remember your cues and resettling routines (see page 617).

14 to 15 month olds, until they need one sleep per day

Please be sure to assess your child's daily sleep intake carefully by this stage. Some average-sleep-requirement babies need to shift to a single-sleep-a-day routine to better suit their overall daily needs (see Routine 1, variation 12 months plus on page 552). If your child will not take the mid-afternoon bridging nap, this indicates they are ready to progress to a single sleep a day and this Routine 2 variation is not appropriate. To try and persist with this routine when they are unable to achieve a late-afternoon bridging nap will result in a very unsettled baby by 5 p.m. due to poor sleep intake and low calorie intake and you may risk causing late-afternoon tears and tantrums and poor eating as well as possibly causing multiple wakings between 7 and 10 p.m. due to overtiredness. Please see ready to move to a single sleep routine (see page 596).

Signs and symptoms that this routine does not suit your baby's need any longer will appear in the form of:

- difficulty settling at mid-morning sleep
- unable to sleep for the rest of the day if they do take the mid-morning sleep effectively
- wake after 40 minutes and are unable to resettle if they do settle well for a mid-morning sleep, to then take a final mid-afternoon bridging nap of 40 minutes
- not taking mid-afternoon bridging nap
- unable to settle at 7 p.m. if they do take the afternoon bridging nap
- wake after only 40 minutes if they do settle at 7 p.m., then needing to be resettled for a minimum of 40 minutes.

If you see any of these symptoms, then your baby's sleep requirement has transitioned and they need to move to a more appropriate single-sleep routine as this routine is not appropriate for their needs.

There is an option for when you offer independent playtime to your child. Depending on your activities for the day, you may opt or find it more convenient to provide this after their lunch or after their mid-afternoon sleep. This is the time to help them become comfortable with being put down to play independently, a skill they need for sleep—think of it as sleep-earning play. If they are not settling down to play remember your flow of communication and follow through (see page 47 and also trouser tug page 374). If you leave the room, remember to say your short-term absence cue 'I'll be back' (see page 94). I usually suggest around 45 minutes to an hour of requested independent play followed by a solid 15 minutes of focus play.

Daily routine outline

6–6.30 a.m.	Natural waking
7	Latest waking. Milk feed
7.30	Breakfast
9.30	Morning tea: fruit and water
10.45	Mid-morning nap: ASR babies take one hour, 45 minutes; HSR babies take two hours, 15 minutes. Once you have built their sleep up to these recommended times, feed your baby when they wake up
12.30–1 p.m.	Lunch: vegetables and protein, plus dessert. A variation in the lunch time exists here to cater for the two different sleep requirement groups waking at either 12.15 p.m. (ASR) or 12.45 p.m. (HSR)
2.30	Afternoon tea: milk feed in a cup and snack
3.30–3.45	Mid-afternoon bridging nap (20 to 40 minutes only)
4.15	Latest wake-up time—no sleeping beyond this point
5.20	Dinner: vegetables with or without carbohydrates
6.30	Milk feed
7	Bedtime for 11 to 12 hours

Daily routine in detail

6–6.30 a.m.	Natural waking. Manage any wakings before 5.30 a.m. with crying interpretation and support (see page 654) and read about how to build their sleep (see page 594). If they are not awake by 6.30 on the first ten days of the routine, wake them. Use your waking routine (see page 622) and offer playtime in cot (see page 609) for 15 to 20 minutes. Before getting them up remember to pack away and use your wait game and cue (see page 74).
7	Latest waking time. Breast or bottle feed but do not allow baby to snooze. Change their nappy (see page 287), and then offer free playtime.
7.10	Prepare baby's breakfast and use pre-emptive and forewarning language (see page 43)—'nearly time for breakfast', 'nearly time to sit down and wait for mummy, yummy apple and oatmeal'.
7.20	Baby's breakfast. Use your meal-time routine (see page 226) and manage their behaviour if they a difficult to feed (see page 255). After breakfast is

finished, dress them for day (see page 287) and then offer free playtime. They'll usually want to 'help' you but allow them to be free to safely venture off once they are mobile if they wish. This might be the time you need to drop off older children to preschools or schools. If you are in the car do not let your little one fall asleep. They need to stay awake until the morning sleep at 10.15 a.m. Prepare cot room for the morning sleep and remember to use your flow of communication (see page 40)—'nearly time for stories, nearly time for nigh' nigh's'.

9.30	Morning tea: fruit and water only.
10.30	Nappy change, then begin settling routine (see page 287).
10.40	Say good night to everyone and complete settling routine
10.45	Morning sleep begins: ASR babies take one hour, 45 minutes; HSR take two hours, 15 minutes. If baby wakes early encourage playtime in the cot until 11.30. Once you have built up their sleep to the time recommended, feed your baby when they wake up. If your baby sleeps for only 40 minutes or less when your first start your program or in the long term you will need to build up their sleep (see Q&A following). While baby is asleep, set-up play stations if you plan on offering independent play at this time.
12.30–1 p.m.	Lunch: vegetables, and protein every day, and they should also be offered a dessert (fruit puree with or without rice cereal, or yoghurt etc.) (see box on page 538). This should be served as close to 11.30 as they wake. Follow your meal-time management routine (see page 226) and use your cues if there are problems (see page 255). After lunch is completed use your wait game and cue (see page 74).
	This is a good independent playtime opportunity if you decide not to offer it later after mid-afternoon nap (see above).
2.30	Afternoon tea: light snack and milk feed.
3.15–3.30	Begin settling routine (see page 609). Depending on how long and how late they slept for their mid-morning sleep adjust this sleep accordingly. For example: if your ASR / HSR baby slept from 10.45 a.m. to 12.30 p.m. then they will be ready for a sleep again around 3.30 to 3.45 p.m. and may sleep for up to 40 minutes (if it does not detract from their capacity to settle easily at 7 p.m.). If, however, they slept longer and later during their mid-morning sleep then they will need a final bridging nap of only 20 minutes closer to 3.50 p.m.
	Offer this bridging nap in the pram where possible.
4.15	Latest nap time—no sleep beyond this point.
	This is a good independent playtime opportunity if you decided not to offer it earlier. Do not expect them to be able to cope with independent playtime at this time if they have been unable to achieve their mid-afternoon

	bridging nap. Please reassess their sleep requirement if required and shift to routine 1 variation 12 months (page 552).
5.00	Use this time to do your final pack away for the day, saying your cues—'time to pack away, nearly time for dinner'. Pop them into their high chair for a quiet time while you prepare their dinner. This may involve their favourite Baby Einstein DVD on TV or books on their tray table in the kitchen while you warm food.
5.20	Dinner: vegetables with or without rice cereal (see box on page 538). Then playtime in high chair (see page 192) as you tidy kitchen, organise your own and the rest of the family's evening meal to be taken after baby goes to bed and prepare their bedroom for the evening. Remember, you must eat a healthy meal at the end of your day to stave off depression and poor sleep, plus it's a good time to connect with other members of your family, so don't neglect this.
6	Nudie playtime (see page 209), using cues for bath.
6.15	Bath time. You need to watch baby the whole time. Remember your cues as you get towards 6.30—'nearly time to pack away, nearly time to get out of bath'.
6.30	Baby out of bath (not before). Everyone in the household should start to calm down with the lights dimmed in preparation for baby's bed time. Dry and dress baby (see page 287), quickly but calmly. As they will be tired you might need to reassure them—'it's okay, bubba, you're just tired. Nearly time for milk and nigh' nigh's'.
6.35	Breast or bottle feed, ten minutes only. Baby must not doze or even zone out at this time as it will interrupt their settling ability at 7 p.m. To avoid tears then, you must keep them awake now.
6.45–50	Begin settling routine. This must start at 6.50 at the latest.
6.55	Final cue—'last page, then nigh' nigh's'—and pack away. Enjoy a last cuddle and complete your settling routine.
7	Bedtime. If your baby cries assess the situation from an adult's perspective (see page 70) and interpret the cries (see pages 654) before you go in to resettle. Remember your cues and resettling routines (see page 617).

16 months until the day sleep is no longer needed

This is essentially the same as Routine 1 for this age group. Once your baby reaches this age, regardless of their sleep requirement, they are usually down to one sleep per day, with one milk feed in the evening. Most HSR babies will need to transition to this one sleep per day.

Daily routine outline

6–6.30 a.m.	Natural waking
7.20	Breakfast
9.30	Morning tea: fruit and water
11.20	Lunch: vegetables and protein, plus dessert
12 p.m.	Midday sleep
2.30	Afternoon tea: milk feed and snack
5.20.	Dinner: vegetables with or without carbohydrates
6.30	Milk feed
7.00	Bed time for 11 to 12 hours

Daily routine in detail

6–6.30 a.m.   Natural waking. Any wakings before 5.30 a.m. are managed with crying interpretation and support (see page 654). Waking routine (see page 622) and playtime in cot (see page 609) for 15 to 20 minutes. Throughout the day remember your wait game and cue (see page 74).

6.30–7   Breast, bottle or cup feed—do not allow baby to snooze. By around 18 months I find most babies are ready to start taking milk in a cup after their breakfast, but only once the early feed is interfering with their ability to eat breakfast. Alternatively, if their breakfast is not being compromised by a lovely snuggle and first feed of the day, carry on merrily. Their breakfast and solid food diet becomes their primary source of nutrition and calorie intake now so you must maintain their ability to eat breakfast here. Remember, they will be consuming far greater quantities of milk during their solid breakfast now, and this will naturally start to take the place of the first morning feed. Change nappy (see page 287), then free playtime.

7.15   Prepare baby's breakfast. Use pre-emptive and forewarning language (see page 43), 'nearly time for breakfast', 'nearly time to sit down and wait for mummy, yummy apple and oatmeal'.

7.20   Baby's breakfast. Difficult to feed (see page 255), use meal-time routine (see page 226). See meal suggestion variation below for more details.

7.50   Dress for day (see page 287) and then free playtime. They'll usually want to help you but allow them to be free to safely venture off if they wish. Prepare cot room for morning bridge, if necessary. Remember to use your flow of communication (see page 40)—'nearly time for stories, nearly time for nigh' nigh's'.

9.00/10   Quiet time in the high chair with favourite DVD or books.

9.30   Morning tea. Fruit and water only. See variation below for more details.

9.45	Independent playtime at play stations (see page 143). This is baby's most active, energy-burning session, so avoid the car or pram at this time if possible. This is also the time to help them become comfortable with being put down to play independently, a skill they need for sleep—think of it as sleep-earning play. It is also the best opportunity for you to do housework and / or cooking (this is when you need to do the whole day's cooking to get it out of the way). The busier you are the happier your baby will be to play independently. If they are not settling down to play remember your flow of communication and follow through (see page 47 and also trouser tug page 374). If you leave the room, remember your short-term absence cue 'I'll be back' (see page 94).
10.30	Be prepared, this is a typical ten-minute tired window for babies. It passes within ten minutes but in the early days of your new routine (maybe five to ten days of the new strategy) if your baby is getting weary and showing it, then a play outside or a little cuddle time (not the kind that might make them more tired) while you play with their favourite toy for a few minutes will help. But put them down again once they calm down.
10.45	Focus one-on-one play (see page 131) for 15 minutes. Give them your undivided attention and don't answer the phones. Remember your cues, 'nearly time to pack away' (see page 42).
11	Pack away toys completely, prepare cot room and wrap for lunch sleep while baby keeps you company and 'helps'. Allow ten minutes quiet time for baby while they watch you do your final lunch preparations. Remember to use your cues 'nearly time for lunch, yummy chicken and vegetables'.
11.20	Lunch of vegetables with a protein (see box on page 538) everyday, they can be offered a dessert (pureed or chopped fruit, yoghurt, custard, etc.). Follow your meal-time routine (see page 226) when feeding them and use your cues if there are problems (see page 255).
11.40	Wait game and cue (see page 74) while you clean up. Change nappy if necessary using cues for sleep—'nearly time for sleep, let's go find our books'. Begin settling routine (see page 609).
11.55	Final page and pack away, using sleep cues.
12 p.m.	Sleep (one and a half to two and a half hours)
1.30–2.10	Natural waking time. Leave baby in cot as long as you can, allowing them to self-resettle if need be. If they wake before 1 p.m., use your resettling routine (see page 617). Once they have had a minimum of one and a half hours sleep and are fully awake, use your waking routine and cues (see page 622). Latest waking by 2.30 p.m. until nights and days are balanced. After ten days see how to build your child's daily sleep intake (see page 594). Allow them independent play in cot up till 2.30 or for 20 minutes.

	Hint: Cook up a large batch of food during sleep time once or twice a week. By the time 5 p.m. arrives, when all children are tired and hungry, it's a dreadful time to try and cook.
2.30	Milk plus snack. See below for suggestions. Snack first, milk follows. This milk feed may naturally go between the age of 12 and 15 months and your child will just have the snack, but you can offer milk in a cup if they are interested.
	Adventure. Time to enjoy the great outdoors in car or pram. No napping allowed—five minutes in the car could mean a 40 minute settle window at 7 p.m. instead of a three-minute one. Motivation enough?
5–5.10	At this time you need to be at home for the first three week of recovery. Use this time to do your final pack away for the day, using cues, 'time to pack away, nearly time for dinner . . .'
5.10	Allow ten minutes quiet time while you warm dinner—DVD or books in high chair or on the couch.
5.20	Dinner (see below) then playtime in high chair (see page 192) as you prepare their bedroom and tidy kitchen and organise your own evening meal. (NB: You must eat a healthy meal to stave off depression and poor sleep, plus it's a good time to connect with other members of your family, so don't neglect this.)
6	Nudie playtime (see page 209), using cues for bath.
6.10	Bath time. You need to watch baby the whole time. Remember your cues as you get towards 6.30, 'time to pack away, nearly time to get out of bath'.
6.30	Baby out of bath (not before). Household should start to become calm and lights dimmed in preparation for baby's bedtime. Dry and dress baby (see page 287) quickly but calmly. As they will be tired you might need to reassure them—'it's okay, bubba, you're just tired. Nearly time for milk and nigh' nigh's'.
6.35	Breast or bottle feed for ten minutes only. Baby must not doze as it will interrupt settling routine. To avoid tears then keep them awake now.
6.45–50	Begin settling routine at 6.50 at the latest.
6.55	Final cue—'last page, then nigh' nigh's', and pack away. Enjoy a final cuddle and complete settling routine.
7	Bed. If baby cries assess the situation from an adult's perspective (see page 70) and interpret the cries (see pages 694) before you go in to resettle. Remember your cues and resettling routines (see page 617).

Variation for 12 to 24 month old

Breakfast:	Rice, barley or Oat or Weet-Bix, oats, semolina, baby muesli cereal and stewed or mashed fruit, or toast fingers (see info on spreads in box on page 538).

Morning tea: Morning tea is a fruit-and-water-only snack (see box on page 538). No other style of food should be offered here.

Lunch: Vegetables, pasta, rice, couscous, meat.

Lunch sleep: This sleep is as per ten to 12 month olds.

Afternoon tea: Between the twelfth and fifteenth month your baby will still be enjoying this breastfeed, but you will see that it may no longer be a primary dietary need as solids start to occupy much of their daily calorie intake. If they choose to take it or not, it will not impact their sleep or happiness. Offer the breast / bottle milk feed and a snuggle, and if they say 'yes please', then go right ahead, but if they 'no thank you' don't force it. If they don't want it, then they should not have to have it. They will need to have a solid snack for afternoon tea, however, to compensate and it will need to be a little more than just fruit—it is a long time between their lunch feed at 11.20 a.m. and their dinner feed at 5.20 p.m. Include yoghurt or finger foods like a Cruskit with avocado, cream cheese or ricotta (see box on page 538). They can eat this while you are out and about for your afternoon adventure but it should only be eaten in the afternoon-tea window. If the milk feed makes it impossible for them to eat some solids at afternoon tea, then they must have their solids first, before the milk is offered. This is vital to help prevent tears, tantrums or stress to your little one. They will not be sustained by milk alone between lunch and dinner. Remember this is about balance, so ensure they have a good snack to get them through. Do not feed them outside the meal-time windows on the recovery plan, food intake and sleep intake are closely linked and these plans are carefully refined to make sure sleep is achieved as easily as possible.

Dinner: Vegetables, pasta, rice, couscous (see box on page 538)—this meal is similar to lunch however does not include meat (see iron warning in box).

Routine 2 wisdom

- Never start before having thoroughly read the philosophy behind this sleep repair program (see page 1).
- Never start your new daily routine without also implementing your new settling, resettling and waking routines (see page 605), and following the interpretation and assistance for crying section of this book (see page 654).
- When you start your new routine it can take up to a week of consistent timing, regardless of their sleep lengths, for the cyclic effect of this program to start to work on a circadian level. Doing something for one or two days only will not achieve your results.

- When you start your new routine, if you keep changing your times based on your baby's wake-up times each sleep, then you will not achieve results. The only way to achieve repair results is to choose your sleep and meal-time windows' plan prior to commencing your program, then maintaining those windows regardless of your little one's possible earlier than scheduled wakings. I do it for a living and achieve stunning results. You can keep them awake; I know, because I can. Work *through* and *past* the old patterns of catnapping and tiredness, and you and your baby's tiring few days will pay off, firstly for your baby, and then ultimately for your entire family.

The effect of today's sleep on your baby's routine

This is a fascinating discovery for most parents. The time you

- put a baby down for a sleep
- allow your baby to sleep until
- and the length of the sleep you allow them to take

affect not only the sleep they take today, but the amount of possible sleep they can take tomorrow at various other linked sleeps. Consider these scenarios:

- The mid-morning sleep affects the following morning's 6 and 7 a.m. waking time, and the length of time they will be able to sleep during this day's coming afternoon sleep:
  - Too early a mid-morning sleep can cause early 6 to 7 a.m. waking times the following morning.
  - Too long a mid-morning sleep can cause a shorter mid-afternoon sleep.
- The mid-afternoon sleep affects their afternoon-bridge sleep or their 7 p.m. settle time that day, and the length of their mid-morning sleep the following day:
  - Too long a mid-afternoon sleep can perpetuate poor mid-morning sleep the following day. This is because a longer sleep is often offered to compensate for a poor mid-morning sleep, thus allowing the body to sustain a shorter morning sleep because it can anticipate a longer mid-afternoon sleep. By waking baby after their balanced, minimum sleep-requirement suggestion, despite their early waking from their mid-morning sleep, you create a demand in the body to sleep longer during the following mid-morning sleep in order to cope with the demand of the *shorter* mid-afternoon sleep being offered.

- Too long a mid-afternoon sleep can also impact on a six- to seven-month-olds' ability to take their afternoon bridge. The roll-on effect is an overtired baby by 7 p.m. who settles quickly but wakes frequently between 7 and 10 p.m. Alternatively, for a baby who is not taking the afternoon bridge, a very long afternoon sleep may impact on a baby's ability to settle at 7 p.m. because they are not tired enough.
- The late afternoon bridging nap for babies between six months of age has a series of side effects when used incorrectly:
  - If the late afternoon bridge is offered beyond it's true need, it can create significant difficulties upon settling your baby at 7 p.m. It can also create a shorter mid-afternoon sleep the following day. This occurs because it is often offered to compensate for a poor mid-afternoon sleep, thus allowing the body to be able to sustain a shorter mid-afternoon sleep the following day because it can anticipate a late-afternoon bridging nap. By limiting the length of sleep offered or holding baby awake until their true sleep time is due (7 p.m.), despite their early wakings in the mid-afternoon sleep, you create a demand in the body to sleep longer the following mid-afternoon in order to cope with the demand of the longer afternoon.

Increasing their sleep requirement

You start with a basic amount of sleep when repairing significant sleep issues for a couple of simple reasons. One is that I'd prefer a slightly tired baby who is ready to go straight to sleep when I offer it, and sleep a decent amount of time at each sleep, than one who may cry because of the above sleep impacts from our miscalculations. The second reason is that you cannot be certain if you are being fair to ask the highest amount of sleep for their sleep requirement group, from your particular baby. For these reasons you start with a reasonable and balanced amount of sleep while they undertake the big new role of learning how to sleep peacefully independently. This means you are freeing them of the exhausting burden of the constant disruption to sleep from needing to wake up crying for your help all the time. This is how you create harmony for your baby. Once you have established your baby's minimum daily sleep requirement, and they are taking all three main sleep windows well, then it will be time, if appropriate, to build their sleep up so they are taking more.

HSR: 7 p.m. to 6 or 7 a.m., one hour, 30 minutes. This is the minimum sleep needed for each of their sleep windows. Now just because your baby is a high-sleep-requirement baby, does not necessarily mean you will achieve

2 x 2-hour day sleeps and a 12-hour night. This 16-hour sleep requirement is tipping the highest end of the scale for this group, and while some can take it easily, others will take on a more moderate, but equally effective version of the routine.

ASR: 7 p.m. to 6 or 7 a.m., one hour, 15 minutes. This is the minimum sleep needed for each of their sleep windows. Now just because your baby is an average-sleep-requirement baby, does not necessarily mean you will achieve 2 x 1 hour, 30 minute–day sleeps and a 12 hour night. This 15-hour sleep requirement is tipping the highest end of the scale for this sleep-requirement group, and while some can take it easily, others will be on a more moderate, but equally effective version of the routine.

For both groups you will not need to build their sleep up if they wake naturally on one or two of their three main sleep windows, as this would indicate that you have reached their sleep need, and to offer more would only steal from other sleeps (see above box on how today's sleep affects them later).

If your baby continues to need waking after every sleep after five days of sleep on the new routine, then it is time to build up their sleep intake using a simple three-step process. You do this slowly, and wait to see if the growth (through adding additional sleep at just one waking window at a time) impacts on your baby anywhere else.

- Step 1. You start with the 6.30 a.m. window, offering another 15 minutes sleep to 6.45 a.m. for three days running and, if you see no effect on the length of sleep they are able to take during their mid-morning sleep, then that adjustment can stay and you can move on to your next window. If you do see it impact, then remove the additional 15 minutes offered, and do not attempt to build their sleep at this window.
- Step 2. You then move to your mid-morning sleep, offering another 15 minutes to the *end* of this sleep (that is, added to the wake-up time) for three days running, and, if you see no effect on the length of sleep they are able to take during their mid-afternoon sleep, or on the time they start to wake at 6.30 / 6.45 a.m., then that adjustment can stay and you can move on to your next window. If you do see it impact, then remove the additional 15 minutes offered, and do not attempt to build their sleep at this window.
- Step 3. You then move to your mid-afternoon sleep, offering another 15 minutes to the *end* of this sleep (that is, added to the wake-up time) for three days running and, if you see no effect on the length of sleep they are able to take during their mid-morning sleep or on the late-

afternoon bridging nap for the six month olds then that adjustment can stay and you can move on to your next window. If you do see it impact, then remove the additional 15 minutes offered, and do not attempt to build their sleep at this window.

You do not ever offer any more sleep for the later afternoon bridge for six month olds.

You have now successfully built their sleep up over a nine-day process. If your baby continues to need to be woken after every sleep on this new routine, then it is time to build up their sleep again using the same simple three-step process. Once you have reached your recommended (HSR) 2 x two-hourly day sleeps, and your 12-hour night or (ASR) 2 x one hour, 30 minute—day sleeps, and your 12-hour night, you should hold and maintain this sleep for three weeks. Ensure they are eating adequately as excessive sleep can be an indication of a slightly lower calorie diet. If they are eating and sleeping well, then you are welcome to repeat the same three-step growth process again until they start to wake naturally on one or more of their three main sleeps.

How to know when your child is ready to move to one sleep a day

This is an important point. A HSR baby could need to transition to one sleep at any stage from the fourteenth to eighteenth month onwards. An ASR baby could need to transition to one sleep at any stage from the twelfth to fifteenth month onwards. Clear signs of this begin to happen after the twelfth month when they are only sleeping effectively on one of their two day sleeps. This means that while one sleep remains longer, the second is reduced to a catnap of 40 minutes or less. This can happen in either order through the day. It is also evident that they are getting ready for one sleep a day when their two, main, day sleep times are interfering with the 6 to 7 a.m. waking time each morning and their 7 p.m. settling time each night, and are constantly needing to be reduced in order to maintain your baby's night sleep pattern.

A final sneaky sign that they may be ready to drop down to one sleep, and this is usually a little difficult to spot without a professional's guidance, is when you start to see prolonged wakings through the night. These prolonged wakings often happen between 11.30 p.m. and 4.30 a.m. and while a baby may not need attending too, they can chat for one to two hours before they are able to go back to sleep. If they are getting iron in their diet in the form of meat about once a day as recommended, then this is an indication that they are achieving too much *accumulated* daytime sleep and you either need to drop down both sleeps to their minimum sleep-requirement recommendation until the night sleep is restored, or move on to a 'single sleep a day' program.

While some are happy to maintain the two sleeps in this slightly unpredictable or shorter format because their baby is still happy and coping, others will identify that it is starting to detract from their little one's happy days and peaceful nights and will be motivated to transition on to the single-sleep program. This is simple actually. Just go to PRM Routine 1 and follow the variations for a baby 12 months old plus to be on a balanced single-sleep routine until the day sleep ends.

Many people ask me if they should transition them gradually, and my answer is simple, 'nope'. Just shift them over tomorrow morning starting at 6.30 a.m., follow my guidelines precisely, stay busy in the morning for the first three days without taking them for long pram or car rides and you're on your way. Simple! Sure, they will be a little tired for two to three days, but on a slow progression plan, where they are tired for three weeks while you try to juggle the changes without impacting other sleeps of the day, it's a no-brainer choice wise. Baby and you will be settled and past the transition tired in hours, not weeks.

Typical triggers for night wakings

Once your child is established on Routine 2, night wakings should be almost nonexistent. But, any imbalance in the day will show up in the night-time sleep cycle of babies on a solid routine. These triggers also have common time windows that indicate behavioural wakings, discomfort, illness, hunger and dehydration, and routine miscalculations (see page 477). While I have never had this officially studied, and therefore confirmed as a science, it occurs so consistently that I have adopted a method of identification to help me accurately finetune routines, and this method of deduction has helped me over the years to determine, with tremendous success, what's happening in the most challenging, unsolvable cases this country has to offer.

Here is a list of possible triggers for night-time wakings. If you have difficulty with your child's sleeping during the following times, these will help you work through the problem to quickly eliminate the cause of the waking the following day, rather than only deal with the crying on an ongoing basis. The following information is to be used for a baby who is on one of my PRMs whose sleep issues have already been successfully solved, and who is sleeping well. It can be used a little while you are 'creating harmony' but be mindful of the fact that there are old habitual patterns that needs to be solved before you can rely to heavily on this chart. This is designed as a way of determining why a child might suddenly experience a disruption at night. You can then work on it the next day to avoid it occurring again, rather than work with the mentality that 'if they cry, this is how I have to manage it'. My strategies encourage you work out why your baby wakes, to resolve that so it doesn't happen or happen again, and only then to deal with any communication or confusion issues that remain to achieve your peaceful nights.

At night, babies should only come to significant partial wakings between 10 and 11 p.m., at around 2 a.m., and between 4 and 5 a.m. All other wakings between these windows are a disruption where they are pulled out of their sleep cycle for one reason or another, and their normal, solid three-to-four-hour window of block sleep is disrupted. Here I highlight the most common triggers that I have observed causing disruption to each solid block of night sleep.

Please remember there are variation in this list to suit those babies on the HSR routine.

Trouble going to sleep initially at 7 p.m.

This is a classic behavioral / association window. They may be having too much of or too late an afternoon sleep. Shorten the afternoon sleep, or make it earlier. Please read your routine variation carefully and see 'The effect of today's sleep on your baby's routine' page 593). If it continues, it's one of two things:

- wrong daily routine—reassess their daily sleep-routine needs and be careful to adopt a routine that suits their *actual* needs, and not necessarily your desire for them to sleep at certain times
- daytime communication is not balanced—if you know they are able to self-settle ordinarily, then it may be that you have not been using balanced lines of communication during the day to ensure they are comfortable with you guiding them.

Wakings between 7 and 10 / 11 p.m.

If they are having trouble after they initially go to sleep:

- They were already asleep when you left—which means you were not honest with them and they were startled when they woke to find you gone. Always let them know by leaving the room before they fall asleep.

- They are too hot—as this is the hottest time in their 24-hour day, it's important to keep them cooler though the first part of their night. A fan or air conditioning is helpful but there is no need to cool them after 10 or 11 p.m. It is most important to be aware of this for babies who are swaddled. Babies who are uncomfortably warm in this first portion of the night are likely to fall asleep and then wake up for short periods of time frequently (around every forty minutes) between 7 and 10 p.m. Babies that are extremely hot are more likely to wake up and stay awake for prolonged periods between 7-10 p.m.
- They are non symptomatic but may be starting to get ill—it's common for a baby to feel unwell and be uncomfortable before they show symptoms of an illness. Often, they will wake momentarily, frequently, without needing intervention. This is when I believe whatever illness they have caught (cold or 'flu perhaps) is taking a hold at the end of the day: their resistance is lower at the end of a long day. If you offer a paracetamol-based analgesic designed specially for their age group and they settle within 20 minutes, or stop waking, you can be sure they are feeling unwell, and that perhaps tomorrow you might have to look a little further into the cause. Always ensure their ears are clear when they are on sleep training

After the initial settling-in period of any PRM is over (after the first three weeks) it would be highly unlikely that your little one will continue to wake for prolonged periods at night without it being a clear routine miscalculation (if they are able to self-settle and self-resettle ordinarily). In this case I would strongly suggest you reconsider your sleep-routine times and, in particular, look closely at your mid-afternoon sleep, and the time that sleep is being offered. When your afternoon sleeps are to blame for prolonged waking in this first windows of the night, they are either too long, or the bridging nap needs to be looked at. The low routine may be more appropriate or, in rarer cases, may be the exact opposite, too short and they have become overtired. If they are overtired they are more likely to wake frequently for short periods of time. If you suspect they may be overtired please see 'The effect of today's sleep on your baby's routine' page 593).

Wakings between 10 and 11 p.m.
This is a classic behavioral / association window. The daytime communication between you and your child is not balanced. If you know they are able to self-settle ordinarily, then it may be that you have not been using balanced

lines of communication during the day to ensure they are comfortable with you guiding them.

Wakings between 11.30 p.m. and 1.30 a.m.
This is a classic illness or discomfort window. A prolonged waking in this window may be because your child is already experiencing symptoms of an illness, unlike the 7-to-10 p.m.'s forewarning of an impending illness. During this window it is very typical to hear from your little one when they are definitely unwell. If you have seen them teething through the day, or they have a cold, or are clearly suffering from an ear infection, tummy bug, etc., they are more likely to run a temperature at this time and be clearly uncomfortable, if not in pain. In this case I try to pre-empt the discomfort they start to feel at this window when the body goes to work healing, growing and fighting illness, and offer pain relief at 10 p.m. so they can peacefully sleep through their body's busy work.

If they have a food intolerance, as far as gut response to wheat, dairy, etc., it will show up at this time. If you introduced a new food the day before or that day and they are suddenly unsettled here, then remove the food from their diet and trial it again in another week's time. If it occurs again, remove that food from their diet for six months before trying again. If it occurs again at your next trial, do not introduce that food until they are at least two years old.

If they are low in iron or, in a more subtle way, not eating enough meat, then they are more likely to have prolonged wakings at this time. If their food intake is unbalanced, their body will wake them to feed here, to supplement the poor nutritional balance from the day. If they are not drinking enough water through the day from six months of age and onwards, then you will suffer from a waking here. In this case you must ensure you are balancing their diet, incorporating meat once a day until the prolonged wakings settle down, and make sure they are getting a good blend of vegetables and fruit. Do not replace solids feeds with milk as their bodies will not be sustained by it through this growth window at night and you will continue to suffer from prolonged waking.

If you know that they are physically well, and you have catered for their dietary and hydration needs, a clear pattern of prolonged wakings at night at this time (three times or more is a pattern) is then a clear sign of excessive accumulated day sleep. Reassess your child's daily sleep requirement, removing the lost sleep from the middle of the night, to determine their true daytime sleep need.

Wakings at or near 2 a.m.

This is a classic behavioral / association window—daytime communication is not balanced. If you know they are able to self-settle ordinarily, then it may be that you have not been using balanced lines of communication during the day to ensure they are comfortable with you guiding them.

Wakings between 2.30 and 3.30 a.m.

This is another classic illness or discomfort continuation window, although it appears to indicate a lesser level of discomfort or dietary imbalance: the tail end of an illness, or the last days of teething or earaches will commonly occur here as opposed to the 11.30 p.m. to 1.30 a.m. window, where a child may still be feeling unwell. See 11.30 p.m. to 1.30 a.m. wakings for guidance. Again, ensure they have a discomfort relief to cover them from 11.30 p.m. to 3.30 a.m. if you know they have been unwell and symptomatic and, therefore, prone to waking for a few days.

If you know that they are physically well, and you have catered for their dietary and hydration needs, then a clear pattern of prolonged wakings at night at this time (three times or more is a pattern) is then a clear sign of excessive accumulated day sleep. Reassess your child's daily sleep requirement, removing the lost sleep from the middle of the night, to determine their true daytime sleep need.

Wakings between 4 and 5 a.m.

This is a classical behavioral / association window—daytime communication is not balanced. If you know your child is able to self-settle ordinarily, then it may be that you have not been using balanced lines of communication during the day to ensure they are comfortable with you guiding them.

Wakings between 5 and 6.30 a.m.

This is when they are waking early and are unable to go back to sleep and there are a number of reasons for this:

- Their mid-morning sleep the day before was either too early or too long
- Your baby is very hungry so their calorie consumption the day before was too low and you need to increase the overall quantity and quality of food you offer at the three main meals of the day—if they are fussy at the meal times, reduce the morning and afternoon snacks to ensure you are not overfeeding them then. Never give them snacks of food with low nutritional value outside the meal-time windows suggested, because it will always detract from their ability to eat meals

of a higher nutritional value at their meal times. Believing that 'something is better than nothing' and allowing snacking on biscuits, milk and snack foods are absolute healthy food–intake destroyers. Don't give them snack foods between suggested meal-time windows and they *will* eat the healthy food you offer them

- They may not have had enough balanced independent playtime the day before, which is when they are developmentally challenged across the board and become tired.
- The first feed of the day, the day before, was given too early, or was too long, too big or a combination of all three.
- They are overeating in the morning in general but, in particular, the food taken the previous morning between 7 a.m. and 12 p.m. could be impacting on their ability to sleep in. They don't need three breakfast, or large morning teas. Remember food is fuel, and sleep provides fuel; if you offer extra food, it's the same as offering extra sleep

Troubleshooting for PRM Routines 2

Q My baby persists waking after the 40-minute mark on the morning sleep. Why and how can I correct this?

A If you have been persisting with your routine sleep times exactly and not offered long sleep-ins past 6.30 a.m. in the morning, or early or longer afternoon sleeps in the afternoon because your baby is tired from their brief morning sleep (see page 593 'The effect of today's sleep on your baby's routine') then you will need to look elsewhere. The first thing I would suggest you assess is the environment. Have you avoided the wrap or tuck-in for some reason? If so, introduce the wrap or tuck-in technique exactly as suggested and try to resettle for the next three days. If you are unsuccessful then your baby is not suited to this routine format and needs to be shifted to the routine variation. Please see Routine 1, and the appropriate age variation for a routine that may suit their needs better.

Q I'm having trouble getting them to eat their lunch. Why and how can I fix it?

A Too much, or too late a morning tea? Refer to your routine for details. There may be behavioural issues with your feeding (please see page 255).

Q My baby persists waking after the 40-minute mark during the mid afternoon time sleep. Why and how can I correct this?

A If you have been persisting with your routine sleep times exactly and not offered more sleep than recommended during the mid-morning sleep, or offered an early or longer afternoon bridging nap yesterday because your baby was tired from their brief mid-afternoon sleep (see page 593 'The effect of today's sleep on your baby's routine') then you will need to look elsewhere. If your baby is over seven months, have you dropped the later afternoon bridging nap yet? If not, it's time. If that has been catered for then the first thing I would suggest you assess is the environment. Have you avoided the wrap or tuck-in for some reason? If so, introduce the wrap or tuck-in technique exactly as suggested and try to resettle for the next three days. If you are unsuccessful then your baby is not be suited to this routine format and needs to be shifted to the routine variation. Please see Routine 1, and the appropriate age variation for a routine that may suit their needs better.

Q I'm having trouble getting them to eat their dinner. Why and how can I fix it?

A Too much, or too late afternoon tea—refer to your routine for details. There may be behavioural issues with your feeding (please see page 255).

Q My baby has been taking a while to settle at this 7 p.m. sleep. Why and how can I fix it?

A If your baby is under seven months, have you been offering more than 20 minutes at the afternoon bridge? If so, drop it back to the recommended time. If your baby is under seven months, have you been offering the 20 minutes at the afternoon bridge all the way up to 5 p.m.? If so, drop it back to ensure your baby is awake by 4.45 p.m. If they are having trouble falling asleep for their afternoon bridge please see 'How their sleep affects their routine' (page 593). If your baby is over seven months, have you dropped the afternoon bridge? If not, it's time! Anything else, please check 'Typical triggers for night wakings' (page 597) or your routine for further instruction.

Q My baby goes to sleep easily at 7 p.m., but wakes 40 minutes later and needs help to go back to sleep. Why and how to fix this?

A Is their room a steady 19 to 21 degrees Celsius. Do you have a fan on them? Are they dressed in the appropriate clothing? This is a possible sign they are hot. Were they still awake when you left the room? If these things are catered for then this is often the result of too much afternoon sleep, rather than too late a sleep time offered. Tighten up the amount of sleep you offer them at the mid-afternoon sleep each day by 15 minutes until this stops happening. Because everyone looks for a medical reason for wakings, a lot of people are concerned that there could be wind. When they pick them up they will burp, so could this be the problem? But in my entire career this has *never* once been the problem despite the parents showing me their baby burping and laying straight back down and going to sleep. The most common reason you see this happen is that babies gulp air when they cry out asking to be picked up. When you pick them up, you satisfy their request so they stop crying (because this is like a negotiation 'you pick me up, and I'll go to sleep' ha-ha!) and because they are upright, the air caused from crying pops out. So, for what it's worth, let me reassure you, it's not wind! Be sure to have dropped the bridge nap by seven months and check your routine for further instruction.

Q My baby has goes to bed at 7 p.m. like a dream but stirs every 40 minutes, rarely needing assistance, but I just hear him. Why and how can I settle him more at this time?

A One of a few things. Is he a little too warm? See above. Is he getting overtired? Under seven month olds need their bridge nap, see 'How their sleep affects their routine' on page 593 to ensure they are taking their bridging nap. Over seven months, are they having a good mid-afternoon sleep? If not, please see 'How their sleep affects their routine on page 593 to ensure they are taking their mid-afternoon sleep well. For all other answers please see 'Typical triggers for night wakings' (page 597).

Q Both sleeps are only an hour. Is this ok?

A This would mean that you have miscalculated their sleep requirement. If they sleep two hours total through the day, and 11½ to 12 hours at night, you are seeing a clear 13½-to-14-hour sleep requirement, meaning they should be on the LSR Routine 1. That said, if your baby is happy, and still coping all afternoon, apart from their little tired window at 5 p.m. until dinner is served, then I see no reason why you should change this pattern unless it is bothering you and you would like them to sleep longer at a single sleep. If that is the case, simply shift them over on to Routine 1.

Q My first child was a low-sleep-requirement baby boy, and my second baby is an average-sleep-requirement baby. Should I expect the same fast turn around that I got when I used the low-sleep-requirement routine?

A The turnaround for LSR babies is extremely fast, in some cases almost miraculous, so it would be nice if that were to happen on this Routine 2 as well. However, the chances of such a sudden turnaround on these 'two sleeps a day' routines are not always as high. You just need to write up your routine, and plan your timing carefully, and stay on track a week and everything will settle. If it does happen really fast, then you can be delighted, but you're better to always anticipate a little bit of work and a tired baby to keep busy.

Q My baby is still a fussy eater even after a few days on the program. Is this normal?

A Lower sleep-requirement babies are naturally better eaters once their program starts, but your child should be improving dramatically with the new routine, and your new meal-time management and communication strategies. If you are still struggling with meal times, please read through meal-time management (see page 226) for more information and read through correcting meal-time difficulties to ensure you are not prolonging unhappy meal times and night wakings by not addressing and repairing some basic behavioural issues quickly.

Q I know independent playtime is important, but do you have to do it every day?

A Yes, it is important, but no. It's designed for the days you are home. For stay-at-home mums or dads this will be during the general working week. On the weekends then you are free to have family time and go out and have fun. For full-time working parents, it's important to note one thing. Just because you do not get to be with them all week, doesn't mean you teach them that when you come home, that they should always be with you non stop. This is not balanced. Sometimes, if you're home and have things to do, set up your play stations and give them a chance to be comfortable with the normal conditions of sleep (playing happily on their own, knowing you are there and they are safe even if you aren't holding them). This will go a long way towards a happy little baby when you are home, rather than a clingy one.

18
Settling, resettling and waking routines

You have one of the most amazing sleep inducers at the very tip of your tongue: your ability to use your voice to soothe, comfort and, most importantly, reassure your child (see page 53). For the purpose of putting your baby to sleep, being able to understand the effect you are having on your little one and how that, in turn, impacts on the way they feel about going to sleep in their cot are your keys to success.

Sadly, however, your confidence will not always reduce tears at bedtime. Some babies cry for only 30 seconds, some only for three minutes (usually these are the ones who are swaddled), while others have a big old cry about the whole scenario and need some reassurance until they get used to it all. They cry because that is all they know; it is what they have been taught to do in the past. If they don't know how to self-settle and have been taught to cry to get some help when they feel tired, it sometimes takes them a while on that first day or two of teaching them how to sleep to understand and accept any change to the conditions of going to sleep. It's not always going to be easy for a little one who has never been able to self-settle to *not* express themselves when exposed to a new situation. So it's normal and healthy for a child experiencing something new to feel a little uncomfortable with the unpredictability or unfamiliarity of the event. Think about it; it's hard even for adults experiencing something new that is slightly out of their comfort zone, so it is perfectly reasonable to expect a child to ask 'I'm not sure about this, I don't feel too comfortable with these surrounding, am I okay, mummy / daddy?' What will your answer be when they ask this question? Before you answer, however, consider the following:

- What will you tell them about this situation?
- What will your body language tell them?
- What will your facial expression tell them?
- What will your tone tell them?

Be honest and be fair

It is not right or fair, or in the best interest of your child to let them think that they are in a situation that is anything other than absolutely safe, and perfectly healthy and normal, because that is the truth. Reread those questions above and think about how you move and look and sound and react when communicating in general with your baby. When you deliver your message, visual and verbal, what tone, facial expression and body language do you use to express it? Do you clutch your child close to you, frantically soothing them like they have hurt themselves or like something genuinely frightening has just happened? Do you tense up, yell at your partner to do something, frown, pull a face, or quickly take them out of the environment reinforcing the fear that it's not safe? Absolutely not! So you must not act this way at all while you teach your little baby or toddler all about what sleep is *truly* like, that they are perfectly okay, that sleep is a truly lovely thing, and that their cot is safe and warm and cozy.

You must stay confident, and sound loving and empathetic to their tired feelings. You must use a tone and make slow, soothing movements that say 'everything is safe, and this place is good, and you are perfectly okay'. This is where you need to assess the situation from an adult's perspective (see page 000). Never react to the new conditions or environment that they may be experiencing for the first time in the same way that your child is responding to the situation, or they have no one to reassure them. They need to be able to ask you if they are okay, and you need to be able to answer them from your adult's perspective and impart your wisdom about the truth of the environment they are in, to them. You are 100 per cent responsible for this. You need to be their solid ground to stand on, so they can feel reassured. You are all they have to gauge if they are or are not okay.

This is what you need to understand about this settling process. Your child *is* okay, and they are safe and much loved. It's just their cot, it's just their room you so lovingly decorated in anticipation of their arrival, and it's just them feeling the physical experience of being tired. They need you to tell them that these are all safe things, that they are okay, and you can hear them, but their room you so lovingly decorated in anticipation of their arrival, and it's just them feeling the physical experience of being tired. They need you to tell them that these are all safe things, that they are okay, and you can hear them, but it's definitely still sleep time, and you *can't* go to sleep for them, and they *can* do it on their own, but you will reassure them for as long as they may feel the need to ask you if they are okay.

Things that can make settling confusing

Two of the most disruptive things to any settling routine are inconsistency and confusing mixed messages. I see many settling routines (both homespun and professionally recommended) that accidentally do both. There are many settling routines floating around that advocate a variety of approaches designed to appeal to a *parent's* need to fix it, or need to stay present while the child tries to work out what is being asked of them. Think about your statements and whether you are defining them correctly (see page 44). If not, then this is what your child might be thinking:

- Why is mummy standing there?
- Am I about to get up?
- Does she want to talk to me?
- Is this a new game?
- Should I stand like she is?
- Is she going to give me a toy?

What is your child learning from you about a particular statement or event you are governing around sleep time?

What can you do to help your baby sleep?

There is only one fair way to help a little one learn how to settle and resettle, and sleep solidly so they do not wake and cry, and feel anxious about their sleep time; that is, address the *reasons* they are having trouble in the first place, empower them with the skills they need to be able to cope with that situation in the future, provide comfort in the cot, and then support them in a non-confusing manner while they learn to settle all by themselves for the first time. So where do you start?

My suggestion is that you read the whole of this book. I know most of you will want quick answers, so here is the *minimum* you should know and read if you want to put your child to bed in the most respectful, honest and empowering way, without going into the reason they fall asleep or stay asleep:

- You must help them become comfortable with being in their cot (see page 175) before you try and ask them to sleep or even lie down in it, so when they are placed in their cot at sleep time they are familiar with and feel empowered in that environment and we know it is not going to frighten them.
- You must help them to learn to trust you when you leave the room, by developing short-term absence language cues (see page 93) that help them predict and feel more comfortable with your absence, making leaving them a far less stressful, unpredictable or frightening event for them. This teaches them that being in the cot without you in their room is actually safe and fine, and a pleasant experience.
- You must teach them that a cot is only for sitting or lying down in if they are having difficulty with sleep—not all babies find sleep difficult so this is reserved for helping unsettled six to 24 month olds. This is done at a non-sleep time while establishing cot play. A simple request to 'sit down' and defining that request with its true definition (see page 44) will make this a quickly understood request. Remember, 'sit down' does not mean 'try to stand up', so preventing them from being able to stand on the first day while they learn to understand this request is important.
- You must teach them that they can predict the new sleep-time request by introducing consistent settling, resettling and waking routines (see pages 609, 617 and 622). This will empower them with a sense of control over the situation and provide security in the knowledge that you will come if they call you.
- You must teach them what to expect before you *ever* ask them to do something as complex as self-settle for the first time. This is achieved by indirectly exposing them to this new settling routine, language and cot room conditions by role playing (see page 631) with a teddy bear in front of them first.
- You should make sure you are not asking them to oversleep during the day, which will make it too hard to sleep at night (see page 534).
- You should make sure their solids / milk intake is balanced with their water intake.
- You need to be able to offer an under-12 month old a feeling of security, as they are clearly requesting when they are not succeeding in going to sleep or back to sleep. This means swaddling them if they wanted to be held before, or providing extra warmth if they needed to be in your bed under the blankets, etc. (see page 424).

- You need to take away the risk of any disruptive, confusing, or tormenting environmental aspects or mixed messages when sleeping. This could be light in their room, excessive noise in the house, open doors, or being able to hear you chatting away when sleep has been a difficult thing for them to achieve in the past (see page 424). Their sights must remain firmly on sleep.
- You need to be able to guide your child without protest from them during the day, so they can accept your guidance at sleep time without stress. If you can't change their nappy or dress them (see page 287), sit them in the high chair or pram (see page 313), or ask them to play independently for a little while, then how could you ever ask them to put themselves to sleep in their cot.

Be aware that many will say strategies like 'control crying', 'total absence from the child's room while they are crying', 'pick up / put down', or 'lying down a hundred times' eventually work, so why go to all that trouble and do anything else? Well, I'll tell you why. Because it's fairer, and the right thing to do, and more respectful of you child's needs. That's why *we* are the ones who need to make the effort, rather than bully children into submission. Don't be in such a rush to get your much-needed sleep that you look for a 'quick fix'. The real solution is quick if you make sure you cater for all your little one's needs first. Read about and understand your child's basic needs first before you try to ask them to go to sleep. Don't have too great an expectation of your baby. Sleep time has probably been just as distressing for them as it has been for you if you are experiencing significant sleep-time disruption, so be prepared to support them.

The settling routine

A settling routine is a set of predictable conditions for your child, leading up to the event of them going into their cot and putting themselves to sleep. It's important that you distance this set of sleep-time conditions from your child's old set of sleep-time conditions, because the old set will be tied up with old expectations and could promote confusion and, therefore, tears. This new set of conditions helps your baby to prepare for bed, to relax and to accept the sensation of being tired at sleep time, and gives them an opportunity to become accepting of your guidance ten to 15 minutes before you put them to bed. This is not what puts a child to sleep though. Only they can do that. The process of putting themselves to sleep is a learnt response after they are put into their cot with these new conditions. You will have skilled them enough to ensure they can start to lie there on your request and begin to accept the tired sensations, all because you will have defined their new settling routine and cues to always mean 'time to go to sleep' and nothing else.

To not provide a new set of predictable conditions around *preparing* for sleep means you perpetuate their expectation that they only need to relax, be still and accept your guidance just moments before you put them into their cot. This is unfair because they won't have time to prepare and relax into feeling tired, and it results in your child fighting you at sleep time. They will, therefore, require intervention to help their body wind down, resulting in the development of learnt dependent sleep associations (see page 399). To create a routine where they have a good ten to 15 minutes to settle into the normal conditions of feeling tired and preparing for sleep means that, if they are going to protest about going to sleep (as some babies inherently do fight the sensation of sleep until they become very familiar with it), then they can have their little 'do I have to go to bed' cry either in your lap during stories or in your arms during singing time. You will be there to reassure them that they are all right and can help them move past that feeling of resistance to accept and relax into feeling tired, so they are truly relaxed for sleep when they are placed in their cot.

The normal conditions of sleep time that your child will adjust to during their new settling routine, to speed up the process of your child falling asleep, will be to be still and to not fight the feeling of being tired. These skills are developed and encouraged in a few really important ways. Their positioning for story time (see page 302) helps your baby to slow down and relax into the feeling of being tired. This is beneficial to them both now and in the future because you will not always be putting your baby down feeling really tired. They will often simply need to go to bed because it's bed time and healthy for them, even if they are not exhausted, so knowing what to expect and what to do when they are in their cot and starting to feel weary is empowering for a child. This still time allows their body's natural mechanisms of slowing down and preparing for sleep to activate. Their body temperature drops, their hormone levels drop off, they begin to breathe through their nose only, one nostril closes and the oxygen supply to the brain is lowered. This process enables a baby to be nicely prepared when you do put them into their cot.

To accept guidance from you is also important because going to sleep independently means you need to *ask* them to go into their cot awake and lie there until they fall asleep. The settling-routine story time allows your child the opportunity to have a protest about you telling them the next step of the day well before you put them into their cot if they are likely to protest. This way you can comfort them and help them relax into your governing line so all protests are over before you put them to bed. This is appropriate from six months of age and younger.

All babies need a ten-minute wind down before bedtime to help them stay calm and learn to accept and cope with the natural body rhythms of hormone and temperature drops, and the sensation of tiredness. Please ensure you have carefully read the 'Sleep basics' (see page 398) and the 'Solving sleep-time blues' (see page 471) sections to make sure your new settling attempt will not be confusing or unexpected for your child, and will fully cater to your child's sleep needs. Always make sure their room and everything you need are prepared before you start your settling routine. Babies on the full recovery program (see page 541) require all recommended comfort items and complete stimulation reduction. For all babies, make sure:

- cot is made ready for the tuck-in technique
- white noise is on
- lights are off in their room, and in all the rooms and the hall near their room
- SafeT Sleep is open and ready
- towel rolls are handy ready to tuck them in with
- wrap or wraps are out on the nearest bed
- books are ready on the couch
- clock or watch is handy
- distractions are turned off and put away.

Always use flow of communication leading up to this settling-routine event. Say your settling cues once they are tucked in with a soft gentle voice, without any sounds of worry or concern, as your child will want to hear your voice even if they are very cross at you. Encourage your baby to settle themselves down by gently patting their tummy / nappy and begin your cues:

- say 'Shh' four times and 'Time for sleep'
- say 'Shh' four more times and 'Mummy and daddy love you'
- say 'Shh' four more times and 'Nigh', nigh''.

Repeat all your cues one more time then turn and leave—don't hesitate—and close the door behind you.

The settling routine comprises:

- reading two books together quietly on the couch with you using your pre-emptive cues and governing line of communication

- baby saying goodnight to others in the room as you carry / lead them out of the room
- wrapping your baby, if doing so, ready for sleep time
- carrying your baby in the cradle position in your arm to their cot after you close their door
- singing 'Twinkle twinkle little star' to your baby
- tucking your baby into bed
- saying your settling cues (as mentioned above)
- you leaving the room.

Outlined here is a full settling routine for a baby aged six to 15 months and who is in the full swaddle. As well, there are also variations for a leg-wrapped baby, ten to 15 months old, and an unwrapped baby 15 months plus.

Swaddled baby, six to 15 months old

For daytime sleeps, go into your baby's room, turn the light on and change their nappy (if required). Take off any bulky items of clothing, down to a singlet and nappy for those being fully wrapped. This is the same for evening sleeps but after final night feed, brush their teeth, then:

- Turn off the light in their room on your way out, saying 'Let's read our books'.
- Go out to the lounge chair where your two or three books are ready for you.
- Sit your baby on your lap, facing the book in your hand (see page 302), and have a lovely read for about ten minutes, or until five minutes before the sleep time. They may challenge you a little when this is new; this is where you are asking them to allow you to govern this next part of their day, and defining that statement (see page 44).
- As you read each book use parent-governed lines of communication (see page 29) and pre-emptive cues (see page 42) like 'wait for mummy', 'turn the page', 'Jake do it' (for lifting flaps or for touching texture books), 'nearly time for sleep', 'nearly time for nigh' nigh'', 'last page, nearly time to pack away', and 'all finished, time to pack away'.
- Five minutes before bed, put the books away and say your cue, 'It's time for sleep', and have a cuddle and a kiss with them. Just remember that this story routine, and final cuddle and kiss are not to be used as a tool to put them to sleep, it's only used as a lovely, calming pre-bed routine that they will begin to rely on to predict what is coming, 'time for bed'.

- They should say goodnight to everyone in the room. As you and your baby exit the room, the others in the room should stay sitting and look away to avoid confusion. Babies and toddlers can get very upset if they think someone is following them, but then do not walk behind them as they anticipated. On those first few days while your little one is adjusting to their new routine, everyone should stay put until baby / toddler is out of sight.
- With five minutes to spare, keep reminding your baby 'It's time for sleep' as you walk to the room they will be swaddled in.
- Point to the wrap (the room should be pretty dark, but you should be able to see just enough to swaddle them) and say 'Lie down', then gently lie them down and follow wrap instructions (see page 439).
- Once wrapped firmly, pick them up and carry them into their room in the cradle position, allowing them to snuggle their face into your neck so they aren't watching the world.
- Once in their room, close the door and walk to their cot, still snuggling them in a cradle position in your arms. Give them a big squishy cuddle and kiss then sing 'Twinkle twinkle little star' very slowly and calmly while you gently and slowly sway with them. Sing slow enough so they can start to calm down and you hear their breathing settle into a calm relaxed rhythm, then quietly give them a kiss and say your goodnight cues: 'Time for sleep, mummy and daddy love you, nigh' nigh''. Then say 'Lie down' *before* you lie them down.
- Lie them in their cot regardless of their reaction.
- Avoid eye contact (not that you will be able to see terribly well). Only say your cues occasionally regardless of their reaction. You are not opening up any lines of negotiation so you must not add any additional language to your cues or additions to your routine or they will think sleep is open to negotiation and this will mean unwanted tears could begin to flow.
- Do up the SafeT Sleep securely and tuck them in firmly, locking bedding in place with cloth rolls to avoid it from coming loose.
- Place a muslin blocking cloth over the side of the cot and bend over so your face drops behind the blocking cloth. This gives them a chance to get used to the independence of the situation while they still have the reassuring and rhythmic settling cues and patting.
- Sing your cues slowly and pat them rhythmically, still avoiding eye contact until they are much better with the routine. Make sure the confident tone and reassuring warmth in your voice tells them that sleep time is a beautiful thing, and that they are loved and safe. It's in your

baby's best interests that you do everything you can to relay this to them through your voice. Smiling can often lift an inflection (see page 58) and you can sound extremely reassuring and gentle by doing so.

- Pause to say your settling cues twice through completely. Your settling cues are also your resettling cues so take the time to make these nice and comforting for your baby in case you need to use them in the middle of the night.
- Stop patting as soon as you say your final 'Nigh' nigh''.
- Turn and leave. Don't hesitate, turn back, or change your mind, you need to make sure your body language is readable and consistent for your baby as they will be taking notice of everything you do and say very keenly.

If you do hesitate, hang around a little too long, say your cues too many times, or in a concerned voice like something is wrong because your baby is unsettled they will anticipate that something is out of place, or misread that to mean you may pick them up, and become very upset when you walk out of the room. Have confidence in your actions and your baby too will feel confident and content in a very short period of time because you are predictable.

Variation for a leg-wrapped baby, ten to 15 months

This strategy is identical to the settling strategy outlined for a fully swaddled baby except for a few minor points. Please remember that movement usually equals crying, so the more firmly you make the tuck-in, the faster they will go to sleep, the quicker they will learn how to settle without difficulties, and therefore the less tears they shed overall.

Please do not fuss around too much with positioning but I never allow a baby under 12 months to lie on their stomach for sleep time. Over that age it is a fruitless venture to try to change a pattern of tummy sleeping if it is well established, but it is a parent's choice and sleeping on their back can still be learnt. In some cases, a 12 month old sleeping on their back has to be re-established because they are simply too unsettled and resistant when placed on their tummy. If you can see that your child is going to fight and try extremely hard to get up when you lie them on their side or stomach, then you must not pursue this avenue. It is best to place them on their back and tuck them in firmly, then manage their positioning as you would for a nappy change (see page 287) until you leave the room.

During the settling routine as outlined above, once you have leg-wrapped your baby (see page 439), you say to them 'Lie down' and cradle them in your arms ready to go into their room, and they must remain in that position in your arms until they are placed in their cot. Because their hands are free they will attempt to grab your shirt and reposition themselves in an upright position. Calmly and firmly make sure you define the statement 'lie down'. This means you may need to keep one of their arms tucked under your arm. If they are physically fighting with you to get up, you will need to calmly but continually hold and release their other hand, or if necessary, hold their hand all the time while you continue on with your settling routine: entering their room, closing the door behind you, walking to the side of their cot and singing 'Twinkle twinkle little star'.

It's very important that your child is given a chance to adjust to the idea of lying down in your arms first, rather than have them fight you if you only say 'Lie down' when you put them into their cot. This is graded exposure to sleep-time expectations and giving them a chance to adjust in your arms is an important tool. Remember to assess this from an adult's perspective (see page 70)—you have only asked them to lie down in your arms. You will need to remember to work up to this request with your flow of communication through the day at nappy time and getting dressed (see page 287) as well as through position requests and the wait game (see page 74).

Once you have finished singing 'Twinkle twinkle little star' to your child, you will then kiss them gently, say your settling cues, including another 'lie down' before you then lie them into their cot. When you do this, please ensure they stay lying down and do not try to get up. If they do, prevent them from being able to get up by quickly tucking them in. Once tucked in, while you begin or continue on singing and with your settling cues, you may still need to request them to lie down a few times and, in some cases, you will need to hold their hands to stop them from trying to get up. If they are still fighting your request to lie down, please use all the strategies you use for a nappy change (see page 287) until it's time to leave the room.

Variation for unwrapped baby, 15 months plus

Once they are this age, a toddler can walk to their room. After reading your books, allow them to say goodnight to everyone in the room, and then they could either walk with you holding their hand (see page 341) out of the room and into their bedroom or be carried by you into their bedroom. With five minutes to spare, keep reminding your child it's 'time for sleep' as you walk to their room. When you are in their room, ask them to close the door. If they are reluctant, help them by using their hand and encouraging them to close the door. Do not allow them to grab it and open it, this will be a confusing message to your child. Stay calm on those first few attempts as they will soon be looking forward to this process and closing the door with great gusto (so watch you get into the room quickly and mind your toes and fingers!). If, after the second day, they are still very unhappy about closing the door, then do not ask them to do this. The role of closing the door will then become your responsibility, but it will be very important to keep role playing this part of the routine with your child, ensuring you close the door when you put teddy to bed.

Once the door is closed, walk them to their cot. After picking them up either snuggle them in a cradle position in your arms, or gently encourage their head to lie on your shoulder. If they will not put their head on your shoulder, then it is important that you lie them down in your arms before you start to sing unless they are extremely calm in the upright position. Often tucking their knees up will encourage them to automatically drop their head on your shoulder so give it a go. Give them a big squishy cuddle and kiss then sing your song very slowly and calmly while you gently and slowly sway with them. Sing slow enough so they can start to calm down and you hear their breathing settle into a calm relaxed rhythm, then quietly give them a kiss and say your goodnight cues. Say 'Lie down' before you lie them in the cot.

Do up the SafeT Sleep and tuck them in firmly, locking bedding in place with cloth rolls to avoid it from coming loose, or lie them down on their back, side or stomach and ensure you define your request to stay lying down if they are not tucked in. Encourage them to get their comfort items saying 'Get your teddy / muslin', etc. (see page 461). If they have a dummy, use your dummy cue and game (see page 467). Bend over so your face drops behind the cot bars if they are not trying to stand up, to give them a chance to get used to the independence of the situation while they still have the reassuring and rhythmic settling cues and patting and your presence. This allows a final opportunity for you to step back visually from them before you leave the room so their focus will shift from watching you to themselves before you have even left the room.

Only say your cues and pat them rhythmically now, avoiding eye contact, until they are much better with the routine. Avoid holding their hand, as they will have to transition out of this just as you leave, making them cry. Also don't allow them to tell you if you can or can't pat them as this allows them to govern the sleep-time routine and encourages tears because you confuse them when you listen to their guidance about when and if you can pat them, but not when or if you can leave the room, or will pick them up. The entire settling routine is a parent-governed line of communication. If you know your baby strongly dislikes being patted, incorporate a 'patting the mattress' variation into your routine and role play this before you offer it as part of their settling routine so you can always maintain your parent-governed line of communication.

If they are flapping, or trying to get up, or fussing with those little hands, then make a clear statement by holding them on their tummy and not allowing the flapping (and be consistent) and calmly say your settling cues until they stop fussing, at which point you can slowly release them to see if they are calm while continuing on with your settling cues. If the fussing and flapping don't stop, though, then hold their hands on their tummy again until they either settle completely or you have completed your settling cues through twice, then release their hands, turn and leave.

Make sure that once they are settled in, and you have paused to say your cues through twice, the confident tone and reassuring warmth in your voice tell them that sleep time is a beautiful thing, and that they are safe and loved. Stop patting as soon as you say your final nigh' nigh' and turn and leave the room.

Resettling routine

A resettling routine is a set of familiar conditions taken from their original settling routine. It is used as a form of understandable communication between you and your baby to let them know it is still sleep time, and that they need to lie quietly until they fall asleep like you always ask them to do. The need for a resettling routine is only relevant when they are learning to sleep through the night, or if there is an illness, or if you travel into a different time zone or other changes of environment that have disrupted your little one's sleep. If you establish a resettling routine when you start your PRM you can always attend to your baby when they need a little reassurance during a change in their life without them becoming stressed, and you can ensure healthy restorative sleep is still maintained in your house.

In order to ensure your baby is comfortable with your resettling routine, you must invest a final minute or so in your original settling routine to lock in some basic cues that tell them you would like them to put themselves to sleep, and that you are about to leave the room. This means you can use the same cues when it's time to go back to sleep and they will know what you are saying, and what they need to do. So, during their original settling process, after you have put them into bed, when they are lying down, just before you leave the room, you establish the set of conditions you can then use later as a resettling routine. I take the time to pause, and then sing my

Troubleshooting

Q My baby complains as I wrap them, what should I do?

A When you lay them down, treat any fussing with the same approach you use during a nappy change (see page 287). Hold them calmly until they stop physically fussing, then proceed with your wrapping. You should stop and hold your position if they start to fuss again, then continue when they stop physically fussing. Make sure you have role played wrapping on your teddy well (see page 631), so you are confident and efficient, firm and fast with your wrapping. If it does not look right, start again. Make sure you are working on nappy change management and positioning at all times during the day to be on top of their usual fussing behaviour and impatience when you lay them down or ask them to wait. Always follow through (see page 47).

Q Once I close the door my baby cries. Is this normal?

A Occasionally this means they are now aware it's bedtime and they may protest in the initial days of learning. If your concern is about their attitude towards the dark, be mindful of not making them frightened of a normal life condition as it is something they will experience for half their day, for the rest of their life. Perhaps role play more, and always role play with the door closed. You can also play peek-a-boo games with teddy (see page 649) so they get accustomed to the dark. Also, be sure that for the entire settling routine in the room, the door is closed and they are in the dark with you. If they do not cry about the dark when you are there, then their crying upon your exit is unlikely to be about the dark, and more likely to be behavioural (see page 654).

Q My baby is quiet until I start to sing. Should I stop singing?

A No, follow through. Only occasionally do I encounter a baby who is really uninterested in their parents' singing and just wants to get straight into their cot. Work through any episodes about your singing for a week, and if they complain *only* when you sing you may then choose to offer two lines of the song as a cue, and then say your other cues and 'Lie down' before lying them down and carrying on with your settling routine.

Q What should I do? My baby is happy until I lay them in their cot.

A Follow through. Stay confident, define your settling routine with the appropriate outcome, and deliver a message that you are not concerned about them being in their cot and that you believe it is a safe environment by the light, confident tone in your gentle, relaxed voice. This will soon pass if you are consistent.

Q My baby is very upset throughout the entire settling routine. What can I do to stop this?

A It is not common but also not terribly uncommon on the first day or two when your little one has previously been fairly unsettled for them to remain unsettled during their new settling routine. Stay confident and show your baby that you trust this routine and you are not concerned. Over time they will settle. Follow through. This will pass as soon as this ritual becomes familiar to them, and they can therefore feel more in control of the situation.

Q How do I get my baby to lie down in my arms during the song?

A It's important that you ask a little baby to 'lie down', and hold them firmly so they don't pull themselves up using clothing or your neck. Hold them firmly and closely to your body and have the arm closest to your body tucked under your arm. You may need to hold their other hand. If they are older and happy to lie their head on your shoulder, and don't struggle with the transition to lying down in the cot, then it is okay for them to stay upright. But remember, the reason for lying in your arms is to prepare them for the expectations of lying down before you put them in the cot. If your baby is going to challenge this request for a minute or two, it is better to have that challenge before they get into bed and allow them to settle down in your arms, rather than them getting upset about this request when you put them in their cot: you can't hold them then to reassure them that they are okay.

Q Is it okay if my baby sings 'Twinkle twinkle little star' with me?

A Oh my, gosh, *yes*! It's adorable.

Q He is trying to pull himself to an upright position in his cot the whole time I am trying to settle him. What should I do?

A Follow through (see page 43) with your request for him to lie down when you ask, just as you would during nappy change (see page 287). He will learn quickly if you are 100 per cent consistent with the definition you give your request to lie down. It can sometimes take a few days of settling routines to establish this clear request and boundary.

Q How do I stop her from trying to nuzzle in for a breastfeed all the way through the settling routine?

A Make sure you are holding her in a position that is not confusing. Hold her further up your arm when in the cradle position so her face is not directly aligned with your breast, and slightly angle her body more upright. Then hold her firmly so she cannot turn and get herself into a nuzzling position again, and carry on. This boundary to not feed during her settling routine will soon become clear to her and she will accept it within the first three days.

Q My baby keeps reaching for the door while I'm trying the settle him. What should I do?

A Carry on with your settling routine. The settling routine is not a time to ask a child what they think is a good idea when they are needing to learn something new to settle down. To not follow through with your settling routine and allow them to ask to leave the routine would only encourage crying as going to bed then becomes a negotiation. If they are never exposed to the new routine, how will they ever discover that they can actually go to sleep peacefully? Follow through *confidently* for three days, without so much as flinching. You will see your little one settle in as little as one day if you make those first settling efforts consistent and well defined.

Q Do we have to follow your settling routine exactly?

A No, not at all, but try to work with the basic flow. Avoid using any language cues or songs that you used to use, as they are tied up in your baby's mind with different associations and will be confusing for them when you behave differently. Otherwise there should be no problems with you designing your own little settling routine, just make it totally consistent every time.

Q Can I read their settling-routine books on a chair in their room rather than the living room?

A I have to say that I am not a big fan of reading in their room at this age, simply because when a baby wakes up they often look at the chair and it triggers the concept of sitting on your lap in that chair and having stories, even at 3 a.m. Because I am all about avoiding tears and tantrums rather than dealing with them, I tend to always remove the reading chair from their room to establish a whole new reading environment.

cues and shush the baby for a soothing minute or more before I then stand and leave them to go to sleep. This is then the basis for my resettling routine. It is consistent with their settling routine, and if they know what to do when you first put them to bed, then the use of these cues and conditions will be a clear indicator of what they need to do to go back to sleep.

It's important that you provide an immediate and distinct message when you first enter their bedroom after they have woken day or night, so they can know immediately, without the risk of confusion, what is going to be asked of them. This is them looking to you for guidance at sleep time and it takes a lot of stress out of resettling for both your baby and you. The resettling-routine conditions of your walking into their room and saying nothing before you promptly close the door behind you compared with their waking-routine conditions (see page 622)—you turning the light on and saying your waking cue 'Good sleeping' immediately—will enable your child to understand your request without any confusion before you even reach their cot. This enables them to predict the situation, giving them a sense of control. This means that within a short period of time, if they ever do need attending to, a simple attendance and your resettling routine and cue should be all you need to see them lie there contently until they drift back off to sleep. Always remember though, you are aiming to remove the need to go in at all because they are happy to lie there awake in their cot and can cope with the feeling of being tired without stress, so be careful to always assess their cries first (see page 654) and only attend to them if necessary.

> In brief, you walk in, say your cues and leave. The whole routine should take no longer than one to two minutes during a resettle.

This is an absolutely achievable result from the time your baby is six months of age and even younger. Resettling routines can only be used as part of a complete PRM. You need to have completely read and understood 'The basics of sleep' (see page 398), 'The settling routine' (see page 609) and 'The waking routine' (see page 622) for each age group to use it to full effect.

In brief, you walk in, say your cues and leave. The whole routine should take no longer than one to two minutes during a resettle. If there is crying after you leave, refer to the crying interpretation and assistance section of this book (see page 654). As for settling above, I have provided a detailed resettling routine for a swaddled baby, six to 15 months old, and variations for the leg-wrapped baby six to 15 months old and an unwrapped toddler 15 months plus.

Swaddled baby, six to 15 months

When *you* determine your baby needs your assistance:

- do not turn on any lights before opening the door
- walk in, closing the door fully behind you
- do not make eye contact with your baby
- with a soft gentle voice, as your baby will want to hear from you even if they are very cross at you, encourage them to settle themselves down by gently patting their tummy / nappy and beginning your cues
- in the same soft gentle voice, without any sounds of worry or concern say 'Shh' four times and 'Time for sleep'
- say 'Shh' four more times and 'Mummy and daddy love you'
- say 'Shh' four more times and 'Nigh', nigh"
- repeat all the cues one more time
- turn and leave—don't hesitate—and close the door behind you.

Variation for leg-wrapped baby, ten to 15 months

All children with a leg wrap should have a SafeT Sleep to maintain consistency of environment during a 12-hour night. This strategy is identical to the settling strategy outlined for a fully swaddled baby except for a few minor points. If your baby is trying to get up, or is overly fussing, please place them back on their back, firm up their leg wrap if necessary, tuck them in securely, then manage their positioning while you calmly and reassuringly say your cues (as above). Then turn and leave.

Variation for unwrapped baby, 15 months plus

If your toddler is standing up, ask them to lie down, or lie them down. Say 'Lie down' and pat them a few times on the back of their hand with one finger, just as a little reminder that you would like them to let go and sit down or lie down. They should be quite accustomed to this request from their playtime in the cot (see page 175), even if they are having a protest about sleep time. If they do not lie down for you immediately, then you will need to sit them down, and then lie them on their back in a fairly fuss-free way, ensuring they do not get up or roll over despite their protests. Remember, you need to be sure you define your request to 'lie down' with its true meaning (see page 44). Once they are lying down, you will need to hold their hand and manage their position as you do for their nappy change (see page 287) if they are challenging you.

Regardless of your child's reaction, use a soft gentle voice, even if they are very cross at you. They will want to hear you and it will encourage them to settle themselves down and to remain calm. Gently pat the side of their nappy or tummy and in a soft and gentle voice, without any sound of worry or concern, say your resettling cues (as above). Then turn and leave. Don't hesitate, even if they stand up straight away. Do not look back at them. It's important that they learn that standing up is not something that gets your attention so they stop doing it the moment they wake up, making it less likely they will fully wake and cry. Close the door as you leave.

The waking routine

A waking routine is important to establish a language stream at this time because, if you are to govern your child when they are going to sleep and going back to sleep, you must also govern the conditions around waking in order to be consistent. If your child governs these areas, imagine their confusion if you respond to their 'I'm awake now come and get me' cry by sometimes asking them to go back to sleep but at other times getting them up. When you have to wake your little one or you don't intend to resettle them when they have woken, you should always observe your partial-waking pause (see page 700) and leave them as long as possible before you use this routine as a clear indicator that it is okay for them to be awake and you don't expect them to go back to sleep, and their day will begin or resume again.

> This waking routine gives your baby all the tools they need to cope with going to sleep and back to sleep by themselves.

The waking routine is, in fact, one of the two most important elements within the entire psychology of sleep (see page 416) as far as I am concerned. The kind of message you deliver at this time will either confuse your child, or be in line with your settling and resettling routine. To confuse your child and damage the careful balance of sleep conditions would tell them to cry to be picked up. It would tell them that as soon as they are awake they should see someone enter the room very quickly or be removed from the cot immediately. It would tell them that the cot is not the place to be when you're awake, and if they want to get up, they just need to call out. This is obviously in stark contrast with the message you are so patiently delivering at settling and resettling times, and can potentially undo all yours and your baby's work in developing trust in a predictable set of conditions around sleep time. You should never be concerned about them being awake in their cot, you want them to know it's normal and to feel comfortable to lie there and play, knowing someone will come and get them when cot time is over.

At settling and resettling times you tell your child to look to you for guidance. You tell them that there is a set of conditions you always follow so there is no need for them to cry because the sleep time runs along these conditions alone (unless they are very unwell of course) and nothing else happens. You tell your baby that it's okay to be in their cot while they are awake, and you tell them that if they wake early to lie there and relax because they may need to go back to sleep. If you were then to come in each morning when they first cried and pick them up straight away, you will confuse them and they will expect the same response from you at 2 a.m. and that's unrealistic. You need to develop predictable sleep conditions by always incorporating a waking routine as well as a settling and resettling routine. To not cause confusion, you:

- enter the room and state if sleep time is over with a simple visual and verbal set of cues
- open the door, turn on the light immediately, make eye contact and smile and say 'Good sleeping, bubba'
- teach them that they need to sit down in their cot, because standing up and asking to be picked up is not something you want to encourage at sleep time
- teach them that they always stay in their cot for a while after they first wake up, and that that time is always a happy time
- teach them that mummy and daddy can come and go from the room when they are in the cot, and it's normal for them to experience this, and that they are okay to be in their cot and in their room alone without you present—this will set them up and equip them with realistic expectations and skills for your resettling routine
- teach them that the process of packing away while still in the cot is what immediately precedes getting out of bed, and not crying, or standing and flapping like a noisy little duckling
- you teach them that you will always tell them when you plan on picking them up by always using your wait game and then saying a predictable 'Up up' (see page 76) when they are doing the true definition of waiting (see page 44).

This entire waking routine gives your baby all the tools they need to cope with the task of going to sleep and back to sleep by themselves. For this reason, I often incorporate the waking routine into a child's day while I'm doing my homework (see page 20) one week before I start my new daily routine, settling routines and cues, and crying interpretation and sleep repair program.

The waking routine in detail

- Walk in.
- Say 'Good sleeping', in a clear voice, not too soft, the moment you open the door.
- Turn light on dimly.
- Walk to cot and make clear eye contact with your baby, give them warm loving smiles, and say your cue again, 'Good sleeping, bubby'.
- Unwrap and undo your little one, and help them sit up by using one hand behind their head and upper back. Don't confuse them into thinking you are going to pick them up by putting your hands under their armpits to sit them up.
- Offer your baby their toys and establish playtime. Ensure your child has plenty of time when they are playing by themselves, this is their independent time, and it is not designed to be time for playing or chatting with you. They will have plenty of time for that while you are busy together during the rest of the day. You want to teach them that, eventually, when they wake up feeling happy they can chat to themselves until you come in to get them.
- Remember, while you are in the room, your little one is not allowed to stand in their cot. This is a simple boundary-setting strategy designed to help them cope with the sleep-time expectation of lying down. Use the cue 'sit down, wait for mummy / daddy' (see page 40). It's also vital to change any habits of standing as soon as they wake up, thus lessening the chances of them accidently waking themselves up early.
- Each time you leave and return use your short-term absence cue (see page 94).
- When their playtime window is drawing to a close, always follow a packing-away ritual so your little one learns that it is the event, and not their crying, that determines when they can get out of their cot.
- Ask them to hand you their toys (see page 328) so you can pack away.
- Fold all the sheets and tidy their bed briefly; remember they must stay sitting down at all times during this.
- Play your wait game (see page 74) before getting them up using your 'up up' cue.

Within a few days, your baby will be relaxed with their settling, resettling and waking routines and your questions about them will all be things of the past, but during the transition they will be important to you. Remember, you must have role played, and role played completely, the whole routine (see page 631) regardless of how insistent your little one is for you to stop, out of their annoyance, boredom, etc. The importance of letting your child know that this routine is followed through, no matter what, is vital. This means that if there are going to be any major tantrums or crying while they get used to you governing the direction of these routines, you will see them appear and be resolved mostly during the week of role play leading up to the start date of your new daily routines, including the settling routine, being implemented in your house. Never introduce the routines until you are prepared to define them using the crying interpretation and assistance technique (see page 654).

On the first day or two of implementing the new routine, your baby will quickly discover that 'these things' all mean 'it's time to go to bed'. It's normal for them to say 'Noooooooooo, I want to stay up and play allllll night with you guys', but it's healthy and crucial for you to say 'you're too little and you need your sleep so, yes, it's bed time for a new little person'. Their response to going to bed does not govern the outcome. You are there to hold them and reassure them, but you need to confidently put your baby to bed with a clear request to them to go to sleep, which means you follow through as calmly and as confidently as if they were lying there silently during their settling and resettling routines.

Most of time the answer to any problems you might come across in these routines is a simple follow through, follow through, follow through. Be entirely predictable. Make sure the settling and resettling routines are not a negotiation, as that's probably what got them into such an imbalanced head space about sleep in the first place. You want and need stress around sleep to end, so you close off the lines of communication and say 'From now on, this is what you can expect at sleep time, and I will always be 100 per cent predictable', just in your actions. Finally, stay confident and calm, and be without hesitation at all times during your routines. Be sure to watch the currency you give certain behaviours (see page 356). If you want certain behaviours to continue, then stop what you're doing and start fussing around when they do them. If you would like your baby to stop trying to negotiate their way out of sleep time however, then give their behaviour no currency and follow through calmly, no matter what. The message you deliver is: 'I love you, I am always here for you, and I will help you for as long as you need help, but it is sleep time because mummy and daddy say you're a baby and need to sleep to keep yourself and this family healthy and happy, and nothing but sleep is going to occur from this point'. The more consistent and relaxed you are, the faster they will relax and accept this time as peaceful, predictable and lovely.

Getting it right!

A quick turnaround in results and preventing wakings is now your number one priority at this point. Once your homework is done and you have embarked on your new daily routine and sleep repair program using your new settling routines, being careful to define them using your crying interpretation and assistance techniques, there are two most important things to keep in mind: consistency and ongoing maintenance.

When things are definitely not okay

Significant clinical depression and / or clinical anxiety in a parent would have to be the number one cause of ongoing night wakings and daytime wakings over all other reasons. I believe this is because a child needs to feel comfortable and know that everything is okay for them to be able to relax enough to sleep. If one or both parents give off a signal that things are not okay, sleep disruptions become a symptom of a shaky emotional grounding during the day. In other words, parents provide the emotional solid ground that a child stands on, but when that ground is not so solid, then the foundation for a child's sense of security is unstable, resulting in unsettled behaviour, clinginess, and a lot of crying. Many of these little ones try to predict the next part of their day by creating it themselves to feel secure. This is when a child-governed line comes forward, and babies under two without a solid parent-governed line of communication are unsettled because they become overburdened thinking they need to govern their day.

The reason I mention all this is to highlight the importance of identifying the causes of sleep problems, and to go easy on yourself and your little one if you are recovering from depression. It is often preferable if you suffer from significant depression / anxiety to seek assistance from a medical professional for the condition while you also gain assistance and guidance to work through your baby's sleep-time issues. You can then comfort your little one, and not stress them, or alternatively, get some much-needed hands-on help with a professional like myself to implement the program for you.

It's a difficult situation because often troubling bouts of emotional stress from either one or both parents can be directly related to their own sleep deprivation. This will be resolved once the baby starts sleeping, but a vicious cycle occurs here and it means you must be as calm and confident as possible as you correct your child's sleep-time issues before you can achieve sleep yourself. Make sure you have solid support yourself, and have read and learnt as much as you can. Being forewarned is forearmed and this will also give you a sense of control as you predict the day and your future progress. If however, you are simply not coping, then it's time to look into getting someone to come in to help you until things settle down. A book is not going to be the solution for everyone, and sleep deprivation has some devastating effects on new parents.

Go easy on yourself and get some support until your baby, and then you, can recover. Know you're not alone. Know there are many people out there, like me, desperately trying to keep up and make a difference to your parenting journey, and never give up on finding harmony in your house.

Consistency

One of the fastest ways to ensure your baby or toddler can settle into their new sleep routine is to remain consistent through your management of the physiology of sleep (see page 403). The importance of maintaining your child's sleep conditions in one set pattern is the only way to prevent stress to the child, avoid tears as much as possible and maintain great sleep without the need to intervene. Some of the conditions that you need to be conscious of maintaining consistently are in the environmental aspects, your communication, the carers you use and their use of your routines, and your honesty.

Environmental

If they go to sleep wrapped, they should stay wrapped (see page 439). This means you need to ensure the wrap is effective enough to remain firm for the entire night, or there are inconsistencies in your baby's sleep environment. If they have a dummy, make sure they have many to ensure this condition stays available to them (see page 461). If the hall lights are going to be off when they wake in the middle of the night, ensure they are off when they first go to sleep. If they have music or white noise to fall asleep to, then they should have music or white noise running right through the night. If you are not going to be in the room when they wake through the night, then make sure you are honest with them and tell them when you leave when they first go to bed.

Communication

Don't change your management halfway through a learning process. To try and work through some crying, then deciding to stop trying because it's been going on for a while, simply translates in baby comprehension as 'if I don't want to go to bed, I need to cry for a long time before I get you up'. If you aren't going to be consistent on those first two to three days of teaching your baby a new way, then don't start in the first place. It's a waste of your baby's time and energy.

Don't change your settling or resettling cues, or open up lines of communication by adding extra lines or asking questions, or looking to your child for guidance at sleep time by obliging demands. Always retain the governing line at sleep time, even if you need to get them up momentarily mid settling routine and change their nappy (only if they have soiled)— 'Mummy change your nappy, up up, time for sleep'—to ensure your baby knows you are governing all the events, rather than thinking that them getting up has something to do with their cries.

Your voice and body language need to remain predictably reassuring and confident and soothing so your baby can trust that, although this feels new on those first few days, they are okay because you are okay.

Carers

You should always use your set of predictable routines around going to sleep, going back to sleep and waking up, and ensure that they are aligned carefully. Make sure your baby or toddler knows who is putting them to bed, and don't chop and change settlers at the last minute. Whenever possible, whoever puts them down, should resettle, and get them up in the morning. Everyone should use the same routines for settling, resettling or waking your baby at home and, where possible, in other locations.

If you plan on going to the shops and leaving them with a carer when they are asleep, tell them, just in case they wake early or if they will be waking up with another carer. Always make sure any carers are there before your baby goes to sleep, so they don't get a surprise if someone else they were not expecting enters their room when they wake up. Imagine how surprising it would be to expect your husband or wife to walk in the front door as usual and have it be your neighbour or, worse still, someone you barely knew.

Honesty

Don't trick them! While this is never the intention of a loving parent, one of the most common but trust-breaking things I see a parent do is put their baby to sleep in their arms, then put them down in their cot and sneak out of the room as quietly as possible before closing the door. This is being dishonest!

Your baby has no concept of sleep, and no concept of time lapsing so can you imagine their surprise when they close their eyes and relax in their mummy's arms or on their daddy's shoulder and open them again to find themselves in a dark room with no one to be seen. Not very fair, right?

Get confident and establish your new settling routine around going to bed, that is more honest and in line with what they will experience when they naturally stir through the night. That means always make sure they are awake when you leave or, at the very least, hear you close the door on your way out should they be impossible to keep awake. Being dishonest creates a situation where a child starts to fight the sensation of being tired at sleep time.

Ongoing maintenance

A part of your ongoing success with this program, once you have established your sleep-time settling, resettling and waking routines, your full daily routine and recovered your sleep, is to then maintain their sleep through always ensuring you are keeping them confident in the three most basic skills they need to keep being able to sleep for you: being able to be in their cot awake, being able to cope with you leaving the room, and being able to accept your guidance with trust.

Independence

For those of you who scoff at the concept of independence in a baby, please be sure that you understand the basic concept I am advocating here. I am not suggesting you loan your baby the car keys, or perhaps leave them at home while you go shopping. I am simply suggesting you look at empowering them with a sense of security and comfort when they are in their 'own space', and help them come to terms with, and not be frightened of, certain 'normal' feelings associated with sleep.

I feel very strongly about the importance of a baby feeling comfortable with being in their cot, and just as strongly about the importance of exposing your little one to the feeling associated with you wandering around the room, and in and out of the room, and *not* thinking they are in danger. So often I have to remind a parent that even though their child is anxious about them leaving the room, they are in fact safe to have a little play in their cot. Parents' response to those anxious emotions expressed by baby should be nothing but reassuring and confident, and certainly not something that would indicate they are in a situation that they need to be rescued from. To become as anxious as the child around these events means you are delivering the wrong message about a safe environment, thus 'teaching' them that it is not safe when it is actually *perfectly* safe.

To avoid gently and confidently working through this simple playtime means you are never exposing them to those normal emotions, thus limiting their ability to grow and become confident with coping with a normal range of feelings that come up around sleeping in their cot, or you stepping out of the room while they put themselves to sleep. Just as important as the emotionally independent sleep tools learnt around playtime in the cot, and you leaving the room for short periods of time, is the ability to cope with the feelings associated with sleep, and the feeling associated with you guiding them at sleep time.

Being able to deal with the feeling that is associated with being tired is something extremely important. How can you expect them to be content to peacefully lie in their cot as they drift off to sleep if they are not comfortable with the feeling associated with being tired? To deal with each of these stages I have developed strategies carefully incorporated into natural parts of their day.

Coping with you leaving the room

There are two basic skills you need to empower your little one with, both in the day or so leading up to implementing your new routine and to maintaining it: the ability to be in their cot when awake and the ability to cope with you leaving the room. This is where you need to implement and maintain playtime in the cot (see page 175) and establish your short-term absence cue (see page 94) during both non-cot and cot playtimes.

The ability to accept your guidance

Finally, this program advocates asking your baby to go to sleep for you. This is definitely not potluck sleep where you hope they are tired enough to accept you guidance, but a very clear, safe, parent-directed request to go to sleep because you think they need a rest. This is obviously why it's important for your baby to be able to be awake in their cot and cope with you leaving the room, and know how to cope with the sensation of being tired. This also means that in order to achieve and sustain great peaceful sleep in your house, you not only need to establish clear and consistent communication where you can guide them through the days leading up to repairing your sleep respectfully, but you also need to maintain the ability to guide them so you can always ask them to go to sleep for you, and they are able to accept and trust your loving guidance.

This is probably the one part of your program that is then ongoing. Please always refer to Part 1, the communication section of this book, to maintain harmony in your house. Your flow of communication (see page 40) and your three lines of communication (see page 29), when used as a general communication style with your little one, will keep you and your family on track to *always* have 'happy days and peaceful nights'.

19
Role playing for sleep routines

One of the most successful tools of my business has been my role-play program. Children learn as much through observing others as they do through exploring. They display more interest in participating in an observed activity and mastering it, than they show in exploring a brightly coloured toy that they have not observed someone else playing with. For this reason alone, your child will love your TV remote, your mobile phone (or any telephone you use for that matter), your handbag, your shoes, the cooking pots and wooden spoons, your car keys, the computer, getting mail from the letterbox, watering the garden, opening and closing the fridge and cupboards, and squeezing the tubes of cream you use when changing their nappy. Think about this for a moment.

What is the biggest mystery of them all? Why a baby finds the box their birthday present came in far more interesting than the actual present. And the reason is because you appeared to play with the box for ten minutes before you pulled something out of it, handing the actual present straight to your baby without playing with it. It is the activity of opening the box that you demonstrated to your child and this is what they will want to participate in, not the object you didn't demonstrate or play with. Why? Because you are the one they instinctively need to learn everything from in this precious first two years of life: they will literally imitate and try to master everything they see you do.

Be very aware, though, this also means they will copy and attempt to master the way you speak to and treat others, your moods, your table manners and eating habits, and your attitude about life, work, education, sharing and helping. What I have done in my role-play program, is use this natural learning tool to help babies and toddlers learn about their new settling and resettling conditions at sleep time.

Role play has long been recognised by hospitals as an effective tool to help young children learn about and be prepared for painful and frightening but essential medical intervention in order to cause as little trauma to the child as possible. The results of these role-play strategies have spoken for themselves. By incorporating role playing when teaching a baby or toddler a new routine at sleep time, I have been able to achieve the quickest and most successful transitions into independent sleep with tremendous results in the reduction of tears in all cases where the emotional foundations of the house are firmly grounded and stable.

Never underestimate the value of role playing

I met the amazing baby Joseph when he was a tiny but boisterous eight month old. He had the loveliest giant, round cloth nappies and did the best one-legged dance I had ever seen. I digress . . .

Joseph was a very unsettled sleeper. Before I met his family, his mother and father had talked to every possible person dealing with sleep-time issues in the country who avoided control crying. After all the homespun remedies and routine and settling suggestions they felt they had no other options left available to them and decided to try control crying. On their first attempt, Joseph cried for three hours, much to their horror. They were told to continue. They did. For four days. And for each sleep it took on average two to three hours to get him to go to sleep, and this did not guarantee he would stay asleep for more than 40 minutes. Eventually, and wisely, they stopped. Then his exhausted mother and father would take turns for hours and hours on end to rock and pat this beautiful big-nappied baby back to sleep.

One morning, Joseph's father saw me on the breakfast television program 7Sunrise, offering advice on how to get babies to sleep, and decided to give me a call. Because they had all been through so much, I knew trust needed to be re-established, especially after the control crying. On the first day, Joseph showed me just how clever he was by picking up his little toy and saying 'octopus'. It occurred to me that even at eight months Joseph was smart and just needed to be told what was going on.

We role played his new settling routine, including wrapping his blue bear, at least three times before I put him to bed for the first time. Joseph needed a firm wrap to emulate his mummy's cuddles but it took him just three minutes to put himself to sleep the first time. It took him 30 seconds to fall asleep that night. And then I was up all night with his mother, who was crying as she was concerned he had been asleep for too long. Joseph's new sleeping pattern has not faltered since, and he has just started school. He just needed to know what was happening, and what to expect.

Role play strategies

There are two forms of role play. One is visual and this is the predominant form I use when dealing with children under the age of two years. The complementary form with this age group is verbal. Verbal role play enables you to re-enforce and replay a previously conducted visual role play with a child while in the car, or while feeding them, etc. This means your baby has the opportunity to run through the process of events indirectly multiple times before ever being exposed to the experience directly. This gives them the opportunity to become familiar with the predictability of the event, start to trust the consistency of you within that event, and learn to cope with the emotions that may arise in this situation by looking to you for your reaction and confidence in that same situation.

Role play is where you show your child what is going to happen during a new event, such as their new settling process by using a teddy bear or doll and acting out the entire scenario word for word, action for action. You must treat the teddy bear with exactly the same affection, love and respect that you will display towards your child when you eventually implement the new routine with them. Your child needs to have seen it from where you stand, and seen your intentions with this new management technique, and how you will respond to their reaction to be able to accept the new routine with less stress and confusion.

This role play needs to be done each and every time someone new, such as a babysitter, is introduced to the routine, particularly when you have a child who has found sleep or any other event a very stressful task to achieve in the past. Role playing is a key strategy in helping your child quickly adjust to new conditions that would normally be stressful when experienced for the first time. This is because it enables us to indirectly put forward our expectations of their behaviour and ensures that we show ourselves to be predictable for our children, which fosters trust.

Role play also helps your child know where you are going to be once you leave their room. To them, based on the role play, it will appear that you will be waiting just outside their door should they need you, and while not accurate, this is a misconception I am happy to allow them to have. This is a comforting thought for your baby, and one that you can safely encourage. Role playing enables a child to experience the new routine while they are being held by you.

How to role play

Where possible, there should be two adults present for role-play scenarios: one to hold your baby or toddler and one to do the role playing with teddy. You and your partner must remain 110 per cent positive, completely identical with your actions and tones, and act as though you love teddy like you do your child, all the while giving off an air that you are really happy, and doing something really positive with teddy. This attitude remains, no matter how your little one reacts those first few times. This is how we replace an existing negative association around an event with a new positive association. Remember, they will learn how to react to their world around them through your role play and attitude to the world around you.

However you would like your child to feel about the routine, you must first role play emotionally to them. For a settling routine you can create a positive association around their room, around going to bed, and around you leaving the room by simply role playing with teddy a confident and happy example as often as it takes for them to understand the game. As you do each role play, you pull the door towards close a little bit more and more until the door is completely closed by the end of the resettle attempts with teddy, all within the same role play. By the third day of role playing, the door will be closed from the very start of the routine as your child will have had the opportunity to get used to, and become comfortable with, those conditions.

The person doing role play with teddy needs to keep their focus on teddy, and not change the pace, tone or sequence of events, regardless of their child's reactions to their new routine. The person doing the role play is not to keep interacting with, or focusing their attention on, their child because we do not want to confuse the baby about who you are putting to bed. This is about the teddy going to bed, and I need you to treat the teddy as though it is your baby.

If your baby has had a difficult time, and finds sleep or any other daily routine particularly difficult, then this strategy needs to be used and taken very seriously from six months of age. The person holding your baby needs to be aware of the importance of the role they have to play through the role play. They need to:

- position the child in a comfortable position before they enter the room and hold them reassuringly and comfortably but not too tightly
- remain entirely focused on the person doing the role play and on the teddy
- not talk to or be distracted by the baby's best tricks or verbal attention-seeking games as this might be where bubba is seeing what they can do to change the line of communication from a parent-directed to a child-directed one

- not fix it for them—if your child cries, just keep holding them without patting, squeezing, rocking, shushing or talking them through it. Allow them to experience the feelings and learn that they are safe and don't need a circus act to fix it, or you risk teaching them they will need that when it's their turn to go to bed.

You need to provide the same conditions your child will experience at a settling routine, and for the settling routine only. You are helping them get used to that unique set of conditions and used to experiencing the emotions that come up around that event, all while you are holding them *and* they need then to find a way, while in your arms, to calm themselves down without your assistance. Just allow them to witness, experience and work through the events independently, all while in the reassuring arms of a loving parent or primary carer.

When their attention is elsewhere

If they are fighting to be put down on the floor or are moving too much in your arms, then turn them to face the front and have their back on your tummy and hold them firmly. If they reach forward and try to climb in, kick off, bite or shake the cot, for fun or another reason, you will need to step back so they cannot reach the cot. If the baby is looking around, don't feel the need to try and turn around to make them look where you want them to. Just stand still, and allow your baby to take in the entire environment: walls, ceilings, curtains, darkness, door closed, mummy, their cot, their level of sight, everything. They will be able to hear so that's important, and in good time the repetitious actions of the person doing the role play will draw their interest and attention anyway.

Stay confident, calm and interested in the role play. Try not to talk at all. If your baby is really enjoying the role play and trying to share that with you, then you can smile and agree and point, but be very careful this is not just one of their tricks to change the attention to them and their line of communication. Remember, you are equipping them with the conditions they can expect at settling time, and that will not include a 'making mummy or daddy laugh' game simply because this is clearly going to involve a child-governed line of communication which cannot be used at sleep time. The idea of trying to direct them back to the role play of the settling routine should be enough if you have a baby who has found going to bed a challenging task in the past. If need be, hold your baby firmly in the sitting position in your arms if they are challenging you.

What to expect and how to help your child through role play

It is normal to see some of the following positive reactions during role play:

- They laugh at your repetitious behaviour and communication—perfect; enjoy the routine with your baby but don't deviate from the routine and make sure you complete the role play before cuddling and kissing them.
- They try to pat the cot—a lovely response; allow them to lean forward and pat the cot, but watch they don't try to climb in, or eat the bars.
- They attempt to climb in the cot with teddy—natural, but not allowed. This is where you are governing all lines of communication, and they need to observe, not tell you what they want to do at sleep time. Them wanting to get in is a great start, but they are not ready yet; they need to know the whole process.
- They reach forward and pat you while you pat the teddy—another lovely response and one you can allow them to have. Don't stop them, or talk to them, just allow it to happen. Don't stop to look at them, or laugh, obviously, or change or lose focus on the flow of the settling routine. Don't ask them to do it either. If it isn't spontaneous, then stay busy role playing.
- They lean towards the door with you to hear if the teddy is crying—a wonderful indication that they are enjoying and participating in the role play; carry on with your role playing, and look really interested in what you are doing.
- They reach for the door handle to attend to a crying teddy—this is fine so long as it's not completely distracting. They cannot tell you to go into the room, however, because that would be a child-governed line being introduced during a settling routine which is always parent directed. Simply carry on with your routine, and open the door when you are ready and it fits into the role play, not when they request or demand you open it. If you have a toddler, perhaps remove their hand from the door before you plan on opening it and say 'Mummy do it!' (This would not be necessary with an under-12 months old.)
- They pretend to cry for the teddy when you ask if teddy is crying—this is fine if you plan on having the teddy cry and role play attending to him, but if you have said 'no crying from teddy', and your child still does the cry anyway, reaches for the handle and insists on you going in, then do not change the line of communication to oblige their demands.

To suggest to a child that they govern this time will only promote tears when you try to put them to bed.

- They clap with you if teddy doesn't cry—excellent; be really excited and clap and cheer, and kiss and cuddle your baby. Lots of praise is always encouraged. We want them to think and feel happy about this whole new routine.
- They shush like you if teddy doesn't cry—again, a lovely response to your role play. Acknowledge their communication with something like 'Yes, shhhhh, teddy has gone nigh' nigh's'. If you are still role playing attending to a crying teddy, baby cannot tell you not to attend. Carry on, even if they get cross at you. This is you retaining the governing line of communication.
- They role play themselves independently without prompting—beautiful; do not disturb them unless they need help reaching their teddy, or putting the teddy in the cot. A lovely play-station idea for a toddler is to set up a sleep-time–style corner at home. Provide a cot (could be something as simple as a box with a pillow in it) and teddy and include any additional environmental things they see you use in your role play. Briefly role play their normal settling routine at the play station and allow them to role play themselves. This will be a wonderfully empowering thing for them to do—them governing the entire scenario themselves, and you not having assumed the line of communication is absolutely fine here.
- They sing or do the actions to 'Twinkle twinkle little star' while you sing to teddy—lovely, cute and okay to just allow to occur naturally. Don't respond to it during the role play; you can perhaps do it together at another time of the day. I have many toddlers who will do the actions to 'Twinkle twinkle little star' as I put them down the first time, even when they used to hate their bed. It does not change the flow of my routine for settling them however.
- They try to touch and see your face in the dark—this is actually quite sweet. They try to see how close they need to get to see you but, alas, they come to realise they can't see at night, no matter how big their eyes are, and no matter how close they get. Don't react to this, just allow them to work through it. This is the whole purpose of role playing in action as we talk it through. Your baby is learning the normal conditions of sleep while they have the security of their mum or dad holding them and, since they can see that you aren't concerned, they can feel safe during this process.

It is normal to see the following poor reactions during role play

Poor reactions to role playing is more difficult for some people to handle than others, and they may feel tempted to stop the role playing but this is not the right thing to do. Remember to always assess the situation from an adult's perspective, and remember your motivation: to help teach your little one a better way to do something that will ultimately mean no tears and a contented, soundly sleeping and well-fed child. There is always a period of transition that feels unfamiliar to the child and this will naturally be met with temporary resistance until it becomes familiar. Re-read the sections on 'Motivation for communication' (page 65) and 'Assessing the environment from an adult's perspective' (page 70) and work through your fears and emotions to find a better way to cope if you need further encouragement.

Here are some common poor reactions and some solutions to help you and your little one:

- They don't want teddy to sit on your lap while you are reading a book to them—do not allow them to take teddy off your lap. Teddy must stay there. The person holding baby stops them from reaching and grabbing teddy. Don't try to fix the way they are feeling, or spend time trying to calm them. This is where they are learning to accept a parent-governed line of communication, and the first time you do it, they will be unfamiliar with the process and try to fight it. Your best move is to proceed with your routine and use your enthusiastic tones to help distract them. It's better you don't confuse them by letting them cuddle teddy even once, or you risk teaching them to demand you let them cuddle teddy at anytime throughout the role play, which ultimately means they are now running the settling routine. Do not change the pace, tone or confident delivery of your routine role play. Try to quickly start to read the book in a really exciting way to teddy; this will likely draw their attention away.
- They really want the book—the same approach as above applies here. They cannot have the book. You should ensure they can see the book but don't try to talk them through it with remarks like 'Look Charlie, here it is' etc. This will rarely stop the demands or tears. The best method is to use your enthusiastic, effective-reading skills to distract them. Carry on with your routine as normal, and allow your partner to manage the sitting or tantrum issues without your intervention, so stay focused on your task. Don't buckle and stop at this point; it doesn't

last long so carry on like I do, and you will get results quickly. (Please see positioning page 302).

- They may think you are putting them to bed—this could occur if you are too focused on your baby. Stick to the routine, remember to use the cues and teddy's name and only look at teddy, and ask teddy to co-operate with you. Keep moving forward with your routine because only time will show them that you only plan on putting teddy to bed when you read and talk using teddy's name, and you only plan on putting them to bed when you read and talk using their name.

- They cry as you put teddy to bed—this is very normal and is them expressing how they feel about the old conditions of sleep and, most importantly, is why you are re-establishing new conditions. Expect this if your child has previously had to go through difficult settles and sleep times. Stay confident, and work your way right through the old emotions until you have laid down the foundation for new, more positive associations with sleep.

- They want to be taken out of the room—if you are the one holding them, you need to stand, hold them, and carry on with your routine while they get used to the conditions of this parent-governed line of communication. A part of going to bed for mummy and daddy does not involve demanding to be taken out of their bedroom. Carry on with the role play. The person holding the child needs to continue watching the one with the teddy without letting the child get down. Hold them firmly.

- They want to attend to the teddy once you leave the room on the first few attempts to role play even after you have said that teddy has stopped crying and you need to leave him to sleep now—this is normal when they are first experiencing a new routine through role play. This is the purpose of such a strategy. But imagine how confusing and stressful, not to mention trust compromising, any new routine would be if the baby did not experience the new routine indirectly first. Again, you need to carry on confidently and complete your role play. Mind your inflection and tone; remember to sound loving, warm, reassuring and confident as you use your language. This ensures you maintain the governing line of communication, and they get the opportunity to learn that they need to look to you for guidance. Once you have indicated that teddy is no longer crying and has gone to sleep, he needs to stay in there until you determine it's time to get teddy up. This does not ever happen because your child is demanding it.

- They want to get into the cot and pat the teddy—they cannot get into the cot with teddy until it is their turn to go to sleep. Remember, you are teaching them that you govern all sleep times, not them, so they are not to change the routine flow, or demand to be in charge of teddy.
- They want you to open the door—if you have assessed that your child needs their door shut while they are sleeping then it would be dishonest to teach them that they can ask to have the door opened at sleep time. They need an opportunity to get used to this and become comfortable with the conditions of the new routine. Remember, you are learning to cater to their true needs over their short-term demands.
- They try to open the door to leave the room—your little one should be being held but if you are on your own, they may not be, so this may arise. Simply carry on with the routine if you know they cannot reach the handle or, if they can reach the handle, go and pick them up and complete the role play while holding them. Stay confident and reassuring throughout the event. Do not change the process of the role play. Complete it as directed.
- They tantrum—this can happen if your little one has very poor associations with their room and going to sleep, or if they are not yet used to the balanced lines of communication where you govern at certain events of the day. Please ensure you are using your communication correctly through the day so they do not feel stressed by you guiding them. Re-read 'Working through the tantrum' on page 122. Carry on and complete your role play. If your child is a tantrum thrower, don't feel alone in this. There are many mums and dads dealing with this. Be sure to have help during the times you are role playing.
- They hit you, the cot, or the person holding them—reposition them so they cannot reach the cot or the person doing the role play, and cannot reach and hit you. Do not speak; simply reposition them, stay calm and follow through with the role play. Remember, we do not want to teach them to hit us if they do not want to go to bed, or teach them that everything stops when they hit you.
- They want their teddy back—this is a good point. You need to be careful about the teddy or dolly you have chosen for role play. If they already have a significant bond with that teddy, then it's understandable that they will want to hold it when they are feeling uncertain, and to not be allowed to ask for it would be not very fair. Choose a teddy they are not too attached to for the role playing.
- They do not want to walk away and leave teddy to sleep in the room—this is about who is governing the situation, and how they

feel about being left in their room. It's important to remember two key things: you are the governing line of communication around all things sleep, and they need reassuring that it is perfectly safe to leave teddy sleeping. You reassure them by responding appropriately to their reaction.

- They try and go off to play in the room while you role play—if they are being held then this is not really a problem, but on your own it might be. You don't want to confuse them and allow them to believe they can toddle off to play at sleep time, and you don't want to waste any precious learning opportunities. Your child may just not know that you would like them to watch you, so it's important to make sure they come and join you, or you have someone there to help you.

When role playing is running well

Remember, that both the person doing the role play and the person holding the baby need to stay focused, confident and interested in the role play and teddy only, and regardless of your child's attempts to get your attention or to change the focus back on to them, the outcome and the parent-governed line of communication should remain the same. This provides your child with realistic expectations for their new sleep routine so you can put them to bed with no battles, and they will happily look to you for guidance, rather than try to guide you.

The following reactions may occur during the role play and there is nothing wrong if they do. Your child may:

- watch teddy during story reading, and try to make eye contact with teddy up close
- try to talk to teddy
- try to make teddy turn the pages of the book
- randomly kiss or cuddle teddy
- get cross at teddy
- look around the room and not always pay attention to you
- try to get your attention using their best trick, including their best funny antics, and a huge repertoire of verbal attention getters
- become familiar with the routine and try to lead the role play
- talk or sing endlessly through the whole role play
- go back to the door once the role play is over to see if teddy is awake or crying
- be so cute as they concentrate and listen to you that you may feel the urge to hug and kiss them endlessly.

In all these cases, please just carry on and complete the role play with minimal interaction with your bub. Once it's done you can have some fun one-on-one playtime with them.

Acknowledge their honesty

It's not unusual for your child to tell you exactly how they are going to react during their direct settling event through demonstrating their response at a role-play settling event. In a toddler, this may be demonstrated by them being happy for mummy to settle teddy but furious if daddy does. This essentially means they are telling you that they will settle for mummy, but be very cross if daddy puts them to bed. You may be extremely surprised at how clever your baby or toddler is, and be so proud you need to call someone to tell them about it. That all being said, please just take on board what your child is telling you, and either practise role playing a little more until they become more comfortable with the role-play process (indicating they will be more comfortable when settled themselves), or prepare yourself for a little bit of a challenge at settling that day or night. After all, they have already told you they might complain about going to bed while you practised putting teddy down.

Going it alone

Even if you don't have a partner, friend, parent, or in-law who can swing by and help you, it is still very achievable to role play on your own. I often role play alone with toddlers, and have on many occasion needed to role play with six to 12 month olds on my own too, so I can assure you right now: rest easy, you can do this.

If your baby is not yet walking, you have two choices, and it is usually depends on your strength and your baby as to which one you choose to use:

1. Carry them while you do the whole role play. It might feel messy, but they get the message.
2. If the child is very stroppy throughout and difficult to carry, you will need to pop them into a safe seat so they can watch you. Placing them in a baby seat, their high chair (if it has wheels so you can move them about as necessary), their pram or the like, is probably the best way to manage them and your role play at the same time.

If your baby can walk you have three choices:

1. Carry them while you do the whole role play. It might feel messy, but they get the message.

2. They walk into the room holding your hand, then you must close the door behind you and let go of their hand and carry on with your role play. If they potter off, it doesn't really matter because it is dark anyway, so they only need to hear you. (Be careful to make the room safe from falling or other injuries if they do enjoy having a potter in the dark.) Each time you plan on leaving the room and listening to teddy outside the room you will need to hold their hand and keep holding their hand, or pick them up briefly until you are back in their room with them.

3. If they are very stroppy, upset and difficult to carry, you will need to pop them into a safe seat so they can watch you. Placing them in a baby seat, their high chair (if it has wheels), their pram, or the like, is probably the best way to manage them and your role play at the same time.

Role-play routine

It generally takes between four and five role plays for your little one to work past their old associations, become familiar with and start to trust the new routine, and learn that they are okay and can predict this part of their day. Always make sure the room and environment is ready before you start your role play with a checklist like this:

- The cot is made.
- 'White noise' is on.
- The lights are off in the room, and in all the rooms and the hall near the room.
- The SafeT Sleep is ready if you are using one.
- Towel rolls are prepared, ready for when you tuck him in.
- The wrap, if you are using one, is out on the nearest bed.
- The book is ready on the couch (only one book required for role play).
- A clock or watch is available for timing.
- All distractions are turned off and put away.

Please exclude any environmental factors that are not appropriate to your tailored program. For some children it is easier if you include a comfort item (like a dummy, muslin, teddy, dolly, etc.) and if it is appropriate to your baby's actual need, keep it, but for other children you will need to exclude it if you plan on not providing it during their new settling routine. If it does not apply, simply remove the item from the environment.

Role-play example for swaddled baby six to 12 months old
All language cues and requests suggested here are achievable for your child from around six months of age, so keep working on them. It will happen.

Troubleshooting

Q I have another child; can they come in?

A Depending on their behaviour and if they can listen to you, it should be fine, but please make sure you put forward an expectation of their behaviour to them before you start; that is, no climbing on the cot, no opening the door, quiet time, no touching teddy. You could ask them to help you sing, 'Twinkle, Twinkle Little Star' when you sing it, and to pat teddy through the bars when you pat teddy. This will make them feel important in the event and give them a target.

Q Can we both role play and chop and change who settles baby on those first few days?

A Absolutely not. One person, usually the primary nurturer or person who is home the most with baby must be the first person to establish the role play and the settling routine for at least the first four days of your repair program. Once they have learnt to sleep for one of you, then the other parent or other carers can become involved.

Q When should my partner start to role play?

A I generally recommend that your partner starts to get involved in the settling routine between the second and the third week. Depending on how difficult a time you have all had, you may just want to invest a little bit of extra time creating this loving, trusting routine with the first parent before you ask your little one to have to learn to settle for the next person. That said, I find that when babies sleep well for the first time in their lives on this program, the person who introduced the settling routine is often too frightened to allow the other parent to try role playing and then settling the baby just in case it ruins everything. I'm here to tell you that you will start to create an inflexibility in your child, that is ultimately a child-governed line of communication around sleep if you remain the only settler. Remember, you are governing sleep and taking the burden off the baby. They may need to go through a little learning process when the other parent or additional carer is introduced to the settling process but that's okay because, just like they did with you, they will learn to sleep for them as well.

Q How long do I need to role play for?

A You should role play for two to three days prior to starting your routine. You should role play at least twice a day, three times if you can find the time. You should also continue role play until your baby stops having difficulty settling on your repair program, which is usually within the first two to three days. Once the initial role play has been done, the second and subsequent carers should only need to role play once or twice on the day of their first settle. Occasionally, if you can see that baby is displaying a strong resistance to that particular person doing the settling routine through a role play with teddy, then that person should role play for one more day before they then embark on their first settling

Make sure your language is nice and clear, absolutely predictable and routine, as it is the predominant tool you use at settling time. This is not meant to be about rocking them to sleep, patting them to sleep, or giving them things that will make them go to sleep. This is about empowering routine with the baby. They should also maintain their role play for a day or so, until things settle down and baby/toddler has learnt that they too are predictable.

Q What about daycare?

A If your baby has been struggling with sleeping at daycare, as some babies do, then you will find your management and routine adjustments at home will be enough to improve their sleep there. Always be prepared and realistic about what to expect when your baby sleeps elsewhere, however (see 'Sleeping when out' on page 741). You can do a role play at daycare one morning before you leave, settling their role-play teddy using your new routine if you like. I know many mums and dads who have done this with great success. But the daycarers will obviously not be able to incorporate the entire settling routine you use at home, but that's okay. All they need to know is how to use the forewarning element of the flow of communication, and the final portion of the settling routine such as the song and the cues. Daycare must not be encouraged to use any of the old associations used to get baby to sleep, like patting, rocking, feeding etc. If you know your baby can put themselves to sleep at home, there is no need for these methods to put your baby to sleep there.

Q Can my baby sit on my lap while I'm doing a role play?

A If there is someone else helping you then the answer is a definite 'no'. The most important thing to remember here is that you need your little one to be able to watch the entire scenario from an observer's perspective. This will assist them when it comes time to experience the routine themselves and help reduce tears. We also don't want to confuse them when they are sitting on your lap at their settling time: they may think you are putting teddy to bed as you usually do when they sit on your lap when role play. For this reason, try to make the distinction quite clear. The child should not move about and tell you they want to sit on daddy's lap, then mummy's lap, then the couch, because this changes the important parent-governed line of communication into a child-governed one.

Where toddlers are concerned I tend to be a little more careful. I start to position them on the helper's lap and if they are resistant then I offer them the option to sit on the couch next to the person doing the role play. If they are resistant here as well, then without a doubt I get them safe and secured on the helper's lap and get reading in my most enthusiastic manner possible, even if they start to tantrum. Within a short period of time they are focused on the book because I am reading it enthusiastically to teddy. If you are on your own and you have a little baby aged six to 12 months, snuggle them safely into the corner of the couch and sit facing them to keep them safe and help them see you, the teddy and the book better. If you have a toddler, sit them on the couch next to you. If your little one is difficult to manage, or a real wriggly worm, then the high chair is the best option to keep them safe, and help them focus on the role play (always fasten buckles on the high chair for safety reasons).

your child with the tools to do this themselves, so they don't have to have a stressful settling or resettling routine, and so you can be at your best—happy, energetic and enthusiastic—throughout the day as the stress of sleep time is lifted. Here you are saying to your child, 'We are getting you ready to put yourself to sleep; getting you things you need to help yourself go to sleep. We love you, and if you need us, we're right outside. Goodnight.'

Remember your flow of communication. Pre-emptive language is a fair warning of what's about to happen: 'Charlie, we're going to play with our blocks, then it's time to put teddy to nigh' nigh's'. Forewarning language is the final prompt before the event begins: 'Charlie, last one, last [state event], then it's time to put teddy to nigh' nigh's'.

Initiate a parent-governed line of communication: 'Okay, Charlie boy, up up'. You or the other parent or helper now picks them up: 'Time to go get teddy and put him into cot for nigh' nigh's.' (Please don't say bed, as your child sleeps in a cot and doesn't know what a bed is at this stage.)

Go and get teddy together, and have a little moment of love with teddy. Pick teddy up and be really happy to see him, 'Oh, hi teddy, cuddles for mummy, cuddles for [person carrying baby], cuddles for Charlie. Oh we love teddy, he's so soft.' From this moment on you talk only to teddy. Always use the same teddy, please.

Turn teddy to face you and say 'Okay, teddy, it's nearly time for nigh' nigh's, let's go read our book'. Take teddy into the lounge room, or another appropriate room where you plan on reading to your child (preferably not their own room) and say 'Sit down teddy, wait for mummy'.

Show teddy the book and read to him. As you progress through the book, remember to use your language cues 'wait for mummy / daddy', 'turn the page', 'teddy do it', '*nearly* time for nigh' nigh's', '*nearly* last page', '*nearly* time to pack away'. As you read to teddy, you can physically make teddy's paw turn the page, and occasionally (with children ten months plus) make teddy try to turn or pull the book down so you can correct this behaviour and set the new boundary and expectation of behaviour by using the 'wait for mummy' cue and action as demonstrated in 'Reading to your baby'. As you reach the last half of the book, be sure to be clear to teddy that it is nearly time for sleep: 'Nearly time to pack away teddy, nearly time for nigh' nigh's'. At the last page, tell teddy, 'Last page, nearly time to pack away'.

Each time you deliver one of these new lines, make it sound a little more song-like by using a higher tone, and drawing out the length of the words: 'Tuuuuuurrrrrn the paaaaaaaaage'. This will help your child tune into your voice even while you are using a lot of vocabulary through the story. After the last page say 'Time to pack away', and tuck the book down the side of the couch or out of view. Once the story is over, you stop saying 'nearly' and start saying 'time for' in your cues; for example, '*time* for nigh' nigh's.'

Turn teddy to face you and with a big smile and clear eye contact say, 'it's time for sleep, teddy. Mummy and daddy love you, nigh' nigh's.' Have a big cuddle with teddy and give him a kiss as you repeat your cues a second time before you stand and start to walk towards the bedroom where you are going to wrap them.

As you walk, calmly repeat the cues every now and again until you reach the side of the bed that has the wrap on it. Turn teddy in your arms so he can see the bed and repeat your cues as you give him a kiss. Point to the wrap and say 'Lie down'. Lie teddy down in the wrap in the correct position so you can be sure to minimise any additional moving you may need to do. Wrap teddy casually, or practise your firm wrap. Occasionally repeat your cues.

Pick teddy up by sliding your correct arm (which will depend on which end his head lies in the cot) under teddy's neck and lift him so he remains in the lying-down position in your arms. Cover teddy's eyes with your cheek or by tucking his face into your neck as you walk from the wrapping room into the cot room. Close the door (refer to closing the door during role play on page 648).

Walk to the side of the cot. If it is very dark, use your hand to find the position you need to be in to lie teddy into the cot in just the right position (but don't lie him down just yet, just get in position) and plant your feet firmly. You need to get comfortable, and slow everything right down. Your voice and the rate and tone you speak with could literally put your baby to sleep so use that tool wisely. Slowly rock from side to side. Very slowly. This rocking should only be about moving your torso, or moving from the waist up. Your feet should remain in the same position, and when I say slowly, I literally mean very slowly. Sing 'Twinkle twinkle little star' in a soft, reassuring lilt and in a slow, slow, sleep-inducing way, but loud enough to be heard. Sing the song through twice, then stop swaying and singing.

It generally takes between four and five role plays for your little one to work past their old associations, become familiar with and start to trust the new routine

Kiss teddy on the cheek or forehead (choose the one you prefer and always stick to it). Say your cues in a gentle, reassuring way without even a slight hint of concern. If you smile, it will slightly lift your inflection and make you sound even more comforting. Even if you don't feel like smiling, try to do it for your baby's sake. Smile and say 'Time for sleep. Mummy and daddy love you, nigh' nigh'. Lie down.'

You should say 'Lie down' before you begin to lie the teddy down. Once teddy is in the right position, pull the extra piece of free wrap material on the top left to ensure the wrap is still firm. Place teddy so he is higher up the bed, then place his lower legs under the firm sheets before you slide him down into the tucked-in bedding. (See tucking in baby on page 453.)

Do up the SafeT Sleep firmly. Tuck bedding in. If you are using a leg wrap only and your 12 months old has a dummy that you have chosen to keep you could encourage (like a puppet) teddy to reach for his dummy and say 'Get your dummy'. (See independent dummy strategies on page 467.) Hand teddy his comfort item, saying 'Take your muslin / dolly / sooky / teddy / cuddly'. Manipulate teddy's free arm, or the preferred arm, by lifting it as though he is taking the dummy or place the comfort object parallel to his side, and drape it over his shoulder. This way is the way you would do it for baby so they can get it themselves.

Pull or attach the blocking cloth to the side of the cot. Bend over behind the blocking cloth, side on to the cot and look at your feet. Reach over the top of the cot side and into the cot and pat teddy rhythmically, 'Sh sh sh sh, time for sleep. Sh sh sh sh, mummy and daddy love you. Sh sh sh sh, time for sleep. Sh sh sh sh, mummy and daddy love you. Sh sh sh sh, nigh', nigh'.'

On the last word of your last cue take your hand away, stand and turn to your baby. Say 'C'mon, Charlie, let's go!' and head for the door. Once outside the room, say 'Close the door' and close it making sure it clicks (because we are learning to be honest with our children about leaving their room). Once outside, make clear eye contact with your baby who is still in your partner's arms and say 'Is teddy crying?' Head towards the door, turn and cover your mouth and make a crying sound. Say 'Oh dear, teddy is crying. Let's go and see him.'

Walk back in the room and your baby and partner follow. Close the door behind you. Walk to the side of the cot and bend over behind the blocking cloth, side on to the cot and look at your feet. Reach over the top of the cot side and into the cot and pat teddy rhythmically, saying 'Sh sh sh sh, time for sleep, Sh sh sh sh, mummy and daddy love you. Sh sh sh sh, time for sleep. Sh sh sh sh, mummy and daddy love you, sh sh sh sh, nigh' nigh'.'

Again, on the last word of your last cue take your hand away, stand and turn to your baby, 'C'mon, Charlie, let's go!' and head for the door. Once outside the room, say 'Close the door', and close it, making sure it clicks. Do the 'is teddy crying?' line, leaning towards the door, turn and cover your mouth and make a crying sound: 'Oh dear, teddy is crying, let's go and see him'.

You will need to repeat attendances to teddy a few times but, after your final attendance, when you say 'Is teddy crying?' lean in to listen and allow a prolonged silence, even if your baby pretends to cry in the appropriate gap. Repeat the question with a little bit of a gasp and a look of surprise, 'Listen, is teddy crying?'

Allow for another pause of around ten seconds. Look happy and excited, say 'Listen, no crying', and pause again.

Repeat one last time, 'No crying! Teddy's gone nigh' nigh's, yeah!' and clap and cheer. Raise your hand to your mouth and gesture and say 'Ssshhhhhh, teddy has gone nigh' nigh's. C'mon, let's go.' And carry on with your day.

For baby not swaddled, six to 12 months plus

This routine is as outlined above up until just before you read the book. Turn teddy to face you and say 'Okay, teddy, it's nearly time for nigh' nigh's. Let's put on our sleeping bag and go read our book.' Place teddy in his sleeping bag, and do up the zipper. Take teddy into the room where you plan on reading to your child and say 'Sit down teddy, wait for mummy'. This step means you will not do the steps involving wrapping the teddy. Continue on with above routine.

For toddler, 12 months plus

Again, steps are as above, placing teddy in his sleeping bag prior to reading. Only teddy is in the cot and you have said 'lie down'. Pretend teddy is trying to stand up. Say a clear, 'No, lie down, teddy'. Repeat this several times if you are anticipating you are going to have this battle with your little one. When teddy is lying still say 'Good listening, teddy, good lying still'. Encourage (like a puppet) teddy to reach for his dummy, 'Get your dummy', and continue on with routine above.

Working through fears or discomforts with role play

Obviously the new sleep routine is only one of a number of skills your child will learn quicker and with less stress if shown through role play first. Another positive application for role playing is that it can be used to help a child work through a fear. This should be done to help a child instil a more positive attitude and feeling about being in the environment they are uncomfortable with or fearful of, such as a dark room. A visual role play of peek-a-boo with teddy in the dark room right from the time your child is 12 months old would be as follows:

'Mummy and Mitchell play "where's teddy?" Mummy close the door', and you gesture closing the door.

'Mummy said, "where's teddy?"' Be very light and airy with your voice as your child will be transfixed by this happy conversation you instigated and which they recognise. They may become still at this stage, perhaps stare off into the distance, turn to look towards the bedroom, point or express their dislike of the feelings associated with the role play by crying. If your child is still concerned throughout a verbal role play, then you need to do as much physical role playing as you can, on and off, throughout the day. Keep continuing on with the verbal role play. This is an excellent opportunity to expose your little one to the emotions of the event indirectly and to instil a new association via your happy tones and fun attitude about the peek-a-boo game you are talking through.

Continue to progress through the events of your role play verbally by repeating the cues and game as they transpired during the physical role play, including your language cues and carefree attitude about the dark, 'Oh, its dark now, mummy can't see teddy, where's that teddy?' Throughout the game, find opportunities to clap or say hurray about the dark and not seeing teddy.

Complete the game with a big hurray and talk through your cuddle with teddy before moving on to another conversation.

Indirect verbal role playing

Once you have physically role played through a particular sequence of events a couple of times, that sequence becomes so predictable to your child that you are now able to verbally role play through it. This gives you a unique opportunity to work through your child's anxieties without it consuming too much of your day. As you drive in the car, or go for a walk in the pram, or perhaps after dinner while they are having a little play in their high chair, you can talk though your role play in the same sequence as your usual visual role play. Your little one will listen, look at you, or stare off into the distance as they recall the visual role-play event. They may or may not get upset at the concept, but you should remain confident and complete the event. If your little one has become so relaxed about the role play and just continues to play and appears undisturbed, then there is no need to repeat your verbal role play as they have indicated that they are comfortable with this event. For those who struggle even with verbal role play, you will need to persist longer until your baby becomes relaxed.

The value of role play can never be overstated (see box on page 632). Take the time to show your child exactly what you will be doing when you put them to bed by doing that exact same routine when you put teddy to bed. Prepare the room, and then expose them to those new environmental conditions during a role play. This will give them a chance to experience the new dark room: the door closed, the night light gone, the new sound machine, the sound of the SafeT Sleep if you are using one.

Let them be a part of leaving the room and closing the door once teddy is in bed to allow them to see what you will be doing when you leave. Let them be involved in listening to see if teddy is crying (yes, even at 8 months of age) so they can have a basic idea of where you might be while they are tucked into their bed. This allows them to see that you are at the door, you are waiting and listening, and if they need help, you will come to them.

Take the time to allow them to experience your feelings about teddy crying. By remaining calm, and confident, and practising your resettling cues, your baby becomes familiar with the cues, allowing them to feel soothed by these when you use them in the real scenario later.

The importance of boundaries

Why do children do some of the things they do, and behave in some of the ways they behave? It's because they don't know the consequences of their actions, or the impact those actions have on others. This is perfectly normal and natural. Sometimes they are very happy to oblige, and at other times they are less than impressed with your plans, even if you thought, or even know, they are good plans and in your little one's best interests.

Children are naturally impulsive, and will happily run onto a road to chase a ball, grab a burning candle because it's attractive to the eye, and turn on a hot tap because they have observed you do it. Equally, they will squirm and tantrum when you change their nappy because they would rather get down even if to allow that could result in a nappy rash and pain. This is because they don't have the capacity to think in terms of consequences; they only respond to the very moment they are in, and it is you, as their guardian and protector, who is responsible for deciding when their impulsive actions are in their best long-term interests.

Some people would have you believe that children behave in certain ways because they 'need' to do all the things they do. I do not subscribe to that school of thinking. I firmly believe that children only do and behave the way they do around certain events because they haven't been shown a better way, or an alternative. They have no way of knowing that the consequences of some of those impulsive actions will be detrimental to them or others.

This same principle applies to basic boundaries that need to be set on any given day, such as those set around sleep and other basic needs like nappy changes, or getting dressed, sitting in the pram or letting you feed them. We live in a time of tremendous judgement and pressure to perform and be a 'perfect' parent and, as a result, I've seen many parents so focused on trying to keep their children happy at all costs that they abdicate their 'knowledge' of what truly makes a child happy. They start to look at a tiny child, not even two years old, for guidance on a subject they could not, being new to this world, know or understand.

This means that some parents just accept certain behaviours, no matter how exhausting, unpleasant to endure or inappropriate they are to the child, the family or those around them, regardless of the long-term effects those patterns of behaviour will have.

I firmly believe that children only do and behave the way they do around certain events because they haven't been shown a better way, or an alternative.

This means a child who needs desperately to sleep because they are tired is still allowed to stay up half the night, or a child who needs to eat nutritious food because they are clearly hungry is still allowed to drink milk whenever they demand it.

This means a child who is screaming and tantruming on a change table is allowed to crawl all over the floor rather than learn how to lie still and be a little calm and patient.

Finally, this means that when the child turns four or five and the parent decides they would no longer like them to do any of the things they have grown up being taught is right, they tell their child to 'grow up and stop acting like a baby'.

A more fair, honest and healthy approach would be to decide, as a family, which behaviours you would like to avoid, or correct, and what the boundaries are within your house and family. Boundaries are good. Let me repeat that statement for those of you who still aren't sure: boundaries are good.

Yep, I'm going to scream it from the rooftops, for the rest of my life. Not only do I think boundaries are good, I think they are the absolute key to happy and balanced babies and toddlers, and essential in preparing a child for life. Boundaries help a child learn patience, persistence, social skills, expectations of others, self-control, empathy towards others, and safety, as well as provide opportunities for you to encourage the great sleep and healthy eating necessary to promote optimum growth and development, so your precious little people can be all they could ever possibly be.

Anyone who says a baby should have no boundaries has failed to see the vitally important role they have in a child's life. To not provide boundaries for a child, particularly around the areas of health and safety, is neglecting your duty of care through failing to provide the best possible state of health so your child can develop and learn at peak capacity. Boundaries act as emotional safety nets, reassuring the child that when they feel out of control or overwhelmed or overburdened in a world full of choices, they can safely turn to you and you will take over, unburden them and keep them safe.

Those safety nets should be set close, like training wheels, while a child is young. As the child matures and starts to develop the capacity to cope with the responsibility of choices and guiding others, the nets should be slowly withdrawn to allow a child to steady themselves and try out their new skills. You will still need to keep an eye on them, though, and if you feel they are tired, stressed or in a challenging position, you may then decide to tighten up the safety nets until they settle down again.

Setting appropriate boundaries or house rules also sets them up to have a healthy expectation of others' respect towards them, and helps them learn what they may expect in return. Our children know nothing of our western culture or its social ways. We function predominantly through the day, and sleep at night. We have cultural and social etiquette and boundaries, and for the most part, we all need to be in a reasonable mood to cope with the day-to-day trials of life. So, unless you plan to move in with the Moiré tribes people, our little children and their mums and dads do need to 'learn' how to live in our western culture, and it is up to us as adults who understand the consequences of our actions to teach our little ones how to function within those boundaries.

It's unrealistic to think that a child will have an automatic understanding of how a toy works when they first see it, or how to go to sleep in their cot, or how to lie still while you change them, or play on the floor while you wash the dishes, so they rely heavily on you, the people who know more about this amazing world they are a part of, to tell them what to do, and how to best do it. You are the ones who need to show them what is going to exact the best results for them when they step out into the big wide world. You are the ones who want to teach them all these things, not a teacher or a nanny. You want to do it with love and respect and patience. They need clear guidance with their play and their behaviour.

It's important to give them a day they can predict, so they can be freed of the burden of telling you how to make them happy. We don't need them to tell us what in general makes them happy because we already know. They need to be loved, they need to feel safe, they need to sleep, they need to be nourished, and they need to feel free to explore and play to enjoy and learn about the world around them. Only an adult can find that balance when things go a little awry.

Be confident: make decisions, and help them through those decisions until they too understand the benefits of some of your ideas and plans.

20
Crying interpretation

Ask just about any grandparent and they will gladly and proudly attest to the fact that parenting seemed less complicated in their day. Not only that, sleep time really wasn't that big a deal for anyone. This is clearly in stark contrast to modern parenting, where it has been reported that more than half the families in this country alone are struggling with persistent sleep-time issues beyond their child's first birthday, and that those problems are considered severe and ongoing. Why, then, is this generation of parents finding putting their babies to bed so much more challenging than the previous generation found it? Why is it, that by six to 12 months of age, some babies today are needing two or three times more night feeds than they needed when they were newborns? Do they truly need that level of milk intake, or are they actually seeking more comfort to feel safe, ironically in an environment that has been nothing but safe and nurturing? Or could it simply be that we are teaching them to need those things—feeding, rocking, pacing, patting—as a solution to feeling tired?

Getting some perspective on crying

I believe there are many causes of the current sleep-time challenge, ranging from changing sleep requirements due to strong healthy pregnancies and great nutritional advice for children and mothers alike, through parents doing less labour-intensive domestic chores due to washing machines, dishwashers, etc., to fewer children being born per household, creating more one-on-one time between parents and their little ones, which occasionally tips the scales to the child being fully entertained and having no quiet times to discover their own place of peace and happiness. I also believe, however, that one of the most relevant and, as far as I am concerned, the ultimate end result of all the varied causes of the current sleep challenge is the fear or anxiety around a baby crying *at all* when it comes time for sleep.

In 1998, some of the causes of cot death were discovered thanks to the wonderful research of the SIDS foundation amongst others. Parents were alerted about potentially dangerous practices that could pose a significant SIDS risk factor for their child. This research has been responsible for saving over 5000 children's lives since the beginning of the campaign—thank goodness. But as a result of it, everyone started putting their babies on their backs to sleep, reducing the layers of excessive warmth and removing cot bumpers. So babies lost the digestive relief that came from lying on their tummies, the natural sense of security they got from the weight and warmth of those extra blankets, and were exposed to more visual stimulation through the removal of the bumpers. Babies were left feeling less settled, more exposed and far more overstimulated when it came time to going to bed. This ultimately led to tears, and lots of them.

Ask just about any grandparent and they will gladly and proudly attest to the fact that parenting seemed less complicated in their day.

When this situation became an increasingly difficult situation for many families to deal with, many healthcare professionals started to recommend a single strategy commonly known as 'control crying'. Some even went a step further to suggest strategies commonly known as 'uncontrolled crying'—it is also called 'controlled comforting' or 'cry it out'. These methods were implemented without with any form of communication, play, independence, emotional foundation work, sleep or meal-time management strategy, and so they were doomed to fail in a good proportion of cases.

This is where I believe the bulk of modern parenting problems lie when trying to understand the difference between what is right and normal when teaching those precious little ones how to go sleep. Yes, *teaching* them how to go to sleep. It has become most definitely a learnt skill for many (but not all) babies these days. While the premise of limiting the level of intervention you offer a child to allow them some opportunity to try and develop independent-settling skills is an important one to consider, the control crying strategy and all its derivatives were sadly used and misused in isolation of any form of teaching, and devoid of any understanding of the causes of crying in the first place. As a result, they failed to prepare or empower a child with the ability to cope with the very great task of going to sleep by themselves.

This ultimately led to many tears and much stress for both the baby and parents going through this kind of sleep training. In addition, due to the failure to understand the mechanics of sleep and the causes of crying in children, the control crying strategy inherently came hand in hand with a very confusing and contradictory strategy: the parent being their child's full emotional solution during the day, perpetuating the cause of crying at sleep time. This is basically teaching your child that you will respond to their cries through the day in one way, and then respond to them in an entirely different way at night. In other words, because the reason for the crying at sleep time is predominantly caused by the daytime management of a child, even after a night full of tears and distress for a baby and their parents, any *learning* (if you could call it that) would immediately be undone the following morning because you completely contradict anything you have taught them, and ultimately cause them enormous confusion.

A classic example of this lies in the fact that control crying suggests that to be successful you must teach a baby that when they ask at night, you will not pick them up and feed them. Yet, control crying does not address the fact that when they wake up at a reasonable time in the morning, despite everything you have spent hours trying to teach them through the night, when they ask to be picked up and fed, you will walk straight in and pick them up, and take them to their feeding chair, and feed and cuddle them, and play with them.

Can you see how to a baby, who does not know 10 p.m. from 2 a.m. from 7 a.m., you are being entirely inconsistent and confusing? One minute you say 'Don't ask to be picked up because I won't pick you up when you cry' yet the next moment you say 'If you want to get up, cry out to me and I'll come and pick you up and feed and cuddle you'. Confusing, huh? This is where control crying and all its derivatives are entirely flawed. They simply do not address the cause of the crying in the first place.

It is important to note that I am not saying that you should not let a baby cry, and nor am I advocating you just let a baby cry. I am simply saying that you need to find a balance by looking more closely at the reason a baby cries in the first place, and then set about trying to empower them with the necessary coping skills before you ask them to try and go to sleep on their own without excessive levels of our help. Crying interpretation is the art of listening and understanding your child and what they are actually saying, rather than interpreting just your fear of crying and what that fear 'might mean'.

As times passed, most parents found controlled crying stressful and, in many cases, unfair and confusing. As a result, they began to move in the opposite direction to more extreme ways of thinking, like avoiding all crying at sleep time, at all cost. This created a situation where any unattended crying by a baby who was tired and going to sleep independently was considered cruel and treated as though it was / is neglectful or unloving. This contributed to the trend of a parent becoming a child's only and complete emotional solution at sleep time and, ironically, this has actually been the cause of so many nights of crying, stress and discomfort for many children and their entire family. You would be saddened to read some of the thousands of emails I have received over the years from parents who had begun to look to a tiny and exhausted little baby for guidance on how they should best go to sleep. For a good portion of babies, their answer so far has been a resounding 'I don't know mummy and daddy, can you show me . . . please?'

I think it's important you recognise that you can't keep doing the same thing, and expect a different result. If you want to see a change in your child's level of peace at sleep time, you need to do something different. Often, it's as simple as giving them some space and time to learn to sleep without the stimulating fuss of always having to guide grown-ups through the night. Change is hard though, and I often see people cling to ineffective strategies and poor patterns simply because of the *fear* of change.

The use of a fully assisted sleep-association approach or an 'avoid all tears' policy can actually be the reason that a baby will need to cry at night. In a parent's effort to avoid their baby crying in the first place, they will actually be causing the incidence of crying through the night because the child is forced to call out and recreate the associations again to go back to sleep. While a baby *does not* always cry when they learn how to settle into the feeling of being tired and going to sleep independently, there are some little people who just do this naturally, whether you hold them or not. It is for the little babies who find falling asleep a bit of a challenge that you need to be careful to not make it even more difficult for them to attain sleep. Some babies become terribly overstimulated by fussing and despite their inability to cope with the conditions being provided, do not know any other way to go to sleep with you showing them first. There are also some babies who, simply because of discomfort from conditions like reflux or any number of things that make lying down painful, have needed extra assistance to sleep until the conditions have been resolved first and foremost. Even when they have been resolved, these little people will have learnt a sleep pattern that you will need to correct to ensure they can start to enjoy peaceful sleeping. Initially, they will be under the impression that the cot or the bed is the cause of pain, and perhaps insist on continuing to lie on your chest on the couch if that is what they have been taught, even after the reflux or other conditions have been resolved.

It is important you help them work past these fears so they do not have to be fretful of things that are no longer difficult for them. Finally, if your baby has been on a program of long efforts of control crying, or they have failed sleep school, or you have tried a homespun version of control crying, or you have had someone come in to implement control crying, and your baby is now crying more than ever, or is no better off, then you are going to have to undo the learnt pattern of crying they have been taught.

My theory on the subject of finding peace and harmony at sleep time subscribes to the thinking that avoiding all crying when learning or relearning how to sleep independently is actually the problem, not the solution. This is where it's important to note that there are only two ways that a child (from birth to five years of age) can go to sleep. Either via:

- a child-governed association to go to sleep—that is, by themselves or
- a parent-governed association to go to sleep—you doing it for them.

It is not possible for a child to learn how to go to sleep or to sleep through the night for 11-plus hours when over six months of age *on their own* if you stay in the room with them. The two just do not go together.

Children are either taught that they can't go to sleep without you, or taught that it's normal to lie in their cot awake after you leave the room without stress or the need to call out for help, and therefore taught that they can go to sleep on their own peacefully. But this sometimes takes a little bit of practice to master, and may or may not involve some tears, and this is where the difficulties lie.

It's your choice how you would like to parent at sleep time. Would you like to teach them to rely on you, or to rely on themselves? Both are effective and easy for a child and, when done correctly, both are loving and in their best long-term interests. If you would like to co-sleep, and your entire family, baby and you are all sleeping well and are happy with the arrangement, then excellent. I always say 'Don't fix what isn't broken'. If, on the other hand, you would like your little one to sleep in their own room (after the first few months), or they are not happy with your assistance or co-sleeping and you are all unsettled at night as a result, then you will need to set about arranging a plan where you are able to step back and allow them the opportunity to settle themselves. They either have

> Change is hard . . . and I often see people cling to ineffective strategies and poor patterns simply because of the *fear* of change.

to rely on your skills (patting, feeding, rocking, etc.) or their own skills (playing with hair, thumb sucking, turning their head, humming, etc.).

The importance of self-settling

The reason that it is so vital that a baby learns how to self-settle when put to bed is because, from the age of four to six months, a baby will naturally stir between 10 and 11 p.m., at around 2 a.m. and again between 4 and 5 a.m., and will expect and need to do the same thing they were doing when they initially fell sleep. This is because they have no concept of sleep or time lapsing. This means they only know the *feeling* of being tired and what you have taught them to need when they feel that way.

There are several common things that I have discussed elsewhere in this book that start to occur when strategies advocating 'avoid all crying' or 'never leave a child to fall asleep alone' or 'always physically put your child to sleep' are adopted, particularly when a baby is learning to sleep:

- a baby who once slept independently could temporarily or permanently loose that ability due to a disruption like a holiday, house guest, illness or growth spurt
- a child is taught that they should never be in their cot awake when a parent holds them in their arms to put them asleep and/or then immediately takes them out of the cot upon waking
- a child can become fearful of the cot, and often cry when they find that the person who put them in the cot to sleep, who was there when they closed their eyes, has disappeared instantly—as far as the child is concerned—when they opened their eyes again
- a child starts to fight sleep

It's time to stop parenting from fear, and to start looking at making choices based on love, and what is in your little one's best interest.

What's your motivation?
Always remember your main purpose is to empower your baby with the ability to self-settle. You are empowering your little one with the ability to sleep a full, peaceful, undisturbed night so they can grow and be healthy, and have happy busy days with happy well-rested parents who can be the best possible parents. You are moving away from surviving as a family and progressing into living as a family. You are moving away from sleep being the main focus of your days, and an attitude of 'whatever it takes', to a more healthy balanced approach where sleep is only a part of your journey, and by no means the one thing the entire family is controlled by.

When you observe a child who knows how to sleep through the night, they will always open their eyes, look around, and feel quite relaxed to be in that environment because it is familiar to them. Eventually, when their body starts to drift back into the next sleep cycle (either in that surface sleep or when the Sleep Bus arrives—see page 675), their little eyes just flutter closed and they go back to sleep. With a baby who is told they should not be awake in that environment without intervention from an adult, they will wake and automatically cry, look for, or call out for whatever it is you have told them they need when they feel tired and want to sleep. A good proportion of sleep-time responses from a child are simply taught or routine based.

Of course there is a need for comfort, health, nurturing, love, bonding, reassurance and responsiveness, but I rarely encounter a home where that is lacking (except in cases of profound depression, or in a house where mother and baby are at risk from stress and exhaustion). In fact, I often find the opposite problem. Parents are sometimes so frightened that they should never do anything else but meet every demand their child makes of them at sleep time, regardless of whether it is a learnt pattern or a true need of the child. Parents will continue to offer up to three or 20 feeds a night when their baby is beyond six months of age. Parents will average no more than an hour's sleep at a time, a maximum of four hours a day, even when they and their baby are becoming physically ill from the level of intervention that is being demanded. This mind-set continues even when a marriage is about to break down due to the stress, and even when they are experiencing dangerous situations like falling asleep at the wheel, or falling asleep or being unable to concentrate while working heavy or dangerous machinery. Yet the irony is this is where a child's overall needs are being ignored. To forgo sleep and focus only on meeting demands, and in doing so allow a baby to wake repeatedly through the night, is not balanced.

If you are not willing to try and encourage solid sleep for your baby because you are frightened they might cry the first time they don't get a bottle to resettle, or you might be criticised by friends who are trying to work within an ideology of raising a baby rather than responding to what the child and their family is needing, then you are parenting from fear or pride, and not from love and what's in a child's best interests.

Change is a challenge, and it's important to not teach your children that change is something to be frightened of. Crying is normal and healthy, and it is a baby's way of expressing a little concern or uncertainty when placed in an unfamiliar situation. They are saying 'This is new, am I okay?' So what is your answer to them when they ask this? You can rarely avoid them crying, if you want to teach a baby, toddler or preschooler how to start going to sleep on their own for the first time after they have been taught something different, simply because children are creatures of habit. You will literally be putting off the inevitable, or making it worse by avoiding making the transition.

It is very clear to me that avoiding crying, by fully assisting a child to sleep because you are frightened of them crying, is one of the very real causes of them waking and crying repeatedly through the night, and catnapping through the day. If you subscribe to the theory that *all* crying when learning how to go to sleep is unkind, your child would never learn how to breastfeed, which often involves tears and frustration while they learn, they would never try something new, they would never learn how to sit in their pram or to wait in their high chair, and they would never eat more than three mouthfuls of food or learn to drink from a cup or eat off a spoon. They would never go beyond their first day at daycare or big school. Eventually your child would be under the impression that whenever they felt anything but happy, they needed to be rescued from those feelings, and that someone else—you—should be responsible for making them go away. This occurs when there is an imbalance. Everything you do now works towards your child's ability to walk off independently into the big wide world, equipped with the ability to cope. Learning how to sleep in the first five years of life is a healthy skill that will change their future in areas of education, personality, confidence, career prospects and more.

Everything you do now works towards your child's ability to walk off independently into the big wide world, equipped with the ability to cope.

Before you start

Once you have developed a clear style of communication and established all the skills a baby or toddler needs to be confident with sleep time, any crying that a child then does when first introduced to the settling process is short lived. They are then ready to learn the final skill that no one can prepare them for, which is trying to actually put themselves to sleep when they are used to being assisted to sleep. Always try to see past any first few trying days of your sleep program, including the slightly tricky part where they may be very sleepy during the day and when they might do some crying during the transition to new routines, because it is so short term in comparison to what may lie ahead if you do not give them a chance to find a more restful way to sleep through.

You should always be mindful of working towards that positive goal of 'soon they will be able to go to sleep and back to sleep peacefully, without the need to call out or become upset through the night'. You must always be mindful of weighing up a couple of days, where there may possibly be a few episodes of crying versus disrupted sleep every night for many weeks or even months or years, next to the potentially great years ahead of peaceful slumber. It will go a long way towards you remaining confident for your child when you settle them.

Before you start to implement any form of sleep-time management however, I need you to consider two things first and foremost. First of all, you should never attempt any form of crying support at sleep time until you have carefully read the Dream Baby methodology on sleep repair and learnt about the many areas in which your child needs to feel comfortable and empowered during the day before you ask them to go to sleep under new conditions.

Secondly, you need to be able to put a normal amount of crying / communication from your child into balanced perspective and be realistic about how normal and reasonable this natural response to new scenarios and situations is for any baby or child. This means, be prepared for some tears if they are unfamiliar with the request, and help them through it with ongoing reassurance until they feel more comfortable about settling off to sleep.

If you start with a realistic expectation of your little one as they experience something new, and have a realistic expectation of your role as you help reassuringly support them work through that change, then if there are no tears, and that is not that uncommon with a baby under two, then it will be wonderful. If there are tears, however, then you will be confident enough to be able to reassure them over a short period (a few days) of time until they learn a new peaceful, long-term solution to wonderful restorative sleep.

So the two important things you need to bear in mind when your child starts to cry are:

1. Not all crying means they are in an emotional state of distress, or that you need to fix it or stop it from occurring. Some cries could simply mean 'hey, I was playing with that', or 'I don't feel like doing that', or 'no', or 'pick me up please, I'm a bit bored or want to see what your doing', or 'I'm feeling a bit tired'. It is important to allow your little one to feel this normal range of feelings and learn that they are nothing you find concerning. The last thing you want to teach your children is

that they shouldn't feel anything but happy, because it's normal and safe to feel tired, and it is nothing they or you should feel frightened of.

2. Your response as a parent to your child's crying when they are feeling any of the natural array of normal daily emotions tells your child if those emotions are normal and safe to feel and something they can cope with, or not normal, are unsafe and something that someone else must fix for them because they are incapable of doing so.

It is when a parent accidentally over responds to a child's cry around natural and perfectly safe feelings of being tired, or of hunger or frustration, that indicate to a child that something unsafe is occurring. This is where a child's response to how they cope with day-to-day events can become imbalanced.

When I talk about how you respond to your baby I am not talking about 'never responding or supporting your child' when they feel any of the natural, normal and safe emotions because that would be equally as imbalanced in the other direction. I am simply talking about 'balancing' your approach to their natural array of emotions. An inaccurate over response to normal healthy emotions is not in your child's best interests, just as an under response is unhealthy. An overly responsive approach is one of the main reasons that babies and young children start to struggle with being able to self-settle because they start to feel stressed about feeling tired or whatever. By six to 12 months of age they should have already been allowed to become comfortable and confident with these feelings, simply through experience. This means they may have learnt to be uncomfortable with a safe feeling simply because they have never been given the opportunity to experience and get comfortable with it, and the message they are being given about that feeling is 'you shouldn't feel like this, someone needs to make it better'.

Obviously, a child being told that adults need to run in and pick them up is a not a true reflection of what they need when they are tired. They need to go to sleep when they are tired. A parent's over intervention in a bid to stop a child from crying will do nothing to empower a child with the coping skills they need to deal with the normal feeling of being tired, or learn how to go to sleep without tears. To tell them anything other than you think the best thing to do is to sit back and relax while reading a quiet book, then go to bed for a lovely long sleep, would be misleading your little one and wasting a wonderfully valuable opportunity as a loving and patient parent to tell them all about themselves, the world, and how to best deal with this natural and healthy situation of feeling tired. This applies to normal and natural feelings at non-sleep times of the day as well, like frustration, boredom, impatience or general irritation at having to do something dull like have their nappy changed *again* when they would rather play, or playing on their own when they would rather you carry them all day.

This same principle *does not* apply to the range of emotions that clearly indicates they need reassurance and comfort to feel better, like when they get a fright, or feel pain, or illness or are feeling sad because daddy has gone to work. It quickly becomes apparent to any child that people will literally run to their aid for an emotion that is too much for them to cope with on their own, like fear, pain, or illness, and will help them work through and past these and other normal natural daily emotions.

Being able to help your child feel comfortable within their own little body and with the huge array of emotions and feelings they will experience for the rest of their life is so important from an early age, and it is one of the magic keys that unlock a child's feelings of security and peace when they are in their own cot or bed going to sleep independently. Look just one stage beyond that and you see when a parent has lovingly equipped a child to feel empowered to cope when they start to spread their little independent wings and experience life out from behind the shelter of their parents' shields. This occurs when they go to childcare, kindergarten, or are cared for by others and head off to their exciting world of school. This is all achieved by simply staying confident and reassuring, stopping yourself before you react too quickly to see what it is that they are actually saying or doing, and waiting to see if they can settle or get past it without too much intervention from an adult if it is not necessary.

By learning to listen to what they are saying, and deciding when it is *truly* appropriate to intervene and assist them through a particular scenario, you give your child a wonderful opportunity to learn to experience, assess and become more comfortable with their natural ebbs and flows physically, emotionally and intellectually. Put yourself in their booties. Imagine if you come home from work and you are upset at a colleague for stealing one of your concepts. Your husband grabs you and holds you and says 'Shhhh', and then makes you a drink. The next night, you come home sad because your friend has resigned and your husband grabs you and holds you and says 'Shhhh', and then makes you a drink. Imagine, then, on the third night you come home really exhausted and drop your keys in a puddle on the way in the door. Your husband grabs you and holds you and says 'Shhhh', and then makes you a drink. Would you not start to think that he wasn't listening to you, and that there was no point expressing your true need? Would you not just start to say 'I need a drink' the moment you walked in the door with anything but a smile on your face, anticipating that is what your husband thinks? Would you also not occasionally get cross at this and burst into tears, and refuse to respond?

This is crucial for managing your child's settling routines. By showing them a way to work through a situation or how to settle down from a natural feeling that doesn't require your full intervention through the day at non-sleep times, they quickly learn that there are some emotions they can actually trust and learn to resolve, which ultimately will no longer feel uncomfortable or unmanageable for them, particularly at sleep time. This is how you equip their emotional tool kit with more than just a bottle, breast, pat, rock or drive in the car. This means that when they have a feeling like tiredness, and they go to their little emotional tool kit, they see mummy, and a breast, and their teddy, and their cot and themselves as a solution, equipping them to cope in a variety of situations.

Sometimes you can let them express frustration at a toy and let them work through it without trying to take that feeling away immediately by fixing the problem for the child. By taking the time to teach them that lying down and waiting while you change their nappy, or sitting and waiting in the pram while you're in the check-out line, or sitting patiently in the high chair after the meal is completed before they get up, are normal, safe, manageable, and with a little practice, no longer even situations that will evoke protests or tears.

This is very important to understand because when you and your child have had the opportunity to feel comfortable with their natural emotional highs and lows through the day, the principle applies to coping at sleep time, by helping and teaching a child to learn how to deal with the scenario and feeling of being tired. When a child is tired and you know (even if they don't) that they are due to take a sleep, you would tell them they are tired and say 'When you're tired we will always read a book, always say goodnight to everyone, I will always sing you this song, I'll always pop you in your bed' and 'I'll always leave you and you will play or lie there peacefully until you go to sleep'. This is said through your normal routine flow and follow through rather than directly. Make this routine repetitious and they will love and embrace it like their favourite book, nursery rhyme or song.

Always assess the situation that is making your child cry from an adult's perspective. If they are in the room you lovingly decorated, in the cot you lovingly dressed in sweet sheets, and under a roof where they are loved and cared for, then they *are* safe, and asking them to have a sleep is not a task that is unmanageable or an unreasonable request to learn, so you should not express anything other than the sound of confidence, love and empathy to their feeling of being tired, and work towards teaching them to go to sleep all by themselves.

When I say empathy, I don't mean 'oh baby, oh you poor little boy, oh no, shhh, please don't cry' (insert panicked sound here). That is not 'confident', it is 'concern', and could easily translate for the child as 'I'm concerned about the environment, too', meaning they have nowhere to gain a sense of security from because their foundation and comfort—you— are not coping, so surely they too are in danger. You need to smile while you settle them, and smile when you sing to them. You need to sound like you're singing a loving and beautiful lullaby as you settle them into their cot, even when they are feeling uncomfortable with the new conditions of a settling or resettling routine. This will reassure them and you will help eliminate a common trigger of tears.

This strategy is well known for minimal tears and quick resolutions for two very good reasons: it is fair, and it treats a child in a manner according to their intelligence.

Before you ask your child to go to sleep once they have experienced difficulties in the past, ensure they are empowered with all the skills they need to cope and are able to feel familiar and comfortable with the process of going to sleep. This means you will have developed appropriate communication and independence strategies and sleep-time routines to cater for their need. You will have:

- assessed their daily sleep requirement or routine miscalculation and have adjusted these according to your child's age and needs
- developed predictable and soothing settling, resettling and waking routines, and have role played them so that the conditions your baby will experience in their cot room are so familiar that they begin to enjoy this process
- adjusted their diet, and fluid intake
- catered for their environmental and emotional need for feelings of security and warmth with the addition of wraps, SafeT Sleep, teddy bears or other comfort items, and dummy pots, etc.
- practised your wrap on a teddy so this is perfect before you use it the first time on your baby
- empowered them with feelings of security around you leaving the room for short periods, using your short-term absence cue
- made them feel comfortable to be in their cot during cot playtime
- taught your child to understand that normal emotions are okay and that they don't need to be rescued from simple feelings like being tired, frustrated, bored or impatient

- taught them how to relax and accept the feeling of being tired independently through the reading of books, rather than just by breast or bottle feeding so they can lie peacefully in their cot when feeling tired, and be able to cope with you leaving the room
- taught your child to accept loving, consistent guidance from you through clear communication during the day around simple requests to sit down in the bath / car seat / pram / high chair or lie down during nappy changes, getting dressed or having a milk feed without stress or resistance
- helped your baby learn they can play independently at their play stations while you do basic chores in the kitchen or around the room.

The emphasis here is on preparation and empowerment to avoid or dramatically reduce crying rather than taking on any inconsiderate sudden action plan like control crying. This is the only respectful way to do it, and the very least you can do to help a child feel in control of a brand-new situation that is notorious with crying.

One thing that is absolutely crucial for me to assess and be comfortable with before I ever assist a parent in helping their child learn how to go to sleep independently, is to make absolutely sure that the parents are prepared to give their child the time they need to learn something new. I need to be sure that a parent will invest a good three to five days to work through daytime tiredness, some crying, and a few protests as the child adjusts to the new balanced lines of communication and a new way of going to and back to sleep. I check that each family has made a conscious decision to invest the time and energy into following the plan 100 per cent to the letter before packing it in. It is a waste of your precious baby's time, energy and learning capacity if you start something you are not willing to follow through on. It's also time to be sure you can use your well-developed coping skills as an adult, and commit to the changes and remain consistent and confident when implementing them, rather than go into the same head space as your little one.

The secrets of sleeping and waking

Understanding what occurs during the process of falling asleep, sleeping and waking up will help you understand what is happening when your little one initially starts to fall asleep, or wakes and starts to cry, and will consequently help you understand what is normal and natural when teaching or observing your little one during any part of their sleep-time process. Here I am going to talk about the times when your child may naturally cry during the night so you can assess whether they need your intervention or not. These times are when your child is:

- falling asleep—known as the ripple effect
- waking up prematurely—the sudden partial waking.

After discussing these two important points, I want to introduce you to the 'Sleep Bus', an important tool to help you to work out when your child will fall asleep when you first put them to bed and again during surface-sleep windows through the night and, finally, how long it may take them to go back to sleep if they do appear to be wide awake in the middle of the night. This will give you realistic expectations of your baby, help you feel less confused and, most importantly, will help you know how to interpret their crying during these settling and resettling periods. The Sleep Bus describes predictable windows of time during which a child's body can fall asleep.

> When I talk about how you respond to your baby, I am not talking about 'never responding or supporting your child' . . . I am simply talking about 'balancing' your approach to their natural array of emotions.

First things first though, let's look at what happens as your baby falls asleep.

Falling asleep—the ripple effect

A child takes around three to ten minutes from the moment they start to drift off to sleep before they fall fully into the deeper sleep cycles. This first three to ten minutes is called a 'surface sleep' (see page 412). A child may intermittently cry briefly through the duration of this falling asleep (three- to ten-minute surface sleep) process. This is why falling asleep is called 'the ripple effect'.

Imagine you have dropped a pebble in a pond, and you observe the ripples it makes. Well this is a good analogy for falling asleep. Where you drop the pebble is similar to the point of origin when falling asleep. If you watch how the ripples move away from that point of origin you will see that they are initially closer together, gradually getting further apart until they are eventually gone. These ripples are a lot like drifting consciousness as a child drifts off to sleep. The peak of each ripple is where the child becomes more conscious of their environment, while the lull between the ripples is where they start to drift into sleep and are no longer conscious of the environment around them. They ripple between the two states for the first three to ten minutes before finally dropping into a deeper sleep. Remembering that a baby has no concept of sleep: whatever behaviour or crying they were doing at the point of origin will be repeated each time they peak at a ripple until they begin to drift again. This is why they may cry briefly, pause for 30 seconds, then cry again briefly, then pause for a minute, cry again briefly for the last time before finally falling into a deeper sleep with no more ripples.

Interfering with your little one as they progress through this pattern will prevent them from going to sleep for a further 20 to 40 minutes, so we need to be extremely mindful of how you manage this falling-asleep process. This surface sleep or ripple effect also happens each time they wake between sleep cycles and is aligned with your baby's Sleep Bus timetable (see page 675). When your little one's Sleep Bus is due, there are two things that could typically happen on those first few days of your new sleep program as your baby adjusts to falling asleep independently:

1. they resist the Sleep Bus approaching
2. they get on the Sleep Bus.

Resistance to the Sleep Bus as it approaches

When your baby's Sleep Bus is due, they will start to feel the natural sensation of being tired. This will involve their body temperature dropping, hormonal changes, irritated nose and eyes as one nostril closes to reduce oxygen supply to the brain, and light-headedness as the oxygen supply to the brain naturally lowers, helping your baby fall asleep. Anyone who has suffered from significant sleep loss will appreciate that the sensation of feeling tired can often be a little uncomfortable unless you are in your familiar sleep place.

As your baby's new sleeping environment is still to become a familiar place to them, they will naturally become more insistent with their request for their old sleeping conditions to be provided as the tired sensation becomes stronger for them. This is when you may hear them call out or cry quite loudly and resist the sensation of feeling tired and falling asleep for a few moments, or even for a minute or two, even yawning between big loud cries. Disrupting your little one by going in and attending to their crying at this time could mean they miss their Sleep Bus and will have to wait another 20 minutes before the next Sleep Bus is due on settling. This is when you must be careful about listening to your baby's cries, and only attending to them at a time that will not interfere with them going to sleep, or going back to sleep as quickly as possible, so there is as little crying as possible on the two or three days it takes for them to become familiar with their new conditions at sleep time.

It is at this point of starting to fall asleep (the point of origin), when their body is *trying* to pull them into a sleep cycle (the ripple effect or surface sleep) that you must be very conscious of not rushing in just moments before they are about to naturally fall asleep (indicated by a slightly louder call out or cry), because a poorly timed attendance will not help them as you would desire. Often, going in moments before the Sleep Bus arrives will mean that their behaviour and crying at the point of origin of sleep with be elevated, causing heightened crying through the ripple effect, making it very possible that they will struggle to be able to settle enough to fall asleep in their three- to ten-minute surface-sleep (ripple effect) window. Any poorly timed attendance because they were crying a little louder as they resisted the sensation of feeling tired would then only serve to disrupt them to the point where they miss the Sleep Bus and have another 20 (settling) or 40 (resettling) minutes before the next bus is due and ripple effect begins again. This is when you must be conscious of your little one's Sleep Bus timetable, and conscious of only attending to the right cries / language, in the right timeframes.

Always remember that within one to three days, this new sleeping environment will be that familiar place for them, and their own clever little practiced self-settling skills will be their new associations, so sleep will become an easy task for them. All the weeks and months of night wakings will then be behind them and you because you will have empowered your baby with the skills needed to be able to go to and back to sleep without stress or the need to call out, and without feeling helpless without your full assistance any more.

Always try to remember: this is an adjustment period. Just as you taught your little one to go to sleep with their old set of associations initially, it is now no different when teaching them a new set. It's no different to a child learning to go to sleep in their daddy's arms for the first time, when they are used to being breastfed by mummy. They just need to find a new way, and all they need is a little time and opportunity with loving predictable support.

The Sleep Bus arrives

So your little one's Sleep Bus has finally arrived and it is over the next ten minutes that you will discover if they are calm enough at the point of origin to catch the bus to sleepland, or miss it, and have to wait for the next bus (see bus table on page 675). Now the bus is there, with the doors open luring them to get on and relax, their cry has changed from that resistant cry to a more sleepy cry—the cry meows or slurs off on the end with what sounds like a downward inflection. Perhaps they are even in a style of cry that clearly becomes a weary 'errr . . . errr . . . errr' but if you were to look at them their eyes would be shut. They would do this on your shoulder or in your arms too if they were resisting sleep, and it is a typical pattern in a baby who has been having a difficult time sleeping for some weeks or months. As this subtle change appears in their cries, they may begin to have brief pauses (the ripple effect) until finally it becomes clear that they are actually drifting off to sleep. You can now officially say that your baby's Sleep Bus has arrived and all they need to do is be relaxed enough to catch it.

During this process you will hear your child starting to fall asleep. This is when they start to drift in and out of moments of consciousness and increasing intervals of light surface sleep, indicated with pauses, for a period that lasts for no more than three to ten minutes before they become fully silent as they fall into a deep sleep.

After a few minutes, they stop surfacing and becoming aware, and they are now officially asleep. As a baby does not know sleep, or time lapsing, if they were in a settling cry before they drifted for a moment, then when they surface at the next ripple peak 30 seconds later, they will resume their settling cry unaware that they had just been drifting. The peaks or surfaces are only brief and may involve five to ten seconds of a little sleepy cry, or whatever cry they were in when the bus arrived (the point of origin). The next ripple will then be a little further away and, despite a one-minute pause, they may briefly resume their settling cry (or whatever cry they were in when the Sleep Bus arrived, or at the point of origin) before drifting again. This will continue for a short period of time, and varies from baby to baby. The surface sleep ends after around three to eight minutes and they finally dip off into a deeper sleep cycle. Either that, or they climb off the bus and miss it.

Occasionally however, even if they are very tired and they do drift on and off while the Sleep Bus is there, if they are finding that first day or two with new sleeping conditions and / or routine a little bit challenging, or they are a fairly unsettled baby, they may cry enough at one or more peaks to not allow their little body to take them off to sleepland, and they will officially climb off the bus and miss it. Occasionally, if they are very certain that they want you to do something, they will remain resistant to the Sleep Bus and not even pause through the ripple effect even though they are slurring and yawning. This will mean that you need to wait for the next Sleep Bus to arrive. Once you know your little one has missed the Sleep Bus, indicated by the window of opportunity ending and their cries returning to the pre-Sleep Bus elevated levels, then you should go in and attend to them after assessing their cries, do your resettling routine, and then continue to support them with consistent visits based on what they are 'saying' to you, until the next bus is due. This means you repeat your resettling routine, based on your interpretation of their cries until the next bus arrives.

If they do miss the bus, don't despair. It is only fair that they may need a little time to adjust on the first few days of learning something new. This is where you need to be patient with them and have realistic expectations if you have previously been having significant difficulties with their sleep. They may just need to say 'this is different, am I okay?' numerous times until they feel certain that they are okay, and you are always there for them, even though things have changed a little, and they will then fall asleep. This scenario is particularly likely if your baby has been terribly unsettled, has had previous strategies like straight control crying used on them with no positive results (so they have learnt to be a resilient crier), or your family or yours or baby's health is at a crisis point. Then this adjustment and processing time is not uncommon but yields the most staggering results of a peaceful, calm and settled little baby within two days of consistent communication and support at this time. It is worth being patient and staying confident that this is the right thing for your terribly tired little baby.

> If they do miss the bus, don't despair. It is only fair that they may need a little time to adjust on the first few days of learning something new.

Waking up prematurely—the sudden partial waking

A baby aged six to 24 months becomes only partially conscious when waking up through any incomplete sleep session, and will not be fully aware of their surrounding for a full three to ten minutes. A child in this state could be standing, sitting, crying or have their eyes open, but will not yet be fully conscious. This is called a sudden partial waking. This sudden partial waking could also function in much the same way as the ripple effect. At the end of this three- to eight-minute window, they will either be fully aware of their environment and awake or will have gone back to sleep. This is a very, very important part of managing their sleep and can make a big difference to your and your baby's success.

This is where the Sleep Bus analogy comes in handy again. The bus pulling up at the bus stop and opening the doors allowing time for people to get on or off the bus is similar to this transitional surface sleep.

Babies naturally cycle through different stages of sleep and subsequent brainwave activity. The four key stages of consciousness you need to be aware of are:

1. fully conscious
2. semi-conscious (surface sleep, see page 412)
3. deep REM (dreamy sleep, see page 413)
4. deep REM (non-dreaming sleep or healthy sleep).

There are more stages of consciousness, and we have discussed the function of some of these stages of sleep such as power sleeps (see page 412) and healthy sleeps (see page 413), but these four stages of consciousness are the only relevant ones for the purpose of understanding your little one's stages of sleep and likelihood to cry during sleep.

Sudden partial waking occurs during the semi-conscious stage, surface sleep. So that you understand this better, it is the same state that you might come to frequently during the night when you adjust your pillow or change positions and immediately go back to sleep. You can go to the bathroom quickly, or grab a glass of water in this state, then, if you get back into bed soon enough, and don't became too simulated in conversation or actions, you will fall asleep again almost immediately. This transitional window only lasts three to eight minutes, is still considered a sleep pattern, and ends as abruptly as it begins.

The key times for these brief surface-sleep transitions, based on a baby going to bed at 7 p.m., are between 10 and 11 p.m., around 2 a.m. and between 4 and 5 a.m. During the day they are in 20-minute and 40-minute cycles. There are two typical responses you can expect from your child if you go into their room during this transitional window:

1. if you go in too quickly you can quite often startle them, which can result in a very distressed cry where you can't seem to console them and this can last for up to 40 minutes
2. if you go in quickly enough and offer a milk feed, or pat on the tummy, or a dummy, you might catch them before they come to a full waking and they will go back to sleep almost immediately.

The problem with the second response is that you are creating for them a learnt pattern of dependence in this semi-conscious state. This means you will need to continue to be required for all resettlings during the surface-sleep windows.

The most important thing to be aware of here is to make sure you don't interfere with that time of their sleep wherever possible. What you are aiming to do is have them learn to go back to sleep, when they come to surface sleep, without intervention using the self-settling strategies you've empowered them with through your new settling routines, cry interpretation and support. Because of the risks associated with attending during the three- to eight-minute surface sleep, you need to ensure you create an initial pause time before going in to resettle only if they have woken midsleep.

This means that over the first five days of teaching your baby how to sleep, you will gradually, as they become more confident with their abilities, increase the pause time before attending to them and only if they are crying in a way that indicates they need reassurance. On day one you will pause for a minimum five minutes; by day five you will pause for a full ten minutes as a minimum based on cries. You must always be careful with your interpretation of their crying in those first ten minutes because your attending to them could actually prevent them from going to sleep within the three- to eight-minute sudden partial waking. The result will be that they are woken up or overstimulated enough in that first ten minutes and

Surface-sleep pause for resettling

When your child is learning how to go back to sleep without intervention during surface sleep, you will need to pause and interpret their crying before deciding to attend to them or not. This process is not about watching a clock; it's about observing their sleep patterns and listening to their cries. Often, the more you fuss the more they fuss, so the idea should be to try and avoid going in during the first ten minutes if at all possible. If they appear upset, however, then turn to crying interpretation (see page 654) to help you determine if you should attend or not. One thing I will say is that if you do need to attend in the first ten minutes, then there is a far higher likelihood that they will get off the bus and you will need to assist them until the next Sleep Bus arrives in 40 minutes' time. The length of your initial pause will increase, in the first few days of learning to go back to sleep, in the following pattern:

Day 1—wait a minimum of five minutes before interpreting their cries, deciding to attend or not, and using your new resettling routine

Day 2—wait a minimum of six minutes before interpreting their cries, deciding to attend or not, and using your new resettling routine

Day 3—wait a minimum of seven minutes before interpreting their cries, deciding to attend or not, and using your new resettling routine

Day 4—wait a minimum of eight minutes before interpreting their cries, deciding to attend or not, and using your new resettling routine

Day 5—wait a minimum of ten minutes before interpreting their cries, deciding to attend or not, and using your new resettling routine

These times are only for when you feel you have no choice but to attend in those first ten minutes, until they have become fully conscious of their environment, or gone back to sleep. Try to remember that the more you fuss the more they fuss.

you will then need to wait for the next Sleep Bus to come, which will not be for another 40 minutes. This is why crying interpretation—your ability to accurately assess their cry and knowing when you should go in or when you should give them some space—becomes crucial.

Important: this is not about watching the clock; it's about listening to your little one. Always listen and determine if your attendance is going to be soothing or disrupting for your baby.

The Sleep Bus
Settling Sleep Bus timetable
When you first put your child to bed awake, their window of opportunity to initially fall asleep lasts for three to eight minutes, and occurs only once roughly every 20 minutes from the time they are put to bed if they are on a regular routine until they finally fall asleep again. For example, a baby who is regularly put to bed at 7 p.m. will have a Sleep Bus timetable pattern like this:

• 1st Sleep Bus arrives at 7.03 p.m.—window lasts from around 7.03 to 7.10
• 2nd Sleep Bus arrives at 7.23 p.m.—window lasts from 7.23 to 7.30
• 3rd Sleep Bus arrives at 7.43—window lasts from 7.43 to 7.50
• 4th Sleep Bus arrives at 8.03—window lasts from 8.03 to 8.10.

This pattern of 20-minute falling-asleep windows will continue in the same way until they eventually catch the Sleep Bus to dreamland. Knowing this helps you to not become stressed when your child is quiet for five minutes between buses, and then makes a little noise again, because you already know they are just lying there awake waiting for the Sleep Bus. This is in stark contrast to that horrible feeling of not knowing and hoping they are asleep, then hearing them again. Many parents dissolve into tears when they think their child has gone to sleep and then discover that they have not.

This will give you realistic expectations and something more tangible to work with. Of course there is a chance you will still hear from them until the next Sleep Bus arrives if they miss the first one. It's important to remember that once the Sleep Bus window has passed, you can then be sure of the fact that they will be asleep, and you can expect to not hear from them. Remember, we are not at all concerned about them being awake in their cot alone, wrapped or not. This is an important skill because it means that when the Sleep Bus does arrive, they will be calm; meaning that what they are doing at the point of origin of sleep is not crying; meaning no crying through the ripple effect; and meaning your baby will be able to fall asleep. Better still, as they have no concept of sleep, then there is a good chance that the next time they wake, they will just be content to lie there through their transitional surface sleep, and not wake fully. This is how your baby can successfully sleep through. This is an empowered, content and peaceful baby. We are definitely not worried about them being awake in their beds without our intervention.

Resettling Sleep Bus timetable

A child's window of opportunity to fall *back* to sleep after waking midway through a sleep session also lasts only three to eight minutes, but this time only occurs once in about every 40 minutes (see variation) for the first 80 minutes of a child's waking. If they are still awake by then, they will return to a single opportunity once every 20 minutes thereafter. This is why night wakings are notoriously long and difficult. For example, a baby who has a sudden partial waking at 11 p.m. will not be fully conscious until after 11.10 p.m. and could fall back to sleep again quite quickly. If they do not fall asleep in that first three to ten minutes, then they will become fully awake and will have to wait for the next night Sleep Bus before they could possibly fall asleep again. The timetable for that is as follows:

• 1st Sleep Bus arrives at 11.40 p.m.—window lasts from 11.40 to 11.48
• 2nd Sleep Bus arrives at 12.20 a.m.—window lasts from 12.20 to 12.28
• 3rd Sleep Bus arrives at 12.40 a.m.—window lasts from 12.40 to 12.48
• 4th Sleep Bus arrives at 1.00 a.m.—window lasts from 1.00 to 1.08
• 5th Sleep Bus arrives at 1.20 a.m.—window lasts from 1.20 to 1.28.

Occasionally, a baby's first bus will come at the 50-minute mark, and then follow the same format as above. This could be because they have a solid 40-minute cycle in addition to their first ten-minute surface sleep. Either way, once you have identified if your child's first bus is 40 or 50 minutes, then that pattern will always remain your child's personal bus timetable. If this 50-minute pattern is your child's timetable, your baby's timetable will look like the following:

• 1st Sleep Bus arrives at 11.50 p.m.—window lasts from 11.50 to 11.58
• 2nd Sleep Bus arrives at 12.30 a.m.—window lasts from 12.30 to 12.38
• 3rd Sleep Bus arrives at 12.50 a.m.—window lasts from 12.50 to 12.58
• 4th Sleep Bus arrives at 1.10 a.m.—window lasts from 1.10 to 1.18
• 5th Sleep Bus arrives at 1.30 a.m.—window lasts from 1.30 to 1.38.

If you are very lucky, after the first 40- or 50-minute pause, their buses will start to come every 20 minutes from then on. The important thing to note is that once you identify your child's timetable, by keeping notes, their timetable will remain the same for them.

This pattern of regular falling to sleep windows continues in the same way until they fall asleep. This means that you have a realistic expectation of when your baby will be able to fall asleep. The predictable timetable helps you to not become stressed when your child is quiet for five minutes, and then they make a little noise again, because you know they are just lying there, and there is a chance you will still hear from them until the next Sleep Bus arrives. Once the Sleep Bus window has passed, you can then be sure in the knowledge that they will be asleep, and you can expect to not hear from them. If they have missed the bus, you can then be aware of when they might be able to next fall asleep.

Locking in your settling Sleep Bus timetable

Locking in your settling Sleep Bus timetable is essential to ensuring your little one is settled each and every time they go to bed. This is done simply

A little history of The Sleep Bus

This is possibly one of the most important observations of my entire career. I have developed and used my Sleep Bus idea since 1993 on children all around the world. It is a simple concept based on years of my recordkeeping while observing children and on the study I have undertaken on sleep. I first noticed the pattern I call 'The Sleep Bus' when I started working with children in daycare, but it was not until 1993/94, when I started comparing the data from my mountains and mountains of observations of different children, that I actually discovered a clear distinction in day versus night and settling versus resettling sleep patterns. I noticed that a child put to bed at a certain time comes back to surface sleep at specific times, so it is possible to predict times when a child will cry naturally during the night.

I named it 'The Sleep Bus' simply because of the different lengths of time it took sleep to come at night when compared with the time it took during the day. I was living in London at the time and as I sat waiting one night at Trafalgar Square to get the night bus home it felt like an eternity, and I was tired and freezing cold and consequently desperate for the bus to arrive. So I got up to check the timetable. What I saw was a mirror image of what I was seeing and using as a prediction method to assist children to settle to sleep, or to go back to sleep, during the day and night. It was ironic to me, because the same desperate wish for the bus to come that was filling me, was just as it is after I wanted a little person to go back to sleep when they have woken during the night, but the bus only comes according to the timetable and I needed to be patient.

In 2003 I introduced The Sleep Bus to all of Australia on the 7 *Sunrise* program, and it caught on like wildfire. I am very proud to release it here completely, and believe it has the potential to change the way sleep time and wakings are ultimately managed everywhere.

by developing a daily routine and following it consistently. This then programs their circadian rhythm to prepare for sleep at roughly the same time each day. Think about it: you can go all night without a sensation of hunger, but suddenly be hungry for breakfast at 7 a.m., or you can cope with being awake until a particular time each night, then suddenly need to go to bed. By following a routine you can help your little one be tired at a particular time each day so they can recognise the feeling of being tired and always associate it with being put to bed and going to sleep. This means that they are always ready for bed when you pop them down on the initial few weeks of their new settling routine. In doing this, you lock in a settling Sleep Bus timetable.

Without a regular sleep routine, your baby will not be as predictable, but even if you are responding to your baby's tired signs as to when to put them to bed, so long as you pop them down when you first identify their approaching Sleep Bus within the same timeframe each day, you will be able to anticipate the same pattern from six months onwards.

As discussed, there are two parts to your baby's Sleep Bus timetable:

- during settling—the predictable sleep times they have each day because of their daily routine
- during resettling—the predictable times when your baby will be able to go back to sleep during their surface-sleep transitions.

The ability to predict when your baby can resettle after a full waking does not depend on locking in a predictable routine. You can basically assess the time they are able to go back to sleep on their waking time. But this entire holistic approach is about avoiding the wakings from even happening in the first place, so you never have to deal with the crying outside behaviour-based or association-based wakings. For this reason, for any wakings outside the typical, transitional, surface-sleep windows of roughly 10 to 11 p.m., 2 a.m. and 4 to 5 a.m. you must investigate the cause to ensure they are in the best possible position to be able to go back to sleep, *before* you embark on any resettling attempts. To discover the cause of your little one's night waking you may be able to prevent them from waking simply through strategic planning rather than ever having to manage crying.

This then only leaves their associations and skills and your communication ability to work with at settling to sleep, and resettling back to sleep through any surface-sleep transition windows' mid-sleep cycle. For this reason you have been doing your homework. For this reason you have adjusted their environment. For this reason you have taught them how to cope with being in their cot awake and cope with you leaving the room as well as developed your ability to ask them to go to sleep for you. This means that, done correctly, it may be instant results you achieve, or results after only a 20-minute settle, or results that take a few settling and resettling attempts over a few days. Whatever the length of time it takes, be it repaired within six hours or repaired within five days, preparing for this correctly and taking every opportunity to prevent the wakings first, then ensuring they can cope with your request to go back to sleep, because you understand the mechanics of sleep, will be what makes this fast for your baby to learn.

The Sleep Bus gives you an opportunity to do two things:

- be realistic about when your baby can physically fall asleep
- know when it would be incredibly destructive to attend to your baby during a surface sleep.

In order to understand this more clearly, let's look in depth at the settling Sleep Bus timetable of a daily routine for a low-sleep-requirement baby:

6 to 6.30 a.m. The Sleep Bus drops child back from dreamland.

8.46 / 47ish Another Sleep Bus arrives but you will need to take them off that bus after their allocated bridging nap time. This means waking them at their allocated nap length. They will happily ride this Sleep Bus for a little or a lot longer time if you let the sleep run its course but then they will not be able to sleep well later that same day, and will sleep poorly that night.

12.02 to 12.05 p.m. Another bus leaves, therefore getting the baby into bed at 12.10 on the first few weeks of their new sleep program is too late and they will become overtired by the time the next bus arrives. It would be a big mistake to wait until 12.20 p.m. to put them to bed as their body will have provided hormones (adrenalin, etc.) that will make them stay awake because they are now even more overtired. If your baby misses this bus their body will send a Sleep Bus every 20 minutes until they finally catch one and go to the land of nod. But note, once you put your baby into bed, they have to stay there until a Sleep Bus takes them to the land of sleep. To give up and get them up will only teach them that your new settling routine and cues mean you would like them to go to sleep but if they would rather stay up then they should just cry. Obviously, without a concept of consequences, a baby would opt to stay up and play with mum and dad any day or night of the week, but we know this is not in their best interests to do so.

The evening bus timetable is as follows:

7.03 to 7.05 p.m. The first Sleep Bus will come, but if your baby is not used to going to bed this early, it could take a couple of nights to establish the need for a bus at that time. You may need to lie them down at 7.00 p.m. each night before their body recognises the need for sleep at that time, as they are already overtired. For the first couple of days, their body will be trying to sustain them as usual with hormones, including adrenalin, and you might have a support session at this time because they are having a little trouble actually winding down to fall asleep. Remember to be cautious about not letting them get hot at this time as they are likely to be at their warmest. This is achieved before bed by cooling the room, by your baby not having too warm a bath, by not overdressing them for the settling routine, and by ensuring there is a fan on in their room on the first few nights. The evening bus timetable on a settling will run to the same format as the midday timetable. A bus will depart about every 20 minutes when you first put them to bed.

10.00 p.m. If they have caught the 7 p.m. Sleep Bus, their first surface sleep will be round about now. They may resettle within the first ten minutes. If not, for resettling attempts during the night, the next bus will come roughly 40 to 50 minutes after the initial waking time, then there will be either a Sleep Bus again in 40 minutes time or, if you're lucky, every 20 minutes thereafter. So if they wake as 10 a.m., the next bus will be 10.40–50, then 11.20–30, then 11.40–50, then 12.00–10, and so on. You need to watch your clock and be cautious about any decision to attend to your child around the time a Sleep Bus arrives.

Being totally consistent with your times is absolutely vital in the first three weeks of any positive routine management. During this time your child will still be learning to fully understand the language and its true definition, so until they are fully able to grasp that concept, work with their body's strong need for sleep rather than just their temperament or their intellectual ability to understand their new cues are not negotiations. After three weeks they will fully understand the language and be completely comfortable with what they need to do, whether they are six months or 22 months old, and they will be then able to comfortably self-settle on request, which will overtake your need to work with their body's biological clock so carefully.

This may feel a little difficult to understand but it's important to watch and listen for signs the Sleep Bus is near. It will give you something to target during a long assistance and, most importantly, help warn you when it might be disruptive to attend to them. If a bus is due, and you are about to attend to your little one, don't go in until the Sleep Bus has passed and you are sure they have missed it. It is a little difficult to establish exactly when your baby is about to go to sleep, but there are some things that are fairly consistent with most children. Just before they are about to go to sleep and you can hear them sounding tired, they may suddenly try to fight that tired sensation. This is the time to resist the temptation to go in. Often this (final fight) results in your baby going to sleep within the next three to eight minutes.

It's important that, when you are trying to resettle your baby during those first few nights, you are prepared for the possibility that it may take you some time and patience to get them to settle themselves off to sleep with your assisted self-settling strategy. Remember there are only two ways for your baby to fall asleep, either by:

- being put to sleep by another (dependent = will need assistance through the night), or
- putting themselves to sleep (independent = will be comfortable to put themselves back to sleep).

Obviously, though, they need to be given the opportunity to learn how to put themselves to sleep.

On your first few nights I need you to be in the right head space. I need you to know that you have worked hard to come to this new place, and this first night or two are really important in your ability to communicate with them, so they are not confused. I need you to embrace this time as an opportunity to communicate and teach your baby a better way to go to, and back to sleep. This is not about letting a baby just cry randomly. This is about a very clear opportunity to communicate with your baby, working with all your new skills, to empower them with the ability to understand this new process. If you put aside fear, and just stay focused on love and staying clear and honest with your baby, you will not only achieve your results but you will change their sleep permanently. Invest a couple of days staying confident and reassuring them (so while this is tricky, you need to be strong because there can be no room for you to get teary or you will frighten them, and we know there is nothing to be frightened about) and your results will be wonderful for your entire family. This means, once you know your little one has fully woken and got off their Sleep Bus and you have therefore begun the resettling process, you should stay up. Don't try to sleep or even lie down between attendances, even if they are quiet and only calling out here and there, because it will make it even more exhausting for you than it might ordinarily feel. Sit up, have a timing device, a pen and a notepad, and work out their Sleep Bus timetable first and foremost, so you have something to work towards. Carefully assess any crying as highlighted in the following chapter, remembering that the more you fuss the more they will cry, and keep notes. As it gets closer, note down when they start to yawn or sound like they are about to settle (which means a Sleep Bus is there). By taking notes you can start to identify exactly how often, to the minute, their personal Sleep Bus comes. Once you have identified it in your child, it rarely changes. If you can bear it, grab a magazine and read or watch TV (don't let them hear it at all though). Just sit it out and be brave.

Once they have been asleep for ten minutes, toddle back to bed and get some sleep yourself. Remember: this should only last one, two or three nights if done correctly and will then be a learnt life skill forever more. If you compare it to your baby waking and crying every night for months or years to come, as many of the families I have met have endured before asking for help, you will know that it is far better to take the opportunity to teach them something that will benefit not only them, but your entire family. Remember: you cannot keep doing the same thing and expect a different result.

The last thing I need to mention is obviously noise or changes to the environment. While you are teaching them to go to sleep it's important that you are considerate of their need to sleep (especially through those old glitches in their rhythm that have them waking regularly). So:

- don't make a lot of noise right outside your child's room
- if you use a bathroom near their room, don't flush for a week at night or during their midday sleep
- most importantly, if they stir through the night, in the early morning, or through the main day sleeps, don't go to the toilet or make a cup of tea
- don't turn on lights that might create even the slightest glow around their door or they may interpret this to mean you are going to come in, and become upset if you don't.

I always say 'No one move during the (ten-minute) surface-sleep pause time', until the sudden partial-waking phase of their sleep passes. To go in to them before this means they are only slightly aware of their environment but still essentially asleep, and you are waking them up. If you wake them up, they are then awake for at least 40 minutes. So you should be fairly reluctant in the first ten minutes unless it is absolutely necessary on the first night. Once the pause time has passed, you can better determine if you need to attend or not. When you know they are fully awake and know you will need to go in and manage their crying, you can quietly go to the bathroom before attending to them.

Interpreting the cries and learning how to respond

My comprehensive PRM sleep repair philosophy is designed to resolve and, therefore, avoid the main causes of crying before the program even begins. For that to happen, you must have locked in consistent settling, resettling and waking routines through role play before attempting to manage crying or asking a child to go to sleep on their own. Once you have done your homework by carefully adopting the recommendations in this book, including seriously considering the wrap and SafeT Sleep, carefully looking at an appropriate routine or at the right adjustments, ensuring your child has eaten well and had enough fluids, carefully worked on your communication skills, and equipped their little emotional tool kit, there is much less chance you will have to deal with many tears. The other thing to be aware of is that, through this process, you are moving away from feeling as though you need to fix everything for your baby if they are awake in their cot. We are not at all concerned about them being awake in their cot when we are not there with them. It's only when they are finding it difficult that you want to assist them, but if they are awake and just calling out then you need to leave them be in order for them to go to sleep independently.

To truly develop a plan that is honest and empowers your child with independent-settling skills, you will need to provide assisted self-settling guidance. This is the part of most routine managements that needs extra attention and time taken to ensure you give your child the best possible chance of learning to cope with the sensation of tiredness at sleep time. Almost all babies or toddlers have a little protest from time to time in their life. The key to your success is to properly assessing the type of cry your baby is in, and when you do, you should start to hear what your child is saying so you can respond appropriately. This means you are actually listening to your baby, and not just listening to your fears. Once you put your baby or toddler to bed, there will be two basic types of crying that you will encounter and, as a result, there will be two different responses that you need to decide between.

You will note that in Chapter 6, I discussed some crying that you will encounter during the daytime and playtime portion of your child's day, and typical triggers and management for those cries. However, assisting a baby while they learn how to sleep independently is an entirely different task and requires careful consideration to do correctly.

During sleep time, if you hear from your little one, their cries will fall into two main groups:

- emotion-based cries—'I'm feeling overwhelmed, please help me'
- communication-based call outs—which sound like cries because crying is a baby's main form of language—as well as singing, humming or rhythmic vocalisations.

When your baby cries, a couple of questions will come to your mind: 'I have heard them, and they are safe, but I still need them to go to sleep and I can't do that for them—do I need to attend to them to reassure and remind them that I'm here'? and 'Do I need to give them a little more space as they are just having a grumble, squawk, or perhaps even a bit of a verbal protest, but are basically starting to settle themselves down without the need of my intervention?'

In answering these questions, you should always be mindful of not creating a pattern where you are attending so frequently that your little one is entirely focused on just calling for you to come in, which will naturally mean they will never just lie down and snuggle in to try and go to sleep or have a little quiet time while they are feeling tired. Ask yourself before you choose to go in at any given time whether your baby has progressed into starting to settle themselves. Will your attendance serve to stimulate or confuse them? If you know that when you attend to them and leave they will be in a more elevated state than when you first went in, then their cries are possibly only communication based and calling out. This is not always something you want to encourage so you should really not be attending too rapidly. On the other hand, if there is something wrong, or they are genuinely feeling overwhelmed, it's important that they know you will always come into them and reassure them, but your request will remain the same and you will help them for as long as they need, but sleep is all you will be pursuing.

Emotion-based cries

You always support your little one if they are in an emotional place. These cries definitely need your intervention because your child is feeling overwhelmed by their feelings. This is when you need to let them know that they are okay and safe, and that you have heard them and you will always come if they need you. The messages you send to them at this time, by the way you sound and how calm, reassuring and consistent you are with your resettling cues, will be two of the most important tools you have, and will have the most profound effect on them.

During their transition from one set of learnt sleep associations to another, you may hear any one of these emotion-based cries:

- distressed cry
- upset cry
- angry cry.

The distressed cry

This is where your baby becomes very upset when you attend to them, or as you leave the room. This is usually only ever the extent of this cry, and you are rarely going to hear it outside those moments, if then. It's a very prolonged cry where they will empty their lungs fully with a strong drawn-out cry and go into a silent cry before they take a big breath and start again.

I virtually never ever hear this cry in the cot but I am highlighting it because most people tag just about every cry as a distress cry. I need you to be able to listen more carefully than that to truly hear what your child is saying. Obviously, if your child is in this cry it will make you want to go in immediately and it is extremely difficult to listen to. You always attend to this cry if it does not subside within a minute and follow your resettling routine and cues (see page 617) very calmly.

If your little one is extremely upset, you can say your cues slowly up to four times through to help them calm down before stepping back again and giving them a little room to try and calm themselves down. If your child is under 12 months, a cry of this level may indicate you have not catered to their need to be wrapped or tucked in firmly enough so they feel secure and held.

The upset cry

This is my least favourite cry to hear. It usually happens at the end of an angry cry session and indicates your baby is tired and wants to go to sleep, but doesn't know how to. This is almost always reserved for the first settling attempt and requires your intervention and reassurance. Remember: your response to them and how confident and reassuring your voice sounds tells your little one that they are safe, and it won't take long before they can go to sleep all by themselves. They just need an opportunity to see that they can relax, and once they have learnt they can relax, then they will be able to self-settle. We always attend to this cry within the times stipulated in 'Supporting your baby when they cry' (see page 694).

The angry cry

This is a very common cry. It is a deeper, raspier cry than others, and sounds more like a furious yell. During this cry your baby pauses only to take a breath between loud and furious vocal cry outs. During this cry, they are obviously calling for someone to come and put them to sleep or pick them up immediately. The deep raspy nature of this cry can quickly dry out their throats and they may cough. This cry doesn't make you want to jump up immediately like the distress cry but is still very difficult to listen to. Your baby is clearly feeling overwhelmed at this stage. Often you may hear them become upset when they are cross and you are not doing what they expect. You always attend to this cry within the times stipulated in the management of crying section of this book. Your baby is not being naughty, or having a defiant tantrum, they are simply feeling overwhelmed, and need your reassurance to help them relax and understand that they are okay.

Just because your child is feeling overwhelmed does not mean you don't maintain your request for sleep. It just means they need you to reassure them more often at this time, and you will need to do that while you remind them it's still time for sleep. Many parents say to me 'But they are momentarily worse once I have attended, and it makes them even more upset. Wouldn't it be easier if I don't go in.' My answer to this is always 'No, it is never easier if you don't go in?' PRM is about communication, and your baby is asking, firstly, 'I don't know about this, am I okay?' and, secondly, 'I'm tired, could you do the old things I am used to?' while they are learning a new way to go to sleep or back to sleep. At no point should you not address their question.

You need to be honest, and show them you will always come for them, but that they need to look to you for guidance and you can't go to sleep for them. If you were to never address this language hurdle, then when you really do need to attend to them to offer medication, check on them, transition them from one sleep location to the next, or for any number of things, the language problem will still exist and they will always cry, and you will always have to walk away and leave them alone until they cry themselves to sleep. That is not balanced, fair or honest and will always be a problem within your communication because you have never addressed the reason for the crying if you just ignore it.

It is far better to attend and teach your little one that you are there for them whenever they need you, but they are to look to you for guidance at sleep time: the single most important reason that all the families that follow this program are able to maintain sleep in any environment and have the freedom to always attend to their child without the fear that they will scream and cry. Once you have balanced the sleep-time scales and your little one learns that mummy and daddy govern sleep time and they need to put themselves to sleep, your child will happily sleep and you also can happily come and go from their room without tears or stress. If you ever plan on transferring them to a bed, your baby needs to be able to accept your clear guidance or they will never stay in their room.

Remember that you won't always have the ability to make them stay in their room. By the time they are two years of age, you most definitely have to have established a clear and respectful line of communication so that your child doesn't fuss and fight and the transition into a 'big bed' can be a wonderful confidence-building experience for all.

Communication-based call outs and vocalisation

The communication call outs are distinctly different from the emotion-based cries because your baby will stop crying out when they hear you approach their room, or turn their door knob, or see the shadow of your feet under the door, or see you enter the room, or when you do as they are requesting, such as pick them up, pat them, or put their dummy back in. These cry outs are often interrupted with frequent pauses to hear if you have heard and are coming as requested, or because they are momentarily distracted, like the typical toddler who is crying out loudly until they hear their favorite garbage truck or airplane passing outside: they stop calling out until it has passed, then resume their loud crying.

You need to be cautious about attending to these sorts of cries as you do not want to encourage crying or disrupt settling. These cries are far more common on this program, and the ability to understand your child's style of communication is something that will be reassuring and eye-opening for any parent. With these cry outs, your child is generally saying something like 'Hey, you usually pat me to sleep, I think you forgot, can you come and do that because I don't know how to go to sleep any other way?' It's during this time, however, when they are calling out because they want to go to sleep, but they are not in a true emotional state, that a child learns to find another way to put themselves to sleep. Over intervening when they are not in an emotional state will actually interfere with this very important process.

It's important to listen closely to your child's language-based cry outs because even when they are insistent and sound very passionate about what they are asking for, or demanding you do, a child in this state can instantly stop the crying out when the desired outcome is achieved. A good sign that they are not in a cry that is overwhelming is if they can completely stop when you come in the room, or smile at you and raise their little arms up to be picked up. But remember, they are not deliberately trying to challenge you, they are just wondering how they can go to sleep without you.

This is why you need to be cautious about how frequently you attend as this can turn into a bit of a game, or you can keep them so focused on trying to get you to come in the room that they are entirely distracted from relaxing and not at all focused on trying to find a new way to cope with feeling tired and going to sleep. This misinterpretation and mismanagement of their communication are two of the main reasons that a baby can cry for prolonged periods of time. They call out, you come, you go, the pattern continues and they have company while they are waiting for the Sleep Bus, and eventually they fall asleep out of exhaustion. This is not the intention of this communication style. You need to teach your little one that it's not time for big conversations and games once sleep time begins, and if they are not upset emotionally, then they need to try and focus more on sleep than telling mum and dad what to do. In other words, you need to set a healthy boundary at sleep time early on. It's okay to tell your children that at sleep time they don't bellow if they are awake. It's okay to ask them to entertain themselves until they fall asleep. You say this by not overly responding to language-based cries.

There is no need to be stressed by these cry outs. It only takes a few days for your child to learn how to focus more on sleep, and learn how to go to sleep, so long as you interpret and assist their crying and communication in an appropriate manner. The main principle with crying interpretation is to help them find a way to self-settle. This means that the more you fuss, the more they fuss. One of the most important tools you can equip them with in their cot is to be okay when they are awake, and to not need entertainment or fussing. This is because when they wake in the middle of the night, when the rest of us would roll over and drift off back to sleep if we were feeling fine, a baby who is taught to call out and expects to be fussed with simply because they are awake, will wake up and cry, and will take a longer time to learn how to go to sleep and go back to sleep than a child whose cries are carefully interpreted and managed by pausing.

If you want them to go to sleep quickly and cry less, be very cautious to assess the cries properly. Always compare them to the daytime awake-time cries, and always listen to them in their natural form, and not through a monitor that is blaring ten decibels higher and louder than your child ever would. It's better to listen through the door, and that doesn't mean you should always stand at the door. Potter over to the nearest room and take a seat and listen carefully and quietly without distractions.

There are two identifiable cries in this category:

- the call out / behavioural cry
- the settling vocal pattern or cry.

The call out / behavioural cry

As mentioned above, these long cry outs start and stop a lot and pause if your little one is distracted. These cries tend to start with an open mouth and sound, and end in the same way. There is rarely a build up in the single cry itself and the call out does not fade off towards the end of the cry. If they do start to trail off it is simply because the sensation of feeling tired is starting to take a hold and even though they are still trying to call out they are feeling quite weary and a little bit distracted. There is a clear difference between this cry and the emotion-based cries and that becomes clear when you attend and their cry elevates to an emotion-based angry or upset cry with you leaving the room without obliging their demands. If you identify that you misjudged a call out and your attendance only caused your little one to become upset, then you must remember this and offer a little more space by being reluctant to attend to this cry next time. You need to be cautious about attending to these language cry outs. Essentially, this is not the kind of communication that gets your attention too quickly, and your child needs to take this opportunity to find a way to relax so they can go to sleep rather than rely on you to relax them in order to go to sleep. Sleep is absolutely achievable from this state, and all your little one needs at this point is space and time to find their way.

One of the most amazing things in my years working with families is just how often a family will call me in the middle of the night and say 'We are having a tricky time, they have been crying for X-long'. At this point, I work through their day to see if we can find any reason for the waking based on behaviour, digestion, environment, excessive stimulation / emotion or timings. This usually takes around five minutes. Then we work through their Sleep Bus timetable together and talk though how they have assisted them to this point. This usually takes us up to around the eight- to ten-minute mark. By the time we have been through all of that, if there is nothing of concern showing up in the daytime assessment, then we usually hear that they have calmed right down. Within those ten minutes, they have been given the space they needed to settle down and focus elsewhere. At this point, they still call out occasionally but feel less irritated and we no longer need to attend to them as they are now coping. By the time the bus arrives they are much calmer and, before we know it, they have caught the express bus to the morning. I'm telling you this to remind you of the important of giving them space to settle themselves down. Sometimes over attending will just irritate and stress them.

Obviously, if you over attend at this language call out your child will remain focused on trying to get you to come into the room rather than trying to settle down. Be cautious about attending to this cry but if it goes on for a long period of time you should think about going in to remind them it's time for sleep *if* the calling out is persistent enough to make you think they might need a little reminder. If they are having long pauses between cries, however (significant periods of time like close to a minute or more), then you really need to give them all the room they need. At this point they are not in any state that needs intervention and are in the best possible position to learn how to settle themselves.

It's so important that you don't interfere at this point. They are doing as you asked and, remember, you are not to be nervous about them being awake in their cot because that is a very healthy thing for any child to be able to do. This is a situation where you want to teach your child that their cot is normal and lovely and peaceful and absolutely nothing to be fretful of, therefore you can't ever be nervous of it for them, even when they are getting used to those new conditions.

This means they may call out on and off for 17 minutes between long pauses before they start to feel angry and need assistance on those first couple of days, and you need to be absolutely certain you remain focused on listening to their cries and not on just ignoring what they are saying and going in as soon as you can because you are watching the clock. This entire approach is about listening and communicating, and not clock watching.

The settling vocal pattern or cry

This cry is when your child is not calling out to you through the door but are vocalising to themselves over a period of minutes. Often babies will use the valuable settling-down tools that you have taught them, such as our rhythmic bottom pat and sh – sh – sh sounds, to help them settle. You may even hear your baby make a cyclic pattern of crying or vocalising as a way of settling off to sleep. This cry will sound like 'cry hic cry, cry hic cry, cry hic cry', or any number of rhythmic patterns. It is often distinguished by a drop off at the end like a meow, or a 'mmm' or 'nnnn' sound. As soon as you hear this sound, almost like a little trailing off or settling themselves, you will know they are starting to feel the tired sensation strongly now and they are very close to falling asleep or trying very hard to use their newfound skills to try and do as you have asked, fall asleep.

You need to be extremely cautious to not interfere with this natural process of falling asleep on their own. It's okay for them to feel a little uncomfortable with feeling tired the first few times you are not there to completely resolve it for them. This is a short-lived expression of tiredness while they get used to the new conditions of sleep. You may also hear this cry throughout the night if they have prolonged wakings where you don't need to attend. This will be your little one repeating the original settling-down patterns they were using when you first put them to bed.

Often, in the early stages of learning how to self-settle, babies are more vocal in their methods to self-settle and use patterns such as 'uh uh uh' or groaning or making a cry that always ends with a meow-like sound as they slowly start to wind down into a sleep pattern. Just because they are vocal at this time it does not mean you should interfere with them. Babies have few methods of creating a rhythmic pattern other than their voice or repeated patterns with their hands, such as rubbing their hair forward. As time progresses they won't feel this need to consciously try to settle themselves (in the way that adults would have previously taught them they needed to be able to fall asleep, such as the very active forms of patting or loud shushing / singing or hair stroking or rapid bouncing I often encounter parents teaching babies). They will start to lie quietly and drift off in a more peaceful manner. On the first few days, a baby or toddler will often self-settle through the night with this type of cry or vocalisation if they have been taught by their parent that singing, or vocalisations, or firm patting or rhythmic movement is the best way to go to sleep.

Occasionally, prolonged settling cries may indicate that they have come free of their wrap or it is too loose. You can generally hear movement in their cries if this has occurred—you'll hear them physically kicking in their cry in the form of a wah-ah-ah-ah-ah sound as they move. In this instance you will need to go in and re-wrap them if it appears they are unable to settle without it. Always be conscious of trying to avoid this happening in the first place as they will continue to focus their attention on getting out of their wrap if they know it is possible. Every baby will, with a little persistence, get free of any wraps, even mine, so make sure you keep yours nice and secure on those first few weeks so they don't learn to do this. It is only when the wrap is allowing kicking or excess movement that they don't settle, so remember the wrap is a huge comfort device that can prevent or greatly reduce tears when used correctly. So do it well.

Responding appropriately to your baby's cries

The different cries are like the steps when climbing on to the bus. The bottom step is their most unsettled cry (distress cry) and the furthest away from going to sleep a child could possible be when lying in their cot. The top step is the settling vocalisation / cry, the direction your baby needs to go in order to be able to fall asleep on those first few independent-settling occasions. This essentially means that your baby is accepting the sensation of feeling tired and preparing to go to sleep, essentially catching that Sleep

Bus. Always remember that every time you attend to their crying, your little one is likely to climb down a step or two as their focus is removed from trying to calm down and go to sleep to trying to get you to pick them up or put them to sleep in the old way. If you are going to attend, you should make sure they are really needing some reassurance, and not just calling out.

- You always attend to any distressed cry within a minute or two when we are sure this is the cry your little one is in and we can see they are totally feeling overwhelmed. This should rarely ever happen to anyone so please make sure you're listening carefully.
- You might decide to repeat your resettling cues and routine three times or even four if it is necessary to help them calm down.
- You always attend to the emotionally upset or angry cries within appropriate timeframes.
- You are fairly cautious around their language call / cry out and behavioural cries and make sure you provide more space and time to focus on the new task of putting themselves to sleep.
- You do not disturb them when they are in a settling cry, even if they occasionally call out here and there.

Each cry needs to be consistent *without pause* for the recommended time before you attend and offer your resettling routine while they learn how to settle themselves off to sleep. Then, as they get better with this skill, you offer a little more time each night and wean ourselves out of the process altogether.

In combination with complete PRM strategies when I assist a family, one in three babies will sleep through without the need for assistance on the first night, another the second night, and the last the third night. Occasionally, some children may take an extra day or so, depending on the extent of their skills before you start the program, or how significant your sleep-time disruption was prior to starting.

Once your child has had the opportunity and practice to discover that they can settle themselves off to sleep, your baby will quickly settle into a peaceful pattern of going through the settling routine and having you say goodnight and leaving the room. They will be feeling confident and familiar enough with the new routine to not cry as they now have found a new way to go to sleep. Always remember that you are not putting your baby to sleep: you are supporting them as they learn how to do it themselves.

If they are just calling out, then you need to remind yourself that they are only one small step away from trying to put themselves to sleep.

So your careful attention to detail when it comes to helping them calm down by attending to the right cries at the right time is absolutely crucial in seeing them settle as quickly as possible and cry for as short a period as possible. Even if your little one is having a big protest, then you hear them starting to decline in intensity or you can hear the odd pause, wait another minute or two, allowing them time to continue to calm down. This is the secret to being able to achieve sleep as quickly as possible: you attend when they need reassurance as often as they need, but as soon as they try to calm themselves down, sometimes indicated by a 'mmm' or 'nnnn' sound on the end of a cry, or the downward inflection like a meow sound, then they are doing really well and settling themselves beautifully considering it is one of their first attempts.

If you have not experienced a dramatic improvement within the first three days, then you need to stop any PRM management and review and revise your plan as something is not quite right.

Remember to not expect too much of them. Learning how to go to sleep all by yourself is a big new task, and does need a little time to adjust to, but with consistent routines and patience from a loving confident mum and dad, you will be amazed how quickly they will learn. Never underestimate how clever they are as they learn this new way of going to sleep, and how quickly they can learn to do that. If you spend the whole time lost in fear and concern because they are crying, you may well miss out on anticipating how well they are actually doing. Stay optimistic, and be confident. Most parents have their jaw on the floor the first day I or they implement the strategies in their entirety.

Finally, there is something very important to note. Once your baby has shown you that they can self-settle, and can resettle also, then the way you assist their crying needs to be even more carefully measured. This is no longer a question of can they do this or, can they cope? Because they can and they can. This means you are now moving into the realm of assessing possible causes for waking, how you are managing your parent-governed line through the day, and asking yourself if this is a behavioural reflection of any inconsistencies through the day on your part where guiding them is concerned. For example, are they learning that a parent-governed line is actually negotiable with lots of tears or tantrums? If so, you will see them challenge your parent-governed line at sleep time. Remember: difficulties through sleep are a strong indication of an imbalance through the day. Once you know they can put themselves to sleep and back to sleep, responding to their cries needs to be very carefully assessed to ensure you are not causing the crying yourself.

21
Supporting your baby when they cry

I always hesitate when parents ask me for timeframes to work with when helping their little ones learn how to sleep, particularly to do with how long you allow a child to cry. As you have seen in the previous chapter, it depends entirely on what type of cry it is and where your baby is on the Sleep Bus cycle. The problem with timings is parents will sometimes watch the clock and not listen to what their baby is saying or doing. So if baby hasn't settled by such-and-such minute they rush in as though the cavalry has arrived and they're going to fix everything. Ultimately, this only caters for the needs of the parents to do this rather than accurately assessing the cries and ensuring they are empowering their child with the ability to self-settle in as brief a period as possible. They can only fall asleep every so often, and you need to support them between those windows, and your visits won't make everything better if you are not listening carefully. In fact, some poorly measured visits will create more tears, rather than resolve them. Please do not fall into this trap. This must remain about listening to your baby, and not watching a clock.

Now having said that, I will provide in this chapter vague windows of opportunity for you to work with but, as the entire concept of sleep repair is designed around *avoiding* the reason for crying or waking in the first place, then *listening* to and interpreting your child's language. Then you can determine when it is best to attend to them or when it is best to give your child some space to experience the normal conditions of sleep and to try and settle themselves down. These timeframes offer the *minimum* windows that you should leave your little one before deciding on further action.

When to attend after an initial settling

Always be conscious of your baby's Sleep Bus (see page 675) and the natural ripple effect of falling asleep on the first few days.

On day one

When initially settling a baby to sleep, wait a solid five minutes after you leave the room and if your child has been vocal during that time you will then need to assess their cries to determine what they are saying and if you should attend to them. If you decide not to attend to them because they are simply in a language-based call-out cry, then you will no longer be following any timed pause windows. Only once they begin to cry in an emotion-based cry where they appear to be finding the situation overwhelming, be it because you are not coming when they call, or they don't know what do on their own when they feel tired, then wait roughly three minutes of consistent crying to be sure you have heard them correctly and to see if they can settle down before assessing their cry and choosing to attend to reassure them, or not. You are just stepping back long enough to hear what they are saying, see if they can calm down, and if not, offer them reassurance and support.

You may need to stop and start your timings because the cry might stop for 30 seconds to a minute, which indicates they are in a language-based call-out cry, rather than an emotion-based cry. It might also just become a clear random call out between blowing raspberries after a period of time, in which case there is no need to continue monitoring the cry, and you would not attend to this. It is important if this is the case that you don't go into their room, or near their room, as you risk them focusing on you rather than sleep. Reserve attending for the times when they are not able to calm themselves down. At no point do you want to encourage them to call out, fuss, blow raspberries until you attend, or yell at you. When it's sleep time you need them to stay focused on sleep, and they can't if you teach them to call out to you until you attend. Attending is reserved for the times when they are finding the new task of sleeping a challenge. To go in during a language-based call out, you literally create the need to cry. You should not worry about them being awake in their bed. This is the skill you are encouraging. You should only be concerned if they are finding it a challenge. To attend to the wrong cries will keep them crying to get you to attend more, and you could prevent them from being able to calm down enough to catch the Sleep Bus.

Ensure you interpret the cry (see page 683) carefully and if, after you leave the room it has remained the same for a consistent four to five minutes, with no pauses or changes and fluctuations of more settled times, then go in and reassure your child using your resettling routine again (see page 617). Do not add to, change or lengthen the settling routine or you will cause a huge problem. You will teach your baby to cry to achieve (whatever change you add) which ultimately turns the parent-governed line of 'I'd like you to go to sleep now!' to 'I'd like you to go to sleep, but if you don't want to, just cry!' I don't know about you, but most children I have met, when told they look tired will automatically say 'I'm not tired' even if their eyeballs are bright red and they're unsteady on their feet. Follow your resettling routine exactly as role played by you, then quickly step out of the room to give them some space to try and focus on the sensation of feeling tired. Repeat this process of assessing their cries and deciding after a consistent four to five minutes of crying if they have been able to settle themselves down or if they need to be reassured.

If your precious little friend is feeling overwhelmed, then of course you attend to them. If they have not been able to settle themselves that would be the appropriate thing to do. Just be cautious of *not* delivering a message of 'If you're awake in your cot, then focus on calling out to us when you're waiting for the Sleep Bus—we'd love to come in 20 times' as this will only encourage and perpetuate a cycle of crying. This methodology subscribes to offering comfort and support when they are feeling overwhelmed by the task, and not if they are just awake or bored or want you to play with them, or are complaining about going to bed. If, when you attend, they are able to completely stop if you do as they ask, this indicates that their cry is purely language based and you need to set boundaries, even at this age, about what you would like from your children when it comes to the request to go to sleep for you.

You need to be honest with your little one and say 'You don't just call out at sleep time, you need go to sleep. If you are having a tricky time we will always be there for you, but if you are fussing and getting stroppy about being put to bed, we won't be overly fussing with you then'. This means that if their cry has not been consistent, or they are having pauses, or are clearly in a call-out cry or settling cry, then stop your timing as you don't need to attend to them. If they are pausing for 30 seconds or more at a time, then they are not in an emotion-based cry (see page 684) and they are coping well enough with the situation for you to give them some more space to settle themselves down. Try to remember that you are not afraid of them being awake in their cot. There is nothing wrong with that, and if they are awake, and communicating with a call-out cry, or just intermittently with a call out or settling cry, or having a little grumble about how boring the prospects of bedtime might be at that particular moment, you do not go in and try to help in those times because they are okay, fine, loved, and just need a little space to settle down on their own. Essentially, you can stop timing their cry unless they start a cry that you interpret as an emotion-based cry, usually indicated by it being consistent, with no changes in crying style, or elevation in crying style.

If your little one starts crying consistently, then start timing the cry again. If they cry on and off for three to five minutes and you have identified that the cry is still not an emotion-based cry, or your baby is pausing enough for you to offer them a little more space and time to try to settle themselves, then you no longer focus on the 'how long': it becomes all about listening and interpreting their cries. But if they go into a consistent cry then you would always attend to them, after timing the cry to ensure you were not disrupting them and stimulating them, which will prevent them from settling themselves off to sleep, particularly when a Sleep Bus is approaching. If at this point they need your intervention, then enter the room as outlined in this book, sing your cues slowly and lovingly and turn and leave. By pausing once you have identified an emotional cry, you ensure that you are standing back long enough to hear what they are saying, and to see if they can calm down by themselves. If there are no changes in the cry, however, in that next three to five minutes, then your little one needs your reassurance and comfort and you would attend.

Once you have attended to your little one's crying after the initial three and four minutes, try to wait for five-minute intervals before assessing the cry and attending or not attending. If you do need to go into their room, consistently use your resettling routine only, then turn and leave. One of the biggest mistakes I see people making is to focus on going in and hoping to make everything better and their baby never having an opportunity to settle down because they are overstimulated and unable to focus on sleep because they are becoming too frustrated by your attendances. This is exactly why babies cry for longer. Please make sure that you are correctly interpreting their cries. If they are tired and just need a little space to settle down, then it's important to listen carefully and determine if they are saying they are not coping, or if they just need to be left alone.

When asked to come and observe a family in distress I often feel sad to see babies pushing parents away, arching their back, kicking, screaming and biting because they are just so tired, yet they have no skills to cope on their own either. This is where, like all of us, sometimes people fussing with you is just too much to cope with and we just need our space. Babies are the same. As romantic as the notion is that you will be the solution to everything, the reality is, sometimes they don't want to be fussed with, and they have said 'no' to the breast five times already and no one is listening to them. This is where your little one needs space. Be mindful of the fact that you should set safe and healthy boundaries around sleep.

Remember, if you keep telling them that if they call out constantly you will always go in to them, then they will always call out. If you teach them that you will always go in when they are not coping, but when you put them to bed they need to not try and talk through the door or walls, then they will start to fill that time between you saying goodnight and them falling asleep with the usual little baby things like sucking thumbs, playing with fingers, twirling hair, turning their head from side to side—the list is endless. I know that the final result, of giving them that freedom and an alternative way of coping when they are tired, is no more upset or overtired baby.

> Be mindful of the fact that you should set safe and healthy boundaries around sleep.

Maintain this management approach of attending to around every four to five minutes of solid uninterrupted, consistent emotion-based style of crying, and stay confident and reassuring during your resettling attempts and cues, while continuing to step back between attendances, and patiently wait for them to settle down enough to catch the Sleep Bus. You *must* ensure you are assessing their cries accurately. If they are not in the right cry, then you are not due to attend. Remember: done correctly, you will teach your baby to sleep on the first day or two and there will be fewer tears.

On day two

Repeat the same crying-support pattern of day one but progress a little further with the time you give them to settle themselves down, knowing that they are starting to learn how to do this and are getting good at it. Be mindful of the ripple effect when initially putting them to bed. Wait a good six to ten minutes before you assess your child's cries to determine if you should attend after you leave the room for the first time. From that point on, wait around four to six minutes before assessing the cry and whether to attend or not. If you have to attend to them a few times, try to wait six minutes before assessing the cry and deciding to attend or not. This is absolutely about listening to your baby and what they are saying, and not about watching the clock and only listening to what you want to do. It's tricky but be mindful of the behaviour you encourage. Attend if they need support and reassurance, but pause longer if they are just calling out or fussing about going to bed.

On day three and onwards

Repeat the same crying-support pattern of day one and day two, only progress a little further knowing that they are really starting to know this process and are getting very good at this. This means you just move forward your *minimum* pause times by one minute. So be mindful of the ripple effect when initially putting them to bed. Wait a solid seven to ten minutes after you first leave their room on day three before you assess your child's cries to determine if you should attend or not. If they start to cry after you have decided not to attend them, then start to monitor and time that cry, waiting a minimum of five to seven minutes before you assess the cry and decided what to do. After a few initial attendances when they have consistently cried with an emotion-based cry, try to also wait seven minutes before assessing the cry again.

After day three, you only continue to increase the initial pause time after you first put your baby to bed by one minute each day until you always give your little one ten minutes to settle, resulting in your baby always settling in the first ten minutes. No time-pause changes are needed after today and all support from this point on will remain the same five to seven minutes. Here is an example of what a crying-support session could look like on those first few days:

7 p.m.	Bubby down after settling routine completed, parent / carer leaves room.
7.02	Call-out cry begins, on and off, pausing often, no need to monitor cry or time.
7.05	Crying escalates to a more intense upset cry; begin timing, waiting three minutes before assessing crying.
7.08	Crying has not calmed, so attend and use your resettling routine calmly, then leave room at the end of two full cycles of your singing cues.
7.09	Baby is crying an angry cry; begin monitoring and timing, but allow a four-minute pause if possible from this point on.
7.12	Crying has continued with no pauses, so calmly attend to them with your resettling routine before leaving and giving them some space to try again.
7.13	Baby was quiet while you were in the room doing the settling routine, but has peaked in volume since you left, with crying being assessed as upset; begin timing and wait four to five minutes if possible.
7.14	Brief pause in crying then a slight change in cry and loud call outs begin.
7.15	Longer pause in crying, one minute in total, so end timing and only start again if the emotion-based crying begins.
7.16	Call out for 20 seconds then pause—don't begin timing.
7.17	Crying suddenly starts again and you assess it as intense upset-sounding cry, so begin timing, waiting four to five minutes, if possible, before attending

7.21   Crying continues with no decrease in intensity and no periods of pause. Attend, do resettling routine and leave quickly. Please note, 7.21 is actually the latest you need to leave the room if you are to give your baby enough time to settle down to catch the Sleep Bus.

7.22   Baby goes into loud upset crying after you leave as they are starting to feel tired, so begin timing again, allowing four to five minutes, if possible, before attending.

7.23   Sleep Bus is due. There is a pause for 30 seconds, a call out for 20 seconds, another pause.

7.24   Pause continues so stop timing.

7.25   Pause continues, then a call-out cry for 30 seconds before another pause.

7.26   Call out crying for ten seconds, then a pause.

7.27   Pause continues, then a call out cry for ten seconds. Pause.

7.28   All quiet. Caught the Sleep Bus.

Note that the Sleep Bus arrived at 7.23, according to this timetable, and the ripple effect started to slowly pull baby down into the surface-sleep pattern before the bus doors finally closed and baby caught the Sleep Bus to snoozeville—and hopefully it's an express! Be mindful of the typical stops the bus will make through the night where the door opens for three to ten minutes and they enter a surface sleep again.

While this is an example, your first or second crying-support session could go on for longer than this, based on the buses coming every 20 minutes or so on settling, particularly if your child is crying often through their sleep time before the program begins. Try to embrace this first day and night as a really important opportunity to be consistent with your new communication, and clear about the new routine's definition and boundaries. This is where babies learn because you are actually teaching them something. So be mindful of being consistent, following through, and doing your routine correctly, ensuring any crying is brief. This is, actually, a really important discussion between you and your baby which helps lift the burden of sleep time off them, helps them relax and allows you to show them a better way to sleep. Remember to be confident about your request so they can see they are perfectly fine, despite things feeling slightly unfamiliar.

Managing sudden partial wakings

Unlike managing your baby's surface sleep from a conscious state, a sudden partial waking occurs when a child comes to a surface sleep from a deeper state of sleep consciousness.

During sleep, as discussed in the 'Crying interpretation', we cycle through four stages of consciousness. The second stage, when we are semi-conscious, is what I call 'surface sleep'. When this occurs mid sleep, it's often referred to as a 'sudden partial waking'. The first time you attend to your child during this state is a very important part of sleep support, and an intricate part of how you manage your child's sleep carefully. In particular your use of the surface-sleep pause (see page 674), during this time can make a big difference to your baby's ability to cope and yours and their success to resettle quickly (within ten minutes) or not (minimum of 40 minutes awake).

On the first day of supporting your baby while they learn how to self-settle, in order to avoid long periods of crying, this pause needs to be carefully considered. While ultimately you are always aiming to pause at least ten minutes, if your baby's cry sounds very elevated, and there is no pausing, then your initial pause before attending could be as short as five minutes. Please do not attend prior to this time. Seriously consider the cries your baby is having, however, and if you can pause at least five to ten minutes, that would be ideal. The reason for this is that once you attend, you can be sure they will come to a full state of consciousness and you will need to support them for 40 minutes before the next bus arrives, at least. Over the days, this initial five-minute, minimum 'wait' window will gradually build up and your surface-sleep pause times, mid sleep, will always be ten minutes. Within this first week, however, your baby will start to learn how to self-settle in this time, without the need for intervention and you will never need to go in as they will always resettle themselves without coming to a full-alert state of consciousness.

Once they get better at going to sleep independently, and the habit of calling out during a surface-sleep pattern becomes less prominent, these brief sudden partial wakings will become silent. Here is a run-down of how these sudden partial waking 'wait' windows will look as your baby gets better at self-settling and therefore self-resettling.

On day one
Before attending to your baby's waking you must wait a minimum of five minutes, with a desire to try and pause ten if possible, then assess the cry and decide whether you need to attend or not. If your baby does not need attending to because their cry is not emotion-based, you can resume your normal crying interpretation and support pause times of three to five minutes as outlined above, after the first ten minutes have passed. If you

do need to attend to your baby, use your resettling routine and cues only (see page 617).

On day two

You increase your initial pause time by one minute, so wait a minimum of six minutes, with a desire to try and pause ten if possible, then assess the cry and decide whether you need to attend or not. If your baby does not need attending to because their cry is not emotion-based, you can resume your normal crying interpretation and support pause times of four to six minutes as outlined above, after the first ten minutes have passed. If you do need to attend to your baby, use your resettling routine and cues only (see page 617).

On day three

You increase your initial pause time by one minute, so wait a minimum of seven minutes, with a desire to try and pause ten if possible, then assess the cry and decide whether you need to attend or not. If your baby does not need attending to because their cry is not emotion-based, you can resume your normal crying interpretation and support pause times of five to seven minutes as outlined above, after the first ten minutes have passed. If you do need to attend to your baby, use your resettling routine and cues only (see page 617).

On day four and beyond

You will wait a minimum of eight minutes initially, with a desire to try and pause ten if possible, and on day five you will be pausing for ten minutes anytime they wake mid sleep before attending. After this initial pause is observed, the five- to seven-minutes' pause as you monitor a consistent emotion-based cry remains the same. There will be times when you won't need to resettle your baby for a long period because their cries don't fit into the range of cries where they need your reassurance. Please don't worry about these longer pauses. This support strategy is designed to promote independent resettling so if they are not getting angry or upset, it simply means they are becoming empowered and trying to resettle themselves, which is why you are giving them the space to learn to achieve this skill. This is a good sign. It's your homework starting to work for your baby.

Try to remember that you should not be frightened of them being awake in their cot. This is a normal part of their life. This is a life skill, that when learnt, means a healthy nights' sleep, and peaceful bedtimes and night times for the whole family. This always results in you never going in before ten minutes have passed, simply because they will settle themselves back to sleep without the need for intervention: this is the natural progression of positive routine management.

The following is an example of the first night-waking pause time followed by the process of interpreting the cries and pause windows you would follow. You will note that once the *initial* ten minutes of waking have passed, there is no longer a need to observe your designated surface-sleep pause window, only your *usual* pause times of three to five minutes on the first night.

11 p.m.	Bubby suddenly wakes after being asleep for some time. Baby is in a sleepy settling cry with the occasional call out. Do not begin timing for this cry.
11.02	Call-out cry begins solidly, pausing occasionally. Do no begin timing of this cry.
11.05	Crying has escalated to an upset cry so begin timing the cry. As this is not the initial cry-pause window anymore, you wait for your usual three to five minutes on the first night before assessing if your baby can settle down on their own, or if they need a little assistance and reminder that you are there, but it's sleep time. It is important to note that once the initial ten minutes have passed your should now aware that they have come to a more conscious state, and are no longer at risk of creating a session of wild thrashing (see page 475).
11.08	Crying has not calmed, so you attend, calmly using your resettling routine and leave within a minute.
11.09	Baby is now crying an angry cry so begin timing, waiting for four minutes if possible.
11.11	Crying has continued with no pauses, so calmly attend to your baby with your resettling routine calmly and leave within a minute.
11.12	Baby was quiet while you were in the room doing the resettling routine, but has now peaked in volume with crying assessed as upset. Begin timing, waiting for four to five minutes if possible.
11.14	Brief pause and slight change in crying; loud call out begins.
11.15	Longer pause, one minute in total, so you end timing and begin again only if the upset crying begins again.
11.16	Call out for 20 seconds, then pause. No timing begins.
11.17	Crying suddenly starts again and you assess it as intense upset cry so you begin timing, allowing a four- to five-minute pause, if possible.
11.21	Crying has continued with no decrease in intensity and no periods of pause. Attend to your baby and calmly use your resettling routine.
11.22	Once you have left the room, baby goes into loud frequent call outs. Begin timing, allowing four- or five-minute pause, if possible.

11.23	Crying pauses for 30 seconds, then call-out cry occurs for 20 seconds.
11.24	Pause in crying continues. End timing.
11.25	Pause continues, then call-out cry for 30 seconds, followed by another pause.
11.26	Call out cry for ten seconds, and pause again.
11.27	Pause continues, then call-out cry for ten seconds.
11.28	Angry crying begins. Start timing, allowing four- to five-minute pause, if possible.
11.32	Crying pauses for 40 seconds, followed by a single call-out cry and another pause.
11.33	All is quiet. Baby lying peacefully in bed, but possibly not asleep yet as bus is not due.
11.39	Sudden angry crying, and then pause.
11.40	Sleep bus due. There is a call out for ten seconds, then a ten-second pause.
11.41	Brief call out for five seconds, then pause.
11.43	Brief call out for five seconds, then all is quiet.

While this is an example, your crying support may or may not go on for longer than this on the first day, particularly if your child is crying often throughout the night already. Please see page 675 for the nights' Sleep Bus timetable.

Some common triggers of prolonged crying to avoid

- Not swaddled when they need it due to parent's incorrect perception of what the wrap represents. I am fairly well known for my immediate results and one of the tools I use as a form of immediate comfort and quick turnaround (one to three days) is the wrap. So dismiss your negative thinking about a wrap because I use it to help a baby not cry, not the other way around.
- The swaddle is not firmly wrapped enough due to poor or reluctant technique. Practise!
- Jumping, leg thumping on mattress, climbing out of cot, legs out of cot bars, kicking walls or thrashing in their cot, excessive movement. This is when an older baby needs a leg wrap or a firm tuck-in and SafeT Sleep.
- Sobbing. Some babies sob before they even cry and it is a part of their natural vocalisation in a cry. While this takes a little longer to work through, it's still important to work through their concerns about going to bed and help them learn how to sleep over a few days, and that way they no longer feel the need to cry when placed in bed, and sobbing at sleep time will be a thing of the past.

- Vigorous eye rubbing can trigger eczema or sore eyes. Babies who do this usually need wrapping if they are under 16 months of age.
- Eczema. It needs treating (see page 711).
- Congestion, such as production of excessive saliva or blockage in nose from crying. Some babies immediately block up with swollen nasal passages after a minute of crying. Unusual, but it is common when one of the parents suffers the same problem.
- The door being open. It is not fair to expect them to go to sleep when they can hear all their best friends (the family) still playing in the lounge room. As they need sleep, close the door so they can settle without the distraction and frustration of an open doorway that they can't walk through. It is fine to ask your baby to go to sleep by closing the door in a home where they are loved and safe, and it is unhealthy and untrue to tell them this represents anything other than a normal, safe time of the day.
- Too many noises disrupting baby—purchase a white noise machine or CD to counteract.
- Night lights being on—turn them off.
- Being able to reach the change table so it is distracting, which is dangerous so please move it or the cot away.
- Not interpreting and timing the cries correctly—get a notepad and pen, and write down what you are *hearing*. Stop thinking a blanket thought of 'I have to get in there and fix it' and start stepping out of your own head space that is full of fear and listen to what your baby is doing. Look for change in the projection so you know if they are standing or, if they are pausing, if they sound like they are moving, standing, lying down, kicking, if the cry is being projected for you, or if they are having a little cry to themselves as they settle into the feeling of being tired. Write down any clear improvements, no matter now small, and watch your Sleep Bus. If you keep an ear out for the 'normal' secrets of falling asleep, it will help you understand what is going on, and if you should or should not attend.
- Attending too frequently—will encourage crying.
- Changes during their day (weekend, visitors, daycare)—be prepared for how easily your little one can be overstimulated. You will note a change in their sleep over the weekend with both parents home, but more commonly, you will see your little one have a difficult time on Monday when there are less people around. Finally, if you go to a big family barbeque or get together where lots of people handling your under-two year old and taking them away from you often, even when they are loving it, it can often trigger a slightly tricky settle.

- Excessive food—make sure food is balanced, and you do not overfeed your child when they sleep poorly. To do so will only help sustain their poor sleep patterns.

Basic guidelines when introducing your new sleep routine

- Have one solid week where you focus wholeheartedly on repairing sleep. Take time off work if you need to, and be sure that you are not worrying about disturbing any grown-ups. If there is someone in your house who needs sleep, either send them to sleep elsewhere, or choose an appropriate time to work on repairing your baby's sleep so that concern is no longer a factor in your family, and everyone, not just one person, gets sleep in the house. It will take a few days to help your little one to not feel the need to wake all through the night and not wake at all, so invest the time in repairing the problem of night disruptions correctly.

- Do not introduce your cues or new sleep times until you are ready to implement your new crying interpretation and support strategy. One of the valuable tools of introducing a change in sleep times through the day when correcting sleep is that it will naturally help your baby feel tired, making the settling process through those early days of sleep repair a much faster and easier process for them, helping your child build their confidence and adjusting with less stress.

- It takes three weeks for your routine to be locked in, so in that time you should plan to stay close to home, not have any big changes (like going away on holidays) and be cautious of having people come and stay. Try to remember that you are saying to your baby, 'It's okay, mummy and daddy will take care of things from now on, you can relax and just be a baby'. It is not fair to ask them to look to you for guidance, yet go away from them often to shop or get your hair done, and leave them with different people. Try to stay close for a few weeks while they learn to settle into a guided day, and when they are more confident, you can start to use clear language to warn them of your impending absences, even when they are six months of age. Make sure carers understand your respectful, language-rich parenting style.

- Keep everything very low key half an hour before sleep time is due. It is unfair to have grandma turn up just before their main sleep of the day and not expect your baby to want to be up and playing with them. Just be mindful of such events and your little one will not have to go through any unnecessary tears. People often ask what effect the arrival of someone coming home from work at the end of the day might have at settling time. Regardless of anyone's timetable, I have a rule: daddy or mummy or anyone else are either there for the settling routine by 6.30 p.m., or they stay out of the scene until bubby has gone to bed, particularly during those first three weeks. This does not mean someone arrives at 6.30 p.m., goes and grabs a bite to eat, then showers and changes and rocks up five minutes before baby is taken to bed. It means whoever is going to be there is sitting down and relaxed by 6.30. So if it means you literally walk in the door, kiss everyone, sit down and feed your baby, still in your work clothes, then quietly enjoy stories, then so be it. Or, you try to get home earlier. If you do get home late, you need to stay calm and slot into the flow of the routine, stay focused on what needs to be done, or you may see tears and tantrums and, ultimately, risk having a very tired under-two year old.

- The settling routine can involve the entire family, or just the settling parent and the baby. If there are people not involved in the settling routine, they need to say goodnight before stories start, and stay away and keep low key—no wandering around and distracting the little one.

- If you make a mistake during your settling routine, carry on. Don't tut, sigh, tense up, start again, apologise, etc. Just carry on knowing you love your baby, and they are safe in your care.

- Surround yourself with encouraging and positive people. You cannot be so worried about another adult not coping that you do not remain 100 per cent focused on the baby. Your baby's need must come first. Stay confident.

- If you have a disruptive older child, it will be important to have your partner read them stories elsewhere on those first few days or, if you are on your own, provide some distraction for them while you do your settling routine. Try to work on your communication with your older child through the day, using the language strategies highlighted in this book, so they can be involved in the process.

- No one is to come into the baby's room while you are putting them to bed. If necessary, place a child safety gate further down the hall to ensure you can enforce that solid boundary with other children and pets without disrupting the flow of your little one's settling routine. Even if your older child tantrums while you settle your baby, continue on with your routine. Close the door, have the white noise on, and do not sound concerned so your baby can focus on your voice, and not their sibling's tantrums. Your baby's need for sleep is a higher need than an older child's tantrum for attention or demands. If this is an issue for an older child, you need to have worked on your short- and long-term absence cues with this sibling through the day while you role play and prepare to start your new sleep program.

- Pets are not to come in the room with you while you settle your baby.
- Whoever puts baby to bed, should be there to get them up.
- Once baby goes down, they need to stay in their cot until they have slept as requested.
- Where possible, try to only resettle a little one during the day when you have a good chance of being successful. This usually means pursuing putting a baby to sleep, but if they have taken at least an hour plus to do so, try to not force the issue unless you can feel assured that they will be able to go back to sleep. Calculate their Sleep Bus windows and decide if it is a worthwhile venture to try to get them to go back to sleep. One thing that I am always cautious to avoid is 'teaching a baby to cry' by having an unsuccessful resettling attempt where the primary message delivered is 'cry for an hour and I'll get you up'. I see this as entirely fruitless. Their tears are pointless and the stress is all for nothing if they ultimately cannot get themselves back to sleep. I do sometimes have to pursue sleep, however, after a shorter sleep of 30 to 40 minutes during a primary, day sleep session and, when I do, I always make sure I pursue the sleep to a positive outcome. Sometimes, it becomes about defining your statement and not confusing your baby, rather than the amount of sleep they can tackle in the end. Occasionally, you may need to resettle right up until the final opportunity for that particular sleep window, and they may finally fall asleep in the last ten minutes. This is now not about the sleep, as they will need to be woken in accordance with the routine, as it is about the request to go back to sleep.
- No matter what kind of sleep session you have, you are nothing but calm, patient, gentle and consistent.
- No matter what kind of sleep session you have, whether successful or unsuccessful, when you have reached your furthest time in that day's sleep window, you walk in and use your resettling routine and 'good sleeping' cues like normal and carry on like normal. You need to always be positive about their ability to sleep. Remember they are a clean slate, and they will be and do everything you tell them they are and do. Always tell them they are good sleepers, even if it's through a gritted grin on those first couple of days of settling into a new routine.
- The most difficult window to resettle your baby in is between 5 and 6 a.m. when they have been asleep for ten hours. If they are close to 6 a.m., I try to hold off as long as I can before attending and just start the day early, but still sticking to the routine. If they wake at 5 a.m. and you do need to resettle, be mindful of the fact that once you have asked them to go back to sleep you will need to follow through until 6.30 a.m. Also, until

you need to attend (based on what your baby is saying), don't go in there unless they are in the right cry because you risk making them very upset because they may insist on getting up, and you will be asking them to go back to sleep. This is where you must listen carefully to their cries.

- Another difficult time is if they wake 20 to 40 minutes after going to sleep at night, or after a brief day sleep that was meant to be longer. Remain calm, work out their Sleep Bus windows based on their waking time, and settle in to help them.

- Be fair, and patient. Don't be so demanding of them for your own sake and expect them to be able to learn something in one sleep session. If it happens that way, then be grateful, but if it takes a little longer, try to remember that they are learning something brand new from what they have done their whole life, and you need to support them patiently and consistently until they are able to understand and feel comfortable with the new way of going to sleep.

- Always make sure your baby knows you have left the room. No sneaking off and avoid putting them to sleep, although in many cases on my set routine, that is the biggest battle. Say your cues louder if you suspect they are drifting off, cut the song short if needs be, shuffle out of the room so they hear you leaving and click the door shut so they hear the door close.

- Never just 'give it a try' when it comes to settling or resettling, only to stop trying if they don't immediately go back to sleep. Be mindful of what definition you are giving your settling cues and any requests to go to sleep or back to sleep. These meanings cannot be made lightly as you will need to follow through until the end of that particular (or typical) sleep window.

- Don't alter the routine backwards or forwards to suit their waking time each morning. If you want to be successful and quickly resolve their sleep, then work with a set window and wait for your little one's body to settle into the predictable pattern. If you are on a suggested routine or you have developed one of your own then be sure to lock in your windows for sleep. Once in a routine, ensure you do not overwork the hours awake between sleeps or tired signs. This results in yoyo days and an unsettled baby. It can also get your baby into a cycle of catnapping again, and lead to an unsettled baby as they don't have the added assistance of a locked-in settling and solid sleep window in their circadian rhythm.

- Never compensate for poor sleep at the right time, with good sleep at the wrong time, or you perpetuate cycles of poor sleep.

Troubleshooting crying

Q What's the best way to avoid crying?

A A well-planned and rehearsed strategy through role play. Role playing your new settling routine for your little one daily, before implementing the strategy. Do your homework first, and work on the areas of the day where your baby is not coping as well (communication, independence, meal times) for a good week before you start your plan. When you are ready, be warm, confident, reassuring and totally consistent with your settling routine, support and expectation to sleep—I call this a 'liquid flow', when you glide through your plan effortlessly and without stress (from books to wrap to singing to tucking-in to cues to leaving) and are consistently the same at each attendance (into room, close door, position them correctly, sing cues calmly and leave calmly). If you are chopping and changing, and rewrapping, or doing and saying something different every time, or sounding worried, or bickering with your partner and chatting about what they need, then you are guaranteed to cause tears because your little one is looking for predictability to feel secure.

Q What if they get out of their wrap?

A I can't tell you how important it is that you prepare correctly to *avoid* this at all costs. Make it a good wrap, it needs to stay on for 11 to 12 hours, so it needs to be good. The idea is that it remains the same through the night so they can wake, feel their comfort and association is in place while they learn how to sleep, then they can drift back off during the surface sleep without coming to a full waking. If they learn early on in the process that they can get out, which any baby can if they 'really' want to, thus you need to be very good with your wrapping, then that is what they will focus on for some time. Practise your wrapping on a teddy over and over and over again, practise doing the tuck-in correctly in the dark; double wrap as a preventative on the first day or two if you suspect you have a little worm.

If you are unfortunate enough to have this happen, don't fear; it even happens to me, and my wraps are solid. Firstly, be prepared, they may take a little longer to settle now which usually means a few more tears, but it is still very manageable. Your little one may focus heavily on 'trying' to get out, rather than going to sleep the next time you put them down. To manage this event, however, there are a couple of things. You will need to rewrap them on a nearby bed. This means lights off (except for a distant dim glow from some far-away room light where the door is mostly closed). All doors and curtains closed, and no extra people about fussing. Take their wrap off them in their cot, and leave them in there while you go to the other room and prepare the wrap. Return and get your little one. Pick them up in the cradle position repeating your settling cues only, and take them to the room. Point to the wrap, and say 'Lie down', then lie them down. Define 'lie down' before you start to wrap them again. Follow normal wrap strategy. Carry them in as usual, and when you get in their room, close the door behind you, and walk to the side of the cot.

Do *not* sing 'Twinkle twinkle little star' again, just use the final step of your usual settling routine from the moment you would have sung the song. So say 'Lie down' before lying them down, tucking them in while saying their cues as usual, and then finally assuming your settling-cues position, and singing your settling cues before turning and leaving. If your baby is always trying to worm out the top of their wrap, be sure to wrap their legs firmly. It's also a good idea to position them close to the top of the cot so they cannot worm right up and out. Place a soft rolled up towel at the top of the cot, but pushed down the gap between the mattress and the cot bar only leaving a soft ridge of towel or blanket showing. This way, when their head reaches that point of comfort, they will not try to wiggle out beyond it. Once you return, simply correct their position without the need to disrupt your settling process.

Q My baby is rubbing her eyes non-stop and crying. Why, and is there anything I can do?

A These babies tend to have either eczema or are dry around their eyes. They are often better off being wrapped to prevent them using their hands to rub more while in the cot. Always be sure to keep their face well moisturised with sorbolene, and their hands well creamed to prevent even more drying out if they do rub. Try to discourage vigorous eye rubbing during the day with a simple cue like 'no rubbing, bubba' said in a patient tone, and defined to mean no rubbing at all (similar to the 'hands down' cue during feeding). This will help you to discourage it at sleep time and hopefully help remove it from their repertoire of usual responses to certain situation.

Q She throws all dummies / teddies out of the cot and cries. Should I pick them up?

A Not unless you know they have accidentally bumped them out. If she is throwing them out of the cot, pointing at them when you come in and asking for them back, keeping them until you leave before throwing them out again, then she is wanting to govern the outcome of sleep. As this is not the correct line of communication for sleep repair, and always leads to tears in babies who find sleep challenging, you do not give her the dummies back to avoid the governing line being transferred from you to her. Simply scoot the dummies under the cot and pursue sleep without them. If you do offer them every now and again, then you will actually encourage the behaviour and encourage crying until she gets them back. If they have accidently fallen out if the cot (and don't cheat here), then pop them back in the dummy pots and carry on without a fuss.

Q If they miss the first Sleep Bus, can I just get them up and put them down ten minutes before the next bus is due?

A Absolutely not. There are two major problems that occur with that approach. Firstly, this is where you risk them being sustained by hormones, including adrenalin, and being unable to catch the next Sleep Bus. If they then become overtired, even if they do first go to sleep they may not be able to stay asleep past 45 minutes to an hour due to the fact that they are overtired. Secondly, you teach them that time for sleep means both 'go to sleep, please' and 'cry and I'll get you up for a while and . . .' This will confuse baby and is guaranteed to create ongoing tears.

Q My baby is kicking the wall and opening the curtains. What should I do?

A Move the cot away from the wall or curtains. Consider using a SafeT Sleep or wrap. Discourage this behaviour during playtime in the cot by staying with them and requesting 'no kicking' and defining that statement. 'No kicking' does not mean 'kick and the I'll stop you after'; it means, 'no kicking', so you will need to prevent them from being able to kick when they attempt to do so, so they understand that no kicking means exactly that.

Q My baby pushes her teddy away and won't hold it. Does that matter?

A No, it's there if they want it, but if they don't want it you don't need to take it away or force them to hold it. Just having their furry little friend in the room may be all they want.

Q My baby sounds more upset when I go in the room? Is this normal?

A It's not uncommon for a baby who has a lot of recovering to do from being very unsettled. Remember you are talking about taking the burden off your baby, and asking them to let you govern sleep time. This can be a slightly challenging adjustment and they will still be quite vocal and try to govern or re-establish the old pattern. It's difficult to establish new communication sometimes because when you do attend they are saying 'pick me up' and you are asking them to 'go to sleep, please'. When you are not responding to the right cries, you create frustration by repeating this argument in a sense. Once you have asked them to go to sleep, your attendances should be for when they are finding it tricky to do, not for when they are protesting and arguing with you about the request. Even at eight months they can be very cross when asked to lie on a change table or sit in the pram, so their cot is no different.

Q My baby hasn't stopped crying by the time I have finished saying my cues twice through. Should I stay with them until they stop crying?

A No. You are not trying to 'fix it', the cues are designed to reassure them that you have heard them, you love them, and you will always come, but that you want them to go to sleep, and you can't do that for them. It's also important for them to note your calm and reassuring tone, so they know that you are okay and not concerned, so they know they are okay. Leave the room and support your baby through the crying by assessing the cry.

Q My baby tries to climb up me when I come in the room to resettle. What should I do?

A Turn them around to face away from you, and lie them down on their tummy before rolling them on to their back and keeping them there while gently saying your cues. Please see 'Independent playtime in the cot' for managing their hands as you approach (see page 175).

Q Can I pick them up during a resettle?

A No, because despite what it represents to you, while you are teaching your little one to sleep, it would be nothing but confusing to add this to the definition of your new cues, and they would cry for longer. This means that to say 'time for sleep' means 'cry if you want to be picked up' will confuse them, and therefore encourage crying.

Q My baby seems to want to skip the singing and just get into bed. Can I do that?

A This is not uncommon. Some babies think that the idea of you singing is just awful, or they cannot wait to get into bed. Fortunately, this has nothing to do with your singing ability, or whether they like your singing or not. Through experience I have discovered that you don't have to an idol to get a baby's nod of approval, but you do need to be calm and gentle and soothing. On the first days of your settling routine, they may naturally resist the singing as they learn that it means it's time for bed, and they are probably saying 'I'd like to stay up for play'. Because of this, it's important to hold them firmly and continue to follow through on your settling routine to help them understand that the routine is predictable. If, however, after a few days you are noting that the 'only time' your little one is getting upset is when you sing, and they stop as soon as you put them down, you can then modify the song to only include the first two lines and then, eventually, just your settling cues and 'lie down'. Alternatively, you can sing as you wrap them.

Q My baby won't lie down in my arms during the settling routine. Does that matter?

A In a little one who is protesting about sleep in general, yes, it is important for you to establish this boundary and request with them while you are able to hold them so they can be reassured. If they will not lie down in your arms, chances are the request for sleep will involve a big old protest. If you leave that protest until they are placed in their cot, then their cot becomes associated with the discomfort of the request, rather than them learning that mummy and daddy need them to listen, and lie down for sleep. It is easier for a little one to accept a request, even after protest, from their mummy and daddy, than to have to deal with a battle when they are placed in their cot. While the settling routine's flow of stories, governed with a parent-governed line of communication, requesting a child listen and sit down generally, eliminates most challenges by the time they are in their room, there may be a brief period (first day or two) where they also challenge or protest about the request to lie in your arms. If your entire settling routine is locked into place, this will be short lived, so it's important that you pursue this request to lie down. Occasionally, once they are 18 months or more, or if you can see that they are happy to drop their head on your shoulder and still happily lie down when asked, then it is okay to allow them to remain upright, without compromising the governing line of sleep time.

Q My baby is jumping. Can I do anything?

A Simply follow the resettling routine and the lying-down strategy outlined in the earlier question regarding a baby climbing up on a parent during an attendance.

Q My baby is not crying, but I know they are awake and I can't relax until I know they are asleep. Is there anyway I can speed up the process?

A No, the most important thing to remember while teaching your baby how to sleep is for them to be happy when they are awake in their bed. You should not be frightened of them just lying there or chatting to themselves, and be realistic about the fact that when they go to bed, they won't be asleep the moment their head hits the pillow. Because your baby wakes naturally through the night, it is important they are comfortable with being awake in their cot. It is a positive outcome if they can lie there and be relatively relaxed. Leave them be. On the other hand, if your baby is awake every night for an hour when you first put them to bed it could signify one of two things: one, their day sleep is excessive, in particular, their afternoon sleep is either too long or too late and needs to be modified; or, two, you have a baby who needs to wind down or debrief at the end of each day. This is rare, but more common with toddlers, and in even rarer cases, in little ones under 15 months. The common thread I have seen with these children who need to run through their day (usually in words or vocalisations or role playing the day's events) is that this need appears to be more prevalent in children who seem to be more advanced in certain areas of their development.

Q Can I sing a song again if they have missed the Sleep Bus?

A So often, people ask if they can start the entire settling process again, and either get them up and do the entire process again from stories, all the way to singing again, or just pick them up and start from their settling process again at song again. My answer to this question again is 'no', you will only confuse them, and taint or confuse the settling cues, and in doing so, will change the governing line of communication at sleep time from a parent-governed line, where you will always attend to them and predictably help them with your resettling routine, to a negotiation. This means you are encouraging your baby to run through other options available to them at sleep time. 'One more' is what you are teaching them, and in doing so, you teach them to not accept your sleep-time request, and to cry if they don't want to go to bed. In reality, because children have no concept of the consequences of not sleeping, just about every child on the face of the planet could think of something more 'fun' than lying quietly in their bed until they fall asleep, but as this is not in their best interests, and you are wise, you have to make sleep time a place of a simple, clear, parent-governed request.

Q Can my partner and I take turns during the settling, or resettling routine?

A I have a rule: whoever puts baby down, supports them and gets them up. This prevents one parent from accidentally undermining the other. If your baby learns that only mum or dad can settle them, then the other parent loses confidence in their ability to settle and, worse still, your baby thinks that they cannot go to sleep for both parents. It is also unpredictable for your baby to have one person put them to bed, and then when they call to that person, someone else entirely walks in the room. Even at eight months, you will see a child react to this strategy by crying significantly more at the next sleep time.

Q If I start to get upset or cry, what should I do?

A This is tricky. I know you're tired, and I know you have never been through so much in such a short period of time, since your baby was born, but I need you to try and take things step by step, and just for today. One day at a time. I'm going to say this: 'first things first'. What is the most pressing matter at hand right at this minute? The answer is to get through this as quickly and as smoothly as possible, so baby can get to sleep with as little disruption or crying as possible. In order to do that you must reassure your baby, and you can't do that if you allow yourself the luxury of falling apart. Don't drop the batten before you cross the finishing line. A day or two and your baby will be sleeping without tears. Just be strong a little while longer, and all this exhaustion will be behind you. If you can, reserve your crying for later when you can just get it all out, uninhibited and for as long as you like. This means, you can have a big cry once they fall asleep, but not while they are trying to learn how to. Hang in there for me for now though, because you becoming distressed and dropping your bundle are possibly two of the most destructive things you can do during a sleep-repair settling or resettling routine. It's frightening for your baby to see, hear or even detect that you are stressed because you are delivering a very negative message about their new sleep-time routine before they have even had a chance to get used to it and, therefore, get comfortable with it. It's also very destructive to your ability to identify the cries and respond in a way that is reassuring. To tell your child that feeling tired or going to sleep is anything other than safe, natural and nothing to be stressed about is not in their best interests and simply not true. Try to stay focused on their cries and ignore your own negative inner dialogue, which is distracting you from the job at hand. If you cannot cope, you should have an objective friend or family member to support you. If all else fails, you will have to hand over support and attendance duties to your partner, but please be aware that this is the least desired outcome because it is catering to your needs over your baby's needs. Swapping carers is unsettling for your child and will cause crying because they will not be expecting the other person, will wonder where you have gone, and will start asking the new supporter to 'pick them up', etc., all over again. That said, swapping is the lesser of two evils when you compare it to having a parent who is upset attend to help them calm down and feel okay about going to sleep. Always remember to assess the situation from an adult's perspective. Is their room or sleep something to be scared of? No, therefore you should not be upset for them. It's just new. Give them some time to get used to it.

Q   What do I do if they climb out of their cot before I am due to go in and attend to them?

A   It's important to have worked through any potential environmental problems before you start your new sleep-time routines. If you know that your little one is a real climber there are a few things that need to be put in place early for safety reasons. Setting boundaries through the day is very important. This means that at no point is your little one allowed to climb in or out of their cot during play, etc. They need to be clearly told that they are not to climb and if they even raise a foot to their cot side, you quickly brush their foot so they go back to a standing position as you say 'No climbing'. Clearly define this cue and be consistent with this request. If you can prevent them from climbing out during the day then there is a good chance that they will not try during night settling. Alternatively, you can taper the bottom of their sleeping bag by sewing the bottom two corners together, making lifting their foot to the side of their cot no longer possible. If your child is more inclined to lean out over the top of the cot side and has the potential to fall head first then you should immediately invest in a SafeT Sleep. It can be used until a child is three to five years old.

It you suddenly discover that your baby is a climber, then you will need to go in and very quickly put them back into their cot and lay them down. This should be done with no rewarding snuggles, eye contact or conversation because, while tempting, this would only encourage more climbing out. When you enter the room, pick them up under their arms and without holding them close to your body say in a clear monotone style 'In your cot' before lying them down promptly. The sensation of being out of their cot when you entered the room should be something that is not rewarding. It should be clear to them that this is something you would like them to not be doing, and it is far more rewarding when they stay in their cot. This action may need to be repeated until they go to sleep. If you struggle with this, then you will need to consider a SafeT Sleep and pop it on them as you tuck them in. You may even need to use a temporary leg wrap to help them feel held and take away their need to want to find someone to make them feel held. The results of this kind of swaddling are almost instantaneous and mean far less fussing, crying or danger, for that matter, in the future.

Q They are standing when I attend to them. What should I do?

A Lie them down immediately, without pausing to do anything else and say with a clear statement 'Lie down'. If their hands are reaching out, take their hands in your hands as you say 'Lie down'. For more information on lying them down see 'Independent playtime in the cot' (page 175).

Q They have cried for a while. Should I give them a drink?

A No, not if you can help it. The emphasis on keeping them well fed and hydrated is focused on during the day time, so you do not have to provide hydration or dietary intake at night time. Any night intake detracts from the daytime intake and perpetuates a cycle of hunger and thirst at night. More importantly, you don't want them to think that going to sleep is a negotiation. The request for a drink on these first few days is no different to 'one more book' and any other typical stalling technique. Though I recommend you do not offer food or water through the night, if you have to or choose to do so anyway, there is one thing you must remember to do: retain the governing line of communication. When you are due to attend next, walk in and say 'Have a drink for mummy, please' and offer them their cup when they are sitting down. Once they have had a drink say 'Ta for mummy' and take the cup back, even if they protest. If you do not, then you will only encourage more tears as they govern when you can have the cup and, therefore, when you can leave the room. Once you have said 'Ta for mummy', that's it. Take back the cup before lying them down as described in your settling routine. Babies in wraps generally should not be offered drinks through the night.

Q What would happen if I just picked them up and cuddled them when they are crying?

A You will teach them to cry to be picked up and they will not be able to focus on settling themselves to sleep because they have learnt that if they would like to be picked up they just need to keep crying. Please don't confuse them. The settling and resettling routine is totally consistent so your little one learns that you will come in and help them and settle them down as often as they would like, but you are always predictable. Sleep time is not a place for discussions, requests or negotiations, particularly while they are learning how to sleep.

Q Can I stay and pat them for longer if they are crying?

A If a child is very upset I tend to stay and say my cues one extra time, or two more times at the absolute outside before leaving. If you pat them until they are asleep, then sneak off, they will not trust those cues, will not calm for them, and will wake multiple times that night looking for you and need to cry to get you back in the room to pat them. You will also teach them to need patting to sleep, and you will teach them to cry. As tempting as it is, remember it only takes a few days and they will have learnt how to go to sleep peacefully and it is a valuable life lesson that benefits both your baby and family.

Q They stop crying when I'm in the room, but cry when I walk away. Is this normal?

A Yes, this is very normal, but it is also very important that you do not avoid going in to reassure them if they are saying it is difficult. This is simply avoiding the communication and request your little one is posing. If you do not answer them by attending and doing your resettling routine then you run the very real risk of creating a pattern where you can rarely attend without tears when you leave. Obviously this is not realistic, as often you will need to medicate or transition your baby and will want to have the freedom of attending, checking in on them, or offering them some support, while knowing that you have established clear, safe boundaries around you leaving again that still enable you to maintain sleep and avoid tears. The crying when you leave is always reserved for the first few days and then it almost always completely disappears permanently.

Q Do I still leave after the settling routine is completed even if they are crying?

A Yes, carry on with your resettling routine as normal.

Q Is there any other way to teach them how to go to sleep on their own without crying?

A This strategy of empowerment and prevention of tears is the best way to avoid crying, but still does not guaranteed no tears, which is only fair for the children. They, like you and I, are not that great with change; it's usually a little uncomfortable, so it's okay if they need a little reassurance while learning something new.

Q Do they have to be really good at cot play for me to start?

A No, if you have used your cot play strategy for a week leading up to implementing your new routine or routine changes, then that is adequate time. Often the settling routine and sleep-time support and repair will help progress your little one's ability and enjoyment of cot play.

Q How long should I keep trying to get them to sleep?

A Until they go to sleep. You will have them sleeping quickly if you manage them well until they go to sleep the first few times. I do not understand the point of even allowing a single cry to escape their lips or a single tear to be shed if ultimately you achieve nothing from theirs and your efforts. Though it has only twice happened to me, if they are still crying at something like the three-hour mark, then something has gone very astray. Please be sure to go back to the how to use this book section and read thoroughly through sleep repair homework.

Q How do I know when I am going in too much?

A If your little one does not calm down, and the cries remain intense, you may not be giving them enough space to calm down. If you keep coming in too frequently, then they will remain focused on you coming in the room rather than trying to focus on their immediate environment for comforts. It only takes once or twice and they will automatically snuggle into a teddy or look for their dummy, or relax and enjoy the comfort of the cuddly wrap and safe, snug tuck-in. Try to listen very carefully for their calling out, and when you attend, if they are able to completely stop when you enter the room, you may need to step back for longer periods of time to ensure they start to focus on trying to settle themselves down. Remember that each time you enter and do the resettling routine you are saying to them that laying calmly is the most peaceful thing to do at sleep time. If you offer a little extra space you will see that they will automatically lie down and try to get comfortable.

Q Sometimes I do not need to go in for a long period of time, even though they are clearly awake and calling out. Is this normal?

A Yes, this is normal, and this is when you are making great progress. Them being awake in their cot and relatively calm and settled (indicated by a language- or behaviour-based cry) is a tremendous achievement and a great milestone in learning on that first day or two, and normal and healthy when it comes to skill of sleep.

Q My baby doesn't like to have a wet nappy as they are used to being changed often. Should I change them during the night?

A I have only come across this a couple of time but I thought it was worth answering here. If you change your baby's nappy every single time they are wet through the day they will quickly learn that being wet is not normal. Obviously for sleep times, it is not possible to always change their nappy every time it becomes damp so it's important to not get too fussy with keeping them totally dry the whole time through the day. It takes around two to five years for a child to be able to retain a full bladder through the night and it would be fairly disruptive to change them when they are sleeping well, so try to be a little balanced during the day. It's okay to leave a nappy on for an hour or so unless they have soiled it. Slowly build up to a new nappy once every two hours and work from there. Once you stop feeding them during the night you will find that their nappy remains fairly dry through the night and very wet during the day. If you use a good quality disposable for the night sleeps this will also help baby feel dry.

Q My baby has soiled their nappy. Is it ok to change them?

A Of course, but try to change them in their cot so they don't misunderstand you getting them up as the beginning of playtime, as this will obviously upset them when you put them back to bed. If they often poo once they go to bed, then it's important to always cream their bottom with a good treatment cream like Bepanthen then a barrier cream. You can be very liberal with the barrier cream, and be sure to check them before you go to bed, and change them in their cot without waking them if possible. If they do not wake, then simply tuck them back in like normal, and leave after a whispered 'nigh' nighs'. If they wake up fully, then literally treat their nappy change with the same style of language you use in your normal settling routine while you tuck them in. This would mean you would 'say' your cues periodically as you progressed through the change and re-tuck-in process.

Q Do I need to check on them through the night?

A When you first help them learn how to go to sleep, you are better to leave them be and not disturb them. You will be upset with yourself if you are responsible for waking them, and if you do wake them you need to manage them with your resettling routine only. If you have a video monitor, then this is a better way of taking a quick peek at them to ensure all is well and the environment is safe and sound. Alternatively, have a good listen to the sound monitor. If you feel that you must go in and you are willing to take the risk, turn off all the surrounding lights, be as quiet as a mouse, go in quickly and have a look without touching if possible, and then leave quietly. The worst times to go in to check are anywhere between 7 and 8.30 p.m., and between 10 and 11 p.m. As much as possible I always suggest you leave them be so they can sleep peacefully without the risk of disruption. An monitor can offer peace of mind too.

Q When I attend to them they are asking for the other parent. Can I send them in next time?

A No, whoever puts them down needs to support them. Remember this is a parent-governed line of communication and if your child says 'No, not you, I want daddy', then you have transitioned the parent-governed line to a child-governed line or a negotiation. This will ultimately confuse your baby, result in frustration and more tears. It will also undermine the original settling, parent-governing line and teach the baby that they don't need to go to sleep for you, but they do for daddy.

When a baby wakes after a good amount of sleep

So your baby has woken at the right time. They have slept what you deem to be a reasonable and healthy amount of time and you are not quite sure whether to wait a moment, or go straight in. It's an excellent question and actually a pivotal part of remaining consistent and predictable with your communication. When you put your baby to bed, you ask them to look to you for guidance and, when they cry, you remain consistent with your reassurance but the request to go to sleep remains the same. This is achieved through the settling routine. Then, in the middle of the night, if your baby wakes up and cries, you ask them to look to you for guidance and you remain consistent with your reassurance but the request to go to sleep remains the same. This is achieved through the resettling routine.

In the morning when your baby wakes up, if, regardless of whether they have slept to the right time or not, you were to then go in and pick them up immediately, this is inconsistent. To go in immediately and pick them up when they cry at one time but not others is entirely delivering the wrong message. It is this pattern that causes a baby to continue to cry at night for a long time when parents embark on a sleep-training progress. You want them to not wake up and cry out to see if someone will come in immediately. This would be a mixed message for the middle of the night where you want them to stir, look around comfortably and relax, know that you will come in soon, so if their body does need them to drift back off to sleep, they are relaxed enough to do so. For this reason also, you need them to be happy to lie there awake for a time when they first wake, because the Sleep Bus has its door open for a good three to ten minutes through the transitional period or ripple effect, so you don't want to confuse them into thinking they need us in that time, or it will keep them awake through future night stirrings.

For this reason it is so important to be consistent. If they wake up and are happy enough, and not in any kind of cry that is concerning, then leave going in to them until the end of that natural sleep window or as close to as possible. For example, if they usually sleep for two and a half hours, and they wake at the hour and a half mark and are only occasionally calling out but are happy to lie in their cot and have a rest for the remainder of the sleep window, then this is best thing for them to do. If they wake at the end of the sleep window, then you would still attempt to leave them for the usual surface-sleep pause (see page 674) of five to ten minutes to make sure they are fully awake and conscious before attending with your waking routine.

Once you have waited the initial pause, or the extended pause, whichever is more appropriate, then you should always enter using your waking cue and routine (see page 622). You should always initiate a playtime in the cot (see page 175), even if it is only brief, as this is the simple routine. Then you are basically telling your little one to relax and trust that you will be so predictable that they can just lay back and leave all the sleep stuff to you. By the time they are six months of age you have three things you generally do like clockwork for your baby at sleep time. They are:

• you either ask them to go to sleep
• ask them to go back to sleep
• tell them it's time to get up.

This leaves your baby totally burden free and ensures there is no confusion when it comes to who is governing sleep time, thus eliminating tears because they are happy to relax and wait.

Imagine how confusing it would be if you went to great lengths on one of their wakings to ask your baby to go back to sleep when they called out, yet on another you simply walked in and picked them up when they called out. This is when children become unsettled as they cannot predict your actions, and as they are creatures of habit, they will then start to create their own little rituals. Often, because they are so tiny, these rituals are not always in their best interests and can leave them overtired and seriously overburdened with having to guide a parent through a predictable set of conditions for sleep time.

The sudden sleep adjustment

It is not uncommon for a family who has had instant success with their routine management to see an almost miraculous increase in their child's consistent sleep intake, and a dramatic increase in their child's overall daily sleep requirement. Everything seems a little too good to be true. Your baby has suddenly gone from sleeping 30-minute catnaps and waking 12 times a night to sleeping for two and a half hours at a time during the day and 11 hours straight at night, and it all happened almost overnight. Now this would be a fairy tale if it lasted but you do need to be realistic.

There is always a little price to pay when things happen really quickly. For those of you who have very little crying support to do initially there is an adjustment period where your baby is just feeling really well slept and will wake for a period through the night. This is not a time to panic or think they have gone back to their old ways or backwards. This is simply a balancing effect. Manage the waking with your settling or resettling routines, and maintain your routine plan, ensuring you don't suddenly offer more sleep, or longer naps, or later sleep to simply compensate for the waking, otherwise you will

> If they wake up and are happy enough, and not in any kind of cry that is concerning, then leave going in to them until the end of that natural sleep window or as close to it as possible.

perpetuate the prolonged wakings and encourage them to continue night after night. If you are on a PRM routine, do not offer an extra or early meal time, or sleep. If you are following on with your own routine, again, do not compensate with excess, early or too much food or sleep.

Once the adjustment days have passed, which is usually on the third to fifth day, you will find your little one settled into a more average pattern of sleep. For those who have some work to do on the first few days, this adjustment period tends to not occur as your child's needs for sleep gradually increases over the one-week window, rather than all at once on the first and second day.

The two- to three-week sleep adjustment

There is a typical adjustment that occurs once all the graduate sleep babies start to catch up on their consistent sleep. It always impacts the midday sleep somewhere between the second and third week for the low-sleep-requirement children, or the second long sleep of the day for the high-sleep-requirement children. At some point over this time the body's need for daytime sleep drops and you will have disruptions during the day sleep when they wake early and it's difficult to resettle them. This is only short lived but there are a few rules to adhere to ensure this period is only short lived.

If it occurs or, should I say, when it occurs, take it in your stride. It is generally a short-lived phase if you follow these general rules:

- they still have to have their playtime in the cot
- they can't have their afternoon milk feeds early
- they don't get to go to bed earlier that night, or sleep more at another sleep window because they didn't sleep well that day.

Never compensate for poor sleep at the right time with extra sleep at the wrong time. That means don't let them sleep in the next morning because they are tired after a poor night. The idea is that if they need more sleep their body has to take it when you offer it the following night or you only perpetuate more poor night, making them tired and unhappy. The night-time sleep cycle should be no longer than 11 to 11½ hours initially as anything more will detract from daytime sleep patterns and can encourage unsettled nights.

Helping a baby who vomits when they cry, day or night

While very few of you will need to read this section, for those of you suffering from this dilemma, I feel for you. Hang in there. I have included this section for you, to help you understand and help your little one if they have been suffering from this difficult situation.

This is possibly one of the most distressing things a parent will have to work through when sleep has gone astray. Fortunately, I have never had to address it when I implement an in-home sleep repair program, other than to correct a pattern of vomiting that is already pre-existing. These patterns of vomiting generally start with strategies that promote leaving a baby to cry in their cot as the only way of managing the sleep problems. Control crying strategies used in isolation do not address the real reason for the anxiety or stress the child feels in the cot. The entire premise of control crying as a single strategy (new routine or not) is designed to address a behaviour-based problem, where a child is supposedly trying to be resistant or manipulative. That is never the case, however. Not surprisingly, a baby put through such rigorous and thoughtless strategies can get so distressed that they vomit. Once a pattern of vomiting occurs, it often becomes a repeated pattern that takes patience and hard work to correct.

Obviously, the first step is to address your child's actual settling, resettling and waking routines, then look carefully at independence issues, and encourage their comfort and confidence in the cot environment. This is done through cot play (see page 175) and independent floor play through the day (see page 143). Assessing their level of comfort with a parent-governed line of communication being used is often the one area that needs the most work. A parent with a vomiting baby at sleep time needs to have thoroughly read and started to work through their communication throughout the day long before ever trying to teach their little one to self-settle. Once you have assessed the overall needs of your baby (see 'Dream Baby Profile' page 5), and worked hard to empower your little one with better coping skills, then you will need to embark on repairing your little one's sleep-time difficulties, just like any other family would. You will only need to take some extra precautions, and use some additional crying-support strategies to help you and your little one avoid vomiting wherever possible or gently manage it with care and confidence.

Understanding the triggers of vomiting at sleep time

There is most definitely more than one trigger of vomiting at sleep time. Obviously every baby is different but for most they can fit into four main causes:

- stress and anxiety
- physiological reasons
- accidental
- attention seeking.

For each trigger, there are some things to consider before beginning to repair sleep. For all triggers, however, there are some environmental things that must be added to help you and your little one move past this situation and achieve sleep quickly.

Stress and anxiety around the conditions of sleep create an elevated level of crying which can easily result in vomiting. This can often be identified by a baby becoming stressed to the point of gagging or vomiting when they enter their room or during a role-play scenario. This kind of vomiting is almost always the result of control crying where their anxieties had not been addressed and misinformation was given to the parents or the strategy used by someone who was not truly knowledgeable about the area of sleep repair in children under five. This vomiting pattern could also happen during the awake portion of the day if the child is exposed to a situation they find stressful. For example, when you are driving and they have started crying to be picked up and you have been unable to oblige this request for safety reasons or otherwise, they may become so elevated in their crying and stressed that they vomit.

A physiological reason would be when a certain cry—usually an angry cry—will vibrate and cause the gag reflex or dry out their throat and trigger vomiting. This can often be identified by a baby almost spontaneously vomiting when they cry out with a low angry yell like a vibrating raspy cry, or after crying or calling out at a lower level without the phenomenon occurring, with any sudden increase in intensity then being enough to result in a sudden vomit. The other common physiological trigger can be a baby that overproduces saliva or mucus in their mouth or nose. This too can often cause coughing and spluttering and, in some more extreme cases, vomiting. You will know your baby has this potential because any attempt, assisted or not to get them to sleep when it did not suit them, would have resulted in some very messy crying sessions where they would cough and splutter on the excessive mucus. This can be stressful for them, so needs to be managed carefully.

Accidental vomiting is more common in babies over 12 months. Some babies will automatically put three or four fingers down in their mouth and rest them on their tongue or hold their bottom jaw while they cry. This is a pattern that often happens from a younger age and would happen if you are holding them or not. It's just their way of crying. These babies are less likely to swallow their saliva as they cry and will either aspirate or inhale the pooling fluid, causing them to cough and vomit. Alternatively, the fingers in the mouth with loud crying or calling out accidentally trigger vomiting because the fingers make them gag. The child does not know it is their fingers triggering the vomiting so do not know to stop doing that when they cry.

Attention seeking is almost always reserved for the 18 month or older age group and often starts off quite innocently. Perhaps the baby had a virus that resulted in vomiting and, after the virus stopped, the vomiting behaviour remained. This can be identified by a child vomiting for one parent only, for instance, or by it becoming a natural part of the tantrum (frustration) process, or by a child spontaneously being able to vomit without crying. Often, if the parent attempts to ignore the pattern, the child will point out the vomit in a bid to achieve a response. It's important to understand that this is not a child being manipulative, but ultimately they are simply (as unpleasant and difficult as it is) expressing themselves in another way.

Each type of vomiting needs a slightly different approach. Prevention before management is my motto, however. Empower their emotional tool kit through the day first. Stress- or anxiety-based vomiting needs to be addressed through communication, solid role-play opportunities for one to two weeks, through predictability in the settling, resettling and waking routines and gentle reassurance and consistent crying support. It's also vital to offer some kind of physical security, be it swaddling and a SafeT Sleep, or just the tuck-in technique if they are older. These little ones will need to be managed carefully during the settling routine so you can stay consistent and help them to find a better way to go to sleep as quickly as possible. This is vital because they shouldn't have to ever feel this way about sleep.

> You should start to make progress within a couple of days if you are consistent.

Physiology-based vomiting needs to be addressed with the above strategy, plus a pre-emptive cry management (see page 694). It is important that you address the reason your little one gets so upset when you guide them at sleep time by ensuring you find plenty of opportunities to guide them gently through the day. These opportunities always appear at nappy change, getting dressed, the car seat, high chair or quiet sitting on your lap. They come up around being asked to play on their own or not being picked up while you are washing the dishes. When you can master the language that will help your child accept your guidance through the day without getting to a loud cry, then they will be far more comfortable with your guidance at sleep time resulting in fewer tears and therefore creating less likelihood of vomiting.

Accident-based vomiting is sometimes a little difficult to work toward eliminating through the day simply because sometimes some babies only have their fingers in their mouth at sleep time and not during the day. This is often because the baby has been taught that when they feel the tired sensation they should have something in their mouth (breast or bottle). The obvious choice for a baby is to put their little fingers in their mouth in an attempt to sooth themselves to sleep. If your child puts their fingers in their mouth it's important you try to discourage the pattern. Simply remove their hand and say 'Hands out of mouth' and then define that statement with patience. You should start to make progress within a couple of days if you are consistent. Other times, despite your best consistent encouragement, this is your baby's way of simply being themselves and you will have to wait until they get used to the settling routine rather than hope to stop the fingers in their mouth triggering vomiting through those first few assisted self-settles. This means that there may be episodes of fingers in their mouth, and you will need to manage this and support them until you achieve sleep. Within one to three days they will be at ease with the request to go to sleep, and the need to comfort themselves with fingers in their mouth will pass as they are now comfortable with the new, predictable sleep routines.

Attention-seeking-based vomiting needs to be addressed through the day first. Looking at managing daytime attention-seeking vomiting is always about remaining calm, and not creating a valuable currency in the behavioural pattern when it occurs. With any attention-seeking behaviour, it is simply the attention that it receives that perpetuates the pattern. Regardless of your interpretation of the attention style you offer (often people think being cross is a deterrent, for example), attention in any form is still attention. It's important to note that at this very young age, your child will not understand anger and, therefore, trying to be firm, cross, or any form of management like that, is entirely fruitless and serves to do little more than exacerbate the situation further.

Once you have addressed the pattern of behaviour through the day they should have less propensity to attempt this style of communication at sleep time. Unfortunately, however, if this is a part of their dialogue repertoire, it does not guarantee you will eliminate it from being a part of your child's communication when first attempting to put them to sleep. Manage your sleep time and repair your sleep quickly to move past this.

For all triggers of vomiting at sleep time

The bulk of the work then lies in your preparation so your little one feels totally familiar with the new settling routine, has had a chance to get confident with being in their cot awake, and has developed a trust in you leaving the room for short intervals. In addition to lots of completely predictable role play and confident parent-governed lines of communication so your baby can trust and accept your loving guidance, this creates the strong foundation for a quick transition into a new, relaxed sleep routine within one to three days.

Any baby or toddler who has had to learn how to put *themselves* to sleep when they feel tired has only achieved this with a little bit of practice, and that has often entailed a little bit of crying. You should not be afraid of this crying because you should expect your child to express themselves, and you would always assist them with your regular visits and resettling routine and cues until they are comfortable to go to sleep on their own.

The bulk of clients see an almost complete turn around within three days with baby or toddler going through the program, but often a baby with a complication as significant as vomiting at sleep time needs a little longer to settle down. I would always suggest you try to seek professional help regarding your plan before commencing any program. Once your plan is in place, it is then time to prepare for a smooth management and transitioning from their old way of settling, into a new and more peaceful routine. This means you may need to jump some hurdles on that first settle or two to remain consistent, smooth and contained in how you manage the situations, and continue to support them while requesting sleep.

Managing the vomiting

It will take you a while to get everything organised to deal with the vomiting so plan ahead and make sure you're not rushed on the day you start:

- Put three sets of bedding layered on the cot mattress, each layer being a mattress protector, fitted sheet and beach towel, so if you need to strip the bed then there is another layer underneath without you having to remake the bed and create more disruption.
- Have a plastic sheet on the bedroom floor that goes under your baby's cot and out into the room, then place a towel over the top of that.
- Have a supply of large towels handy in case you need to change the floor towels.
- Have some small towels in the main bathroom ready to assist your baby if you need to on the first night or two while you establish the new pattern.
- Have a supply of extra nappies, long-sleeved T-shirts and long, light, cotton pants in the main area of the house so you can take a change of clothes in with you rather than be scrambling around in the dark looking for them.
- Have a little wash basket outside your child's bedroom door.
- Try to have another wrap or comfort item handy just in case you need one.
- Have a large beach towel or even a bowl out in the storytelling area in case your little one feels unsettled by the concept of sleep when they start to understand the flow. That way you can just carry on and not overreact or break the flow of your storytelling. While this has only happened once for me with a very stressed baby, having the bowl ready allowed us to calmly managed the way we felt and reassured them with our calmness through the storytelling process. It enabled us to move past

this vomiting within one day. It's important to note that even in this more extreme case, where the baby boy had been throwing up upon entering his room for nearly three months prior to me being contacted, his sleep-time anxiety was fully repaired within 24 hours. Stay confident, and work smoothly and calmly through the situation to help your little one calm down and rely on your comfort and reassurance, rather than become more frightened by your reaction to their concerns.

In my experience, I tend to see really stressed children throw up once or twice during the storytelling and in their cot once or twice. After this, which happens within the first 24 to 48 hours all the symptoms settle down, and the stress is alleviated by the comfort the predictable routine provides.

As no lights can be on in their room, only dimmed lights from the hallway or a distant bedroom should be used, and while it may be a little difficult to see, you should be okay to work quickly by this light when following the instructions.

When they are in your arms

Continue your singing or cues and don't even change the tone of your voice. Lean your little one when they throw up so it goes anywhere but on themselves, you or the cot, and carry on with your routine. Break your flow to say a gentle 'oops, little vomit, mummy wipe you' then wipe their little face momentarily *as you continue* to sing and go on with the entire routine as calmly as normal. This means your little one can vomit if they feel a little stressed and you can reassure them that they are okay by staying calm.

If they are in the cot

Walk in armed with a change of clothes, a damp cloth to wipe them and a dry cloth to wipe the cot bars and throw these towels in the wash basket at the door while you assess the environment. If they have only thrown up on the floor then fold the towel on the floor and throw it into the basket outside their door and replace the towel. Then simply lie them back down and carry on with your resettling routine.

If they have thrown up a little on themselves or the cot and you can wipe it and just remove the beach towel, then that is fine. Say 'Oops, little vomit, mummy / daddy wipe it'. Even if it leaves a few little damn spots, that is less disruptive than to completely change them and their bedding (when it is warmer, those small patches will dry quickly). Wipe down the cot bars quickly, then simply lie them down and carry on with your resettling routine. At no point do you get them out of the cot.

If they have thrown up significantly then say 'Oh dear, Ruby had a vomit, mummy fix it. Sit down, mummy change you.' Then start with the bedding. Ask them to sit, or place them at one end of the cot as they are not to get out. They can wait at one end while you strip the other end of bed and strip them down. Give them a quick wipe down and wipe the bars. Move your little one to the dry, clean end of the bed and take the soiled bedding and clothing to the wash basket outside the door. Tell your baby 'It's time to get dressed, time for sleep, mummy and daddy love you'. Dress them quickly in the cot, while repeating your cues. Lie them down once you have said 'lie down' and carry on with the resettling routine as normal.

If you would like to offer them a sip of water, it needs to be within the process of the changing and reassuring and it should be predictable for them so it doesn't become too much of a child-governed line of communication during the resettling routine. Before you redress them, always instigate that drink time with 'have a drink for mummy please, bubba' and complete that drink time with 'ta for mummy' so you can retain the communication stream to ensure you aren't being inconsistent or confusing. You need to be careful about retaining this line as to not keep it would only result in tears.

Additional crying support

Some babies vomit when their voice / pitch or the vibration of the vocalisation reaches a certain point. This might be an angry yell for a toddler, or a high-tone cry for another. It's different for all babies but the one constant thing is that it is always a certain cry that triggers the vomit and rarely would they vomit unless it is triggered during that particular vocalisation. These little ones could cry for ten minutes without a problem because they don't make the sound that triggers their gag reflex. Yet, at another time they could make that sound and immediately throw up in as short a window as ten seconds. This could happen in their cot, their pram, in your arms or anywhere when your child goes into that type of trigger cry. It is fairly common for accidental vomiters to do so when they get upset in their car seat as they are often asking the same thing—'pick me up', or 'I want to be upright'—and often getting the same response—'you cannot be upright at this particular time'. This is often similar to what happens at sleep time when a parent is trying to nurse, rock, pat or settle a baby to sleep. This is why practising and becoming comfortable with positioning is vitally important for these little ones in particular.

Obviously then, in this situation, your role is to identify the cry that always precedes your child's vomiting and enter the room quickly but calmly and follow your resettling routine as per usual. This means that you should be waiting outside their door but be sure that they cannot see you, or hear you during the pause. Try to wait as long as you can but, as soon as you hear their trigger cry, step in and close the door behind you and carry on with resettling as usual.

Vomiting is generally a condition that goes away as their little body becomes less responsive and sensitive to the vibrations that certain cries make to stimulate the gag reflex. The purpose of this is to train the gag reflex to be less responsive to normal cries, so it's important to allow them to express themselves naturally through the day. You respond with your usual crying-support strategy. This means that you are only immediately responsive to this particular cry when you know they might vomit at sleep time. Remember, though, when your little one has been asleep all night and has woken early there will probably not be as urgent a need for this pre-emptive intervention as their tummy will be empty.

Troubleshooting

Q If they have been sick, can I take them out of their cot?

A Whenever possible you need to make the management as smooth and uncomplicated as you can. Because you need to be extremely cautious to not teach them that they need to vomit to be picked up, always go out of your way to change them and the bedding and clean the cot while they remain in their cot.

Q My baby did a very big vomit. Should I feed her again?

A No, simply carry on as usual. It is your child's overall food intake through the day that will impact on their hunger, not the last meal or milk feed of the day as many believe. If you have achieved a good breakfast and a decent lunch and made sure that they are well hydrated they will be fine. They will keep throwing up if you keep filling their tummy.

Q How can I be sure it's not teething that is making them put their fingers in their mouth?

A This is a good question. It is such a common enquiry and my answer is always the same. Did they suddenly start to teeth when you put them to bed? If they have not been exhibiting this behaviour during the day, and they have not been teething through the day, then teething is not the cause of this behaviour. Fingers in the mouth for crying is common. If your little one is teething, you are more likely to hear from them in the middle of the night between 11.30 p.m. and 1.30 a.m. or 2.30 and 3.30 am. If your baby has been teething through the day, then offer pain relief or teething gel half an hour before bed time, and keep the doses up at any required attendances through the night. This is appropriate and fair.

Q Can I offer them a drink of water after they have been sick?

A If you offer water, do it using a spill-proof cup. Make sure you retain the parent-governed line of communication by saying 'Have a drink for mummy', and when they have finished say 'Ta for mummy, mummy take the cup'.

Q My child is asking for things (food, drink, milk, toys, other parent, etc.) when they are sick. What should I do?

A Just as in any normal resettling routine, don't negotiate at sleep time while you teach them how to go to sleep without crying. If you allow for negotiations at sleep time, you no longer hold the governing line of communication and this will only result in elevated crying when you ask them to go to sleep. As with any resettling routine, there is a very clear, loving and gentle routine that you do not deviate from. If they have been sick, you can offer water as highlighted above, then carry on with your resettling routine.

Q In the morning, when my baby wakes, they go into that trigger cry but don't vomit. Do I still need to pre-empt it and rush in?

A No. Only respond to their cries as described in crying interpretation support and management (see page 694).

When the long three-week settling period is over

Finally you have reached the time in the routine management where you can predict your baby almost by your watch and everything has settled into a smooth, relaxed rhythm. It's time to sweep away the eggshells and gradually reintroduce normal household sounds into their sleep times. When it is time to introduce noise, don't go out and deliberately make a lot of noise because you want them to get used to it. All you need to do is not be too worried about chatting near their room or as you wander around the house.

For the most part, just be considerate. Think of your baby as you would a houseguest who is really tired and needed to go and take a nap, and if you are using a white noise CD it will take care of the rest. Gradually over time it will be fine to reduce the volume setting of the white noise CD so it is just audible. If, however, your little one is particularly sensitive to noise and you notice that they are stirring more frequently, keep the volume up high for another three months and then try again.

Just remember that they are your greatest fan, so if they hear you talking they will naturally want to come and be with you. Be cautious of the obvious sounds that they will know are yours, such as loud kitchen clatter and cleaning, walking down the hall, flushing the toilet, or showers.

This is the time that you can also start to relax about when and where you take them. Obviously the rule of 'no sleep outside routine sleep times' applies, and, of course, their routine sleep and meal times still apply, but you can choose to give them any of their day sleeps in the car, in the pram or at another house. I always suggest that if you plan on having them sleep somewhere else at night or for that dominant daytime sleep then make sure they have familiar smells around them—worn cot sheets or perhaps one of your used pillow cases placed under their fitted cot sheets should do the trick. Be absolutely consistent with their settling routine and your cues and your support of them while they settle. This is their framework that says it's sleep time so they will need this to be the same in order to go to sleep and stay asleep.

The framework of the settling routine is language based and designed to be used anywhere. Predictability is what makes children comfortable. One of the biggest mistakes you can make is to change their environment *and* their settling routine. The whole world around them can change, but if you stick to the language framework of your settling routine, they have predictability and they can cope.

Now you can go back to having dinner parties and street parties but know that the reality of having a young baby is that they are often disturbed by loud laughter and talking. Don't be tempted to bring them out if they wake to show them off, regardless of the peer pressure you may receive, unless you are really confident with retaining a parent-governed line of communication so you can pop them back to bed. Remember that it takes three weeks of consistent management to lock in a good sleep pattern and just one inconsistent resettle to confuse them and create problems again.

You will need to settle them as usual using the crying-support technique I have shown you. If you are not prepared to maintain management in front of other people because you are concerned about their reaction, then you will need to rethink having guests over until your child is a little bit older. For the most part they will learn quite quickly that your expectations won't change and they will settle themselves off as usual.

I always suggest that five out of seven main daytime sleeps should be in their cot until you are well-practiced and confident in settling them. There is a seven-day theory: one in seven will be a little unsettled—so don't over-analyse if one day is not so good.

You should stay on your toes for the next three months. Be cautious that everyone involved in settling your child is informed of their routine management. If you have not trained them into the settling techniques and support of crying strategies, they should not be putting your baby to bed. They can undo all the good work you have done and will be doing your baby no favours changing things around when they are just too little to understand.

After all those months of no sleep or stress around going to bed, and the time and effort that you and your baby have put into your routine management it is always a tremendous relief to finally have your baby sleeping. I find, however, that this can make the relieved mums or dads very tentative about introducing the settling routine to the other parent. I can understand this, but now is the time to get brave. If you have not already introduced the settling routine to the other parent, then you must do it by the three-week mark. Remember, the parent who hasn't done any settling will need to role play several times in front of bubby and have talked constantly with you about the settling routine before they can confidently put baby to bed for day sleeps first. Once they are confident with the day-sleep settling, you can start to settle your little one on alternate nights.

> Just remember that they are your greatest fan, so if they hear you talking they will naturally want to come and be with you.

The general rule of keeping your baby active in the morning should always apply, as they will have good, solid night sleeps from now on. If you plan to go away and sleep somewhere new they should always have their own room; it is too difficult for babies to sleep in the same room as their parents and a lot of my clients' problems started on holidays when the baby shared a room with them.

Relaxing the routine

Once you and your partner have established a trustworthy, reliable, consistent parent-governed line of communication around sleep you will have earned the freedom to be more flexible. There will soon come a time when you won't always be able to, or you may not want to, put your child to bed at their designated sleep time because of an appointment or special occasion. This is obviously essential for most families but still very much a break from 'the norm' when it comes to a sensitive sleeper. This is fine to do, and I do encourage people to explore their little one's coping boundaries as the entire premise of this management strategy is designed to help you learn how to communicate with your little one about sleep time so they can go to sleep when you ask, and you can relax about when you put them to bed.

The entire program is designed to help you know how much sleep your baby is capable of taking and, therefore, help you plan day sleeps appropriately so you can avoid problems that night. It will also give you the insight into knowing exactly what might happen when your child doesn't sleep their usual amount, and how best to recover the following day, so you don't have to see your baby or toddler unsettled and tired for days. I always suggest that a LSR baby can be placed on a modified HSR routine (one hour, 15 minute sleeps) to accommodate special times such as for a party or christening, or on a day when you regularly go out, such as to church. Just be sure to return to your usual routine the following day. Equally, a HSR baby can be placed on a modified LSR routine (30 to 40 minute bridge naps) to accommodate a special occasion, but be sure to return to your usual routine the following day and maintain it to recover quickly.

Coping with illness while they are learning how to sleep

It is quite common for a child who is suddenly sleeping for the first time in their entire life to get a cold, particularly a child who was sleeping very poorly before the program began. It's not unlike the response our body has when you go on a holiday after being a little run down and not as well rested as you should be. If this does occur and your little one only gets a cold, offer relief medication half an hour before sleep times, and through the night at regular intervals for the first few days of the illness, and carry on with your program as per normal. You may need to use saline drops and an aspirator to clear their nose before feeds or before they go to bed.

If on the other hand, your baby suddenly gets a serious tummy bug or a painful ear infection or a sudden raging temperature, then naturally, you should stop if you little one is clearly not coping and needs help. It's not uncommon for a baby who is not well to just want to sleep, so you may choose to continue on your new routine flow as usually, but if they are sleeping more or looking tired then do not wake them and allow then to wake naturally. If you are unable to put them down without offering assistance, then once you do change the way you manage your baby at sleep time, and become their way of them going to sleep or back to sleep, I strongly suggest that you *stop* using the usual settling and resettling routines and *stop* using the new language cues as you do not want to taint them.

Always remember that the definition you give language, by the actions you take once you make a statement, is what defines each word or statement, and you do not want to confuse your baby and tell them that your new settling cues also mean you are going to stay and pat them, etc. To do this would cause your cues to become unuseable, inconsistent streams of communication that your child will associate only with your help, and this alone will stress your baby once they recover and you try to go back to your new self-settling routine. This means, if they are really unwell and you cannot leave them, you are best to sleep on the couch with them so as to not confuse them about expectations in their cot. You would say something like 'Takoda feels sick, mummy help you fall asleep'. The important thing to note here is that as soon as they have 'started' to recover, you return to your program, and follow through as usual.

Coping with illness once your child has learnt how to sleep so you do not lose sleep again

It has always been important that you take the time to establish settling and resettling routines to give you the freedom to come and go from a child's room so you can check temperatures and offer medication without causing your baby distress when you leave again. It's so important that I urge you to invest a little bit more time into your parent-governed, language-based sleep-time conditions so you have this freedom for management of mild and common illness.

First and foremost, you need to use your instincts when it comes to your child's illness.

Obviously if they have the common cold, are teething, or are generally off colour then it's important to retain their normal routine. Offer them prolonged discomfort relief in the form of approved medicines for sleep time only, if that is possible. Try and give it to them half an hour before you plan to put them to bed and help them to settle down with regular attendances, when you can repeat your cues up to four times if they are having a little trouble when you put them to bed initially. Ensure that you keep the pain relief doses up (as per the instructions on the medication) through the night time if they are inclined to get upset during the night. Be mindful of typical discomfort windows and align medication relief to be at its best through those windows.

The most important thing to maintain during the day is hydration, and there is certainly nothing to be concerned about if they indicate that they do not have an appetite for food. This is generally the body's way of focusing on healing rather than digestion and growth, and should be accepted. If, on the other hand, you know that they are finding swallowing painful because of an ear infection, blocked nose or sore throat, offering pain relief 30 minutes before a meal is important so they can eat, and is always a considerate thing to do.

Making sure they have the opportunity to drink and stay hydrated (through water and even juice if they are not eating terribly well) is important, as is making sure they are in the best possible position to eat by offering their favourite food, food that is easy, and in a very casual way with distractions around. When dealing with colds, tilting the bed can help, and a vaporiser is extremely useful to reduce coughing if you keep the room slightly warmed (if it is appropriate to do so without overheating your little one), and then of course water and sleep are the final keys to healing.

If, however, they are running a new significant temperature and you don't know the cause, I suggest you keep vigil. If they are very hot, lying in bed with two hot bodies is not going to help them. You're best to stay in their room with them and help them go to sleep that way. If you have any doubt about their condition at any stage during the night always seek medical help. You have nothing to lose by asking some advice from a qualified professional.

> At the end of the day you will have to use your instinct and / or a doctor to determine whether you think they are recovering or not.

All through history there are tales of parents sitting up by their children all night while they were unwell, and this is still a very normal part of parenthood. The important thing to remember is that they would have to be quite unwell to need that kind of attention. Do not apply this sleep support to all forms of common illness. If they are that unwell, no doubt you would have already taken them to the doctor.

While they are unwell you may choose to put on less clothing or allow them to sleep longer in the morning or take all the sleep they want at whatever time during the day. If they have an ear infection, laying flat can be painful. Always prop their mattress up and give them pain relief at the times suggested on the bottle for their age. Just remember that *as soon* as they start to get better, get back on track.

It is important that as soon as you start to see a change in their condition, as soon as they start to get better, you put your little one straight back on to your routine. Don't wait until they have fully recovered as by then bad habits can reform and you will have a bigger job on your hands than normal. If you can keep the routine as close to normal as possible, then it is best to do so. Expect that there will be a few little battles to overcome when you initially go back to your normal routine but your success will lie in how consistent and clear you are on the first day back into the routine. It should only take a day to get them back on track, maybe two or three at the most, but if you try to introduce things gradually or in bits and pieces it will all go pear-shaped on you (spoken from experience). You need to be consistent to help them recover and start to sleep peacefully free of confusion.

At the end of the day you will have to use your instinct and / or a doctor to determine whether you think they are recovering or not. From my experience, parents have an amazing sixth sense when it comes to their baby; always listen to your intuition when it comes to illness.

22
SURE sleep

As adults, we find the prospect of travel a thrilling and wonderful thing and are able to anticipate with excitement a different environment. But babies and young children, who are such creatures of habit and who love to feel in control of their surroundings simply by being able to predict them, sleeping elsewhere can be a very challenging task. This is why I always suggest, to make it as easy as possible and to help your baby be as flexible as possible, a language-based framework during their normal event and daily routines. This means your baby relies predominantly on your communication and a transportable series of actions around any normal daily event, like a settling routine for instance, so you can literally pick up their predictable framework and take it with you anywhere you go.

A language-based framework means you use your flow of communication around typical times of the day like sleeping, bathing, eating, nappy changes, getting dressed, going out and playtime. This ensures your child does not become heavily dependent on the home environment as the only set of visual conditions in which they feel comfortable when given a particular request. Just because there is a cot in a new room does not mean the child understands that that new room and cot are somewhere you would like them to sleep. The same goes for a foreign high chair, an unfamiliar change mat or a tent, caravan or cabin that they have never been in before.

Classic language-based routines that are transportable and that have been discussed in this book include:

- your flow of communication to keep them well informed
- the settling, resettling and waking routine for sleep time
- your sit down / lie down cues for the car seat, pram, high chair and change table, bath, etc.
- the role-play game and teddy-bear attachment.

In addition to the communication needs of your child being provided for, you also need to ensure you cater for the environmental needs of your baby in a new place. You do this by:

- making the sleep environment smell familiar by using their two-days' worn and unwashed cot sheets, pyjamas, wraps and comfort items, and placing one of mum's or dad's used pillow cases under their fitted sheet to allow familiar, safe smells to permeate the cot environment
- getting them used to their travel cot at home before you use it in a foreign environment
- having environmental aids that are transportable
- creating a darker environment or darkening a room elsewhere so they are less likely to wake up and, forgetting they are somewhere new, become disorientated. The best thing to do is to limit their view of the foreign room for the first two days.

Once you are comfortable that you have developed trust in their language-based settling routines and listening skills at home, and you have catered for the environmental needs of your child by making sure the room smells and feels familiar to them, you must always prepare and orientate them when you arrive at the new destination. They should see their familiar travel cot constructed, or their bed made with their usual things once they are eight months plus. They need to be told it's their cot for nigh' nigh's. By making a statement like 'look, William's cot for nigh' nigh's', or 'oh, nice cot, this is William's time for sleep cot', then he will quickly understand the statement because these words are a small of part of their usual settling cues: 'time for sleep', 'mummy and daddy love you, nigh' nigh's'. This means you are able to talk to your child, and explain that this is where they will be sleeping well before you put them to bed, and this alone goes a long way towards being able to settle them when they go to bed awake.

The second thing you always do is role play a full settling routine with your baby. I find role playing is essential from around six to eight months onwards. This gives your child an opportunity to become familiar with the going-to-sleep process, learn that they can not only predict you, but pre-empt and ultimately feel in control of the settling process because it is so familiar. Role play is really the only way you can accurately explain something to a child under two years of age. It gives them an opportunity to indirectly experience the exact scenario they will encounter at sleep time in the new environment while you are still holding them. They can see and experience going to sleep in a new room with all the familiar environmental conditions by listening to the usual songs, seeing their teddy being tucked in, and hearing their normal settling cues, then see where you will be once you leave the room. This gives you a valuable opportunity to express that you are happy and confident while you put teddy to bed in this new environment. This is one of the most important messages you can pass on to your baby or toddler. If mummy and daddy are okay, then they can relax and trust the new situation with ease.

> Just because there is a cot in a new room does not mean the child understands that that new room and cot are somewhere you would like them to sleep.

Always remember that role play is a predictable pattern, and like anything else that is predictable in early childhood, it becomes a thoroughly enjoyable game and the associations linked to the settling process as a result are often feelings of warmth, fun and relaxation simply because they know the scenario so well. Just as a child develops a strong sense of pleasure around a familiar book, toy or routine with a grandparent or parent, taking the time to establish and present a predictable game around teaching them the settling process can make bedtime in any environment an absolute breeze.

In this encyclopaedia I'm going to give you more practical information to help you guide your little one in the following scenarios:

- moving room / house
- sleeping when out—car sleep, pram sleep, plane sleep, or sleeping in your arms
- sleeping in hotels / other houses
- adjusting to daylight saving
- changing time zones
- going back to work / others caring for your child.

Moving room / house

While some babies and toddlers may not be terribly bothered by all the commotion and stress of moving room or house, others will find this a very challenging time. It can be particularly difficult because unpredictability is what makes them feel insecure. Their entire universe under the age of two years generally consists of their primary carers (those living with, and taking full-time care of them) and the room they sleep in and the house they live in. When they start to predict the flow of behaviour of the people in the house, they feel relaxed. When that suddenly changes, it can leave them feeling insecure, and you find they need to cling on to adults in order to feel more comfortable when experiencing unfamiliar events and environments.

Based on this knowledge, imagine how it must feel when the whole house is being prepared and packed ready for the big move. Not only is the environment changing, but a parent is no longer following their usual routine. They are usually busy racing around doing important sorting and preparing for the big move. The normal flow of the day is disrupted with phone calls, packing boxes and rushed-feeling days. This is the perfect recipe for an unsettled and clingy baby, and disrupted sleep is almost always a by-product. The following steps will help you calm your baby, keep them well informed and ultimately help you maintain sleep through a house move:

- keep them well informed of what is going to happen using your flow of communication—break it down to small ten-minute increments of the day if they appear stressed
- in the lead up to the move, visit the new house as often as you can
- start to talk about your homes in 'Drew's new house' and 'Drew's old house' terms as you visit and manoeuvre between them so your child has a sense of which 'home' they are going to
- always sound very positive and happy about the 'Drew's new house'
- if your child is 12 months plus, allow them to see you packing away their room to go to 'Drew's new house'
- if they are 18 months old or more, allow them to pack a box with their favourite things to take in the car to the new house
- try to have someone care for them on the day of the actual move so they don't need to be a part of the stress, or take them away and allow others to move you
- set up your child's main areas of the new house first:
  - make their room look and feel as close to their old cot room as possible—you can change it around later if you like, but for the initial few days, it's nice for them to have predictability
  - always make the cots with used sheets, and dress them in used sleepwear, wraps and comfort items so they have familiar smells when settling down the first night

- prepare the bedroom so it will be darker than the old room for the first week or so to help prevent them from becoming confused when they first wake up and forget they are in a new house
- set up the lounge room and play areas next
- be sure to get the kitchen and their eating environment organised for their feeding times

- introduce them to the new set up before you expect them to sleep, play or eat in that new environment, and sound really enthusiastic
- role play your sleep settling routine with teddy several times before you put them to bed in their new room the first time
- stay with them to play during morning play sessions for the first few days if they are a little unsure, and really enjoy exploring their new environment together
- keep them close until they are ready to move away from you rather than just expecting them to be fine
- stay confident and relaxed, even if they are feeling a little stressed, because your response to the environment will tell them if their feeling of concern is shared by you or not—even if they are feeling a little unsettled, you will need to be the one who lets them know that everything and everyone is okay because you indicate that you are okay; to fret openly when they fret or it will lead them to think that there is definitely something to be concerned about. Be their rock, and stay positive and encouraging until they settle down
- be patient and attend to them as often as they need, but remain consistent. Their settling routine and your usual pattern of behaviour are the two truly predictable things left during a big change so don't change that on them too—most parents think they should be different as it's a new place, but this only unsettles a child even more.

Sleeping when out
Car sleep

Asking a child to sleep in the car is something that is achievable from six months of age if you continue to work with their normal settling routine, regular sleep times and your predictable communication. Most people just hope their baby will konk out once they start driving, but it is also possible to ask your little one to go to sleep, and help them to understand they need to do what they usually do to fall asleep but, this time, in the car. This is possible because you have taught them a clear set of language cues, and attached strong associations to those cues at home first through the use of a predictable settling routine. This means they understand you and know what to do.

Encouraging sleep time in the car is useful for many reasons. It is more pleasant for them on long trips to utilise their sleep time so the trip appears faster for them. It enables you to go on school runs with older siblings and means that, if you need to, you can communicate your desire for them to go to sleep, and they will actually try to go to sleep for you. The following tips will help you encourage sleep in the car:

- if you are planning a two- to three-hour car trip, leave it until their longest daytime sleep session
- tell them 'It's nearly time for nigh' nigh's' 'nearly time to sleep in car'
- do your normal settling routine at home before you leave, reminding them during the stories that it's 'nearly time for nigh' nigh's in mummy's / daddy's car'
- once you pop them in the car, buckle them in and offer their comfort items to them (teddy, dummy, dolly, etc.)—use a dummy chain and clip if they have a dummy, and encourage them to get their dummy by using the language cue 'get your dummy'
- they obviously can't be wrapped for a car trip so, once they are buckled in, snuggle the muslin around their legs and over them like a sheet—the familiar smell, texture and contact of it while you use your settling-routine language will trigger all the usual sleepy feelings
- say your settling-routine cues as normal, then close off all lines of communication once you have said your cues and hop in the car and begin your trip, being caution to stay quiet for a while until they drift off to sleep
- on a long trip, play their usual CD or one of their white noise CDs as these might trigger the old sleepy feelings
- if you have left earlier than their due sleep time and it is a family outing, get someone to sit in the back seat with them and keep them awake by playing and having some fun games until it's time to stop for lunch—if they are due morning tea, it can be had on the move (unless it is a breastfeed, naturally) but always try to stop for a leg stretch and little run around at lunch time, maybe in a café or park, before heading back to the car for their settling routine—after which both parents can be in the front seat again and can sit quietly, not talking to baby but quietly to each other, until bubby goes off to sleep
- if your child becomes upset, respond to their cries and communication as you normally would when assisting them to self-settle. If you do need

to offer some support and remind them it's sleep time you should only do it by singing your cues without turning around so you can always maintain your management if you are driving alone, without becoming distracted from watching the road

- continue to have appropriate crying pauses, and offer some support when necessary, but remember to always listen to what they are saying and assess the environment and request from an adult's perspective; stay confident, loving and calm until they settle down
- if they chat happily to themselves, don't worry, just relax and enjoy your trip knowing that they will eventually drift off to sleep
- when they wake up, wait your initial surface-sleep pause to ensure they are fully awake and not about to drift off back to sleep then use your usual waking cues and have a lovely chat with them so they know your sleep-time request is over
- if you plan on transferring them to a cot, if they wake when you stop the car, say 'Time for sleep' and carry on as usual with your settling routine. Be sure to have set up their room and wraps at home before you left, knowing you may come home and transition them into their cot—this is far more achievable at night than during the day but can be achieved in the day on a longer sleep window if they have not been asleep for too long (longer than one hour, 15 minutes)
- do not leave them unattended in the car—if you want them to continue sleeping, either take the scenic route until the sleep time is complete or stay in the vehicle with your child with the air conditioning running in a safe, well-shaded place until they wake up at the appropriate time
- make sure your little one is wearing sunscreen for long car trips, and provide a shade cloth on the window nearest them for both sun protection and from being blinded by glare
- bridging naps are great sleeps for the car when you have older children that need to be taken to school, even if you need to take a little detour to make your trip home a few minutes longer. It's a great opportunity to drop the children off, let your baby have their bridge nap until you arrive at the shops to get any little grocery items you may need for the day, then head home in time for morning tea.

Transferring your sleeping baby to and from your car

This is a fairly difficult task for some babies and toddlers to achieve during the day. Some transfer beautifully, others do not. Night transferring is far easier, simply because it is dark and during a baby's longest sleep sessions. Below are the strategies will make the movement of your little sleepyhead happen more calmly, but I strongly suggest you master the transfer method at night first, but always make sure your baby is able to go to sleep for you ordinarily with the settling routine and not cry if they are awake for a short period and ensure they can play happily in their cot before you attempt to transfer them during day sleeps. If they do wake up during the transfer for day sleeps, what you are aiming for is them lying in their cot quite contentedly until the end of their usual, natural sleep session.

Okay, so you're at your parent's house and your baby was bathed and put down for their usual 7 p.m. sleep time before all the adults settled down and ate together. The evening has come to an end, and it's now time to go home. You need to make sure your baby is disrupted as little as possible when getting them from a bed to the car. To do this, you need to say your goodnights to everyone, get yourself organised and pack your car before you go in and get your baby. When it's time to make the move, make sure just mummy and daddy are involved. Granny and grandpa are way too lovely and exciting to ensure your baby sustains sleep so they should have already said goodbye when they said goodnight before baby first went to bed. If you know your little one is sensitive, ask the adoring grandparents to peep at baby from a distance as you leave so your child can't see them.

As you pick up your baby quietly say 'Time for sleep' and hide their face in your neck while you cradle them to guard their eyes from light or other stimulation. If they are older, encourage them to lay their head on your shoulder by tucking their knees up on your chest and quietly whisper your cues to them. Don't worry if they wake up, just repeat your cues and calmly buckle them into their car seat telling them 'You're going home for nigh' nigh' in your cot'. This ensures they know your intention is to put them in their cot. If they stay asleep while you put them into the car, only quietly say your cues to them if they need it.

You will need to unwrap a swaddled baby first to pop them in their car seat, but just try to keep all stimulation, including talking and eye contact, to a minimum. Respond to any cries they have as you would if they were in their cot, and only use your language cues in the usual way of repeating them twice before staying quiet again and giving them an opportunity to settle down. The cues are meant to reassure them and remind them it's time for sleep, not designed as the tool to make them go to sleep. Only they can do that.

Remember, the more you fuss, the more they fuss; so be calm and consistent, and keep fussing and stimulation of any kind to a bare minimum. If they wake up fully and are happily looking around all the way home, don't worry; it's okay for them to have a little awake window, but if you become stressed about this they will pick up on your mood and will then become difficult to resettle. Remember: you have taught them through their settling routine that it's normal to go into their bed awake, so there is nothing to be anxious about if your baby wakes up during transfer. That is the beauty of developing a language-based self-settling routine that your child is fully empowered to cope with.

Before you left for your evening out you should have prepared their sleep environment, including wraps out on the bed, lights off, etc., so that everything is ready for your settling routine when you walk back into your house. When you arrive home, if they are asleep, just say your settling cues once as you lie them into their cot, then tuck them in as usual and whisper a gentle 'Nigh' nigh"—because you are always honest about leaving the room—then turn and leave, closing the door behind you. If they are awake when you get home, tell them 'It's time for sleep'. When you unbuckle them, either cradle them, shielding their eyes, or carry them, encouraging their head on to your shoulder, and only say your cues to them as you would after stories while you walk to their room, and nothing else. If they are awake, you pick up the settling routine from the point *after* you've read your books, and respond to any crying in the same way that you would during an ordinary settling routine. Please try to remember that once you have practised and mastered this for a good week or two at their usual bedtime, then your baby will be familiar with the routine, so there really should be no tears if you stay confident and remain consistent.

Remember, if they are asleep when you take them from the car, stay quiet and take them to their wrap environment to swaddle before going to their room, or take them directly to their room if not swaddling. Close the door and follow your normal settling routine. If they remain really very sleepy, then skip the song, and just follow your normal settling routine from the tuck-in or lying in the cot portion onwards. Only say your cues once before you leave. Manage any subsequence crying consistently with your usual resettling routine until they settle. Try to remember their Sleep Bus, and their surface-sleep window. Be realistic, if they do stir and become partially aware of their environment then you have ten minutes only to get them into bed and to leave them to get them to put themselves to sleep. If they do not resettle within the surface-sleep window, then please refer to the resettling Sleep Bus timetable for a realistic idea of how long your baby could stay awake for (see page 675).

> Remember, the more you fuss, the more they fuss; so be calm and consistent, and keep fussing and stimulation of any kind to a bare minimum.

Pram sleep

Just like car sleep, most people think it's pot luck if your baby or toddler falls asleep in the pram. But once you have established settling, resettling and waking routines, and your child understands the cues, without doubt you can step out and *ask* your baby or toddler to go to sleep for you on request, and they will be able to fall asleep with relative ease. This is communication with your baby, where you are able to tell them that they need a sleep, and they are empowered with the skills they need to take that sleep without stress. Almost every baby I have worked with, who has never slept in their pram before, is able to do so the first day I attempt pram sleep with their settling conditions if I remain calm and consistent with my routine, environment and support. This means sleep stops being hit-and-miss; it is a clear and simple request your precious little one will feel empowered to be able to do independently in any situation so long as you provide their predictable language-based routine.

If you have a child under 12 months of age who still needs a super-snuggly wrap for sleep time at home, then they will need the consistency of being wrapped in the pram too. Once they no longer need the wrap in their cot, they will no longer need the wrap in their pram. It's important to also relieve any stress to make the task of going to sleep easier by both reclining the pram and reducing visual stimulation completely. All under-two year olds should be given the consideration of having a pram that can be covered so they can go to sleep with as little disruption as possible. I always suggest you use two muslins in the initial training stage, one that is white and a second that is navy blue, to darken the pram by draping them over the pram. A mesh sun cover also has the added advantage of providing your child a clear signal that it's time for a little snooze, and they will learn to clearly read this sign. Once they are asleep, you can lift the mesh cover and allow them to sleep under the muslin. Remember, when a baby or toddler is tired they become extremely sensitive to stimulation, which is why they become so unsettled. Often, time in the pram is the most stimulating part of the day because there is so much to look at, so if you can reduce that distraction, a tired baby will be able to calm and settle themselves quickly.

A baby that knows how to go to sleep at home will happily chat to themselves or lie peacefully in the pram until they drop off to sleep. The golden rule of sleep in any new environment is to always ensure you have prepared your little one well. For pram sleep you make the environment clear to them, and ensure they understand your intentions and what you would like them to do. Any new sleep environment must feel familiar to them, and they must be able to cope with the skills required for sleeping or being in any particular environment. So before you ask your baby to sleep in the pram, help them be comfortable with just sitting in the pram on request, and being still (see page 316). Obviously sleeping in the pram is harder than sleeping in the cot, so they must be well versed with going to sleep in their cot with your settling routine at home before they experience the request to put themselves to sleep in the pram for the first time.

For those babies on a PRM routine, you will need to role play the settling routine with teddy in the pram—while at home—in much the same way that you would do for the settling routine in the cot, but cover the pram as opposed to closing the door during cot sleep-time role play. When you first try to help your little one sleep in the pram I usually suggest you stay close to home, and do it during a cooler time of the day. If you are outside, always walk in the shade so there is not too much direct light on the pram, and the pram stays cool for them. If it's too hot, perhaps head to a local mall that is air conditioned.

There is no need to use the full settling routine for the pram when you are out and about, but the use of your flow of communication (see page 40) and their normal settling cues and comfort items are important to help them predict the upcoming events. 'Nearly time for sleep, bubba, nearly time for nigh nighs' said five minutes before you begin your settling routine in the pram will be enough to help them be relaxed when you say 'It's time for sleep' at the beginning of their sleep time. Once the pram-settling routine (wrap, sing, cues, cover over) has been completed, if they continue to have a difficult time, use your normal resettling routine and cues and support of crying technique to help them settle down and accept the new sleep conditions.

If, however, you are planning on taking a walk around your local neighborhood, then you can do the full settling routine (see page 609) at home the first few times you attempt a pram sleep before following through with settling them in the pram, then saying your cues and covering them over. Be ready as this means you can head straight out the door and they are in the best possible position to go to sleep as the full settling routine will help them relax. I would always attempt this kind of settling routine for pram sleep before I attempt to settle them in a more foreign environment without the added benefit of calming them right down with books.

Always make sure you are ready to walk out the door as soon as you ask your baby to go to sleep. Have your shoes on, bags packed, house keys and mobile phone in your hand, or watch on, so you know the time. They will usually need to be walked off to sleep for a pram sleep, but if you can park your pram and they will self-settle without any serious difficulty then lucky you, and it should be encouraged too. This is not for every baby though, so don't feel that this is something you need to do. If you want to help them drift off to sleep in the pram for a deliberate pram sleep by pushing them in a covered pram then, by all means, go ahead.

If your only intention of settling them in the pram is to just teach them how to sleep in places other than their cot, before going on a holiday for instance, then once they are asleep you can park them quietly under a cool tree where you can see them, or stop at a coffee shop and let them snooze or even come home again and wheel their pram into their room for them to complete their sleep session in the pram. Because the pram is covered, the environment will not have changed. This means they are already used to sleeping in these conditions and, because they have learnt to sleep in their cot at other times of the day, these sleep associations will not be foreign. So they will be able to continue sleeping even if you park their pram in their room or under a tree. Always apply the pram brake when the pram is stationary, and never let them out of your sight if they are not in a house with you.

Try to always settle your little one in the pram to sleep for their normal sleep-time duration but be realistic. Babies do not sleep *as* well in their prams or any other environment as they do in their cot or usual sleep location. Always expect them to sleep about half the normal amount of sleep they would ordinarily take. If they sleep two and a half hours at home in their cot for instance, then expect about one hour, 15 minutes. Don't worry about the shorter sleeps, just stick to your normal daily routine and you will find they will be perfectly okay.

Pram sleep for an evening meal at a restaurant

If you are going out to dinner and you need to drive to the location of the restaurant, allow a little extra time so your baby or toddler can be walked off to sleep in the pram before you take them into the restaurant. Do not let them go to sleep in the car on the way to the restaurant as this could be seriously problematic for a baby who has previously has difficulty with settling. Take them out of the car once the pram is set up with their usual comfort items, including their sleeping bag, and then take your baby out of the car to wrap them, if doing so. If you have a car with a hatch back or door-opening rear, you can wrap them on a soft blanket in the back of the car and have lots of room to do so, otherwise wrap them in the pram. Ensure you use your usual pre-wrapping and wrapping language cues so your baby isn't fazed by the unfamiliar wrapping environment. Once wrapped, cradle them in your arms, say your settling cues and sing your settling song before asking them to 'lie down' and placing them in the pram.

Make sure you have all your bags ready and have locked the car before you say your goodnight cues so you can start walking as soon as you cover the pram. Once they are asleep (which won't take long—about five to ten minutes for a baby in a good routine) you can head to the restaurant and tuck their pram neatly beside you. I tend to choose an outside table in summer as it's a little quieter, or a corner table so they can be shielded from the bulk of the restaurant chatter by being placed near the wall.

If your baby wakes, try to leave them for the first five to ten minutes in the pram to resettle *if possible*, and then offer a gentle rock of the pram. If they cry quite loudly immediately, you can start to offer a gentle rock as soon as you deam necessary to keep them asleep. If you need to use your cues, then just pop your hand in under the cover and pat them and quietly shush and repeat your cues before continuing the pram rock. If they appear very awake and the chances of resettling them are remote, then you have a few choices. You can get them up using your waking cue and allow them to sit and play in their pram. Or, if you know they really need to sleep, someone could go for a bit of a stroll with baby until they drift off again. This is why it's always best to practise pram sleep, and park them quietly under a tree and read a book well before you brave a restaurant with a previously troubled sleeper. If your baby is generally not a troubled sleeper, then you will need to do a lot less preparation for this kind of event than others with sensitive sleepers.

Once you have enjoyed your meal out, and hopefully your little one has slept peacefully, remember to not over fuss. If they are sleeping, leave them be and don't keep peeping in or disrupting them. Once you need to transfer them back into the car, you will need to follow the instructions for car sleep above to transition from one sleep environment to the next. The biggest obstacle you face when it comes to helping your baby become flexible with their sleeping environment is your own fear of it not working. If you adopt an attitude of 'I'll give it a go, it can't hurt', then you can't really go wrong. You will then discover your child's true limitations and can plan around those. Some children are just better off sleeping in their cot peacefully with a babysitter than coming to a restaurant with you, but if you go on holiday, pram sleep is a really valuable skill to have taught them, and very achievable with a bit of persistence and practice for even a previously poor sleeper. There's also that 'my baby can sleep anywhere' thing that any mum or dad with a baby who can do this, is usually really proud of. It's just knowing that they can take their baby on a rare, fun night out that means the world to some, even when they don't go out very often, or dare I say it, ever!

Plane sleep, or sleeping in your arms

Once a daily settling routine has been established at home, one of the biggest problems most parents report is keeping their little one awake while they complete their routine song and tuck baby into bed. Well, plane sleep time is a perfect opportunity to utilise the soothing approach you have adopted at home to encourage your baby to calm down for sleep time, but this time you will allow them to fall asleep in your arms without putting them down. Getting a baby to sleep on a plane is usually a task most people find daunting but, really, there are only two positions in which they can go to sleep: in your arms or in a basinet if you are fortunate enough to get that spot on the plane. If you face a particularly long flight, it might be worth your while checking in online as soon as it opens or getting to the airport as early as possible to secure the bassinet seats, but if this is not possible it is easy to have your baby fall asleep in your arms.

> The biggest obstacle you face when it comes to helping your baby become flexible with their sleeping environment is your own fear of it not working.

There are many other occasions when it could be useful to hold your baby while they drift off to sleep: an evening concert like carols by candlelight, at a family barbeque where a pram sleep is not possible, a wedding reception, as well as sleep on a tour bus. To ensure you and your little one have an enjoyable flight, one of the most important things you can do is prepare them for the conditions they will encounter on the plane. Predominantly, position is the issue here. The most basic skill they will need is to know how to sit calmly on your lap and accept your guidance so you can entertain them, or they can entertain themselves. Remember that they will need to remain buckled at least for take off and landing, and whenever seated for safety reasons, so the ability to calmly sit will ensure there are no tears or stress for baby. Just as the ability to sit happily on your lap is vital for a peaceful and pleasant flight for both child, parent and other passengers, it is equally as important for your baby / toddler to be able to happily lie in your arms while you sing to them. This is one of the reasons I incorporate a song into my settling routines.

Before your little one settles in for a nice, long sleep in your arms, make sure you have been to the bathroom and you are good and comfortable so you can bear the full weight of your arm and baby. I always ask for a couple of flight pillows or blankets and get myself warm and cosy before the settling routine even begins. Use your pre-emptive language, 'nearly time for sleep', as you read them their stories. Complete your stories and pack away as usual, then get them to say goodnight to daddy or mummy or whoever is sitting next to them before putting on their sleeping bag or wrapping them casually on your lap if you are able to—it's a good idea to practise this at home so they are used to you wrapping them this way—then say 'Lie down' as you cradle them in your arms as for the usual settling-routine song. For safety reasons, always ensure their seat belt is fitted to yours and placed around them after they are zipped into their sleeping bag wrapped. Then you won't have to disturb them by putting it on mid sleep if the captain requests it. Draw the window blinds and drape a muslin over your shoulder and your little one so they are only able to see your face and the wall of the plane or the back of your seat if you are not near a window, then begin your settling song. As you sing ensure they stay lying in your arms, even if they resist for a little while until they drift off to sleep.

For any protests to be short lived or nonexistent on the plane, you must ensure you have been consistent with your routines at home first. If you know your little one is likely to resist you, there are a few positioning things you can practise at home first to minimise problems. Your child needs to be able to lie in your arms as you sing the settling song to them. They cannot get up again during or after the song, or insist on getting into their bed before the song is complete. Practise sitting on a chair in their bedroom for their song for a week prior to the flight so they are familiar with this request. Ensure you sing the song through twice fully before you place them in their cot. Be very consistent with your request to 'lie down' in your arms at home and be sure to define that statement with its true definition when it is just the two of you and they are in your loving home. This means any little challenges to sit up will have been worked through at home and they will happily accept your request to lie down for the song on the plane as a result. Ensure you have not created a situation where a child can negotiate endlessly about who is putting them to bed or they will chop and change settling parents ten times in ten minutes on the plane, and sleep will not come peacefully as a result.

On the plane, you will need to be consistent. Remember to not worry about others and what they may be thinking if your little one is having a temporary protest, even if it is a passionate and somewhat blush-making loud one. Carry on and know that they will settle down when they can see that this is one of those times when mummy and daddy are governing the situations calmly and consistently. Once they are asleep and settled, you can either place them calmly into their bassinet if you have one, or get them comfy on the pillows on your lap and free both your arms so you can eat, read or stretch.

Sleeping in hotels / other houses

Your settling routine at home is pivotal to your ability to transfer your request for your baby to go to sleep independently without tears in a new location. You must have already established and be maintaining a parent-governed, consistent settling routine to be able to ask your little one to go to sleep happily without the need to over fuss. The second thing you must be conscious of is making their sleep environment as familiar and safe as possible. This is done in two ways: catering for the environmental needs, and through role playing.

There is much that can be done to ensure sleep is achieved by making your little one's new sleep environment as familiar as possible:

- use unwashed (but not dirty) cot sheets, one of mum's or dad's used pillowcases under the fitted sheet, and used wraps, pyjamas or sleeping bags for familiar smells
- get your baby used to sleeping in the travel cot at home first
- ensure your little one has their own room or space in the new environment—you can achieve this by giving the baby the room you were all offered at, say, a friend's house and you sleeping in the lounge room, or by placing a visual curtain up to separate your child's sleep zone from your own; or at a hotel put up some temporary hooks on the wall and drape a dark sheet over some fine fishing wire to provide a visual block
- take any comfort items, white noise or CDs that you use at home with you.

In addition to catering to the environmental needs, it's important to make sure you make going to sleep as easy as possible. Because this entire routine is designed to empower your child to be able to lay happily in their cot awake after you have said goodnight so they can put themselves to sleep calmly, so you will need to be considerate and not expect them to go to sleep in a room with a television on, lights blazing and adults chatting all within eyeshot. This will deliver a mixed message to your child and they will not see your clear request to put themselves to sleep because this sleep environment will be very unfamiliar to them. A simple, full visual block like a dark sheet will simulate a normal independent sleep environment and make settling a much easier task for your little one.

Naturally though, before they are put to bed for the first time in a foreign environment, it's important to role play (for children six to eight months and older) with your normal role-play teddy and their usual settling routine. This means they will be aware that if they cry, you will come, they will know where you will be (the other side of the sheet) and they will understand your request to go to sleep. If you are in a hotel, your settling routine will need to be followed through in the same way as it is at home. All distraction turned off, two books, and the normal, complete settling routine and assisted self-settling through the interpretation and support of crying.

If you are staying at a friend's or relative's house, allowing grandparents, cousins or friends to run around while they are settling may make going to bed a bit of a challenge. I tend to suggest that your baby enjoys a fun bath time with their grandparents, friends or cousins but, whether they are six months or two years old, they need to say goodnight before their final milk feed and settling routine, which needs to be conducted in a room away from any distraction. Once their settling routine begins, they should not see any of the other house guests until their sleep time is complete. This takes any confusion out of the settling request, and gives them around 15 minutes to settle down and get used to a less stimulating environment, making placing them in their cot awake and saying goodnight a less stressful or difficult event for them.

If your little one is upset, it's important to be consistent. When things around them change, it's important that you don't take away the only predictable thing they have left, which is you and your normal behaviour and communication style. Many people make the huge mistake of changing the way they support their children when everything in the environment changes because they feel bad that they are in this position, but to change yourself and what they can expect from you actually stresses the child even more. Remember to always assess the environment and request from an adult's perspective, and decide if they are or are not safe. If they are safe, then it is absolutely in their best interests for you to convey that by remaining calm, confident, reassuring and consistent to help your little one settle quickly. This means you now do in this new sleep environment just what you would do at home.

You need to use the same resettling routine and crying-support plan, and the same waking routine and 'playtime in the cot' routine before you pack away and get them up for the rest of their day as at home. This ensures they can rely on you for guidance, can see that everything is predictable, and are able to see that you do not consider this changed environment as anything to be rescuing them from, thus enabling them to feel more confident about the changes. Your confidence and consistency tell them if they are okay or not in a new environment. If they say to you 'This feels a little uncomfortable because it's different' by crying, and you suddenly reacted by doing everything differently and rescue them from a safe environment, then you have told them that change is not safe and you're the only one to fix that feeling. This could cause them to struggle when coping with change and become clingy and anxious every time they are exposed to it.

It's important to maintain your confident parent-governed line of communication and keep them well informed and be the one consistent thing in an inconsistent environment. If you are okay, they too will be okay.

Adjusting to daylight saving

You know how it goes: in spring we 'spring forward', in autumn we 'fall back'. On a Sunday morning in spring we turn our clocks forward one hour, from 2 a.m. to 3 a.m. On a Sunday morning in autumn we turn our clocks back one hour, from 3 a.m. to 2 a.m. It's only an hour, but for a little one who does not understand time, it can pose a few problems.

When daylight saving begins—spring forward

The warmer months when we have daylight saving are a lovely time of the year. Because of the movement of the clock, it doesn't feel as hard to wake up or as though there is no day left to yourself when your beautiful children go to bed at the end of a long day. The sunrise is at a more social hour of the day (6 a.m. instead of 5 a.m., or sometimes earlier), and your precious little one's natural alarm clocks (the birds, sun and traffic) peep and zoom happily when the sun comes up, which, conveniently, is the time when your body wants to wake up, and not before.

Before daylight saving begins in the wee small hours of the Sunday morning, I suggest your normal day routine runs as usual the day before you change your clocks and, just before you go to bed on the Saturday night, you turn your clocks forward an hour. Try and go to bed earlier on that Saturday night because you will, in effect, be losing an hour's sleep because that Sunday will only be 23 hours long.

For those of you on a PRM or any time-managed routine with your little one, the transition is actually a simple one. Pre–daylight saving, your baby was probably rising a little too bright and early by the clock because the sun was rising earlier, so they will now wake at a more reasonable hour for you by the clock because the sun will be rising later. So set your alarm for your child's designated wake-up time according to the new adjusted time. This means that if your baby has been waking too early, like 5.30 a.m. (normal standard time) because of the light or birds, then the daylight-saving's change will see them now waking 6.30 a.m. If they do not wake naturally by 6.30 daylight-saving's time, then you will need to wake them, if this is their latest waking time according to their routine.

Without wanting to complicate things, your baby is waking according to their normal routine, or old waking time, but everything on their routine during the day will actually be shifted forward an hour. Where you fed them at 7 a.m. before daylight saving, it will now be 8 a.m. old time, though the clock will say 7 a.m. after daylight saving starts. Once you have woken your little one at their routine waking time, you need to follow through with your routine according to the new clock time. Bear in mind that everything will actually be an hour later than their natural body clock tells them, so don't fret if they take a little while to fall asleep initially and they are a little off their food and yawning at odd times through the day. This is to be expected, and it does not change the outcome of your management. Their body's natural rhythm will settle into the new pattern within one to three days. Remember it always takes around three weeks to lock in a new circadian rhythm pattern so be careful to stick to your usual routine times for the next three weeks to ensure the best results.

When you don't have daylight saving

For those of you who do not have daylight saving but are suffering from the early morning starts of summer, I have a few handy hints to help you get that much-desired sleep in past 5 a.m.

- Reduce the light in your little one's room with blackout curtaining (see page 428). Ensure you start with the room being extra dark and then, gradually, as they start to sleep in longer, you can begin to introduce more light if your baby can tolerate it.
- If your little one is woken by birds chirping happily in the weeeeee early hours of the day, desensitise your baby to the noise by using a white noise machine—simply adjust the device to eliminate the sound of the birds chatting without creating a sleep association.
- Don't compensate for a poor sleep at the right time with a good sleep at the wrong time. This is a problem in many houses that I go into. The best plan with a little one over six months old is to find a standard routine that suits and stick to it, regardless of when they wake. This will take a couple of days and require patience on your part, but will prevent your baby from waking at 5 a.m. and going back to bed *by* 7 a.m. to take the remainder of his or her sleep that should have actually happened *between* 5 and 7 a.m.

End of daylight saving—fall back

This is the most challenging of the two time changes and it is more likely to result in early wakings and tired babies for a few days. Stay strong, be patient, and know that this is only temporary. You are turning the clock back one hour so 6 a.m. (daylight-saving's time) will become 5 a.m. (standard time) again. In effect, there are 25 hours in this one day.

Based on the standard time, adjust their first, day sleep window by pushing it out 30 minutes (see example below). Based on the new time, the adjustment on their second sleep window will be another 30 minutes (see example below). An example of this for babies on LSR morning bridge follows.

Daylight-saving time (old time)	Standard time (new time)	Strategy
6 a.m.	5 a.m.	Ideal situation: your baby wakes at 6 to 6.30 a.m. and you maintain your routine with no changes. You don't need to read any further. Just run your day according to their routine, based on the new clock. Worst-case scenario: your baby wakes at 5 a.m. thinking it's 6 a.m. You will need to push out their next sleep-window start time by 30 minutes (see below). Any further changes below are designed to get them through the day if they have started it an hour early.
8.45	7.45	For LSR morning bridge, begin sleep window half an hour earlier at 8.15 am, standard time.
1 p.m.	12 p.m.	For babies who go to sleep at 12 p.m., keep them up now and they will go down at 12 p.m. standard time. Expect them to be tired. Their morning would be one hour longer than normal, if they wake at 5 a.m. and you have to push their sleep windows out.
2	1	Worst-case scenario: your baby could wake before 1 p.m. They will need to be resettled until 2.30 p.m. standard time. Any early waking at lunch can only be corrected by putting them down at the right time for the next sleep, according to the new adjusted clock. Either 4.15 p.m. (if bridging) or 7 p.m. (if not bridging).
	4.15	This window is now adjusted. Put your baby down at 4.15 p.m. standard time. Maintain your routine according to your personalised chart.
		Evening bedtime should be at standard time as per your positive routine management.

The full adjustment has now been made by the end of the first day. Remember that this is just an example, so adjust the times according to your baby's personalised routine management.

If they are the babies that wake at 5 a.m. new time, thinking it is 6 a.m., then don't fret. Just expect that they will be a little tired and weary on the first day or two while you make the push into the new clock after a few days of early wakings. Their circadian rhythm (internal clock) will still flow in its old pattern for a few days yet so don't be alarmed when they still show tired signs (those waking early for a few days) or alert signs (those who are waking at the normal time but have to adjust their circadian hunger and tired rhythm to new clock times) according to old daylight-saving's times. You will need to work your way through this patiently; make play time after dinner longer to pep them up, and even the trusty walk in the garden to find the 'birdies' can be pulled out of your bag of tricks until those sleep waves pass (they should only be ten minutes' long), then you can carry on as normal.

Do not be tempted to put them down early on the first night back on standard time. Their little body won't shift into this new time and you will have the same battle on your hands the next morning. This will promote a cycle of early wakings resulting in a tired baby through the day again. Babies can make the shift very quickly and be back on track by the next morning if you stick to your plan. This is a new rhythm and, like with all other changes to the body's rhythm, you will need to be consistent with your new times until the pattern is established (usually one to three weeks).

Changing time zones

When you have significant time-zone changes to make, or you are transitioning through multiple tims zones in a short period of time, then there is always a little bit of juggling to help your baby settle into their new surrounding and help you all recover from the jet-lag effects of time-zone transitions as quickly as possible. This kind of strategic planning is not necessary for everyone. Some babies and some parents are very relaxed and don't feel it's necessary to plan ahead, while others find it absolutely necessary. If you do not mind when they wake or fall asleep on your holiday, and your child has always been flexible with sleep, then these measures are more than likely unnecessary and you will all fall into a natural pattern without the need for planning ahead.

If, on the other hand, you have had a very difficult time with sleep in the past, or are particularly anxious about your child's sleep on holidays from past experience or for other reasons, then these kinds of plans are extremely helpful and comforting and, in some cases, absolutely essential in ensuring a holiday does not turn into a disaster zone for all concerned. The strategies highlighted in this book are always about catering to your individual needs, and finding a balance based on yours and your child's needs.

There are two common scenarios I encounter often in both domestic and international travel:

• multiple time-zone changes
• single time-zone transitions.

Multiple time-zone changes

In multi-stopover trips I always suggest you shift your baby's routine into the time zone of the place you are going to stay the longest, rather than change it too often. So if you are travelling from Perth via Melbourne (for one day) and Sydney (two days) then up to Brisbane for a two-week holiday, for instance, you would work on Brisbane time during the three days in Melbourne and Sydney so your baby is well adjusted and settled by the time you arrive in Brisbane.

To do this, the morning your holiday begins, wake your baby so they start the day on your destination time. This might mean you have to wake them at 4 a.m. You then run your routine for the rest of the day based on the times at your destination, even when you are in the stopover places. This may mean that your baby goes to bed for the entire night in the first stopover at 6 p.m., which may be 4 p.m. at home but 7 p.m. in your final destination. This of course is your ultimate goal, and the reason for waking them early on the morning of your intended travel day: to shift your baby's body clock quickly rather than have them waking at odd times for up to seven days before their body adjust to the new times.

Some parents would like their children to sleep in longer on holidays, and go to bed later at night for convenience's sake, but sadly it doesn't always work this well. What may happen is your baby will end up waking with the sun occasionally, and sleep in on other days, which throws their body clock completely, and makes them tired. When I travelled with the families in Europe or Australia, the ability to transition the children quickly into the new time zone was the key to a happy holiday right from the start.

Whether it's a trip from London to Turkey, or Perth to Sydney, slight changes in times zones are best dealt with by shifting over into the new time zone on the morning you plan on leaving for your holiday. Bear in mind, you are aiming to achieve a full night's sleep from 7 p.m. (new time zone) to 6 or 7 a.m. (new time zone). Once you have a base to work with (the night settling time on 7 p.m. new time zone, for instance), then you can arrange their day sleeps in the right pattern to encourage them at their normal, daily nap intervals.

If the transition is in the reverse order and you have a time shift that requires your baby to sleep in until 9 a.m. in order to fall into a new time zone of 7 a.m., then this is clearly not always an easy task for your children. I tend to adjust the routine from the afternoon / evening before and try to achieve a later settling time to push them into the new pattern. With a six- to 12-month-old baby this can be achieved by offering a late nap, between 6 and 7 p.m. of around 20 minutes (low-sleep-requirement babies) or 40 minutes (high-sleep-requirement babies) to help them achieve a later settling time the night before. If they are 12 months plus, you can offer them a bridge nap at 5 or 6 p.m. for 20 minutes to encourage the later settling time.

The later afternoon bridge would ensure your baby will stay awake until 9 p.m. to encourage a later sleep in, and a faster transition into the new time zone. If your little one still wakes at their usual 6 to 7 a.m. time on the morning of your trip, you can feed them and resettle them to encourage a wake-up time closer to the time you are wanting to achieve. You will need to adjust their meal plan as well as their sleeping plan. The two run parallel to each other when it comes to adjusting their circadian rhythm. This may mean your little one may be up a little at night when you make a stopover, and may sleep more during the day, but this will give you the flexibility to explore the new places as they sleep in their pram, and have some fun evenings out to enjoy late evening meals and walks.

The most important thing to remember with multi-stopover travel when the transition is the reverse order (9 a.m. = 7 a.m.) is to adjust their nights' sleeping pattern to align with your destination's time zone the evening before you plan on arriving, even if this means their final night cycle happens on the airplane. Be sure to plan your arrival time a little carefully. Arriving in the middle of the night or at 4 a.m. in the morning is never a good thing when you want to adjust their body clocks quickly. Precious days could be wasted with an exhausted baby and exhausted parents before you all settle into a good rhythm. Book a flight that will have you landing first thing in the morning, preferably or, at the very least, some time during the day so you can always work your previous, evening sleep cycle around that.

If you land in the morning, it will work in your favour as you can check into your hotel, get their sleep environment organised, and head out for the day, encouraging appropriate day sleeps at appropriate times in the pram, and not fall prey to the ever inviting jet-lag day sleeps that ruin your and yours child's chances of quickly adjusting to the new time zone by discouraging a good, first, full-night's sleep.

For example, if you are on a 24-hour flight that lands in Italy at 7 a.m. their time, then ensure during the first part of the flight you keep your baby going with naps and healthy snacks and well-spaced meal times. Then you settle them down for a full night's sleep for the final ten to 12 hours of the flight. Alternatively, if your flight lands at 5 p.m. Italian time, then ensure they have been up for the day and progressed through the normal breakfast, lunch, dinner time and all their usual sleep times for ten hours prior to landing. This way, they will ready to go to bed at 7 to 7.30 p.m. Italy time after you have checked in, set up their cot and role played through the settling routine.

The final leg of your flight is carefully aligned with your destination time zone and means that by the time you land, your child and you will have already started to adjust, and the chances of your little one being awake all night and wanting to sleep all day during your holiday will be less likely. Obviously, in order to adjust their body clock, you will need to wake them after appropriate lengths of time, and feed them and provide naps rather than allowing long, full-night sleep patterns through the day, to help you achieve the transition into the new time zone adequately.

Single time-zone transitions

If the amount of time you are going to spend in the first time zone exceeds three days, then you should transition them into the first stopover's time zone in much the same way you would for domestic or international travel with a single time-zone change. This is done in two ways depending on whether the time zone you are moving into is earlier or later than your city's time zone:

1. you provide an extra nap later in the day to help them stay awake longer for a late settle time
2. you wake them earlier the morning of your travel so they can go to bed earlier in the afternoon for their usual full-night cycle in the new time zone.

This is done in the same way as described in the international zone transition. Plan the previous day to align their night sleep cycle to be in the destination's time zone and ensure their meal times through the day would run in direct correlation with those sleep times. For example, your child's routine at home may look something like this:

6 a.m.	wake
7	feed
7.30	breakfast
9	nap
9.30	feed
11.30	lunch
12 p.m.	sleep
2.30	feed
4.15	nap
5.30	dinner
6.30	feed
7.00	sleep

If your destination is three hours behind these times, to adjust theirs and your body clock quickly, adjust them into the new time the morning you plan on flying out for your vacation. This may appear daunting, but you will have to make the transition anyway, so you are best to adjust on the day of your travel, than waste a day of your travel adjusting their body clock, or worse still, have a baby or toddler that becomes overtired or is overwhelmed by inconsistent sleep on a number of days.

To do this, you adjust your leaving day's routine to:

4 a.m.	wake
5	feed
5.30	breakfast
7	nap
7.30	feed
8.30	lunch
9.00	sleep
11.30	feed
1.15	nap
2.30	dinner
3.30	feed
4.00	sleep

But your destination's routine clock will read:

6 a.m.	wake
7	feed
7.30	breakfast
9	nap
9.30	feed

11.30	lunch
12 p.m.	sleep
2.30	feed
4.15	nap
5.30	dinner
6.30	feed
7.00	sleep

This means that your little one's body clock will be adjusting, and now you will simply have to adjust them to the new environment with ease and as little stress to them and you as possible.

Going back to work / others caring for your child

Returning to work and leaving their child with a carer is often a great concern for any parent who is planning on maintaining their career. Regardless of a mother's or father's preconceived ideas of what returning to work will be like, the realities of doing so can be an extremely daunting and emotionally difficult step to take. The primary concern of any parent I talk with is how their precious baby, who has virtually been with them from the moment he or she was conceived, will cope without them there to cater to their emotional needs.

Obviously, there are so many choices of environment and care that you can choose for your child, that even that decision can feel overwhelming. You can have your child cared for at home, at a family member's house, at a friend's house, in family daycare or in a childcare centre. You can have your child cared for by a nanny, a grandparent, a friend, or a trained childcare worker or teacher in a centre. You can have your child in care full time, part time, or cared for as little as half a day a week.

There are some things that you should be very conscious of to make the transition as easy as possible for your little one, when returning to work:

- continuity
- predictability
- frequency.

One of the more difficult scenarios that you can place a child into when they are having to adjust to their primary carer going back to work is when there is a lot of inconsistencies in their new week. To have to adjust to three or more carers in a week, and multiple environments can leave a child feeling unable to establish themselves in any one environment and unsettled as a direct result. Sleep will always suffer when a child is feeling that there is nothing predictable in their day.

As far as possible, try to limit their carers to you and their other parent, plus one other carer. As far as possible, try to limit their care environment to home plus one other location. When placing a child into care, consecutive days are almost always easier for them initially to adjust to and recover from each week, than to have staggered days.

When placing a child into a childcare situation with other children, a minimum of two days is more highly recommended that one single day. After working in childcare centres and preschools for many years, the most difficult and slow adjustments I witnessed children having to make was when they were only attending the centre one day a week. On the single attendance days, they took longer to become familiar with the carers, the children and the routine flow of the day.

When placing a child into care in any environment other than home, take the time to have an orientation and slow introduction to that environment. Spend time exploring and enjoying the environment together and start to develop a predictable but brief arrival routine, and a departure routine. An example of an arrival routine could be something as simple as:

- greet their carer enthusiastically
- unpack their milk cup / bottles / food into the fridge together
- unpack their sleep comforters, whether they are dummies, a wrap or sleeping bag, or their dolly / teddy and place them in or near their cot
- put their bag away and play two activities together before saying good bye—I usually do a little something fun like a lipstick kiss on their hand, a little stamp if they are 12 months or older, and a funny little song as the last thing you do before confidently saying your cheery bye bye (long-term absence cues) and heading off to work.

Once you go, you should actually go and give them a chance to be comforted by their temporary primary caregiver. If you teach your baby that when they cry you will return, they are more likely to naturally want you to stay simply because they love you, so may be more inclined to cry expecting this style of communication to yield the same results of you returning each time. This makes it harder for them to accept comfort from their carer and almost always promotes crying and clinginess while you are in that environment. This will obviously become confusing for them and for you, so make sure you give your child and their new carer a good opportunity to find a way together. In my experience, most children settle down very quickly when distracted and will quickly bond with an attentive carer.

Always remember to assess the environment and situation from an adult's perspective. If they are safe but feeling a little unsure of the changes, your response should be empathetic but really reassuring by remaining confident and happy even when they are expressing a little concern. Your confidence will be the most reassuring and comforting thing you can provide for them in this situation. If their mummy and daddy are okay, they will generally be able to trust and accept the situation far more quickly then they would if their parent appeared as concerned or unsure as them.

Before you would ever actually leave them for the first time however, you will need to be sure they are familiar and confident with the new environment and their carer. They must be able to cope with you slowly pulling back your involvement during their play, and learn to eventually cope with short absences while they play, before you leave for gradually longer intervals.

Initial absences could be as brief as a trip to the toilet using your short-term absence cue that you have already established and practised at home. Gradually you will step out to make and enjoy a cup of tea, remembering to use your short-term absence cues as always for an absence of under 15 minutes. Eventually you will build this time and leave them for a few hours in the morning before returning to take them home for a sleep, or attempting a sleep in that environment (depending on where they are being cared for).

If their care environment is a place that you often visit as a family as well as have them cared for there (such as a grandparent's, aunt's or friend's house) be sure to establish a clear language cue for the two different scenarios they will encounter at that house. One cue for your work days, that you can use as a part of your flow of communication so they can have forewarning that you are planning on leaving them there, and another that will enable them to predict the occasions you will stay with them.

These cues should be a simple language cue like 'it's mummy's working day today, Bell's turn to play', or a little routine like a song to the tune of 'This is way we clap our hands' on the way like:

This is the day mum goes to work, goes to work, goes to work,
This is the day mum goes to work
And Bella has a play day.

For the occasions you do not plan on leaving your baby, I would ensure I had a very different language cue so your little one can predict your movements and will not become clingy for the entire visit to the house in anticipation of you leaving them.

When looking for an appropriate centre, I always suggest you look for the more obvious signs of a settled and well-flowing environment as well as for good accreditation. Often, people are really impressed with the programming and planning done by long daycare staff and can become easily sold on these points. But we are blessed to have wonderfully high standards of care that are continuously assessed to ensure our children are catered for in the best possible way.

Some of the things I would always look for when visiting a new centre are:

- staff communication dynamics, including staff–parent, staff–director, director–parent, staff–children and children–staff relationships
- environment—art displayed well with names and dates, and looking as though it's circulated regularly; toys put away, and the general environment tidy and organised. (If they don't have time to pack away correctly, or clean up after meal times in a reasonable timeframe, then the staff may be under tremendous pressure and not have enough time to really invest in the care of the children and their other duties. This is generally problematic because this can mean staff are not happy and, if they are overly stressed or distracted, this can impact on the children indirectly. This is generally not a staff problem; this is a management problem or perhaps a communication problem.)
- a good staff-retention rate
- well-established and practised system of communication between staff and with the parents including daily events, routines and weekly programs
- happy children busily exploring their environment
- flexibility to accept transferable communication; that is, predictable routines that can be transferred from you (their parent) to their new primary caregiver, which is a really lovely way of helping your child feel comfortable and able to predict their day even when their mummy and daddy aren't there for a little while.

First and foremost, I would always establish a sleep-time settling, resettling and waking routine. I would ensure there was a predictable environment for them to sleep in, and I would make sure that where possible I had role played through their usual settling routine for the child in the new cot environment. In addition to developing a language-based settling, resettling and waking routine and teaching it to their carers, I would also ensure I had worked hard on a long- and short-term absence cue, and some basic forewarning and guiding cues around sitting down or lying down for the typical events like nappy change, meal times, pram play and getting into the car.

Other carers and your child's sleep

This is a really important consideration when deciding who will care for your child. If you are like many of the clients that I have dealt with over the years, and sleep time was a very challenging thing for you to repair, maintaining good sleep and your child's trust in their sleep routine and environment will be a priority for your family. As mentioned in this section already, the importance of role play and consistency cannot be under estimated in children from eight months onwards, but is still a valuable tool from six months in a child who has found sleep particularly stressful in the past. Once your new carer (in any environment other that a childcare centre) is familiar with the settling routine, your child should be given the opportunity to witness them settling teddy so they can see that this is a normal set of condition to expect from this person, and so avoid tears when they experience it for the first time with their new minder while you are at work. Even if your carer has raised six children or had mountains of experience, this is not a reason to allow everything to become unpredictable for your baby. You have established a predictable set of cues and events that empowers your baby, and it is much easier for your well-experienced carer to have to adjust to change and settle baby a new way, than it is for your baby to adjust to change and settle the way your carer wants to do things. Stick to your sleep routines, and train anyone settling your baby into them. If they are experienced, this should be a simple task for them.

> Even if your carer has raised six children or had mountains of experience, this is not a reason to allow everything to become unpredictable for your baby.

Obviously, as I have a business that has a primary focus on parenting skills and sleep repair, I come across many different types of sleep-time challenges that a baby or toddler struggles to cope with. If you have a carer who wants to let baby guide sleep time again, you can run into serious problems. Once you have corrected your sleep-time difficulties by re-establishing a confident guiding style of parenting, it can be quite confusing for a child to have to deal with a sudden reversal of roles again at sleep time, particularly in those first few months after their sleep disruption has been repaired.

By this I mean that finally they are burden free at sleep time, and can relax knowing that mum and dad will be predictable and do all the things they know mean sleep time. Often, however, when they go into care with some new carers, they suddenly have to go back to having to guide an adult at sleep time again through crying and fussing.

Now while I have a golden rule of 'grandparents privilege' when it comes to how a child is cared for by grandparents (within healthy and respectful boundaries of course), I do think that it is very important to maintain their full sleep-time program and management in order to help a child stay calm and relaxed. This also ensures they do not become upset when they come home and have changed sleep association, even if their grandparents are caring for them.

Obviously though, that is often easier said than done, and there are certain cultures that I have come to understand very well over the last nine years (you know who you are) where even the concept of asking the grandparent to put the child down for sleep time would be a laughable suggestion. This means that unless your carers (grandparents or otherwise) are willing to maintain your little one's new peaceful sleep program, that it is probably much easier on the child in the long and short term that you find someone who will be able to provide the predictability your now-settled and well-sleeping child needs.

The end result of someone physically teaching a child to rely heavily on others to settle again during the day, particularly after they have learnt the skills of independent settling and been able to go to sleep and stay asleep peacefully, is that your child will suddenly become unsettled again day and night, and will cry when you put them to bed. Try to make sure the person caring for you child understands the difficulty your little one may have had in the past and is respectful of not taking your baby or toddler back to the old ways that made sleep time so difficult for them.

If your child is in a daycare centre environment, obviously time is far more precious to the carers and while all good centres are happy to accommodate your daily sleep routines and incorporate certain aspects of your settling routine, it is reasonable to assume that no centre could afford to allocate one entire staff member to a ten-minute settling routine that we luxuriously enjoy in the home settling. Stories are not necessary but pre emptive language such as 'it's nearly time for sleep / nigh' nigh's' and your little one's normal sleep-time song and settling cues are all absolutely reasonable to expect a staff member to be able to do when they are putting your baby / toddler to bed.

If, while in daycare, your toddler or 12-month-plus baby is on a little mattress out in the main room with the 'big babies' then there is always a chance that the staff may assist them to settle off to sleep with a pat or hair stroke. In a situation where your child has just recovered from unsettled sleep patterns and is now able to self-settle, it's important you request the staff use your usual cues and requests to lie down, etc., but do not assist them to sleep through patting or stroking as this could create old patterns of expectation and make sleep at home challenging again.

If your child is upset you can suggest that they can sit next to them, perhaps have a hand gently resting on their back for reassurance, or even sing the sleep-time song to help them settle down, but try to stop all those aids and just sit quietly next to them once they have calmed and are starting to fall asleep.

What to expect when you collect your precious baby after care

While all our children are so unique, there are also some very predictable patterns of behaviour that I have witnessed hundreds and hundreds of times when a parent goes to collect their child from care, whether they have been there for two hours or a full day. Most people write the behaviour off as tiredness, and in some cases that is most certainly accurate; it can take a good one to two full days to get your little one to settle back down and stop being so reactive or grouchy after daycare.

In my experience, particularly with children who have been very unsettled and have finally relaxed through balanced communication and confident guidance at home through the PRM program, they transition from their parent guiding them to the burden of being much more self-directed in childcare or care in general. This makes going back to accepting balanced guidance a little challenging for them at the end of the day.

I always say it's a little like handing them the reins when you drop them at daycare and saying 'Here you go, it's all yours'. Often this is a little bit of an adjustment, but through the experienced guidance of their new carers they build their confidence and enjoy the feeling of freedom that comes with being separated from their primary carer. This is a healthy and normal transition as they start to spread their little wings and test out all the wonderful life skills you have been busily equipping them with since they were born.

The transition back to sharing those reins with mum and dad again can occasionally be a little tricky when you come to collect them at the end of their exciting independent day. Often, the emotions of seeing mum and dad can be a little overwhelming and a mixture of laughter and by a few tears greets you and your baby's strong desire to have a big cuddle is quickly followed by them pushing you away. All of this can make the first few minutes a little bit unnerving for even the most confident of parents.

Remember to never assume why these things are occurring. In baby terms, they are just a little overwhelmed by the emotions of seeing you and are not sure what to do with themselves when they feel this way, but for a parent's active and occasionally guilt-riddled imagination, images and buzz terms like resentment, abandonment and anger are often the first things they think a child is expressing. Stay confident, smile and take the pressure and focus off them by taking the time to sit and have a little play with their toys until they settle down and come to you for a cuddle or to join in.

Now is the time to put in place your flow of communication so you can resume guiding them, but empower them (right from six to eight months of age) with what is coming next so they too can feel in control. Always maintain your usual arrival and departure routine and keep them well informed and well involved in the process. You do this through the use of the flow of communication (see page 40)

When they resist, which they invariably do as they transition from independently holding those little guiding reins of their day, to sharing them with their mum or dad again, it's really important that you remain consistent, confident and follow your flow plan of defining your statements clearly and following through. If you re-assume your usual, confident, guiding-parenting role, they will quickly settle back into sharing the control of their day, and you will not have the 24- to 48-hour transition of grouchy and teary or challenging behaviour until they settle back down.

Acknowledgements

This book is the culmination of my life's journey and faith; an amazing mix of upbringing, environment, education, inspiration, experience, belief and trust. These bound together with my life's most essential ingredients: family and friends, and the children and their parents. Unsuspecting individuals, young and old, who came into my life for years, months, days or even a fleeting moment and left a lasting impression. All those encounters enable me to now pay it forward. I only have room to acknowledge a small fraction of those amazing driving forces that have touched my life in one way or another, but to everyone, thank you.

To my parents, my gratitude and love towards you both is immeasurable. I am so grateful you are my beautiful, loving, and endlessly dedicated mum and dad, who I can still rely on for wisdom and confident encouragement and guidance every day of my life

To my favourite girls in the world, my extraordinary and wonderful sisters Simmeone and Brooke. Your love, support, encouragement and beautiful natures inspire me to be a better woman. Thanks also to your beautiful partners Jeff and Kris. A very special thank you to Jeff for the role you played in inspiring me and helping me pitch and put together this book.

To my beautiful nephew, Gage—you're the absolute best! I am so proud of you. You will always be the treasure of my life. And to my precious 'angel' nephew, Caleb. You changed the world in your short stay. What an amazing little cherub. I love you so much and I miss you every day.

To Drew. Thank you for your support and encouragement, and especially for your enormous heart. You are an inspiration.

To my beautiful friends Mez (freckle P) and Tez (Steeeeve), Jessy (poodles), Tina and Mark; to my very special little friends Joseph (sparkles) and his beautiful baby brother, Daniel; and to Lamar and little Billy Chops amongst many others. Thank you all for always going way, way, way above and beyond the call of duty with your love, support and encouragement.

To Allen and Unwin for this amazing opportunity. I am so thrilled my book is with my dream publishers. Thank you for the freedom to write this book and your patience as I fine-tuned my life's work. To the lovely Joanne Holliman, my ridiculously patient editor. Thank you so much for taking it on, and for your patience as I learnt how to be an author.

To the team, past and present at The Australian Baby Whisperer: Kris, Lisa, Chris Headford, Jessica Teni and Tamara. Thank you all for investing time, love and energy into making The Australian Baby Whisperer what it is today.

And thank you to the producers, hosts and crew at 7's *Sunrise* for six years of amazing loyal support and encouragement.

The wisdom, clarity, abundance and unshakable love and devotion I feel in my life every day is due to my faith. It has given me wings to fly, eyes to see and ears to hear. I am truly blessed.

Index